THE ULTIMATE EVIL

The Search for the Sons of Sam

MAURY TERRY

QUIRK BOOKS

PHILADELPHIA

For Robert and Joseph Terry;
to those who were always there;
and in memory of the innocent slain

Library of Congress Cataloging-in-Publication Data
Names: Terry, Maury, author.
Title: The ultimate evil : the search for the Sons of Sam / Maury Terry.
Description: Philadelphia : Quirk Books, [2021] | Originally published in 1987;
revised in 1999; with new introduction. | Summary: "Maury Terry's investigation
into the Son of Sam murders"—Provided by publisher.
Identifiers: LCCN 2020049444 (print) | LCCN 2020049445 (ebook) | ISBN
9781683692843 (trade paperback) | ISBN 9781683692850 (epub)
Subjects: LCSH: Berkowitz, David Richard, 1953- | Manson, Charles, 1934-2017.
| Mass murder—United States—Case studies. | Satanism—United States—Case
studies. | Conspiracies—United States—Case studies.
Classification: LCC HV6529 .T47 2021 (print) | LCC HV6529 (ebook) | DDC
364.152/320973—dc23
LC record available at https://lccn.loc.gov/2020049444
LC ebook record available at https://lccn.loc.gov/2020049445

ISBN: 978-1-68369-284-3

Printed in the United States of America

Typeset in Adobe Garamond Pro

Designed by Andie Reid
Production management by John J. McGurk

Quirk Books
215 Church Street
Philadelphia, PA 19106
quirkbooks.com

10 9 8 7 6 5 4 3 2

Contents

Introduction

by Joshua Zeman

I first learned of Maury Terry in the summer of 2008. At the time, I was directing my first documentary about five missing children and the man linked to their disappearances in my hometown of Staten Island, New York. My interest in the case was sparked by a local legend I'd heard years before about a boogeyman named Cropsey. According to the kids in our neighborhood, Cropsey was an escaped mental patient who lived in the tunnels beneath the old abandoned Willowbrook State School and came out late at night to snatch children off the street.

For most of my childhood, Cropsey remained nothing more than a cautionary tale—until the summer of 1987. That was the summer I turned fifteen and Jennifer Schweiger, a twelve-year-old girl with Down syndrome, disappeared from our neighborhood. After more than six weeks of searching, her body was found on the grounds of the same Willowbrook State School. Though I didn't know it back then, Willowbrook had a nefarious history. For decades, the "snake pit institution," as Bobby Kennedy called it, had been warehousing hundreds of developmentally disabled children in a real-life house of horrors, until a 1972 exposé by Geraldo Rivera finally led to its closure. In the days following Jennifer's discovery, the police arrested a man named Andre Rand. He wasn't a mental patient, as the urban legend suggested, but a former orderly who often lived in a campsite on the school grounds. The police revealed that Rand was suspected in the disappearances of four other missing children going back to the early '70s. For the kids on Staten Island, the legend of Cropsey had turned into something very real and truly terrifying.

Eventually, Rand was sent to prison for the kidnapping of Jennifer Schweiger, and I moved away. In 2004, Rand returned to Staten Island to stand trial for another missing child, and I came back as well, now as an adult and a filmmaker, to find out what really happened to those disappearing children and to see if my childhood boogeyman was real. However, as I tried to reconcile one urban legend, I soon uncovered another—or, at least, what I thought was a legend.

While interviewing Staten Island residents who had searched for Jennifer back in 1987, I documented rumor after rumor of "devil worshippers" who supposedly roamed the island's woods and held ceremonies on Willowbrook's grounds. At the time, Satanic Panic was sweeping the nation. In 1988, Geraldo Rivera, the man who sparked the school's closure, would bring the hysteria to its frenzied peak with the highly sensationalized prime-time special *Devil Worship: Exposing Satan's Underground.* I still believe most of those "sightings" were nothing more than devious teenagers who took an understandable pleasure in tweaking their parents' anxiety. However, at some point during our filming, *something* happened. The stories began to change.

The legends turned strangely specific as people told tales about a cult operating on the island, which was ultimately responsible for these missing children. Most intriguing, this cult was said to be connected to the infamous Son of Sam murders. Of course, I knew the story of David Berkowitz, the madman who claimed a demon dog had commanded him to kill couples in parked cars during the sweltering New York City summer of 1977. Considering my film was about both "childhood" and "adult" urban legends, I continued to dig deeper.

Piecing together rumors of this so-called Son of Sam cult, I soon found a local reporter who could confirm a few errant facts—a name, a date, a local house that the police had looked into. He passed me on to an eccentric lawyer who only added credence to my growing list of clues. Finally, I found a truly credible source: a veteran detective from the NYPD's Cold Case Squad, a man who had been trained to compile evidence, not conjecture. After much prodding, the detective agreed to tell me the source of these rumors. One night, he sat me down with two other detectives as they revealed a secret, one that had swirled through the squad rooms of the NYPD for decades: David Berkowitz, the infamous Son of Sam, did not act alone.

I learned there were a number of detectives in the NYPD, past and present, who had come to believe, based upon their own investigations, that David Berkowitz had accomplices and that the allegations of a so-called cult were true. While they didn't think Staten Island's missing children were connected, they still believed the group was responsible for numerous other unsolved murders throughout the metropolitan area. Many of the detectives had passed along their findings to a journalist named Maury Terry, who went on to write a book about his own investigation called *The Ultimate Evil.*

To this day, I consider *The Ultimate Evil* one of the most terrifying books I've ever read, and I know I'm not alone. I consider myself a skeptic, a debunker of things that go bump in the night, but I do believe there is something uniquely unsettling about *The Ultimate Evil.* Maybe it's the fact that the book hovers between the believable and the unbelievable. As hard as it is to fully accept Terry's allegations, it's just as difficult to completely dismiss them—much like the enigma of the Process Church, a group profiled by Terry in this book. To some, they were a doomsday cult responsible for a series of ritualistic murders that spanned the country. To others, they were nothing more than an oft-maligned church whose bizarre theatrics led to their scapegoating. Regardless of their true intentions, it seems Terry had found the perfect adult urban legend.

My fascination with *The Ultimate Evil* comes from a desire to explore how people conflate different shades of evil. I've always been interested in experts of the occult for their fascinating knowledge, but also for their gross misinterpretations. Terry is no different. Though the term *satanism* is used quite liberally in this book, I believe Maury finally came to realize that true Satanists are not devil worshippers. In fact, far from it. True practitioners of satanism are far more aligned with atheism and libertarianism than with any religion. Still, that doesn't mean there aren't individuals, whether Catholics, Jews, Muslims, or even Satanists, who use their religion, or lack thereof, as a means to morally justify or simply conceal their aberrant behavior.

I first sat down with Maury in the fall of 2010, in a cramped attic apartment in Yonkers. Maury wore an oxygen mask as he battled acute pneumonia, in no small part due to decades of incessant smoking. He refused to leave his apartment so instead I brought him tuna sandwiches. As we ate, he would regale me with stories—not just about Son of Sam, but of other unsolved crimes that echoed through New York City lore. It was then that I realized I had found something special: a knowledgeable mentor and an unreliable narrator woven into one.

Though I befriended Maury Terry, I remained skeptical of his story—what he called "the Son of Sam Conspiracy." I think he knew it, too, which is why he was forever trying to prove its veracity—undoubtedly, because so many had called him a crackpot over the years. Tragically, those claims only pushed him to double down, to become even more fervent, which in turn only made those crackpot claims seem somewhat true.

During our friendship, Maury would pester me to do a documentary on his investigation, and for years I refused. I found the cult story fascinating, but I wanted to turn *The Ultimate Evil* into a fictionalized series instead. Maybe I was concerned about what I would find—that much of his story was untrue. Or maybe I knew what I know now: that Maury was far too close to his story. He had fallen down the rabbit hole of his investigation and was ensnared in a trap of his own creation. In essence, he had spent so many years trying to uncover one conspiracy that he had created another.

It is this tragedy that brings us to the ultimate question: Is Maury Terry's story true? I've spent the past decade asking myself that same question and the last five years trying to answer it. It's what led me to finally embark on the documentary that Maury always pestered me to do. Of course, if I were being clever, I would say you have to watch the documentary to find out, but in many ways our series only scratches at the surface of the truth. The best I can say is that if none of it were true, I wouldn't be here writing this introduction. Instead, all I can offer is a challenge to you, the reader: approach this book with a dose of healthy skepticism as well as an open mind. See if you can answer the mystery that I, and so many others, have spent so long trying to solve. But before you do, consider this a warning . . .

The Ultimate Evil is a fascinating read, an investigation of epic proportions. But it is also a cautionary tale about what it means to become obsessed with true crime.

Though we now associate *true crime* and *obsession* with a weekend lost in the twists and turns of our favorite new case, for Maury Terry it was a descent into the abyss— an investigation, spanning more than four decades, that eventually led to his demise.

I don't think Maury ever truly believed in the devil, but I know he believed in the power of the devil as a unifying force that could be harnessed to create a so-called network, or what he called a conspiracy. Yet, while there is no denying that some use religion to legitimize their deviance, I take issue with Maury's notion of conspiracy. I think we believe in the specter of organized evil to make sense of aberrant behaviors we don't understand, and to protect us from a far more unsettling notion: that this malevolence we fear does exist, and it lives deep inside each and every one of us, waiting to emerge. In the end, is it not more terrifying to accept that there is no grand conspiracy—no structure, no organization, no method to the madness that haunts us all? That there is only rudderless chaos? To me, that is the ultimate evil.

It's often been repeated that, "The greatest trick the devil ever pulled was convincing the world he didn't exist." But I say different. I think the greatest trick man ever pulled was convincing *himself* that the devil was real. Of course, you, the reader, will come to your own conclusions. But I caution you against staring too deeply into the darkness. You never know what you might find.

PART I

ON TERROR'S TRAIL

We had pure panic. The city was exploding around us.

—Steve Dunleavy, *New York Post* columnist

I am still here. Like a spirit roaming the night.

—Son of Sam letter

. . . the pinnacle of Heaven united with pure
hatred raised from the depths of Hell.

—Robert DeGrimston, satanic cult leader

I

Satan at Stanford

At 11 p.m. on October 12, 1974, the lush, sprawling campus of Stanford University was alive with the sounds of Saturday night partying. Exuberant bursts of harmony, laughter and the *thump, thump, thump* of reverberant bass guitars drifted from dormitory windows and doorways as the student population unwound from a week's worth of classes, study and football fever.

A love affair with big-time sports was enjoying a resurgence at the university, long known primarily as a bastion of academic excellence. But Jim Plunkett's Stanford Indians had ridden a dark horse out of nowhere to upset the world in the Rose Bowl game on New Year's Day of '71. Four seasons later, the pride still burned with the memory, and the fervor lingered yet on autumn Saturdays.

And although it was mid-October, Columbus Day—a time of smoldering dry leaves and ripening pumpkins in the northern reaches of the country—it was a clear, pleasant evening in Palo Alto. A light breeze gently rattled the gum trees and palms that studded the campus and bore the musical merriment from one distant corner of the sparkling complex to the other.

There were many such nights in the friendly climate of California's Silicon Valley, which nestled some forty miles to the south and east of San Francisco. The Valley's nickname, and the whole of Santa Clara County, which enveloped it, spoke of tomorrow, progress and affluence.

The general vicinity of Palo Alto, including nearby San Jose, was home to a considerable number of high-technology corporations—such as IBM—which had erected laboratories or development centers for the manufacture of advanced computer circuitry. Silicon is a nonmetallic element critical to the production of semiconductors: hence the Valley's label.

And since Stanford graduates were harvested annually by the area's corporate residents, the school functioned as an integral component of a community that was science- and academia-oriented, a domicile of the prosperous and an enclave of both the scholar and the pragmatic business executive. Although Stanford and other local institutions were regarded as hallmarks of philosophical liberalism, the Valley itself was considered a refuge of conservative mores and politics—especially when compared with its raucous northerly neighbor, San Francisco, or to that hissing viper vat located a more reassuring 350 miles to the south—Los Angeles.

To Valley citizens, nearby Frisco was the site of 1967's "Summer of Love"—and the haven of the gay community, flower children, hippies, freaked-out bikers and Jefferson Airplane acid-drooling rock. It was a breeding ground of occult deviance and satanism, and the harborer of the notorious North Beach section, where Carol

Doda and friends would shake their booties and other such things nightly on the sweaty stages of Big Al's and the Condor Club.

* * *

To nineteen-year-old Bruce Perry, studying on this October night in a campus apartment at Stanford, those activities were as foreign as the Latin he'd soon have to master as a diligent second-year pre-med student.

Around him, out of doors, the sounds of Saturday were faint in the wind, and only remotely tempting. Bruce Perry was dedicated to his work, and a weekend with Hippocrates was as normal to him as was an evening with Led Zeppelin to some of his less industrious counterparts across the campus.

Not that Bruce was always serious. He did have his moments. But for the immediate future, they seemed as long ago and far away as his hometown of Bismarck, North Dakota.

By all accounts, Bruce Perry was an all-American boy from an all-American town whose family nurtured him with a Norman Rockwell Americana upbringing. The son of a comfortably set dentist, Dr. Duncan Perry, the handsome, curly-haired Bruce was a standout in both the classroom and sports in Bismarck. His days at Bismarck High School had been alive and full.

When he graduated in 1973, he was the honored holder of a smattering of track and field records in North Dakota—including the state mark for the quarter-mile. He was popular, deeply religious, and participated in the Fellowship of Christian Athletes, both in school and at summer camps. In short, Bruce was a sure-shot pick to succeed in the world. And even more than that, since August 17, 1974, Bruce was a married man.

His young, blond bride, also nineteen, also from Bismarck, and also immersed in religious causes, was his high school sweetheart, the former Arlis Dykema. As Bruce labored over his assignments that October night, Arlis busied herself around the small but cozy corner apartment the couple shared on the second floor of the university's Quillen Hall, a residence for married students.

As it neared eleven thirty, Arlis gathered up some letters to Bismarck family and friends and told Bruce she was going out to mail them. Bruce shrugged at his bride, then decided to pack up his work and get outside for a while himself. He realized Arlis was showing signs of restlessness and that he hadn't done very much to liven up her evening.

* * *

Bruce was still adapting to the idea of being married. Marriage was adjustment, his parents advised, and was subject to growing pains. Not that he didn't love Arlis. He was happy she was with him and they shared long hours of contentment and caring. In many respects, they complemented each other. But Bruce regretted that he'd seen so little of his fiancee the previous year. He had been alone at Stanford while Arlis remained in Bismarck, working with her religious friends, attending Bismarck Junior College and squirreling money away for their wedding.

During their months apart, the couple maintained regular contact, but it wasn't the same as being together. People can grow in any number of ways in the year after high school.

Bruce took the concept of traditional marriage to heart; his religious background wouldn't have permitted otherwise. Arlis, he was confident, felt the same as he did. Life would be good, Bruce believed, with children and a comfortable home. But first they had to survive Stanford and cope with the added demands that came with preparation for a career in medicine or dentistry. Bruce had a high hill to climb, and he knew it. But he was optimistic he'd make it, and Arlis would be there to help him.

Arlis herself was an Everyman's vision of Middle America. She was a studious young woman who'd also served as an enthusiastic cheerleader at Bismarck High for three years. Rounding out her life, she was a devout, practicing Christian who swelled with a religious ardor that was almost a quaint artifact of a simpler, more compassionate past in the U.S.A. of 1974.

A friend to many and confidante of some, Arlis was a pretty girl; tiny, almost fragile in stature. She had a quick smile, an inquisitive, probing nature and that overriding passion for the lections of the Lord.

Always in motion, she passed some of her idle hours at Stanford with frequent, long walks around the campus—sometimes jogging to release her pent-up energy. She had shoulder-length, wavy blond hair, wore glasses and—being fallible—was possessed of an occasional streak of self-righteousness that could grate on the nerves of those less enthralled with the Holy Word than she was. And more than anything else, religion seemed to dominate Arlis's life.

Like her future husband, Arlis belonged to the Fellowship of Christian Athletes in Bismarck. She'd also joined Young Life, a student evangelical society whose members taught Sunday school, studied the Bible and strove to spread the Message to the masses. Included among those masses was the North Dakota drug culture.

And since Arlis didn't employ halfway measures when it came to her faith, she was an outgoing, insistent missionary of God.

Maybe it was there, in that consequential corner of her being, that she angered the devil.

*   *   *

There had been a boy in her life before Bruce, friends say, but they don't reveal much about him. Only that it was puppy love—hearts and flowers long consigned to a scrapbook by the time she and Bruce fell in love.

Their bond was their religion. Slowly at first, they were drawn together, and then the romance gathered steam. There was a period of dating and courtship; a year of long-distance engagement while Bruce scrambled through his freshman year at

Stanford; and finally, a picture-book wedding ceremony held at the Bismarck Reformed Church on August 17, 1974.

Then, after a week's honeymoon at a rustic cabin owned by Arlis's parents, it was back to business as the new Mr. and Mrs. Bruce Perry drove west and settled into their California home as September began.

Several weeks later, on October 1, one of the couple's major concerns evaporated when Arlis was hired as a receptionist at a Palo Alto law firm, where she listed her part-time experience at the Bismarck dental office of Duncan Perry as a reference.

The supplemental income would ease the financial strain, and Arlis also now had a way to fill her days while Bruce attended classes. In her free time, she continued to explore the expansive campus, often stopping to pray at the large, decorative Stanford Memorial Church in the quadrangle. Bruce, when his schedule allowed, would accompany her there.

* * *

Whether or not Arlis was slightly bored is impossible to determine. But she did miss her Bismarck family and friends. She was young, not accustomed to being away from home, and Bruce's responsibilities—which included tutoring freshmen in math—occupied much of his time.

In one letter to North Dakota she lamented: "Friends are hard to find here. Many times, I've been tempted to go knock on doors asking if anybody needs a friend. But I guess we just have to appreciate each other and trust the Lord for new friends, too."

Arlis also discovered pronounced lifestyle differences between the Dakotas and California. "Nobody [here] is very personal at all," she wrote. "They don't even say hello when you ride up the elevator with them."

Arlis was indeed a long way from home.

The Dakotas are ruggedly beautiful in their simplicity and remoteness. Ironically, while that inaccessibility has helped maintain a low crime rate, it has also contributed to the lawbreaking that does exist. Young people everywhere tinker with drugs and liquor, but in North Dakota experimentation sometimes lingers on because the state, and others like it, are devoid of the diversions available in more populous areas with major metropolitan centers. In short, some people can become burdened by too many "wide open spaces" for too long a time.

On the other hand, the Dakotas have been spared the incredible amount of crime which bubbles in the big cities, where low-income neighborhoods and industrial districts provide a conducive backdrop for organized mayhem of every variation: major-league narcotics dealing, murder, rape and mugging.

This new and fast-paced world was overwhelming to Arlis, who, like so many before her, suddenly found herself a small fish in a sizable pond. Bruce Perry empathized with his wife's adjustment phase, having endured it himself a year earlier. Sensing her mood that Saturday night, he decided to join her on the walk to the mailbox.

*   *   *

At about 11:30 p.m., apparently in good spirits, the young couple strolled from the high-rise campus apartment building. Engrossed in conversation, they ambled across the school grounds and suddenly began to argue. The reported subject was minor; ludicrous, in fact, unless other matters were occupying their minds at the time. A tire on their car was slowly losing air, and each thought the other should have filled it.

The bickering continued as they strode in the direction of the Memorial Church, which loomed before them in the distance. It was about 11:40 p.m.

Ostensibly miffed at Bruce, Arlis halted abruptly, faced him and emphatically stated that she wanted to be alone. She told her husband she intended to visit the church and would see him later at the apartment, which was about a half mile away.

Equally annoyed, Bruce turned from his wife and hastened back across the campus, oblivious to the sounds of revelry wafting around him as he walked. He didn't notice whether anyone was watching him.

At approximately 11:50 p.m., Arlis Perry pulled open the massive outer doors of Stanford Memorial and entered the foyer, where another set of portals offered access to the main body of the church.

Stanford Memorial is ornate and somewhat imposing. It is a decorous, breathtaking edifice, and as Arlis stepped inside she saw a veritable rainbow of scarlet and gold. There were rich velvet tapestries of red and purple, and montages, sculptures and candelabra of immaculately polished, glistening gold. Above it all was a magnificent golden dome.

In front of Arlis, and elevated several steps from the floor of the church, was the main altar. To either side were rounded alcoves which contained additional pews, all angled to face the altar. In rough outline form, the building resembled a thick, three-leafed clover, with the altar alcove in the center.

*   *   *

The church, as always, would be shuttered at midnight by a campus security guard. And since it was nearly twelve, only two other worshippers sat in a silent vigil of prayer. These young people, who occupied a pew to the right of the center aisle in the rear of the church, noticed Arlis in the subdued perimeter lighting as she softly padded down the main aisle, eased her way into one of the front rows on the left and knelt to pray.

For her nocturnal visit, Arlis dispensed with formality. She wore a dark brown jacket, a blouse, blue jeans and a pair of beige wedge-heeled shoes.

Bruce Perry, having returned to Quillen Hall, was still fidgety about the altercation with his wife. He probably gave no thought to the futility of mailing letters late on a Saturday night—Arlis's stated reason for wanting to go out. With no Sunday mail collection at Stanford, the letters wouldn't be processed until Monday morning.

It is also unlikely he considered the possibility that Arlis might have wished to go out alone and used the letters as an excuse for doing so. And he probably didn't reflect on how their argument grew so out of proportion—resulting in Arlis continuing to the church by herself. But there was no reason for Bruce Perry to have been analyzing such thoughts as he paced the apartment and worked out his irritation.

Back in the church, as Arlis meditated at midnight, the two worshippers behind her rose to leave. It was now closing time. Looking over their shoulders as they departed, they saw that Arlis hadn't moved from her pew. She was now alone in the cavernous house of worship.

Outside, a passerby spotted a young man who was about to enter the building. He was casually dressed and had sandy-colored hair which was parted on the left. He was of medium build and wore a royal blue short-sleeved shirt. He appeared to be around twenty-three to twenty-five years of age. For some reason, the witness noted the man wasn't wearing a watch.

*   *   *

Security guard Steve Crawford was a few minutes behind schedule when, at 12:10 a.m., he stood in the rear of the church, looked for stragglers and saw none. There was no sign of Arlis or the sandy-haired stranger. Crawford then spoke aloud into the apparently empty, dimly lit church: "We're closing for the night. The church is being locked for the night now. If anyone is here, you'll have to leave."

He was answered by his echo rebounding off the muted statues and shadowed walls and rolling slowly back to him. Satisfied, Crawford shut the doors, locked them and walked away—leaving Arlis Perry alone with the devil. In the house of God.

Almost certainly, she was already in Satan's grasp when Crawford voiced his notification. From wherever she was being hidden, she would have heard him calling out, listened to the great portals clanging shut and heard her heart pounding in the deathly stillness that followed.

But she probably never believed she wouldn't leave the church alive.

*   *   *

At about that moment, Bruce Perry was nervous. He disdained arguing over trivia. He was unhappy that his bride was alone somewhere on the campus after midnight, and he didn't take to cooling his heels waiting for her in the apartment.

So he hurriedly set off to rendezvous with Arlis. If the church was closed, their paths would cross on the way. But they didn't—and Bruce found himself puzzled and slightly concerned. It was now 12:15 a.m., and he stared at the front of the darkened church. The doors were locked. And where was Arlis? He walked around to a side entrance, which was also secured, and then circled to the rear of the building. But she wasn't there either. Bruce then decided to comb the campus and left.

At about this time, a passerby thought he discerned some noise inside the church, in the vicinity of the choir loft. But he was uncertain and kept walking.

Bruce's tour of the campus was futile. Growing increasingly anxious, he abandoned his search and returned to Quillen Hall. But Arlis wasn't there. He didn't think his wife had been *that* upset. And since she didn't know anyone at Stanford yet, she couldn't have just dropped in on some party. No, Bruce reasoned, she must be walking it off, calming herself down before coming home. And so Bruce Perry waited and worried.

At 2 a.m., on his next series of rounds, security guard Steve Crawford again checked the church. He tried all the doors and assured himself they were locked; he said later that he also walked through the building—as he was supposed to—and saw and heard nothing.

Across the campus Bruce Perry was in a quandary. At 3 a.m., he finally had enough and reached for the telephone. He dialed the Stanford security police and reported his wife missing, telling the dispatcher Arlis might have fallen asleep in the church and been locked in at midnight.

Responding to the call, Stanford officers went to the church. They would later say they examined its outer doors and found them locked. Unfortunately, that action was irrelevant. The police didn't go inside, which was the only way to learn if someone was indeed asleep in one of the pews. If they had, and if their statements and Crawford's account are correct, they would have met the killer.

This is so because, when Crawford next returned to the church at 5:30 a.m., a door on the right side was open—forced from the inside. His discovery suggested that someone broke out of the church after the 3 a.m. visit by the Stanford officers, which is possible but unlikely.

What is more credible is that Crawford, despite his statement, never entered the building at 2 a.m. and that the Stanford police didn't check all the doors an hour later. The time of Arlis's death would be fixed at approximately midnight, and it is improbable the killer or killers loitered in the church for three hours afterwards.

But now, at five thirty, alerted by the forced side door, Crawford cautiously entered the chapel. In the faint light, he quickly appraised the main altar to determine if anything valuable had been stolen. But nothing appeared to be disturbed, and so Crawford began a slow, wary walk around the perimeter aisle, peering apprehensively into the pews. It was then he discovered the missing Arlis Perry.

He wished he hadn't.

*　　*　　*

In the words of a church official who later viewed the scene, the sight was "ritualistic and satanic." And indeed, it was a vision from hell. Arlis was lying on her back, with her body partially under the last pew in the left-side alcove, a short distance from where she was last seen praying. Above her was a large carving which had been sculptured into the church wall years before. It was an engraving of a cross. The symbolism was explicit.

Arlis's head was facing forward, toward the main altar. Her legs were spread wide apart, and she was nude from the waist down. The legs of her blue jeans were spread-eagled upside down across her calves, purposely arranged in that manner.

Viewed from above, the resulting pattern of Arlis's legs and those of the inverted blue jeans took on a diamond-like shape.

Arlis's blouse was torn open and her arms were folded across her chest. Placed neatly between her breasts was an altar candle. Completing the desecration, another candle, thirty inches long, was in her vagina. But that wasn't all: she'd also been beaten and choked.

However, none of that butchery caused her death. Arlis Perry died because an ice pick had been rammed into her skull behind her left ear; its handle protruded grotesquely from her head.

None of this explicit information would reach the public.

* * *

Crawford, gagging at the horrible sight, fled the empty church and summoned his superiors. They, in turn, immediately called the Santa Clara County Sheriff's Department, which had criminal jurisdiction over the Stanford campus.

A team of uniformed officers and six detectives sped to the scene. Undersheriff Tom Rosa, viewing the body, quickly characterized the slaying as the work of a sexual psychopath. As the officials secured the church, other detectives went to the Perry apartment, believing, logically enough, that Bruce was a likely suspect.

In fact, when he opened the door for the police, he was nearly arrested on the spot. And not without reason. Bruce Perry was covered in blood.

The horror-stricken young athlete was told of his wife's death and questioned about the events of the night before. Through tears and agitation, Bruce tried to convince the detectives that the blood staining his shirt was his own. He explained that he was prone to nosebleeds when upset and said his anxiety about Arlis set off an attack. He pleaded with the police, who were skeptical, to put it mildly.

But a polygraph test and a check of the blood type would soon tell the story: it was indeed his own blood. Or at least, it wasn't Arlis's.

Most of the specific details about the murder were withheld, including the exact location of the stab wound and the fact that the weapon was recovered. Police will routinely conceal some pertinent information as a way to separate truth from fiction in the event a suspect is identified, or as a means of eliminating "bedbug" confessors. And in this instance, particulars weren't disclosed because of the revolting violation of the victim.

It was now a couple of hours past dawn, and the morning was blossoming into a bright and sunny Sunday. The air was clear, the sky was cloudless, but the night had yet to relinquish its grip. The damage done by the powers of darkness was still apparent as word spread across Stanford that something terrible had occurred in the church while the campus slept.

In a few hours, the Sunday service was scheduled to begin. But not this Sunday; not inside the church. Police and coroner's investigators sealed it off and pored through it looking for something—anything—that could lead them to the killer. The devil had claimed this Lord's day as his own.

Three members of the choir appeared at 9 a.m. to prepare selections for the fifty-member choral group. But they weren't allowed inside to retrieve their music until 10:15, when Arlis's body was finally rolled out on a gurney by downcast coroner's investigators.

As worshippers assembled for the 11 a.m. services, they mingled with a burgeoning crowd of media, police and curious, shocked students. Voices were hushed; occasionally a police radio crackled. Rev. Robert Hammerton-Kelly, dean of the church, had seen Arlis in death and was aghast. Visibly shaken, he was determined to hold the service out of doors in the rear of the church, where he told the congregation about the murder, saying the ceremony wasn't canceled because he "wasn't going to let evil triumph."

At four thirty that afternoon, the interior of the nondenominational church was turned back to God as Fathers John Duryea and Robert Giguere celebrated a Roman Catholic mass which began with a blessing scripted to reclaim Stanford Memorial from the forces of evil.

*   *   *

The Santa Clara Sheriff's Department was mounting its own campaign against the "forces of evil"—mainly by failing to see they existed. From the outset, the department's superior officers directed a hunt for a local sexual psychopath. Such preconceptions aren't unique to Santa Clara County, but in the Perry case they cost the police a realistic chance to locate the killer, or killers.

The top possible suspects at the beginning, of course, were Bruce Perry and security guard Steve Crawford. Ranked behind them was the "unknown sexual psychopath," who most probably was the sandy-haired young man seen entering the church at midnight.

That man's existence was withheld from the public, along with other details which might have dampened the sex crime theory. The fact that the murder occurred in a church meant little to the police, who didn't believe in symbolism—even when coupled with Arlis's own active religious background.

Also kept under wraps was the knowledge that FBI technicians in Washington, D.C., lifted a perfect palm print from the candle found in Arlis's vagina. That discovery finally eliminated Crawford and Bruce Perry as possible suspects, and eventually inspired the police to fingerprint more than a hundred other individuals who ranged from students and university employees to local sex deviants.

And yet, the biggest clues eluded them.

*   *   *

On Tuesday, October 15, the Stanford church was the setting for a memorial service for Arlis Perry. Bruce, his skin crawling at the prospect of walking into the scene of his wife's slaying, nonetheless swallowed his repulsion and attended. Seated in the front row with his father and uncle, who had flown in from Bismarck, Bruce and some hundred and fifty other mourners heard Rev. Hammerton-Kelly eulogize Arlis as a "member of the Body of Christ who was cut off as she prayed."

His voice ringing from the pulpit beneath the golden dome, Kelly noted that Christ, too, was "cruelly murdered by cruel and perverse men. He was a victim. Arlis, in her death, was like her Lord. I assure you that Arlis is with Christ in glory."

"Violence," Kelly intoned, his voice dropping, "has swept to the very altar of God."

The mourners then joined in several choruses of solemn hymns. Some wept open-ly; others dabbed their eyes with handkerchiefs; and more were on the verge of tears. Many in the church were classmates and friends of Bruce. Arlis hadn't been on the Coast long enough to make any friends—or enemies—of her own.

As the sorrowful throng waited for Bruce, his father and his uncle to file out after the service, one of the acquaintances Arlis had managed to make in the six weeks of her California life was startled. Mark Connors*[1] was looking at Bruce, and something was wrong.

Bruce Perry wasn't who he was supposed to be.

*　　*　　*

Mark Connors worked at the Palo Alto law firm of Spaeth, Blaise, Valentine and Klein, where Arlis was hired as a receptionist just two weeks before her death. In the church, Connors strained for a close look at Bruce. He met him outside, expressed his sympathy and then he knew for sure: Bruce Perry was not the man he believed was Bruce Perry.

Contacting the sheriff's office with a story that should have turned the investiga-tion around, but didn't, Connors recounted a dramatic event from the afternoon of Friday, October 11—the day before Arlis died.

It was noontime, and Arlis was behind her reception desk when a visitor appeared. Connors assumed it was Bruce Perry since Arlis was so new in California, and newer yet at her job. Who else would know where she worked?

Connors watched as Arlis and the young man engaged in a fifteen-minute con-versation he described as "serious and intense." He speculated that Arlis might have been angry at Bruce for coming to the office so soon after her hiring. Regardless, he decided, Bruce was a nice-looking young man who seemed to be in his early twenties. He was wearing jeans and a plaid shirt, and was husky, broad-shouldered and athletic-looking. He stood about five feet ten and had curly, blondish hair of "regular" length. He wasn't a hippie freak.

As the earnest discussion ended, Connors was surprised that Arlis didn't introduce him to Bruce. But if the topic of their talk was as important as it appeared to be, then perhaps Arlis reasoned this wasn't the time or place for social niceties, Connors thought.

---

1   Every person named in this writing is real. Only the names of certain confidential witnesses and living sus-pects have been changed, and those will be noted by an asterisk.

When the young man left, Arlis resumed her duties. She said nothing to Connors or anyone else about the visitor, leaving him with the impression that the young bride's husband dropped by unannounced to settle a pressing matter. Until the memorial service, Connors believed he had seen Bruce Perry. But now, he stated that it certainly hadn't been him after all.

The detectives took down the information and asked Bruce if he'd stopped at the law firm. He hadn't; and Bruce further advised the investigators that Arlis asked him not to call or visit there until she'd settled into the job.

Did she mention a visitor the day before she died? the police inquired. She hadn't, Bruce replied, adding that it wouldn't be unusual for Arlis to keep something from him if she thought the knowledge would be upsetting to him. (Arlis's friends in North Dakota would later make that same observation. Five years later.)

Well, the detectives continued, does this man sound like anyone you'd know? Bruce Perry shook his head. No, it didn't.

The police knew what Bruce was unaware of, but they disregarded the fact in their single-minded quest for a random sex pervert: the description of Arlis's visitor was similar to that of the man seen entering the church the next night. Surprisingly, they didn't assign a police artist to draw sketches of the two men for comparison or identification purposes.

And the questions that should have been asked were unspoken. Who was this man at the law office? Who knew Arlis was in California? Who knew where she worked? Could the killer have come from *Bismarck?* Is it possible the slaying wasn't the work of an area psycho after all? Could Arlis have actually known her killer? Is it possible this guy was from Bismarck, didn't know Bruce, but learned where Arlis was from others in North Dakota? Could he have known her family or Bruce's, who were among the few who did know that Arlis had recently found employment? Or could he have just known she was at Stanford, followed her around until he learned where she worked and then dropped in on her? And *why* did he materialize only a day before her death?

Could Arlis have known Bruce would have disapproved of whoever this was and consequently arranged to meet him secretly at the church and fabricated the letter mailing and argument to get Bruce out of the way? Or did she tell this guy to split when he came to the office—but he followed her the next night, saw the altercation with Bruce and seized the chance to kill her? If so, *why?*

There was no question that he had murder on his mind. The killer carried the ice pick into the church. It wasn't a weapon of opportunity. So was this a premeditated slaying and not a random sex crime at all?

But the questions weren't asked, or at least weren't pursued.

* * *

As the police hunted their Jack the Ripper in California, Arlis Perry returned to North Dakota.

She had left Bismarck in Bruce's automobile. She came home in a box.

The Bismarck Reformed Church, where the couple had been joyously married two months before, was the site of the funeral on Friday, October 18. As the bells pealed mournfully, about three hundred friends, relatives, former schoolmates and hangers-on filed into the church. Virtually everyone who had attended the wedding to wish Arlis a long and happy life gathered again to see her to her grave. There is a chance someone involved in the murder was among them.

It was a crushing experience for those close to Arlis. The wedding day was still fresh in their minds, too recent to have yet become a memory. Most hadn't even seen the bridal pictures yet. Arlis's parents, her sister Karen and brother Larry reacted to the death with total shock and disbelief. Bruce Perry found himself at the second service for his wife in three days. He'd lived the equivalent of a lifetime in eight weeks.

As he listened to the eulogy with his head lowered heavily onto his chest, Bruce heard Arlis described as a deeply committed Christian who lived a life dedicated to God and her fellow man. Her own words, now so distant and of yesterday, were spoken aloud by Rev. Don DeKok, who read from verses Arlis had underlined in her Bible and from marginal notes, such as "very nice."

As DeKok talked of Arlis, her friend Jenny closed her eyes and envisioned a golden day and an unseen California hill and meadow, from where Arlis had penned a letter on October 6, the Sunday before she died: "We're on a picnic right now. It's about 90 degrees and we're suntanning in the hills. Bruce is studying and I'm writing letters." Then, in a poignant irony, Arlis explained: "We went to the Stanford Church this morning. Maybe you remember me telling you about it. The guest speaker was Malcom Boyd, maybe you've heard of him. He's the author of *Are You Running with Me, Jesus?* I've never read the book, but I'm going to be sure to now."

No, Arlis, the crestfallen Jenny thought. You never got the chance.

In the pulpit, DeKok recalled a time when Arlis enunciated what Christ meant to her. She'd once thought of God as a judge seated behind a huge bench who pointed a finger down at her when she'd done wrong, the pastor remembered, quoting Arlis as not believing she could be significant to "such a big God. But when I realized he really does care for me," she said, "it was like a choir of angels bursting into song."

But Arlis's song had been stilled forever.

*   *   *

Throughout Bismarck, as the reality set in, grief succumbed to fury as people asked why. Murder was an intrusion in Bismarck, an aberration. Murder belonged in the big cities—not in their territory. More people were killed in New York City in a week than in Bismarck in a year, they said. And they were right. And the bitterness intensified.

Inevitably, California was raked over for spawning the slime that would brutally murder a young girl—and in a church, besides. A double desecration. And indeed, it was. But as righteously as California could be indicted for a century of sins, there were those hints, those indications, that perhaps this time wasn't one of them. The families didn't know that; neither did the press or the public. The Santa Clara detectives knew; but seeing, they were blind. They were running their own game, working their own leads—convinced the killer was from the neighboring area.

But the signs were there. They weren't totally in focus, but the faint lettering which appeared read: "Bismarck."

First, of course, was the puzzling incident of Arlis's visitor, who entered her California life just thirty-six hours before it ended. The police considered that he might merely have been a delivery man or a prospective client of the law firm, but that couldn't hold up for various reasons. But most important, the intense, fifteen-minute discussion demonstrated that Arlis either knew the young man or else he was bearing a message from someone she did know.

Where did the people whom Arlis knew live? They resided in North Dakota, not on the West Coast. And if there in fact was a motive for the killing, it would be hidden in Bismarck, not Palo Alto. But the sheriff's investigators didn't make the connection.

They still didn't budge two weeks later, around Halloween, when another bizarre incident occurred which should have sent the red flags flying. And it even happened in Bismarck.

At Arlis's grave.

At the time of her burial, a temporary marker was placed at the site until a permanent stone could be readied. It was stolen. Random vandalism was ruled out as no other markers were disturbed. Only Arlis's.

A sick souvenir? It certainly was. Santa Clara detectives already knew of two other "souvenirs" involved in the case: personal possessions of Arlis which were removed from the murder scene by the killer or killers. Trophies. Reminders. Proof that the job was done by whoever was supposed to do it.

The public didn't know this, just as it wasn't aware of the visitor to the law firm or the man at the church. But the police did know. And yet they reacted stoically to the news of the theft in Bismarck. That wasn't the only time information was backburnered. There was still another incident, just as ominous, which was halfheartedly pursued—and dropped.

The details were provided by Bruce Perry's parents. They'd heard a story, a tale which unsettled them, and they wondered if it was possibly connected to the murder.

According to word on the streets in Bismarck, Arlis and a girlfriend—whose name the Perrys didn't know—had crossed the river from Bismarck to neighboring Mandan one day to try to convert members of some satanic cult to Christianity. That sounded like Arlis.

The unknown girlfriend, the Perrys believed, was probably a member of Young Life, the student religious organization. The incident was said to have occurred during the year Bruce was at Stanford and Arlis in Bismarck. Yes, the Perrys agreed, it might only be a rumor. But in light of Arlis's death in a church and the theft of the grave marker in Bismarck, they felt the California police should be aware of it.

The Santa Clara detectives were 1,700 miles from Bismarck, and they lacked the manpower or budget to conduct an intensive investigation in North Dakota. And they still believed the killer was a local sex marauder. So with some degree of routine assistance from Bismarck authorities, they made a cursory check to try to solidify the information. A number of Young Life officials were questioned about the incident. Interestingly, people *had* heard of it, but no one seemed to know exactly when it happened or the name of the girl who allegedly accompanied Arlis that day.

And so it died; and other details which could have proved vital to the investigation would also lay dormant for years.

Time crept by, and except for periodic "anniversary" stories, Arlis's name disappeared from California news columns. In the Sheriff's Department, her file gradually drifted to an "open but inactive" drawer. Detective Sergeant Ken Kahn and his partner, Tom Beck—who weren't assigned to the case at its outset—were now appointed to monitor the search and pursue new leads, if and when any surfaced.

About every six months, Arlis's parents would phone the sheriff's office to learn if any progress had been made. Bruce Perry, who eventually graduated from Stanford and became a doctor, would do the same. But the answer from Kahn and Beck was always no. There was nothing to report—then.

It was still several years before the chilling handwritten clue, "arlis perry: hunted, stalked and slain. followed to california," would be scrawled across a page in a book about satanism and secreted from the confines of a forbidding New York prison.

But those haunting days were yet to dawn.

And as of the summer of 1977, the murder of the young Christian bride remained unsolved.

The Gun of August

Slowly, because that's the way it was done, he crept closer. Quietly, trying not to make a sound. Stealth, he knew, was essential. His quarry was elusive and easily spooked. He'd already missed several opportunities this day. But not this time. This one was ready to be taken. Now.

He dropped the net and the blue crab slithered mindlessly away.

"Son of a bitch," George Austin muttered. He raised the net again and slammed it into the water in frustration.

"These things are made for fish—not crabs! Don't you know that?"

Behind him, nearer to shore, I started laughing. "They're gonna recall your Gold Glove award," I shouted. "You'd better stick with the clams. They don't move as fast."

Austin, thirty-one, a brown-haired insurance broker and a friend for five years, turned around, grumbled unfavorably about my lineage and began inching a path farther out from Davis Park, Fire Island, into the Great South Bay. I decided to join him, and soon found myself just as luckless in the quest for a seafood dinner.

If the summer of 1977 was such a bountiful one for crabs, then where the hell were they? The bay water was warm and glistening in the late-day sun as we waded along, nets in hand, probing the shallow water for the slowly propelling shadow that signaled supper was near.

"I feel like an antisubmarine pilot," George complained.

"Yeah, this is different."

It wasn't this way in Rockaway Beach in the early fifties, when, as a child of six, I'd go crabbing daily while on vacation. Rockaway, in those days, was the borough of Queens's halfhearted answer to the New Jersey ocean resorts. All the Irish in Yonkers rented bungalows in Rockaway then, it seemed. But crabs never swam like this in Rockaway Bay. In fact, I couldn't remember them swimming at all.

My father, my grandfather and I would stand on a pier, drop collapsible wire nets over the side, let them hit bottom and open. Then it was a matter of waiting for the crabs to crawl onto the wire and nibble at fish bait tied inside. Raise the line, the cage closed, and hello, dinner. Times had certainly changed. And so had I.

I was nearing thirty-one that summer of 1977. In the nine years since college, I worked at IBM in Westchester County, in the northern suburbs of New York City, as an editor and feature writer for a number of the company's publications. It was good, decent work and it paid fairly well, but I found myself restless—a wayward wind skimming the land for something new; something more.

For as long as I could remember, I sought challenges. And that sometimes bothered me because I felt I should be more settled. Many of my contemporaries were secure with their jobs and families. Content with nine to five. I wasn't. Why that was so, I couldn't answer. But that quizzical trait would soon involve me in the most bizarre, frustrating and yet rewarding experience I'd ever known. In a short time, my career and life would be changed forever.

I'd joined IBM rather than write for the Westchester newspaper chain. As a varsity baseball player and golfer with a competent background in football and basketball, I landed a part-time sports-reporting job while still in college. But I became terribly disillusioned in the aftermath of Martin Luther King's murder in April 1968.

Working alone that night in Port Chester, New York, for the *Daily Item*, I returned from covering a basketball tournament to find a two-block stretch of downtown in shambles. Fires, rioters and looters ran wild. The police and firefighters seemed helpless as they ducked bricks, bottles and garbage being tossed at them from rooftops and tenement windows. I stood with them on the street that night, all of twenty-one years of age, and went back to the paper to write the story.

The *Item* was a small afternoon paper then, and I manned the office alone at night. So I let myself into the darkened building and typed the piece as I'd seen it.

There had been extensive property damage, some nineteen arrests, and several dozen others could have been booked. But the editors killed the story, compiled their own and buried it around page ten with a headline that said, in effect, "Sporadic Violence Hits Village."

The next day I drove with my girlfriend from my home twenty miles away in Yonkers just to obtain a copy of the paper that didn't print my story. I then took her through the urban battlefield so she could satisfy herself that I wasn't hallucinating. She was stunned, and we both learned a lesson we wouldn't forget. I saw how the game was sometimes played and gladly accepted IBM's offer. Since that time, the ownership of the Westchester newspapers passed to the Gannett Corporation, and standards changed for the better. But it was too late for me. Or so I thought.

Within the corporate world I survived, even prospered; a victim and yet a beneficiary of this compulsion to explore new horizons. I also did some freelance work in the music and travel businesses and was a partner in an investigative sports journalism TV project that almost—but not quite—made it to the air.

But full-time employment did have its advantages, such as paid vacations. And that's what I was doing on Fire Island on Saturday, July 30, 1977—enjoying the last two days of a leisurely ten at a friend's beach house.

*   *   *

"What's new with Sam?" George Austin cut in, knowing my fascination with the sensational series of murders that was immobilizing New York City. It was a guaranteed conversation starter. I wasn't the only one engulfed in that drama. Everyone, it seemed, was following the saga very closely, including George "McCloud" Austin, so nicknamed because of his resemblance to Dennis Weaver's TV detective.

I didn't have any special knowledge of the case. I wasn't then part of the media or law enforcement fraternities. I was an outsider reading the newspapers, watching television and listening to radio to absorb all I could about Son of Sam. Like thousands of others, I was trying to figure out who—or what—he was; and where he was.

It was an incredible time, for never before had one, single ongoing criminal investigation captured the attention and dominated the thinking of an entire metropolitan region the way New York was mesmerized and terrorized by the Son of Sam slayings.

Looking west across the Great South Bay in the general direction of the distant, invisible city, George continued: "The sun'll be down in a few hours. Nothing happened last night when they thought it would. Maybe tonight . . . ?"

"I don't know. If I had that answer I wouldn't be playing Sea Hunt now. But sure, it could be tonight. Maybe the bastard caught the flu yesterday, or maybe he chickened out. Or maybe he died. Or maybe—shit, I don't know. I'll tell you, though, I don't envy those cops. This is one hell of an unbelievable case."

"Yeah." George nodded. "The big anniversary day is over. Maybe he won't venture out tonight either. But he's over there somewhere on the mainland. . . . Just as long as he doesn't take the ferry out to here," he added dryly.

*   *   *

On Fire Island, the terror consuming New York seemed far more removed than a ferry ride. It seemed a continent, a lifetime away—rather than the forty-five or so miles it actually was into the outlying boroughs. For the past five months, since early March, the city had been aware that a deranged psychopath was on the loose; shooting down young girls and couples as they embraced in parked cars on lovers' lanes or near discos, stood on porches or walked the night streets. The toll was holding at eleven: five dead, six wounded.

Son of Sam, or the .44-Caliber Killer, had begun his work on July 29, 1976, a year and a day earlier. But the New York City Police Department had taken more than seven months—five separate attacks—to decide it was chasing one gun; that all the shootings were related. As public recognition of the menace grew, so did the fear. The newspapers, particularly the tabloid *News* and *Post,* fanned the flames and outdid themselves on the anniversary date of the first shooting.

That was yesterday, and the killer hadn't struck, although he'd hinted at an anniversary attack in a macabre letter sent in June to *Daily News* columnist Jimmy Breslin. "What will you have for July 29?" he teased.

New York's mayor, Abraham Beame, up for reelection, knew what *he'd* have: the biggest dragnet in the city's history blanketing the boroughs of Queens and the Bronx—Son of Sam's exclusive hunting grounds. This was well and good, but Beame chose to make the announcement in full view of the ever-watchful eyes of the cameras, resulting, some thought, in a direct dare to the killer to strike on that night.

If that was so, Son of Sam decided to pass; and the twenty-ninth of July oozed by without incident.

However, the sounds of silence on the twenty-ninth didn't abate the deathwatch over the city, which had been operating on the fringes of mass hysteria for months. Thousands of girls with long hair were still cutting it short—because all the victims happened to have had long hair. And since that hair happened to have been brown in color, blond wigs were still selling out in stores from Floral Park in Queens to Van Cortlandt Park in the Bronx. And television crews were still stalking beauty parlors across the city to record the shearing and bleaching for showcasing on the nightly news broadcasts.

The tastelessness spread to the citizenry, too. Because of the extensive publicity surrounding the case, the NYPD's suspect file was bulging with an inconceivable seven thousand names. Some were young men whose jilted girlfriends were determined to even a score, or loan sharks whose clients were hopeful of short-lived reprieves while the police investigated the tipsters' allegations.

Other suspects were sons believed by their elderly widowed mothers to be exhibiting abnormal behavior. And some were genuine loonies whose names were forwarded to other police jurisdictions for future reference, if and when the detectives who checked the original information remembered to do so. Often, they didn't.

In one case, a young woman from Westchester contacted authorities to advise she was certain her ex-husband was the killer. To quote from the official report:

> She said that just before her divorce he told her that one of the things he will miss is her long brown hair. She also stated that he loved Italian girls [most of the victims to that point were Italian-American]. He has sexual hang-ups and wanted her to get into the sadomasochistic scene with ropes.

In addition, this suspect, from whom police *did* obtain a handwriting sample to compare with the block-lettered Son of Sam notes, also went to discos and topless bars; wore a wig; was brought up in the neighborhood of two of the shootings; owned guns; "shot" at the TV when he thought no one was around; thought his sexual equipment was under par; and besides all that, looked like police artists' sketches of the Son of Sam. Or so the wife said.

In yet another incident, two Westchester residents believed they knew the gunman's identity, so they took it upon themselves to drag him to his father's grave to coax a dramatic confession from him. He refused to admit his guilt, however, so they decided to beat him with baseball bats to "get it out of him." Still no go. The "killer" was seriously injured, and the two vigilantes were promptly arrested.

In other graveyard occurrences, police were sent to investigate reports that men were seen dancing on the graves of two .44 victims; one at a Queens cemetery, the other in the Bronx. A Bronx cemetery worker was questioned and released. No one was identified in the Queens incident.

*   *   *

Each of these leads, no matter how outlandish or unlikely, had to be investigated, to some degree at least, by the Police Department's task force, whose burgeoning ranks included many of the elite of the city's detective corps. The problem was, they weren't doing much detecting: they were pushing paper and chasing wild geese all over the metropolitan area. It was demoralizing; and as those on the inside knew well, there was little guidance and barely any communication between teams and shifts.

Detectives would find themselves tuning in the TV news to learn what had happened that day in their own investigation, for, eager to see their faces on camera and their names in print, some task force supervisors were perfectly willing to discuss the case at length with the media.

On most days, the task force headquarters at the 109th Precinct in Queens resembled a Hollywood set with camera and sound equipment scattered about.

Internally, the special command was known as "Omega." "As in 'watch'"—watch TV to find out what's going on—was the derisive dismissal of the group's effectiveness by some who were there. Nonetheless, by late July about three hundred police, a force larger than most departments in the United States, would be punching their clocks at Omega.

And all the while, the panic was spreading. Coveys of psychics visited crime scenes and issued mystically inspired descriptions of the killer and his getaway cars. Numerologists, soothsayers, magicians and housewives from Queens were tying up police phones for hours pushing their own theories on the killer's identity and motivation.

Motivation. That's where the psychiatrists came in. From studying the incidents and the letter to Breslin, every psychiatrist in the Manhattan Yellow Pages, it seemed, had an opinion on the case; and many of those analyses wormed their way into the newspapers. One of the more popular offerings went like this:

> *Son of Sam was a loner. He hated women and was killing young girls with long brown hair because he'd been rejected by such a girl. His .44 was really a surrogate penis, and when he was firing it he was really copulating. He was a quiet type who blended right into the crowd. He was religious, and alternately felt he was doing God's will and possessed by demons. He attended Catholic schools. The name Son of Sam was a play on "Samson"—whose hair was cut off by a woman. Son of Sam was emasculated by a woman.*

The press, anxious for stories on the slow days between attacks, dutifully gave gobs of space to these scatter-gun diagnoses. On one occasion the *Post* even carried a story about a misguided but well-meaning priest who offered himself as a hostage to the murderer.

Also during that summer, it seemed as if the media were running a "Surrender to Me" contest among the city's journalists, as Breslin and Pete Hamill of the *News*, the *Post*'s Steve Dunleavy and a couple of TV reporters all appealed to Son of Sam to turn himself in—to them.

Even the *Times,* the aristocratic gray lady of 43rd Street, was dipping her crumpet in the killer's cup, devoting extensive space to the investigation. That must have flustered its editors, who liked to consider "the paper of record" above such things as mass murder. But by late June the *Times* realized the killer was "fit to print" in a big way and joined the fray in earnest, along with *Newsweek, Time* and other publications from coast to coast and in Europe.

It was difficult not to become immersed in the hysteria, particularly when a number of citizens' groups, media outlets and corporations began offering reward money that totaled $40,000. But much of the panic was overreaction. The odds against a particular person being shot were immense. There were eleven victims as of July 30. Out of how many millions? Still, it was a horrible, grim lottery.

"Hello from the gutters of N.Y.C. which are filled with dog manure, vomit, stale wine, urine, and blood," Sam had written Breslin in early June. Then, with words that might have flowed from the pen of Poe, he reminded the world: "I am still here. Like a spirit roaming the night. Thirsty, hungry, seldom stopping to rest."

The letter was fascinating in its flawless horror and vivid imagery. The case itself was hypnotic. It was the greatest manhunt in New York history, a deadly game between the hunted and the hunters. The letter to Breslin topped it off.

Usually, people don't learn of a crime until after it is committed. But with Son of Sam it was much different. People were looking over their shoulders, knowing he was out there *before* he struck. He was terror with a name, an identity; the equivalent of the dreaded great white shark stalking the ocean shores. People in New York felt the fear and became personally involved in the case. The victims were young, white, middle-class and Roman Catholic, it so happened. Sam had invaded the bedrooms and watering holes of working-class New York.

The discos in his two targeted boroughs thus far—Queens and the Bronx—were empty. Businesses were suffering. The streets were deserted by midnight.

New York, on July 30, 1977, was a city under siege.

But how did it get that way?

* * *

According to what the public knew at the time, it had begun quietly on Thursday morning, July 29, 1976, in the northeast Bronx as Michael and Rose Lauria were returning to their roomy, fourth-floor apartment at 2860 Buhre Avenue in the predominantly Italian-American Pelham Bay section. It was 1 a.m.

Lauria, a bus company employee in Manhattan, and Rose, an administrative worker at New York Hospital, also in Manhattan, were coming home after attending a wake and stopping briefly at a local restaurant, the Chateau Pelham.

As they neared their building, they recognized the 1975 blue-and-white Oldsmobile double-parked in front. It belonged to Jody Valente, nineteen, a student nurse and close friend of the Laurias' daughter Donna, eighteen. Jody was behind the wheel talking with Donna, who sat beside her in the passenger's seat. Donna had medium-length dark hair and light brown eyes. She was a pretty young woman, popular, and dated often. She was currently on the "outs" with a boyfriend.

The two girls were back from an evening at a discotheque in nearby New Rochelle, located on the Long Island Sound in southeastern Westchester County. The disco's name was Peachtree, and in time it—and New Rochelle—would figure prominently in the Son of Sam story. Donna and Jody, who herself was a pretty girl with shoulder-length, flowing brown hair, were regulars at Peachtree's Wednesday night backgammon tournaments.

The Laurias paused to speak with the girls, and Mike reminded Donna to come upstairs soon because she was due at work in the morning. As he looked up from his conversation with his daughter, Mike Lauria noticed a yellow compact-sized auto double-parked across the street and about twenty yards behind Jody's car. It was occupied by a lone male driver.

Unknown to Mike, neighbors had spotted a similar, unfamiliar vehicle cruising the area several hours before—at about the time Donna went out.

"Make sure you don't stay down here too long," Mike advised. He was understanding of the comings and goings of his sons, Louis and Michael, but was more protective of Donna, his only girl.

Donna offered a compromise, saying she'd wait with Jody while her father went upstairs and brought down her poodle, Beau. Then they'd walk the dog together. Mike Lauria agreed, and he and Rose entered the tan brick apartment building and rode the elevator to the fourth floor. On the street, Donna and Jody continued their conversation.

Donna, who'd been sickly as a child, had blossomed into a healthy young woman. Perhaps remembering her past, she chose a career in the medical field and was now employed as a technician by the Empire State Ambulance Service in Manhattan.

Jody Valente, the student nurse, was a neighbor as well as a friend to Donna and her family. She lived with her parents just three blocks away, at 1918 Hutchinson River Parkway.

*   *   *

At 1:10 a.m., Donna bid good night to Jody and turned to open the door of the double-parked Olds. As her hand pulled the latch open, she saw a young man standing on the curb about eight feet away, toward the rear of the car. Donna was startled. "Now what is this . . . " she started to say. They were her last words.

The man on the curb pulled a gun from the brown paper bag he was carrying, put both hands on the weapon, crouched slightly and fired three shots into the car. Donna raised her right arm as the bullets shattered the closed passenger's window. One of the slugs entered above her right elbow, traveled downward through her forearm, exited beneath her wrist, entered her back and killed her instantly. Donna tumbled from the car and hit the pavement with a sickening thud.

Another bullet, apparently aimed at Donna as well, tore into Jody Valente's left thigh. The third missed.

His work done, the killer turned and walked around the corner of Buhre and Mayflower avenues and into infamy.

Rose Lauria looked directly down from her kitchen window on the fourth floor in response to the noise below. She heard Jody Valente's horn blaring and she watched curiously as Jody crawled from the car and hobbled back and forth in the middle of the street, shouting at the top of her voice. Then it dawned on Rose: Jody was crying for help.

Mike Lauria was in the stairwell with the poodle when he heard the series of explosions. He raced outside to Jody's car and she screamed to him, "Donna! Donna!" Mike Lauria looked down to the pavement and saw his stricken daughter. He rode with her in the ambulance, holding her hand and pleading with her not to die, but it was too late.

As for the wounded Jody, her mental anguish was more severe than her thigh injury, which was promptly treated. When police visited the hospital, she was nearly hysterical. But after a time, she provided a detailed description of the gunman:

> Male white, 30s, 5'9", 160 pounds. Curly, dark hair; mod style. Clean-shaven. Light complexion. Wearing a blue polo shirt with white stripes. Dark pants.

Although no one knew it, the Son of Sam case had begun.

* * *

There are typically more than 1500 murders in New York City annually, and many of them—because of their "routine" nature, or because the victim was a drifter, or a bum, or even a minority—get short shrift in the newspapers. But a young white girl from a middle-class family who was slain in a car for no apparent reason was unique enough to be reported in some detail by the city's press corps.

Still, within days the story of Donna's death faded from the public consciousness.

The name of Donna Lauria wouldn't surface again until February 1, 1976, six months later.

For the police responsible for bringing her killer to ground, Donna's name remained an important one. The investigation of her murder was handled by the 8th Homicide Zone, which covered the Pelham Bay area. At that time, homicide detectives were a breed apart, the elite of the NYPD. The city was divided into districts or "zones" of homicide, with the detectives assigned to each responsible for the slayings that occurred within those boundary lines.

The homicide cops worked only murder cases. Other officers handled robbery, burglary, vice, organized crime, etc. It was an efficient system, allowing for much-needed specialization in homicide investigations. It has since been discarded.

But at the outset of the Lauria probe, the police knew two things. One: Jody Valente said she didn't recognize the killer; and two: the ballistics examination indicated the weapon used was a large-caliber handgun—a .44-caliber Bulldog revolver—not a common firearm in New York.

A powerful weapon that fires five rounds, the Bulldog is designed for only one purpose: to kill people. And, at close range, it is effective. Its drawbacks are that it is difficult to control because of a strong recoil, or "kick," and it isn't very accurate beyond a distance of some twenty feet—after which the velocity of the bullets also decreases markedly.

For want of any other apparent motive, the detectives believed that one of Donna's former or current boyfriends was somehow involved in the killing; or that the attack was the result of an organized crime mistake—a "hit" on the wrong person. There had been some mob-related activity in the general vicinity in the preceding few months, including a couple of shootings. The police speculated that some contract killer may have shot Donna in a case of mistaken identity. Such things had happened before.

Much to his chagrin, some detectives began to insinuate that bus company employee Mike Lauria was himself "connected" to organized crime. Mike, to understate the issue, was livid.

These theories never reached the public, however. The existence of the double-parked, compact yellow car and the sighting of a similar auto several hours before the shooting were also withheld.

The investigation, after some promising early leads evaporated, went nowhere. And as of October 23, there was no progress to report in the Lauria case and, barring new developments, the folder would find its way to an "open but inactive" file.

*   *   *

At 1:15 a.m. on Saturday October 23, Rosemary Keenan, eighteen, the daughter of an NYPD detective, and Carl Denaro, twenty, a former department store record salesman and security guard at Citibank in Manhattan, left a Flushing, Queens, bar called Peck's and rode a half dozen blocks in her navy blue Volkswagen to a darkened spot in a residential area near the corner of 159th Street and 33rd Avenue.

With brown shoulder-length hair, Denaro had tried to picture himself as he'd look in a week's time, after the Air Force—which he'd just joined—trimmed his tonsorial splendor to meet military regulations.

Keenan, a student at Queens College, knew Denaro casually before their late-night encounter at Peck's, where Denaro was toasting his final days as a civilian. Invited to join the party, she had; and now the two were escaping the madding crowd for a few moments alone before Rosemary's curfew time.

Denaro was in the passenger's seat as the bug slowed to a halt on the quiet, tree-lined block. After turning off the engine, Rosemary glanced in her rearview mirror and noticed the passing of a solitary jogger as he crossed her line of vision.

Then, for a short five minutes, their world was still—until 1:30 a.m., when it exploded around them in a shower of glass.

As the couple reflexively ducked in shock and surprise, both the driver's and the passenger's window blew out with a deafening roar, and the speedometer suddenly shattered—its needle jolting forward and jamming stuck at "30."

Large-caliber bullets whining through the front passenger's window were causing the eruption. Other slugs slammed into the right side and roof of the VW as the gunman apparently struggled to adjust to the weapon's recoil. In contrast with the Lauria shooting, the assailant was having some trouble.

But neither Rosemary nor Denaro knew they were being fired on—not even when Denaro felt the force of something slicing through the back of his head on the right side. Instinctively, he reached behind and put his hand into his own warm, seeping blood.

"Get out of here! Get out of here!" he screamed.

Rosemary lunged for the ignition switch, clicked it on, ground the Beetle into first gear, and the car lurched forward as she struggled to regain her composure and cope with the reluctant clutch.

Shaking, crying, she stared at Carl and was horrified to see he was covered with blood. Disoriented, not thinking clearly enough to drive to a hospital, she sped the six blocks back to Peck's, where they both staggered inside. Denaro, still not knowing he'd been shot, collapsed.

He would spend the next three weeks in Flushing Hospital and return there for an additional ten days on January 20. As Jimmy Carter was taking the oath of office as President of the United States, doctors were implanting a steel plate into Denaro's head.

Rosemary Keenan escaped unhurt. The attacker, perhaps mistaking Denaro for a woman because of his long hair, had vented his fury at the young man instead of the short-haired college student.

If Carl Denaro had been less of a "hippie," Rosemary Keenan might not be alive today.

The Queens detectives from the 109th Precinct assigned to the case learned from the NYPD's ballistics laboratory that a .44-caliber handgun was used to shoot Denaro. Beyond that, the ballistics technicians were stymied due to the deformed condition of the slugs. They couldn't determine any particular make or model of .44.

All of the NYPD's ballistics work was performed in the same lab in Manhattan, whether a shooting occurred there or in Queens, Brooklyn, Staten Island or the Bronx. So into a file went the slides and bullets recovered from the Denaro assault. The evidence obtained from the Lauria scene in the Bronx already lay in another folder in the lab.

With no answers forthcoming from the ballistics examination, the detectives pursued other avenues. Rosemary Keenan's father, Redmond, a second-grade detective with more than twenty years' experience, participated in the probe. But there were no witnesses to the attack, and nothing in Denaro's background—or Rosemary's—surfaced as a possible motive. So, as with the Lauria case three months earlier, the inquiry went nowhere.

Lack of apparent motive aside, no one noted the similarities between the shootings: young people, late at night, shot in cars for no discernible reason. No one pointed out that some type of .44 revolver was used in both incidents. The attacks, which occurred in boroughs separated by the short spans of the Throgs Neck and Whitestone bridges, might as well have happened six thousand miles apart.

Carl Denaro's wounding was in and out of the newspapers in the course of one day.

The next assault in the lengthening string would in time develop into one of the most critical and telling episodes in the saga of Sam. This was so because, in contrast to the Denaro case, there were witnesses—three of them. Two would look straight into the shooter's face from less than ten feet away. He would even speak to them. These were the two young victims, who would survive to describe the event in detail and provide descriptions of the gunman which would differ markedly from Jody Valente's eyewitness portrayal of the man who murdered Donna Lauria.

*   *   *

Saturday, November 27, 1976, began with a blustery binge as a chilling wind whipped through the canyons of midtown Manhattan carrying scraps of paper, debris and yesterday's headlines through the midnight air.

On various street corners in the Broadway area, the hardiest of vendors—wearing ancient woolen caps with earflaps lowered—huddled near their carts of roasting chestnuts. The smoldering aromas, tipped skyward by the wind, blended with the assorted litter gusting its way from gutter to sidewalk to doorway.

Leaving the movie theater, the two young friends bundled themselves against the sudden cold and hastened for the warmth of the underground station. Soon a graffiti-splashed subway train, clattering and swaying on its path beneath the East River, took them home to Queens.

In their borough again, they left the train at 179th Street and Hillside Avenue and boarded a bus that brought them to the corner of Hillside and 262nd Street, less than a block from Joanne Lomino's house.

Joanne, eighteen, graduated from Martin Van Buren High School the preceding summer and was seeking a job as a secretary. So far, she hadn't found anything to her liking. But since she lived at home with her parents, the pressure to find regular employment wasn't excessive—although her family was hopeful she'd find full-time work before the new year began.

Her companion, Donna DeMasi, was sixteen and still enrolled at Van Buren. She was tall, slender and attractive, and her long dark hair contrasted with Joanne's, whose blond tresses were shorter.

After stepping from the bus, the girls walked leisurely down 262nd Street, talking animatedly as they went. It was a good time of the year. The family get-togethers of Thanksgiving were just two days previous, and the girls were now anticipating the Christmas season.

When they reached the front of the Lomino home—a small, two-story dwelling with a modest front yard cut by a walk which led to a tiny cement porch—Joanne and Donna continued their conversation on the steps. Across from the house a powerful streetlamp cast a reassuring halo of light on the immediate area. Now mindless of the cold, the two teenagers chatted on for several more minutes.

And then they saw him.

Actually, Donna spotted him first. But as he strode onto the grass and halted just eight feet from the girls, Joanne—who'd been facing sideways with her back to the man—looked over her shoulder to study him also.

He was dressed in what appeared to be a green form-fitting, three-quarter-length coat, perhaps an Army fatigue jacket. He was slim—about 150 to 160 pounds—and stood about five feet eight. His hair was longish, straight, parted and dirty blond in color. His eyes were a piercing dark brown.

The girls were somewhat nervous, but not frightened by the man, who seemed to be lost. As if to confirm their speculation, he began speaking in a high-pitched voice: "Can you tell me how to get . . . "

He never finished the question. Instead, he yanked a revolver from his coat and began firing. Joanne, still with her back to the gunman although her face was looking into his, was jarred sideways as the first slug tore into her spinal cord and continued on, puncturing a lung.

Donna, on a lower step, was struck next as she lunged away from the spitting gun. The large-caliber bullet entered the base of her neck and barely missed her spine.

Like fragile, broken mannequins, the two girls tumbled from opposite sides of the porch and into the surrounding bushes. The attacker kept firing, the remaining bullets splattering the front of the house and smashing the living-room window.

His weapon finally empty, the gunman fled down 262nd Street toward 81st Avenue as a witness, who heard the shots, ran outside and watched closely as he hurried by, carrying the gun in his left hand.

*   *   *

Donna DeMasi lay in Long Island Jewish Hospital for nearly three weeks recovering from her wound and wore a neck brace for months afterward. Joanne Lomino wasn't as "fortunate." Her stay at Long Island Jewish lasted three months and was followed by another 120 days at the Rusk Institute in Manhattan, where she underwent rehabilitation therapy. She was now a paraplegic and would live the rest of her life in a wheelchair.

The investigation of the assault fell to the detectives at Queens's 105th Precinct. Once again, the ballistics people were unable to be of much help since the recovered bullets were too deformed for any precise comparisons to be made. Beyond the conclusion that the slugs came from some model of .44 revolver, the laboratory analysis was fruitless.

And as in the cases of Donna Lauria and Carl Denaro, background checks on the victims uncovered no apparent motive for the attack. Still, no one connected the three incidents. As the Christmas season came and went, there were no further developments in any of the cases.

Three composite sketches had been prepared: one from Jody Valente's description of the Lauria killer; another from a combined effort by Joanne Lomino and Donna DeMasi; and a third from the witness who saw the assailant flee that scene.

The two Queens sketches were very similar, differing primarily on the location of the part in the attacker's long, straight, blondish hair. The girls remembered the part was on the left side; the witness recalled it was on the right. But that a part *did* exist was not in question.

In any event, the drawings looked nothing like that of the man who murdered Donna Lauria—whose hair was dark and curled into a bushy "perm." That man was also younger and heavier than the Lomino-DeMasi shooter; and his nose, eyes and mouth were shaped differently from those of the Queens assailant.

And still another Queens resident would be the next to fall to the nameless force behind the .44. And she would die.

*   *   *

The new year, 1977, was the "Year of the Cat," and Al Stewart's haunting hit of that title climbed the charts in the early months. It was midwinter, and it was freezing, bitter cold. On January 29, the mercury in New York registered a scant fourteen degrees above zero as midnight neared. Three thousand miles to the west on this Saturday, comedian Freddie Prinze had just died from a bullet wound in the head— self-inflicted in a "tragic accident."

In Forest Hills, Queens, in the shadow of the West Side Tennis Club—then the site of the U.S. Open—Christine Freund, a twenty-six-year-old secretary, would become victim number six. Several years later, the events surrounding Christine's murder would provide pivotal clues in the search for the conspirators who aided David Berkowitz in the shootings. But for the present, the following highlights will outline the story:

Austrian-born Christine Freund, a diminutive five feet two, was a beautiful young woman with long, dark brown hair that cascaded over her shoulders to a point mid-way down her back. Her parents, Nandor and Olga, emigrated to the United States when Chris was five and found a new home in the bustling Ridgewood section of Queens. Soon after their arrival, Olga gave birth to another daughter, Eva. Together, the sisters were the spark of the middle-class Freund household and both were now employed in secretarial positions in Manhattan.

In 1972, Chris was hired by the Wall Street firm of Reynolds Securities, and currently worked out of its office at 2 Broadway, in the heart of the financial district.

For a short time, she'd taken courses at Lehman College in the Bronx. But as her relationship grew with her boyfriend, John Diel, her interests changed.

Diel, thirty, was a soccer aficionado who earned his money as a bartender at the Ridgewood III, a neighborhood watering hole. He and Chris had survived an up-and-down relationship and were planning to announce their engagement in two weeks—on Valentine's Day.

On that frigid Saturday evening of January 29, Diel called for Christine at her Linden Street home in his blue Pontiac Firebird and they drove to the Forest Hills Theatre to watch Sylvester Stallone conquer the world in the original *Rocky*. It was Chris's second consecutive evening in a theater.

The night before, she remained in Manhattan with two girlfriends and attended the Broadway production of *Godspell*.

Twenty-four hours before meeting the devil, Christine had joyously sung "Day by Day" with Jesus.

* * *

Following *Rocky*, Chris and Diel trekked the snowy streets to the Wine Gallery restaurant on nearby Austin Street. After a light meal and some Irish coffee, the bundled couple began to walk to Diel's car, which was parked several blocks away in Station Plaza, near the Long Island Rail Road tracks. Their next stop was to be a Masonic dance, at the hall where they first met seven years before.

At the corner of Austin and Continental Avenue they passed a lone hitchhiker with an orange knapsack, and neighbors saw a man in a small green foreign car drop off a passenger with a suitcase at the train station at about this time.

Back in the car, Diel revved the engine and let it warm up for about two minutes in the cold night air. He inserted the latest Abba tape in the stereo and the sound of the newly released "Dancing Queen" filled the auto. Chris nestled close to John, and they hugged briefly.

"God, it's cold," she remarked. The couple then sat back and prepared to leave.

At that moment, the first of three .44-caliber slugs crashed through the passenger's side window.

"Chris! Chris!" Diel hollered, pulling her down as two more shots roared into the car. One passed through Christine's shoulder and entered her back; the other missed and blew out a hole in the windshield on the driver's side.

And then, it was over. Diel, quaking in fear and anguish, kept his head down until he was sure the onslaught had ended. Reaching for Chris, he pulled her to him. When he took his hands away he saw they were covered with blood.

"Chris, Chris!" he shouted again. But Chris didn't answer. Frantic, Diel propped his fiancee up in the seat and fled the car, running madly to Continental Avenue for help.

Waving his arms wildly, he rushed to a couple stopped at a red light. "My girl's been hurt! Please help me!" he blurted. The couple took him back to his car and, as

Diel leaned in to check on Chris, they left.

Diel then glanced across Station Plaza, saw a man entering the Forest Hills Inn and let out a rather interesting cry: "Mister! Mister! They shot her! They shot my girl!" The man stared at Diel and kept going. "They shot my girl!" Diel yelled again, as two neighbors heard him and phoned the police.

But on the street, Diel, alone again and with no help in sight, jumped into his car. Seeing that Chris hadn't moved, he floored the Firebird and squealed to a halt in the center of the Continental and Burns avenues intersection, blocking traffic. Finally, he had help.

But it was too late for Christine Freund. She died shortly afterwards—at 4:10 a.m.—in St. John's Hospital. The shooting had occurred at 12:40 a.m., January 30, 1977. The cause of Christine's death was a bullet wound in the head. Diel had dragged his girlfriend down one shot too late.

Finally, the Police Department began to rumble. The ballistics tests failed to link the bullets fired at Christine to any other shooting. But once again, it was noted that a .44-caliber weapon, identified as a Charter Arms Bulldog model, had been used. Not "one particular .44 Bulldog to the exclusion of all others." But "a" .44-caliber Bulldog.

On February 1, Peter Bernstein of the *Daily News* wrote:

> *More than 50 detectives are investigating possible links between the murder of Christine Freund in Forest Hills, Queens, early Sunday and three episodes last year—two in Queens and one in the Bronx.*
>
> *Two young women have been killed and three were wounded, one of them seriously, in the four incidents.*
>
> *"We are leaning toward a connection in all these cases," said Sgt. Richard Conlon of the Queens 15th Homicide Zone.*
>
> *In each of the cases, a single gunman, acting without apparent motive, emerged in the early morning darkness to shoot down his unsuspecting victims.*

Accompanying the article, which erroneously stated that Carl Denaro hadn't been injured, were a photo of Chris and Diel, a map of the three Queens shooting sites and the police composite sketches from the Lauria and Lomino-DeMasi shootings.

The drawings differed so widely the caption referred to more than one suspect: "Police sketches of suspects in Lomino-DeMasi shooting in Queens and slaying in the Bronx last July."

The most critical words in the article were Sergeant Conlon's "leaning toward a connection." Simply, the police weren't sure. The circumstances of the attacks led them to suspect a single gun was behind all of them—a relatively uncommon .44 Bulldog. But they had no evidence. And more importantly, they certainly had no proof that one particular man was responsible: their own composites clearly indicated otherwise. In addition, there were *other* possible motives for Christine Freund's slaying—motives which would remain hidden within the Police Department.

But despite the cautious approach chosen by the police in February, March would whirl with a pungent wind that would blow all that rightful reticence into the gutter.

From that point, when the bosses and politicians bulled into the case, there would be *one* man and *one* gun, regardless of what the facts were. But New York's press and citizenry wouldn't know that. The media and the public would believe that a single, crazed psychopath was prowling the nighttime streets.

It was nearly time for the birth of the .44-Caliber Killer.

III

"Knock on Coffins"

March 8, 1977. A Tuesday. The first, faint scent of spring tantalized New York as temperatures crept to the high sixties, signaling the coming end of a long and bleary winter whose February blizzards piled deep, frosted blankets of snow throughout a glazed and desolate metropolitan area. For all its life in the other seasons, New York in winter evoked the specter of an ancient gray freighter ice-locked in a barren harbor: creaking, shuddering, rusting and waiting for the April thaw.

Unlike some of its volatile adjoining neighborhoods, the enclave that was Forest Hills boasted a low crime rate, and its affluent residents were determined to keep it that way. The fact that the police investigation of Christine's death was seemingly stalled in low gear tainted the locality with a sense of apprehension and a bitter taste of vigilance.

John Diel, back tending bar at the Ridgewood III, was—he knew—once considered a possible suspect in the murder of his girlfriend, as was the "unknown psychopath." There were, as mentioned, other possible suspects, too. But none of that would matter.

*   *   *

At seven o'clock in the evening of March 8, the thermometer still hovered at a balmy fifty-two degrees as eighteen-year-old Amy Johnson* left her Forest Hills home on Exeter Street for a customary nightly jog in the company of her thirteen-year-old brother, Tony.* Beginning her run less than four blocks from the scene of Christine Freund's murder, she traveled west to 69th Avenue, turned left and continued south to the next block, Fleet Street. Turning east on Fleet, she and Tony trotted to the corner of busy Continental Avenue, where they again veered left, following a rectangular route back to their home.

As Amy jogged north on Continental to the corner of Dartmouth, the image of the Freund homicide formed in her mind, and she involuntarily glanced across Station Plaza, where the murder occurred five weeks before.

Especially wary of strangers since that night, Amy looked back to her left and saw a young man standing by a small play area at the corner of Continental and Dartmouth. Now, as he stared at the approaching Amy, his eyes studied her in what she termed an "eerie, threatening manner," and she became alarmed.

He had wavy, dark hair combed straight back, and his hands were jammed into the pockets of the beige three-quarter-length raincoat he was wearing. He stood about six feet tall and weighed approximately 175 pounds.

Unknown to Amy, this same man was loitering in the area before her arrival. He'd frightened another young girl, Peg Benson,* just minutes earlier.

Now, as he glared at Amy, she shivered and quickened her pace, passing him and turning east onto Dartmouth Street. Off the sidewalk, she kept to the middle of the narrow road, and gestured to her younger brother to do the same. Together, they maintained a hurried gait down Dartmouth Street, which was lined with Tudor-style and stucco buildings and dimly lit by turn-of-the-century-type streetlamps.

When Amy and Tony reached Tennis Place, near the stadium, they swung left and aimed toward Exeter Street, their own block. They would be home in a few moments.

Incredibly, at the corner of Exeter and 70th, she again spied the same man standing on the sidewalk, and again he was staring at her. How did he get there? she wondered. Although she'd been running all the while, he somehow managed to get in front of her and was waiting for her to pass. Did he drive, or had someone driven him ahead of her?

Now very frightened, she and her brother ran even faster. They scurried past the man—who made no movement—and safely reached the front of their home. Catching her breath, Amy looked around and saw that the stranger was walking away— heading east on Exeter toward Tennis Place and Dartmouth. It was about 7:25 p.m.

* * *

Virginia Voskerichian was late coming home from Columbia University in Manhattan. It was nearly seven thirty when she climbed the subway stairs at the Continental Avenue stop in Forest Hills and began the short hike to her house at 69-11 Exeter Street.

Walking south on Continental to Dartmouth, she turned right and began striding west on the same route her neighbor Amy Johnson had followed just fifteen minutes before.

Virginia, nineteen, had long, wavy brown hair. She was attractive, well liked, and was currently dating one of her Columbia teachers, a twenty-seven-year-old Russian-language assistant named Vladimir Lunis.

Virginia was born in Bulgaria and emigrated to the United States with her parents, brother and sister at the age of eleven. An intelligent girl, she soon mastered her adopted tongue and was officially welcomed as an American citizen on July 29, 1975—a year to the day before the murder of Donna Lauria in the Bronx.

After two years at Queens College, Virginia transferred to Barnard College at Columbia, where she was a B-plus student majoring in Russian and planning a career in political science. As she walked to her home, she carried a calendar and some schoolbooks in her arms.

As she neared 4 Dartmouth Street, an apartment house, Virginia noticed a short, youngish-looking figure in a watch cap and sweater approaching her from the opposite direction.

As Virginia and the youth closed to within five feet of each other, she moved slightly to her right to allow the stranger to pass on her left side. Then, for the briefest of moments, everything froze.

Virginia cried out as she saw the gun pointing into her face. Desperately, she ducked and frantically raised the schoolbooks to her face to ward off the coming attack.

When the killer fired, the bullet ripped through the textbooks and entered Virginia's head on the left side of her upper lip, knocked out several teeth, tore through her skull and lodged in the base of her neck, cracking vertebrae.

Slain instantly by the .44 slug, Virginia pitched sideways into the row of hedges fronting 4 Dartmouth.

Down Dartmouth Street—back in the direction from which he'd come—the killer ran. At the corner of Dartmouth and Tennis Place, the gunman pulled the watch cap over his face as he hurtled by a startled Ed Marlow,* a fifty-nine-year-old civil engineer.

"Oh, Jesus!" the killer exclaimed, covering his youthful features with the cap. But Marlow had seen the face, if only briefly. The person looked to be only about sixteen to eighteen years of age, was stockily built, clean-shaven, and wore a ski jacket, or sweater, and a cap—which was either brown or blue, and striped. He appeared to be about five feet seven.

* * *

Now, it happened. Someone in the NYPD either panicked, manipulated, or stretched opinion to merge with fact. Whichever, the results would have a profound impact on the public's perception of the case for years to come. Just who actually endorsed the decision is still not known with certainty, but it bore the imprimatur of the Queens detective command and the highest officials in the Police Department, as well as that of the mayor of the city of New York.

At the pyramid's pinnacle were the new chief of detectives, John Keenan; the police commissioner, Michael Codd; and Mayor Abraham Beame, who was facing a doomed-to-die reelection campaign.

Somewhere in this alliance, which would later enlist Deputy Inspector Timothy Dowd, whom many regarded as a career bureaucrat, the answer lies today. For it was this group, acting on information gleaned from the ballistics unit, that created the .44-Caliber Killer, subsequently known as Son of Sam. Together, they misled the press and populace and stoked a panic the likes of which New York had never seen.

To be sure, there absolutely *was* reason for great alarm, because some unknown force was definitely gunning down young women in Queens and the Bronx. But the authorities would now package opinion about the .44 revolver and label it as "fact"; they would inflate the ballistics findings.

As a result, they would *underestimate* the menace. And in doing so, they would box themselves in on the .44 killings and their aftermath—a scenario that would include the deaths of many more young people, innocent and culpable alike.

There isn't a definitive answer for why it happened.

What was known unequivocally in March 1977 was that the Police Department was in the midst of a serious morale crisis. Since 1971 and the Knapp Commission corruption scandals, the detective division, once regarded as a fiefdom in the NYPD, had seen its elite ranks dwindle from 3,000 to 1,800 when Son of Sam began to march through the city streets. In fact, no policemen had advanced to the detective corps between 1974 and mid-1976 and promotions were scant for those already there.

Procedural changes and budget cuts were responsible for the trimming. Adding to the department's disenchantment, the city had laid off some 1,700 cops as it struggled to emerge from the fiscal mire.

What all this meant is that the NYPD was dismayed at its sinking status and an absence of recognition and public support. The Department sorely needed a shot in the arm. Or maybe a shot from a Charter Arms.

* * *

On March 9, the day after the Voskerichian shooting, the newspapers and television stations accurately reported that the police, logically, were tracking a "chubby teenager" in a ski (or watch) cap as the prime suspect in the crime. This was Ed Marlow's suspect, who attempted to hide his face from the surprised witness as he fled. Other neighborhood residents also spotted this individual lingering in the area shortly before the slaying.

And although the incident occurred barely a block from the Freund homicide, police told the *New York Times* there was "no evidence" to positively link the two killings. That was true, but it was also one of the last of the Police Department's concise statements about the .44 case.

None of the following was ever revealed to the public, but here is what happened:

In the morgue, a "large-caliber deformed lead bullet" (as stated in the autopsy report) was extracted from the body of Virginia Voskerichian. Although the slug passed through her books and her head, cracked vertebrae and flattened considerably, police ballistics were still able to identify it as having been fired from "a" .44-caliber Charter Arms Bulldog revolver; again, a relatively rare weapon in New York.

The police now had evidence that *a* .44 revolver was used in all the assaults, and that a Charter Arms Bulldog model was used in at least two or three of them. And they had legitimate investigatory reasons to believe the attacks were related, given the common circumstances of each.

But one gun and one gunman they did not have.

There was no certain, positive match between the Voskerichian bullet and those recovered at virtually all the previous .44 shootings, due to the deformed condition of those bullets. In other words, the police had no irrefutable proof that the same gun was used in all the incidents.

More importantly, they had even less evidence to demonstrate that the same individual, acting alone, committed the crimes. In fact, they had accumulated considerable data which indicated that the opposite was likely. The composites drawn from the Lauria, Lomino-DeMasi and Voskerichian shootings (there would be two people sought in the Voskerichian case) showed that at least three and possibly four persons were involved. This information held regardless of whether or not the same .44 was used each time.

A police claim of a ballistics match is not an indisputable edict, and such determinations are vulnerable to courtroom challenges. Aware of this, the NYPD recommends that two technicians concur before accepting a finding. It is not known if that procedure was followed in the .44 case, or if the ballistics lab was pressured.

For all the benefits of ballistics it is an inexact science which often calls for conclusions rather than final statements of fact. Like fingerprints, ballistics evidence has become sacrosanct to many minds. Not true.

A cliche in crime dramas, fingerprints, for example, are often effectively useless as investigative aids. A perpetrator would have to leave behind a fair number of clean prints before law enforcement computers could identify an unknown suspect. One, two, even three prints are simply not enough. However, when a suspect is under scrutiny, fingerprints become important because at that time a particular individual's prints can be compared with any number found at a crime scene. With a suspect in mind—fine. Otherwise no, unless he leaves a sufficient number behind and his prints are on file in the first place.

New technology available in some jurisdictions is enabling police to work with fewer samples. But the equipment has not yet been installed throughout the country.

As for ballistics, a bullet recovered at a typical New York shooting scene or in a hospital or morgue is forwarded to the NYPD's ballistics lab. There, on the premise that no two gun barrels are precisely identical, the bullet is analyzed microscopically and compared with a "clean" bullet which has been fired into a tank of water from a suspected gun. The bullets pick up tiny, unique markings from inside the gun's barrel as they are fired, making it sometimes possible for them to be matched to a particular weapon.

As with fingerprints, the job is infinitely easier if a suspected firearm is available from which to obtain a "clean" bullet, via the water tank, for comparison purposes. However, in the .44 shootings there was no such gun in police custody. The killer still had it. Thus, any comparisons had to be attempted through analysis of the bullets recovered from the five crime scenes or from the victims' bodies.

These bullets were all deformed. Similarities did exist and indeed they would exist in any number of Charter Arms .44 Bulldogs manufactured in the same plant, perhaps even with the same machines. In fact, due to a manufacturing quirk, the Bulldog produced an unusual "right six" twist because Charter Arms, in boring its barrels in twenty-four-inch lengths, clamped one end while the other hung free. So, as the cutter trimmed the barrel to the actual length that would be part of the gun, it vibrated slightly, leaving an impression that would be picked up by bullets fired through it.

But this trait was peculiar to the Bulldog revolver itself, not to only one particular Bulldog.

Out of the seventeen bullets fired in the attacks the comparison effort was narrowed to the projectile which killed Donna Lauria and the single bullet fired at Virginia Voskerichian. The other fifteen slugs must have been useless. If they hadn't been, a match could have been obtained much sooner. And in light of what the police were about to announce, that point, which concerns the Denaro, Lomino-DeMasi and Freund shootings, is a relevant one.

Years later, NYPD ballistics detective George Simmons would say: "The gun wasn't in good shape, so the matches were hard."

Queens district attorney John Santucci would phrase it differently: "Based on the reports we later obtained from the Police Department, the bullets were similar but weren't conclusively matched. Maybe the same gun was used; maybe not. In terms of evidence, the reports were inconclusive."

* * *

On March 10, two days after the Voskerichian murder, the police and Mayor Abraham Beame convened a press conference to publicly state there was a ballistics match between the Lauria and Voskerichian bullets; i.e., that both were fired from the same—to the exclusion of all others—.44 revolver. It was possible the same gun was used in those attacks. But even if that was so, there was no evidence to lay the murders at the doorstep of a single individual, acting alone.

The officials would further allege that although test results weren't as definite—meaning no match at all—in the Denaro, Lomino-DeMasi and Freund cases, they were nonetheless "certain" that the same gun, fired by the same man, was also used in those attacks.

The press conference was held at the 112th Precinct station house in Forest Hills, where Codd and Beame proclaimed the birth of the .44-Caliber Killer to an anxiously waiting world—represented by every newspaper, television and radio reporter who could wheel his or her way to Queens on that chilly afternoon.

There was yet another surprise in store. Codd and Beame took pains, by implication, to impart the message that the .44 fiend was *not* the man in the ski or watch cap, so far as they knew—a position they would sorely regret taking five months later.

Oh, Ski Cap was still wanted for questioning. But, carefully couching his words, Codd revealed that his men were primarily seeking a white male, about six feet tall, 180 pounds, wearing a beige raincoat, and with dark hair combed straight back.

This, the police knew (but the public didn't), was the man who frightened jogger Amy Johnson and Peg Benson shortly before the shots were fired. The statements of the two girls were kept under wraps, where they remained until this writing.

Here is what the citizens of New York, and consequently the nation, were told: From the *New York Times*:

> *Mayor Beame and Police Commissioner Codd, in a joint appeal to the*
> *public for help, disclosed yesterday that the police were seeking the same*
> *man for the "senseless" killings of three young women since July 29, in-*
> *cluding two recently from Forest Hills.*
>
> *The conclusion . . . was based on ballistics examinations that showed*
> *the same .44-caliber revolver had been used for the three killings.*
>
> *The commissioner gave the following description of a person wanted*
> *for questioning in the murders: male, white, between 25 and 30 years*
> *of age, between five feet ten inches and six feet tall, medium build, well-*
> *groomed, with dark hair combed straight back.*
>
> *However, when asked if this person was believed to be the murderer,*
> *Mr. Codd replied, "I can't say he is a suspect."*

Then *what* was he? And what about Ski Cap? The press had the opportunity to pin Codd and Beame to the wall. Why were you hunting one guy yesterday, another today, and two people in total, Commissioner? And what about the other sketches that look so different from these descriptions? What makes you so sure one gun means one killer?

If those questions were asked, or answered candidly, the house of cards may have crumbled and the .44 case might have assumed an entirely different dimension.

From the *Daily News*:

> *The man who killed coed Virginia Voskerichian on a Forest Hills,*
> *Queens, street last Tuesday also killed a woman in January less than 100*
> *yards away, murdered a Bronx woman last July, and has wounded at*
> *least two other women in the city in the last seven months, Mayor Beame*
> *and Commissioner Michael Codd disclosed yesterday. . . . Ballistics estab-*
> *lished that the same .44-caliber Wild West revolver had been used in all*
> *five shootings, Codd said.*

Outside of the already mentioned misrepresentations, the .44 Bulldog wasn't exactly Wyatt Earp's type. It was a short-barreled weapon designed primarily for police use and had been available commercially since 1974. Why Codd described it as a long-barreled, Wild West weapon is another, possibly telling, enigma.

The truth—that the police were making a judgment call—remained a closed secret, and the media and public pressure soon gave the NYPD brass and the mayor what they wanted: a task force. Initially, the group was comprised of about fifty detectives and uniformed officers, a combination of the Bronx and Queens cops already working separately on the various investigations.

At first, Captain Joseph Borrelli was put in charge, with Lieutenant John Power and Sergeant Joseph Coffey right behind him. But the case was getting too big for a captain, at least in the public-appearance sense. A month later, after a number of officials turned down the assignment, Deputy Inspector Timothy Dowd, sixty-one, was named to head the squad. Borrelli, Coffey and Power would remain, and report to Dowd.

With the mayor now involved, the case had become a hot political issue. The link with City Hall started the flow of money and manpower, but it also engendered pressure and interference. Beame was in a political dogfight. He wanted publicity. He wanted to be aligned with such an important case and known to the voters as the public servant whose personal intervention and concern cleared the path for a quick, efficient solution to the matter of this lengthening string of homicides being committed against young, white, middle-class residents of Queens and the Bronx.

March soon surrendered to April, and with April came spring weather and Easter on the tenth, and still the killer didn't resurface. Reporters routinely interviewed detectives, psychologists and police supervisors involved in the probe.

On a real-world level, the investigation was riding a rail to nowhere. By determining that the killings were all committed randomly, the police had dropped their probes of potential suspects with possible motives for the individual crimes. After all, a "deranged individual" had been doing all the shootings at random, right? And the deranged don't have *real* motives.

And now, in the search for the psycho, the police were at square one. No suspect. No motive. Frustration. The investigation desperately needed some impetus.

Impetus arrived in the early-morning darkness of April 17, 1977—the Sunday after Easter.

* * *

Prominently displayed in the living room of the large, tastefully furnished high-rise apartment at 1950 Hutchinson River Parkway in the Bronx's Pelham Bay section, the impressive oil painting revealed a young, attractive girl in a formal, yet still soft and vulnerable pose. Regally resplendent in her gown, perhaps someday she would become an actress. That was her ambition.

At nineteen, Valentina Suriani had her vision, and she had no reason to believe she wouldn't live to see it fulfilled.

A 1976 graduate of St. Catherine's Academy, Valentina, daughter of postal employee Frank Suriani and his wife, enrolled at the Bronx's Lehman College to study her chosen profession.

Five feet five inches tall, Valentina had short brown hair, brown eyes, a lively temperament and a strong will to succeed in her field. Outgoing with those she knew well, she was—like many people theatrically inclined—still somewhat shy and insecure around strangers. In April 1977 she was seeking a photographer to capture her essence for the portfolio she'd need as a budding thespian.

Valentina's boyfriend, Alexander Esau, six feet one, was twenty, but the long, curly brown hair which framed his baby face made him appear to be about sixteen. The son of immigrant parents, he was employed as an operator's helper with Luna

Brothers Towing Service in Manhattan.

At 3 a.m. on April 17, the young couple, who'd been to a movie in Manhattan and later stopped at a party, pulled up and parked along a chain link fence on the west side of the darkened Hutchinson River Parkway service road opposite number 1878—about two blocks south of Valentina's home and less than a short city block from Jody Valente's brick house on the same street.

Out of the millions of people in New York and its thousands of roadways, Valentina and Alex would die within four blocks of Donna Lauria—and less than two hundred yards from where Donna's wounded friend lay sleeping.

As the young couple embraced in the borrowed Mercury Montego, Alex was behind the wheel. Valentina nudged close to him, and then sat on his lap with her legs stretched out across the seat in the direction of the passenger's door.

As the lovers kissed, Valentina was face to face with Alex. Then, through the closed front passenger's window, a .44-caliber bullet shattered the glass and smashed into Valentina above the left corner of her mouth, passed downward through the base of her neck and exited below her right ear. Immediately, a second shot hit her above the left ear, traveled downward through her brain and lodged in the back of her skull on the right side. The shots came so rapidly Valentina didn't have time to fall between them.

Alex, meanwhile, tried to escape the roaring rampage. Reflexively, he attempted to dive away from the shots. But not being able to judge where the noise was coming from, he instead bent straight into the path of the next two missiles—both of which hit him in the top of the head and tore their murderous path into his brain.

And then it was quiet.

The two young lovers lay motionless in the car. Valentina was still sprawled on Alex's lap, and his upper body was slumped toward the passenger's door. Their blood was mixing together.

Valentina was already dead. And Alex, despite a frantic effort to save him, succumbed hours later at the Bronx's Montefiore Hospital.

With the morning light, old women from the row of brick homes across the street in this Italian neighborhood sadly carried buckets of water to the scene to wash away the horrors of the night before. It was a tender gesture, made out of respect for the dignity of the dead couple.

But nothing would eradicate the stain that was now spreading across New York.

The gunman had been astonishingly accurate, even considering the close range. Four fatal head shots were fired with a weapon known for its significant recoil. Who he was remained an agonizing mystery. But before he fled, he did something that hadn't been done before—he dropped a macabre calling card in the road beside the victims' car. It was an envelope, addressed to Queens Detective Captain Joseph Borrelli.

Inside the envelope was a letter which gave birth to Son of Sam.

* * *

On Monday, April 18, the New York newspapers screamed the return of the homicidal night stalker. "BRONX GIRL SHOT TO DEATH IN CAR, GUN LINKED TO THREE OTHER SLAYINGS," read the banner headline in the *Daily News.* Underneath was a large photo of a smiling Alex and Valentina, both dressed formally for a prom or wedding.

By the next day, the *News,* through its network of sources in the Police Department, learned that a letter was left at the scene. "KILLER TO COPS, I'LL DO IT AGAIN. TAUNTING NOTE IS FIRST SOLID CLUE," the paper shouted on page one. Beneath the headline were two composite sketches—both from March's Voskerichian murder.

The drawings were of Ski Cap and the man wearing the beige raincoat, and the caption revealed that the two were being sought for questioning. The police already claimed only one man was behind the killings and were now publicly labeling Ski Cap a witness.

At this point, it is reasonable to say that the man in the beige raincoat was David Berkowitz, as, among other things, a comparison of the sketch and Berkowitz's photo clearly illustrates the strong resemblance. However, it is not so reasonable to say Ski Cap was a man. Ski Cap, a "witness" who never came forward, may well have been a woman.

Something else was at play here. Not that the police were thinking otherwise, but the Borrelli letter dropped at the Suriani-Esau scene negated the presence of two people at the Voskerichian murder simply because it was ostensibly written by one person claiming credit for the slayings. The police wanted one man? Then they'd have one man.

The *Daily News,* quoting a police source, said the letter advised authorities that the murderer lived in a "nightmare world of blood-sucking vampires and Frankenstein monsters." The *News* also reported that the letter contained words in "a Scottish accent" and the phrase "too many heart attacks."

That coronary wording would set police poring through hospital records because they believed the killer's father might have been mistreated by brown-haired nurses after suffering a cardiac arrest, thus igniting his demented offspring into a murderous onslaught against brown-haired young women. Moreover, Donna Lauria was a medical technician and Jody Valente a student nurse. This fueled the theory, although how police reconciled the killer's possible knowledge of the victims' professions in a supposedly random series of attacks was never explained.

The letter also caused police to believe the killer attended Catholic schools, a point worthy of remembrance.

The people of New York never knew why authorities entertained these thoughts because the note was withheld. The *Daily News* hadn't seen it, either, and so the police were able to deny—falsely—that the assassin warned he would strike again.

The rank and file members of the task force also didn't view the correspondence, several have since stated. Borrelli and Dowd wouldn't show it to them. And these detectives were responsible for catching the killer. It was a very closed circle at the top.

In any event, the withholding of the Borrelli letter was a significant error because the note contained important clues which, if released, might have led to an arrest months—and several victims—sooner.

The letter, four pages in length, was printed in capitalized, slanted block letters:

> *I AM DEEPLY HURT BY YOUR CALLING ME A WEMON HATER. I AM NOT.*
>
> *BUT I AM A MONSTER.*
>
> *I AM THE "SON OF SAM." I AM A LITTLE "BRAT."*
>
> *WHEN FATHER SAM GETS DRUNK HE GETS MEAN. HE BEATS HIS FAMILY. SOMETIMES HE TIES ME UP TO THE BACK OF THE HOUSE. OTHER TIMES HE LOCKS ME IN THE GARAGE. SAM LOVES TO DRINK BLOOD.*
>
> *"GO OUT AND KILL" COMMANDS FATHER SAM.*
>
> *BEHIND OUR HOUSE SOME REST. MOSTLY YOUNG— RAPED AND SLAUGHTERED—THEIR BLOOD DRAINED— JUST BONES NOW.*
>
> *PAPA SAM KEEPS ME LOCKED IN THE ATTIC, TOO. I CAN'T GET OUT BUT I LOOK OUT THE ATTIC WINDOW AND WATCH THE WORLD GO BY. I FEEL LIKE AN OUTSID- ER. I AM ON A DIFFERENT WAVE LENGTH THEN EVERY- BODY ELSE—PROGRAMMED TOO KILL.*
>
> *HOWEVER, TO STOP ME YOU MUST KILL ME. ATTEN- TION ALL POLICE: SHOOT ME FIRST—SHOOT TO KILL OR ELSE.*
>
> *KEEP OUT OF MY WAY OR YOU WILL DIE!*
>
> *PAPA SAM IS OLD NOW. HE NEEDS SOME BLOOD TO PRESERVE HIS YOUTH. HE HAS HAD TOO MANY HEART ATTACKS. TOO MANY HEART ATTACKS. "UGH, ME HOOT IT URTS SONNY BOY."*
>
> *I MISS MY PRETTY PRINCESS MOST OF ALL. SHE'S REST- ING IN OUR LADIES HOUSE. BUT I'LL SHE HER SOON.*
>
> *I AM THE "MONSTER"—"BEELZEBUB"—THE "CHUBBY BEHEMOUTH."*
>
> *I LOVE TO HUNT. PROWLING THE STREETS LOOKING FOR FAIR GAME—TASTY MEAT. THE WEMON OF QUEENS ARE Z PRETTYIST OF ALL. I MUST BE THE WATER THEY DRINK. I LIVE FOR THE HUNT—MY LIFE. BLOOD FOR PAPA.*
>
> *MR. BORELLI, SIR, I DON'T WANT TO KILL ANYMORE NO SIR, NO MORE BUT I MUST, "HONOUR THY FATHER." I WANT TO MAKE LOVE TO THE WORLD. I LOVE PEOPLE.*

*I DON'T BELONG ON EARTH. RETURN ME TO YAHOOS.
TO THE PEOPLE OF QUEENS, I LOVE YOU. AND I WANT
TO WISH ALL OF YOU A HAPPY EASTER. MAY GOD BLESS
YOU IN THIS LIFE AND IN THE NEXT. AND FOR NOW I SAY
GOODBYE AND GOODNIGHT. POLICE: LET ME HAUNT
YOU WITH THESE WORDS:*
   I'LL BE BACK!
   I'LL BE BACK!
   *TO BE INTERRPRETED [sic] AS—BANG, BANG, BANG,
BANK, BANG—UGH!!*

> *Your in murder*
> *Mr. Monster*

If "I'll be back" isn't the equivalent of "I'll do it again," then the NYPD is owed an apology.

With regard to its other contents, the letter was loaded with salient leads, such as references to a house, garage and attic—which implied a residential, suburban-like location; an old man named Sam who drank and was beset with a heart condition, who was prone to violence, who had a family and who apparently spoke with a Scottish-sounding accent. There also was an allusion to a dog, and to a yard of some type "behind our house."

In addition, the letter clearly indicated that an attack had been *planned* to occur in Queens—rather than the Bronx—and was to have been carried out the week before—Easter. That is, a shooting scheduled for seven days earlier in Queens was delayed and transferred to the Bronx. This evidence was at variance with the official psychological profiles of an obsessed murderer whose pent-up internal rages exploded unpredictably.

If it had been released, there is every reason to believe (and *without* the benefit of hindsight)—particularly in light of events which will be detailed later—that someone in the Greater New York area might have read the letter and provided vital information about "Sam" and his murders.

But no one, with the exception of a handful of police officials and consulting psychiatrists, would see the correspondence, except for Jimmy Breslin, columnist for the *Daily News.*

Breslin would slip in a July 28 column devoted to the anniversary of Donna Lauria's death, when he would write that the killer, who referred to "women as wemon," might let the anniversary pass as he sat looking out "his attic window"—direct references to the secret Borrelli letter.

Breslin would see a note the police brass wouldn't even share with the detectives working on the case. But perhaps the powers in the department thought it only fair to show Breslin their letter. After all, he was going to show them his.

*   *   *

As Memorial Day neared, six weeks had elapsed since the murders of Valentina Suriani and Alexander Esau. But the police, now bolstered by a task force of more than
150 officers and detectives, were making no progress in the case. The investigation
was centered on current and former mental patients, sex criminals who had demonstrated a hatred of women and candidates culled from the growing list of suspects
phoned into the police .44 hotline number.

On the twenty-sixth of May, the NYPD released a new psychological profile of the
killer. It described him as neurotic, schizophrenic and paranoid—dime-store defini-
tions resulting from remote analyses by the psychiatrists. The profile also suggested
that the killer might regard himself as a victim of "demonic possession."

That little nudge from the Department would emerge as significant.

On a more realistic level than the police profile of the killer, the detectives were
trying to trace and test-fire the fifty-six Charter Arms .44 Bulldogs registered in the
New York area. This was eventually accomplished, but produced no results.

From that starting block, Inspector Dowd ran a nationwide marathon to locate every .44 Bulldog ever manufactured—all 28,000 of them. Some 670 had been stolen
from Charter Arms and weren't even available for a possible trace. It was a hopeless
mission but was illustrative of the lack of progress and sense of desperation pervading
the NYPD.

The police were scrambling. They had decoy teams necking in parked cars and
dummies posed in other vehicles; they were consulting psychics and investigating the
thousands of tips received from citizens and other law enforcement agencies. Things
were not going well. It was time for a little encouragement.

On May 30, Memorial Day, encouragement was dropped into a mailbox in Englewood, New Jersey. The box was located in proximity to a large apartment complex in
the affluent suburb, which was just a few miles across the George Washington Bridge
from upper Manhattan. Specifically, the mailbox sat on the corner of Myrtle Street
and Lorraine Court, something the police were privately able to determine because,
on account of the holiday, the letter was hand-canceled at a local postal substation.

The envelope was addressed to one Jimmy Breslin, the Count of Queens Boulevard and a controversial columnist for the *Daily News*.

At forty-seven, Breslin was a success, and not undeserving in many respects. He
was a colorful, earthy, man-of-the-streets writer, and a good one. He'd authored a
number of well-received novels and would later become familiar to many Americans
for his self-caricature in the Piels beer commercials: "It's a good drinkin' beer," he
would observe, cigar in hand.

But notoriety bred a degree of pomposity and, some said, a touch of journalistic
ambivalence. Breslin, a crime aficionado, had taken a keen interest in the Son of Sam
slayings and produced a number of his trademark pounding-the-pavement-with-
the-cops columns about the investigation. He was also well plugged in to the Omega
task force.

When the letter for Breslin arrived at the *Daily News* building on East 42nd Street in Manhattan, the paper milked it for several days with teasing, circulation-building articles before finally making its contents known. When ultimately published, the note set off an explosion throughout the entire metropolitan area.

More than anything else, the Breslin letter set New Yorkers spinning, sleuthing and trying to solve the case. The reason for this was simple: the missive contained four aliases of the killer, names which triggered hundreds of leads in the public mind.

Beyond the clues, the letter was a chilling masterpiece—graphic, flowing and literally bubbling with vivid imagery. It was the work of a creative, intelligent writer. It was mailed in Englewood, but as its opening lines said, it really rose from the gutters—and the dank, mist-shrouded back alleys and entrails of the city. And from the deepest recesses of the human brain from which the most horrifying nightmares ooze.

> *Hello from the gutters of N.Y.C., which are filled with dog manure, vomit, stale wine, urine, and blood.*
>
> *Hello from the sewers of N.Y.C. which swallow up these delicacies when they are washed away by the sweeper trucks. Hello from the cracks in the sidewalks of N.Y.C. and from the ants that dwell in these cracks and feed on the dried blood of the dead that has seeped into these cracks.*
>
> *J.B., I'm just dropping you a line to let you know that I appreciate your interest in those recent and horrendous .44 killings. I also want to tell you that I read your column daily and I find it quite informative.*
>
> *Tell me Jim, what will you have for July twenty-ninth?*
>
> *You can forget about me if you like because I don't care for publicity. However you must not forget Donna Lauria and you cannot let the people forget her either. She was a very, very sweet girl but Sam's a thirsty lad and he won't let me stop killing until he gets his fill of blood.*
>
> *Mr. Breslin, sir, don't think that because you haven't heard from [me] for a while that I went to sleep. No, rather, I am still here. Like a spirit roaming the night. Thirsty, hungry, seldom stopping to rest; anxious to please Sam. I love my work. Now, the void has been filled.*
>
> *Perhaps we shall meet face to face someday or perhaps I will be blown away by cops with smoking .38's. Whatever, if I shall be fortunate enough to meet you I will tell you all about Sam if you like and I will introduce you to him. His name is "Sam the Terrible."*
>
> *Not knowing what the future holds I shall say farewell and I will see you at the next job.*
>
> *Or should I say you will see my handiwork at the next job? Remember Ms. Lauria. Thank you.*

In their blood
and
from the gutter
"Sam's Creation" .44

Here are some names to help you along. Forward them to the inspector
for use by N.C.I.C:
"The Duke of Death"
"The Wicked King Wicker"
"The Twenty Two Disciples of Hell"
"John 'Wheaties'—Rapist and Suffocater of Young Girls."

PS: J.B. Please inform all the detectives working the slaying to remain.

P.S: JB, please inform all the detectives working the case that I wish them
the best of luck. "Keep 'em digging, drive on, think positive, get off your
butts, knock on coffins, etc."

Upon my capture I promise to buy all the guys working on the case a new
pair of shoes if I can get up the money.

Son of Sam

On the back of the envelope, in the same professional style of block lettering, was written:

Blood and Family Darkness and Death Absolute Depravity .44

Beneath that was the Son of Sam graphic symbol. It was one hell of a return address; and was withheld from the public.

Besides the accomplished printing style, the Breslin letter incorporated techniques normally used by someone familiar with graphics, such as centering and "hanging indentations."

Once the letter was published, police phones rang off the hook. People were turning in journalists, artists, draftsmen, cartoonists, men named John, boys nicknamed "Duke"; and the police themselves arranged for a screening of a Scottish film, *The Wicker Man*, which revolved around Druid sacrifices in flaming wicker baskets.

The police said they believed the graphic symbol at the letter's end utilized the universal signs for male and female. This was incorrect. The symbol had its origins with nineteenth-century occultist Eliphas Levi. And the "signs" were actually the astrological renderings of Mars, the god of war, and of Venus—goddess of the Roman sewers, who was also known as Placida.

* * *

Three weeks later, Judy Placido, of Wickham Avenue in the Bronx, was celebrating her graduation from St. Catherine's Academy—the same high school attended by Valentina Suriani a year earlier. Judy, seventeen, didn't know Valentina, but a friend of hers did. And another fact that would be kept confidential: Judy had attended Valentina's funeral with the friend. The .44-caliber world was certainly a small one.

On Saturday, June 25, Judy, in the company of three girlfriends, drove across the Whitestone Bridge from the Bronx to party at a Queens discotheque named Elephas, which was located on Northern Boulevard in the Bayside section. Elephas, a Latin word, means elephant. In the occult, the elephant is the demon Behemoth—a reference contained in Son of Sam's April letter to Captain Borrelli. The implication is clear—and significant.

It was a warm, rainy night, and the combination of inclement weather and mounting fear of the .44 killer turned the normally overflowing Elephas into something of a wasteland.

The night dragged on, but by 11 p.m. the crowd increased somewhat and it was then Judy met Salvatore Lupo, twenty, a gas station attendant from Maspeth, Queens. Lupo, with a styled haircut, a mustache, a love of sports and a flair for disco dancing, was immediately attracted to the vivacious Judy, who herself was a shapely, pretty girl with long, wavy brown hair and an enthusiasm for the disco scene.

Judy, who lived with her aunt, was the youngest of three children. Her mother had died of Hodgkin's disease nine years previously, and her father subsequently remarried and kept a home nearby with his second wife.

At 2 a.m., Judy's friends agreed they'd had enough of Elephas. Judy, however, decided to stay and continue her getting-acquainted effort with Lupo. Lupo's friend Ralph Saccante was a bouncer at Elephas and had driven Sal there that night. Lupo informed Judy that Saccante and he would drive her back to the Bronx if she wanted to wait until the disco closed. After talking about the situation with her girlfriends, Judy consented.

At 3 a.m., after another hour of dancing and conversation, Lupo showed Judy the keys to Saccante's maroon 1972 Cadillac and suggested they wait in the car until Saccante finished for the night. The auto was parked about two blocks from Elephas on residential 211th Street, near the 45th Road intersection.

Hand in hand, the young couple left the disco and walked directly to the Cadillac, entered and began to talk. A few minutes earlier witnesses spied another Caddy, an older one—gold in color with a black vinyl roof and rear-end damage—slowly cruising the neighborhood. A white male in his twenties or thirties who had short black hair and a thin mustache was behind the wheel.

Inside Saccante's car, Lupo and Judy lit cigarettes while they conversed and Lupo, who was in the driver's seat, affectionately eased his right arm around the back of Judy's neck. They passed a quiet ten minutes. Ironically, their conversation turned to the subject of Son of Sam.

And then Son of Sam decided to join in.

The first shot, aimed at Judy's head, shattered the front passenger's side window, smashed Lupo's right wrist and hit Judy in the neck. It continued downward, exited her neck and embedded in the seat cushion. A fragment of flying glass sliced into Lupo's right leg.

Lupo dove below the front seat, looked toward the window and was able to see the gun, which kept spitting red flashes. The second shot hit Judy in the head, but miraculously only grazed her skull, penetrating the skin and traveling along the surface of her forehead before settling just above her right eyebrow.

The next missile pierced Judy's shoulder and, like the first shot, deflected downward and slammed into the cushion.

The barrage was now over. Lupo flung open the car door and fled toward Elephas, trailing blood from the gash in his leg. Judy was left alone in the Cadillac.

Stunned, and not knowing she'd been shot, Judy sat dazed for several minutes before staring into the rearview mirror and seeing she was covered with blood. Now overwhelmed by panic, she crawled from the Caddy and stumbled along 211th Street, trying to focus on the distant lights of Elephas. At the corner of 45th Road, her strength was drained and she collapsed in the rain-soaked street.

Quickly now, the neighborhood came to life and Judy was soon draped with a blanket as a concerned crowd gathered. Police and ambulances were immediately summoned, and Lupo, after telling the Elephas doorman about the shooting, returned to the fallen Judy.

Minutes before the shots rang out, an unmarked car containing Detective Sergeant Joseph Coffey and his partner drove from the neighborhood. Hearing the radio call, the two furious cops hastily sped back to the scene.

Three blocks south of the site, a witness observed a stocky white male clad in dark clothing running along 211th Street, heading away from the shooting location. Another witness saw a well-dressed young man with sandy-colored hair and a mustache jump into a yellow or gold Chevy Nova type of car and leave the neighborhood with the car's headlights extinguished. A partial plate number was recorded but would lead nowhere. It was believed this man watched the shooting and fled in the same direction taken by the killer—but this information was kept confidential. (A similar vehicle was double-parked across the street from the scene of Donna Lauria's murder in the Bronx. Later, evidence of this type of car's presence at yet two more Son of Sam shootings would be uncovered.)

At the hospital, surgeons patched up Lupo's wrist and gashed leg. Judy Placido recovered, which was nothing short of a miracle. However, neither she nor Lupo was able to describe their assailant to the police.

*   *   *

The headlines following the attack fed the massive feelings of fright creeping through the city of New York. Adding to the fear was the fact that the police were admittedly making no progress in the ever-widening investigation. More officers were promptly assigned to Dowd's Omega force and in early July Mayor Beame announced he was allocating even more cops to the case and would step up patrol activity in anticipation of July 29—the anniversary of Donna Lauria's death in the Bronx.

In the letter to Breslin, Son of Sam had written: "Tell me Jim, what will you have for July twenty-ninth?" Beame acted in response to that question, but he was criticized for "speculation" by some, including the *New York Times*.

On the twenty-eighth, in a column titled "To the .44 Killer on His First Death-day," Breslin wondered if Son of Sam would strike: "And somewhere in this city, a loner, a deranged loner, picks up this paper and gloats. Again he has what he wants. Is tomorrow night, July 29, so significant to him that he must go out and walk the night streets and find a victim? Or will he sit alone, and look out his attic window and be thrilled by his power, this power that will have him in the newspapers and on television and in the thoughts and conversations of most of the young people in the city?"

Two of the city's young people, twenty-year-old Stacy Moskowitz and her sister, Ricki, fifteen, were as aware as any New Yorkers of the July 29 anniversary.

On Thursday, the twenty-eighth, the sisters left their home in Brooklyn's Flatbush section and drove to Beefsteak Charlie's restaurant on Ocean Avenue in Sheepshead Bay.

Stacy, a petite five feet two, was employed as a color coordinator at the Minella Shoe Corp.'s offices in the Empire State Building in midtown Manhattan. An attractive, brown-eyed blonde, she had attended Brooklyn's Lafayette High and the Adelphi Business School before landing the job with Minella.

Stacy was a lively, outgoing girl and had just returned to New York from a Mexican vacation. Her father, Jerry, had met her at John F. Kennedy Airport and was immediately surprised with a box of Cuban cigars she had purchased in Acapulco. Stacy was like that.

As she and Ricki conversed idly while waiting for their dinner to be served, a tall young man with dark hair and a mustache approached their table and asked if he could join them for a minute. The two sisters glanced inquisitively at the handsome intruder.

"O.K." Stacy nodded, and Robert Violante slid into the booth.

At twenty, Violante was a graduate of Brooklyn's New Utrecht High School and had been employed at several retail clothing jobs. He lived with his parents on Bay Ridge Parkway and was taking a summer vacation from the menswear business but planned to resume work after Labor Day.

He'd gone to Beefsteak Charlie's with two friends and noticed Stacy and Ricki when they entered the dining room. Deciding he wanted to meet them, he initially focused his attention on the younger Ricki. But Ricki, realizing he was too old for her, steered the conversation toward Stacy, and Violante quickly caught on.

Ultimately, he invited Stacy to go out with him. She was attracted to the confident Violante and reasoned that her work in the shoe business complemented his background in retailing. So she agreed to a date, and Violante scribbled down her phone number and address and said he'd call for her at 8 p.m. on Saturday, July 30.

* * *

In a suburban Yonkers apartment building high above the Hudson River, a young man named David Berkowitz used the anniversary date for his own purposes. He knew what was in the wind, and he knew how it could end for him. He wasn't sure there'd be another opportunity, so he didn't dare procrastinate. His July 29 "celebration" would be poignant. Little did he know, or think, that the letter would be suppressed by authorities. Nearly four years would elapse before it came into my hands:

> *This is a warning to all police agencies in the tri-state area: For your information, a satanic cult (devil worshipers and practitioners of witchcraft) that has been established for quite some time has been instructed by their high command (Satan) to begin to systematically kill and slaughter young girls or people of good health and clean blood.*
>
> *They plan to kill at least 100 young wemon and men, but mostly wemon, as part of a satanic ritual which involves the shedding of the victims' innocent blood . . .*
>
> *Warning: the streets shall be run with blood.*
>
> *I, David Berkowitz, have been chosen, chosen since birth, to be one of the executioners for the cult.*
>
> *He who hath eyes, let him see the dead victims.*
>
> *He who hath ears, let him listen to what I say.*

July 29 came and passed without incident.

IV
Her Name Was Stacy

The 6:15 p.m. ferry from Patchogue, Long Island, to Davis Park on Fire Island was nearly empty as it nudged the narrow pier, reversed its coughing engines and was secured in place with thick mariner's line by the small crew of teenaged deckhands.

It was Saturday night, July 30, and as the gangplank rattled noisily landward, only a handful of casually dressed passengers alighted onto the aging wooden dock, which was sometimes known as Presbyterian Dock, most likely for a patently ungodly reason hidden in the weathered structure's colorful past.

The scene was in stark contrast to the previous evening, when the Friday ferries swelled to capacity with beach-house shareholders—or "groupers," as they were cynically termed by homeowners and renters who could afford the price of a summer place without the assistance of co-contributors.

As a National Seashore and weekend retreat on the Atlantic Ocean, Davis Park, and all thirty-two miles of Fire Island, had a direct, human link to the city proper that was never severed for more than five days at a time. Beginning late on Friday afternoons and continuing until the last ferry slipped into the marina at 11 p.m., the hottest news from the "Apple" was borne by the harried secretaries, admen, artists, writers, accountants and other white-collar types who emerged from the steaming bowels of the summer city to decompress in the salt air and sun until Sunday nights, when a reverse exodus veered toward the distant, unseen metropolis.

Mostly, the summer people were young. And because they were, they were personally affected by the Son of Sam killings. Their jobs, weekday lovers and analysts they left behind, but they carried their dread and preoccupation with Sam off the ferries with them—a fact evident from the tone of conversations which drifted through the Friday swarms as the weekenders loaded groceries and baggage onto squeaky red wagons which they lugged behind them as they slowly trekked to their homes.

Cars weren't permitted on Fire Island, a restriction that would spawn more than one morbid joke that weekend: most of Son of Sam's victims had been shot in parked autos. There were also few sidewalks in Davis Park. Instead, six-foot-wide elevated boardwalks, bearing rustic names like Beach Plum, Spindrift and Whalebone, weaved through the sandy landscape.

The home I rented was perched midway between the bay and the magnificent beach on the Atlantic side of the island and was no more than two hundred yards from water in either direction.

Vacations on Fire Island were always good, affording total escape from the concrete, cars and hustle of the "mainland"—as Long Island and the rest of the metropolitan area were collectively known.

* * *

But on Saturday, July 30, the mainland was on our minds. George Austin, my wife Lynn, and I stood on the dock and mingled with the oil-glistened hordes of day-trippers who were leaving on the six fifteen ferry's turnaround run to Patchogue. Lynn was departing, too; returning to Westchester to visit her recently retired parents, who'd just arrived in New York from their new home in Florida. George and I would remain for the weekend, spruce up the house and leave the beach on Monday, August 1.

"Stay on the parkways when you go through Queens and the Bronx," I dutifully reminded Lynn as the ferry prepared to sail. "And above all, don't pick up some guy and go parking with him."

Lynn managed a weak laugh while George, who was accustomed to such comments, just shook his head.

"I'll phone you in a few hours," I added, "after you've had enough time to get home. It's still early. If anything's going to happen tonight it won't go down until late. You should be home before ten, so no sweat."

"I'll be fine. Don't worry a bit," she replied.

"I'm not worried about you—I just don't want to be pulled away from this island until I absolutely have to go, that's all," I deadpanned.

"Bastard." She grinned and boarded the boat.

We waited as the ferry, a wheezing blue-and-white aberration knighted the *Highlander* many years before, slowly inched its way into the deep-water channel it would follow on its six-mile voyage across the bay. Lynn waved from the stern of the top deck as the ship slid past the marina boundaries and opened its throttle with a gurgling roar as it cleared the outlying channel marker.

With all the guests who'd visited during the vacation, I must have seen eight ferries come and go. This one, for an unsettling reason, felt different. One of *us* was going back; leaving the safety and serenity of the summer hideaway on a night just about all the smart money in town thought Son of Sam would strike. The apprehension seemed foolish, I knew, but I also knew that it was real. These were frightening times in New York.

And if I also knew how close the case actually was to me—even on that night—I'd have departed the island myself and driven directly back to Westchester. But that knowledge was yet to come.

It was still cocktail hour in Davis Park, and as we ambled down Center Walk small clusters of brightly dressed people were gathered on front decks sipping gin and tonics and nibbling on pepperoni, cheese and crackers and steamed or cherrystone clams—standard pre-dinner fare at the beach. Some 30 percent of the clams harvested in the United States were dug from the bottom of the shallow Great South Bay. So what might have been a five-dollar decision to ponder as a restaurant appetizer elsewhere was as common as potato chips to Fire Islanders.

"I wonder if anybody else managed to get crabs for dinner," George chided, mindful of the afternoon's futile crawl through the bay.

"No, smart-ass, they'll get their crabs later—after dancing the night away with the loves of their lives."

"Speaking of rock and roll, when do you want to go out tonight?" he asked.

"Around eleven, I guess. Nothing much going on before then. We'll fritz around the house a while."

Indeed, it was far too early for any serious socializing, so we busied ourselves with the supper dishes and TV. Later, I sat in a canvas director's chair and scanned the newspapers, which were filled with Son of Sam articles. I'd also brought a collection of earlier clippings with me, which I'd previously read fifty times, and spread them out on the ancient oak table and devoured them again. Like many others, I'd become addicted to the .44 case.

"Just what do you think you're going to find in all that?" George inquired after an hour elapsed. "You know all that stuff by heart as it is, and you've watched every news program that's been on for the last week. What's going to happen is going to happen and we can't do a damn thing about it. Nobody can, like it or not. And what do we know from mass murder anyway? You don't write about it and I sure as hell don't analyze it in the insurance business."

"Well, I don't know a hell of a lot," I agreed. "But it doesn't look like the NYPD knows very much either. This shit's been going on a long time. A year yesterday. And they have zilch. They must have a million cops out tonight because of this anniversary thing."

"In Queens and the Bronx, right?"

"Yeah. I wonder why only Queens and the Bronx. Sam, I mean. He must know the streets."

"All the shootings happened near the parkways," George suggested. "They think that's significant. Easy access and escape with a car. Meaning he uses a car. That's a pretty safe bet."

"But they don't have any car ID'd," I cut in. "They've probably got a couple of 'possibles,' but nothing firm at all. There was something about a mustard-colored car at the disco in Queens. But that's it; nothing solid that's hit the papers."

I held up a dog-eared map of the shooting sites from the *Post*. "A lot of people are trying to make some sort of design or pattern by drawing lines between the different spots where he hit. It can look like a triangle if it's done a certain way. They think they might be able to predict where the next one's going to be by plotting out the pattern."

"Well, if that's so, where's he going to hit tonight?" George challenged. "God damned if I know."

* * *

In Brooklyn, forty miles to the west of the lazy idyll of Davis Park, Robert Violante arrived at 1740 East 5th Street in the Flatbush section and parked near a fire hydrant in front of the brick three-family home. From the second-floor terrace, Jerry

Moskowitz gazed curiously from his lounge chair as Violante emerged from his father's 1969 brown Buick Skylark and, reading the address through the gathering dusk, opened the small iron gate and climbed the front stairs.

Nice-looking kid, Jerry thought, as behind him in the apartment the doorbell rang. And on time, too. Jerry, fifty-three, a burly, graying truck driver for the Dolly Madison Ice Cream Company, looked at his watch. It was 8:05 p.m.

"Hey, Neysa," he called in to his wife. "Tell Stacy her date's here." Neysa Moskowitz, forty-three, a vivacious, outspoken, auburn-haired woman with a keen interest in anyone her daughter went out with, hit the buzzer and opened the door to let Violante into the apartment.

Stacy's younger sister, Ricki, who met Violante two nights before at Beefsteak Charlie's, remained in her room while her parents and Violante made small talk as they waited for Stacy.

"What are you kids going to do?" Jerry queried. "That Son of Sam guy is all over the papers and TV . . ."

Violante quickly assured Jerry that they'd probably go to a movie in Brooklyn before stopping for food or dropping by a disco. At that moment, Stacy appeared from her room.

"I'm glad you've all met already," she announced brightly, and asked Violante to sit for a minute. This time, Neysa asked their destination, and Stacy let Violante answer again: "We're probably going to see *New York, New York* at the Kingsway and then get something to eat."

"That's sensible," Jerry observed. "I don't want you kids getting anywhere near trouble out there."

"We won't. I'll call you, Mom," said Stacy, who always made it a point to touch base with her mother during her evenings out. With that, the young couple rose to leave.

"Now I want you to have a good time, but remember that Son of Sam," Neysa warned.

"This is Brooklyn, not Queens. And anyway, I'm a blonde. We'll be just fine," Stacy remarked, and tossed her mother a reassuring smile.

Jerry and Neysa, who were now joined by Ricki, stood on the terrace as Violante opened the passenger's door for Stacy before letting himself into the driver's side of the car.

"Look at that, Jerry," Neysa gushed. "She hasn't stopped talking about him for two days. She said he was a real gentleman. When's the last time you saw that?"

"Yeah, it's been a while." Jerry nodded. "He seems like a nice kid. Must come from a good Italian home."

Together, the Moskowitzes watched the Skylark pull from the curb and rumble down East 5th Street until it disappeared into the twilight.

*   *   *

In the city of Yonkers, some forty miles north of the Moskowitz home, David Berkowitz was cognizant of the growing darkness. He knew it was time to be on the road.

This night would be one of motion for people who were, or would become, part of the case. At 8:20, the Omega task force was fanning out from the 109th Precinct in Flushing, Queens, to blanket the residential and disco areas of that borough and the Bronx. About three hundred cops were on exclusive Son of Sam watch that night and thousands of others, on regular duties, were also on top alert for the elusive night wind with the snarling Bulldog .44.

Lynn Terry was nearing the Whitestone Bridge, which connected Queens and the Bronx, on her way back to Westchester. Stacy Moskowitz and Robert Violante were driving through south Brooklyn, deciding whether to view a movie in Manhattan or queue up at the local Kingsway. On Fire Island, George Austin and I were discussing Son of Sam's escape routes.

And David Berkowitz was edgy in Yonkers.

The "nondescript postal worker," as he'd soon be labeled, was eight weeks past his twenty-fourth birthday. He stood about five feet eleven and weighed approximately two hundred pounds. His eyes were steely blue, and his hair was short, dark, and curled in a "perm." He had lived in the tidy, top-floor apartment at 35 Pine Street for fifteen months—since April 1976. To most who knew him, Berkowitz, outside of a brush with born-again Christianity that turned some people off, was a nice guy. Quiet, not pushy. A follower rather than a leader. Just one of the guys.

An Army veteran who was discharged in June 1974, he'd held a handful of jobs since returning to civilian life. He'd been a security guard, a construction worker and a cabdriver for the Co-Op City Cab Company in the Bronx, where he formerly lived. His life was different then.

Dressing to go out, Berkowitz donned a short-sleeved grayish shirt, a pair of black half-sneakers, blue jeans and, despite the searing July heat, a blue denim jacket.

Passing up the elevator as was his habit, he trotted down the seven flights of stairs to the lobby of 35 Pine, a newly refurbished high-rise building. Opening the glass door, he bounded up the front steps to street level and walked to his car, a 1970 four-door Ford Galaxie, which was cream-colored with a black vinyl roof and black-wall tires. The car, as it frequently was, was parked a block north and east on hilly Glenwood Avenue.

Sliding behind the wheel, Berkowitz cranked the engine, which needed a tune-up, and climbed east on Glenwood to Park Avenue, where he made a left. He drove one block to Lake Avenue, turned right and drove down a slight incline and past a row of stores before making a right on Ridge Avenue and beginning to descend the steep hills of Yonkers as he angled toward the Saw Mill River Parkway.

Finally entering the parkway on Yonkers Avenue, Berkowitz veered south toward Manhattan, paralleling the Hudson River. He played with the buttons on the Galaxie's radio, alternating between rock music and all-news WINS and WCBS. The broadcasts were highlighted by reports about the .44-Caliber Killer.

Within hours the radio would be crackling with another report—that of what would become the most sensational homicide and follow-up investigation in the history of New York; and also one of the most infamous and controversial shootings in the annals of recorded crime in the United States.

Into Manhattan now, Berkowitz exited the West Side Highway at the construction site at 56th Street and followed the detour to 34th. He made a left at the traffic light and soon found himself in familiar territory—a location of the Universal Car Loading Corp. where he'd once worked as a guard for IBI Security.

At 34th and 9th Avenue he turned right, continued south for several blocks, again turned right and came out on 10th Avenue. At 31st Street, he looked for a parking spot, found one and walked to a food stand, where he ordered a quick dinner-on-the-fly. He didn't have much time to spare. He had a rendezvous in Brooklyn.

*   *   *

At 8:45 p.m., Robert Violante and Stacy Moskowitz had themselves arrived at a joint decision concerning dinner. They opted to skip having a meal before going to the movies; and would stay in Brooklyn. They also agreed to drive down to Gravesend Bay to watch the ships in the harbor before catching the 10 p.m. showing of *New York, New York.*

The young couple, enjoying each other's company immensely, drove west on the one-way Shore Parkway service road in Bensonhurst and stopped under a streetlamp opposite a playground and softball field at 17th Avenue. This stretch of Shore Parkway was known as a parking spot for couples, a sporadic dumping ground for abandoned cars and a place where on-duty police would occasionally "coop" for coffee breaks.

A high, bent chain link fence separated the service road from a greenbelt and the rush of traffic on the Belt Parkway. Behind the couple's car, a pedestrian footbridge rainbowed the highway and led to an esplanade where a handful of park benches faced Gravesend Bay, a sadly appropriate name for the body of water.

In the distance, the necklace of lights from the Verrazano Narrows Bridge twinkled in the near darkness; and beyond the span loomed the distant purplish hulk of Staten Island. Several tankers lolled easily in the bay, riding quietly at anchor. A full moon was rising.

After an hour of talking and a stroll down to the water, Violante and Stacy drove to the Kingsway Theatre at Coney Island and Kingsway avenues. From the lobby, Stacy phoned her mother to report she was having an excellent evening. At 10 p.m., the couple settled into their seats, hoping to be entertained by the multiple talents of Liza Minnelli.

*   *   *

After watching the eleven o'clock news, George and I walked to the marina, where I called Lynn from a phone booth outside the police substation. Inside, two bored Suffolk County officers were leaning back in wooden chairs.

"They're sure as hell not on the task force," George cracked. "Life at the beach does go on and on, doesn't it?"

Lynn answered the phone after just two rings and reported her trip back was uneventful. But she noticed what appeared to be a number of unmarked police cars near the tollbooths on the Whitestone Bridge.

"Great," I replied. "If *you* can spot them, do they think the killer can't? What'd they look like?"

"Well, they had no chrome on them, no whitewalls, four doors . . ."

"Bingo. The whole country knows about the dragnet, and their unmarked cars might as well have neon lights on them. Next we'll have the Goodyear blimp over Forest Hills . . ."

In fact, Lynn's observations were correct. The Whitestone and Throgs Neck bridges, which linked Queens and the Bronx, were high on the police priority list. They were reasonably certain the killer had a car and used the spans to travel between the boroughs. They were right.

After the phone call, George and I headed for the only night spot in town, the Casino, which was always an annoying wall-to-wall crush on Fridays and Saturdays. But on a positive note, if one wanted to find the action in Davis Park, one knew exactly where to look.

But that night, surprisingly, the crowd was more subdued than usual. Between Jimmy Buffett's "Margaritaville," jukebox disco and Rita Coolidge covering Jackie Wilson's classic rocker, "Higher and Higher," conversations were almost all concerned with Son of Sam.

"Jesus, he's really out here, too, isn't he?" George observed as we exchanged theories on the killer with some friends at the bar. Around us, other discussions were as animated.

Hypotheses were flowing as fast as screwdrivers were being poured into the plastic cups that passed as Casino crystal. Girls were comparing the guy who'd just asked them to dance with police composites that were indelibly branded in their brains. Anyone who came across as even a little "different" aroused suspicion.

We'd never seen anything like it, but it was sure that similar scenes were being played out in night spots all over the metropolitan area—except in Queens and the Bronx. Those singles bars were empty.

"This is a little much," I said. "What the hell do they think he's going to do—shoot them and escape in a speedboat?"

"It's not that," explained Don Bergen, a tall, husky fuel-oil dealer from Sayville, Long Island, who was renting a house with his family for the month of July. "It's just that everyone who's come out from the city is now so used to being paranoid that it's become part of them. They can't even forget out here."

"How I spent my vacation—jumping at shadows. I feel for them," Don's wife, Connie, remarked. "This is quite the unusual summer."

That was an understatement.

Later, at about 1 a.m., a small group sat on the dune stairs near the Bergen home on East Walk. Edith Kelly, whose husband, Carl, was a New York City cop working that night in Manhattan, joined us, along with her recently widowed friend, Barbara Newman.

For a time, no one spoke. The light slap of the waves on the shore below was the only intrusion. Thoughts turned inward.

"Carl says the whole force is going crazy," Edith quietly said, breaking the silence. "Vacations are being canceled; everyone's on overtime to cover for the manpower on the task force. The guys all hate it. This kind of thing is like a domino effect. It's upset the balance of the whole Police Department."

"I wouldn't want to be the owner of a disco in Queens," added Don Bergen, ever the businessman. "I keep reading how those places are really hurting."

"And maybe some other places after tonight," said George. "It's gotta be tonight. It's so damn peaceful here. We're so close to that zoo over there but still so far from it all. I'd say tonight's the night."

"Who the hell knows," I said. "But it damn well sure could be tonight unless they scared him off with that dragnet."

"Well, maybe he'll go somewhere else," Barbara Newman stated.

"Could be." I was enjoying my role as a student of the case. "Maybe into New Rochelle, somewhere just across the Bronx line."

I believed Sam lived in lower Connecticut, Westchester or the north Bronx. There was no specific reason for this opinion. It was just a feeling based on the escape routes and the fact that the first shooting occurred in the northeast Bronx. Perhaps Sam, unsure of himself on his maiden flight, hadn't ventured too far from the nest.

"Well, why not Brooklyn, good old Brooklyn?" Connie Bergen, a native of the Bensonhurst area, where her parents still lived, was tentatively serious when she spoke.

"I haven't thought about Brooklyn since the Dodgers left, and I don't know anyone else who has either," Don said, laughing.

"Yeah. But maybe *he* has," I countered. "Wherever it is, if it's tonight, they're going to learn a lot about this guy. By where he hits or doesn't hit. About his ego, his subconscious, his intelligence.

"If he tries to defy them and do it in Queens or the Bronx, that will show one thing—omnipotence. If he just cools it and stays home, like last night, that's another thing. He doesn't subconsciously want to get caught. And if he goes to a new area to outsmart them and beat the dragnet, that's another indication of how smart and powerful he feels and that he doesn't want to get caught—subconsciously or otherwise."

"Thank you, Doctor." It was George.

"Screw it. Everybody on the damned East Coast has a theory on this freaking case. I might as well throw mine in, too."

"Why do you think those pictures they released—the sketches—look so different from one another?" Connie wanted to know.

"1 have no idea," I replied. And I didn't.

"We'll know soon enough on who, where and when, I guess," said Don, ending the night's discussion of Son of Sam.

*   *   *

On the Shore Parkway service road in Connie Bergen's old Bensonhurst neighborhood, at the same location where Stacy Moskowitz and Robert Violante had parked four hours before, a young Brooklyn resident named Robert Barnes* was becoming annoyed with his wife, Paula.* The couple, who were temporarily living with Barnes's parents, had themselves driven to the block for some private moments together. They'd walked into the 17th Avenue playground and down the cobblestone path that separated the softball field and handball courts from the swings and bocce courts. Upon returning to their car at 12:45 a.m., Paula noticed she'd lost her bracelet.

Robert and Paula were two of a considerable number of Brooklyn citizens who were about to enter the Son of Sam saga. The story that is now ready to unfold has not been told before. It would take me nearly three years to piece it together. And it was only accomplished after more than thirty interviews; months of in-depth analysis of the events and the scene; confidential correspondence with David Berkowitz; and the assistance of highly placed official law enforcement sources in Brooklyn. Much of what follows has been culled from secret NYPD files that were never intended to reach the public.

The public itself was told one story—a false story—by New York City authorities who, for their own reasons, decided to whitewash the events of July 31, 1977. The time of the shooting, as established by neighbors' calls to the NYPD's 911 emergency number, was 2:35 a.m. But the scenario actually began to unfold ninety minutes earlier.

*   *   *

1:10 a.m.

Paula Barnes was determined to find her lost bracelet. So, dragging her reluctant husband with her, she reentered the 17th Avenue park and proceeded to search for it. They returned to their car, which was parked on the service road near Bay 16th Street, shortly before 1 a.m.

Paula and Robert, talking in their car, look down the service road and observe a yellow Volkswagen Beetle pull up to the park's entrance and watch as *two* people emerge from the car and walk into the park. The Barneses continue their conversation and leave the area at about 1:15 a.m. But they wouldn't be the only people at the scene; other couples were now beginning to arrive at the urban lovers' lane.

*   *   *

About 1:30 a.m.

Dominick Spagnola,* parked on the south side of the Shore Parkway service road near where the Barneses had stopped, sees what he believes to be a 1972 yellow Volkswagen Beetle parked by the entrance to the playground. It has a black stripe above its running board and what Spagnola thinks are New York license plates.

Robert Martin,* another Brooklyn resident, is, at this time, driving west on the adjacent Belt Parkway. While passing the pedestrian footbridge opposite the park's entrance he sees a man standing on the parkway's greenbelt near the overpass. The man appears to be trying to cross the parkway to the esplanade near Gravesend Bay on the other side. He is wearing sunglasses, dungarees and a white shirt, which is out of his trousers. He is carrying a brown paper bag—an item previously used by Son of Sam to conceal the .44 Bulldog.

Mr. and Mrs. Frank Raymond,* walking their dog on the service road near the overpass, notice a similar man by a hole in the fence which separates the parkway greenbelt from the service road. Seeing the Raymonds looking at him, the man ducks back behind some shrubbery.

Mr. and Mrs. Frank Vignotti,* a young couple, are parked a short distance east of the park's entrance, near the fence and overpass. While talking, they watch a man, coming from their left, walk off the parkway overpass—returning from the Gravesend Bay esplanade. He walks in front of the Vignottis and crosses the service road to the yellow VW. He approaches the driver's door and stops, as if to open it. But he now notices the Vignottis and decides to enter the playground instead.

He is white, stocky and short—about five feet seven—with dark, short-cropped hair. He is wearing dungaree pants and a light-colored shirt which is tucked into his trousers. The shirt's long sleeves are rolled up. His arms are well defined and muscular. He has a golden tan.

*   *   *

About 1:45 a.m.

Tommy Zaino, nineteen, is seated with his date, Debbie Costanza,* in a borrowed blue Corvette which is parked adjacent to the fence opposite the playground, a short distance ahead of where the Vignottis were parked a few minutes earlier. Zaino, the co-owner of a Coney Island auto repair business, was formerly parked directly under the sodium streetlamp near the overpass but pulled forward two car lengths to a darker spot.

It is his first date with the seventeen-year-old Debbie and, unlike some of the other couples in the lovers' lane, Zaino and Debbie are simply talking. At about 1:45 a.m., Zaino hears the distinctive sound of a Volkswagen engine and notices a yellow roof roll by as the VW moves past him on the one-way service road.

A few minutes later, Robert Violante and Stacy Moskowitz, returning after the movie and a stop at a disco, pull into the vacated space three car lengths behind

Zaino and Debbie. They are in Zaino's former location under the streetlamp. With the illumination from the light and the added effect of the full moon, the Shore Parkway service road is almost as bright as day.

*   *   *

2:05–2:10 a.m.

NYPD officer Michael Cataneo, on motor patrol with his partner, Jeffrey Logan, turns off the service road two blocks east of the Violante auto and begins to drive onto Bay 17th Street, a quiet one-way avenue of red-brick garden apartment buildings. The police travel north about half a block and notice a cream-colored Ford Galaxie with a black vinyl roof parked slightly behind a fire hydrant in front of No. 290, on the west side of the street. It is Berkowitz's car. He had arrived at his rendezvous in Brooklyn nearly an hour before.

Berkowitz, in a courtyard between the apartment buildings, watches as Cataneo alights from the police cruiser, walks to read the address on the wall of 290 Bay 17th and returns to the curb to begin writing a traffic ticket. He inscribes the 2:05 time designation on it and then inserts the ticket behind the Galaxie's windshield wipers. He reenters the police car and the two cops leave, only to stop again to ticket two double-parked autos further up the street, near 262 Bay 17th.

Berkowitz, seeing the police about to ticket his car, reacts swiftly. In one of the most startling, significant and ironic moments in the entire Son of Sam story, *he decides to stop the planned shooting from occurring. Hurrying back to the park, he confronts at least two accomplices and tells them his car is at that moment being ticketed and that the attack should be canceled or moved to another location.* Berkowitz explains that the traceable ticket will make him vulnerable to arrest.

An animated discussion ensues, which Berkowitz loses. The alleged reason why he is overruled will be explained later, and it is a shocking reason purportedly involving special plans in effect this night. Berkowitz, chagrined, is told to return to Bay 17th Street and to make sure that the police clear the area. He leaves the park at about 2:10 a.m.

*   *   *

2:10–2:20 a.m.

A young neighborhood girl, Michelle Michaels,* is riding her bike on 17th Avenue near Bath Avenue—two blocks west of Berkowitz's car and three blocks north of where Violante and Stacy are parked. Looking behind her, Michelle notices she is being followed closely by a man in a small yellow car, model unknown. After keeping pace with Michelle for two blocks—heading in the direction of the park—the man pulls alongside and stares at her. Pedaling faster, she reaches her home and runs inside. But the man remains in front of her house for a few moments before continuing south toward the park area. Despite the hour, he is wearing sunglasses—like the man who was standing by the parkway overpass a half hour earlier—and has brownish, short hair, high cheekbones and a pointed chin.

Mrs. Cacilia Davis, forty-nine, a widow and native of Austria, is returning from a night out with a friend, Howard Bohan.* She is riding in the passenger's seat as his car turns off the Shore Parkway service road onto Bay 17th Street and slows while they look for a parking space.

They initially think they can squeeze into the spot in front of Berkowitz's Galaxie, but, seeing the ticket already on his windshield and noting the proximity of the hydrant, they continue about seventy-five yards up the block and triple-park near Mrs. Davis's building, No. 262, blocking the one-way road. Their car is now between Berkowitz's Ford and the police car, which is still on the street near 262 Bay 17th.

While talking with Howard, Mrs. Davis, aware that their car is blocking the avenue, keeps an eye on the road behind them. She suddenly sees a young man emerge from a courtyard, lean across the Ford's windshield and—like any motorist preparing to drive off—angrily remove the ticket. He is wearing a denim jacket and pants. The man opens the driver's door, which is against the curb, and puts the ticket inside the car. He then defiantly, openly leans against the ajar door and watches intently for several minutes as Patrolman Cataneo, laughing and joking with his partner, Logan, writes the second and third tickets on Bay 17th Street that night. When Cataneo finishes, he climbs back into the police cruiser.

Mrs. Davis, meanwhile, has invited Howard inside for coffee and asks if he will accompany her while she walks her dog. Howard declines, *looking at his watch* and pointing out that it is already 2:20 a.m. and he is due at his supermarket job early in the morning.

As the police, who are in front of Howard's car, start to drive off, Mrs. Davis sees the young man down the block quickly enter his Galaxie and speed up behind her and Howard. Clearly agitated, he blares his horn loudly several times to get by.

Mrs. Davis climbs out and walks behind Howard's car, and in front of the Ford. As Howard drives off, she stands on the curb, looking at the profile of the impatient young man in the Galaxie as he passes. She notices the denim jacket and the dark, short-cropped hair.

The Galaxie follows both Howard and the police across the Cropsey Avenue intersection, where it passes Howard—who observes it going by. Still on the trail of the police car, the Ford continues to the next intersection, Bay 17th and Bath Avenue, where both vehicles turn right. They are heading many blocks north and east of the Violante auto and the park. It is approximately 2:21 a.m., just fourteen minutes before the shooting will occur, and David Berkowitz is leaving the scene on the heels of the police.

Mrs. Davis, who has watched the disappearing cars, then enters her first-floor apartment.

* * *

2:20–2:33 a.m.

At about the exact time the Galaxie is leaving the area—but two blocks away—Robert Violante and Stacy Moskowitz stroll into the park through the Shore Parkway entrance.

Stacy and Robert, after arriving at the lovers' lane at about 1:45, talked in their car for about twenty minutes before walking across the footbridge to Gravesend Bay. Returning, and now into the park, they walk a path that separates a ballfield and handball courts on the east from the swings and bocce courts on the west.

Leaning against a restroom building in the shadows beneath a broken park light near the end of the path is a man Violante terms a "weird, grubby-looking hippie." His hair is dark, curly and "all messed up, down over his forehead." He is stocky and wearing either a bluish denim shirt or jacket with a T-shirt underneath. *His sleeves are rolled up.* He is unshaven, tanned, and has "piercing dark eyes."

Robert and Stacy pass within ten feet of the man, who continues to lean against the restroom building as the couple turn left to enter the swings area. Together, they ride the swings "for about five minutes" before returning to their car—parked beneath the streetlamp—at about 2:25 a.m. They do not see the man as they leave.

Zaino, who notices the couple return, will later agree with Violante's estimate of the time, as will Donna Brogan,* who is parked with her boyfriend, John Hogan,* opposite the Violante auto and slightly behind it. Donna had seen Robert and Stacy "enter the park, stay there five minutes" and return to their car about 2:25. Donna and John, in a red Volkswagen, will depart at about 2:30 and drive to a store for sandwiches. When they return at 2:40, the shooting will already have occurred.

Meanwhile, at about 2:22, Mrs. Davis had leashed her white spitz, Snowball, and prepared to take him for a walk. But because neighbors' guests were leaving and the dog sometimes barks at strangers, she delayed her departure. She heard them outside complaining about the parking tickets they'd received minutes before.

When the guests have driven off, Mrs. Davis begins her walk. It is approximately 2:23 a.m. She leads Snowball down the west side of Bay 17th Street and specifically notices the vacated space at the hydrant where the ticketed Galaxie was parked.

At the corner of Shore Parkway, she turns west, or right, and walks through a hole in the fence near the overpass. She then unleashes the dog and lets him scamper on the greenbelt for a minute.

Looking at the service road, she sees three occupied cars: Violante's (whose owners had just returned from the park), Zaino's and a third auto, a Volkswagen "bus"—a van. Donna Brogan has already left. The time is approximately 2:30.

* * *

About 2:33 a.m.

After they have walked back to the front of her apartment (a timed recreation would later show the entire trip took a minimum of ten minutes), the dog hesitates. Mrs. Davis, giving in to her pet, turns and retraces her steps toward Shore Parkway.

But about 125 feet from her apartment she sees a young man "leaping the curb" to the sidewalk on her side of the block. He appears to be coming from the other side of the street—the side away from the park. (The man, whom Mrs. Davis later positively identifies as David Berkowitz—whose auto was also positively identified by the parking ticket—is just returning to the neighborhood after following the police car. He has been away from the area for a crucial thirteen minutes. Moreover, he's been away from the park for twenty minutes.)

But now, Mrs. Davis understandably doesn't connect him with the Galaxie driver, who'd left the area, but she notes he appears "similar" to him. As he walks by, less than five feet separates them. He is wearing a dark blue denim jacket with the *sleeves rolled down*. He has on a shiny, gray-colored Qiana shirt which is tucked into his denim trousers. His stomach is large and he is wearing what seem to be blue deck shoes—half-sneakers. His hair is short, dark, curly and neatly combed. He looks so tidy Mrs. Davis initially thinks he is "out on a date."

Berkowitz's right arm is held stiffly at his side, and as he turns to enter a courtyard between the buildings Mrs. Davis sees something "metallic" partially hidden up his right jacket sleeve. She thinks it is a portable radio.

Berkowitz glares at her and, knowing he is not a neighborhood resident, she becomes "a little frightened." She hurries the forty yards to her first-floor apartment—more than a two-block walk from the Violante auto—where she immediately unleashes her dog. She then opens a newspaper, and at that moment hears a loud "boom" and a car horn blaring in the distance.

*   *   *

2:35 a.m.

While Mrs. Davis is still entering her apartment, Tommy Zaino, who is parked two car lengths ahead of Violante's auto on Shore Parkway, sees a man standing by a bench near the park's entrance, which is across the street and slightly behind him. With the excellent lighting conditions, Zaino gets "a very good look" at the man, who is stationary—gazing at the Violante car.

He is twenty-five to thirty years of age, "short, about 5'7" tall," stocky and with long, straight, messy blondish hair which is covering his forehead and part of his ears. "It looked like a wig," Zaino will later say. The man is wearing a grayish, uniform-type shirt with long sleeves. The sleeves are rolled up to his elbows. The shirt is out of his denim trousers. He is unshaven.

Zaino, who'd been looking out the Corvette's passenger window, now shifts his gaze to the rearview mirror as the man peers up and down the street, crosses the pavement and approaches the Violante auto. Stacy and Robert are necking, oblivious to the nearing menace.

The blondish-haired man stops about two feet from the car, pulls a gun from beneath his shirt, crouches and fires four times through the open passenger window.

Zaino, watching the entire incident, is frozen in place as he sees the gunman's hands "go up and down" between the shots.

The attacker stops firing, turns abruptly, "runs like hell" into the darkened park and disappears. Zaino thinks he's never seen anyone run that fast.

About a hundred yards away, on the opposite side of the park—at the 17th Avenue exit—a beautician, who is seated in a car with her boyfriend, sees a "white male with dark eyebrows," possibly wearing a denim jacket, and wearing "a light-colored, cheap nylon wig, exit the park at a *fast* pace, enter a small, light-colored auto," and speed away.

"He looks like he just robbed a bank," she exclaims to her boyfriend, and reaches for a pencil. Concentrating on the license plate, she writes down as much as she can discern. It is, she thinks, - - 4-GUR or - - 4-GVR. She isn't able to read the first two numbers.

At the same time, Mrs. Robert Bell,* a 17th Avenue resident, sees a car, whose make she can't identify in the shadows, pull away from the park "20 seconds after the shots were fired." Likewise, a visiting nurse tending to a patient on 17th Avenue also hears the shots and looks out to see a yellow Volkswagen speeding north on 17th Avenue, away from the park. She, too, records a partial plate number—463—but is unable to read the letters that follow.

At the corner of 17th Avenue and the first intersection—Cropsey Avenue—the yellow VW, with its *lights out* and the driver's left arm hanging out the window as he struggles to hold the hastily closed door shut, speeds through a red light and nearly collides with a car being driven east on Cropsey by another witness, Alan Masters.*

Both autos come to a screeching halt in the center of the intersection. The VW driver leans out his window and screams, "MOTHERFUCKER!" at the astonished Masters, then straightens out the car and roars west on Cropsey. Infuriated, Masters swings a sharp U-turn and takes off in pursuit.

The VW driver, not realizing he is being chased, now turns on his headlights. But he quickly extinguishes them when he spots Masters bearing down on him. Masters, in a vain attempt to read the VW's license plate, hits the floor button for his high beams. He thinks the plate may be a tan New Jersey plate, lighter than New York's amber, but he isn't sure.

The pursuit continues west on Cropsey to 15th Avenue, where the yellow VW Beetle makes a hard left turn at high speed and again accelerates in an attempt to lose Masters, who is closing the ground between them. At Independence Avenue, the VW abruptly turns right, veering wildly down the narrow one-way street in the wrong direction with Masters still in pursuit.

At the end of Independence Avenue, the VW swerves to the right onto Bay 8th Street. The driver then swings a hard, one-motion U-turn and heads straight back at Masters. The Volks passes the witness and hurtles up the access ramp to the Belt Parkway.

The chagrined Masters also executes a U-turn but is stopped at the ramp's entrance by another car leaving the parkway. Seconds later he speeds up the ramp, which

offers entrances to the Belt in both east and west directions. He slows, looks east toward Coney Island and sees no taillights or cars, so he enters the parkway westbound
toward the Verrazano Narrows Bridge.

But by the time he reaches 4th Street, he realizes the elusive VW has escaped.

Masters may not have been sure of the license plate's state of origin—but he wasn't
the least bit uncertain about the description of the VW's driver. He was male, white,
twenty-eight to thirty-two years old, high cheekbones, face narrow at the bottom.
Slight cleft in chin. Flattish nose. Shadowy, unshaven face. Narrowish, very dark
eyes. Hair messy, stringy and brown, combed left to right.

The VW driver also was wearing a bluish-gray, long-sleeved shirt with the sleeves
rolled up to the elbows—a feature Masters spotted at the time of the near-collision
when the VW driver's left arm was extended out the window as he tried to hold the
door shut.

Mr. Masters was a hell of a witness. His observations were as concise as a cop's.

*   *   *

Even as the VW driver was fleeing from the top of the park, two neighbors were
witnessing events that would receive little attention from the police but would, in
time, prove to be extremely important.

First, on the immediate east side of the park, in her Bay 16th Street apartment
which faced the playground, Mrs. Mary Lyons*—within seconds of the shooting—heard cries for help—Violante's—and the sound of a car horn blaring—also
Violante's. Investigating, she looked out her window. She saw a man, ignoring the
pandemonium, walk casually out of the park's handball courts and continue to stroll
across Bay 16th Street toward her building.

She described a man identical to the one seen by Mrs. Davis, who was face-to-face
with Berkowitz directly behind Mrs. Lyons's building less than three minutes earlier.
Mrs. Lyons noted a "male, white, 25–30, dungaree jacket, dungaree pants, and dark
brown, curly hair." Berkowitz would later say he left the scene by precisely this route.

In the second report, Mrs. Thomas Valens* observed yet another car leaving the
scene in a highly suspicious manner. Mrs. Valens lived on Bay 14th Street, the block
adjacent to the park's western side. She was standing in front of her home shortly
after the shots were fired when she saw a small yellow car with its headlights flashing
on and off speed past her. (The headlight-flashing technique is not a routine normally employed by innocent citizens. It is used when one wishes to prevent one's license
plate numbers—which are illuminated by bulbs—from being read. The lights are
turned on to enable the driver to quickly appraise the road ahead before shutting
them off again.)

*   *   *

As the gunman disappeared into the park, Robert Violante knew he was hurt badly.
He looked at Stacy. He heard her moaning, but he couldn't see her. A .44 bullet,

which smashed his left eye and severely damaged the right one, had blinded him. He was bleeding profusely. Violante immediately leaned long and hard on the Skylark's horn. He then stopped, climbed from the car and, wrapping one arm around the streetlamp, began to cry for help and pressed the horn again.

Tommy Zaino, in the Corvette in front of Violante, had remained stone still during the shooting and watched the gunman until he disappeared into the park. His date, Debbie, had seen nothing—and in fact didn't know the explosions she'd heard were shots. Now, however, the smell of gunpowder hung heavily in the humid night air.

"That was the fucking Son of Sam!" Zaino yelled, frantically reaching to start the Corvette's engine. "What the fuck are we doing here?!"

Debbie started to speak but Zaino admonished her to shut up and peeled away from the scene. He turned right on Bay 14th Street and began to reason things through by the time he reached the corner of Cropsey Avenue. He'd just missed the fleeing VW and the pursuing Alan Masters, and apparently also missed the yellow car Mrs. Valens saw speeding on Bay 14th with the flashing headlights.

Zaino turned right on Cropsey, looked down both 17th Avenue and Bay 16th Street and saw nothing. He knew a police station was only several blocks away, so he drove directly to the 62nd Precinct on Bath Avenue, passing all the traffic signals en route.

Seeing a cop standing on the corner by the station house, Zaino squealed to a stop in front of him. He blurted out there'd been a shooting on the service road near the park and then hurried back to the scene.

When Zaino arrived on Shore Road, Violante was lying on the street and off-duty Port Authority officer Richard Sheehan was standing over him. Sheehan, a resident of Bay 14th Street, had heard the shots and rushed around the corner to the Violante car.

As Zaino slowed down, Sheehan waved his badge at him and Zaino halted the Corvette. Together, they covered Violante with a blanket they found in the back of the victims' car. Stacy, gravely wounded but still conscious, was sprawled across the Skylark's front seat.

In a few moments, sector officers Cataneo and Logan, who may have made a routine stop at a diner after being tailed by Berkowitz, pulled up at the shooting site.

Cataneo looked into the car and saw Stacy. She didn't know she'd been shot in the head. "I just got sick in the car," she muttered.

If only that could have been so.

The Son of Sam had made his choice. He'd outwitted the hapless Omega dragnet and struck in Brooklyn. He was the devil playing God and the New York City Police Department seemed powerless, to stop him.

Police Commissioner Michael Codd, acknowledging that the force's blanketing of Queens and the Bronx was a disastrous failure, said, "We've got an entire city to protect now. Sam is telling us he can strike anywhere."

*   *   *

The description of the yellow VW driver provided by Alan Masters would dovetail perfectly with Tommy Zaino's portrayal of the gunman—a key point—right down to the unshaven face and rolled-up sleeves. It was also very similar to Violante's sighting of the "grubby-looking hippie" in the park. And, with the exception of the hair, it matched the description the Vignottis would supply of the man who approached the yellow VW on the service road an hour before the shooting.

But in no way would the descriptions provided by Masters, Zaino, Violante or the Vignottis—whose suspect was of noticeably short stature and not wearing a jacket—match Mrs. Davis's account of the man who would turn out to be David Berkowitz; he of the roving Galaxie. He who was clean-shaven, carefully coiffed, wearing a dark blue denim jacket with rolled-down sleeves and who was so neat Mrs. Davis first thought he was "out on a date."

Critical elements of timing and movement also would be missed by the police—afterwards, when it really mattered. To explain: Berkowitz, by his own statement to authorities, would acknowledge he watched his car being ticketed on Bay 17th Street—at 2:05 a.m., the time on the ticket. He would further state he removed the ticket from the car's windshield, just as Mrs. Davis—who didn't know the specifics of the unreleased confession—had seen. This occurred between 2:10 and 2:15, according to her and to Howard Bohan—who'd looked at his watch a few minutes later.

Berkowitz also would confess that he next stood watching the police; again, just as Mrs. Davis said he did.

To close the loop, the first of the two other parking tickets written on the block after the Berkowitz summons was timed at 2:10 a.m. Then, still another ticket was written by the police as they leisurely conversed in front of Mrs. Davis's building. And, she said, they also examined two additional cars without ticketing them. Together, these actions could easily account for at least another five to seven minutes beyond 2:10.

Berkowitz, in his 1977 confession, would say he stood watching the police for "about 10 minutes." And he was right, since he returned to Bay 17th from the park at about 2:10 and Howard Bohan's watch pinpointed 2:20 as the time the police began to depart. As of this point, all the statements and the physical evidence complement each other.

However, the Davis, Bohan and Berkowitz accounts would now differ drastically, as they would have to for Berkowitz to claim he was the gunman.

Berkowitz would confess that after removing the ticket and watching the police he returned to the park; sat on a bench; watched Stacy and Violante enter the park and ride the swings; saw them return to their car; waited "about 10 minutes"; and then shot them at 2:35—the time established by the calls to the 911 computer.

There are significant factual contradictions in his account. For one thing, Berkowitz would say he was "far down" in the park and seated on a bench. Violante, however, said he and Stacy passed within ten feet of the man who was leaning against the restroom building—not hidden far down in the park or seated on a bench.

"He saw us and we saw him. We went right by him," Violante would tell me. "And he was leaning against the park house. He wasn't near a bench at all."

But even more importantly, Mrs. Davis and Howard both state the Galaxie—driven by Berkowitz—left the neighborhood at 2:20, following the police car blocks from the park. There is no question that the Galaxie moved. The car was in fact ticketed, and Berkowitz and Mrs. Davis agreed that he removed the ticket and stood watching the police after that.

She and Howard then saw the car as it approached and blared its horn behind them. And they saw it again when it passed Mrs. Davis as she stood on the curb and then went by Howard at the corner of Bay 17th and Cropsey Avenue.

Also, while walking her dog, Mrs. Davis specifically noticed the vacated spot at the hydrant where the Galaxie had been.

What this means is that by *all* accounts, even Berkowitz's, he could not have been the man seen by the victims in the park at 2:20—a time established by Violante, Zaino and Donna Brogan. Even allowing for a minor miscalculation on the exact minute, Berkowitz, *by his own statement,* would have been away from the park for an entire twenty minutes—from 2:05 until 2:25. The man in the park, moreover, was already lounging against the rest room when the victims entered; he didn't show up midway through their ride on the swings.

But beyond that, Mrs. Davis put Berkowitz totally out of the area beginning at 2:20, when she saw him leave to follow the police. And he was *still* away from the park at 2:33—just two minutes before the attack—when he passed Mrs. Davis on foot while she was walking the dog.

Her second sighting of Berkowitz would highlight yet another major contradiction in his confession. If, as he claimed in 1977, he removed the ticket, went back to the park and didn't leave it—what was he doing two blocks away on Bay 17th Street *again* at 2:33? There is only one credible answer: he had just returned to the area from following the police and hadn't been in the park at all since the argument with his accomplices at about 2:10.

But Berkowitz, as noted, would claim he was the man in the park; the man seen by the victims; the man police believed was the killer. Why did Berkowitz do so? Because he *had to become that man* in order to confess to sole responsibility for the crimes. By making himself that person, he accounted for that individual's presence on the scene.

The intricate detail provided in this explanation of July 31, 1977, is necessary. The facts, some subtle, involve mass murder, and it is vital to document and explain them as explicitly as possible.

And there is one more relevant fact concerning the murder and who actually committed it: When Mrs. Davis re-created her walk with the dog for me on two occasions, a stopwatch showed she could not have passed Berkowitz on foot before 2:33, at the earliest. This conclusion was determined by her actions and the distance she walked after Howard left at 2:20—a time all the principals agree on.

Then, further timing of her movements demonstrated that only one minute and ten seconds elapsed from the moment she saw Berkowitz disappear into the courtyard and the instant the shots rang out—which she heard as "a long boom." In several timed reenactments, while walking at a brisk pace over the route Berkowitz would have had to travel if he was the gunman, my stopwatch showed he still would have been *more than a minute and twenty seconds away from the Violante car* at the time Mrs. Davis heard the shots.

Simply put, he couldn't even have arrived there in time—let alone discard his jacket, pull his shirt from his pants, roll up his sleeves, change his hairstyle and stand stationary at the park's entrance for about ten seconds—as Zaino saw the killer do—before approaching the victims' car and firing.

The Brooklyn scenario had a beginning—the 2:05 ticket—and a computer-logged ending at 2:35. With those bookends, Howard Bohan's watch, numerous interviews and the timing of the movements of the principals and measurement of the distances traveled, this final re-creation of the last two minutes was accurate. This, too, was a step the police never took.

But with the actual story of July 31, 1977, described here for the first time, it now becomes possible to compare these confidential reports, facts and other information with the subsequent police investigation; an investigation which would, in eleven days' time, end with the arrest of Galaxie driver David Berkowitz as the "lone" Son of Sam killer. The man who, sources close to him say, tried to stop the killing of Stacy Moskowitz would be arrested as her murderer.

The yellow VW, the eyewitness descriptions, the timing and movement contradictions and Mrs. Davis's account of the Galaxie's travels (Howard Bohan was never interviewed by the police) would be ignored or forgotten—as would the conflicting composite sketches, additional evidence gathered at other .44 scenes and evidence virtually begging to be uncovered in Berkowitz's own life and activities.

What was David Berkowitz's role that night in Brooklyn? Who owned the yellow VW? And who pulled the trigger? The second and third questions will be addressed later. But as for Berkowitz himself, all available information demonstrates that he functioned as a lookout responsible for the "east sector," near Bay 17th Street. It is apparent that when the police arrived, he went back to the park to argue his case for postponing the shooting. Failing, he returned to Bay 17th and followed Cataneo and Logan to make sure they'd left the area.

Returning after following the police, Berkowitz parked in an alleyway between 18th Avenue and Bay 17th; passed Mrs. Davis on foot; reached the outer fringes of the playground and signaled an "all clear" to the gunman—who in fact was the man in the park, just as the police believed. The killer then approached the Violante car and fired.

As the murderer fled and the VW chase began, Berkowitz—as seen by Mrs. Mary Lyons from her apartment window—calmly walked away from his vantage point in the corner of the park.

None of this information would come to me for several years.

V

Countdown: The Final Week

Stacy Moskowitz and Robert Violante were rushed by ambulance to Coney Island Hospital and then promptly transferred to Kings County Hospital because doctors believed their severe head wounds could be better treated by the team of neurological specialists there.

As word of the attack filtered rapidly through the media grapevine, a host of television, radio and print journalists converged on Kings County while others hastened to the Shore Parkway shooting site. The scene at the hospital was one of pandemonium. The *News*'s Jimmy Breslin and later Steve Dunleavy of the *Post,* both of whom were prominent in Son of Sam reportage, joined the crush of reporters jamming the corridors outside the emergency room.

The three television networks and their New York flagships sent crews to Kings County, as did local TV outlets WOR, WPIX and WNEW. The Associated Press and United Press International dispatched representatives, who melded with reporters from *Time* and *Newsweek.* Both national newsweeklies had already devoted substantial space to the .44 killings, and would do so again.

Radio reporters from more than a dozen stations also arrived, along with staffers from the *New York Times,* Long Island's *Newsday,* New Jersey's Bergen *Record* and other newspapers. Even the European press was represented by members of several publications' New York bureaus.

On the fringes stood the victims' families. Overwhelmed by fear for Stacy and Robert and stunned by the sudden media explosion, the Moskowitzes and Violantes were on the precipice of shock and collapse. Hospital administrators recognized the precarious situation and directed the couples to a more private area. Still, bedlam reigned.

Behind a curtain in the nearby emergency room, Stacy remained conscious, frequently calling out in pain for her mother. Neysa ran to her daughter's side, but aides gently escorted her from the room. "Baby, baby, you'll be O.K.," the anguished Neysa called back over her shoulder. Stacy's right eye was swollen shut and the lid was a morbid black-and-blue.

Before the doctors could operate, they first had to control her bleeding. Dr. William Shucart, chairman of the neurosurgery department, was reached at his Westchester home by Dr. Ahmet Oygar, chief neurosurgical resident, after he and Dr. James Shahid conducted a preliminary examination of Stacy. Shucart consulted briefly with his colleagues, then dressed and drove to Kings County to direct the operating team.

Meanwhile, Violante was wheeled into surgery. His left eye was completely shattered, but specialist Dr. Jeffrey Freedman hoped to save his life and, if possible, also preserve a degree of sight in the right eye.

An agonizing deathwatch, which through the media presence would be observed by an entire nation, had now begun.

* * *

At the same time, the NYPD was engaged in a mad scramble. The Omega task force members, who could by now count every jagged sidewalk crack in Queens and the Bronx, were preparing to shut down for the evening when news of the shooting arrived at the operation's headquarters at the 109th Precinct in Queens at about 2:50 a.m.

At first Omega commander Timothy Dowd discounted the attack as being Son of Sam's. He simply refused to believe the murderer would thwart the dragnet and strike in Brooklyn, even though the parked-car setting was indicative of the .44-Caliber Killer's *modus operandi.*

But Dowd was persuaded when detectives on the scene radioed that the bullet hole in the Skylark's steering column was large—consistent with that of a .44 slug. Only then did Dowd react. In total, nearly an hour elapsed before a decision to set up roadblocks at the bridge and tunnel exits from Brooklyn was communicated to the field. An advisory regarding the yellow Volkswagen also was transmitted, as at least two neighbors who lived near the shooting site told detectives of the VW's flight from the top of the park.

Grim-faced cops, revolvers at the ready, halted cars for more than two hours at various bridges and tunnels: scanning drivers' faces; trying to spot a gun on a floor or back seat; looking for something—anything—that might indicate the man behind the wheel was the murderer. It was all in vain.

Other detective teams had a dozen of the department's top suspects under surveillance. And as the night wore on, the depressing news became apparent: all were accounted for; none were near the shooting scene. And frustration exploded.

Two detectives, parked outside a high-priority suspect's home, heard the "shots fired" report over the Omega force's special radio band. They'd been investigating the man for weeks, sticking closer to him than did his wife's mother. He'd eluded them the night of the shooting at Elephas, and they'd caught fifty pounds of hell for it. Now they were positive he was in his house—but they had to make sure. What if he'd evaded them again and gone out a back window?

The cops rang the bell. No answer. Maybe he *had* slipped away, gone to Brooklyn and done the shooting. The detectives knew they'd be pounding the pavement in Staten Island. They rang the bell again. Now there were sounds of movement inside.

Revolver drawn, one of the detectives stepped away from the doorway. Then the door opened and the sleepy, somewhat inebriated "suspect" stood in front of them— and the other detective promptly punched him in the mouth. Anger and frustration. It was the worst of all nights for Operation Omega.

The Omega detectives were good, professional cops—among the city's best. Many worked long, grueling hours and volunteered even more time than that. Some suffered family and personal crises because the case was so demanding, time-consuming and obsessive. Personalities changed. Resentment simmered until anger boiled over—sometimes at home, sometimes on the job, sometimes in the smoky, beer-charged atmosphere of a neighborhood bar in Queens.

As dawn broke on July 31, 1977, it was a sour summer Sunday. The police were back at square one, no closer to snaring the killer than they'd been in July 1976.

* * *

At Fire Island, we awoke at nine in the morning on July 31 and heard the news of the shooting on the radio.

"Brooklyn," I exclaimed to George over breakfast. "Goddamnit, the bastard went into Brooklyn!"

"This guy is one smart son of a bitch," he replied. "You've got to wonder if they'll ever get him now. What's that—thirteen victims? It's unreal. How much can they take over there? The city must be going nuts."

Eyeing the kitchen clock, I hurried to meet the 10 a.m. ferry, which carried the morning newspapers.

The trip was hardly worth it. Since the attack occurred after the newspapers' deadlines, recap stories and updates on the task force were all that appeared. The *Times,* its foot firmly in its mouth, reported that the killer's warning of an anniversary attack had gone "unfulfilled." "PROBE FIX RING IN N.Y. COURT" was the *Daily News's* page one banner. The murderer had rendered the papers obsolete before they were delivered. So radio and TV became the main news sources of the day at the beach.

* * *

Robert Violante survived his surgery; his life had been saved. But the doctors, who knew going in that his left eye was gone, were guarded in their prognosis for the right one, through which he could only distinguish a gray haze of light. The surgeons hoped that the faint glimmer indicated he might regain at least a semblance of vision in the right eye; but they weren't optimistic.

The operation Shucart and his team performed on Stacy had at best a remote chance of success. One slug had grazed her scalp, causing minimal damage. But a second bullet entered the left side of her head and traversed downward through her brain before embedding in the base of her neck. The damaged brain portion, which influenced motor functions, was removed in the course of an heroic, eight-hour operation. Her condition was stabilized, but the surgeons knew the outlook was bleak. Later that night, it was reported that Stacy was returned to the operating table.

* * *

There were no deadline problems for the newspapers on Monday, August 1. "44-CAL KILLER SHOOTS 2 MORE, WOUNDS BKLYN COUPLE IN CAR DESPITE HEAVY COP

DRAGNET. 12TH AND 13TH VICTIMS OF SAM," the *Daily News* proclaimed. The *Post*, seizing on comments from Dowd and Commissioner Michael Codd, truthfully but sensationally shouted across page one: "NO ONE IS SAFE FROM SON OF SAM." The *Times* also displayed the story prominently on its front page and continued with extensive coverage inside.

The *News* picked up on the yellow VW, but only vaguely—saying merely that two witnesses reported the killer fled in such a car.

The paper did have a gem inside, the story about Michelle Michaels (whose real name was withheld) being followed by the man in the yellow car as she rode her bike shortly before the shooting. The *News* seemed confused, mentioning again, as it had in its lead article, that other witnesses saw a VW flee. The first inklings of a second car were there, but the paper didn't know what to do about them. And the police, normally very cooperative with the press on the .44 case, weren't about to help. Not this time. The VW chase and other important information would be kept from the public.

The *Post* included a scene map in its layout, correctly showing the escape route through the park to a car waiting on the opposite side. They'd drawn the killer's auto one block too far to the north, but were in the right arena. These points are mentioned because, when the arrest occurred ten days later, no one carefully studied the scene or investigated inconsistencies in the announced police version of the events of that night.

*   *   *

Three words can sum up the police investigation in the wake of the Brooklyn attack: Volkswagen, Volkswagen and Volkswagen.

Out of the public eye, this was the entire focus of the probe—along with interviews of Alan Masters, Violante, Tommy Zaino, the Vignottis and later Cacilia Davis in an effort to arrive at an accurate composite sketch of the killer. It would be a hectic and confusing week for the police, who themselves would be shocked by the arrest of David Berkowitz on August 10.

The attack had occurred in the 10th Homicide Zone. Normally, the detectives from the 10th would have been absorbed by the Omega force; and indirectly they were. But for the most part, Dowd and his assistant, Captain Joseph Borrelli—with the concurrence of the PD's top brass—allowed the 10th a free hand while the Queens detectives began investigating new suspects from the deluge of tips that were now flooding the .44 hotline number at the rate of a thousand busy signals per hour.

In the aftermath of a major crime, it is routine to check traffic tickets in the event the perpetrator happened to receive one and because a witness might be located among those cited at the approximate time of a given incident.

A police supervisor claims that sometime during the morning of July 31 the two sector officers, Cataneo and Logan, were asked if they'd handed out any tickets in the vicinity of the assault. Both had responded to the scene and to the hospital. They were drained. Allegedly, they replied they hadn't written any summonses—when of course they had done so. The two officers later acknowledged they had no recollection of writing any, but have been unclear as to whether or not they were asked if they had.

The tickets wouldn't be found until August 8. It is possible that no one checked for summonses. It is also possible that Cataneo forgot to submit them until later in the week. Or it may have happened that he inadvertently left the ticket book in the patrol car, where it was later discovered and turned in by another officer. Whatever, it would be Mrs. Cacilia Davis who would alert the police to the fact that summonses indeed were written on her block shortly before the shooting.

David Berkowitz certainly knew tickets were issued—he had one. Back in Yonkers the same day, July 31, Berkowitz calmly sat down, opened his checkbook and in a clear, steady hand wrote check #154 from his account at the Dollar Savings Bank in the Bronx. The draft was made out in the amount of $35, payable to "Parking Violations Bureau N.Y.C." to satisfy the hydrant infraction noted on summons #74 906953 2. Berkowitz inscribed the number of the citation and that of his license plate, 561-XLB, across the top of the check.

Berkowitz's action would seem to be an uncharacteristic one for a so-called "mad, salivating, demon-possessed monster"—as the police would have liked the public to believe—to take just hours after allegedly gunning down two young victims with the clamor of infernal deities pounding in his brain.

Berkowitz mailed the summons and the check, which was cashed on August 4 by the city of New York.

* * *

But, still on July 31, police officers and detectives from the 62nd Precinct canvassed the Bensonhurst neighborhood, jotting down the license plate numbers of some two hundred cars in the immediate vicinity of the shooting. This was done on the chance the killer fled on foot, leaving a car behind; or had arrived in one auto and left in another already waiting for him, with the intention of returning for the second car. The canvassing also was a way of locating potential witnesses.

In addition to logging licenses, the detectives knocked on doors in the area. In doing so, they met several key witnesses—including the Vignottis, Donna Brogan, Mr. and Mrs. Raymond, Mary Lyons, Paula and Robert Barnes and others. Gradually, a picture began to develop.

Also on July 31, an interesting discovery was made a few miles east of the shooting site. A map was found in a phone booth at a Mobil gas station at Flatbush Avenue and Avenue U. According to a confidential police report: "The major access routes in Bensonhurst, Sheepshead Bay, Flatlands, Canarsie and Greenwood Cemetery sections of Brooklyn were outlined in heavy, colored ink. The Bensonhurst section, which is outlined in red, has a number '1' pointing to the spot near where the commission of this crime took place."

The other neighborhoods mentioned surrounded Bensonhurst, and the number "1" coincided with the time the yellow VW arrived there with its two passengers.

The map's presence in a phone booth implied a telephone call to someone; perhaps a conspirator, perhaps not. But the police weren't looking at a conspiracy angle. And with the avalanche of reports coming in, it is likely the potential relevance of the map was overlooked. Berkowitz, incidentally, would later admit to being within two blocks of that gas station the night of the attack.

*   *   *

The next day, August 1, Alan Masters came forward to Detective Roland Cadieux and Sergeant Gerard Wilson and told of the VW chase. He was questioned a second time by three members of 10th Homicide—Detective Ed Zigo, Detective John Falotico and Sergeant William Gardella.

Armed with Masters's information, other detectives traced the escape route. At Independence Avenue, the narrow, one-way block through which the cars sped in the wrong direction, they rang bells up and down the street, seeking witnesses who might have spied the VW or its plate number. No luck.

Continuing on, they arrived at nearby Fort Hamilton, situated off the Belt Parkway on the route Masters said the VW traveled. There, they obtained data on all VW owners with access to the base, as well as to Fort Totten in Queens and Fort Tilden.

The U.S. Coast Guard was then contacted as police attempted to learn shipping schedules along the Brooklyn and New Jersey waterfronts on the theory the VW driver—Son of Sam to the police—might have been a merchant seaman. If he was a crewman, coming and going with his ship, it could have explained the irregular lapses between .44 attacks, the authorities reasoned. Plus, the VW had indeed escaped along the waterfront.

Other reports on yellow Volkswagens were filed throughout the day, and neighborhood residents continued to advise the police as to what they had, or hadn't, seen. Tommy Zaino, who gave his first statement to Detective John Falotico on Shore Parkway forty minutes after the shots were fired, was questioned again at one thirty that afternoon.

His description of the gunman was consistent, concise, and his recollections were vivid. He was one of the best witnesses the detectives had to work with in the .44 case. Zaino was placed under police protection and housed in a motel across the Verrazano Narrows Bridge on Staten Island. Zaino's existence, but not his last name, was leaked to the *Daily News* by Brooklyn police. The paper referred to him as "Tommy Z.," adding that he was parked directly in front of Violante and Stacy.

Why the police, in whispering Zaino's name to the *News,* didn't call him "Tommy X" is a matter to be questioned. Zaino was known in the area, and the police had no way of being sure that Son of Sam didn't write down the Corvette's license number, which, although the car was borrowed, could have led back to Zaino. And although Zaino was under a police umbrella, the protection wouldn't have lasted indefinitely.

After a few weeks he'd have been on his own again, and a potential target.

That wouldn't be the only time the 10th Homicide detectives played roulette with a witness. Cacilia Davis would endure the same experience a week later.

The blinded Robert Violante was himself questioned in the intensive care unit at Kings County Hospital on August 1. He described the grubby man in the park, but told police he didn't see the gunman as he pulled the trigger.

It was a busy, eventful day for the NYPD. But the police and the entire metropolitan area ground to a halt late that afternoon when the announcement came that Son of Sam's double assault in Brooklyn had now become a single assault—and a homicide. At 5:22 p.m. on August 1, some thirty-nine hours after the shooting, Stacy's heart stopped beating.

The "Deathday" anniversary may have arrived late, but it was observed.

The toll now stood at six young people dead, seven wounded.

*　　*　　*

With the announcement of Stacy's death, the lid blew off New York's already boiling pressure cooker. Several incidents of mob violence erupted, with crowds attempting to attack suspicious young men in yellow cars or bar patrons who spoke eerily or offensively to teenaged girls.

In Brooklyn's Sheepshead Bay section, a group of vengeful tavern customers rushed into a street as police arrested a man who sat with two revolvers in a yellow car. Screaming and shouting, "Kill him! Kill him!" the crowd surged at the police and the suspect, whom they believed was Son of Sam. The cops quickly handcuffed the man, flung him to the floor of their patrol car, and squealed from the block.

In suburban Mt. Vernon, the cemetery incident occurred in which two young men dragged an innocent third to his father's grave and attempted to beat a confession out of him. In the Bronx and Queens, fearful residents phoned police to report sighting men dancing around the graves of two .44 victims.

Throughout the city, the situation was explosive.

It was also a time of questionable taste. Vendors began hawking T-shirts which read: "Son of Sam—Get Him Before He Gets You." Another entry, stained with splotches of red dye, contained a facsimile of several paragraphs of the Breslin letter. And a rock group released a recording called "The Ballad of the .44-Caliber Killer." Cynics said it was "number 44 with a bullet" on the charts.

Now, too, the reward money was posted. Donations from the *Daily News,* WABC-TV and a number of corporations and fraternal organizations rapidly reached $24,000. The total would rise steadily to $40,000 by the day of the arrest.

The case was now daily front-page news, and the nightly TV broadcasts also hammered hard at the story. In City Hall, Mayor Abe Beame was feeling intense heat. The Democratic primary was barely a month away, and the city was blowing up around him and was at the core of a national media storm. He was already trailing Ed Koch in the polls, and this .44 madness, which made both him and his Police Department appear incompetent, was now out of control. Rather than wearing heroes' laurels, Beame and the police brass were accumulating funeral wreaths. Something had to be done.

Trying to grasp a greased rope, Beame announced that he was authorizing the immediate rehiring of 175 of the cops who'd been laid off in the fiscal crisis. He also ordered the strengthening of the Omega task force, and the group's ranks were increased to 300 overnight. Son of Sam had to be caught.

*   *   *

For a number of reasons, Tuesday, August 2, would prove to be the most pivotal day in the police investigation. As detectives continued to interview Bensonhurst residents, handle telephone tips and search for the yellow Volkswagen, Cacilia Davis met with her friends Steve and Tina Baretta* and discussed what she'd seen early Sunday morning. She explained that the previous police sketches didn't resemble the man who passed by her just before the attack. By then, Mrs. Davis realized the "long boom" and horn she'd heard were the sounds of the shots and Violante's reaction to them.

She was frightened. She was upset. Her dog, Snowball—or Snow, as she called him—was a distinctive white spitz; the only one in the area. If the killer decided to eliminate a key witness, he'd have little trouble locating Cacilia Davis. She wanted to help, but she didn't know how to go about it and needed to talk it through with Tina and Steve.

The Barettas convinced her she'd be safer speaking to the police than remaining in a fearful silence. Mrs. Davis agreed, and Tina called 10th Homicide during the evening of August 2. She was remotely acquainted with Detective John Falotico and asked if he was in.

Falotico had been engrossed with witness Tommy Zaino and police artist William McCormack, trying to arrive at a concise sketch of Son of Sam that would join the drawings compiled from the other attacks. With interviews of Violante, Alan Masters and the Vignottis—who saw the short-haired man approach the yellow VW—already in hand, the detectives were considering it likely that the killer wore a wig.

Detective Joseph Strano, thirty-six, a strapping police veteran of fifteen years, advised Tina that Falotico wasn't available. Tina thought about hanging up, but decided to tell the story to Strano. Strano liked what he heard. Accompanied by Detective Jim Smith, he immediately drove to the Barettas' apartment. There, a nervous Cacilia Davis sat waiting.

After some small talk designed to allay the widow's fears, Strano began his questioning. A review of his detective division report (DD-5) reveals that Mrs. Davis told him about the ticketed Galaxie and said that she barely reached her front door before the shots were fired. The fact that she observed the Ford leave Bay 17th Street before the shooting was inconsequential to Strano, who, like the rest of the NYPD, was looking for a yellow VW.

He was much more concerned with the physical description of the man who passed Mrs. Davis on foot at 2:33 and what he appeared to be hiding up his jacket sleeve.

After writing down Mrs. Davis's detailed description of what the man on Bay 17th Street was wearing, Strano zeroed in on the object he was carrying up his sleeve. Mrs. Davis, as Strano's report reveals, thought it was a portable radio, but "perhaps a gun."

However, Strano then put his own .38 service revolver up his sleeve—barrel first, with the butt, or handle, facing backward—and Mrs. Davis remarked that yes, it did look like that. And Strano wrote the word "gun" in his report.

But was that a positive identification? Hardly. And why a weapon was supposedly carried in such a bizarre manner by an experienced shooter has never been explained. At other Son of Sam shootings, and in Brooklyn as well, the killer pulled the .44 from beneath a shirt or coat, or carried it in a bag. That was the *modus operandi*— why would this time be different?

It is also difficult to believe that Berkowitz would have called attention to himself by blowing his horn and following a police car if he had the infamous Bulldog in his possession.

And if the gun was under his shirt—as seen by Zaino two minutes later when the killer approached the Violante car—why would he have so brazenly, and awkwardly, displayed it two blocks away?

Because he was thinking of shooting Mrs. Davis? No. Even in his own muddled confession, Berkowitz, in becoming the man in the park, would recount spying on Stacy and Robert as they rode the swings—an action that occurred twelve minutes *before* Berkowitz's encounter with Mrs. Davis on the street. Berkowitz wouldn't, couldn't, confess to his presence on Bay 17th just prior to the shooting. He had to become the man in the park—the killer—in order for his confession to have the slightest chance of being accepted. He would say he was sitting in the park, watching Stacy and Robert with the gun in his jacket pocket.

So if he wasn't carrying a gun on Bay 17th, what was the object hidden in his rolled-down sleeve? It might have been the flashlight that would be found in his car the next week. A flashlight could have been used to blink an "all clear" signal to the man in the park. Or it might have been the hand-held police scanner which would be found in his apartment. Or it might have been a portable walkie-talkie, although none would be found. In any case, it is highly doubtful he was carrying a gun. And it appears reasonable to suggest that Mrs. Davis, who originally thought the object was a radio, was swayed by Strano's demonstration.

* * *

Back at 10th Homicide, Strano filed his report. The detectives in Falotico's camp, who were familiar with Zaino's description of the actual killer, his clothing and that of the VW driver, thought Strano's witness was off the wall. And when Mrs. Davis's comments about the tickets were discussed, several police were further convinced she was in error. There weren't any tickets.

Strano spoke to his witness again. She remained adamant: tickets were indeed written. The police didn't believe her. Mrs. Davis threatened to contact the media anonymously and tell reporters the police refused to search for the summonses.

She was frightened, and angry. She'd come forward, and now most at 10th Homicide were ridiculing her. But not Strano. This was his witness, his big break. With the approval of his supervisor, Sergeant James Shea, the detective returned to Cacilia's apartment the next day—Wednesday, August 3—with police artist Bill McCormack. There they began to work on a profile sketch.

Later, Strano and Mrs. Davis took the first of several shopping trips in Brooklyn, trying to locate a denim jacket identical to the one the man wore. It was fruitless, except that they ultimately learned the coat was similar to those worn by Alexander's security guards. (Berkowitz had been employed as a guard by IBI Security.) The day ended with the completion of the profile sketch and a promise from Strano that the hunt for the parking tickets would continue.

It is important to remember that at no time were the summonses connected to Son of Sam himself. Son of Sam was in the yellow Volkswagen at the top of the park, the police believed; not in a Ford two blocks away on Bay 17th Street. Yes, a Ford was ticketed at the hydrant. And yes, Mrs. Davis said that car later moved. But that revelation meant nothing because she didn't connect the Galaxie driver with the man who later passed her on foot, although they appeared similar to her. Moreover, she knew the police believed the killer drove a yellow VW, knowledge which further disassociated the Galaxie and the man on the street in her mind.

The tickets were of interest to the police for two reasons. First, a potential witness might be found. And even more importantly, the discovery of the summonses would confirm Mrs. Davis's story. Their existence would guarantee she was on the block at the right time on the right night. Without the citations, her entire story was suspect. And so, the search continued.

* * *

The press knew nothing of Mrs. Davis and nothing about the massive, all-out hunt underway for the yellow Volkswagen. At a press conference on August 1, Chief of Detectives John Keenan calculatingly said the reports of a yellow VW appeared to be of little significance.

Deputy Commissioner Frank McLoughlin added: "We have nothing more substantial than a general description [of the killer] and possibly a yellow Volkswagen." McLoughlin also stated: "Some neighbors thought they saw more than one car." There it was, a heady comment. But it wasn't pursued.

Instead, the media extensively covered Stacy's death and funeral arrangements. The *News,* however, by virtue of another leak from Brooklyn, reported that Violante and Stacy had encountered a "weird onlooker" in the park shortly before the attack and that police believed the man was the killer.

The paper, quoting the police allegedly quoting Violante, said: "He kept staring at us, almost scowling, and just stood leaning against a tree or something." This was a false kernel of com purposely planted by the police. The man wasn't leaning against a tree; he was lounging against the brick restroom building. The real killer would know that, and if and when he was arrested, the police could use that fact as a "key" in determining if a confession was legitimate.

Berkowitz would say he was sitting on a bench, and he'd be allowed to get away with it.

* * *

On August 3, Howard Blum of the *New York Times* wrote an article encapsulating the police investigation. Deputy Inspector Dowd was quoted, but he carefully avoided mentioning the VW chase or any of the numerous solid leads the police were working on.

Although through no fault of Blum, who was only reporting what the police were thinking, the article actually said eyewitnesses to the various shootings provided descriptions that "have resulted in four different drawings by police artists of the killer. In these composite sketches, the suspect is a white male between 20 and 35 years old, whose height ranges from 5 feet 7 inches to 6 feet 2 inches and who weighs anywhere from 150 to 220 pounds. The descriptions are so varied that the police are now considering the possibility that the killer wears various disguises, including wigs and mustaches, and has gained weight to complicate further his identification."

Didn't anyone think it was possible that the descriptions were so contrasting because more than one, solitary gunman was responsible for the shootings?

* * *

On August 4, police artist Bill McCormack and Cacilia Davis completed a facial view of the man on Bay 17th Street. Now the police had two sketches, front and profile, based on Tommy Zaino's description of the killer, another drawing from the recollections of VW chaser Alan Masters and the two Davis composites. The detectives sought out the Vignottis for the second time to ask again about the man who approached the yellow VW on Shore Parkway an hour before the shooting.

The young couple, the report says, "picked out Sketch #301 as being the description of the Son of Sam." This clearly demonstrated that the police believed the man who walked to the VW was the killer.

The sketch chosen by the Vignottis was the profile sketch drawn from Mrs. Davis's description—showing a clean-cut, youngish man with short, dark, wavy hair. The difference between the man the Vignottis saw and the one spotted by Mrs. Davis—Berkowitz—was that Berkowitz was noticeably taller and wore a denim jacket with rolled-down sleeves while the Vignotti suspect was clothed in a light-colored shirt with the sleeves rolled up. Significantly, the Vignottis added that the nose of the man they saw was "flatter" than that of the original Davis composite.

The media were clamoring for the release of a new sketch, and police officials wanted to accommodate them. But not yet, not without the tickets and not with the controversy raging over who saw what, and whom.

On August 5, reporters Carl Pelleck and Richard Gooding of the *Post* wrote a page one story under the banner headline "SAM: COPS GET HOPEFUL." The article said that officials had arrived at a "new, more exact composite drawing of the most-wanted man, which police expect to circulate publicly today. . . . Sources who have seen the new sketch say it bears a close resemblance to an earlier one based on a description by Joanne Lomino after she and her friend Donna DeMasi were gunned down Nov. 27 . . . in Floral Park."

That was a long-haired sketch; and the *Post's* source was noting its similarity to the Zaino description from Brooklyn. But the source was premature. Zaino's composite would be held back and a combination VW driver-Davis sketch would be released four days later. But the article is illustrative of the confusion in police circles at the time—a confusion born of trying to turn two distinct people into one person.

*   *   *

In the end, the police decided to believe all the witnesses. But first, they had to develop the proper scenario and have it fit only one man—Son of Sam—not "*Sons of Sam.*"

Mrs. Davis wasn't pleased with the flat nose the adjusted composite showed, maintaining it was actually sharper and "hooked, like an Israeli's or an Indian's." But Zaino, Masters and the Vignottis all said the nose was flat—and that feature would survive and remain on the composite. (Berkowitz's nose *is* pointed, as Mrs. Davis said.)

Then there was the issue of the killer's hair. The Vignottis and Mrs. Davis each portrayed a man with short, dark, curly hair. Zaino and Masters both totally disagreed. Violante's description of the "grubby hippie" in the park was similar to theirs.

On August 6, the beautician called the task force in Queens to report the man she'd spotted fleeing the park wearing "a light-colored, cheap nylon wig." That phone interview helped settle the matter, although the police already were leaning toward the wig theory.

Now, with the beautician's statement, the police thought they had a complete picture: The Vignottis saw the man shortly after he arrived. He was scouting the area and was about to enter the VW when he spotted them and decided he'd better get away from his car. He was not wearing the wig at that time. Later, with the wig on, he was seen in the park by Stacy and Robert. A third police interview with Violante produced the following comment: "It could have been a wig."

Then, for some reason, the man wandered over to Bay 17th Street and, with the wig in his shirt, walked past Mrs. Davis. Returning to the park, he put on the wig, shot the young couple and fled. The beautician saw him running from the park, still wearing the wig, and it was still in place when he nearly collided with Masters at the red light up the block.

Zaino's sketches were withheld, as was that of Alan Masters. Police believed those witnesses, and Violante, saw the gunman with his wig on, and thus prepared to release the short-haired composites instead. But the face would remain that of the VW driver, primarily, and the nose would stay flat.

After the arrest, many observers would remark that, with the exception of the hair, the final sketch—purportedly Mrs. Davis's—didn't resemble Berkowitz. It didn't because the police unknowingly took two men and turned them into one composite. But the fact that they did is yet another example of how certain authorities were that the VW driver was the killer. And that drawing would be released August 9, only one day before Berkowitz's capture.

*   *   *

Still to be resolved was the issue of the killer's clothing. Zaino, Masters and the Vignottis all said the man was wearing a long-sleeved, light-colored shirt with rolled-up sleeves. Violante agreed on the sleeves but, in the darkened park, was uncertain as to whether the gunman was wearing a shirt or a denim jacket.

Mrs. Davis insisted that her suspect was wearing a dark blue denim jacket with rolled-down sleeves—an observation police didn't challenge since the sleeve, which hid the supposed gun, was an obvious and critical element of her story.

Apparently, the police didn't consider the implications of the scenario they were creating: The killer had worn a shirt with rolled up sleeves at 1:30 a.m. on the street, and was in the park with the sleeves still rolled up at 2:20. But now, two blocks away at 2:33, they were down—and he was now wearing a denim jacket. Then, two minutes later, the jacket had disappeared and the sleeves were rolled up again on the light-colored shirt as he pulled the trigger.

It is stretching credibility to believe that one man was accomplishing all these wardrobe adjustments. But the fact is, the police missed the significance of the sleeves. Strano had written in his report that Mrs. Davis's suspect was carrying a gun. Some detectives didn't believe that, but the brass did, so that made Mrs. Davis's man the killer. And it also made him the VW driver.

Beyond that, the Police Department had concocted a single murderer months before, and that's the way it would remain. To justify their position, Strano told Mrs. Davis the man she saw had a large stomach "because he stuffed the wig in his shirt." And after the arrest, when Berkowitz, claiming to be the killer, said no wig was worn—ever—the police suggested to Zaino that Berkowitz might have "doused his hair with water to make it look long and straight."

At no time were the witnesses in contact with one another. None knew the others existed. Zaino later said to me: "How could that Mrs. Davis say he was wearing a jacket? He was definitely not wearing a jacket."

Likewise, Violante was astounded: "How could she say he looked so neat? The guy I saw looked like a bum."

But after the police combined the descriptions into one sketch, they still waited, pending the discovery of the elusive parking tickets which would substantiate Mrs. Davis's story—and her suspect.

Meanwhile, the search for the yellow VW was building to mammoth proportions.

The Vignottis didn't know the model year of the yellow Beetle they saw by the park when "Son of Sam" approached it. Neither did Robert or Paula Barnes, who noticed two people climb from the car at about 1:10 a.m. How the police were dealing with the "two people" is unknown. Maybe they decided the couple were mistaken about its multiple passengers. Or perhaps the police didn't know what to think.

In any event, Dominick Spagnola, who was parked on the service road at about 1:25 a.m., was a tow-truck driver by trade. The police interviewed him on two occasions, and Spagnola decided the car was of either 1972 or 1973 vintage with New York plates and a black stripe above the running-board area. Alan Masters also described the VW he chased as a Beetle-type car.

But then something happened. It is unclear exactly what it was, but the police, on about August 5, decided the vehicle probably wasn't a VW bug at all—but was likely a 1973 yellow VW Fastback. At night, and from the rear, the cars were similar in appearance. And a rear view is what most witnesses had. Moreover, with its taillights extinguished, as the VW's were, the Fastback—which is a few inches longer than the Beetle and has a somewhat different trunk configuration—was even more easily confused with the more familiar bug.

However, my investigation later determined the car apparently *was* a bug—a 1971 model—faded yellow in color and with a front bumper that hung low on one side. But *if* a Fastback was on the scene, it may have been the auto flashing its lights on Bay 14th Street, or the car that followed cyclist Michelle Michaels.

But what appears to have happened is that the police, in an attempt to learn the VW's plate number, put chaser Alan Masters under hypnosis (apparently he came up with the numbers 684) and out of that session arrived at the Fastback conclusion.

An August 7 police report sums up details about the car, which also contained a CB radio and a long antenna, that were uncovered in that apparent hypnotic experiment. The following functions were performed utilizing . . . printouts, available information and resources:

A. Search NJ Printouts VW   198 combos 4-GUR,
                                 4-GVR, no VW fastback

B. Search NJ Printouts VW   72 combos 684-GUR-
                                 GVR, no VW fastback

C. Search NY Plates Computer   12 combos 684-GUR-
                                 GVR, negative results

D. Search NY Plates Computer   684 GUR-GVR, 2 hits,
                                    registered owners

E. Inquiry NCIC [a federal   99 combos 4-GUR, 2
crime data bank]   plates stolen

F. Hand Search NJ Printouts, all 1973 VW fastbacks, BG
[beige], TN [tan], YW [yellow], 300 of 200,000 [300 of the
described autos out of a total of 200,000 VWs]

The following items are in the process of being completed as of this date:

A. request printouts 1973 fastbacks NYDMV (possible 600–400,000
   autos)
B. Personal observation of each 1973 VW fastback from NJ & NY
   printouts (possible 900 autos)

This was a remarkable document. The police were planning to "personally observe" *900* VW Fastbacks from New York and New Jersey—an awesome task—in a massive, all-out effort to locate the car and the killer. How serious was the NYPD about the yellow VW? That strategy adequately answers the question.

The other license plate combinations available were 463, which was observed by the nurse who saw the VW fleeing on 17th Avenue.; and 364. The 364 was a number the police apparently ignored because its significance was missed.

The 364 was written on the back of an anonymous postcard, postmarked in Brooklyn, that was mailed to the Moskowitz home on August 4. It was turned over to the police. The numbers were scrawled in the center of the card; below them were the words "Son of Sam." It was the exact reverse of the nurse's 463 and a common visual interpretation of the "possible 684" the police already had. Somewhere in these combinations was the key to the actual plate number.

But it was already August 7. The arrest of David Berkowitz was only three days away and would occur before the police got very far with the leads on the license plate numbers. And after the arrest, the investigation was immediately halted.

In the interim, teams of detectives began to scour the metropolitan area, checking VWs and other small yellow cars whose plate numbers were similar to those reported by the witnesses.

Other detectives drove to the NYPD's photo bureau, where, under job #2361, they obtained several thousand photographs of a yellow VW for possible mass distribution in the event the department decided to reveal the entire focus of its case. But the arrest would occur before the pictures were released.

*   *   *

It was now August 9, and the wayward tickets were finally discovered in the 62nd Precinct. Officers Cataneo and Logan had written four in the Bay 17th Street vicinity shortly before the shooting. One of those had been slapped on the windshield of a 1970 four-door Ford Galaxie, cream-colored, black vinyl roof, New York registration 561-XLB. At 2:05 a.m. on July 31, a half hour before the attack, the car was tagged for parking too close to a fire hydrant in front of 290 Bay 17th Street, a brick garden apartment building in Bensonhurst, Brooklyn.

With the tickets at long last located—nearly a week after Mrs. Davis told Strano of their existence—the widow's story was substantiated and the police quickly released the final composite sketches. When the drawings, a frontal view and a profile, flashed across television screens, about 200,000 young Hispanic males dove for cover, as the full-face sketch bore a resemblance to any number of young men of Spanish origin. And as many observers also noted cynically, the picture looked strikingly like Herman Badillo, a U.S. congressman from New York City.

The sketches were at such variance with composites released after earlier .44 attacks that Chief of Detectives John Keenan held a press conference to disclose the thinking of the NYPD's top officials. Keenan explained the drawings were primarily the result of the recollections of a single witness which were corroborated by several others. Keenan stated that *the NYPD believed the killer had been wearing wigs all along.*

Son of Sam's new face was spread across the front pages of the city's newspapers. The *News* incorrectly reported that "Tommy Z." had provided the latest description and "was so close to the attack that he was able to describe tiny, kidney-shaped designs spaced three inches apart on the killer's bluish gray Qiana shirt."

Interestingly enough, this shiny Qiana shirt, which Mrs. Davis said Berkowitz had worn under his shirt, in no way resembled the coarser, uniform-type gray shirt observed by Zaino, Masters and Violante. This contradiction was beyond the jacket-off, jacket-on, sleeves-up-down-up discrepancy noted earlier.

The *Post,* getting closer to the truth through its own police sources, responded with a banner front-page story which was headlined "NEW WITNESS SAW SAM CHANGE WIG." Written by the able Carl Pelleck, the article said a new "secret witness . . . has been able to describe him without the wig or wigs cops now believe he's been using all along as a disguise. . . .

"Police would not say whether the witness saw the killer without his wig before he attacked or after the shootings.

"There were other witnesses to the Moskowitz killing who saw different stages of the attack. . . . The others saw him as a man with long, disheveled hair which police now believe was a cheap, light brown wig."

Thirty-six hours later, the Police Department would deeply regret that proclamation when Berkowitz, claiming to be the killer, would assert that he never wore a wig. And he was right: *he* never did. But he wasn't the man who pulled the trigger either.

But on August 9, the pressured hunt for the killer's yellow VW continued in earnest. The media knew nothing about it, and in fact knew none of the details which led to the NYPD's conclusion about the wig. If the press had been aware of some of these facets, the arrest of Galaxie driver David Berkowitz might not have been so readily accepted as the total solution of the case.

But the media and public were misled. With the secret aspects of the investigation now revealed, this much can be said about David Berkowitz as the "lone" .44 killer:

For Berkowitz to have been the slayer of Stacy Moskowitz, the entire hierarchy of the NYPD—and the total thrust of the monumental investigation—had to have been 100 percent wrong.

* * *

Keenan's press conference was over, the sketches were on the street and tomorrow was coming. And to Detective James Justus, the night of August 9 was shaping up in routine fashion in the offices of 10th Homicide in Brooklyn's Coney Island section. Justus was a veteran detective who was normally assigned to Brooklyn Robbery. But he was temporarily pitching in at the 10th during the Sam investigation.

Working the evening shift, Justus was looking at a computer printout which listed the owners of the cars ticketed on Bay 17th Street the night of the shooting. It was Justus's job to contact the car owners to ask if they'd seen anything of value while in the neighborhood.

Dialing the phone, Justus eliminated two of the owners, and at about 7 p.m. he typed up DD-5 #271. A great deal of false information would later be released about the events of this night, and some would exaggerate and distort them for obvious, but insidious reasons. But here is what actually happened:

At the typewriter, Justus wrote:

Subject: INVESTIGATION AS TO POSSIBLE WITNESSES TO THIS CASE:

1. Check of summonses served in the area of this crime disclosed there were four (4) served thereat as follows:

   A. 0210 hrs. . . . F/O 262 Bay 17 St. reg #XXX-XXX. Registered to Robert E. Donaldson* of 20 First St.,* Staten Island. Phone EL-0-0000.
   B. 0210 hrs. . . . F/O 262 Bay 17 St. reg #XXX-XXX. New reg not in computer as of this date.
   C. 0205 hrs. . . . F/O 290 Bay 17 St. reg #561-XLB. Registered to David Berkowitz of 35 Pine St., Yonkers NY. Phone (914) 000-0000.

2. Check re Donaldson disclosed that owner is deceased and the auto was being used by the son of Mrs. Donaldson. Son was alleged to be at a party in Brooklyn on the night of this crime.

Son's name is James, DOB 1/3/53. A message was left thereat for the son to contact this command regarding this case.

3. Check with Berkowitz disclosed that there is no answer on phone.

The thought of what Justus might have been told had he reached "potential witness" Berkowitz is, despite the seriousness of the subject, amusing to ponder. But that didn't happen. Instead, about ninety minutes later, at 8:25, Justus called Berkowitz again. Still no answer. Justus was tired of dialing the phone, so he decided to let the Yonkers Police Department give *him* some assistance.

Justus called the information operator and obtained the listing for the Yonkers Police Department's main switchboard. The phone was answered by a female dispatcher:

"Police Headqurters, 63."

"Hello, this is Detective Justus, Brooklyn Police Department."

"Yes?"

"We would like to get a notification made up there in Yonkers."

"Yes, all right. Hold on."

In a moment, operator 82 would come on the line, replacing 63.

David Berkowitz was now just twenty-four hours from his appointment with destiny.

VI

Catch .44

Detective James Justus had absolutely no idea that anything of interest was about to come his way as he waited for the Yonkers police operator to return. To him, this call was strictly routine. He'd tried four times to reach Berkowitz without success. For all he knew, the man was out of town. The supervisors wanted this witness thing cleared up, so he'd ask the Yonkers cops to notify Berkowitz and have him call the 10th. Then Justus could get on with more pressing matters in the investigation; specifically the matter of the yellow VW. In a moment, a new Yonkers operator was on the line.

82   Police Headquarters, 82.

JJ   Yes, this is Detective Justus from the Brooklyn Robbery Squad, New York City Police Department.

82   Yes . . .

JJ   I'm working in the 10th Homicide Zone now, on the .44-Caliber Killer.

82   Yeah . . .

JJ   And I'm trying to contact a party that lives up in Yonkers who is possibly a witness to the crime down here. That's a Mr. David Berkowitz . . .

82   Oh no . . . oh no . . .

JJ   Do you know him?

82   Could I . . . I was very involved. This is the guy that I think is responsible . . .

JJ   David Berkowitz? [Justus must have thought he'd wandered into the Twilight Zone. Berkowitz drove a Ford, not a VW.]

82   . . . is responsible. My father was down there yest—Saturday.

JJ   Yeah . . .

82   . . . and you also got information regar— . . . Is he at 35 Pine Street?

JJ   Yes, dear.

82   David Berkowitz. I don't know how you, or what, but my father went down to the 109th and you also . . . someone received information through our police officers and that's because of some incidents involving shooting where we have reason to believe this person is responsible. He also has written sim-ilar-type threatening letters to the sheriff's investigator who recently moved into his apartment. So, I don't . . .

JJ   Do you know David Berkowitz yourself?

82   I don't know him. I, really, because of a shooting incident at my home and a firebombing and threatening letters . . .

JJ   At your home . . .

82   . . . and through investigation found out that this is probably the person.

JJ   Did you notify the Police Department on it?

82   Oh, yeah, there are numerous reports on it, and information regarding this guy was given to your department on Saturday.

JJ   Yeah, well, I am doing it another way. He got a summons down here that night, right in the vicinity . . .

82   Oh my God . . . he . . . he . . . you know, because we have seen him and he fits the description. This is why my father went down there with his whole file of copies of letters we have received from him. And I believe the Westchester County Sheriff's Department is now investigating him because he threatened a sheriff's investigator . . . My dog was shot with a .44-caliber bullet.

JJ   Oh, really?

82   At least that's what it was supposed to have been. The people who have seen it claim it was a .44 . . .

JJ   Ah . . .

82   [Laughing] . . . He, he just scared me to death . . . now you are telling me he's a witness.

JJ   Well, we don't know. A *possible* witness. And from what you're telling me, a possible perpetrator.

82   . . . And he owns a yellow car.

JJ   He has a yellow . . . yeah, I'd say a yellow Ford, I believe it is . . .

82   Yeah . . . yeah . . . do you—the 109th, is that Brooklyn?

JJ   No, that's Queens. We're working on it out of the 10th Homicide Zone in Brooklyn.

82   O.K. . . . well, he went . . . my father went to the 109th on Saturday. Last week someone was up here at our intelligence unit and at that time spoke with officers Intervallo and Chamberlain and they gave him information . . . just on a long shot, now, because he does resemble the picture. I don't know him personally.

JJ   All right, so you know *of* Berkowitz . . .

82   Right.

JJ   Through . . . ?

82   Incidents that have occurred that I have reason to believe that you could prove in court that he's responsible for a shooting incident at my home . . .

JJ   Yonkers had at home and believes Berkowitz responsible . . .

82   He happens to be . . . He either was or is now employed as a rent-a-cop, like a security guard.

JJ   Rent-a-cop . . . you use the same terms we use down here, huh?

82   Yeah.

JJ   Your dog shot . . .

82   With a large-caliber bullet. It's never been confirmed because you know how it happens, right? Seventeen people have seventeen different jobs and nobody gets together and it's only in the last week that these two cops and I got together and put all the reports together and got the DD [detective division] reports where he is doing everything . . .

JJ Let me ask you something, honey. With his name, do you have a pistol license bureau up there that would . . .

82 O.K., supposedly he has a permit to shoot by New York City or has an application now being processed in relation to this . . .

JJ . . . in New York City . . .

82 He holds no permit in the city of Yonkers at this time.

JJ But possibly here in New York City . . .

82 Possibly, because he was employed as a security guard. Well, you know who you should get in touch with? And if you will hold on a minute, I will find out when he's working . . . all right . . . it is either police officers Chamberlain or Intervallo who for their own reasons put this all together, just because it happens to be their sector where I live.

JJ Chamberlain or Intervallo?

82 Yes.

JJ Would you be able to do me the honors, please?

82 Well, I'll find out where they are. They are not working right now. I know that. Can you hold on a minute?

JJ All right. [Justus, on hold, speaks to people in his office.]

JJ I have something beautiful here. I wanted to talk to this guy about a summons . . . lives up in Yonkers. I was talking to Yonkers to get a notification made and she says, "Oh, not him, he shot my dog with a .44 about a month ago. He's crazy! He's sending threatening letters to the deputy sheriffs office . . . "

82 Could I get your name and have someone call you back?

JJ All right. My name is Justus. Uh, I'm thinking about what the hell number to give you. I'll give you this one, 946-3336, and that's a 212 exchange . . . . Can I ask you a favor, honey? Operator 82, can I get your name, please?

82 Sure. My name is Carr. C-a-r-r.

JJ First name, honey?

82 Wheat . . . W-h-e-a-t. Now, my father, my father is Samuel Carr. He went down there with all the information the other day.

JJ Where do you live, Miss Carr?

82 316 Warburton Avenue, and that is immediately behind—the back of his house and the back of mine . . . face each other. There is also a Westchester County Sheriff's Department investigator because he wrote letters to this investigator who has the apartment beneath him saying that my father planted him there and he is going to get us instead. But I'll have Pete or Tommy call you back . . . I'll call them at home . . .

JJ Do you know how to spell the last guy's name? Not Chamberlain . . .

82 I-n-t-e-r-v-a-l-l-o. Just like it sounds.

JJ Okeydoke, honey.

82 Thank you a lot.

JJ Thank you very much, dear.

82 Bye-bye.

This transcript of the actual conversation between Wheat Carr and Justus hasn't been made public before. It vividly shows what role the NYPD believed Berkowitz played in the Son of Sam saga and invalidates numerous police proclamations which followed the arrest, when authorities claimed they initially were highly suspicious of Berkowitz.

Wheat Carr was a police and gun buff—owning a .357 Magnum, a .25-caliber revolver and a .22-caliber pistol. She had a mother named Frances and a black Labrador retriever named Harvey. She also had a brother named Michael, twenty-four, a freelance advertising stylist, photographer and designer who was a ranking member of the Church of Scientology.

At that minute, her other brother, thirty-year-old John Carr, was on the road. New York was far behind him as he crossed the midwestern United States, angling north. John Carr had his reasons for vacating the metropolitan area. And his reasons involved David Berkowitz.

After hanging up from her conversation with Justus, Wheat called her family home at 316 Warburton Avenue—a rambling, old three-story frame house where her father, Sam, operated an answering service.

Warburton Avenue, once a thriving middle-class thoroughfare of private homes, apartment buildings and small businesses, had gone downhill since the early 1960s. Its southern portion, in which the Carrs lived, was somewhat seedy. High above, at Pine Street, the neighborhood changed for the better. David Berkowitz's building was newly renovated and well maintained and commanded a majestic view of the Hudson. The apartment house, contrary to Wheat Carr's implication, was not situated very close to the Carr home. The impression given was that the two dwellings were practically back to back. No so. About two hundred hilly yards consisting of trees, the Croton Aqueduct path and Grove Street separated Berkowitz's apartment from the Carr home far below.

Sam Carr, sixty-four, a thin, gray-haired, chain-smoking retired Yonkers Public Works employee, who himself owned several guns—including revolvers—listened as his daughter repeated the essence of her exchange with Justus.

Carr hung up and called Justus in Brooklyn. About two hours later, at 10:30 p.m., Wheat Carr reached Yonkers police officer Tom Chamberlain at his home and Chamberlain, too, called Justus. Bit by bit, the NYPD was learning about potential witness David Berkowitz, and the story Justus was hearing was a fascinating one.

*   *   *

In mid-February 1976, David Richard Berkowitz, then employed as a guard with IBI Security, moved from a small apartment at 2161 Barnes Avenue in the Pelham

Bay section of the Bronx to a room over the garage in the private home of Jack and Nann Cassara at 174 Coligni Avenue in New Rochelle, Westchester County. The Cassaras, an elderly couple, occupied the well-kept colonial house with their son, Steve, nineteen.

The Cassaras' other children were grown and living their own lives in the Westchester area. Jack Cassara, still short of retirement age, worked at the Neptune Moving Company in New Rochelle.

Berkowitz, a model tenant, had complained about the barking of the Cassaras' German shepherd dog, but otherwise was friendly and no bother to the family. He paid his $200 monthly rent on time. However, he abruptly moved from the Cassara residence in April 1976, leaving his $200 security deposit behind. He'd been there only two months.

Berkowitz left New Rochelle for apartment 7-E on the top floor of 35 Pine Street in northwest Yonkers. Nobody seemed to know how he'd found the Cassara home or the Pine Street address. His Yonkers rent was $237 a month, which he paid punctually.

On May 13, 1976, a Molotov cocktail firebomb was tossed at a second-floor bedroom window in the home of Joachim Neto, 18 Wicker Street, Yonkers, a two-family, wood-frame house located down the hill from 35 Pine and no more than fifty yards south of the Carr home. Neto, his wife, Maria, her mother, and their daughter, Sylvia, thirteen, lived on the first two floors, and a construction worker occupied the top floor by himself. The Netos received a number of abusive telephone calls and at least one threatening letter, which Mrs. Neto's mother destroyed.

On October 4, 1976, at about 4:40 a.m., someone threw a Molotov cocktail through a window in the Carr home. Sam Carr, awake at the time, extinguished the flames before the firefighters arrived.

Eleven weeks later, on Christmas Eve, the Netos were entertaining a large gathering of family and friends when several shots, fired from a car through a chain link fence fronting the house, slammed into the dwelling, barely missing a window behind which young Sylvia Neto was playing the piano. But on the front stoop, the family German shepherd, Rocket, lay dead. A bullet from a small-caliber weapon had sliced through its neck.

On April 10, 1977—Easter Sunday—a handwritten letter was mailed to Sam Carr asking him to silence the barking of Harvey, the black Labrador retriever. On April 19, another letter—written by the same hand—was sent to the Carr residence. This missive was more threatening in tone than the previous one.

On April 27, at about 9:30 a.m., somebody made good on the threat. Harvey was wounded by one of the several shots pegged into the Carr backyard from the aqueduct path some twenty yards behind the house. Carr got a glimpse of a man in blue jeans and a yellow shirt running north on the aqueduct. The shooting was *not* done with a .44, as Wheat Carr implied it was.

Next, on June 7, Craig Glassman, a nursing student and volunteer deputy with the Westchester County Sheriff's Department, received the first of four threatening letters mailed to his apartment at 35 Pine Street, where he'd moved in March from around the corner on Glenwood Avenue to apartment 6E, directly below David Berkowitz.

Two days later, on June 9, the Cassara family in New Rochelle—Berkowitz's former landlords—received a get-well card in the mail. The card, which was decorated with a drawing of a puppy, told Jack Cassara: "Sorry to hear about the fall you took from the roof of your house . . . " Cassara had taken no such fall. The card was signed: "Sam and Francis" [sic], and the envelope was embellished with the return address of the Carrs, whom the Cassaras didn't know. Both annoyed and curious, Mrs. Cassara located the listing for Sam Carr and phoned him to discover why the card was sent. The Carrs said they knew nothing about it; but Sam Carr told Nann Cassara about the letters he'd received and the subsequent wounding of Harvey, who still had a large-caliber bullet in his body. It was deemed too risky to remove it, Carr said.

The two couples agreed to meet, and on June 9, at the Carr home in Yonkers, they compared the handwriting on the Carr letters with that on the Cassaras' get-well card. The samples matched.

Something was happening in Yonkers. Something strange. The Carrs and Cassaras had something or someone in common. But they couldn't decide who, or what, it was.

Back at home that evening, Nann Cassara talked about the Yonkers visit with her son, Steve. Hearing about the attack on the Carrs' dog, Steve suggested: "Remember that tenant we had who didn't like our dog barking? Maybe it's got something to do with him."

Recalling the incident but not the tenant's name, Nann Cassara checked her records. David Berkowitz. She next looked in the Westchester telephone directory and noticed a listing for a David Berkowitz at 35 Pine Street in Yonkers. She phoned Sam Carr.

"Is Pine Street anywhere near you?" she asked. Bingo.

The next day, June 10, Carr went to the Yonkers Police Department's detective division with the information he'd received. To say the Yonkers detectives mishandled the case would be to understate the matter. But, in short, nothing happened. This was on June 10, sixteen days before the Elephas shooting and seven weeks before Son of Sam attacked Stacy Moskowitz and Robert Violante.

*   *   *

Volunteer sheriff's deputy Craig Glassman, meanwhile, had carried his June 7 threatening letter to his superiors in White Plains. Nothing happened there either. Glassman received another mailed threat, postmarked July 13. He again showed the letter to his superiors. If someone had bothered to check with Yonkers police, they would have learned the handwriting on Glassman's letters matched that on the Cassara get-well card and on the Carr letters about Harvey. But no one bothered.

But on Saturday August 6—a week after the Moskowitz-Violante shooting—everyone began answering reveille's bugle. At seven thirty that morning, someone started a garbage fire in front of Glassman's door at 35 Pine Street and flung about two dozen live rounds of .22-caliber bullets into the flames for good measure. Luckily, no one was injured.

One of the Yonkers police officers who responded to the blaze was Tom Chamberlain, who was familiar with the Carr and Cassara correspondence. He asked Glassman if he'd received any mailed threats. Glassman showed him the two letters he'd received as of that morning and Chamberlain immediately recognized the handwriting. This was not a monumental feat: Berkowitz's writing is distinctive and easily identifiable.

And more than that, Glassman's June letter *contained the return address of the Cassaras* and the July 13 note *actually had Sam Carr's last name in it.*

Glassman's notes also were spiced with references to blood, killing and Satan. Suddenly, everybody wanted a piece of David Berkowitz.

*   *   *

The stories related by Chamberlain and Sam Carr to the NYPD's James Justus were of interest in the waning hours of August 9. But despite the violence, gore and bizarre conduct loose in Yonkers, the Brooklyn supervisors weren't overly impressed—although they'd later claim they were. There were, they knew, thousands of borderline psychotics in New York, and Berkowitz—if he was indeed guilty of the war being waged in Yonkers—might only be another in a long list of erratic citizens whose names were being forwarded to the Omega task force every day. Moreover, this blatant, wild activity didn't at all jibe with numerous psychiatric portraits of a low-keyed killer who "would melt into the crowd." On the surface—Joe Ordinary. And that was, and is, an important point.

The NYPD did not storm into Yonkers that night; nor would they unleash a battalion of detectives the next day. They'd send two—only two—detectives to conduct a routine check of "potential witness" Berkowitz, who was of interest because of the ticket and the allegation that he was now suspected of violent behavior involving a weapon as well. He didn't drive a yellow VW—the killer's car—and he didn't borrow it: his own Ford was at the scene that night. But it was remotely possible he somehow switched vehicles. Anything was possible.

*   *   *

It is interesting to note that on Wednesday, August 10, Police Commissioner Michael Codd was out of town. Not in Europe or China; just out of town. John J. Santucci, district attorney of Queens, site of five of the eight Son of Sam attacks, would later offer this observation: "If you knew beforehand that you had identified your suspect, you just would not make the biggest arrest in the history of the Police Department without the commissioner available. It's simply not done. They didn't know until the very end it was Berkowitz they were after."

At around noon on the tenth, Detective Sergeant James Shea of the 10th Homicide Zone asked veteran detectives Ed Zigo and John Longo to drive to Yonkers to look into the Berkowitz situation. Strano and Justus, who'd carried the issue to this point, were excluded from the excursion—another indication that Berkowitz wasn't believed to be the killer. If an arrest was thought possible, the two cops who built the case probably would have been on the scene.

Arriving in Westchester, Zigo and Longo used a street map for reference and cruised along North Broadway in Yonkers, turned left on Glenwood and proceeded down the hill to Pine Street. They stopped, walked around the area and spotted Berkowitz's Galaxie parked on the west side of the narrow road about twenty-five yards north of the entrance to No. 35. Zigo gazed through the car window and spied a duffel bag in the back seat. A rifle butt was protruding from the bag.

There is no law in New York that prohibits possession of a rifle. Rifles aren't considered concealed weapons, and it isn't even necessary to obtain a license before owning one. Zigo, peering through the window, knew that. He also knew he could see only a butt, or stock, and nothing more. In other words, he had no reason to think any illegal material was in the vehicle.

Regardless, he entered the car. Opening the duffel bag, he saw the rifle was a semiautomatic Commando Mark III capable of firing thirty bullets from any of the assortment of clips that were also stashed in the duffel bag. The gun, although not of the type normally owned by hunters or "average citizens," was not illegal.

Popping the glove compartment, Zigo came across an envelope addressed to Omega commander Timothy Dowd and the Suffolk County, Long Island, police. Reading the enclosed note, Zigo knew what he'd found. The text, in longhand, promised an attack in Southampton, the exclusive summer resort on Long Island's south shore, not far from Fire Island.

Zigo and Longo were thunderstruck. They'd located the Son of Sam. Or had they?

*   *   *

David Berkowitz had spent an eventful, busy week. Plans were formulated and enacted. Wheels were set spinning. An elaborate mystique had to be created. It had been difficult to accomplish, but it was done.

While Zigo poked through the Ford, Berkowitz—whose apartment didn't face the street—paced the living area. Earlier that morning, he'd gone downstairs and put the duffel bag into the car and jammed the hastily scrawled note into the glove compartment. The letter was written in longhand. There hadn't been time to copy the stylized, slanted, block-letter printing of Son of Sam. He'd also plagiarized a poem—apparently inspired by another individual—adapted it to Craig Glassman, wrote it on a manila folder and drawn the Son of Sam graphic symbol beneath it. He sketched the symbol incorrectly, reversing the Mars and Venus sign positions from the original used in the Breslin letter and adding arrows to the ends of the "X." (A

Yonkers police official would later find pieces of paper on which Berkowitz practiced drawing the symbol.)

Berkowitz's printing also faltered in his attempt to mimic the Son of Sam method. Unlike the letter to Breslin, which contained only capital letters, the ode to Glassman was sprinkled with several lowercase letters done in the normal Berkowitz style of printing. One would have thought "Son of Sam" knew his own techniques.

The poem said: "Because Craig is Craig, so must the streets be filled with Craig (death). And huge drops of lead poured down upon her head until she was dead. Yet the cats still come out at night to mate, and the sparrows still sing in the morning."

But why all the haste and hurry with the poem and letter?

David Berkowitz, sources close to him say, *knew that the police were coming to Yonkers that day. He'd been tipped off.* The implications of this revelation are staggering. Was Berkowitz really alerted? At this point, it is perhaps better to answer that question with several other questions: Did a means exist through which Berkowitz could have been alerted? Is it logical to believe that the infamous, ingenious Son of Sam—who'd eluded the biggest manhunt in New York history for so long—would leave a valuable, potentially incriminating weapon exposed in his own car which was parked in front of his own home in broad daylight? And with that weapon so displayed—inviting a break-in such as Zigo's—would that killer then leave a Son of Sam letter within easy grasp in his glove compartment? And would he do so in light of a parking ticket he knew would eventually lead the police in his direction— knowledge that should have led him to be doubly cautious?

* * *

In actuality, the initial preparations had been in the making since the day after the Moskowitz-Violante shooting. The parking ticket, the sources close to him state, had assured Berkowitz of the nomination, and the VW chase had cemented his election. He couldn't claim an innocent reason for his presence in Bensonhurst because doing so would have kept the police investigation centered on the yellow VW driver, who, it would be learned, was deemed more important in the conspiratorial hierarchy than David Richard Berkowitz. The police were after only one killer. Berkowitz could be tossed to the wolves—as the result of his own mistake. And the truth could remain a secret.

Berkowitz, the sources say, wasn't at all happy with the situation. But he had no choice. At first, it was hoped there was a remote chance the police wouldn't investigate the ticket at all—and he *had* paid it immediately. But it was far more likely they would pursue the matter routinely, so Berkowitz had to be ready.

On about August 4, less than a week after the Brooklyn attack, Berkowitz—with some assistance from his accomplices—removed his possessions from the Pine Street apartment in the dead of night. They included a bed, a couch, a bureau, a dinette set and assorted clothing. An expensive Japanese-made stereo system he'd purchased while stationed with the Army in Korea was disposed of by other means.

The clothing and furniture were loaded into a van rented from a Bronx gas station and carted to the Salvation Army warehouse in Mount Vernon, Westchester County, about five miles from Pine Street. The contents were piled in front of the building where they could be discovered when the facility opened the next morning.

Then, a series of "insane" notes had to be written and strewn about the apartment to enhance the illusion of a lone, demented Son of Sam. These letters railed against the Cassaras, the Pine Street neighborhood, Sam Carr and others.

Next, a number of weird ramblings and obscenities about Sam Carr, demons and Craig Glassman were slapped onto the apartment walls with Magic Marker. A hole was punched into one of the walls and surrounded by other bizarre writing.

The intent was plain: he was to feign insanity; and the "demonic possession" angle provided in May by the NYPD itself would serve as the motive for the slayings.

There were some mistakes made, but they would be missed or ignored by the police, who didn't concern themselves with any kind of follow-up investigation.

It was, all in all, a brilliant hoax to pull on the naive NYPD. But as Berkowitz would later write to me in a modest vein: "It wasn't all my idea, and I'm certain you know this."

The police, under intense pressure, were so desperate for an arrest they'd believe almost anything, Berkowitz was told. Accurately. Nobody would challenge the story because nobody would *want* to do so. Accurate again. Politics was involved. The city was in shambles. You can tell them anything and they'll go for it just to bring this to an end. Berkowitz listened to the milk and honey, and he thought hard. There wasn't much he could do. So he bought the arguments about politics and the desperation of the police.

And he agreed that he could get off on a "not guilty by reason of insanity" plea and be put into a mental institution. There, he was told, he'd either be released as a "cured" man in five to seven years' time—or else his friends would break him out. He knew *that* part was bullshit.

But it is not known what he thought fifteen months later when, unknown to the public, a loaded .38-caliber revolver was mailed to him at the Central New York Psychiatric Center in Marcy. The package, postmarked in Bayside, Queens, was intercepted by Center officials before it reached Berkowitz's hands. But he knew it had arrived for him.

*   *   *

As far as Berkowitz was concerned on the afternoon of August 10, 1977, everything had gone wrong since May. At that time, sources say, a meeting of conspirators was held and the possibility of someday having to donate a scapegoat to the police was discussed. No one was picked out then. Ideas were tossed back and forth, but nothing was resolved. It was thought that perhaps some innocent, hapless junkie could be set up.

But Berkowitz made his own decision that day, and he began to implement it in

June immediately after the publication of the Son of Sam letter to Jimmy Breslin—a letter that tended to set up someone called "John 'Wheaties'—rapist and suffocater of young girls," more than anyone else.

But in Berkowitz's mind, there was one certain way to ensure *he* wouldn't be the fall guy: he'd get himself arrested for something else—as a writer of threatening letters.

Thus, carefully, calculatingly, he sent the get-well card to Jack Cassara with Sam Carr's return address on the envelope on the morning after the Breslin letter was printed in the *Daily News*. The very next day, he mailed the first threat to Glassman—and put Cassara's return address on this envelope. Berkowitz, in other words, wrote *his own* most recent former address on the threatening letter to his downstairs neighbor, Glassman.

Obviously, he was deliberately tying a loop around himself—linking himself to Cassara, Glassman, Sam Carr and the dog letters. He was, the sources add, confident that the Yonkers cops or the Westchester Sheriff's Department would identify him and arrest him. He'd then be off the streets, effectively, probably under psychiatric observation, and out of the picture in the event of a Son of Sam setup.

But, to his dismay, nobody followed Berkowitz's explicit trail—not even when he wrote the second threatening letter to Glassman in mid-July, sixteen days before the widely heralded "Deathday" anniversary. In that second note, Berkowitz actually included "Captain" Sam Carr's name in the text. He even added "Command Post 316" to the return address; and Carr lived at 316 Warburton Avenue. But once again, nothing happened. Berkowitz was amazed. He couldn't understand it. The Yonkers Police Department and the Westchester sheriff's investigators had to be totally incompetent, he decided.

But Berkowitz didn't stop there, according to the sources. He simply shifted gears. After the Moskowitz murder—when it was determined *he* would be offered to the NYPD because of the ticket and the "value" of the VW driver—Berkowitz went all the way with the insanity scheme. While its original intent was to save him from a .44 arrest, he now, with the encouragement and counsel of his accomplices, used the already laid foundation to build an insanity defense to lessen his legal culpability for the crimes.

In addition to the steps previously described, he mailed two more letters to Glassman in that final week—*both* on August 5—and set the fire at the luckless deputy's door the next morning. It was a period of frantic activity, and that fact alone is indicative that something was in the wind.

For example, the last two notes to Glassman went much further than the preceding pair in June and July. "True, I am the killer," one even claimed. And Sam Carr's full name and return address were plastered across the envelope. It was as explicit as he could possibly be, Berkowitz knew, and it also linked him back to the other crazy letters and related incidents and was a definite boost to the now-certain insanity scam. (But it *still* wouldn't be enough to get him arrested by the Yonkers police or the Sheriff's Department.)

Why didn't Berkowitz run? He felt safer opting for police custody than with the prospect of hiding from his fellow conspirators—who specifically told him that his family members would be murdered if he crossed them and changed the plan, the sources say.

His final preparatory move was to place the duffel bag and Southampton letter in his car on the morning of the tenth after, the sources say, he received the tip that the NYPD was on the immediate horizon.

But there was one more step. Unknown to his mentors, he left behind—hidden in the pile of irrational ravings—the letter concerning "at least 100" murders planned by the cult which he'd written before the Moskowitz killing. And he also left behind a list of fascinating phone numbers. Just the numbers—no names attached. He was trying to cover all the bases. He'd be insane and claim responsibility for all the crimes, yes. But with a little luck the police would delve into the case and he'd come out an insane individual who was *not* responsible for all the shootings. That would be the best of both worlds.

He was sure that the NYPD would check out the letter and phone numbers and discover a trail that led to rather high places. But Berkowitz was wrong. The numbers wouldn't be investigated until they came into my hands in 1983—and they *would* lead to high places. But on August 10, 1977, Berkowitz's work was done.

It was almost time for the conclusion. As Berkowitz himself predicted—with reason—just five days earlier in his final, anonymous threatening letter to Glassman: "I believe that the end of the reign of terror is near."

Ed Zigo and John Longo, puppets in the game, rapidly retreated from Pine Street. Rushing to a telephone, Zigo called his supervisors in Brooklyn.

"We've got him," the tall, middle-aged detective reported.

Sergeant Shea was not amused. "What the hell do you mean—you've *got* him?"

Zigo, an experienced second-grade detective, quickly explained the results of the Yonkers trip. When he mentioned entering Berkowitz's car, Shea saw visions of the case bouncing out of a courtroom and down a stairway to the street.

The two detectives were promptly ordered to stay away from Berkowitz's car and to take action only if he tried to drive away. Even then, they were advised *not* to arrest him, but instead to hold him for questioning—a procedure that didn't require a warrant. In the meanwhile, the NYPD hierarchy would be informed of the sudden turn of events and support teams and brass would travel to Yonkers. The police still weren't quite sure how Berkowitz fit into this newly formed, VW-less scenario, but they'd concern themselves with that later.

While Zigo and Longo awaited assistance, the police telephone lines were humming. Inch by inch, level by level, the news from the outlying reaches of the hills of Yonkers snaked through the chain of command, ultimately reaching Chief of Detectives John Keenan at One Police Plaza in lower Manhattan.

The 10th wasn't about to share this now probable arrest with Operation Omega, and Keenan backed them up. Borrelli, Coffey, Power et al. were cut out. So were Joseph Strano and James Justus, the two detectives from the 10th itself who'd brought the Berkowitz matter to this point.

Sergeant William Gardella, thirty-four, a boyish-looking supervisor with a marked talent for police work, was assigned to drive to Yonkers with Detectives John Falotico and Charlie Higgins, also from the 10th Homicide Zone. Shea was ordered to remain at his desk in Brooklyn to coordinate the phones.

At about 6 p.m., an aging, unmarked police car containing Higgins, Gardella and Falotico turned onto Glenwood Avenue. Pine Street, which ran one way north to south, was about seventy-five yards down the incline.

Standing near the corner of Glenwood and Pine was an NYPD contingent consisting of Zigo, Longo, Deputy Inspector Bernard McRann and Captain Harold Coleman, also from Brooklyn. The two supervisors had arrived in Yonkers shortly before the reinforcements from the 10th.

McRann, who was in command, assessed the situation and recognized the need for a search warrant. He ordered Gardella to take charge on Pine Street and would leave Longo, Falotico and Higgins with him. Zigo was instructed to accompany McRann and Coleman to Yonkers Police Headquarters to begin the paperwork that would be necessary to obtain a warrant from a Yonkers judge. At this moment, the Yonkers Police Department itself had no idea of what was beginning to unfold in the city.

While the conference among the detectives was in session near the corner of Glenwood and Pine, neighborhood residents noted the obvious: there was police activity on the block. What an interesting way to pass a summer's twilight, they reasoned. So out came the lounge chairs and folding chairs and lemonade and beer; and the good citizens of Glenwood and Pine Street settled back to enjoy the drama being performed in front of them. Only it was more of a farce than a drama.

*   *   *

Four detectives would now be responsible for maintaining surveillance of a large building which, counting garages, side doors, stairwells and the like, had at least four exits. Behind it, a wooded area dipped sharply toward Wicker Street (*that* Wicker—as in "Wicked King Wicker" in the Breslin letter). The escape possibilities were numerous.

Moreover, the public display of police pondering had alerted the neighborhood. Berkowitz himself might have seen them: the police didn't know if their suspect's apartment overlooked the river or the street.

Beyond that, in the Breslin letter the killer had suggested a blazing finale when he wrote: ". . . perhaps I will be blown away by cops with smoking .38s." They'd already found a semiautomatic rifle in the car. What might he have stored in the apartment? Considering the circumstances and background, the force left to monitor 35 Pine was small and ill-prepared.

Gardella, cognizant of the predicament, told Higgins to join Falotico in a car parked two autos behind Berkowitz's on the west side of Pine Street. His car's presence suggested Berkowitz was at home, but it was hardly conclusive. No one thought to call him and do a "sorry, wrong number" routine to verify that he was in fact inside the apartment.

*   *   *

At about 6:30 p.m., a blue-and-white Yonkers police car turned onto Pine Street and stopped directly in front of Berkowitz's building. Two uniformed cops, carrying paper bags, climbed from the car and walked into the lobby of the red-brick apartment house. Gardella knew that the squad car's appearance could alarm Berkowitz.

Agitated, the young sergeant radioed the NYPD on the detective band and asked that Yonkers be notified and told to move the cruiser. A few minutes later, the bewildered officers, who'd been on a dinner break with a friend, came out, looked around uncertainly and drove away. This incident alerted Yonkers police to the Pine Street stakeout. No one from the NYPD had advised them beforehand of the activity.

Shortly afterwards, darkness was falling—and so was the elevator at 35 Pine as it slowly rumbled to the lobby. Inside was a solitary passenger, Craig Glassman. Now aware of Berkowitz's existence as the suspect in his apartment fire, Glassman had decided to play detective. The volunteer deputy ambled from 35 Pine, sauntered nonchalantly up the block and stared into the passenger's window of Berkowitz's Ford. He'd been given the car's description and plate number by Yonkers officer Tom Chamberlain after Saturday's fire.

Seeing Glassman at the car, Higgins and Falotico—who in another example of the woeful state of police preparedness didn't even know what their suspect looked like—jumped from their auto, drew their guns and raced down the street. In another auto, Gardella, Zigo, Longo, Coleman and McRann—who still hadn't left the block—watched intently. The idly curious on their porches snapped to attention.

Glassman, who didn't remotely resemble a single police sketch of the killer, finished his observations, turned from the Galaxie and began heading back to his building. But New York's Finest didn't know whom they were supposed to be grabbing as the most notorious slayer in the city's history.

"Hey, Dave. Dave. Hold it a minute," Falotico called out. It was the age-old police ploy. If he's the guy you want, he'll turn around. Of course, Glassman turned around.

Seeing the revolvers, he had second thoughts. "I'm not David! I'm not David!" he blurted. The dismayed detectives wanted proof, so Glassman cautiously reached for his wallet.

It is depressing to contemplate what might have happened if Berkowitz chose that moment to emerge from 35 Pine. For one thing, lives could have been lost.

*   *   *

After Glassman showed the detectives his identification, the disgusted cops sent him away. Also disappointed, the neighborhood spectators slumped back in their chairs.

False alarm.

Glassman had assumed Falotico, Higgins and the others were Yonkers police ready to arrest Berkowitz for the fire at his door. He never thought to ask where they'd come from, and they hadn't bothered to tell him. Then, Glassman went back inside and began to do his laundry.

But by 9 p.m., the bulky volunteer was back on the street, his gun now tucked into his cutoff jeans and hidden beneath a shirt that hung over his belt. In the interim, McRann and Coleman had left the area, and Zigo drove off to obtain a search warrant. Longo and Higgins were now stationed on the roof of 35 Pine, and Gardella joined Falotico in the car on the street.

Seeing Glassman lumbering toward them, Gardella and Falotico winced. Glassman leaned into the unmarked car and asked if he could be of assistance, reminding Gardella that there were numerous exits from 35 Pine—a valid point. Gardella, who in the real world was a good, professional supervisor, was growing frustrated with the situation and by the awareness that he needed more help.

NYPD brass were flocking to Yonkers Police Headquarters at this time. But the Pine Street outpost was a lonely one, with four detectives and a volunteer deputy staking out the vicious Son of Sam without a warrant to arrest him or search his person or premises.

Besides the nonsupport, Gardella, Falotico and their partners on the roof had the other little problem concerning their ignorance of Berkowitz's appearance. Falotico, a veteran officer, asked Glassman if he could identify Berkowitz. Glassman told the stocky, white-haired detective that he'd caught a glimpse of the suspect driving his Ford at seven thirty that morning and yes, he thought he could recognize him.

Gardella then asked Glassman to hop into the police car. But Glassman, still standing conspicuously on the street, said he needed permission from his superiors in White Plains before he could participate in any investigation. Still not knowing he was dealing with the NYPD and the Son of Sam case, Glassman went back to his apartment, phoned White Plains and received approval to join this stakeout of whoever for whatever.

The Pine Street grandstanders had by now grown weary of the Craig Glassman Show, and most retired to their homes before he returned to street level at about 9:45 p.m. When he climbed into the unmarked car, the radio suddenly broadcast a dispatch on the New York City detective band. Only then did Glassman realize the police in the front seat weren't from Yonkers. It dawned on him: the suspicions voiced by Yonkers officers Chamberlain and Intervallo were right.

Berkowitz had to be the Son of Sam.

* * *

The so-called Son of Sam was ready for his fate. He donned a pair of blue jeans, a light-colored, short-sleeved dress shirt with pinstripes and brown work boots. He put the .44 Bulldog—*his* .44 Bulldog, that is—into a paper bag and slowly descended the stairs to the lobby of 35 Pine. Walking through the glass doors, he bounded up the steps to street level and began to stride north to his car. Unknown to him, the Galaxie was hemmed in tightly. Gardella had earlier asked a neighbor to roll his van flush with the rear bumper of Berkowitz's car. With another auto barely three feet in front of the Ford, Berkowitz wasn't going anywhere. It wouldn't have mattered: Berkowitz would later recall that the car would have stalled had he tried to drive it away in a hurry. It badly needed a tune-up.

Not even looking around, Berkowitz entered the street, reached the driver's door of the Galaxie, opened it and squeezed his fleshy frame behind the wheel.

"Is that him?" Falotico asked Glassman as Berkowitz neared the car.

"I'm not sure. I can't say for certain," Glassman reportedly answered.

At that, Gardella and Falotico had reached their limit. Followed by Glassman, they jumped from the car and ran along the sidewalk—Berkowitz's blind side—until they reached the rear of the Ford. Falotico then cut to the street while Gardella crept to the passenger's window. Berkowitz, fumbling with the keys, found the ignition and started to crank the reluctant engine. He looked up to see Falotico's .38 revolver pointing at his head.

On the passenger's side of the car, Gardella aimed his gun through the glass.

Berkowitz looked at Falotico and smiled. It was a long, slow, sweet, knowing smile. His blue eyes twinkled with amusement.

Falotico was shaken at the sight. What the hell do I *have* here? he wondered.

* * *

The early editions of the next morning's *Daily News* were already on the street by the time Berkowitz was arrested at 10 p.m. Fortunately for her, Cacilia Davis, cowering in fear inside her Bay 17th Street apartment since the Moskowitz-Violante attack, didn't see the first press runs. If she had, she might have boarded the first flight out of New York. The police, by leaking information to a reporter from the *News*, had potentially placed Mrs. Davis's life in danger.

Although the origins of the material can't be proven, this much can be said: One of the three journalists who shared the August 11 byline was William Federici. He was said to be a close friend of Detective Joseph Strano, the homicide cop from the 10th who developed Mrs. Davis's story. On August 10, which apparently was the day the *News* received the confidential information, Strano was not sent to the scene in Yonkers. He remained in Brooklyn, still pushing his witness's value—and consequently his own—in the investigation.

Mrs. Davis was the owner of a white spitz, the only such dog in her neighborhood. She, and the police, knew she'd seen a man believed to be the killer. And that man had certainly seen her. But had she gone to the police? Could she identify him? There was no way that man could know—until the police leaked the following to the *News*:

Police officers have been assigned as bodyguards for a middle-aged woman who came face-to-face with a man described as the .44-Caliber Killer . . . before he struck . . . on July 31. The woman, who was walking her dog, . . . told police she had seen a man with curly hair dressed in light blue jeans, blue denim jacket, blue shirt and deck shoes. The man acted strangely and the woman went home feeling fearful . . .

The message was clear: Mrs. Davis was a star witness. As was the case with Tommy Zaino nine days earlier, the police jeopardized Mrs. Davis's safety. Several hours later on August 11, another chapter would be written in the Davis saga.

But first the Son of Sam suspect would create his own news.

*   *   *

David Berkowitz, guarded by Falotico and Detective Charlie Higgins, and with Craig Glassman in the front seat to provide directions, was driven to Yonkers Police Headquarters on St. Casimir Street to greet his public—Timothy Dowd of the Omega task force and Chief of Detectives John Keenan. Sergeant Bill Gardella remained on Pine Street with Berkowitz's Ford, and John Longo went upstairs to maintain security outside apartment 7-E. Pine Street was now evolving into a boisterous block party as residents poured from their homes. Other police, from both Yonkers and the NYPD, began arriving at the scene.

Berkowitz had been arrested without a warrant. Ed Zigo, who was commissioned to acquire the crucial piece of paper, was still somewhere in the depths of the Yonkers court system waiting for Judge Robert Cacace to sign the hastily composed request.

Berkowitz had offered no resistance when he looked up to see the revolvers pointing into his face. He'd come quietly. "You got me," he wisely said. And then he uttered a fascinating comment, "What took you so long?"

In the parking lot at the Yonkers Police Department, Dowd approached Berkowitz and asked him if he knew whom he was speaking to. Berkowitz shocked Dowd by replying in a calm and friendly manner, "Sure. You're Inspector Dowd. I know who you are." Like Falotico, Dowd was taken aback by the relaxed demeanor Berkowitz displayed.

After an expected amount of confusion and some brief, off-the-record questioning at Yonkers Police Department, Berkowitz was charged with unlawful possession of a firearm—the legal .45 semiautomatic rifle—and a convoy assembled for the victorious journey to police headquarters in Manhattan. First, however, Berkowitz had to tell the police where the all-important .44 Bulldog was. In all the excitement, the gun was left behind in the Galaxie. The weapon was hastily retrieved.

Mayor Abe Beame, asleep at Gracie Mansion, was awakened and told of the arrest. Beame issued a statement that said, "The people of New York can rest easily this morning because the police have captured the person known as Son of Sam."

Berkowitz had yet to be questioned formally, and the first prejudicial bricks were already being laid. There would be many more from the police and the media. Berkowitz would essentially be convicted before he opened his mouth. The Berkowitz bandwagon was rolling now. His mentors had been correct: New York officials were so desperate for a solution to the case that they'd accept almost anything, or anyone.

When the suspect arrived at One Police Plaza he was welcomed by an overflowing mob of photographers, reporters, camera crews and curious cops and citizens. Hundreds of people barred the path as Gardella and Falotico, who were now joined by a camera-conscious Ed Zigo, struggled to escort a smiling David Berkowitz through the sea of flashing lights and flying questions. Berkowitz, as he would say later, was smiling with amusement at the photographers fighting for favored positions from which to capture the image of this now-recognizable terror for front pages and television screens throughout the world. The night-stalking phantom suddenly had a face, a name and a background.

With Berkowitz's arrival at the rear of One Police Plaza, TV programs were interrupted by bulletins in cities as far from New York as Los Angeles, London, Tokyo and Frankfurt, Germany. The next night, for example, ABC's network newscast would devote *more than half* of its nationwide broadcast to the arrest. The tight formats of the network newscasts usually allow even major stories only a minute or two of airtime.

Berkowitz also became headline news in a multitude of foreign newspapers, in addition to those in the United States. Further, he would appear on the cover of *Newsweek* and be featured prominently in *Time,* the *Washington Post,* the *Los Angeles Times,* the two big Chicago dailies and hundreds of other newspapers and magazines.

In New York, where Son of Sam would remain a front-page story for years to come, the *Post* and *Daily News* would break all previous circulation records with their coverage of the arrest. The *News* hastily published an "extra" edition and the *Post* bannered the headline "CAUGHT!" in red ink across the front page above a large photo of the suddenly infamous postal clerk. In the *New York Times,* the story of the arrest dominated page one and continued across two entire pages inside.

At year's end, the story of Son of Sam would be chosen by wire service executives as the ninth-biggest story in the world that year, dwarfing countless other political, military, social and economic events.

The biggest case was reaping the biggest publicity.

*   *   *

But even as the photographers jockeyed for strategic points from which to record his essence on film, there was a feeling about this suddenly real specter of David Berkowitz that drifted through the crowd—a feeling of disbelief. Many who were there that night stated even then that something didn't seem right. Familiar with police composite sketches and generally knowledgeable about other aspects of the investigation, some media members on the scene were hit with the gut reaction that something was wrong. Berkowitz didn't seem to fit at all.

But the police would endeavor to take care of those doubts in a hurry. This was now going to be a police performance, in the grandest sense. The triumphant entrance to Police Plaza was itself a tip-off as to what was going on. There was no regard for security. Berkowitz could have been shot, quite simply, by anyone who had a mind to do so. He wasn't sneaked into the building. He was paraded in front of the journalists—and anyone else who happened to be there.

In addition, Berkowitz was arrested by Brooklyn detectives for a Brooklyn crime. What was he doing at Police Plaza in Manhattan? Not a single Son of Sam shooting occurred in Manhattan. Maybe he was there because it was easier for the networks, newspapers and wire services—and the mayor—to convene at Police Plaza than at 10th Homicide in the Coney Island section of Brooklyn.

While the police awaited the arrival of the mayor to preside over a late-hour press conference at which Berkowitz's guns and other paraphernalia would be displayed, the suspect himself was taken upstairs, where he was subjected to all of a half hour's worth of informal questioning by about ten detectives who competed for the chance to query the most infamous criminal in New York history. Berkowitz allegedly had been advised of his rights, and he reportedly answered the superficial questions put to him. However, there apparently was no recording or transcript made of this thirty-minute chitchat with the police. In effect, it was "off the record."

Eight attacks had occurred. Thirteen people were shot, and six of those were dead. The police questioning of Berkowitz, by any professional standard, should have lasted many hours. The detectives would have allocated more time to question a routine mugging suspect. And the questioning certainly should have been on the record.

But the police didn't care. Berkowitz sat there and said he did it all and was commanded to do so by old Sam Carr, who was really a six-thousand-year-old man who spoke to David through his demon dog, Harvey. The police promptly leaked mountains of information about Berkowitz's insanity and sole guilt to the media. All of this was based on thirty minutes of bedlam, but it served its purpose. The newspapers, radio and TV stations ate it up, and by the next morning, amid the champagne corks popping as the police celebrated, Berkowitz's fate was sealed. He was guilty, he was alone and he was crazy. And he had *still* not formally confessed to anything.

After the session with the detectives, it was finally time for Berkowitz's formal statement to be made to representatives of the district attorneys of Queens, Brooklyn and the Bronx. The questioning would be conducted by assistant district attorneys, but one DA, John Santucci of Queens, made an appearance. And he didn't like what was going on. "I wasn't happy with the whole case from the minute they brought Berkowitz in and I saw him," Santucci would tell me three years later. "I had questions I wanted answers to and I had doubts that were troubling me. It was all too smooth, too easy. I didn't like it."

Santucci must have blanched the next day when he saw a *New York Post* photo of a beaming Timothy Dowd writing "Case Closed" across a police blackboard. Case closed—the night of the arrest.

Berkowitz's confessions would begin officially at 3:28 a.m. on August 11. The packed downstairs press conference was over; Berkowitz was on his way to international celebrity—and sole guilt—and only now were the assistant district attorneys gathering to interrogate him on the record.

Berkowitz, my sources would say, had rehearsed his lines and, as an active conspirator besides, knew enough details to satisfy any surface questioner. He was hoping that with the immense pressure to bring the case to an end the interrogation would be light. Too much detail could blow the whole thing wide apart.

Berkowitz needn't have worried. The questioning would be superficial and devoid of trick questions designed to trap a false confessor in a lie.

Berkowitz's answers would contain numerous factual errors. But they would not be challenged. To the contrary, officials would tell the media that Berkowitz had given them a detailed, "blow-by-blow" description of the crimes.

VII

Confession

It was shortly after midnight on August 11. The night was muggy, the air conditioning faulty, and the rushing sound of cars speeding by on the expressway near the White Plains apartment weakly mimicked the relaxing roll of the Atlantic's waves on Fire Island.

I was attempting to doze off to a radio talk show, and was tuned to the talented, sandpaper personality of Bob Grant, who was fielding questions from listeners concerned with the Son of Sam killings.

About a week before, Grant was unnerved by a caller who had credibly passed himself off as the gunman. But the police, after studying a tape of the conversation, decided it probably was an impostor. As New Yorkers offered their theories on the case to Grant, I was startled to full awakeness when he announced he'd just received a report that a suspect was under arrest.

I turned on the TV in time to see Berkowitz escorted through the crowd at One Police Plaza. At this moment, in another part of the country—Minot, North Dakota—one John Carr was also watching television. He'd just driven to the small northland city from New York and was sitting in his girlfriend's civilian apartment on the U.S. Air Force base near Minot when a bulletin about Berkowitz's arrest flashed across the screen.

"Oh, shit" is all he said.

Back in New York, someone else was responding to the capture. According to Berkowitz, an individual connected to the case and whose name neither he nor the police have revealed, phoned Police Plaza, somehow got through to Captain Joseph Borrelli and asked the task force supervisor if Berkowitz was implicating anyone else in the killing spree.

"The telephone conversation bothered Borrelli. This was obvious," Berkowitz would later write. But Borrelli, perhaps thinking of the champagne on ice, then shrugged off the incident.

The spirits may have been bubbly at the NYPD, but several cups of warmed-over coffee were the extent of my celebrating as I absorbed the unfolding developments through the early-morning hours. I was intrigued that Berkowitz resembled none of the composite sketches and that he resided in my former hometown of Yonkers. I'd heard of Pine Street, but was unable to fix its location. After four hours of sleep, I phoned my father at 7:30 a.m. and asked him about it. Though not in the city, he knew the Yonkers streets better than I did.

"It's off Glenwood, down the hill, just below North Broadway. It's a small, one-way street. You've seen it a thousand times," he said.

"What are the other streets around there?"

"Funny you asked that. Remember last week when you were talking about the aliases in that letter? Well, Wicker Street is right behind Pine, running down to Warburton. That sounds like your 'King Wicker' thing to me."

I was very interested in Pine Street itself, and even more struck by the realization that the Breslin letter's "Wicked King Wicker" alias apparently was a clue to the name of a street. The information was significant because I'd been doing a little "roadwork" of my own the preceding three days.

Since leaving Fire Island on August 1, I'd made a full-time evening job of researching the case, having paused only on Saturday night, the sixth, to take Lynn out to dinner at a restaurant along the Saw Mill River Parkway in Elmsford. Returning at midnight, I dropped her at the door before parking behind the apartment building. The residence was but a block from the Cross Westchester Expressway, and we were cognizant of the killer's penchant for striking near the parkways.

Later, I'd learn that a Berkowitz letter received that same day by Craig Glassman in Yonkers warned that "the streets of White Plains" would run red with blood. It was another small irony; but one I wouldn't forget.

* * *

The next morning, Sunday, August 7, the *Daily News* reprinted the entire text of the June letter to Breslin. Reading it over, I was struck by a hunch, a feeling—whatever—that the letter contained more than met the eye.

It was the note's second P.S. that drew my attention. Whereas the body of the letter was flawless in its "correctness" and formal tone, these five phrases (keep 'em digging; drive on; think positive; get off your butts; knock on coffins) were disjointed and top-heavy with slang. They simply didn't blend with the rest of the wording. Moreover, by inserting them into a postscript, the killer had set them apart and called even more attention to them, I thought. But why?

It was, I finally reasoned, quite possibly a list of five items. As I read the P.S. again, the words "keep," "drive," "get off" and "knock" suddenly seemed to spring off the page.

"Directions," I said out loud. "Maybe they're a set of directions. 'Go here, do that, turn off.'"

The letter's aliases were clues; so why not the P.S. as well? Why not include a set of directions disguised in code form? The ultimate come-and-get-me? It was widely known that the killer was said to be taunting, daring the police to capture him. The more I looked at the wording, the more sensible it seemed.

For the remainder of Sunday, the seventh, and for another five hours the night of the eighth, I experimented with any kind of system that came to mind; I even went to the library and checked out books on World War II and other ciphers. I added and subtracted letters to words, substituted letters and tried dozens of combinations—none of which made any real sense. A few times I thought I was on to it when one or two words melded together. But then the other phrases wouldn't fit in.

I called two friends, Bob Siegel and Ben Carucci, and asked them to give some thought to the breakdown. Both men began to experiment with the phrases, and I was glad they did, because I was stumped. It had been draining work. I was still convinced the answer was lurking, but gazing around the apartment—with books, crumpled papers and overflowing ashtrays everywhere—I doubted I'd ever find it.

"You're burning yourself out," Lynn warned. "Take a break from it and clear your head."

She was right.

*   *   *

On the night of August 9, after a daylong respite, the waters suddenly parted. With hindsight, it seemed ridiculously simple. But in that simplicity lay the system's strength. I had been looking too deep, bypassing the obvious. The solution was a combination of two "codes"—word games, actually. One piece consisted of basic word association, a crossword puzzle type of system. The other element was based on a ploy I'd come to learn was a common Satanist trick: spelling words backwards.

I looked at the first phrase, "keep em digging." Why, I wondered, would the ever-careful Son of Sam, so language-conscious throughout the letter, slip into "em" instead of using "them"? Maybe it wasn't a slip: "em" backwards spelled "me." The word preceding it, "keep," then became "peek"—as in "look for" or "see." The next word, "digging," couldn't be reversed, but using the crossword or word association approach, it did become "home." In the United Kingdom, as the dictionaries pointed out, a "digging" is a home (often shortened to "digs"). The first phrase now read: LOOK FOR ME HOME.

The next expression, "drive on," offered two possibilities. Reversing the word "on" resulted in "no."—the abbreviation for "north." If "drive" was left as it was, the phrase became: DRIVE NORTH. However, using word association, a "drive" was also a street, an avenue, a roadway or broadway. So the phrase could have said: NORTH AVENUE (street, roadway, etc.).

Continuing, with "think positive" word association was again the key. "Think" became "head," as in "mind," "brain," etc.; and "positive," after eliminating several other possibilities, became "right"—as in "certain," "sure," etc. The phrase read: HEAD RIGHT.

I was now looking at what I was sure was a set of directions. My failure, as I'd later learn, was not to have looked at the "Wicker" alias in the same way. But with the next expression in the P.S.—"get off your butts"—I soon saw that the only word Son of Sam had toyed with was "butts." Via word association again, "butts" became "ash"—as in cigarette butts. The reconstructed phrase said: GET OFF ASH.

Finally, through picking and choosing, "knock on coffins" translated to KNOCK ON PINE—a coffin being a "pine box."

The process, once I'd caught on to the system, went rather quickly, consuming about five hours. I sat back at the kitchen table and printed it all out at once:

LOOK FOR ME HOME . . . NORTH AVENUE (street, roadway, etc.) . . . HEAD RIGHT . . . GET OFF ASH . . . KNOCK ON PINE.

At 10 p.m., I called both Siegel and Carucci. "It's got to be right; it's got to be right," I emphasized. When I explained the breakdown rationally, each man agreed the decoding made sense.

I told them I was going to check street maps of the entire metropolitan area to try to confirm the analysis and to develop a list of possible addresses. But after I hung up from the calls, my mood changed. I started doubting myself. I also began to rationalize that the NYPD, with access to coding professionals, had assuredly traveled this road before me.

Within an hour, despite encouragement from Lynn, I'd convinced myself that I was wrong about the entire matter. I also knew the police were being deluged with well-meaning tips, and saw myself being filed in the "crackpot" folder.

* * *

Now, with Berkowitz having been arrested twelve hours earlier, I studied a street map of Yonkers. I located Pine Street and backtracked across the page with my finger: North Broadway . . . Ashburton Avenue. It was all there. But rather than elation, I felt stupid. I had been familiar with all these Yonkers streets for years; yet I hadn't even thought of them in the search.

But from the map, the trail was clear: to reach David Berkowitz's apartment from any of the major routes out of New York City—site of the investigation—one would exit the parkways or thruways, drive across Ashburton Avenue, head right off Ashburton onto North Broadway and proceed to Pine. Despite what the map told me, the entire idea of a code sounded so bizarre that I wanted more assurance. But where to get it?

Once again, I was sitting close to the answer. I contacted Benoit Mandelbrot, a respected Ph.D. in mathematics, and asked him about the odds of the analysis being correct. Gun-shy, I refrained from telling him the question concerned Son of Sam. Instead I simply asked about the probabilities that five phrases could, in order, lead to a particular address if the writer had *not* intended to incorporate such a ploy.

Mandelbrot, who had a reputation for graciousness and patience with the uninitiated, explained that the series of phrases could be likened to a mathematical progression. The odds against one phrase being accurate were small; against two being on target they increased dramatically; and so forth. Finally, the odds against all five—in order—leading step by step to the *right* address were almost impossible to calculate as a coincidence or an unintentional happening.

"So," Mandelbrot intoned, "it's not a coincidence. What you have done is correct. If you sent me a letter, what do you think the odds would be that I could get step-by-step directions to your house out of five successive phrases if you *didn't* intend to word your writing in such a manner?"

By using layman's language, Mandelbrot hit home—in more ways than one.

In the coming months, a long-term friend of Berkowitz's, Jeff Hartenberg, would tell the press: "David always liked to play word games." Berkowitz himself, in discussions with doctors and others, would state that "hidden messages" and "hints" on where Son of Sam could be found were contained in the two letters. However, he would consistently refuse to discuss the matter of who actually *wrote* the Breslin letter, or at least provided the wording. This subject would eventually evolve into one of the strongest pieces of conspiracy evidence. But that was in the future. On August 11, I was left to ponder the implications of the "code."

*   *   *

David Berkowitz was doing precious little pondering on the eleventh of August. Instead, in the hours following his arrest, he was amazing the assistant district attorneys with his "encyclopedia" memory as he readily confessed to all the .44 shootings. He also confessed to wounding a woman in Yonkers with a rifle. The police had no record of any such incident. This development should have raised questions about the other confessions—but didn't.

"His recall appeared marvelous," Queens assistant district attorney Herb Leifer said three years later. "It was almost as if it was all scripted ahead of time; and it probably was. There were holes in his statements when they were compared to established information. The DA [Santucci of Queens] never liked it; but he didn't take the statement, and there was no access to Berkowitz afterwards for the prosecution. He was turned over to the psychiatrists. And of course Santucci had no control over Brooklyn or the Bronx," said Leifer. "So what we had was a command performance by David—and they wanted to believe everything he said anyway."

Leifer was referring to the inconsistencies and contradictions that dotted Berkowitz's confessions. Primarily, major flaws appeared in the Berkowitz version of the shootings of Robert Violante and Stacy Moskowitz in Brooklyn and the Queens attacks on Joanne Lomino and Donna DeMasi, Christine Freund and Virginia Voskerichian.

Other problem areas, including the Bronx shootings, may also have existed. But in some instances, without witnesses or other evidence to contradict Berkowitz's original statements, no one knew for certain.

In total, there were significant discrepancies in the confessions to fully half the .44 attacks—an astounding fact when one considers that the NYPD and the Bronx and Brooklyn district attorneys took no action to investigate the case after the arrest—except to clear up a handful of "loose ends," as the police put it.

The confessions will be published here for the first time; and all crucial passages will be included—especially those relating to the incidents at which contradictions appeared.

It will be possible to identify many of the inconsistencies and to see—from the slant of the questions to Berkowitz—the areas which even then were troubling the assistant district attorneys themselves.

* * *

It was shortly after 3:30 a.m., August 11. Berkowitz, who had been awake for about twenty-one hours, was nonetheless showing no signs of confusion or exhaustion, as might have been expected. A large number of detectives and assistant district attorneys had gathered in the conference room of the chief of detectives at One Police Plaza.

First up would be Ronald Aiello, head of the Brooklyn DA's homicide bureau. He would be followed by William Quinn, an assistant from the Bronx, and Martin Bracken, an assistant to Santucci in Queens. Aiello would open the session because Berkowitz was arrested by Brooklyn detectives as a result of the Moskowitz investigation. From this point, the Brooklyn DA's office would ride herd over the case.

Aiello finished his introductory querying of Berkowitz, who had waived his right to an attorney, and was now ready to ask the curly-haired postal worker about the Moskowitz-Violante shootings.

Q. David, on July 31, 1977—where were you living at that time?

A. The Pine St. address.

Q. That's up in Yonkers?

A. Yes.

Q. Who were you living with?

A. Myself . . .

Q. How long had you been living there?

A. A little over a year.

Q. Do you live with anyone, David?

A. No.

[Berkowitz then said he'd eaten dinner that night at a Manhattan diner and drove out toward Long Island. Aiello, very much aware of the yellow VW saga, then asked the suspect about the type of car he drove.]

Q. What kind of car do you have?

A. 1970 Ford Galaxie.

Q. What color is it?

A. Yellow.[2]

Q. How long have you had that car?

2   The car was actually a faded yellow, almost beige or cream-colored, t Berkowitz claimed in 1977 that his relationship with Sam Carr was only "mystical"—that he didn't actually know him. Yet even in this early post-arrest comment, he acknowledged knowing that Sam had a daughter named Wheat.

A.   About three years.

Q.   Is the car completely yellow?

A.   No, a black vinyl roof . . .

Q.   Is that a two-door or four-door?

A.   Four-door.

Q.   Were you using that car on the 31st?

A.   Yes, I was . . .

Q.   Were you with anyone, or were you alone when you were having your dinner on 10th Avenue?

A.   I was alone.

Q.   Where did you go from there—out to Long Island?

A.   Yes. Long Island, Brooklyn.

Q.   Did you have any purpose in going out on Long Island? Just to take a ride?

A.   Purposely going out killing somebody.

Q.   Did you have anyone in mind at that time—or anyone you might come across?

A.   Whoever would just come around—when I was told who to get.

Q.   Who told you who to get?

A.   Sam Carr.

Q.   Who is Sam Carr?

A.   My master.

Q.   Where does Sam live?

A.   In Yonkers.

Q.   Is Sam the father of Wheat Carr?

A.   Yes.

Q.   How long have you known Sam, approximately?

A.   Probably—well, as Sam, I'd say just a little over a year; a year and a half.

Q.   Is that his actual name—Sam Carr?

A.   That's the name he goes by, yes.

Q.   Did you have any discussion with Sam that particular day, about finding someone to kill?

A.   I just had my orders.

Q.   Do you want to tell me how you got those orders?

A.   Yes, he told me through his dog, as he usually does. It's not really a dog. It just looks like a dog. It's not. He just gave me an idea where to go. When I got the word, I didn't know who I would go out to kill—but I would know when I saw the right people.

Q. Did you have a location in mind, David?

A. Let's just say the area I was in, Bensonhurst, was one of several I rode through . . .

Q. About what time did you reach the Bensonhurst section?

A. Two o'clock. No. Yeah. Two o'clock, about two o'clock . . .

Q. Where did you park?

A. On Bay 17th, between Shore Parkway and Cropsey Ave.

Q. Are you familiar with that neighborhood?

A. I have been there before.

Q. On what occasion were you there?

A. I'd say the past week.

Q. Prior to going there that night you were there?

A. Yes.

Q. What brought you there on that occasion?

A. I had to go and kill somebody—what can I tell you?

Q. . . . Do you recall where you parked your car exactly on the block?

A. Up by a fire hydrant, midway between Cropsey and Shore Parkway.

Q. Did you realize you parked your car by a hydrant?

A. Yes. I saw the police give me a summons.

Q. How did you see that?

A. I was walking away. I saw a police car coming up Shore Parkway and turn onto Bay 17th, going up that street. I had a feeling they would go by my car. . . . I saw the policeman give me a summons. Then, they went slowly up the block near Cropsey Avenue, and pulled over again. I watched for about ten minutes. They got out of the car. I don't know what they were doing, but I went back to my car. There was a ticket on it.

Q. What were you wearing that night?

A. Blue denim jacket, blue dungarees.[3]

Q. What did you have on under your denim jacket?

A. A light brown shirt.

---

3   This is how Mrs. Davis described Berkowitz's attire, as did Mary Lyons, who saw him after the shooting.

Q. When you went back to your car . . . did you take the ticket off the windshield?

A. Yes.

Q. What did you do with it?

A. I put it inside the car.

Q. Tell me what you did from there.

A. I was still walking around the area, went back to the park, sat down for a while.

Q. Where were you sitting—on the bench?

A. Sitting on a bench.

Q. Did you have a weapon with you at that time?

A. Yes.

Q. What weapon?

A. .44 Bulldog.

Q. Then what did you do, David?

A. I saw that couple, Stacy Moskowitz and her boyfriend. They were by the swings; they went back to their car. I don't know how much time elapsed, maybe ten minutes or so. I walked up to their car . . .

Q. Were there other cars parked, or did other cars come eventually?

A. Eventually.

Q. You say you saw this Stacy Moskowitz car and then you saw the one up in front of them?

A. No, the one up front was there before.

Q. Then Stacy Moskowitz came afterwards?

A. Yes.

Q. Did you see them get out of the car?

A. No, I was too far down in the park. I saw them walking. I saw a couple by the swings. I didn't know it was them. I saw them go back to the car.[4]

Q. Then what did you do?

A. I just—I don't know. I waited for a time. I don't know how much time elapsed. I just went up to the car. I just walked up to it, pulled out the gun and put it—you know—I stood a couple of feet from the window.

Q. Were the windows open or closed?

---

4 In a later letter to a psychiatrist, Berkowitz contradicted this statement by saying: "I saw her and her boyfriend making out in the car. Then, they walked over the walk bridge and went along the path by the water . . . and then came to where I was by the swings."

A.   Open, and I fired. [Berkowitz then described how he "sprayed" the car with bullets.]

Q.   Then what did you do?

A.   I turned around and I ran out of the park through those town houses [the garden apartments where Mrs. Davis and Mary Lyons lived].

Q.   You say you ran through the park. You came out of the park eventually?

A.   Yes.

Q.   Did you go out an exit or hole in the fence?

A.   There was a hole in the fence.

Aiello now had several more problems. Berkowitz, who said he'd arrived in the neighborhood at 2 a.m., also said he knew Tommy Zaino's car was at the scene before Violante's, and at a location Berkowitz said he hadn't walked to yet. Violante had pulled into the parking spot between 1:40 and 1:45. Moreover, Berkowitz had told the police that Zaino had been the original target, but was spared when he pulled forward. This action occurred at approximately 1:35, a full twenty-five minutes before Berkowitz said he parked two blocks away.

This wasn't simply a matter of confusion regarding the time: Berkowitz said he arrived just before the police ticketed his car—an action recorded by the 2:05 time on the ticket.

Aiello was also faced with Berkowitz's saying he left the scene in a different direction from that of the man who ran through the park exit and entered the yellow VW.

Certainly concerned about the VW chase, Aiello then asked Berkowitz how he left the area. Berkowitz confounded the issue even more by saying he drove as far north as he could on 18th Avenue, a street located east of Bay 17th. This route took him in a completely different direction from that of the VW driver.

Aiello then concluded his questioning by asking Berkowitz about the variety of weapons he owned, and about the origin of the .44. Berkowitz said his Army pal Billy Dan Parker had purchased it for him while Berkowitz was visiting him in Houston in June 1976.

*   *   *

Aiello's interrogation about the most infamous homicide in New York history had lasted thirty-two minutes. He did not follow up on the obvious discrepancies in Berkowitz's account.

Berkowitz's statement that he removed the ticket from his windshield was confirmed by Mrs. Davis, who saw him do it. However, Mrs. Davis—whose account was supported by her companion, Howard Bohan—insisted that Berkowitz didn't even return to the park at that late time, 2:20, but instead left to follow the police car.

Also, at no time did Aiello ask Berkowitz to explain why, if his confession was accurate, he was back over on Bay 17th Street *again* at 2:33 when he passed Mrs.

Davis as she walked her dog just two minutes before the shots were fired. Berkowitz, simply put, claimed to be in the park the entire time, while Mrs. Davis's account *twice* put him well away from the shooting site.

Beyond these and the other footnoted contradictions were, of course, the matters of the yellow VW, the clothes the killer wore and the gunman's physical appearance and hairstyle—radically different from Berkowitz's.

"Nobody wanted to upset the applecart," Herb Leifer would later say. "They didn't want to go into any areas that might upset David or rattle him into changing his mind about confessing."

Indeed, the only "trick" question Aiello threw Berkowitz concerned the bench sitting; and Berkowitz fell for it. The actual killer, according to Violante, had been leaning against a restroom building and not seated on a bench when the two victims walked within several feet of him—another encounter Berkowitz failed to confess to.

Berkowitz would later create still another version of the shooting that again contradicted established fact. After telling Aiello he'd simply walked up to the passenger's side of the victims' auto and fired into it, as the killer actually did, he told a psychiatrist: "I walked straight to the car. When I got to the rear of it I looked around, then stepped onto the sidewalk." (There was no sidewalk.) "I moved right to the driver's side and pulled the gun out." (Violante and Stacy were shot through the passenger's window; in fact, not a single Son of Sam victim had been fired on from the driver's side.)

*   *   *

Aiello, who is now a New York State Supreme Court judge, gave way to William Quinn, an assistant district attorney from the Bronx. Quinn managed to better Aiello's interrogation time record, consuming only twenty-seven minutes to question Berkowitz about three murders: those of Donna Lauria, Valentina Suriani and Alexander Esau.

There was little noteworthy information in these confessions, except that Berkowitz had Suriani and Esau seated in the wrong positions in their auto—a mistake he probably picked up from erroneous newspaper reports. He also forgot to mention that a letter had been left at that scene; but Quinn was quick to suggest the answer:

Q. Now what did you do after you fired the four shots?

A. I ran to my car and got in my car and drove off.

Q. Did you leave anything at the scene?

A. Oh, yeah, right. The letter. I had it in my pocket. It was a letter addressed to Captain Borrelli.

Quinn had some concern about the Breslin letter, and a few other matters as well:

Q. Did you write a letter to Mr. Breslin?

A. Yes, I did.

Q. And you wrote it yourself?

A. Yes.

Q. Why did you mail it from New Jersey?

A. I was there at the time, hunting.

Q. Did you ever admit to anyone before tonight what you had done in relation to the Bronx cases?

A. No.

Q. To anybody at all?

A. No.

Q. . . . Did you write any other letters besides the two we mentioned?

A. Not addressed to anyone.

Q. Ever mail them?

A. No.

Q. Ever call the police?

A. No.

Q. Ever identify yourself as Son of Sam?

A. No.

In speaking to Quinn about the Suriani-Esau killings, Berkowitz had known, without prompting, that the words "Chubby Behemoth" were contained in the letter left at that scene. Since the note was not made public, Quinn had reason to be satisfied Berkowitz was involved in the shootings.

In his confession to the murder of Donna Lauria and the wounding of Jody Valente, Berkowitz stuck close to the facts of the case. Still, Quinn had some concerns:

Q. Did you have the same hair[style] as you have now?

A. Yes.

Q. You didn't have a wig?

A. No.

Q. . . . Had you followed either one of those two girls earlier in the evening—nine or nine-thirty? [This was a reference to the suspicious yellow car, smaller than Berkowitz's, cruising the area at that time.]

A. No.

Martin Bracken, an assistant district attorney from Queens, began his questioning at 4:34 a.m. by asking about the wounding of Carl Denaro as he sat on the passenger's side of Rosemary Keenan's navy blue Volkswagen, which Berkowitz incorrectly stated was "red."

He said he fired five times at the car and that he intended to kill "just the woman. I thought she was in the front seat, passenger's side. It was very dark."

There were no witnesses to this shooting. The person who pulled the trigger, however, had fired wildly—unlike the Lauria shooter. The remainder of the questioning about this attack was sketchy, and Berkowitz's answers were brief and apparently factual.

The shootings of Joanne Lomino and Donna DeMasi were another matter. It was this incident which resulted in two composite sketches of a gunman who didn't remotely resemble Berkowitz and a report from a witness that the shooter had fled carrying the weapon in his left hand. Berkowitz is right-handed.

Q. Who did you fire at?

A. The two girls.

Q. And where were they seated?

A. They were standing by the porch of one of the girls' homes.

Q. . . . Did you walk up to the location where they were seated?

A. Yes.

Q. . . . Do you recall what you were wearing that night?

A. No.

Q. Do you recall the weather conditions?

A. A bit chilly, clear.

Q. And could you describe what happened when you came up to the two girls?

A. I walked up and I was going to shoot them. I tried to be calm about it and not scare them, but they were frightened of me and started to move away. And I asked them—I didn't know what to say to calm them down—so I said I was looking for an address. I'm looking for a certain address or something like that and at that time I was a few feet from them, and I pulled out the gun and opened fire.

Q. . . . What position were you in when you fired?

A. I was at maybe eight or nine feet from the steps or something.

Q. And did you go into a crouch position at that time?

A. Well, I just picked up the gun—they were like running up the steps. I stood upright.

Q. And how many times did you fire?

A. Five.

Q. And did you use both hands or one hand to hold the gun?

A. Both, I believe.

Q. And when you fired, did you hit anyone?

A. Yes. Both girls.

Q. Did you see what happened after you fired?

A. No, they just fell down.

Q. . . . When you fired the shots at the two girls, were they face-to-face with you or were their backs to you?

A. Face-to-face.

Q. And were they standing still or running?

A. They were running.

Q. In which direction were they running in relation to you?

A. Towards the door, but they were on the top and the door wouldn't open. They looked at me, facing me.

Q. Do you recall what you were wearing that day?

A. No, I don't.

Q. Did you have the same hairstyle?

A. Yes.

Q. Anything physically different about you on that day?

A. No.

Q. And did you see anybody besides the two girls as you were getting out of your car?

A. Yes.

Q. Who?

A. An elderly woman at the porch of her house and I think she was putting on or turning off a porch light.

Q. Now, did she say anything to you at this time?

A. No.

Q. Now, did she look at you?

A. I believe she did, yes.

Q. . . . Did you ever have occasion to get out of the car prior to the first time you went to the girls?

A. Just to urinate or something.

Q. Did you get out around Hillside Avenue and 262nd [Street]?

A.   No.

Q.   Now, did you use the same gun that you used on the prior occasions, the one in Queens and the Bronx?

A.   Yes.

Q.   Now, did you use the same ammunition that you purchased in Houston?

A.   Yes.

Berkowitz twice said the girls were running up the steps. However, Joanne Lomino stated to prosecutors: "We were standing by the sidewalk talking. We walked over to the porch and we were standing for about five minutes. I heard a voice, then turned around and the guy pulled a gun and started shooting at us."

She added: "I turned around and the gun was already out and he was firing." The girls weren't running anywhere.

Berkowitz also confessed that the victims were face-to-face with him. Joanne Lomino, struck first, was shot in the back. She further stated: "I had my back turned towards him . . . and he just had the gun out and he fired it. My back was towards him, though."

Bracken's question to Berkowitz as to whether he'd gotten out of his car at Hillside and 262nd was based on the girls' observation of a suspicious man, possibly the gunman, hiding behind a telephone pole at that location, which wasn't far from the shooting site. His question about whether or not the same .44 had been used related to the lack of ballistics evidence linking the bullets from this shooting to any others.

Berkowitz later told a psychiatrist that he "just popped out" of "the lot around the corner" before approaching the girls. There is no such lot.

* * *

Bracken, who conducted the most comprehensive of the three assistant district attorneys' interrogations, then shifted gears and began to question Berkowitz about the murder of Christine Freund as she sat in her boyfriend's car in Forest Hills on January 30, 1977.

This Berkowitz confession also went unchallenged. Later in the narrative, the in-depth follow-up investigation of the Freund murder will be explained in detail. These are among the key areas of the confession I would be analyzing:

Q.   Where did you park your car?

A.   I parked on a street that runs parallel to the Long Island Rail Road. It's a small winding street. I don't know the name of it.

Q.   . . . And did you get out of your car at that time?

A.   Yes, I did.

Q.   And where did you go?

A. In the vicinity of Austin Street.

Q. . . . And can you tell me in your own words what happened?

A. Yes. I was walking in the opposite direction. I saw them walking down [from the restaurant to their car, parked in Station Plaza by the railroad station], we just passed each other, we crisscrossed. We almost touched shoulders.

Q. You passed by them?

A. Yes. They got into their car and I saw Mr. Diel get in and he reached over and opened up the door for Miss Freund and I was standing four or five feet away. And I watched them get in the car, and I guess a minute went by, and I opened fire.

Q. When you approached them, did you approach from the front or the back?

A. Back.

Q. . . . And what were you wearing on that occasion?

A. Heavy winter clothing.

Berkowitz then described how he fired three shots through the passenger's window, aiming only at Christine Freund. He said he used only three bullets, rather than four or five as in most other incidents, because "I only had one person to shoot." Later, Bracken returned to the "shoulder touching" occurrence:

Q. In relation to the car where Diel and Freund were sitting, where did you first see them when you crisscrossed or almost touched shoulders?

A. 71st and Continental. [71st and Continental are the same street, with two names. Berkowitz actually meant to say Continental and Station Plaza.]

Q. And they were walking towards their car?

A. Yes.

Q. And you were where at that time?

A. I was coming from walking parallel to the railroad.

Q. I see—so they went diagonal past you. Would that be correct?

A. Yes.

Q. And where was your car parked in relation to the railroad?

A. You have those winding streets. It was in there.

The murder of Virginia Voskerichian took place less than a block from the Freund shooting at approximately 7:30 p.m. on March 8, 1977:

Q. What happened that night when you were in that area?

A. Just walked around all night.

Q. How long were you walking around?

A. Maybe an hour and a half.

Q. And then what happened?

A. I saw Miss Voskerichian, and I had to shoot her. She was coming up—we was walking in opposite directions.

Q. . . . And when you saw her, what did you do?

A. I pulled out the gun from my pocket and fired one shot into her face.

Q. And what did you do after that?

A. I turned around and ran towards my car.

Q. Do you recall what she looked like?

A. Vaguely.

Q. Could you tell us, please?

A. She had a long, pretty face. There was a shadow effect; long wavy hair.

Q. . . . Showing you this map, you see where the tennis courts are at the top. Where were you parked in relation to the tennis courts?

A. Adjacent to the tennis courts. The same street as the railroad.

Q. . . . Now after you shot her and to the point that you got to your car, did you see anyone?

A. Yes, there was an elderly man walking. I ran by him.

Q. Did you happen to see anyone jogging in the area? [This was a reference to Amy Johnson and her brother.]

A. No, I did not.

Q. . . . Did you say anything [to the elderly man]?

A. I said, "Hi, mister."

Q. . . . And what were you wearing on that occasion?

A. I think my ski jacket, dungarees.

Q. Were you wearing a hat?

A. A watch cap.

Q. And what type of a hat was that?

A. A brown watch cap. [The shooter's cap was also striped.]

Q. And was that in your duffel bag that was taken by the police today?

A. Yes.

Q. Do you remember the type of evening it was—the weather conditions?

A. Cold.

Q. . . . Can you describe what she [the victim] was wearing and doing at that time?

A. She was just walking home from school. She had on a long coat and boots. She
was carrying her books.

Q. How far away from her were you when you fired?

A. About two feet.

The glaring problems with this Berkowitz version are evident. Primarily, the Police
Department, after initially nominating "Ski Cap" as the killer, changed course and
said Ski Cap was a witness and the Berkowitz look-alike who followed jogger Amy
Johnson and her brother, Tony, was its prime target. That person—almost certainly
Berkowitz, as the composite sketch illustrated—was hatless and wearing a beige rain-
coat—not the type of clothing Ski Cap wore.

Now, in custody, Berkowitz was trying to claim *he* had been Ski Cap and had
indeed done the shooting. The scenario was totally confused and contradictory. Berkowitz was trying to become another individual—a person he didn't resemble, who
was some three inches shorter and who was dressed differently—just as he'd done in
confessing to the Brooklyn shooting.

The Police Department, which had initially done an about-face on its prime suspect, now would do another one, accepting Berkowitz's version and *still* leaving one
suspect—actually the shooter—unaccounted for.

There were other discrepancies, too. Berkowitz said he pulled the gun from his
pocket; he later wrote it was in a plastic bag. He said the night was cold, when in
fact it was springlike. He said he spoke the words "Hi, mister" as he ran by Ed Marlow. Marlow, however, had reported Ski Cap as saying, "Oh, Jesus." Berkowitz also
confessed that Miss Voskerichian was wearing a "long coat," whereas, police reports
show, the garment was actually a short jacket.

Berkowitz's statement that he was in the area for more than an hour is consistent
with the reports of Amy Johnson and others, who had seen both the Berkowitz
look-alike and apparently Ski Cap in the neighborhood well before the shooting.
It is worth remembering that the Berkowitz look-alike had somehow managed to
again appear ahead of Miss Johnson and her brother after they'd passed him the first
time—and they were jogging. The scenario strongly suggests he was driven ahead of
the pair and dropped off.

Berkowitz also confessed that after the shooting he ran to his car, which was
parked near the railroad tracks only about a block from the shooting site, He later
contradicted that account by telling a psychiatrist he was parked several blocks further west, in another direction.

*　*　*

Martin Bracken's final set of questions concerned the wounding of Judy Placido and Sal Lupo as they sat in a borrowed car near the Elephas discotheque. Berkowitz simply said he parked two blocks south and four blocks west of the disco, wandered around the area, saw the couple seated in the car, approached, fired and then ran back to his own auto and fled.

The troublesome areas regarding this attack involved the "man with the mustache" and his yellow, Nova-sized car, as well as other factors described in Chapter III. However, after the arrest, a friend of Lupo's told the *Daily News:* "This guy [Berkowitz] was definitely in Elephas five minutes before the shooting." He added he'd seen Berkowitz speak with a young woman, then turn around and say aloud to "a few people: 'That girl is a snob.'" If this identification was correct, it seriously compromised Berkowitz's confession to this shooting as well.

*   *   *

It was now 5:20 a.m., and the questioning of Berkowitz was over. Bracken had spent forty minutes interrogating the suspect about five different shootings. The "verdict" was now in, and the newspapers churning off the presses were already telling the story—as relayed by the police. Berkowitz was crazy. He acted on the orders of a barking dog who was the intermediary for Sam Carr, who was really a demon—Berkowitz's "master." Berkowitz had acted alone. The biggest case was over.

*   *   *

In the early morning hours, Mrs. Cacilia Davis was awakened by loud knocking on her door. "We're from the police," the voice behind it said, according to Mrs. Davis. Releasing the latch, she was greeted by *Daily News* reporter William Federici and a photographer. Federici's name had appeared on the byline of the "Make Mrs. Davis a Target" story that was on the newsstands at that moment.

Federici, said Mrs. Davis, had been a longtime friend of Joseph Strano—the detective from 10th Homicide who took down her account of the night of the shooting and later accompanied her on the shopping trip during which they unsuccessfully searched for a jacket identical to the one Berkowitz had worn.

Now, having obtained Mrs. Davis's name and address from some source or other, Federici was inside the comfortable, beautifully furnished Bay 17th Street apartment ready to hear the prized, confidential witness's own first-person story. Hesitant at first, but reassured since the killer was now arrested, Mrs. Davis agreed to pose for photos with her dog and to accompany Federici to the offices of the *Daily News* in Manhattan.

Mrs. Davis picks up the account: "I went with them. They told me Strano said it was all right to talk to them. So I told them what happened that night."

I interrupted: "Did you tell them about Berkowitz's car moving, leaving the neighborhood, blowing the horn and all that?"

"Yes," she replied. "I told Federici all about it. Strano already knew about the car. Strano knew, and then I told Federici about it."

Before the arrest, the significance of the car's leaving the area was minimal. The action occurred fifteen minutes before the shootings, and no one knew the owner of the flagged auto would turn out to be Berkowitz—the alleged killer. But the Galaxie's departure now took on a new—and very damaging—significance.

"Federici took down what I told him, and it was typed out. I looked at it, and it was just as it had happened," Mrs. Davis continued. "And then Strano came in."

According to Mrs. Davis, Detective Strano appeared at the *Daily News,* read the draft of her "first person" story and then suggested Mrs. Davis might be hungry. She then accompanied a female reporter "downstairs for something to eat," she said. "When we came back up, the part about him [Berkowitz] taking off the ticket and blowing the horn and all was taken out."

*   *   *

The next day, Friday, August 12, Mrs. Davis's story (under her byline, no less) appeared on page two of the *News.* There was no reference to her earlier sighting or the Galaxie's pre-shooting maneuvers—which of course occurred at the time Berkowitz claimed he'd been stalking his victims two blocks away in the park.

Strano also knew from his own DD-5 report that Mrs. Davis had barely entered her apartment when the shots rang out. He'd written that she heard the gunfire while unleashing the dog. If someone—as I later did—thought to measure distances and check time factors, serious questions would also arise.

In fact, in a "special" edition of the *News* published the morning after the arrest, a detective was quoted as saying: "She was standing on her stoop, unleashing her dog, when she heard the shots and the squeal of a horn." This account was inaccurate by about twenty seconds, but the red light was definitely flashing. Unless Berkowitz was a track star, the police had problems.

Accordingly, in Mrs. Davis's story the following day, the issue was avoided thusly: ". . . it was strange to see somebody with a [leisure] suit on in that heat. Before I went to sleep, I started reading the paper, and I heard what sounded like a long boom and then a horn." Through clever writing, the story implied that Mrs. Davis was lounging around her apartment for some time before hearing the shots; which wasn't true.

In still another article in the *News* that *same* day, on which Federici—Mrs. Davis's ghost writer—shared a byline, the story was further embellished and distorted: "He [the killer] walked away. She went home. *Fifteen minutes later* [emphasis added], she went to her window to turn on the air conditioning. She heard a loud bang, and then the sound of a horn blowing."

This article managed to contradict the other—even though both appeared in the same newspaper on the same day with the same reporter directly involved in both versions. One said the witness heard the shots as she opened a paper (which was technically true); the other said she'd heard them while turning on her air conditioner.

The stories, through inaccuracies in one and a writing device in the other, effectively submerged the critical time-and-distance factors.

* * *

What actually transpired between Federici and Strano in the city room while Mrs. Davis was downstairs isn't known for certain. Perhaps the inaccuracies were simply the result of mistakes in the writing process. But it's more likely that they weren't.

A Brooklyn assistant district attorney, Steven Wax, later confirmed that Mrs. Davis told him Berkowitz's car drove away before the shootings. Wax said he didn't hear of the incident until the day before Berkowitz pleaded guilty in May 1978—nine months later—when Mrs. Davis explained it to him.

It seems the Brooklyn DA's office hadn't bothered to interview its own witnesses during all that time—no lineups, no checking or verifying statements from Berkowitz, etc. This lack of follow-through is illustrative of the authorities' aversion to perhaps compiling information they didn't want to address concerning what lay beneath the surface of the case. The now-you-see-it, now-you-don't intense hunt for the yellow VW is another example of this syndrome.

The fact is this: the Brooklyn district attorney's office acknowledged receiving evidence from a star witness that seriously undermined the veracity of Berkowitz's confession. This information, which went hand in hand with the yellow VW evidence already known by the authorities, was obtained before Berkowitz pleaded guilty. But the Brooklyn DA did nothing to halt or delay that proceeding, or to mount an investigation.

When I asked Strano about this matter, he claimed that the May 1978 session was the first time *he'd* heard about the Ford leaving the area. I suggested to Strano that perhaps he was making this claim because, for a variety of reasons, he'd not told the DA's office about the incident immediately and had no choice but to plead ignorance in Wax's office that day.

This suggestion was denied by Strano.

Mrs. Davis simply says that Strano is not telling the truth.

When Mrs. Davis was first interviewed by me in the spring of 1979, I was accompanied by Marian Roach, an editorial employee of the *New York Times,* and freelance reporter James Mitteager. Mrs. Davis's attorney was also present at the interview, as was a friend and neighbor of the witness.

Until that moment, Mrs. Davis wasn't even vaguely aware of the technical details of Berkowitz's confession—which hadn't been released publicly—and had no idea of the importance of her account, which was supported by Howard Bohan, who was also interviewed.

It was only during the course of this and subsequent meetings, when the reconstruction of the murder scene was explained to her, that Mrs. Davis came to realize her sightings effectively eliminated Berkowitz as the gunman that night.

The knowledge made her fearful; she was apprehensive of retaliation from the "real killer," as she put it. And she was also concerned that her testimony might free Berkowitz.

"He's still a killer, I don't want that to happen," she said on several occasions. She was assured the intent wasn't to free Berkowitz, but to bring his accomplices to ground if possible.

Ironically, the police's own star witness had almost destroyed their effort to depict Berkowitz as a lone, demented killer.

Meanwhile, the Brooklyn district attorney's office steadfastly refused to act. District Attorney Eugene Gold would turn a deaf ear to the mounting evidence and continue to endorse the Berkowitz-alone position.

*   *   *

As for Strano and Federici, one is free to arrive at an independent conclusion. Federici subsequently left the *News* for a job in private industry. Strano, along with twenty-four other members of the NYPD, was promoted just nine days after Berkowitz's arrest in the largest advancement ceremony in the history of the New York City Police Department.

Down and out in March, the NYPD was now basking in the glow of its success in the Son of Sam case. Its status was restored; its rating was sky high in the public mind. And the promotion ceremony topped it off.

In coming months, a split would develop within the previously united legions of 10th Homicide. Some detectives, including Strano and John Falotico, became somewhat concerned as Detective Ed Zigo—who was attempting to obtain a search warrant at the time of the capture—sought to claim a considerable amount of undeserved credit and fame.

This knowledge is firsthand, as I spoke with Strano and others, including Zigo, on several occasions during this period. Zigo was moving in his own direction, but in conversations with others, subtle questions and hints concerning books and movies invariably were present. Mrs. Davis also said that a fight had erupted between members of the opposing camps at an awards function in Brooklyn, at which she was present.

Zigo, who may or may not have landed any blows at this alleged "Policemen's Brawl," did beat the others to another punch at least. After retiring several years later, he collaborated on a supposedly factual TV movie about the case with producer Sonny Grosso, himself an ex-member of the NYPD. The film, which first aired on CBS in October 1985, was titled *Out of the Darkness*. But rather than shedding any new light, the movie distorted and fictionalized the investigation, the events surrounding the arrest and Zigo's role in each.

CBS wasn't the only victim of a whitewash. In 1981, author Lawrence Klausner published a book which purported to tell the "true" story—which of course meant that Berkowitz was a salivating, demon-haunted madman who acted alone. Klausner was fed a large plateful of distortions by a handful of task force supervisors and others—all of which he dutifully digested and reported as fact. He literally canonized Captain Joseph Borrelli, Sergeant Joe Coffey and other Omega task force members, whose investigation was, despite Klausner's platitudes, an expensive failure.

* * *

But these subplots were beyond my vision of the future on August 11, 1977—the day after the arrest. I was in White Plains, holding clues from the Breslin letter I suspected were beyond Berkowitz's ability to concoct, based on background information that had already surfaced.

I was also troubled that he didn't remotely resemble some of the composite sketches of the killer and that reports I'd read of the Moskowitz murder and Mrs. Davis's role seemed contradictory.

Following that trail, I'd looked up all the "Carr" listings in the telephone book and learned, to my considerable interest, that a number for a "John Wheat Carr" existed at Sam Carr's address. John Wheat and the "John 'Wheaties'" alias in the Breslin letter—the discovery was intriguing.

In an older directory, I noticed another listing—that of a Carr III Studio. That heightened my interest because the Breslin letter was said to have been printed in the style of an illustrator or cartoonist.

The first seeds of the conspiracy investigation were now planted. There was no way of knowing that official hindrances and roadblocks would result in a long growing season.

VIII
"Sam Sleeps"

"Kill him! . . . Kill him! . . . Kill him!" A crowd of several hundred frenzied New Yorkers chanted outside a Brooklyn courthouse as Berkowitz was arraigned and ordered held for psychiatric testing. Later, at Kings County Hospital, another throng shouted for the immediate execution of the alleged Son of Sam. Telephoned death threats swamped the hospital's switchboard, and five young men were arrested in the outdoor melee, suspected of plotting to put a bomb inside the large medical center.

Upstairs in a small cell in the prison ward, a heavily guarded Berkowitz paced the floor. In another wing of the hospital, Robert Violante lay quietly, still recovering from his blinding head wound.

It was now Friday, August 12, and a forty-eight-hour immersion in the media left me resigned to the belief that there would be a difficult, if not impossible, mountain to scale if I sought to resolve any questions about Berkowitz's sole guilt. But I was determined to give it a try.

After compiling the initial information about the Carr household, I followed a hunch about the "John 'Wheaties'" alias and phoned around to find someone who knew the family. Since I'd grown up in Yonkers, I was able to obtain referrals, and after about five calls I located a contact who was acquainted with them.

The conversation was revealing. By the time it ended, my adrenaline was working overtime.

"You're right, it's more than a phone listing. John Carr's nickname was Wheaties," I was told.

The contact, whom I will call Jack, added: "The nickname may have originated with the listing, which was probably a number for both John and Wheat when they were kids. Old man Sam runs an answering service, so there's lots of lines into that house. They probably just never changed it in the book," Jack suggested.

"Based on what you're telling me, John Carr was an alias of Son of Sam," I said slowly. "That's heavy stuff."

"Well, his nickname was Wheaties," Jack replied.

"But how could Berkowitz, if he wrote that Breslin letter, know John Carr's nickname if he didn't know the Carrs?" I asked. "He says he didn't; they say he didn't, and he's supposed to be this loner with no friends anywhere. He's only in that neighborhood since last year, not all his life. And he's the original Herman's Hermit. So how does he know the nickname of someone he doesn't even know?"

Jack added some more fuel: "John doesn't even live in New York anymore. He's back and forth a lot but he's been in the Air Force for years. He's somewhere in the Dakotas last I heard."

"That's even more curious. Now he knows the nickname of a guy who's only around here sporadically. . . . What do you know about this Carr studio in that house?"

"Nothing, but I'd guess that's Michael. He's some sort of a designer, I think."

Jack knew little else, except that John was about thirty and Michael "about five years younger. . . . I think you're raising some interesting questions, but Berkowitz says he was alone, and so do the cops."

"I know. I don't know where this is leading, if anywhere. But they do have him convicted already. I've been reading the papers."

*　　*　　*

Indeed, I'd been absorbing every detail I could in the aftermath of the arrest. Pages and pages of newspaper reports and countless minutes of television and radio time had successfully transmitted the official message to the nation: "Crazy David Berkowitz heard a barking dog and killed for his master, Sam."

There were many myths published about Berkowitz in the weeks following his apprehension. For instance, it was widely reported that the arrest halted him as he prepared to drive to the Hamptons to shoot up a discotheque with his semiautomatic rifle and "go out in a blaze of glory." This story was leaked by police officials and immediately bannered in hundreds of headlines. It was false. Berkowitz said he'd driven to the Hamptons *the weekend before* his capture, thought about shooting up a disco, but changed his mind. But the inaccurate story, which did have a grain of truth in it, served a purpose: the NYPD had, in the nick of time, saved many lives.

Another item which received widespread publicity held that Berkowitz apparently shot and killed a barking dog behind an apartment building where he lived in the Bronx in 1975. This wasn't true either, according to building superintendent James Lynch, who knew Berkowitz at that time.

Lynch would tell me in 1984 that a neighbor actually shot the dog—his own dog, at that—in a drunken rage one night.

Another false story seeping from that same Barnes Avenue address also garnered extensive attention. It involved some "threatening notes" Berkowitz supposedly slid under the door of an elderly woman because she played her television too loudly.

Once again, Lynch told me otherwise: "I saw those notes. The woman—she's dead now—showed them to me. She didn't know who wrote them, and neither did anyone else. But *if* it was Berkowitz, there was nothing threatening about them at all. They were simply polite requests to please try to lower the sound."

Small matters? Not really. These are but three examples of many which, put together, painted a distorted picture of Berkowitz that made later efforts to uncover the truth even more difficult than it already was. First impressions linger, and in the Berkowitz investigation, reversing them was akin to plowing through a brick wall. The story of the loud television, for instance, appeared in hundreds of newspapers and was included in *Newsweek*'s cover story of the arrest.

* * *

So, who was David Berkowitz? He was born in Brooklyn on June 1, 1953, and given up for adoption shortly afterwards. His mother's name was Betty Broder, a Brooklyn resident of the Jewish faith. She had been married years earlier to a man named Tony Falco, who left her. Sometime later, Betty Broder began a long-term affair with a married Long Island businessman named Joseph Klineman, also of the Jewish faith. Klineman, who died of cancer in the early 1970s, never left his wife for Betty Broder Falco—but that didn't impede him from fathering Richard David.

Betty, however, already had a daughter, Roslyn, from her marriage to Falco. She couldn't keep her infant son without the willing support of Klineman, who apparently demurred. And so the baby was put up for adoption.

The media reported Berkowitz was half Italian and half Jewish because Tony Falco was listed as the father on the adoption papers. Betty put Falco's name on the document because she knew she couldn't use the married Klineman's name.

So the child was actually 100 percent Jewish and was then welcomed into the modest Bronx apartment of Nathan and Pearl Berkowitz, a childless, middle-class couple who lived on Stratford Avenue in the Soundview section.

The baby was renamed David Richard Berkowitz. His new father, Nat, owned a hardware store on the Bronx's Melrose Avenue and worked long hours to maintain his business. He was serious about his faith, and young David received religious training, was bar mitzvahed and led a basically normal childhood.

David possessed above-average intelligence and was capable of doing well in school when he applied himself. He enjoyed sports, particularly baseball, and cultivated a small circle of childhood friends.

In October 1967—when he was fourteen—his adoptive mother, Pearl, died of cancer. David loved her deeply and was hurt greatly by the loss. Thereafter, his relationship with Nat, while cordial, was occasionally strained due to the father's child-rearing attitudes and David's reactions to them.

In late 1969, David and Nat moved from Stratford Avenue to a new home in the Bronx's Co-Op City, a huge high-rise complex in the eastern area of the borough. There, David, who was attending Christopher Columbus High School, accumulated a new group of friends. Prominent among them were four boys his age, some of whom he maintained contact with until his arrest.

Berkowitz liked uniforms, joining the auxiliary police at the 45th Precinct in the Bronx in 1970, while still in high school. He was also instrumental in the formation of an unofficial volunteer fire department at Co-Op City.

By his own admission, his teenage love life left something to be desired. He professed to like girls and said he'd had a few dates, but no relationship, with the exception of one with a girl named Iris Gerhardt. Berkowitz implied the affair was significant, and it apparently was to him. Iris viewed it as a basically platonic friendship. She reported liking David as a person; and Berkowitz kept in touch with her throughout the early 1970s, writing her frequently after he joined the Army.

David graduated from high school in 1971, a few months after his father remarried. David resented the intrusion of his new stepmother, Julia, who had children of her own. One daughter, Ann*, had an influence on David's life that, if his story is correct, is shadowed with dark overtones. Berkowitz later wrote that Ann was very interested in the occult. He called her "a witch."

But with Julia in his life as an unwelcome stepmother, the Army suddenly appeared attractive to David. Nat thought his son should attend college, but David opted for the military and enlisted in June 1971, shortly after his high school graduation.

David's soldiering career was unremarkable. He was not sent to Vietnam, but did spend a year in Korea. He was later stationed at Fort Knox, Kentucky, before being discharged in June 1974.

While in the service, he received routine firearms training, achieving a mid-level competency grade as a marksman, and was brought up on minor disciplinary charges twice. While in Korea, Berkowitz said, he experimented with LSD on several occasions, as did many of his fellow GIs. The Army did change Berkowitz in one major respect. He went in a hawk but came out an anti-military dove.

*   *   *

But it was during his period at Fort Knox, beginning in January 1973, that a symptom of the mind-set which would later leave him susceptible to untoward influences became manifest. Berkowitz, born and raised a Jew, began to attend Beth Haven Baptist Church in Louisville.

He said he enrolled in every program, and often remained in the church for the entire day on Sundays. He listened to religious broadcasts incessantly, studied numerous liturgical writings and began to try to convert his fellow soldiers and some of Kentucky's civilian population from a street-corner pulpit.

This was "fire and brimstone" old-time religion, and when David returned to the Bronx after his discharge in the late spring of 1974, Nat Berkowitz reached for his tranquilizers. His Jewish son was sounding as if he'd just strolled out of a cobwebbed chapter of *The Scarlet Letter*.

Naturally, David's new beliefs led to some difficulties with Nat. On top of that, David's inner feelings of resentment toward Julia intensified. He needed a place of his own. So, with Nat's help, he located the apartment at 2161 Barnes Avenue and moved there in late 1974, bringing along a fair amount of furniture Nat gave him.

David enrolled at Bronx Community College, and was hired as a guard by IBI Security, working in Manhattan. He also resumed contact with his friends from Co-Op City, several of whom professed to have been "put off" by his religious proselytizing.

Early in 1975, Nat Berkowitz retired from his hardware business, and he and Julia retreated to a condominium in Boynton Beach, Florida. Ann, Julia's daughter, apparently drifted off to California and became involved with a commune.

David, who had philosophically separated from his father months before, was now physically distanced from him as well. The pressure cooker was simmering.

The recipe's final seasoning was added in May 1975. David, feeling terribly alone and without purpose, begin a search for his real parents. He joined ALMA (Adoptees Liberty Movement Association), attended several meetings and then began his quest in earnest.

His "David Berkowitz" birth certificate led him to the Bureau of Records in New York City, where he discovered his real name was Richard Falco. He then called all the Falcos in the Brooklyn directory, and came up empty. An ALMA counselor subsequently steered him to the New York Public Library's collection of old telephone books. He found a "Betty Falco" in the 1965 Brooklyn edition and learned she was still at the address, albeit with an unlisted number. Berkowitz still wasn't sure this Betty Falco was his mother, but he decided to chance it.

On Mother's Day 1975 he stuck a card in her mailbox. It said: "You were my mother in a very special way." He signed it "R.F.," for Richard Falco, and wrote his phone number on the card.

He drove back to the Bronx nervous, apprehensive and yet excited at the possibility that he'd at last discover who he really was and be united with the woman who'd brought him into the world. Since the death of his adoptive mother, Pearl, in 1967, there was a well's worth of emptiness in David; a hollow pit he was desperate to fill.

Several days later Betty Falco called, and mother and son soon met for the first time since David's infancy. Berkowitz, edgy but hopeful, was ultimately crushed. He learned he was illegitimate, discovered Betty had a daughter, Roslyn, she'd not given up and absorbed other details about his heritage and Betty that further dismayed him.

He never voiced his torment, however. He instead sought to begin and maintain a relationship with Betty, Roslyn, Roslyn's husband, Leo, and their young daughters—whom David genuinely adored. He attempted to live a normal life.

But the hurts had piled too high. The lid was ready to blow off the now boiling pressure cooker.

*   *   *

About nine months later, in February 1976, Berkowitz inexplicably moved from the Bronx to the private home of the Cassara family in New Rochelle. Superintendent Lynch told me Berkowitz was "in the middle of a lease" when he left Barnes Avenue. He was also still working in New York City for IBI Security, and his Bronx rent was lower than that in New Rochelle.

So, on the surface, the move made no sense in terms of reducing his commute or any other reason usually associated with a relocation. The Cassaras would tell me they only advertised the room in the Westchester newspapers, and Berkowitz never revealed how he came to know about the rental.

Regardless, Berkowitz was out of the Cassara house just two months later. Much media noise was made of the belief that he suddenly fled the residence because of his aversion to the Cassaras' barking German shepherd dog.

Berkowitz may not have appreciated the animal, but he hadn't "fled." Records show that he applied for an apartment at 35 Pine Street in Yonkers *a month before* his move. His application was approved and he moved into apartment 7-E in mid-April. And so another widely reported Berkowitz myth now dies.

If Berkowitz's move to New Rochelle was mysterious, at first glance his journey to Yonkers seemed even more curious. This relocation didn't ease his commute either. Pine Street was also off the beaten track, and as such wouldn't be known to a boy from the east Bronx who most recently lived on the opposite side of Westchester County in New Rochelle.

Logically, however, Berkowitz certainly must have had some reason for choosing to live in that northwest Yonkers apartment—where the rent was also about forty dollars a month more than he was paying in New Rochelle and nearly a hundred dollars higher than his cost in the Bronx.

That reason would concern me for quite some time. I had my suspicions, but wouldn't be able to confirm them for several years.

In May, incidents of violence erupted in Berkowitz's neighborhood, as detailed in Chapter VI. There is no question that Berkowitz was involved in these crimes—but not as a sole instigator or perpetrator.

In June, just two months after arriving at 35 Pine, Berkowitz visited his father in Boynton Beach, Florida, and then drove on to Houston, Texas, where Billy Dan Parker, his Army buddy, purchased a .44 Bulldog revolver for him at a local shop. Six weeks later, the Son of Sam shootings began.

Berkowitz also found new employment in the summer of 1976 as a cabdriver in the Bronx, and later as a sheet-metal apprentice in Westchester.

In March 1977, Berkowitz joined the U.S. Postal Service, having passed the required civil service exam a year earlier. He worked in a large postal facility on the Grand Concourse in the Bronx. His hours encompassed the second shift, from approximately 3:30 p.m. to midnight. It was his last job.

*   *   *

The *New York Post,* a recent acquisition of Australian publishing magnate Rupert Murdoch, was heavily involved in coverage of the Son of Sam case. At times, it was guilty of sensationalism, but so were the rest of the media. The *Post* was losing money when Murdoch took the reins, and he immediately laid claim to the .44-caliber investigation, engaging the *Daily News,* particularly, in a battle of headlines as the probe continued. It was said in New York that Murdoch "hung his hat on Son of Sam."

Two weeks after Berkowitz's arrest, I sat in the office of Peter Michelmore, the *Post*'s metropolitan editor, and elicited his interest in the subject of John Wheaties Carr and the Carr illustration studio. The *Post* was headquartered at 210 South Street, near the Seaport, not far from the Brooklyn Bridge. Its city room reflected the paper's financial struggles, which antiquated typewriters and general disarray in evidence.

Murdoch had imported a number of Australian writers and editors to work at the *Post;* people he knew well from his overseas operations. Michelmore, a distinguished-looking, gray-haired man of about fifty, was one of those.

"I think this John Carr thing is good stuff," he said, after I explained what I'd discovered. Michelmore summoned columnist Steve Dunleavy, another Australian, and assigned him to work with me to develop the story. Dunleavy was about forty and had just written *Elvis, What Happened?,* which would become a best seller. Elvis Presley had just died, and Dunleavy was fortuitously working on the book with a couple of the King's ex-bodyguards at the time.

Dunleavy decided to visit my apartment in White Plains, where we discussed the case at length.

"We're going to have a hell of a time with the cops, mate," he warned. "They're not going to like this stuff at all."

Dunleavy said that he knocked on Sam Carr's door the morning after the arrest. "He had a gun underneath a towel and he pointed it right at me. I almost dropped dead on the spot. The cops say there are guns all over that house."

I showed Dunleavy the breakdown of the P.S. in the Breslin letter. We agreed it was on target, but also concurred that its publication would open the door to charges of speculative reporting, which neither of us wanted to endure.

"The cops will deny this. We need more about John Carr first. Do you know where he is?" Dunleavy asked.

"No. He's just supposed to be somewhere in North Dakota."

The meeting ended with an agreement to pursue John Carr. Dunleavy would check his sources in the city; I'd do what I could in Westchester.

A week later I heard from Peter Michelmore, who asked me to drive to his office for another session. "I think we can get something on Carr," he said.

"How?"

"We've got a man in the hospital."

"In Kings County? You've got access to Berkowitz?"

"Yes," Michelmore answered, but he didn't reveal who it was. I knew Berkowitz was being guarded closely, segregated from other prisoners and patients.

"It's got to be a doctor or a guard or someone like that," I said. "That's fantastic. Maybe we can get somewhere."

There was an ironic justice in this development. The police no longer had access to Berkowitz while I, an outsider, suddenly did—indirectly at least.

But there was no time for self-congratulation. Michelmore asked for a list of pertinent questions which the source could put to Berkowitz one or two at a time. Dunleavy, meanwhile, would use some of my information in a letter he was composing to the alleged .44-Caliber Killer. It was agreed that John Carr wouldn't be mentioned in the note: we wanted the hospital source to handle that one personally, so he could observe Berkowitz's immediate reaction.

I liked Dunleavy and Michelmore. Michelmore was low-keyed and professional;

Dunleavy was hell on wheels. He was bright and incisive. My only difficulty was in trying to slow him down. Sometimes, it seemed as if Steve's attention span could be measured in nanoseconds. He was also occasionally prone to a "headline mentality"—an inclination to view everything as it would appear in 72-point type on page one. He, on the other hand, believed I was too methodical, and too willing to consider fragmented data as relevant to the investigation. Our contrasting traits managed to mesh, however, and we developed a healthy respect for each other.

The *Village Voice,* a Murdoch weekly in New York that was often critical of the *Post,* once referred to Dunleavy as "Son of Steve." I jumped on that label, and took to using it in our conversations.

Within three days of this second meeting at the *Post,* I sent a list of questions to Michelmore. Primary subjects were the Son of Sam letters, John Carr and Berkowitz's movements at the Moskowitz-Violante shootings.

"He was supposed to be in the park," I explained to Michelmore. "So what was he doing on Bay 17th Street just before the shots rang out?"

The contradiction was news to Michelmore, but I was driving a few of my neighbors crazy with that same question. Several nights, after dinner, I'd relaxed outside my apartment with them. Invariably, the case was discussed. Usually I'd draw a map in the dirt, showing Berkowitz in the park and Berkowitz on the street at the same time. "It's impossible. Something's wrong; very wrong," I'd say.

Tom Bartley, a news editor for the Gannett Westchester-Rockland Newspapers, became "Doubting Thomas" Bartley. "You must have read [the *Times*] wrong; there's no way he didn't do it," he'd say over and over, night after night. Bartley's attitude bothered me. Healthy skepticism was one thing, but his demeanor was one of "Don't confuse me with any facts." As he was a journalist, I thought his reactions might have been more inquisitive than they were.

Time and again I'd enunciate the discrepancies, but I couldn't reach him. "Sooner or later this thing's going to blow apart and you and Gannett are going to look foolish," I finally said after two weeks of futility elapsed. "Berkowitz lives in your circulation area and nobody up here wants to investigate this."

Bartley always had an answer. "You haven't shown me anything that's not just some coincidence," he'd say, pointing at me with the twig I'd been using to outline the Moskowitz scene on the ground. After a while, my ire would mount and heated debates would erupt.

"He enjoys busting your chops," another neighbor cut in one night. "Don't fall for it. He doesn't know what the hell he's talking about."

At that moment, the neighbor's dog flopped down on the map.

"That does it," I shouted. "It's a sign from a goddamned demon dog. Berkowitz and his dogs, and now yours." I laughed. "I give up! He did it alone!"

Bartley roared. "At least he didn't dump on it—he could have, for all it's worth!"

"We'll see, you mule-headed bastard," I replied. "We'll see." Tension broken, we switched to something we all agreed on: the lousy season the football Giants were certain to have.

Bartley, for all his bravado, underwent a slow conversion. Within a year he'd become a staunch ally and would later share a byline with me on a series on the case published by Gannett. But until that time, he plied me with regular doses of frustration.

* * *

Drawing maps in the dirt wasn't the only crawling around I did while waiting to hear from the *Post* contact at Kings County. Satisfied that vital clues were hidden in the Breslin letter, I obtained a copy of the unpublished Borrelli note from Michelmore and began to apply the same crossword, word association system to that communication.

A copy of the book *The Story of the Woodlawn Cemetery* was recovered by police in Berkowitz's apartment. Woodlawn, located in the northeast Bronx, was a beautiful, sprawling burial ground landscaped with thousands of trees, running brooks, winding roads and a swan-populated lake.

In studying the Borrelli letter, I thought some of its phrases might have hinted at specific gravesites in Woodlawn. Since Berkowitz had the book, it was possible something might be hidden at one of them.

Many notable Americans were entombed at Woodlawn, including George M. Cohan, Bat Masterson, F. W. Woolworth, Nellie Bly, financier Jay Gould, Oscar Hammerstein, Damon Runyon and others. A map available at the cemetery office pinpointed these sites.

On three successive Saturdays in September, I wandered through Woodlawn with my friend Bob Siegel and his son, Larry, rooting around tombstones and mausoleums that possibly were linked to the wording in the letter. By the second weekend, the caretakers began to take notice.

"These guys must think we had some very important ancestors," Larry cracked. "Or else they're going to arrest us for grave robbing."

"Yeah," I answered. "The invasion of the body snatchers."

The hunt was futile. The analysis was wrong—absurdly wrong—and after a time the beauty of Woodlawn was shrouded by the eeriness of what we were doing. In short order, the Great Woodlawn Clue Caper came to an end.

* * *

Steve Dunleavy, meanwhile, was having better luck. Berkowitz answered his letter, in a fashion, and the *Post* made plans to publish it on Monday, September 19. Acting on the Carr illustration studio lead, Dunleavy also located a couple of Berkowitz's former friends from Co-Op City. Both agreed that the writing ability manifest in the Breslin letter surpassed Berkowitz's, and they stated that the printing style didn't resemble his either. These were important building blocks, adding to the credibility of my suspicions.

Michelmore called me the night of the eighteenth. "We're going to fire the first of the big guns tomorrow," he said, and then read me the text of Berkowitz's letter to Dunleavy.

In it, Berkowitz was still following the party line. He called Sam Carr "one of the devils of Satan . . . a force beyond the wildest imaginations of people. He is not human . . ." The dog, of course, was "a demon from hell." Then Berkowitz gave Dunleavy what he was looking for: "When I killed, I really saved many lives. You will understand later. People want my blood but they don't want to listen to what I have to say. . . . There are other Sons out there—God help the world."

I wasn't overly thrilled with the letter's contents. "He sounds just as crazy as the cops say he is. I think it's an act. So what good are we going to do printing this?"

Michelmore explained that the letter would provide a basis for raising the questions about the handwriting and composition ability. "This gives us an opportunity to go into these things. And [Berkowitz] did say there were 'other Sons' of Sam."

Michelmore was true to his word. The next day the *Post* hit the newsstands with a banner headline: "BERKOWITZ WARNS OF MORE 'SONS.' LETTER TO POST SUGGESTS ACCOMPLICE."

The handwriting issue was addressed; the possibility of a co-conspirator was mentioned; and Dunleavy managed to squeeze an admission from a police source that officials "haven't had a real chance to question [Berkowitz]."

And then the police discredited the article. The *Post* had dared to swim against the tide.

"We told them privately about John Carr and that graphics studio, and they said they'd look into it. But I don't think they will," Michelmore lamented. "They shafted us. And now they're pissed off that we went with this piece."

"What now?" I wanted to know. "Did the hospital guy get to ask Berkowitz any of those questions yet?"

"No, but he's working on it. Look, Maury, the cops are going to deny anything we come up with now. We're going to have to lay low until we get something they can't shoot down. You stay in touch with Steve, and I'll let you know when we hear from Kings County."

I was somewhat disappointed by the outcome of what was essentially a trial balloon story, but I wasn't despondent. At least the questions were raised publicly. More work could bring more results. An hour later I spoke to Dunleavy, who'd carried the cause to a couple of morning TV talk shows as well.

"We did what we could, mate. I'm convinced there's something to all this. We've got to keep plugging on it. Just stay the hell out of cemeteries, will ya?"

"It's a big puzzle, Steve. I'm only looking for the right pieces to fit. Who the hell knows where they'll be?"

"You may be right, but for now forget the tangents. You got the John Carr thing— focus on that. He's yours all the way."

Dunleavy was right, but I was having no luck in the search for John Carr. The game had now evolved into one with the authorities on one side, us on the other. So I wasn't about to approach the Yonkers police for assistance; and Michelmore already recited the weather report from the NYPD: frigid.

Still, I had to do something, and decided to delve into the Son of Sam letters once more and to keep an eye on Pine Street and the Carr house. I didn't really know what I was looking for, but planned to take down license numbers and observe anything else which might prove to be valuable, or lead to the elusive "John Wheaties."

* * *

The next day, September 20, an event occurred in Yonkers which received no publicity. I wouldn't learn of it for more than two years. Its implications are considerable.

Andrew Dupay, thirty-three, lived on Lincoln Terrace, less than a block from Berkowitz and the Carrs. Dupay was a family man. He was married to the former Laurie Heaton and was the father of two young daughters, aged five and three. Dupay worked as a mailman. And he not only lived in the Pine Street neighborhood; he also delivered the mail there—to Berkowitz's building, the two houses on Wicker Street and the Carr home, among others. Stated another way, he lived and toiled in a war zone.

It is not known if Andrew Dupay read the Berkowitz article in the *Post* the day before. If he did, it may have affected him. But he may not have read it, because, since early summer, something had been troubling him; occupying his mind.

An outgoing, cheerful young man who reveled in his family, Dupay suddenly began to act frightened and worried in July. His family noticed the change, as did his co-workers. He said nothing to his wife, but told a couple of friends at work that he had a big problem: Dupay said he feared for his life.

"It just wasn't like him at all. He was not a paranoid person by nature. He said he was afraid for his life, but he never said why," said one associate, who requested anonymity because of his managerial position in the Postal Service.

Dupay's mother-in-law, Mary Heaton, told me in 1981: "It was all so strange, so unlike him. There was no history of mental or physical problems. He didn't gamble; the marriage was fine and he lived for his family. In July and August he began to act fearful and edgy, but he wouldn't say why."

There was, perhaps, a strong clue contained in a letter sent to the Gannett Westchester-Rockland Newspapers after I began publishing articles there about the conspiracy. The writer, who was a neighborhood resident on Dupay's route, said: "One day [in July] he told me, 'Sometimes a mailman learns things about the people on his route he'd be better off not knowing. And he sees things he'd be better off not seeing.'" Dupay, the writer added, did not explain what he meant.

On September 20, at about 5:30 p.m., Dupay and Laurie were bathing their two young daughters. Dupay excused himself, saying he was going to the basement to bring up something for the girls.

At the bottom of the stairs, Dupay wrote a brief note. He then took a shotgun and killed himself.

*   *   *

"It was only later we learned from his friends at work that he said he was afraid for his life," Mary Heaton said.

In late August, about two weeks after Berkowitz's arrest, Dupay "drew very close to Laurie and the girls—closer than usual," Mary Heaton recalled. "He took them on a fishing trip then. He usually went on those vacations without them."

Dupay apparently didn't want to leave his family alone.

In his suicide note, he left another clue to his dilemma: "Remember that day at Glen Island with the Italian family? I think that it's their doing." Glen Island is a Westchester County park located on the shore of Long Island Sound in New Rochelle. In June, three months before his death, Dupay, Laurie and the children were in a picnic area where grills were provided for public use. An Italian family was gathered in the grove at the same time, and they and Dupay got into an argument over who had first rights to a particular grill.

"It was a minor argument and it was forgotten," said Mary Heaton. "I can't believe he thought it went back to that."

Indeed, it stretches plausibility to think that Dupay's life was mysteriously threatened by people he didn't even know a month—and longer—after a verbal spat about a barbecue. It's possible Dupay believed this was the source of the threats; but not likely.

A more revealing insight was contained in that letter from the neighbor on his mail route—a route Dupay strode daily to 35 Pine Street, Wicker Street and 316 Warburton Avenue. That note, quoting Dupay's own words, related that something he'd seen or learned along his rounds had frightened him. And the timing of all these events, so proximate to Berkowitz's arrest, is also telling.

Then there was yet another letter mailed to me:

"I'd have contacted the Yonkers police with the information I have, but I think you know as well as I it would have been another mistake—considering the force employs two members of the Carr family, sister Wheat and brother-in-law John McCabe [then Wheat's husband and a Yonkers police officer].

"The mailman, Andrew (I forget his surname) knew them [the Carrs and Berkowitz] and this was never brought out. He committed suicide a few years ago after a meeting with an unnamed man in the Pelham Bay Park area of the Bronx. He said 'they' were threatening him [the "they" is unknown] and were going to get his family. Shortly after, she found him dead of a bullet wound."

The "unnamed man" Dupay was said to have met with in the Bronx remains unidentified. The letter writer had nothing more to offer about that incident.

Dupay's co-workers were aware that he feared for his own life; but he hadn't mentioned threats were also directed at his family, as stated in the letter. But Dupay's actions prior to his death lend credence to that statement.

He took them away on a fishing vacation when he usually went without them. He withheld telling his wife about any threats at all; and in the final moments of his life he was bathing his two daughters—hardly the impetus for immediate suicide. But it is reasonable to suggest that being with them, and his wife, in that intimate, loving situation may have overwhelmed him with a very real dread that something might imminently happen to them—and he took his own life to protect them.

Why Dupay didn't report the threats to the police is unknown. He may have believed police protection would be inadequate, or of short duration. It may have been for a more sinister reason.

What could Andrew Dupay have seen or learned on his mail route to put him in such jeopardy, to convince him to take the threats so seriously that he would take his life rather than attempt to resolve the situation in another way?

It will be remembered that threatening letters were flying all over that neighborhood that spring and summer—sent through the mail and delivered by Dupay. And perhaps other correspondence, which identified the senders, was also received. It is also possible Dupay observed culpable people coming and going from a particular residence, or saw Berkowitz in their company.

Also, in 1983 a human skull, that of an unidentified elderly male, would be found in a wooded area across the street from Dupay's house. The skull's presence at the site would be dated to the approximate time of Dupay's death. Its origin would remain unknown, but it may have been stolen from a cemetery and used in rituals. And in the summer of 1986, the head of another elderly man was stolen from a coffin in a nearby Mount Vernon funeral home. Whether the incidents are related isn't known.

But to this point, no one knows what or who it was that Andrew Dupay encountered on his postal route. Someday the answer may be found. In the meantime, a widow and children are left to wonder why he died.

*   *   *

Over the next two months I pursued a variety of leads, none of which proved fruitful. I was just beginning to consider the occult references in the Sam letters when Michelmore finally called with the news I'd been waiting for.

"Our contact got us a few answers from Berkowitz. I think you'll be pleased with what he came up with."

"Come on, Peter, I've been waiting a long time. Don't make me jump through the phone to find out." I was affecting a casual attitude, but was splitting apart inside. Michelmore already thought me too impatient, and I wasn't about to stoke his fire.

I had endured a long wait, and had grown increasingly pessimistic as various courtroom proceedings continued. Berkowitz was at first found incompetent to stand trial by a team of psychiatrists who gobbled up his demon story. Later, he was tested again. This time, largely through the analysis of Dr. David Abrahamsen—who was hired by Brooklyn DA Eugene Gold—he was ruled capable of assisting in his defense. Abrahamsen didn't buy the demon tale at all.

Not that there was going to be anything resembling a real defense. Berkowitz's attorneys intended to plead their client not guilty by reason of insanity.

But as the battle of the psychiatrists was being waged, a transcript of Berkowitz's sessions with the doctors was obtained and published by the *Daily News*.

The documents read like excerpts from a witch doctor's cookbook: dogs, demons, blood, monsters, etc. As I read them, my heart sank. I believed the situation was getting too far out of hand. That was why I was anxious to hear from Michelmore. I wanted to balance the private Berkowitz with the public one.

"Well," Michelmore said, pausing for effect, "he says Berkowitz answered that there were messages of some kind in the letter, but he won't say what they were. Berkowitz also refused to answer any questions about whether he actually wrote the letter or not."

"Unreal," I said.

Michelmore continued: "He also won't answer your questions about whether or not he was alone at the Brooklyn shooting."

"What do you mean, he won't answer? What did he say?"

"He was asked several times, on several different occasions. Each time he said he wouldn't talk about that; that he didn't want to go into it."

"But he didn't say he was alone and 'why are you asking me that stupid question?'"

"No."

"I think that says a lot, just like ducking the questions about who wrote the Breslin letter."

"Yes, I agree with that," Michelmore said. "But it isn't proof yet. We don't have enough to print it."

"I understand, Peter—what about John Carr?"

"This is the best of all. He was handed a slip of paper. Written on it was: 'We know you're involved with John Carr.' Berkowitz read it, turned white as a sheet, fell back on his cot there and looked like he was going to faint."

"Holy shit. This is home-run city, Peter. Did he say anything after that?"

"No. There was a concern he might need medical assistance for a minute but he recovered and wouldn't say a word."

After a few more minutes of related conversation I asked Michelmore what we'd be doing next. "We keep trying to get our hands on Carr. And we'll see if Berkowitz has anything else to say."

*   *   *

I next heard from Peter Michelmore at noon on Friday, December 2. "I've got someone here I think you should get together with," he said. "I think the time has come. We're about ready to drop the other shoe."

"What other shoe?" I asked.

"It involves Cassara."

"Jack Cassara, the New Rochelle landlord?"

"Well, it's connected to him in some way," Michelmore answered. "I'm not saying it's him directly. . . . Let me put this person on here."

"Who is it? Is it the guy from the hospital?"

"Yes. His name is Jim."

Jim Mitteager was my age, thirty-one. He'd been a member of the New York City Police Department for three years before resigning to pursue what he'd always wanted to be his career—that of an investigative reporter.

After a brief conversation on the telephone, I gave him directions to White Plains, and he arrived at the apartment at 3 p.m. Initially, he was as suspicious of me as I was of him. But as the afternoon turned into twilight, we began to feel more comfortable with one another.

"I was afraid they sent you up here as a plant to find out what I haven't told them," I said.

Mitteager laughed. "I thought they were setting *me* up by sending me up here to see you."

"I knew about you, but I didn't know who you were. They never told me," I said.

"Yeah, they told me that they had some top contact in Westchester who was supplying them with these questions and the information about Carr. But I didn't know who you were either."

"The mysterious man from the hospital—finally," I said. Here I received a surprise. Mitteager wasn't actually *the* hospital source. Someone else was in the picture, too. Mitteager, when a member of the Police Department, had been assigned to the Kings County Hospital area. As a result, he knew his way around the facility, knew how it functioned.

After Berkowitz's arrest—that same night—he'd gone to the hospital, reasoning that Berkowitz would be incarcerated there. Mitteager wasn't working a conspiracy angle at first. Instead, he hoped to provide the media with tidbits about Berkowitz's routine.

"I found a source," he said. "A source who agreed to help me if Berkowitz was sent there. I went to the *Post,* told them what I had and we began to work together. Then you came along."

Mitteager wouldn't reveal the name of his contact. "He's got access to Berkowitz, and he's reliable. That's all I can say."

I asked if the Berkowitz comments, as repeated to me by Michelmore, were accurate. "Hell, yes. And he did almost keel over when that John Carr thing was put to him. My source thought for a minute they'd have to call the doctors."

"So . . . the source isn't a doctor," I said.

"No, but look, I can't tell you."

I decided the contact was either a guard or an orderly, but didn't voice my opinion to Mitteager.

"How do I know he exists at all?" I asked instead.

Mitteager reached into a travel case and pulled out an assortment of letters—copies—that were plainly written by Berkowitz since his arrest. Some were requests to religious organizations asking for material on demonology; another was a note to Mayor Abe Beame warning of the dangers of "Sam."

"O.K.," I said. "You're on the level. Now what's this about Jack Cassara from New Rochelle?"

Mitteager explained that Cassara, from whom Berkowitz rented a room in early 1976, was a co-worker of Fred Cowan—an avowed neo-Nazi who murdered six people before killing himself during a daylong siege at the Neptune Moving Company in New Rochelle on Valentine's Day 1977.

Moreover, Berkowitz kept a file of news clippings on Cowan in his Yonkers apartment and had referred to him as "one of the Sons."

"Did you know that?" Mitteager asked.

"Yes. I found that out in August. I've been saying up here that if I was Cassara I'd have written a first-person article for *Reader's Digest* on 'My Most Unforgettable Characters.'"

Mitteager laughed, and then turned serious. "What do you think the odds are that one guy, Cassara, would have Son of Sam living in his house and work with Fred Cowan during the day?"

". . . and then have Berkowitz with a file on Cowan," I cut in. "I'd say the odds were incalculable. And we don't know how the hell Berkowitz ended up finding Cassara's place either."

Mitteager was on the edge of his seat now. "Maybe Cowan knew from Cassara the room was available and that's how Berkowitz found out."

"It makes sense. It's certainly possible. I think there's a lot of smoke there. And there just might be a fire to go with it."

Mitteager and I agreed that if the scenario was correct, Jack Cassara, then in his mid-sixties, was almost certainly an innocent link between the two murderers. But we also concurred that it was too much to think there was no connection between Cowan and Berkowitz, especially in light of Berkowitz's comments about the Hitler-worshipping killer.

Mitteager didn't surprise me with the Cowan information, but there was more to come. Reaching into his bag again, he pulled out a handful of pictures. "Take a look at these."

The photos were of a familiar figure: Berkowitz. But these weren't police photos. There was Berkowitz, in hospital garb, sitting on his cot. Another showed Berkowitz writing at a table in what appeared to be a dayroom. Yet another showed the alleged killer fast asleep on the cot in his cell. Others were variations of the same poses. Some were even in color.

"Where the hell did you get these?"

"The source," Mitteager replied. "With a tiny spy camera."

"For what purpose?"

"For the *Post*. They're going to run them on Monday, along with some of those diary notes you saw."

Suddenly dawn broke in my mind. "Jim, as soon as these pictures are published there's going to be a stink the likes of which you've never seen. Berkowitz has been talking to your source. After this, no one is going to be able to get near him. We'll blow our access and whatever progress we can make. There'll be a goddamned investigation of *this*."

Mitteager wasn't so sure. "My source is pretty well insulated. And besides, I don't run the *Post*. If they want to print them, they print them."

I disagreed. "All these months they've kept us apart until today. Why today? Don't you see? They know the party's over—they know we'll be losing access to Berkowitz. So they figure there's nothing to lose by putting us together now."

Mitteager wasn't concerned. "You're set in a full-time job; and that's fine for you. My goal is to get a job at the *Post* and to help solve this case if I can. I think there will be a small storm over this, and then it'll die down and we'll get to Berkowitz again."

I knew that Berkowitz—who wasn't facing the camera in any of the shots—wasn't aware the photos were taken. So he wouldn't be of assistance to any investigation— not that he would have cooperated anyway.

"He likes my source. They get along. He calls him 'Sly Fox One' and I'm known as 'Sly Fox Two.' Don't sweat it," Mitteager added.

"I don't think it's a good idea, but I understand where you're coming from. I just wish to hell there was another way. . . . Anyway, it looks like it's going to be you and me from now on. I guess we'll start on Cowan—and, of course, John Carr."

Mitteager said he'd drive up from his Staten Island home the next week, and together we'd begin to look into some leads in New Rochelle. "Then I'd like you to take me down to see Berkowitz's place and the neighborhood there," he said.

"No problem. I've gotten to know that block pretty well lately."

"I'll give you a call on Monday," Mitteager said. "Don't worry about the pictures. It'll all work out all right."

* * *

On a scale of one to ten, the explosion was a twelve. On Monday morning, as the metropolitan area groggily shook itself awake, its citizens peeked in on Berkowitz, who was still dozing away in a blissful dreamland—in a huge photo that covered the entire front page of the *Post*. Above the picture was a large headline. "SAM SLEEPS." Inside, in a two-page spread, the other photos of Berkowitz I'd seen were displayed in a layout enhanced with excerpts from his jailhouse writings. Of course, the usual photo credits were missing from their customary place beneath the pictures.

Official reaction was swift as several investigations were launched into this blatant breach of security. The Brooklyn district attorney's office, the Department of Cor- rection and the State Special Prosecutor's office—responsible for ferreting out official corruption—all entered the fray. Media response was likewise intense.

Critics castigated the *Post* for tawdry sensationalism, and some publications almost gleefully reported that probes into "Operation Photo" had begun. One out-of-town paper even superimposed a rifle sight on the picture of the sleeping Berkowitz to illustrate the possible consequences of such dire security lapses.

I called Michelmore late in the afternoon. "You were looking for a big Berkowitz story and I guess you sure got one, Peter."

"Christ, we didn't expect this kind of reaction. All we did was print some pictures and notes."

"Well, I guess you could always say you were 'framed,'" I suggested.

Michelmore didn't appreciate the pun, but I felt he had it coming. He quickly changed the subject.

"What did you think of Jim?"

"I liked him. He's been a cop; he's street-smart; he knows his way around. We'll get along fine. . . . One thing, though—we don't think Cassara is dirty. We think he might have been an innocent link between the two of them."

"Yeah, that's what I thought, too. . . . Keep at it and let me know how you're doing. I've got to get going. It's a little hectic here, as you probably can imagine."

I stood looking at a dead phone. Although I was dismayed at the obvious loss of access to Berkowitz, I didn't say so to Michelmore. I thought Peter might have been squeezed on the photo deal, pressured to run with the story.

Whether or not Michelmore was responsible, one thing was clear: someone at the *Post* tired of the conspiracy search, which had yet to produce printable results, and opted instead for "The Big Sleep."

I turned on the six o'clock news, and there again was sleeping Sam. In spite of myself, the image of all those officials scampering about like so many little Dutch boys trying to plug a leaking security dike brought a grin to my face.

But after a few minutes, I realized I'd reached a turning point, and began to reflect on what transpired since August. I entered the case a wide-eyed, eager neophyte. I had, in fact, uncovered a considerable amount of relevant information despite being restricted to part-time work on the case. That was a plus. I'd also gone from completely outside the media and investigation to the inside. But still, during those four months, I'd stumbled through a lot of learning mistakes.

I was right about the Brooklyn killing; right about John Carr and perhaps Michael Carr; right about the authorship of the Breslin letter. I *knew* I was. I was on the brink of being capable of breaking open a story of immense proportions—but what did I have to show for it? Nothing, except the knowledge that I'd have to continue on to build a stronger case—and a sneak preview of Berkowitz doing a Sealy mattress commercial.

It was time to put this recent battlefield education to work and to stop circling around the case as if I was content just to be part of it. If the *Post* wanted to be serious, fine. If not, there'd be another way of getting the story out.

I reached for a pad and composed a short list: "Find John Carr. Get with Mitteager on Cowan. Check occult references in Sam letters."

Three items, only three. But within the next eight weeks there would be major developments in two of them—developments which would greatly expand the scope of the case.

I was sliding the list into a briefcase when the doorbell rang. I wasn't in the mood for business. I'd called George Austin and was on the way to meet him for a drink at Olliver's in White Plains, a favored oasis of ours.

I put on my coat and headed for the stairs as the bell rang again. It was my neighbor Tom Bartley, the news editor from the Gannett papers.

"Ho-ho." He smiled, squinting in the darkened doorway. "What might you happen to know about a certain set of pictures published in your favorite paper today?"

"Well, you caught me. I took them a year ago on a movie set. Even then, I knew what he was involved in, and I wanted to be ready ahead of time. He graciously offered to pose. He's a fine gentleman. You didn't really think they were taken at Kings County, did you?"

Tom laughed. "Naw, I thought you'd hired a stand-in."

"You mean a lie-in, don't you?"

"You son of a bitch. You do know something, don't you?"

"Tom, I had nothing to do with the taking of those pictures."

That was a true statement.

"Look, I'm going down to Olliver's to have a pop with George. Why don't you come along? I want to talk to you about the occult."

"So now you're after those dead dogs."

"Something like that."

"You think Rip Van Winkle was in a cult?"

"I don't know yet. Maybe he was."

Indeed.

The Stanford Memorial Church, a site of brutal murder. (*Stanford University*)

Arlis Perry, a bride of only eight weeks.

Son of Sam victim
Stacy Moskowitz.
(*Moskowitz family*)

Christine Freund,
slain in a pivotal
.44 attack.

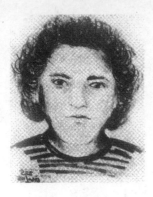  

The slayer of Donna Lauria.

The Lomino/DeMasi shooter.

The Lomino/DeMasi shooter.

"Ski Cap" from the Voskerichian homicide.

The Berkowitz lookalike, Voskerichian murder.

Unreleased profile sketch of Moskowitz/Violante gunman.

Unreleased sketch of yellow VW driver at Moskowitz scene. Note the long hair.

Profile of compromise Moskowitz/Violante sketch, released to public.

Front view of compromise sketch. (*New York Daily News*)

A smiling David Berkowitz, 24, is led away after arrest at apartment house in Yonkers Wednesday night

Under arrest, a smiling David Berkowitz is escorted by NYPD Det. John Falotico. (*DeLorenzia; Gannett Westchester-Rockland Newspapers*)

In bold red type, the *New York Post* flashed news of the arrest. (*New York Post*)

The Pine Street neighborhood in Yonkers. Berkowitz's apartment building is in the background. His windows were on the top floor, right rear, near the fire escape. The descending road at right is Wicker Street. A German shepherd was shot and a firebomb tossed at the house at the top of Wicker. At the bottom left, the white house with the garage-like structure behind it is the Carr house on Warburton Avenue. Behind the Carr property is the Croton Aqueduct path, where slain German shepherds were found before and well after Berkowitz's arrest. The aqueduct path continued (left) to Untermyer Park, about a mile from the Pine/Wicker area. (*Deutsch, Gannett Westchester Newspapers.*)

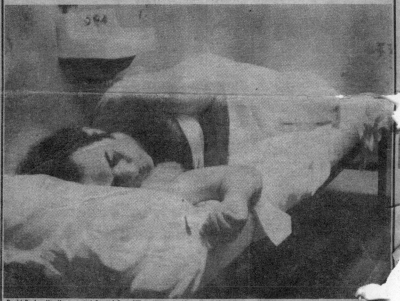

NEW YORK POST

MONDAY, DECEMBER 5, 1977 25 CENTS © 1977 The New York Post Corporation Vol. 177, No. 16

METRO
TODAY'S RACING

LAST MONTH'S
DAILY PAID
CIRCULATION **630,091**

SAM SLEEPS

David Berkowitz, the accused Son of Sam killer, sleeps in his cell at Kings County Hospital prison ward in this dramatic photo of a series obtained exclusively by The Post. Other photos, and excerpts from Berkowitz' jailhouse diary, start on Page

Opening night with Clive Barnes
The Post's new critic reviews Neil Simon's new play • Page 20

This infamous front page cut off access to Berkowitz
and resulted in a criminal indictment.

This occult symbol, drawn by a nineteenth-century black magician, was linked to the Son of Sam in late 1977. The key area on the original was near the "X" in the center. Further, a Berkowitz nickname, "Berk," was contained in "Berkaial"; and Sam Carr's name spelled backward, a common satanic practice, was hidden in "Amasarac" on the circumference of the original sign.

John Carr, circa 1975.

Body identified as John Carr's, as found by North Dakota police. Note the position of the rifle.

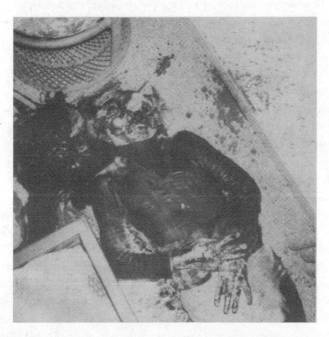

Body identified as John Carr's, turned over by police. Note blood smudges on wall and apparent blood-writing on baseboard. On Carr's hand, although not visible in this photo, the remnants of numbers "666" appeared, carved into the drying blood.

IX

The Process

Looking back, I realize the indications were present all along. I never ignored them, but did keep them at a safe distance those first four months—slightly out of focus on the horizon. Publicly, I'd hold them sequestered for two years. The reason I did so wasn't complex: the idea of satanic cult involvement in the .44 killings was initially too bizarre for me to even want to consider.

Such groups certainly existed. There was ample documentation from across the country. But my entire thrust was aimed at uncovering the presence of a single accomplice. Frankly, I didn't want to confront the implications, or face the consequences, of still more conspirators. As a result, I kept steering away from the signs. But inevitably, I was pulled back into the web. And after a time, I came to accept the unacceptable.

* * *

The path of the old Croton Aqueduct in Yonkers passes between the rear of the Carr home and Berkowitz's apartment building. At one time, the aqueduct—an underground pipeline approximately eight feet in diameter—carried drinking water from the Catskill Mountains watershed region to New York City via the Croton Reservoir in northern Westchester County. It was now obsolete. Above it, at ground level, one could walk a wide path which snaked for miles through numerous Westchester communities.

In the early 1900s, some Yonkers residents dug tunnels from nearby basements and managed to tap into the water supply. Although most were later sealed, apparently some of the old tunnels still existed, offering access to the now-empty pipe from the cellars of a handful of aging homes in the area. Also, at select locations on the surface, entrance to the subterranean passage could be gained through hidden and long-forgotten maintenance portals.

Once inside the aqueduct itself, it was possible to walk for at least several miles beneath the ground. The pipe was damp and musty, groundwater seeped through the rust at points, and vision was impossible without a flashlight or candles.

Behind the Carr home, the aqueduct path cut through a wooded area. A mile to the north, it traveled through the lower reaches of Untermyer Park—a sprawling, formerly lavish estate that had fallen into considerable disrepair. Once owned by Samuel Tilden, a U.S. presidential candidate who lost the 1876 election to Rutherford B. Hayes, the land was purchased by wealthy attorney Samuel Untermyer in 1903. Untermyer, whom a British magazine labeled a Satanist, imported stone and statuary from England to embellish the landscape.

After Untermyer died in 1940, the grounds were assigned to the city of Yonkers. Partial restoration was accomplished, but crumbling stone outbuildings, weathered Grecian- and Roman-style columns and sculptures, and acres of overgrown gardens, vineyards and woodland dominated the site. The estate's main entrance was on North Broadway, but the property then sloped dramatically toward the Hudson River far below.

* * *

On August 11, 1977, two young boys, ages eleven and fourteen, were walking along the trail somewhat south of Untermyer Park. They weren't out for a relaxing walk on the warm summer's day. Searching through the tangled brush adjacent to the aqueduct behind Berkowitz's apartment, the youths were on a specific mission. They were looking for a grave.

The previous Christmas, they found three dead German shepherd dogs at the site, lying together in separate plastic bags. The boys had buried the animals but now, hearing of Berkowitz's alleged hatred of canines, they believed their find might be connected to the case.

At first, the police weren't interested. Yonkers Det. Leon Wyka said he thought NYPD wouldn't be concerned with the animals. "They're satisfied—they got their man," he told the Yonkers *Herald Statesman*.

However, after some publicity about the matter, Yonkers PD picked up the skeletal remains and had them autopsied. Two of the shepherds, which still had chains around their necks, were strangled; the third was shot in the head.

At this same time, Laura Pisaturo, sixteen, reported that Berkowitz had walked up and stared at her at twelve thirty one night a few months before the arrest as she waited for her boyfriend in the parking lot behind 35 Pine. Laura, who had seen Berkowitz before, said, "I smiled at him because I was scared. He didn't smile back."

At first glance, Laura's statement appeared to be of little consequence. It wouldn't be unusual for Berkowitz to be spotted in the parking lot of his own building. And the 12:30 a.m. time estimate meshed with an hour he'd be at home since his postal shift ended earlier. But there was a twist to the girl's account, a nuance missed by the police. She said Berkowitz was walking a dog that night.

Berkowitz, however, didn't own a dog. So whose animal was it and why did he have it? The three German shepherds on the aqueduct had been slain—two of them strangled. Was that the intended fate of this dog? If so, it would have taken a considerable effort for Berkowitz to try it alone. German shepherds don't passively resist strangulation attempts.

Additionally, if Berkowitz in fact hated dogs and regarded them as fearful demons, it was incongruous to think he'd be out for a moonlight stroll with one. I'd already learned that he had a dog, Lucky, as a child, and that he also got along well with the guard dogs at IBI Security. So, what was going on?

As for Laura, she knew Berkowitz by sight before this incident; and her account was credible in other respects. In analyzing the case, I noted the dead German shepherds and the dog-walking observation with large asterisks. (At this time, I didn't know of the satanic cult letter found in Berkowitz's apartment, or that still more German shepherds were slain in the area.)

Several days after the police removed the bodies of the shepherds in Yonkers, yet another Berkowitz-dog incident surfaced.

*   *   *

Mrs. Florence Larsen, a portly, pleasant Bronx housewife, was active in a volunteer agency known as PAWS (People for Animal Welfare Society). Mrs. Larsen had come by an unwanted German shepherd, named Big Boy, in her neighborhood and transported him to a kennel in Mamaroneck, Westchester County. She then placed an ad in the Westchester newspapers advising that the dog was available for adoption.

On Monday, August 8, someone calling himself David Berkowitz phoned her to inquire about the German shepherd. As Mrs. Larsen later told me:

"It was about ten thirty in the morning. He said his name was David Berkowitz and that he lived on Pine Street in Yonkers. We always try to screen the callers, so I asked him about himself. He said he once had a dog and gave it away to his girlfriend, and he now wanted another one. He told me he was in the service at one time.

"He sounded like a nice person, a responsible person, so I told him where the dog was being kept. He said he would drive up to Mamaroneck to see the dog."

And then another call came, later the same day.

"This person told me his name was Jeff and that he fixed cars behind Pine Street in Yonkers. I thought it was very strange to get two calls about the same dog that both mentioned Pine Street in Yonkers. He also said he'd go to see the dog."

Berkowitz was arrested two days later.

Said Mrs. Larsen: "I had his name on a piece of paper. I told my husband, 'Hey, this guy called me about a dog. He'll never get one now.'"

Mrs. Larsen then called the Mamaroneck facility to ask if Berkowitz had in fact shown up there. Jay Baldwin, a veterinary student at Cornell University who was working at the kennel during the summer, told her he thought the alleged killer had indeed visited the premises in the company of another young man.

Police were then called in by kennel employees, but NYPD soon determined Berkowitz didn't visit the shelter after all. I would later see a photo of the man police decided had appeared at the kennel—and he did resemble Berkowitz. The man's companion, first thought to be a possible .44 accomplice, was also identified, although this information was withheld from the public. I have no disagreement with this assessment by NYPD.

But, in ruling out the Berkowitz visit and proclaiming at the same time that no accomplice existed, NYPD Chief of Detectives John Keenan conveniently forgot something of importance:

"The police came back to me and told me Berkowitz didn't go to the shelter," said Florence Larsen.

"Okay," I answered. "But did you question them about the phone call from Berkowitz or someone saying he was Berkowitz?"

"I sure did. I said, 'Well then, who called me?' They told me someone just must have used his name."

"Someone just must have used his name—really?" I was shaking my head in bemusement. "And what about the second call about 'fixing cars behind Pine Street'? He could have meant C-a-r-r-s, you know; they're behind Pine Street. Didn't they think it was curious that you'd get another call mentioning Pine Street which inquired about the same German shepherd?"

"They didn't say anything about that call," she replied. "They just said he didn't go to the shelter and someone must have used his name in calling me."

". . . Two days before the arrest," I interjected.

"Yes, that's the day it was. You can see when the ad ran in the paper."

"I know. I already have."

*   *   *

Whether Berkowitz actually visited the shelter constituted only half the story. The police apparently neglected to see that the important issues of the phone calls remained. Someone—two days before his arrest—gave Berkowitz's full name and address to a third party in a conversation which linked him tightly to German shepherd dogs, a breed of animal that had been turning up dead with distressing regularity around Pine Street.

It reeked of a setup; yet NYPD discounted it.

Berkowitz, writing two years later, would say he didn't visit the kennel. But as for the phone call: "Someone must have used my name. Yes, I will agree with this." He refused to nominate any candidates.

In the course of four interviews, I found Mrs. Larsen to be an entirely credible witness. Sometime later Det. Capt. John Plansker of NYPD would interview her again, in the wake of an article I published.

"She was believable. I have no reason to doubt what she said," Plansker would acknowledge. "Her story was consistent and her memory was excellent."

Later, another important connection would be established between Berkowitz and an animal shelter—this one in Yonkers.

*   *   *

There was, I reasoned in mid-December 1977, a considerable log of accounts linking Berkowitz to dogs, especially German shepherds. Carr's dog, which was wounded, was a black Lab; but that was an exception. The Neto dog, shot Christmas Eve, 1976, on Wicker Street—the day before the boys discovered three more—was a German shepherd, as were others previously referenced.

Satanic cults sacrificed animals, including dogs and cats. But why only German shepherds in Yonkers? Research had led me to the knowledge that groups of dead German shepherds, presumably sacrificed, were found in recent years at scattered locations across the U.S.—including Houston, where the .44 was purchased. Both northern and southern California authorities reported similar finds, as did police in New England. And I would learn that several more were found in Minot, North Dakota.

A total of eighty-five skinned German shepherds and Dobermans were found in Walden, New York, between late October 1976 and October 1977. Officials believed a cult was behind the killings. The site was only an hour's drive from Yonkers, and people later connected to the Son of Sam case were known to have frequented that vicinity.

Cults dispatched animals for a number of reasons. Sacrifice to Satan was a prime incentive. Blood was also used in fertility rites and was often consumed from a chalice stolen from a church. When found, the animals might be skinned, hanged, shot or even strangled. The strangulation often occurred because the animal was hanged from a tree limb and its throat cut to drain the blood.

Body parts were sometimes removed for mixture in a potion or because they were thought to possess magical powers. As abhorrent as these practices sound, they aren't the product of the mind of a demented Hollywood scriptwriter: they are real, and are being performed today. Law enforcement officials across the country can attest to that statement's veracity.

Dale Griffis, retired police captain of Tiffin, Ohio, and a recognized authority on cult practices, told me: "The public is generally not prepared to accept the fact that these killer groups exist, and neither are many law enforcement people. Some police agencies—who have dealt with cults—learned the hard way how real they are, and how elusive they also are.

"But the activities are so bizarre, so apart from the norm, that many—police and public alike—will contrive any explanation at all to rationalize away crimes that are obviously cult-connected. There is a massive education program to conduct," Griffis said.

Berkowitz himself astutely observed that society's reluctance to face up to the fact that cults are slaughtering animals—and humans—is one of the movement's greatest strengths, a primary reason killer satanic groups are able to flourish.

"If you don't want to deal with something, pretend it isn't there," he said.

*   *   *

But "it" is indeed there. There has been no census of the number of witchcraft and satanic cults active today in the United States. But the number is certainly in the thousands. Fortunately, the majority of these groups are benign, or "white," witchcraft covens, as they are often termed. But not all of them.

The witchcraft phenomenon began in Europe in the Middle Ages. In time, it surfaced in America, and anti-occult hysteria triggered the infamous Salem trials in Massachusetts in 1692.

Legends and beliefs concerning the powers of witches abound in folklore, and to many in the United States, the stories are just that—fables fueled by superstition. But there are believers, and those who practice the "old religion," as it is sometimes called. Some devotees operate alone, others join a coven. In total, there are many thousands of witchcraft advocates casting their spells in modern America.

As indicated, the preponderance of these are relatively harmless. Purists point out that a murderous devil cult should not be confused with the numerous benign covens which dot the landscape of the United States.

To an extent, that admonition is accurate. Not everyone who smokes marijuana advances to heroin addiction; nor does every social drinker become an alcoholic. But just as addicts are initiated on pot and alcoholics emerge from the cocktail party set, hard-core Satanists frequently earn their stripes in the lower ranks of occult curiosity or "white" witchcraft.

Witchcraft, per se, is not illegal, and most covens ostensibly operate within the law. There has been an ambitious public relations effort undertaken in recent years to present witchcraft in an acceptable light. But the fact remains that while some groups claim to celebrate "nature," many others pay homage to Satan. That is their tradition; and they honor it.

A typical coven consists of thirteen members, but that number varies often. The group will meet regularly, usually at the full moon. These gatherings are known as "sabbats." Several times each year, according to witchcraft calendars, Grand Sabbats—major festivals—are celebrated. Grand Sabbats occur, for example, on All Hallows Eve—October 31—and on April 30—Walpurgis Night.

For the purpose of blasphemy, some major holidays coincide with important Roman Catholic holy days. Others mark the dates of old pagan festivals.

As mentioned, covens pay homage to Satan, just as traditional religions honor God. Accordingly, in defiance of the Catholic Church, the concept of the Black Mass evolved during the Middle Ages. In the Black Mass, satanic prayers were substituted for those contained in the Catholic service; the Lord's Prayer was recited backwards; crosses were inverted; black vestments were worn; chalices and hosts stolen from churches were used in the rituals.

Elements such as feces, urine, vomit and animal blood were also employed. The host was sometimes smeared with feces or vomit, and urine was frequently poured into a chalice, and consumed.

Animals, such as dogs and cats, were sacrificed to Satan and their blood drunk in fertility rites or for other purposes. Some covens, questing for the ultimate sacrifice, offered humans to the devil.

Some contemporary witches, trying to distance themselves from their own traditions, discount the volumes written concerning the Black Mass and human sacrifice. Others readily acknowledge that such rites existed at one time. Some will

even concede that militant, drug-ridden, hard-core Satanist covens active today have
carried those practices into the 1980s.

It is that element that is of concern in this narrative.

*   *   *

I raised the subject of the dead German shepherds with Larry Siegel—he of the
Woodlawn Cemetery Caper—while visiting his home in mid-December. Larry,
twenty-seven, was a well-informed researcher and professional writer. He'd offered to
spend some time checking into the occult, and was ready with an opinion.

"You've heard of the Process, right? Well, the Process kept German shepherds."

"The Process? I've only heard a little about them. But we want someone who killed
German shepherds, not kept them."

"You've got to remember that cults split up and change their names. They're as
varied as other religions. They worship one deity, but they do it under different
names and practices."

"Like the Great Schism in the Catholic Church, or like the dozens of Protestant
sects that started, really, when Martin Luther nailed his complaints to that door?"

"Yes," Larry responded. "That's the basic idea. They keep what they like, discard
what they don't like, and sometimes adapt a practice that's just the opposite of the
parent group's."

Following Larry's reasoning, I asked if we might be looking for a Process splinter
group that, instead of keeping dogs, was killing them as an act of defiance or a sign
of independence.

"That could make sense," Larry agreed. "These Satan cults are religions, too. Perverse and sick, but still religions."

"Yeah, and in that context, since shepherds are a strong breed they might also
represent a higher or more pure form of sacrifice, like the offering of the virgin in
pagan days," I said.

"They're also known as police dogs," Larry added, emphasizing that satanic cults,
like organized religions, begged and borrowed ideas from other sources. "So there
might not be a blueprint. It might be a mixed bag of philosophies. And just what do
you know about the Process?"

"I'm just getting my feet wet in all of this," I answered, explaining that I knew
the group had been in California and a few other U.S. locales after emigrating from
England in the 1960s. I told Larry that the cult was barely more than a name to me.

"A dangerous name," he stated.

Larry gave me an apprehensive look.

"This *already* involves mass murder," I reminded him. "It's already in that league."

"But *we're* not. If all this is true, it could get pretty damn unnerving before it's
finished."

"What are you saying?"

"I'm saying that we're off on this great adventure here, but these people think nothing about blowing heads off." Larry paused and shook his head. "I don't know what I'm trying to say."

I could see he was uncomfortable with the course the conversation was taking, so I narrowed the discussion to the reason we had convened this December Saturday, five days after the sleeping Berkowitz photos appeared. I'd gone through about a dozen books on witchcraft and the occult and found some close parallels to the Sam letters.

Taking the Breslin and Borrelli notes from a folder, I spread them out on the dining room table. Larry produced a set of notes and a stack of occult books. The information we'd uncovered, it turned out, was nearly identical. When we finished comparing the data, we were convinced satanic references peppered the letters.

"A crazy guy who imagines demons is a far cry from somebody who's up on occult terminology," I said.

"Yeah," Larry concurred. "Whoever did these letters knows a lot about satanism and witchcraft. But couldn't that have been Berkowitz just reading up on this stuff like we did?"

"It could have been. But if that was so, we'd have to forget about the handwriting problems, the composite sketches, the Moskowitz scene, John Carr and the dead sheps."

Larry sat back in his chair. "Then I think there's a cult involved."

"Are you sure?"

"As sure as anyone can be with what we have to work with up until now."

"What kind of cult?"

"Not some hocus-pocus group of witches, but something like the Process or those Satanists who dug up that British cemetery a few years ago and drove stakes through corpses' hearts."

"Well, I think we've got a cult here, too—in some form or another. But we have no proof at all—zip. The clues are all over the lot, but we'd get destroyed by the cops if we tried to push this now; and I'm sure the *Post* wouldn't go for it either."

We also didn't know if the suspected cult planned the .44 attacks with all its members involved, or if it only served as a catalyst, or an inspiration for Berkowitz and someone else—like John Carr—to do the shootings.

"If they were all in it, we'd be dealing with thirteen, right, if it's a typical coven?" I asked.

"That's the traditional number," Larry answered. "But some stick to it, some don't. This doesn't sound like people who pay strict attention to tradition."

Larry picked up the Breslin letter. "See this alias? I think that may be the answer."

It was, "The Twenty Two Disciples of Hell."

* * *

As we had discussed, the Sam letters were sprinkled with occult references. In the Borrelli letter, they included "wemon," as in demon; "brat," as in imp or small devil; "outsider," the title of an occult book; "Beelzebub," the demon known as Lord of the Flies; "the hunt," a reference to the goddess Diana, queen of the Black Sabbath and leader of the Wild Hunt; and "I'll be back, I'll be back," words identical to those spoken by Satan in the book *Black Easter*. In addition, the Borrelli letter contained obvious references to blood drinking, a satanic practice.

When we reached the name of "Behemoth," the infernal watchman and demon of gluttony, I asked Larry, "Do you know how Behemoth is depicted in the occult?"

"As an elephant, right?"

"Yes—and do you know the Latin word for elephant?"

"No."

"It's *elephas*—does that ring a bell?"

Larry let out a long whistle. "Sure, the Elephas disco in Queens, where the shooting occurred."

"Yeah. This letter was left at the April shooting in the Bronx. The *next* attack happened outside the Elephas."

Larry nodded. "And look at this," he blurted. "The next paragraph talks about the 'wemon of Queens.' It's Elephas and Queens back to back. If this stands up it knocks down the random-shooting idea the cops are pushing."

"Exactly. It would at least mean a location was chosen in advance."

"And who knows who or what else might have been," Larry added.

"That's the point," I said. "The police have built a house of cards, and we're trying to prove it's just *that* flimsy. We don't have to come up with *all* the answers. If we can show Berkowitz didn't do *one*—just one—of these shootings we've knocked down the whole thing."

"Like who really wrote the letters . . . ," Larry said.

That was another thing. The Borrelli letter sounded as if it was written inside the Carr home. The text was clearly from the viewpoint of someone in that house, not from Berkowitz's apartment high on the hill behind it. The telling phrases included: "Behind our house . . . locks me in the garage . . . look out the attic window . . . ties me up to the back of the house." And there were also some extremely personal references to Sam Carr's health and habits in it. I was certain that someone who knew Sam Carr well—and hated him—had a hand in the composition of the Borrelli letter.

"What do you think—John or Michael?" Larry asked.

"I don't know who printed it. But I'd bet you anything one of them provided the words, at least some of them. He spelled 'honor' the British way, too, with an *o-u-r*. Does that sound like Berkie from the Bronx?"

"No, it doesn't." Larry laughed. "I'd also say whoever wrote this was stoned on something when he did. It sounds so crude when compared to the Breslin thing. It's just off the wall."

Larry then reached for an occult work entitled *The Book of Ceremonial Magic*. "You talked about Behemoth and Elephas being the same thing," he said. "Take a look at this."

On the cover of the book, a large, circular symbol of obvious occult derivation was staring at me. I shrugged and asked Larry what he was getting at. "Look inside the circle, near the center," he advised.

It looked like the graphic symbol on the Breslin letter. It wasn't exact, but all the elements were there. It was very similar to the Sam symbol and was identified as "The Goetic Circle of Black Evocations and Pacts." On the inside pages, I read a section which explained the symbol's origin. I almost dropped the book. The symbol was created by famed nineteenth-century occultist Eliphas Levi. It was another Eliphas link.

"The Elephas disco and Eliphas Levi," I said slowly.

"It's spelled with an *i* instead of an *e* but I don't think that matters," Larry said.

"It doesn't matter a bit," I agreed, and studied the Levi symbol more closely. On the outer perimeter of the circle, there were several words written at intervals around the circumference. One was "Berkaial" and another was "Amasarac."

"One of Berkowitz's nicknames is 'Berk,'" I advised Larry. "And we know how backward words and phrases are part of satanic practices—like saying the 'Our Father' backwards."

"So?"

"So look at 'Amasarac' backward. It's Car-a-sam-a—or Sam Carr."

"Jesus Christ," Larry exulted. "When they found this symbol they must have flipped. It ties to Elephas and now this. It was perfect for them to base the Sam symbol on it."

It was. We'd found a symbol almost identical to Son of Sam's that was drawn by Eliphas Levi and contained Berkowitz's nickname and Sam Carr's name. Then, the shooting that immediately followed the use of the symbol in the Breslin letter occurred outside the Elephas discotheque.

"I say they hit at Elephas as some symbolic act and cutely tipped their hand with the symbol in the Breslin letter and the behemoth-elephas reference in the Borrelli note," I stated. They were letting it out in advance where they were going to hit."

Larry's response was subdued. "If the symbol and the disco were both named 'Jones,' that'd be another matter. But not 'Elephas.' We're beyond coincidence. I don't like this feeling I'm getting. It's like we're inside somebody's head out there. Somebody that scares the hell out of me."

We quickly went through the remainder of the Breslin letter. There was another allusion to blood drinking, along with the phrase, "spirit roaming the night." However, the most important satanic clue was contained in the letter's first sentence: "Hello from the gutters of N.Y.C., which are filled with dog manure, vomit, stale wine, urine, and blood."

These elements, as listed in numerous occult books and explained earlier, were used in the satanic Black Mass, a full-scale mockery and debasement of the Roman Catholic mass. And the allusion to stale wine implied more than was apparent: "stale" was also a synonym for animal urine. In other words, animal urine was drunk instead of wine in the ritual.

"So now we've got the Black Mass, too," Larry said. "It's like they were hinting all the while, but no one picked up on it."

"I don't think anyone wanted to," I observed.

I was sure people in the occult underground understood the meaning of the Breslin letter. But they either remained silent or the police didn't listen. I recalled that on the preceding Halloween, the CBS nightly news had wrapped up its broadcast with a lighthearted feature about a parapsychology convention being held in New York City.

"Right there, on camera, was a flip chart with the Sam symbol on it and wording about the occult influences in it," I said. "This was a camera pan; they didn't talk about it. But there it was, on national TV, and nobody catches it. But this association obviously knew about some of the references. . . . I guess it just sounds so damned unreal."

"To us in the mainstream it does," Larry countered. "It's a whole other culture. There are people out there who take this stuff very seriously—and it looks like we've run into some of them."

"Wonderful."

As if to illustrate his point, Larry reached for another book, *The Encyclopedia of Witchcraft and Demonology.* "We're new to this, these people aren't," he said, indicating a passage for me to read:

> In New York, the covens have become largely warped and perverted. A twisted sexual element has crept in more and more until today they are sado-masochistic . . . and are using the occult as an excuse.
>
> Criminologists studying these matters suggest that when such people tire of their "staged" activities, they are liable to turn to ritual, motiveless killing. The alarming fact is that many such murders occur in the United States today.

The warning was plain, and was echoed in other publications we studied. And during the ensuing years, its validity would continue to ring out through the course of the investigation.

"New York and California seem to be the spots these authors highlight more than anyplace else," I noted. "This is all hitting me right in the face, yet I'm still antsy about it."

"Yeah," Larry agreed. "Knowing and proving are two different things. But you just can't go out and infiltrate a cult."

"Hell, we don't even know where it is," I said. "These people don't put ads in the papers. This is middle-of-the-night stuff. We find what they leave behind, like the dogs. But where the hell are they?"

"We've got to keep looking," Larry observed.

"And keep it quiet."

Larry chuckled nervously. "You don't have to worry about me saying anything. Living has become a lot of fun the last few years."

* * *

The talk of murder and death was disconcerting. We simply didn't want to believe we were in treacherous waters; in fact, I refused to acknowledge that we might be. The atmosphere had a decidedly surrealistic spice to it. We were circling the beast, observing it, and trying to maintain it could never move against us.

I had seen enough Hollywood depictions of witchcraft to rebel at the reality. The temptation to laugh it off was there, but on the other hand so were the documented references and other evidence we'd found. Now, despite my anger at the police, I suddenly understood their reluctance to sail the river Styx to the realm of Satan. There was a lifetime's worth of conditioning and prejudice to overcome, and it wasn't easy to accomplish. Nonetheless, I still couldn't excuse the official unwillingness to investigate a Son of Sam conspiracy, per se. Accomplices, whether Satanists or truck drivers, were still accomplices.

Larry and I concluded our session by comparing the dates of the .44 shootings with a satanic/witchcraft calendar which listed the major occult holidays—occasions that called for some form of sacrifice to Satan. The police had been puzzled because there seemed to be no discernible pattern to the Son of Sam attacks. But we found one: with one exception, the shootings occurred proximate to occult holidays, of which there were only about ten each year.

"If there was one a week, this wouldn't mean a thing," I said. "It's still not positive proof, but along with everything else, we're building a strong circumstantial case, at the least."

The attacks hadn't occurred exactly on the holidays, but we reasoned that the shootings were public displays, and the cult may have done other things privately on the days themselves.

"They needed to find victims. Maybe they failed on the actual days or only intended that the hits happen as close as possible to them," I offered.

Larry had a further explanation, suggesting that the group may have had to report on a shooting at a cult meeting; to do the deed and then describe it to the assemblage. He also believed that the cult met at least once a month, on the full moon, and convened again on the major holidays.

"You know too much," I joked. "Why don't you confess now so we can get this over with."

For all his professionalism, Larry understandably had a weak stomach regarding this subject.

"Can you imagine those people drinking urine and dog blood? They've *got* to be high on acid or something to do it. . . . Here, take this damn list. They've got a holiday coming up. You can have fun and stake out Pine Street at midnight—send me a telegram if they show up."

In fact, the upcoming December 21 (St. Thomas's Day) was a satanic feast. The Son of Sam shootings, compared with the witchcraft holidays, or sabbats, appeared in the following manner:

SON OF SAM	WITCHCRAFT HOLIDAY
July 29, July 31	August 1 (Lammas Day)
October 23	October 31 (All Hallows Eve)
November 27	November 30 (St. Andrew's Eve)
January 30	February 2 (Candlemas Day)
April 17	April 24 (St. Mark's Eve) and April 30 (Walpurgis Night)
June 26	June 23 (Midsummer's Eve or St. John's Eve)

Larry and I were aware that some cults celebrated Good Friday, so we considered it possible that the April shooting (the Borrelli letter left at that scene mentioned Easter) might actually have been geared to that feast day. The March 8 murder of Virginia Voskerichian matched no occult festival, however.

"That shooting broke both the weekend and time-of-night pattern," I noted. "Maybe they went off their schedule for a reason we don't know about."

"It could have been a leader's birthday," Larry said. "That's always the highest of all holidays, on an individual basis."

Our meeting had been successful, resulting in the discovery and confirmation of significant occult connections to Son of Sam. But the information, while strong, was still circumstantial. There was more work to be done.

Essentially, there were several directions to travel, each of which could lead to the corroboration we sought:

1. We could find the cult itself, and link it to Berkowitz.
2. We could uncover evidence that put someone involved in the case—Berkowitz, one of the Carr brothers or someone whose name was still unknown—into a cult.
3. We could continue to accumulate evidence which demonstrated Berkowitz didn't act alone, whether that evidence was linked to a cult or not.

The paths were separate, but at the same time they theoretically converged at a point in the future. As repugnant as the idea of a satanic cult was to me, I knew I'd be as remiss as the police if I disregarded the information we'd assembled. I knew it was accurate; the research material we'd obtained was in black and white. But there was still a considerable number of unknown factors.

Back at home in White Plains, I phoned Jim Mitteager and briefed him on the newest developments. We arranged to meet the following week.

When Mitteager arrived on Wednesday evening, December 14, we drove to New Rochelle, where we unsuccessfully attempted to pursue the Cassara-Fred Cowan-Berkowitz connection. The case was now branching out in many different directions, and we were few in number. We risked spreading ourselves too thin on what was already a part-time effort for all of us.

As Christmas neared, I made several phone calls to North Dakota, seeking John Carr. I found two people with the same name, neither of whom was "John Wheaties." I represented myself as an old, distant acquaintance from the Air Force, but the John Carrs I spoke to were Army veterans.

We also phoned authorities in Los Angeles, where the Hillside Strangler killings had begun. "It can't hurt," Mitteager said. "He was called a rapist and suffocator in the Breslin letter, and that's what's happening out there. Maybe in a stroke of blind luck it'll turn out to be him, or maybe they'll at least be able to locate the bastard."

John Carr, however, wasn't in Los Angeles.

Mitteager and I also visited each of the Son of Sam crime scenes, where we sketched maps, noted nearby streets and tried to develop indelible mental images of each location. To enhance the project, we took a number of photos and reenacted the circumstances of each shooting as best we could.

The trip to the Brooklyn scene was my third. Earlier, I dragged George Austin, and later another friend, to the site. Each time, as I explained the scenario, my companions agreed serious contradictions existed in the official version of the shootings.

Mitteager, an ex-police officer, voiced similar sentiments and decided to pursue the matter further. He arranged for us to meet with 10th Homicide detectives three days after Christmas.

In the meantime, I endeavored to learn as much as I could about the cult Larry and I discussed: The Process. There undoubtedly were other satanic groups we could have considered (and subsequently did consider); and there assuredly were still others of which we had no knowledge at all. If Berkowitz was a member of a small, strictly local group, with no ties beyond Yonkers, we'd have to approach the investigation differently.

But the dead German shepherds were a tangible parcel of evidence, and that breed of animal was in fact linked to the macabre group formally known as the Process Church of the Final Judgment. And so it began.

*   *   *

Initially, I was surprised to learn that most of the occult writings I perused were bereft of any substantial information about the cult. Most references were vague. Later, through extensive field research and personal contacts with reliable sources in California, and elsewhere, I was able to complete the biographical picture that is painted here.

Among my advisers was Ed Sanders, author of *The Family*—a superb study of the Manson clan—who graciously sat with me in a wild blueberry patch in an upstate New York meadow one summer afternoon and significantly added to my knowledge of the shadowy cult.

We convened in the open air at Sanders's request. "It's too distasteful a topic to go into anywhere else but out here—where the setting and surroundings are as far removed from what those people stand for as we can get," he explained.

Sanders is not given to hyperbole. He is a thoughtful, sincere man; and an accomplished writer, poet and musician. His band, the Fugs, became well known in the late 1960s, and the group still plays reunion tours on occasion. Sanders spent eighteen months probing the grotesque world of Charlie Manson while researching *The Family*, and he hasn't forgotten what it was like. Neither, for that matter, have other sources—who are still fearful of the group—erased the memories of those days when they came to know of the Process.

The following is an overview of the organization which I, and others, consider to have been one of the most dangerous satanic cults in America.

The Process, as far as is known, has now officially splintered, and its offspring— while still active—have gone underground. But before the Process divided, it spread seeds of destruction throughout the United States. Those spores were carried on winds of evil across the 1970s and into the present. The terror still reigns, with far-flung subsidiary groups united by the sins of the father.

But in the beginning, there was a man and a woman; and they came together in London, England. The year was 1963...

*   *   *

Satanic cults lurk in various guises, and their recruitment techniques also differ. Some harvest via pseudo-legitimate counseling or "self-awareness" groups—actually fronts—which frequently flourish around campuses or military bases or in major cities.

An unsuspecting youth, already possessed of a mindset ripe for manipulation, will enroll for a series of courses, seminars or therapy sessions allegedly intended to put his or her life into focus. What follows is a period of careful screening and weeding out. In time, the chosen few find themselves drawn deeper and deeper into a web of deceit, rejection of traditional values, and conversion to the twisted beliefs of the group's leaders.

At its outset, the Process was one of these groups.

The Process Church of the Final Judgment was born in London, England, in

1963–64, the Damien-child of two ranking members of the Church of Scientology who split with the parent organization following some philosophical differences with the teachings of L. Ron Hubbard, the developer of Scientology.

The founding couple of the Process, Robert Moore and Mary Anne MacLean, had met while receiving advanced training at the Hubbard Institute of Scientology on London's Fitzroy Street. Divorcing Hubbard, they married one another and adopted the cult name of DeGrimston for themselves.

Robert Moore DeGrimston was born in Shanghai, China, on August 10, 1935; David Berkowitz would be arrested on DeGrimston's birthday. DeGrimston, a tall, bearded blonde who affected a Christ-like appearance, was an educated man, studying at Winchester in England and later pursuing a career in architecture at the Regent Street Polytechnic Institute.

His bride's background was checkered. Mary Anne MacLean DeGrimston was born illegitimately in Glasgow, Scotland, on November 20, 1931. She reportedly endured a frustrating childhood, punctuated by tenure in a reform school.

Mary Anne subsequently entered the United States, where she managed to meet former boxing champion Sugar Ray Robinson and became engaged to him. However, the relationship ended and Mary Anne returned to England, where she worked as a dance-hall hostess.

At a dwelling in London, she became romantically involved with several prominent British citizens during the days of the John Profumo-Christine Keeler prostitution scandal which rocked the British government in the early 1960s. At least one of those linked to the Profumo affair, Dr. Stephen Ward, was an occult adept. Ward soon died, an apparent suicide.

It was during this tumultuous period that Robert Moore and Mary Anne MacLean met while immersed in profound mental exercises at the Hubbard Institute of Scientology.

On their own, and with their new cult names, the DeGrimstons began to experiment with sophisticated mind-control games. They started a center to study what they termed "Compulsion Analysis"—for research into and elimination of compulsive behavior. They preached a doctrine of free choice, declaring that individuals were completely responsible for their own fates, actions—and afflictions. Mary Anne, for instance, reportedly believed that Jews *chose* the gas chambers; and even birth defects were said to be freely selected and carried into the present from past lives—as the DeGrimstons also believed in reincarnation. The gods they worshipped were two in number: Jehovah and Lucifer.

Not surprisingly, the fledgling Process attracted a following. Young, searching and disturbed men and women were drawn to the group like metal to a magnet. The DeGrimstons also actively recruited, particularly from the ranks of the young and wealthy.

This cult *modus operandi* is an important one, worthy of remembrance. Monied recruits served two purposes. First, they could be tapped for sizable donations that would allow the cult to expand and its leaders to maintain an appropriate lifestyle. Second, wealthy converts often held top jobs or had important connections, enabling the cult to gain entry into powerful business, entertainment, government and financial circles—laying the foundation for an influential, cultic "old boy" network.

In March 1966, the DeGrimstons, flush with success, leased a mansion on Balfour Place in London's fashionable Mayfair section. Now totally absorbed in their power trip, they brought twenty-five groveling followers into the house with them. Here, the German shepherds entered the picture as the DeGrimstons each obtained a large Alsatian, a breed of German shepherd. To mirror their leaders, the acolytes also purchased German shepherds, and the canine corps grew to over thirty in number.

The DeGrimstons weren't content with a limited operation, however. In the tradition of egomaniacal gurus everywhere, they decided to expand—internationally. Accordingly, they, along with eighteen disciples and a number of Alsatians, embarked for Nassau in the Bahamas in June 1966. They lolled in Nassau for six weeks before leasing a large tract of land on the beach in Xtul, Mexico, which is situated on the Yucatan Peninsula.

The Mexican period was a significant one because while in Xtul the Process's two gods, Lucifer and Jehovah, were joined by a third: Satan. For the first time, the group began conducting moonlight satanic rituals. Also at Xtul, the notion of founding a formal Process Church evolved. To Process members, the Xtul experience was the equivalent of Christ's forty days and nights in the desert.

Returning to England, the group sought out the famous, striving to convert the Beatles and the Rolling Stones, among others. A bookstore and coffeehouse were opened, and a *Process* magazine rolled off the presses.

The cult was enamored of bloodshed and war, and its magazine reflected this obsession. Hitler was considered a noble gentleman worthy of admiration—and worship. In this, the era of flower power, the Process briefly managed to entrap singer Marianne Faithfull, a close companion of the Rolling Stones. In one issue of *Process* magazine, she was pictured supine, as if dead, clutching a rose.

In late 1967, Robert DeGrimston published a book, *As It Is,* which spelled out the Process's philosophy:

> *Christ said: Love thine enemy. Christ's enemy was Satan and Satan's enemy was Christ. Through love, enmity is destroyed. Through love, saint and sinner destroy the enmity between them. Through love, Christ and Satan have destroyed their enmity and come together for the End. Christ to judge, Satan to execute the judgment.*

The key to this treatise is contained in the sentence which says that Christ and Satan have joined forces to bring about the end of the world. Christ, according to the Process, was employing Satan as a hit man. So worshipping Satan was akin to worshipping Christ. And killing in the name of Satan was actually killing for Christ: a divine mission.

Naturally, DeGrimston was thought by Process members to be Christ, and they, in adoring Satan, were the agents of God working under divine orders to save the world from itself by hastening the day of the Second Coming. In the end, the cult would survive to build a new world of satanic glory.

From the Bible, the signs of the Second Coming were evident: the fires of Armageddon, death, chaos and confusion. The Process firmly believed its divine duty was to hasten the arrival of the Final Days—and bastardizing the Bible told them how to do it. This was a blueprint for murder, butchery and other crime cloaked in religious justification.

Would the disenfranchised, rebellious or power-hungry swallow this perverse theology? Most assuredly, the DeGrimstons believed, and they prepared a go-ye-forth-and-teach-all-nations crusade which swept into the United States in late 1967.

*   *   *

"My prophecy upon this wasted earth and upon the corrupt creation that squats upon its ruined surface is: THOU SHALT KILL."

It is not known if Process members seeping into San Francisco in the autumn of the "Summer of Love" distributed pamphlets containing that quote from Robert DeGrimston's book *Jehovah on War.* But arrive they did, bringing their German shepherds, magazines, recruitment raps and twisted theology with them.

In the United States, this was the era of burgeoning student unrest. The Vietnam War was igniting protests; parental values were under siege; psychedelic music was the rage; dope was rampant; the hippie movement's flower children were in full bloom. The summer of 1967 and the crossroads of Haight and Ashbury transformed San Francisco into Mecca. Timothy Leary was advising youth to "turn on, tune in, drop out." It was an age of "do your own thing," free love and transcendental meditation. Even the Beatles were grooving on the Maharishi and singing "All You Need Is Love."

This was fertile ground for the Process to plow.

The cult was at this time arranged into three subgroups, which represented its three gods. The Jehovahs were straitlaced and uncompromising, the Puritans of the sect. The Luciferians, in contrast, literally embraced each other—advocating sensuality, tranquility and the free use of narcotics. Finally, the Satanists believed what Satanists everywhere believed in: gore, violence, sacrifice and devil worship.

New Process members were free to select the discipline of their choice. This option mattered little to the DeGrimstons since, according to their preachings, all three branches would converge for the Final Judgment, which would mark the end of the world as nonmembers—the "Gray Forces" of moderation—knew it to be.

For Processans, no matter which god they bowed to, it was a joyous time. The End was coming, and they, as the Chosen People, were going to be part of the big event.

Landing in California, the Process was just another group of proselytizers hawking their wares in an already teeming marketplace. They attracted little official attention, since law enforcement authorities lumped them into the same category as other messianic minions littering the streets with their literature.

But there was a difference here. The Process was dangling a carrot seasoned for a variety of taste buds, and thus was able to entice a sizable number of recruits. Death and violence advocates were attracted by the Satanist wing and the promise of upcoming end-of-the-world rampage and destruction. Free-love and dope aficionados were seduced by the Luciferians; and self-flagellating hairshirts were drawn to the strict, forbidding Jehovahs.

The Christ-Satan duality was very appealing to an aging flower child by the name of Charles Milles Manson. Manson's considerable connections to the Process will be explored later. However, it would not be inappropriate to reveal at this point that Manson was heavily influenced by the group.

In San Francisco, the Process set up house on Cole Street, and later moved to a more amenable residence on Oak Street. In March 1968, after spreading the news in the north, a contingent consisting of thirty members, accompanied by more than a dozen Alsatian dogs, drove down the coast to Weirdness West—Los Angeles.

In L.A., they rented a large house on South Cochrane Street, from where they descended on Sunset Strip like so many vultures in quest of cadavers. There, they vacuumed up new disciples from the swarms of runaways, castoffs, bikers, dopers and other outsiders for whom the Strip was "home."

But true to form, the Process approached the elite as well as the down-and-outers. Singer John Phillips of the Mamas and the Papas, Mama Cass Elliot herself and Terry Melcher, son of Doris Day and a TV and record producer, were among those in show business sought out by the group—apparently with mixed success.

*   *   *

The Process, not surprisingly, was fond of the color black. They wore black capes, some with the Mendez goat of Satan stitched in red on the back. Underneath, they donned black robes, or suits and turtlenecks, and adorned their necks with silver crosses. Some wore a Mendez goat pin. The official Process symbol, paying homage to the idolized Hitler, was a form of inverted swastika.

On the streets of Los Angeles in the spring of 1968, the Process was distributing the "Sex" issue of *Process* magazine. Its front cover displayed a photo of a satanic ceremony, showing a naked girl lying on an altar surrounded by a band of hooded cultists. An inverted cross shadowed the scene.

The back cover contained a rendering of a winged skeleton suspended over a pile of naked bodies. The humans, mouths gaping, apparently were either dead or in hell, or both. The inner pages of this charming piece of literature contained articles relating to Black Masses and necrophilia—the practice of performing sexual or other violations on corpses.

A subsequent issue of *Process* magazine was devoted to "Fear." On the back cover of this publication, a band of marching Nazis spewed from the mouth of a fiery pink skull. The Nazis were trampling on a group of people being consumed by fire. Elsewhere in this same illustration, the face of Hitler appeared in a fun-house mirror and a human being was shown burning to death.

At the top of the page, a legend promised: "Next Issue: DEATH."

The magazine's centerspread was devoted to the Unholy Alliance of the Lamb of God and the Goat of Satan. A caption read: "The Lamb and the Goat must come together—pure love descended from the pinnacle of Heaven, united with pure hatred raised from the depths of Hell."

Other articles of great interest in the "Fear" issue included a page of quotes about fear from members of the Hell's Angels biker group (the Process actively recruited bikers, considering them the frontline troops of the great war to come), an essay entitled "Satan Is Fear," and a picture of twenty-four Process Alsatian dogs menacing the camera.

Regarding the obsession with fear, it is not a coincidence that one of Charlie Manson's favorite lectures to his followers revolved around the expression "Getting the Fear."

As incredible as *Process* magazine was, its rantings could only be considered routine, coming as they did from a group whose leader, Robert DeGrimston, wrote in *Satan on War:* "Release the fiend that lies dormant within you, for he is strong and ruthless and his power is far beyond the bounds of human frailty."

Was a more divine trumpet of violence ever blown?

What the Process had managed to do was envelop isolated individuals from various social backgrounds and mix them together. It was a volatile brew, and the common cause resulted in long-standing alliances being sealed.

I have spoken to several professional people, including educators, who remain sympathetic to the group's theology, so any impression that the cult managed to attract only society's misfits would be erroneous.

* * *

In terms of inner ranking, there were six levels of membership in the group, which borrowed from the family structure for its inspiration. In fact, the Process referred to itself as "the family," as Manson did with his group. It is yet another interesting link between Manson and the Process; and there are many more. For instance, cult names were substituted for legal names once initiates reached a certain level of Process indoctrination. This was another practice Manson utilized for many in his "family."

The lowest level in the Process was that of acolyte, followed by initiate and messenger—the rank at which the recruit acquired his or her cult name, such as Brother Tom, Sister Rebecca or Father Jonas. From the rank of messenger, the aspiring cultist graduated to prophet, priest and ultimately master.

At one point in the journey, all members—regardless of their chosen god—were required to enter a long period of satanic worship, which reportedly included blood rituals and sacrifice. Accepted Processans then formally convened twice each month to summon their three gods, who would then "speak" through the mouths of the gathered cult members.

Most of the original cultists were British citizens who apparently came to America on ninety-day visitor's visas. Some extensions of time were granted, but eventually—in the summer of 1968—many of the group suddenly dropped from sight. Some, it was said, returned to England, but others appear to have remained in the United States clandestinely.

The DeGrimstons themselves headed for New York City, where a Process Church was established on Cornelia Street in Greenwich Village in late 1968. In addition to the church, numerous members lived in a building on East 12th Street, while the DeGrimstons stayed in Brooklyn.

As in California, the Process recruited among the artists, poets and hordes of counterculture youth who frequented the Village. Later, a cult spokesman told United Press International that more than two hundred Americans were fully converted to the "faith." Process contingents subsequently materialized in New Orleans, Dallas, Toronto, Chicago and Cambridge, Massachusetts, among other locations.

In a development that is critical to this story, once the group's leadership turned over the reins to local disciples in Los Angeles, power plays and political infighting inevitably resulted. Differences in philosophy and theology also arose.

As the cult went underground there in the aftermath of the assassination of Senator Robert Kennedy (perhaps concerned that law enforcement would hear of Sirhan Sirhan's occult interests and alleged acquaintance with a Process member), secret Process chapters, or spin-offs using other names, were established in northern and southern California.

Not so coincidentally (since certain members' movements were traced), authorities soon began finding the bodies of mutilated, decapitated or exsanguinated dogs—including numerous German shepherds—in the Santa Cruz area south of San Francisco. Some of the animals were skinned, prompting a humane society official to comment on the killers' abilities with knives.

Reports of human sacrifice were also relayed to the police, including one from a gentleman named Stanley Baker, who was himself arrested for an out-of-state murder. Baker, who said he was a member of the Santa Cruz cult, carried a finger bone from his recent unfortunate victim in a leather pouch.

Upon his arrest, he delivered one of criminal history's epic comments to authorities: "I have a problem. I am a cannibal."

Baker, who sported a swastika tattoo and other occult emblems, said he was recruited from a campus setting in Wyoming. He participated in blood-drinking rituals there, was further programmed and then joined the California activities.

Concerning this particular victim, Baker told the police he murdered the man, cut out his heart—and ate it.

Baker, and at least one other witness, told authorities the Santa Cruz group later headed back downstate, where they resumed their obnoxious rituals—including murder—in the O'Neill Park area of the Santa Ana Mountains, south of Los Angeles.

This cult, a Process splinter group, was said by the witnesses to call itself the Four P Movement, or "Four Pi." Its leader, alleged to be a prosperous L.A. businessman or doctor, was known as the Grand Chingon. Interestingly, Ed Sanders stated that on several occasions—in his presence—Manson family members referred to Charlie as the Grand Chingon. However, Manson was under arrest at that time and the cult was still functioning, so he was not the Grand Chingon.

But a key question remains: how did Manson's followers know the cult name of the leader of this top-secret slaughter society? (It should be mentioned here that there is no evidence available which implicates the DeGrimstons themselves in these alleged Chingon cult crimes.)

Shortly after the Four P cult relocated to Los Angeles in early 1969, another split apparently occurred. Some Four P members decided there was too much emphasis on sacrifice and devil worship and not enough sex. This faction apparently went off on its own, leaving the Grand Chingon and his remaining followers to carry on their business of draining and drinking the blood of sacrificed dogs and humans.

There is a curious similarity here to differences which arose in the parent Process between the sensual Luciferians and the hard-core Satanists.

According to the witnesses, including Baker, the Chingon cult practiced its rituals on the basis of a stellar timetable and employed its own cultic terminology. The group also was alleged to possess a portable crematorium to dispose of victims' remains, an ornate wooden altar and a specially designed sacrificial knife with six blades.

A biker who belonged to the cult did provide the police with one name, Erickson, but authorities were unable to find him. And as many in cults go by names other than their own, or by first names only, rounding up perpetrators is at best an extremely difficult task. Moreover, such underground groups are mobile, often meeting at a variety of remote locations in the dead of night. And informants are scarce, due to the fear factor and blood oaths of loyalty often taken by members. Plus, of course, almost any informant was likely to have been an active accomplice in murder himself and as such would have little incentive to provide information to the police.

Baker, incidentally, did not renounce his satanic proclivities when sentenced to prison for the brutal heart-meal murder he acknowledged committing. Authorities report that he actively and regularly conspired to organize a devil-worshipping cult among his fellow inmates. Apparently an otherwise model prisoner, he was eligible for release in mid-1985. But his parole board, for whatever reason, was finding it difficult to locate a halfway house willing to accept him.

Lower-ranking Satanists such as Baker often literally believe in the havoc they wreak, but cult leaders are likely to be motivated as much by power and greed as they are by infernal incantations. It is possible to visualize the structure the Process left in place—the network of cult contacts between various cities. And it is also possible to envision how such a structure, staffed by willing satanic slaves, could be employed for purposes that could greatly benefit a handful of leaders—both monetarily, in terms of drug distribution and child pornography, for instance—and personally, in terms of power, influence and immense ego gratification. To those leaders, allegiance to Satan is a secondary, convenient avocation.

*　*　*

The Process and its secret offshoots didn't have the Southern California or U.S. occult scene or philosophies to themselves. Master black magician Aleister Crowley, who died in 1947, had written of a unification of God and Satan. That precept, and other Crowleyisms, found their way into Process doctrine.

By sharing Crowley's beliefs, the Process also blended those of the Order of the Golden Dawn. The Golden Dawn was an English occult society to which Crowley belonged in the late nineteenth century. The Golden Dawn believed in cabalistic magic and taught that the will could be trained to accomplish paranormal effects, including astral projection. The Golden Dawn also strongly believed in symbolism, teaching that certain symbols, or thoughts, had the same meaning for all human beings.

After internal dissension, elements of the Golden Dawn more or less merged into the Ordo Templis Orientis (OTO), a German occult society founded in 1902. The OTO accused Crowley of revealing one of its most secret precepts: that sex could be employed for the purposes of magic.

But, after mending some fences, Crowley won permission to head a British OTO branch, and the teachings of the OTO entered the United States with Crowley in 1916, during World War I in Europe.

Later, during World War II, Crowley helped establish an OTO lodge in Pasadena, California, and OTO branches subsequently sprouted in a number of U.S. cities, including New York and Houston. In effect, a loose network was formed and already functioning via occult shops and bookstores, newsletters, ads in the underground press and other methods—including personal contacts—by the time the Process arrived in 1967.

In fact, many believe that the entire occult underground in America today can be traced back to the formation of that Crowley OTO operation in Pasadena.

The Process, then, incorporated the ideas of a number of its ancestors and current occupants of the occult landscape, including the OTO. Accordingly, there was intermingling of philosophy, membership and networking among the groups. This arrangement makes labeling a difficult, restrictive measure. Charles Manson, for example, was exposed to the practices of a renegade OTO lodge in Southern California as well as having been influenced by the Process.

*　*　*

During the Christmas season of 1977, my research of the Process, its offspring and allies was not nearly as complete as presented here. At that time, I had merely learned enough about the group and network to consider it a definite possibility that Berkowitz may have been involved somehow with a branch of that treacherous English society or one of its OTO counterparts.

But I was still facing the task of finding corroboration to buttress the occult clues in the Son of Sam letters and the dead German shepherd connection. In order for the cult or overall conspiracy suspicions to stand up undeniably, we either had to find the group itself, put Berkowitz or John Carr into such an organization or uncover other evidence demonstrating a conspiracy existed—evidence that was either cult-related or tied to the .44 crime scenes themselves. Simply stated, that is how the entire investigation was structured to try to find the proof we needed.

As the year drew to a close, Christmas Day would bring some unexpected information about John Carr. And after that, there would be murder in the wind. But as we wound down for the holiday, no one could have foreseen that this was to be the last Yuletide for a number of people connected to the Son of Sam case.

For them, the "final judgment" was near.

X

Into the Maze

On Wednesday morning, December 28, Jim Mitteager and I linked up near the Verrazano Narrows Bridge, which unites the borough of Staten Island and the south shore of Brooklyn, and veered east on the Belt Parkway toward Coney Island. As we passed under the footbridge crossed by Stacy Moskowitz and Robert Violante that fatal night five months earlier, Mitteager remarked that someone had hung a crucifix on the light pole the couple parked beneath.

"Someone also sent a letter to the 60th Precinct that week before," I answered. "It warned of an attack in Coney Island or Seagate. It was taken seriously and diverted some attention from this spot."

"That's slick planning if it's connected," Jim said. "Maybe we'll find out before this is over."

A few miles to the east, we pulled off the highway and stopped at a local deli where Mitteager picked up eight containers of coffee and an assortment of pastries. "I was a cop, remember? The last guy in always picks up the coffee and rolls."

I wanted to ask how someone knew he would be the last to arrive for duty, but I let it go. Once inside 10th Homicide, which was located on the second floor of the 60th Precinct, we were greeted by Sgt. Bill Gardella, the young supervisor who participated in Berkowitz's arrest. I took a liking to Gardella, finding him perceptive and intelligent. We were then joined by Lt. Robert Kelly, and, later, Ed Zigo materialized briefly.

We summed up the purpose of the visit, and painstakingly went through the Moskowitz scenario as we then knew it. (The most important evidence was not yet discovered.) Surprisingly, with the exception of Zigo, the detectives were not unreceptive to the sales pitch.

"You've done your homework," Gardella said. "You've caught some things no one else in the media did. There are some unanswered questions about the shooting; we won't deny that. But sometimes, like it or not, those questions are never answered."

Kelly added: "All we know is that we had probable cause to arrest Berkowitz. Once the arrest went down, the files were out of here. Everything was turned over to the DA. It's his case now. We have nothing more to do with it."

"Between here and Westchester there are quite a few unanswered questions, to use your phrase," I said to Gardella.

"I can't talk about Westchester," he responded. "We're here in Brooklyn. We don't know anything about these incidents going on up in Yonkers, and we honestly never heard of John Carr until now."

Mitteager pulled out a copy of a note Berkowitz wrote at Kings County Hospital which mentioned John Carr. "That's John Wheaties," he pointed out. "He's real, not just an alias."

Zigo leaned forward, looked at the note and grudgingly said, "That's Berkowitz's handwriting all right. Where'd you get this?"

Jim brushed off the question, and Zigo, evidently bored with the discussion, soon left the room. But Kelly and Gardella remained attentive. "I think you brought up some interesting things here," Gardella remarked. "We want you to see the DA." I looked at Kelly, who nodded in agreement.

"Gold?" Jim inquired.

"No, Shelly Greenberg. He's the chief assistant and he's coordinating the case for Gold."

"I don't know if we'd get anywhere," I said. It was more a question than a statement.

"We think you should see them," Kelly responded. "We'll call over there and tell them you're coming in about an hour."

Mitteager readily consented, but I had reservations. I wanted to hear Jim's impressions of this conference before committing to another and asked the detectives to tell Gold's office that we'd call for an appointment in a few days. On the way back, we rehashed the morning's events and agreed to carry the information to the DA.

"I think we touched a nerve," Jim said. "I wonder if we just might be running interference for a few people with integrity at the Tenth?"

"Maybe. They weren't just patronizing us. You were right to set this up. We're right into the damn lion's den now."

Mitteager had been urging just such a strategy and had accused me of undue caution. He was right to an extent. I was acutely conscious of the mountain we were trying to move and wanted to be as secure with our facts as possible before presenting them to the authorities. We weren't espousing a popular cause; we were going against the established grain. One slip, one error, and our budding credibility would be eagerly destroyed. We couldn't afford to let that happen.

I then told Jim about a Christmas Day conversation I had with my cousin, Mary Ellen, whom I hadn't seen for several months. In describing what we were working on, I mentioned John Carr and said I knew very little about him. Mary Ellen chided my faulty memory.

"You knew John Carr. He was in our freshman class in high school."

"Are you serious?"

"He was in another homeroom," she explained. "He was thin, had light, sandy-colored hair, and he was always cutting up. This was high school, and yet he was always throwing spitballs around and doing other antics that were more like a kid in grammar school would do. But he obviously thought it was all funny."

As Mary Ellen spoke, I was starting to remember John Carr. "What else do you recall?"

"Not much. He wore a red blazer a lot, and I can remember that he wanted to join the Piper's Band."

With the mention of the Piper's Band, my mind switched to the Borrelli letter.

The sentence, "Ugh, me hoot it 'urts, sonny boy," was written with a Scottish inflection and was a puzzle the police were unable to solve. They couldn't explain how Berkowitz, allegedly the letter's author, had come up with a Scottish phrase; or, more importantly, *why* he did. However, John Carr was interested in playing in a bagpipe band, complete with kilts, while a high school freshman in Yonkers.

"Did he actually join it?" I asked.

"I don't know if he did or not. But he liked the whole idea, and he may have tried out or gone to one of their meetings. Do you remember him now?"

"I think so."

When I pulled out an old yearbook later, I put the name and face together at once. I had indeed known John Carr for one year. But I hadn't seen or thought of him since we were freshmen, sixteen years before. My memories were vague. He was just someone I would occasionally spend some time with between classes or during lunch breaks. We didn't socialize after hours, and Carr transferred to Gorton High the next year. Our paths hadn't crossed again—until now.

I also recalled that he attended Holy Rosary grammar school in Yonkers and, despite the puerile conduct my cousin spoke of, was an intelligent person.

"Catholic schools," I thought, remembering the police belief that the writer of the Borrelli letter had received a Catholic education.

The yearbook picture was too old to be of much use; Carr was only fourteen when it was taken. Nonetheless, his hair color, eyes and cheekbones approximated those in a Son of Sam sketch released after the Lomino-DeMasi woundings. At least the photo didn't rule him out. Little pieces were slowly coming together.

* * *

When I related the Carr story to Mitteager, I did so sheepishly, saying that I should have remembered him.

"Why?" Mitteager asked. "A kid you knew casually sixteen years ago? You didn't even hang out with him after school. Screw it. We've got the information now, and that's more than we had before. We're starting to get a feel for this guy."

We were also starting to get a handle on another early suspect, and the source of the information was former football star Kyle Rote. Rote was a collegiate all-American and Hall of Fame gridiron standout from Southern Methodist University who later starred with the great New York Giants teams of the fifties and early sixties. After retiring, he was a Giants assistant coach for two seasons before branching out into broadcasting, working at WNEW radio and WNBC-TV in New York City. He was also a color commentator on NFL games broadcast nationally by NBC.

We met in 1972 and became close friends over the succeeding years. In November 1977, I was having dinner with him and his wife, Nina, in their Manhattan apartment. While talking about Son of Sam, the Rotes recalled an incident that happened in September, just a month after Berkowitz's arrest. At a business dinner they were introduced to a salesman from Westchester who, as the night passed, inexplicably engaged Nina in a discussion of mysticism and black magic.

"He then lowered his voice and said, 'Son of Sam was in a satanic cult in Yonkers and they helped commit the murders,'" she explained. "I didn't believe him, so I asked him how he knew about it, and he said he was acquainted with some people who were connected to it."

The relevance of this statement by the salesman, whom I will call Roger Flood, is that the assertion was made only weeks after Berkowitz's apprehension, when the public was universally satisfied that Berkowitz was a lone killer. It was long before any reference to a satanic cult was made. Flood also claimed that the group operated in Yonkers. It would turn out that this statement was accurate, too.

Flood would be questioned in the future by investigators for the Queens district attorney's office, who tracked him down on the West Coast. And while he admitted that the meeting with the Rotes occurred, he denied any knowledge of the cult. Since Flood was in California, authorities were left with limited legal means through which to pursue his purported links any further. He either made an extremely accurate guess, or he was in fact aware of the cult's activities. At this time, the answer remains unknown.

* * *

I had just completed compiling some preliminary data on Flood's job history when I received an unexpected phone call on the night of January 3. Bill Gardella wanted to know if we'd contacted the Brooklyn DA's office yet, which we hadn't.

"We talked to them and they're expecting you," the detective sergeant explained. "If you don't call, we're going to make the appointment for you." Gardella was being friendly, but it was apparent he was also serious. I was reasonably certain he, and presumably Kelly, thought we might be on to something. But I also believed he couldn't come out and say so. I decided the phone call spoke for itself, and simply thanked him for his interest.

"I'm just doing my job," Gardella said. "You came in with information that we think should get into the right hands." He gave me Sheldon (Shelly) Greenberg's extension, and said he would learn of the meeting's outcome from the prosecutors.

On January 5, Mitteager and I convened with Greenberg, the chief assistant district attorney, and Ron Aiello, head of the homicide bureau, in Greenberg's office in the court complex in Brooklyn.

Greenberg was a large, assertive man of forty-one. Aiello, who was younger, was more amiable than Greenberg, who opened the ninety-minute meeting by reminding us that a court-imposed "gag order"—which prevented principals from speaking publicly about the case—was now in effect. While the edict applied to comments to the press, we weren't there in that capacity. I thought Greenberg was hiding behind the order, and said so. But he insisted his hands were tied.

"Think of me as a big sponge. I'm here to *absorb* information, so let me soak up what you've got," he pronounced grandly.

Jim and I looked at each other. "And just what do we get in return?" Mitteager asked.

"Nothing. I can't say or release a thing."

For a moment, we were sorely tempted to say sayonara to the "sponge." But we opted to stay, hopeful that in the course of the meeting something would slip out anyway.

We told the prosecutors about John Carr, the Moskowitz scene, the occult references, the dead dogs and Roger Flood's statement about the cult. Both men asked numerous questions. When Aiello saw the Eliphas Levi occult symbol and compared it with Son of Sam's, he whistled: "I'll bet this knocked your socks off when you found it." At another point, Greenberg stated: "I once talked to a girl who knew John Carr."

The hints were dropping, but we wanted more; and we pressed hard to get it. Greenberg kept walking the tightrope. Finally, he blurted: "Don't you think I'm not pissing in my pants wanting to talk to you? I *want* to talk to you—but I can't. So if you don't stop pushing, we'll call this off right now."

"We're not here to fight, Shelly," I said. "We're supposed to be on the same side."

"Look, here's where I stand. We'd like to copy your material, and we want to listen to the rest of your ideas. More than that, I can't do. If you don't like it, you can leave. Otherwise, we'll continue," Greenberg stated.

After nearly five months of work, Greenberg's position was infuriating to us. Aiello attempted to mediate, but he was unsuccessful. After some more bickering, I was clutching at straws.

"Would you at least tell us if you know where John Carr is—just *if* you know—so we can stop looking if you do?"

The bulky prosecutor rested his head on his hands. "For all I know, he's on the moon. . . . Does that answer your question?"

"Shit," Mitteager muttered.

"No, wait," I interjected. "It might answer the question at that. You *don't* know where he is, do you?"

"No comment."

"Look, Shelly," I went on, "your time is valuable and so is ours, believe it or not. We've put in a lot of hours on this, and we came forward to you people. We haven't tried to exploit what we found. All we want to know—without any details—is if there might be some value in all this. Just tell us if we're wasting our time and money pursuing this." I was trying for any left-handed confirmation I could get.

"Word games," Mitteager spat. "Everybody in this room is playing games. It's a bunch of garbage. We're out there trying to get to the truth and you guys sit there like you're anointed. You represent 'the people'—well, we're the people, too."

Greenberg shifted in his chair, pushed his glasses to the tip of his nose and glared at Mitteager. "I will respond to your associate's question by saying that if good citizens feel they have reasons to continue to check on certain things, we're here to listen.

That's listen—not share—listen."

Mitteager groaned.

"That's noble of you, Shelly," I said. "But would I be reading something incorrectly if I took your statement to mean we're *not* wasting our time?"

"No comment. Let me read this gag order to you just in case you haven't heard about it."

Our frustration level had peaked. Fortunately, Aiello chose that moment to take our typewritten material to a secretary for copying. Five minutes later, as we walked to the car, I exploded.

"Those bastards. They danced around the whole time. They took our information and we have zero except for some hints that we're moving in the right direction. They're just trying to cover their tails. I thought Aiello was willing to be reasonable, but Greenberg was the ringmaster in that circus."

"Now *you're* the one who's mad," Jim answered. "You kept the lid on pretty good in there."

"It wasn't easy."

"Well, it wasn't so bad, at least not a total disaster. They did give us a few things. And they would have laughed us out of there if the case really was a lock; they wouldn't have sat there debating with us."

"I don't think there even would have been a meeting with those two if they were so sure Berkowitz was alone," I offered. "First, Gardella calls me; then we meet with Gold's top people—not some fifth-level assistant. And they asked a hell of a lot of questions."

Jim stopped walking and said, "You know, it's possible, just possible, that they didn't know much at all, and that we knew more than they did."

"Who knows? I did hear some nondirect confirmations, and they didn't give us the ten-minute brush-off. But if anything ever comes of this, they'll pretend they did it all and we never existed."

"No, they won't," Mitteager answered. He opened his camera case and pulled out a small tape recorder.

"I don't believe this—you taped them? In Greenberg's own office!"

"Only about two minutes' worth. I wanted to be able to prove we were there. And I wanted John Carr's name on there to prove we warned them about him."

Jim turned on the machine, and we heard ourselves discussing the missing John "Wheaties." Greenberg's pants-wetting comment also was recorded. When I heard that statement, my anger and tension broke and I began to laugh.

"I'm sorry," I stammered, "but the image of him sitting there blustering away and wetting his pants at the same time is too much for me to deal with."

Mitteager grinned. "That arrogant son of a bitch. Maybe he'd like to hear himself saying that on the six o'clock news."

In truth, less than two minutes of conversation appeared on the tape. "If they were up front with us I'd never have turned it on at all," Jim explained. "But once I caught

Greenberg's act, I thought they'd take everything and shaft us the first chance they got if the case ever breaks. Two can play their game."

"O.K., but please, no more of that. Besides not being kosher, it's also risky."

"For all we know they were taping us, too. At least we're even."

At this time, we weren't aware of the confidential police reports and other information available to the DA, or of the office's failure to interview its own witnesses, such as Cacilia Davis. But with this meeting, the Brooklyn district attorney was advised of a probable John Carr and satanic cult link to Berkowitz. The notification was formal, and on the record. And soon, another police agency would receive the same advisements.

I subsequently spoke to Ron Aiello twice. Each time, while evasive, he indicated Mitteager and I weren't chasing the wind. And through another contact in Gold's office, I learned several assistants were shown copies of our material, and that John Carr's whereabouts were unknown by the Brooklyn prosecution.

* * *

There would be fallout from our excursion. Inquiries would be made, rippling a heretofore placid pond. In six weeks the swell would reach significant proportions. But first, an incident that grabbed our attention occurred in New York.

On Friday, January 6, the day after the Brooklyn gathering, the bullet-riddled body of Robert Hirschmann, twenty-five, was found a hundred feet off the Taconic State Parkway in East Fishkill, an hour's drive north of Yonkers. Hirschmann, who had a minor theft record, was shot at least six times. He worked for a moving company and lived in Queens.

The next day his wife, Mary, twenty-three, was found slain in a vacant lot near Flushing Airport in Queens, about sixty miles from where her husband's body was discovered. Fully clothed, she was slashed, stabbed and strangled.

The couple were married seven months earlier and then separated for a time. But three days before the killings, they checked into a room at the Aqua Motor Inn in Queens, near Aqueduct Race Track. They were last seen there the day before their deaths. Hirschmann's body was adorned with tattoos, one of which was a swastika with the words "Brother Tom" beneath it. Hirschmann's first name was Robert, but "Brother Tom" was consistent with a Process ranking and name-change practice.

This double homicide wasn't the first outburst of violence I noted since the arrest of Berkowitz. In October, Suzette Rodriguez, twenty-two, who had a shoplifting record in Yonkers, was shot in the head three times at point-blank range as she stood on a sidewalk in Elmsford, New York, a Westchester village several miles north of Yonkers. Curiously, Rodriguez, who may have been thrown from an auto before being shot, was found dead on a lawn next door to the home of Elmsford's police chief, who heard the shots and saw a light-colored car speed away.

Rodriguez was wearing an occult coiled-snake ring and another ring police euphemistically described as being "popular with gypsies."

Six years later, in the northern New Jersey town of Mountain Lakes, another coiled-snake-ring victim would be found stabbed to death. The young woman, who was unidentified, also wore a satanic pentagram type of ring, which had a crescent moon mounted beneath the star-shaped pentagram. The woman was killed just days before Lammas Day, a major satanic holiday, and she was the fourth woman slain in that area during an eight-month period.

On November 21, 1977, a rifle-toting sniper gunned down thirteen-year-old Natalie Gallace as she stood in her ground-floor apartment in New Rochelle. A family friend, Susan Levy, thirty-eight, was seriously wounded in the 10:40 p.m. attack. A full-sized dark green car with a white vinyl roof was seen racing from the site. Not released by police, and perhaps not even known by them at the time, is the fact that six months earlier—during the height of the Son of Sam spree—a full-sized dark green car with a white vinyl roof was also observed at another bizarre sniper incident in Westchester County. That victim also was a teenaged girl, and she also was shot with a rifle through a ground-floor window. But unlike Natalie Gallace, Lisa Gottlieb survived.

Lisa, sixteen, lived in Greenburgh, a township in central Westchester about fifteen miles from New Rochelle. On a warm night in late May 1977, she was dropped off at her house at 1 a.m. by several friends. The teenagers noticed an unfamiliar, full-sized dark green and white-topped auto parked near Lisa's home. Moments after she entered her residence, a rifle shot—fired through a ground-floor window—wounded her.

Because of the similar green cars, the other common circumstances and the unusual, apparently motiveless nature of both crimes (which remain unsolved), they were noted by me as I looked for something resembling a cult pattern. Their potential importance was raised appreciably three years later when I learned of the satanic cult letter Berkowitz had left behind in his apartment. The wording warned of random attacks on "at least 100" young women and men in the tri-state area of New York, New Jersey and Connecticut.

* * *

What sparked my initial interest in these ground-floor sniper attacks was another series of similar assaults which took place in the same general time frame—with a dart gun.

The assailant was known as the infamous Westchester Dartman (a depiction of "Death" in the Middle Ages), and before he (or they) disappeared, twenty-three women, almost all of whom lived in ground-floor residences, were wounded by inch-long steel darts fired into their heads, necks or chests from a dart gun.

The Dartman prowled the night, selecting ground-floor victims and shooting into their homes in several communities in Westchester—including Yonkers—and Rockland County, which lies across the Hudson River from central and northern Westchester. The Dartman attacks preceded Son of Sam and overlapped other bizarre

Westchester events—commencing on February 28, 1975, in Yonkers and ceasing May 13, 1976, in the Rockland community of Nanuet. It was a strange time, indeed, for Westchester County.

"Strange? Not strange. This is incredible," Mitteager exclaimed as I briefed him on the county's recent crime history. "All of this completely off-the-wall stuff going on at the same time. Fred Cowan shooting up New Rochelle; Son of Sam; dead German shepherds here and eighty-five more an hour away; sniper killings and woundings; a girl with an occult ring blown away in front of a police chief's house; and a god-damned Dartman from out of the fifteenth century or somewhere."

"Oh, and let's not forget the Westchester Child Rapist," I added. "Between April and November of '76 there were about fourteen attacks on young girls between the ages of about ten and eighteen. Most were under fifteen. They got somebody on that."

"Did he do all of them?"

"It's still in the courts. You know how it goes—whether he did or didn't, they'll try to wipe the books clean. What is unusual is that this guy supposedly was driving about five different makes of cars."

"So maybe he didn't do all of them," Mitteager said. "And John Wheaties was called a rapist of young girls."

"I hear you. But all of this wacko stuff going on at once does tend to be curious. And these are just the things we know about. Who knows what we might have missed? None of this has ever happened before."

Mitteager was incredulous. "A Dartman—a Dartman who wounds twenty-three women? This is like the Twilight Zone around here. How many murders occur each year in Westchester?"

"About twenty or twenty-five; no more than that. This is peaceful suburbia."

"Well, it looks like somebody decided to start a war," Mitteager observed. "Some of these things would seem like they'd almost have to be connected, especially if the crime rate is usually steady and the types of crimes aren't as unique as these are."

"I would tend to agree with you. Unfortunately, we have no proof yet."

"Does Dunleavy know about all of this?" Jim asked.

"Not in this context—except for Fred Cowan and the sheps."

*　　*　　*

Steve Dunleavy, in fact, was preoccupied with a phantom telephone caller who was regularly regaling him with lurid tales of a satanic cult to which she insisted Berkowitz belonged. The woman, who contacted Dunleavy several times, had the *Post*'s flamboyant columnist convinced she was at least sincere.

"She's driving me batty, mates. I don't know if she's crazy or not, but she's naming names. I haven't been able to get anywhere with it. Do you think you can find her or any of these people?"

"But she's never given her name. How are we supposed to find out who she is?"

Mitteager complained. "The world goes beyond this city room, Steve. There are millions of people out there."

"But it would make sense if we could locate her before going off on what could be a fool's errand as far as these other conspirators go," I said. "It's funny, though, there's not a word about Westchester in here."

The story merits repeating because its future implications would be considerable. Briefly, the mystery lady charged that Berkowitz belonged to a devil cult operating in Queens and Staten Island. She claimed that a station wagon belonging to a girl named Jane was used in the Moskowitz murder and then abandoned in a pile of rushes adjacent to Little Neck Bay, off the Cross Island Parkway in Queens. Jane had then been chopped up and dumped into the bay.

She named a former NYPD detective as one of the cult's dope suppliers, and said he could be found by surveilling the Blue Dolphin diner in Queens. More murders were planned. The cult's leader was said to be an accountant and former drug user, whom I will call Reeve Carl Rockman.* Rockman maintained two addresses, one of which was very proximate to the Son of Sam killing ground in Forest Hills. A major cult "safe house," complete with Black Mass ceremonies, was said to be located at an address on Van Duzer Street in Staten Island.

The information was too detailed and specific that Dunleavy rightly was intrigued by it. With a copy of the woman's latest letter in hand, I met George Austin after work at Gambelli's restaurant in White Plains on January 25, a Wednesday night. After reading the note, he asked, "What are you going to do about all this? She talks about a mutilation murder three years ago and says they used a hairbrush on the girl—and Berkowitz witnessed it?"

"That's just the thing, George. That crime *did* happen. We checked it out today—and the hairbrush part was never made public."

"So she knows?"

"She sure as hell knows something. Jim lives on Staten Island, and he's sniffing around that Van Duzer house tonight. He'll get plate numbers, but no one's going near that front door. Who knows what the hell is going on in there?"

"And you have no idea who wrote the letter?"

"Not a hint. She told Dunleavy on the phone that she knew people in the group and was getting out of town in fear of her life."

"What about the police?"

"No way. They don't want to hear about any conspiracy, and if we turned it over to the Brooklyn DA, we'd never know what happened. We're staying on our own from now on."

"Why not the Queens DA, Santucci, or Merola in the Bronx?"

"For what? It's all a big runaround. Everyone we've seen so far is stonewalling. It's horseshit trying to get to the bottom of all this and seeing the 'public protectors' covering their butts. Mitteager's right. He says the truth doesn't count—it's politics and perception that's important. The system takes care of its own. All this work we're doing is outside the system's appraisal of the case."

My evaluation was based on more than our Brooklyn experience. I had made one additional pilgrimage, and it would soon prove to be a consequential journey.

Not at all convinced that Brooklyn would follow up on the local Yonkers activities we suspected, I spent more than an hour with Sal D'Iorio, the Westchester Sheriff's Department's chief of criminal investigations, to inform him about the satanic cult connections we'd uncovered concerning Berkowitz, John Carr and the dead German shepherds.

I explained to D'Iorio that despite contrary statements by the Carrs and the NYPD, we strongly suspected that Berkowitz and John Carr, at least, were acquainted, and that both may well have belonged to a Westchester-based satanic cult. John Carr, I told D'Iorio, was our top suspect. I gave D'Iorio a copy of the material we'd earlier provided to Brooklyn, and explained that while I knew the .44 homicides weren't in his jurisdiction, any regionalized cult activities or crimes were in his domain. It was hoped that both investigatory ends could meet in the middle.

I also discussed another topic with D'Iorio. It concerned his department's investigation of the four threatening letters Berkowitz anonymously sent to volunteer sheriff's deputy Craig Glassman. I was very interested in confirming that a certain return address—that of Berkowitz's former New Rochelle landlord—appeared on one of those envelopes. D'Iorio avoided that issue.

The meeting transpired in mid-January, shortly before Jim and I received the Dunleavy letter. When I left D'Iorio's office in Valhalla, I didn't know that he would soon begin a quiet investigation, which meant—strictly speaking—that the .44 case was reopened then on at least a limited, local basis. Among other things, the department would begin to make inquiries about John Carr. D'Iorio, whom I contacted occasionally thereafter, never revealed that a John Carr probe had begun. I later learned why.

D'Iorio would attempt to wash his hands of any culpability, but he would become, perhaps unwillingly, a player in the game of cover-up which was about to begin anew. Technically, he would claim noninvolvement on jurisdictional grounds, but one will be able to judge the extent of his responsibility—with the cloak of territorial innocence removed.

In fairness to D'Iorio, it's possible he protected his standing in his department's hierarchy by adhering to Son of Sam marching orders dictated by the man who was then his boss, Sheriff Thomas Delaney. Delaney was a former captain in the New York City Police Department. The NYPD was engaged in an all-out battle to protect its "sole killer" interests in the .44 case, and Delaney's ties there were numerous.

We didn't know it, but the clock had now begun to wind down on Mr. John Wheaties Carr. We had set it in motion ourselves.

*   *   *

Standing at the bar in Gambelli's, George and I continued rehashing the frightening Dunleavy letter as the night wore on. At about 8 p.m., an acquaintance named Jim Duffy took over our side of the serving area as the bartenders changed shifts. Duffy, thirty-two, wore glasses and sported curly brown hair and a friendly demeanor. He knew of my involvement with the Sam case, and asked me how the conspiracy hunt was going.

"Tell him about the letter," George suggested.

"Yeah, this is the latest entry in the sweepstakes. Some unknown woman is calling Steve Dunleavy and sending him letters about this Satan cult. It's eerie stuff, to put it mildly."

"What's she saying?" Duffy asked.

"Blood, gore, murder and mayhem. She names a couple of people and says there's some supposed cult house out on Staten Island."

"Staten Island?"

"Yeah, my partner lives out there and he's checking on it now."

"Where on Staten Island?" Duffy wanted to know. "I used to go to college there, at Wagner."

"Well, I don't know Staten Island, but this address is on Van Duzer Street."

Duffy's eyes widened like globes. "Where on Van Duzer? I used to live on Van Duzer. It's a small residential street."

"Really? Then maybe you'd know where this is. It's number 583." Duffy dropped the bar towel. "*That's* the house I rented a room in!"

George opened his coat like a cop flashing a badge. "You're under arrest. . . . Search this man for dog biscuits."

I was laughing. "Great collar—put him on the chain gang."

"Yes, as soon as we shepherd him out of here."

"Hey, you shitheads—I really did live at 583 Van Duzer Street," Duffy insisted.

We weren't buying the story at all. There were millions of addresses in the New York area, and it was statistically impossible that the second person I'd tell about 583 Van Duzer would have lived there at one time. Moreover, it was at least forty miles from White Plains. But Duffy remained adamant. After another five minutes of deriding him, I decided to put an end to his joke.

"You claim you lived there nine or ten years ago when you were in college. Who owned the house then?"

"The Meehans."

"First name?"

"Jack—actually John. John Meehan."

I went to the pay phone and dialed information to learn if a John Meehan still resided at 583 Van Duzer in Staten Island. In a minute, I was back at the bar. I gave Duffy a quizzical look. "You'll be interested in knowing that they're still there."

George was startled. "Jesus Christ, it's for real—could your old landlord be running a cult house, Duffy?"

Duffy was suddenly as mystified as we were. In the right-wrong debate about the address itself, he'd forgotten why the subject was broached in the first place.

"Awww, no. No way. They're a nice family. They couldn't be involved in any of this deranged stuff."

"The letter says they are. Maybe something snapped out there since you lived in the house, or maybe they've got some boarders into this thing and the Meehans don't even know about it," I suggested. We were all still shaken by the incalculable coincidence.

"Hell, after tonight anything's possible, I guess," Duffy replied. "But I still can't believe the Meehans—I can't believe *any* of this is happening!" It was time for a plan. Without Duffy, we could be staking out the house for months. We needed to get inside, and Duffy could provide a way in—through the front door. I asked the stunned bartender if he'd accompany us to Staten Island the next night, and told him Mitteager, who had police experience, would come along.

"You know them," I explained. "We'll all knock at the door. You can say you were visiting Jim and me and stopped by to say hello for old times' sake. We'll play it by ear from there."

"I don't know. That letter sounded pretty specific. If it's accurate it could be dangerous out there."

"Come on," I said lightly, "the Meehans know who you are. They're not going to butcher you in the basement. Even killers take a night off now and then." I was smiling, but didn't feel any mirth. The potential for danger did exist.

Duffy thought for a long moment. "O.K. I'll do it. This might be something to tell my grandchildren someday."

* * *

The next night, after convincing Mitteager that he, too, wasn't being set up for some diabolical joke, we knocked on the door of 583 Van Duzer, a quaint wooden house on a narrow street. Before approaching, we took down plate numbers of all nearby cars and looked around the back of the house. The Meehans, to our relief, seemed like a pleasant, middle-aged couple. But we wanted to meet their children, and then there was the matter of any boarders in the house.

As the Meehans and Duffy talked over old times, Mitteager and I, trying to appear unconcerned, took in as much of the surroundings—and the Meehans—as we could. At one point, their son arrived, and we eyed him cautiously. Finally, after a prearranged signal, Duffy timidly mentioned that Jim and I were reporters who wanted to discuss "something" with them.

I grimaced. Duffy was supposed to ask the first tentative question so as not to alert or alarm the couple, but he tossed the ball to us instead. Fortunately, Jim was ready for it.

"Have you had any kind of trouble recently with anyone in the neighborhood?"

It was a safe, nonthreatening question, and if it struck the right nerve, a floodgate could open.

"Now that's something out of the blue. How did you know about that?"

"We'd rather hear it from you, Mr. Meehan, if you don't mind," I responded.

Meehan and his wife, at ease because Duffy was with us, said that a "strange woman" who wore "long robes" had lived in the neighborhood until several months previous. The woman, they said, would "stare at the house all the time" and stop their son and say, "I know who you are and what you're involved with. Don't think you're going to get away with it."

"When did this start?" I asked.

"Last summer. She wasn't really threatening to us, she was just very strange," Mrs. Meehan answered.

I then threw out the name of another Staten Island resident—from a different neighborhood—whom Dunleavy's caller accused of being a cult member.

"Do you know a Mike Wollman*?"

"Yes, of course we do. He's a good friend of our son."

"Does he come to this house?" Jim asked.

"Yes."

After another series of questions to both the Meehans and their son to satisfy ourselves they were being truthful, we knew right where we stood.

"Do you happen to know the name of this 'strange' woman and where she lived?" Jim inquired.

"No," Mrs. Meehan replied. "We don't know her name, but she lived down the street. An elderly woman named Erna owns a two-family house. This woman, her husband and I think a black girl lived on the other floor. They rented from Erna, who is a sweet, harmless old lady. I don't think she'd know anything."

"Would you show us the house and introduce us?" Jim questioned.

"Sure, Jack will take you down there."

Jim and I had been circumspect about our reason for talking to the Meehans. But as we left their house, Jack Meehan asked, "So what's this all about, fellows? Is this woman in trouble?"

"It wasn't her, Mr. Meehan, it was you," I replied. "You're supposed to be David Berkowitz's accomplices and hold Black Masses in your basement."

Meehan, flabbergasted, stopped dead in his tracks. After we summarized the allegations, he was enraged at the letter-writing "strange woman."

"She should be thrown in jail," he stormed. "And telling this to the newspapers! God knows who else she slandered us to!"

"We're not sure it's her yet," I said. "But *you* just found out about this tonight. She's been haunting Dunleavy for months—that should make you feel at least a little better."

"I'm afraid it doesn't," Meehan said.

"It would if you knew Dunleavy," Jim deadpanned, but Meehan just gave him a blank stare.

"Don't worry," Jim added quickly. "We're upset about this, too. We're not sure yet it's this woman, but we're going to try to find out."

Erna Wagner was a frail, white-haired woman well into her eighties. She was infirm, hard of hearing, and couldn't understand much of what we were saying. Her home was filled with statues of various saints and the Blessed Virgin. She kept no records, and couldn't remember the name of her former tenant. We were about to give up when I asked if she'd ever heard from the lady again.

A spark of recognition lit the old woman's eyes, and she hobbled to a bureau and produced a letter. On the envelope was a name and return address in Bayside, Queens. The enclosed message was rife with crosses and symbols and mentioned the Meehans, Son of Sam, bodies in Little Neck Bay and Black Masses on Van Duzer Street. The writer claimed she was on a "secret mission" for the police. "Hush, Erna, you must not tell anyone," the letter warned.

"We got her," I exclaimed. "And she's got this poor old woman caught up in this dreadful stuff." I looked at Ema. "Are you O.K.? Does any of this frighten you?" I asked, indicating the letter.

Ema shrugged her sloped shoulders. "I don't see so well," she whispered. "You mean you weren't able to read this?"

"Only a little. But she told me about bad people."

"And how did you feel about that?" Jim almost shouted.

Erna gestured toward her myriad statues. "I pray."

We asked Ema if we could take the letter and envelope with us, and she handed them to Jim. As gently as possible, we told her there was nothing to fear in the neighborhood; and Jack Meehan came in and assured her he'd stop by frequently to see how she was getting along. And then we left Ema Wagner; alone and feeble as we'd found her, but perhaps with a sense of security she hadn't felt in months.

*　　*　　*

"Veronica Lueken? Are you guys sure?" Steve Dunleavy was shocked that we'd solved his five-month mystery in two days. "How the hell did you ever come up with this? This is great work, mates."

"Just good detective work, Steve."

"How'd you ever figure out it was her?"

"That's a long story," Jim said. He and I decided to refrain from telling Dunleavy about the ten-million-to-one shot involving Duffy.

"After we found out it was her, we went looking for this Jane Jacklin* who was supposed to be fish food in Little Neck Bay," I continued. "It turns out Jane is still alive; we found her, too. She told us the cops practically broke down her door a few months ago because someone called to tell them a murder was taking place."

"Then we went to Lueken's house in Bayside," Mitteager explained. "Her husband let us in. He seemed O.K., like he didn't know what was going on. Their number is unlisted, but I asked to use the phone and copied it off the dial. She was in the house, but wouldn't come out of the bedroom—the chickenshit bitch."

Dunleavy was astonished. "What about the cult and this Reeve Carl Rockman who's the leader?"

"If there's a cult she knows about, it's not in that house on Staten Island," I said. "We checked out Rockman. He does exist, with two addresses under two different names—which is interesting. In one listing he's 'Reeve C. Rockman' and in the other he's 'Reeve T. Carl.' But what does it all mean? This whole thing is Lueken's hallucination."

"That's right," Jim said. "She had a chance to explain when we went to her house, but she dove under the bed."

Dunleavy was shaking his head in disbelief. "Hey, Steve," Jim said, "the letter did sound legit; it had a lot of detail and specifics. It had all of us going. But it's bullshit."

"Christ, but you guys didn't talk to her. She was driving me crazy with these phone calls and this sinister plot. She sounded believable; she really did."

"To her, it probably *seems* real," I added. "That's why she was so convincing. I'd love for us to write something about all this, but it would only hurt the investigation. But can you see the headline? 'FAMOUS SEER OF BAYSIDE EXPOSED.'"

* * *

In a real way, Veronica Lueken was in fact famous. Since 1970, the heavyset, middle-aged housewife and mother had been known to countless New Yorkers and others in the United States and Canada as the woman who periodically packed the former World's Fair grounds in Queens with devout believers who listened to the Virgin Mary and Christ speak through the mouth of—Veronica Lueken.

Lueken's legions numbered in the many thousands. Busloads of the faithful would depart for hallowed Queens from points throughout the country when they received "the word" that Mary or Her Son was about to enlighten them with a new series of messages transmitted through Lueken's trancelike meditations, which took place in full view of the hordes of pilgrims.

One cannot help but wonder how the multitudes would have responded had they known that this living embodiment of Mary and Jesus was filling her idle hours with scurrilous accusations.

Lueken's society, which did not discourage contributions from believers, issued a variety of literature, including a newspaper called *Michael Fighting*, which was named for the Archangel Michael. The publications fervently reported the Sacred Word, as spoken by Veronica, who foretold of World War III, the end of civilization, earthquakes, floods and other natural disasters unless humankind reversed its evil course.

During these public pronouncements, thousands of ears heard and thousands of eyes read the Blessed Mother's kind words for Veronica herself. This phenomenon would occasionally spawn another minor miracle—the simultaneous opening of hundreds of wallets and purses.

Veronica-Mary-Jesus frequently bemoaned the dangers of temptation in the modern world, and did so by reminding her disciples that Satan was very much about in the twentieth century. The evil serpent, who lost a heavenly battle to the Archangel Michael, was seeking an earthly inroad via infiltration of the media, the entertainment business and certainly world government.

Veronica's visions, which she vividly described to the throngs of believers as they were occurring, would invariably involve great flashes of light in the sky—which only Veronica could see—before the Virgin or Christ appeared. Frequently, the Blessed Mother would shed tears as she recounted, through Veronica, the dark times to come unless mankind chose the path to salvation. The Communists and Russia were also routinely discussed on the heavenly hotline.

Lueken was shielded from her disciples during her visionary sessions by a carefully chosen honor guard of white-bereted followers. She counts among her membership a number of police and fire officials.

Not surprisingly, Lueken's preaching has been viewed with a measure of disdain by the Archdiocese of New York; and she and her followers have caused headaches for the NYPD and other law enforcement agencies over matters such as crowd control, freedom of assembly, trespassing, permits and the like. Scuffles have been reported occasionally as her followers surged against the white-beret platoons of bodyguards.

And now Veronica had been feeding us vile information—anonymously, she had thought—about the Son of Sam case. Dunleavy, Mitteager and I consigned her allegations to a circular file in early February 1978. Little did we know she would surface again.

*   *   *

The determination that the Lueken allegations were false had taken but a few days, but its depressing effect lingered. The anticipation that a break might have been in the offing was high; the ensuing crash discouraging. With his shining star, Lueken, burned out in a flash of futility, Dunleavy became temporarily moribund. There also was no word from Brooklyn or the Sheriff's Department in Westchester; and we were now of the belief none would be forthcoming.

John Carr, our chief suspect, was still among the missing, and prosecution efforts to convict Berkowitz as a lone killer were grinding through the judicial system. Essentially, we were nearly out of options. We'd made the attempt, but were now on the brink of failure.

On the eighth of February, a blizzard buried New York and my downstairs neighbors threw an open-air fish fry in defiance of Mother Nature. On the ninth, I ventured through the snow to see *Saturday Night Fever,* whose Brooklyn discotheque setting reminded me of the previous summer's .44 shootings. Given my state of mind, I could have done without the flashback.

I saw the film with a new acquaintance, a pretty physical therapist from

Mamaroneck whom I was seeing socially because my wife and I had separated a few months before. We'd made a sincere effort, but the mutual magic had eroded. We did, however, remain friendly.

On Saturday, February 11, I cut through the remaining snow drifts and drove by the Carr home in Yonkers for the first time in more than two weeks. In the large driveway, I vacantly noted the usual assortment of autos, most of which belonged to operators who worked for Carr's telephone answering service. There was one vehicle I hadn't seen there before, a blue 1971 Mercury. Unlike the others, it was still covered with snow—to the extent that I couldn't read its license plate. I was about to drive on when I started to think about that snow, which suggested the car hadn't been moved for at least several days.

Looking around the street, I saw no one. It was dusk, it was cold, and most people were indoors. I took a small pad and a pen from my glove compartment, pulled over and cautiously ventured up the driveway. Quickly, I knelt out of sight of the house and scraped the snow from the rear license plate. It was North Dakota plate number 462-653.

I had finally found John Wheaties Carr.

XI

Blood in the Badlands

I was too young to remember that October day in 1951 when Bobby Thomson hit the dramatic ninth-inning home run that lifted the New York Giants to a stunning, come-from-behind pennant win over the Brooklyn Dodgers in one of the most emotional moments in sports history. But through film clips, the past comes to life: the line drive hooking into the Polo Grounds' left field stands; Thomson dancing around the bases as players and fans flood the field; announcer Russ Hodges screaming, "The Giants win the pennant! The Giants win the pennant!"

It was a Polo Grounds in miniature that roared in my head as I drove from the Carr home with the treasured plate number safely in hand. From the depths of the valley, the pinnacle was suddenly visible through the clouds. It was time to begin stalking John Carr.

I immediately contacted Mitteager and we formulated a plan. During the next week I cruised by the house nightly, hoping to catch a glimpse of the elusive suspect. The strategy was to stick with him if he went out, on the chance he might lead us to others. We also hoped to photograph him from a distance. But by the following Friday, the car, still laden with snow, hadn't moved. Still not discouraged, Jim and I decided to maintain the sporadic surveillance for as long as it took.

Since neither Brooklyn nor Westchester authorities contacted us again, we returned the favor by not informing either agency that Carr was located. But I'd later learn that the Sheriff's Department, in the course of the secret probe we sparked, noticed the auto, too.

On Saturday, February 18, I was preparing breakfast when the phone rang. It was my mother on the line, calling from the family home in Connecticut.

"What's new in your little corner of the world?" I asked.

"There's something you need to know," she replied.

"What is it?"

"John Carr is dead."

*   *   *

At first, I refused to believe it. Then slowly, like an insidious rip tide, the realization slapped at my heels, rose up suddenly and swept me away with a thunderous crescendo.

"What the hell . . . John Carr dead . . . How do you know?" The questions flew in a staccato burst of confusion and panic.

"I don't know. I don't know. There's a little death notice in this morning's Westchester paper. It's not a full obituary——just a small paragraph in that column of notices. No details or anything. Just that it happened Thursday in Minot, North

Dakota."

"Dakota? Thursday? It must be somebody else. His car is sitting in the driveway on Warburton Avenue. I've been watching it all week."

"No, it's him," she insisted.

"Then are you sure it doesn't say he was *from* North Dakota? He's been out there on and off for years."

"It definitely says *in* Minot, North Dakota. What are you going to do now?"

"I don't know. I never would have expected this to happen. I've got to reach Jim. I'll get back to you."

Mitteager, in the midst of a lazy Saturday on Staten Island, was astounded, upset and excited all at once.

"He's *dead?* For six months you chase a guy. He lives all these years just fine, and just like that he's gone after we turn him in to Brooklyn and Westchester. This is one hell of a development."

We then realized we had to learn just what happened to Carr. For all we knew he had been ill or hit by a bus. Mitteager volunteered to contact the Minot police to find out. A long, nervous hour later he was back on the phone.

"Listen to this carefully 'cause you're not going to believe it. It was violent—gunshot. And they think it's murder, although there's a chance it could be suicide. But they're treating it as a homicide! Either way, the guy is dead violently right in the wake of our handing him over."

I was too startled to answer.

"You know what this means, don't you?" Jim prodded.

"Yes, but for Christ's sake, what a way to find out for sure."

"If he was murdered, and he was Berkowitz's accomplice, that would mean there's someone else out there, too," Jim continued. "Someone who shut him up."

"Yes," I agreed. "Either somebody caught up with him before we did or he heard something, freaked out and knocked himself off. There are no other choices here."

"Hell no. Not with this timing," Jim concurred. "And they've got no motive out there. Now, we've got to pull all this together and get the story out. With any luck, everyone else will miss that little death notice and nobody knows he's John Wheaties, anyway. That Greenberg in Brooklyn will croak over this one."

"I'm down there watching the guy's car and he's out in Dakota disappearing from the planet," I said quietly. "It just doesn't seem possible. Why in hell is his car in Yonkers?"

"Because he just flew back to Dakota from here the other day. In a hurry," Jim answered.

"Damn. I wonder if I was seen in the driveway."

"I don't know. But son of a bitch, we're in the middle of the biggest of them all," Jim stated.

It took several hours for the import of Carr's death to register fully. On the one hand, it vividly demonstrated the plausibility of my long-held suspicions. But for the first time, the fear factor also surfaced. Someone—some unknown force—had likely emerged from the netherworld of the investigation and struck down John Carr. But why now? Had that person heard of our work, and would he look for us next?

For months, I'd believed my analysis of the case was accurate, but it was frequently an academic exercise—written reports, interviews and remote observations and digging. Not anymore. Now, the crushing reality of death set in.

Moreover, if Carr was in fact slain, there was a conspiracy of at least three. But how many more? The specter of satanic cult involvement loomed ominously over the investigation.

For the next four days, we scrambled to tie the story together. On the afternoon of the twentieth I phoned Sal D'Iorio at the Sheriff's Department to tell him Carr was dead. D'Iorio said he just heard about it and asked what we'd discovered. I briefed him and wanted to know what, in light of our meeting of a month before, he was going to do about the Carr connection. D'Iorio acknowledged that his office was now looking into the occult in Westchester County. "But we're not into the Sam case per se. That's someone else's case," he said.

D'Iorio was evasive and didn't tell me that his force's inquiry had already widened. But he confirmed that a conversation occurred between his department and the Brooklyn DA. "They're not dismissing any of this, but they won't admit it to you," he hinted.

I'd later learn there was a significant exchange between Westchester and the Brooklyn prosecution.

Meanwhile, implying he was an official investigator, Mitteager cultivated a source within OSI, the Air Force police agency. OSI was involved in the case because Carr's death occurred in the bedroom of a housing unit on the Minot Air Force base. Carr, it turned out, had left the Air Force sixteen months earlier. The home was that of his girlfriend, Linda O'Connor, whose estranged serviceman husband, Craig, had moved off the base.

The information we received was sketchy. But we did learn that Carr closely resembled the Son of Sam composite drawing released after the Lomino-DeMasi shooting, and that he owned a fatigue jacket and was left-handed. The gunman fled that scene carrying the .44 in his left hand and appeared to have worn a fatigue jacket.

The OSI source also reported that Carr wasn't despondent before his death, which pointed to murder; had expressed a "passing interest" in witchcraft and that his brother, Michael, "counseled people in Scientology."

On the night of the twentieth, Jim and I staked out the Yonkers funeral home where Carr was being waked, writing down license plate numbers. Unknown to us, the Sheriff's Department was doing the same thing; we probably flagged the plate numbers of an official car or two.

Fortunately, the rest of the media missed the death notice, and at 6 p.m. on February 21 Mitteager and I sat at adjacent typewriters in the *Post* city room to pound out the copy for the next day's editions.

But something happened along the way. Somehow, the probable homicide turned into an "apparent" suicide as Dakota officials suddenly steered our inquiries away from murder. Mitteager and I fought to keep the muddled circumstances intact in the story, but were overruled.

We also knew that Minot authorities had received calls from Westchester Sheriff's investigators, the Yonkers police, and the Brooklyn DA's office and 10th Homicide, where our recent visits were clearly remembered. The "closed" .44 case was ajar, after all. However, those details were also edited from the story, as was a sidebar piece that raised other questions about the Son of Sam case, including the contradictions at the Moskowitz scene.

The *Post* was jittery and chose extreme caution—especially since a call to the DA's office produced a comment that Gold's people "tended to discount any connection" between Carr's death and the .44 case. That was a fallacy, and we knew it. But we lost a concerted battle to publish a comprehensive story.

On Wednesday, February 22, the compromise version of the article appeared on page one under the headline: "SON OF REAL SAM KILLS HIMSELF." To our dismay, the death was called a suicide, the result of last-minute editing after Mitteager and I left the paper.

The story reported that Carr left North Dakota in late January and drove to New York, telling Minot friends he wouldn't be back for months. (Like us, he was unaware that authorities, because of our initiative, were now interested in locating him.) But then, said Ward County, North Dakota, Sheriff's Lt. Terry Gardner, "He suddenly changed his mind and flew back here. We don't know why. We don't know what went on in New York."

Carr was in Yonkers for just ten days before leaving his Mercury behind and flying into Minot in the early evening hours of Tuesday, February 14. Two nights later he was dead.

Carr's skull was demolished by a bullet fired into his mouth from a .30-30 Marlin rifle on the night of the sixteenth in Ms. O'Connor's home while she was out for the evening, the story said.

The rifle, which was owned by Linda's husband, belonged in the house. It was found lying in a peculiar position, on top of the dead man's leg. No suicide note was written.

The article described the "John Wheaties" alias in the Breslin letter and compared it to the John Wheat Carr listing in the Westchester telephone directory.

The story also mentioned that official sources in New York City discounted any link between Carr and Berkowitz, but Gardner was quoted as saying: "If I were them, I'd be interested in that angle, but that's not my jurisdiction. Our own investigation is completed."

No, it wasn't. Gardner deliberately played with the truth, but it would be eighteen months before I'd learn why he did so.

*   *   *

That night, with the story on the streets, I watched the early evening newscasts, which reported the information as it appeared in the *Post*. Later, I joined Tom Bartley, his wife, Madeline, and other friends for a Westchester nightclub performance by the Drifters, a well-known rock group of the late fifties and early sixties. Our table was festive, my date enjoyable, and even Bartley had praise for the work done on John Carr.

"You may really have something here, after all," he said.

I arrived home late, only to be awakened by a 7 a.m. phone call from Mitteager's wife, Carol. She was close to tears.

"Where were you?" she asked. "I was trying to get you until three this morning. There's big trouble."

"Take it easy, Carol. Tell me what's up," I soothed, still weary from the night's celebration.

Carol broke down and began sobbing.

"Jim's been arrested!" she cried.

Suddenly I was wide awake. Not nine hours after the Carr story appeared, and while I was out singing "Under the Boardwalk" with a gathering of friends, Jim was hustled off to jail and charged with bribery of a guard in the "Sam Sleeps" photo epic.

The investigation was conducted by the Department of Correction and the State Special Prosecutor's office, which was mandated to root out corruption in official agencies. The timing of the arrest was highly suspicious, although authorities said the indictment was secured some days before. Still, it wasn't acted on until the article was published in the *Post*.

In effect, Mitteager was removed from the conspiracy probe, and his reputation and credibility were tarnished by the charges, which carried a possible prison term of up to seven years.

He was held overnight in a Manhattan jail before being arraigned and released on his own recognizance pending a trial. Hearing the numbing news from Carol, who at this time didn't know if or when Jim would be freed, I was speechless. The mercurial emotions of the last thirteen days, beginning with the discovery of John Carr's auto on February 11, had finally taken their toll. I hung up the phone immobilized, not knowing where to turn or what to do.

At the same time, officials in New York City and Westchester were pointedly denying the relevance of the *Post* article and privately castigating the paper for speculative reporting. The story was dead in a day. The rest of the media reported the denials, and the *Post*, stung by the reaction, would back away from the conspiracy hunt and not venture forth again—even though information I uncovered that day showed Carr was being sought for questioning by New York authorities at the time of his death.

After several hours, I summoned the presence of mind to call Peter Michelmore at the *Post*. I told him of the arrest, which he already knew about, and informed him that I just learned New York authorities had wanted to question Carr. Michelmore wasn't interested.

"We got blasted by every cop and prosecutor in town for running that story," he said. "I think we're right, you think we're right and Dunleavy thinks we're right—but they've pulled the rug out from under us. We've got nowhere to go on this anymore. It's over."

"And what about Jim?" I asked. "You had him at Kings County, me up here, and you people were coordinating the whole thing. I never wanted those damned pictures to run, Peter. I swore it would cut us off from Berkowitz, and it sure did that. And now Jim's in goddamned jail over it." Michelmore was sympathetic but unmoved. "Jim wasn't working for us. He was working for himself. As a freelance reporter, he supplied information and was paid for it."

I realized what Michelmore was saying. "So you're cutting yourselves off from him—no legal assistance, no standing behind him?"

"I'm sorry about it, but he was working for himself. We didn't know anything about any arrangements between him and this guard."

"I find that a little difficult to believe, Peter."

"Well, that's the way it was and that's all there is to say about it."

"And what about Son of Sam and Carr?"

"Like I said, we're dead in the water. They got us good on that story." And so the conversation ended.

Later in the day, Mitteager vehemently denied that the *Post* was unaware his source was a Department of Correction guard.

"They knew all along. They even supplied the spy camera used to take those damn pictures. I told the photo editor to preset the damn thing because the guy taking the pictures was an amateur and wouldn't know how to work it otherwise."

I was ignorant of any financial agreements between Mitteager and the *Post* or between Mitteager and the guard. Money was a subject we never discussed. In fact, it was mid-January, six weeks after the photos were published, before Mitteager even told me a guard had taken them. He didn't offer any other details, nor would I have expected him to do so. I did learn, however, that the reason it took so long to receive Berkowitz's replies to my questions was that the guard, Herb Clarke, had only sporadic access to the alleged .44-Caliber Killer.

"They got along well," Mitteager explained. "And Clarke would often be in Berkowitz's area and say hello and all. But he needed to be alone with him to get the questions answered. That's why it took so long."

In fact, Clarke's inability to sit with Berkowitz more often set the stage for Mitteager's apprehension. Jim asked if Clarke knew a guard who had more access to Berkowitz, and Clarke recommended Frank Jost. Mitteager met with Jost in a Staten Island restaurant and told him he was hopeful Berkowitz could be enticed to unravel the conspiracy. He asked if Jost would deal with Berkowitz and get the information out. Jost reported the conversation to his superiors.

At the same time, authorities had become suspicious of Clarke and confronted him. Clarke was then offered immunity from prosecution in exchange for his testimony against Mitteager. With his permission, Clarke's phone was then tapped and officials monitored his conversations with Mitteager. Among them were comments Jim made about the Carr case before the *Post* article appeared, which included information he'd gleaned from the OSI source in North Dakota.

"Why they would give immunity to a civil employee, a guard who did act improperly, to go after a writer is something I'll never understand," Mitteager said. He insisted he was advised by the *Post* that his work was within the law. He prepared to mount a defense based on the contention that he acted as an agent of the paper in his dealings with Clarke and was made a scapegoat—singled out for "selective prosecution."

"I never thought of it as bribery," he said. "I was after a story and trying to help crack this case open if I could. I told Clarke, and it was on their tapes, that I knew I wasn't doing anything illegal and I hoped he was sure he was covered in that respect."

Mitteager said the photos, which had no connection to the conspiracy probe, were taken at the urging of both Clarke and the *Post*. "Clarke wanted money; so he pushed for the pictures. And the *Post* wanted them, too. I was in the middle of it. I did want a full-time job at the *Post,* and I was trying to earn a living. The money from the pictures did help me out there."

*   *   *

With the *Post* out of the picture, so to speak, Mitteager under indictment and the John Carr link officially denied, I was left without a partner, a suspect or a public forum. I continued some halfhearted work on the case, specifically on Michael Carr, but my main preoccupation was with the fatal reversal of fortune. It was almost as if John Carr never existed. But he did.

*   *   *

John Charles Carr was born in Yonkers on October 12, 1946. He shared a birthday with the notorious black magician and cultist Aleister Crowley.

Carr attended Holy Rosary Grammar School in Yonkers, spent one year at a Catholic high school there and then graduated from Gorton High. He apparently enrolled at an upstate New York college, but left to join the Air Force, where he remained a dozen years. He was discharged—allegedly for drug and disciplinary reasons—on October 13, 1976, the day after his thirtieth birthday. Carr had been stationed in Thailand, Korea and Panama City, Florida, before transferring to the large Strategic Air Command (SAC) base outside Minot in the summer of 1972.

His military specialty was aircraft maintenance, and at Minot he was assigned to the 5th Fighter Interceptor Squadron, performing mechanical work on the F-106. He took some courses, including accounting and psychology, at Minot State College while in the military, and was a staff sergeant at the time of his discharge. After leaving the service, Carr shuttled back and forth between Minot and Yonkers.

Authorities placed him in the New York area at the time of at least four, and probably five, Son of Sam attacks, including the Lomino-DeMasi shooting, whose composite he closely resembled. He was also in New York at the time of the Christine Freund homicide in January 1977 and the shooting outside the Elephas discotheque on June 26 of that year. He also was believed to have been in New York at the time of the Donna Lauria murder in July 1976 and that of Stacy Moskowitz on July 31, 1977.

Carr was married and divorced by 1974, and had a daughter who was five years old at the time of his death. (Her name, and that of her mother, will be withheld here out of respect for their privacy.) Friends dated Carr's deteriorating slide to the aftermath of the divorce.

Carr's ex-wife remarried and moved to Beaumont, Texas—near Houston, site of the .44 purchase. Carr was known to visit that area, and his brother, Michael, told Linda O'Connor that John was in Houston on June 12, 1976—the day Berkowitz obtained his .44 Bulldog.

Carr, police said, was a moderate-to-heavy user of marijuana and psychedelic drugs, and he was hospitalized on three occasions in 1976–77 for drug overdoses. Police also stated that Carr dealt drugs in Minot, and perhaps in New York, an assertion supported by several of his friends who admitted buying narcotics from him on a regular basis. He was also a heavy drinker—a fact which I'd later learn was known by Berkowitz, who considered him "unstable" and "a weak link."

In the months preceding his death, Carr received drug therapy and underwent psychiatric counseling as well. A bottle of Haldol, a powerful prescription drug used to treat psychiatric disorders, was found in the O'Connor home in Minot. It was Carr's medicine.

In the months before his death, he was on the move. He was in New York for several weeks in June 1977, where, among other things, he attended a circus with a Long Island friend. He returned to Minot, traveled to Austin, Texas, for unknown reasons in mid-July and apparently was back in New York at the end of the month. He arrived in North Dakota just before Berkowitz's arrest on August 10, when he made that "Oh, shit" comment as news of the capture flashed on the TV screen.

In December 1977, Carr left Minot and traveled to the Houston area, where he dropped in to see his daughter in Beaumont. His ex-wife told us it was the first time she'd seen him in several years, although he'd been in Houston in the recent past. Returning to Minot, he decided to leave for New York again in late January. He packed some belongings in the '71 Mercury, which was registered to the Carr home in Yonkers—not North Dakota, which made tracing the plate futile—and departed for New York on January 31. It is certain he didn't know he was now being sought for questioning.

On February 10, he sent a Valentine's card to Linda O'Connor, and conducted a lengthy phone conversation with her the night of the eleventh, several hours after I spotted his car. I would later learn that during this conversation with Linda he said, "the cops were hot on his trail and he'd have to leave [New York] for a while." He told Linda he'd contact her soon.

On February 14, leaving his car behind, he unexpectedly flew into Minot, and he died forty-eight hours later. He hadn't planned to return to Minot for months.

John Carr was running.

*   *   *

The information we uncovered convinced us Carr was involved with Berkowitz, but there was nothing we could do. The authorities in New York had shut us down. I finally called Sal D'Iorio at the Sheriff's Department and was told: "There are indications of cult activity in Berkowitz's neighborhood, but we can't prove it."

This was a strong comment, supporting what I'd been working toward all along. But D'Iorio offered no specific information, and revealed nothing about the death of John Carr, although I'd later learn there was a lot of data in hand.

I also tried to elicit cooperation from North Dakota authorities, but was rebuffed there as well. With nowhere to turn, I delved heavily into my corporate job, hoping to hide my frustrations in the pages of the magazine I edited. But the case kept gnawing at me, and I commiserated weekly with friends at Olliver's in White Plains, where the bartenders also chimed in with suggestions and bits of information they'd picked up.

Ironically, two of them, Dave Spence and Steve Sturz, were friends of Norman Bing, the young supervisor Fred Cowan was gunning for when he terrorized the Neptune warehouse in New Rochelle a year before. Bing, who was in frail health, escaped injury by hiding under a desk that endless day, but his condition had steadily deteriorated since. He appeared at the bar on occasion, a shadow of his former self. He'd die several years later, effectively the final victim of neo-Nazi Fred Cowan.

But despite some encouragement at Olliver's during the dreary late winter of 1978, it was starkly evident that most people *wanted* to believe Berkowitz had acted alone. The dread was still very much alive.

In mid-April, I began dating an attractive brunette secretary named Georgiana (Gi), a former Queens resident. At twenty-four, she'd been affected by the fear that engulfed New York's women a year earlier, and to my surprise she expressed interest in the later developments. It was a welcome change from the setbacks and blank stares Jim and I often endured.

On our first evening together, we went to dinner at Thwaite's restaurant on City Island in the Bronx—a quaint finger of land on the edge of Long Island Sound which harbored marinas, bait and tackle shops and a number of excellent seafood establishments. On the way back, I realized it was the first anniversary of the Suriani-Esau murders and we drove to that scene and to that of Donna Lauria's death a few blocks to the east.

I pulled into the same darkened spot on the service road where Valentina and Alex parked, and explained what had happened that night. Rather than feeling fright, Gi was inquisitive and struck by a somber reverence. The narrow street was deserted and the dim light from a distant streetlamp flickered in the haze as we talked.

"One year ago tonight," I said quietly. "And in the next instant they were gone. What's that song out now—'Dust in the Wind'?"

"I close my eyes; only for a moment and the moment's gone," she recited.

"Yes, that's it. And who's here in their place exactly one year later and up to his damned neck in all of it? I never would have believed it. I used to live a normal life. And now Berkowitz is only a couple of weeks from taking the fall for everything. It's almost finished—dust in the wind."

"It's not over for you yet," Gi replied. "I think you know that."

"I don't think I make a very good Don Quixote," I answered. "I have an aversion to windmills."

"Don't you think you owe it to yourself, to Jim and maybe even to the victims who died here?" she asked.

For a long moment we sat in silence. A thousand images of that shooting and the past eight months spun in my mind. Nothing was clear; there were only fractured flashes of myriad events.

"I just don't know anymore," I finally said. "I simply just don't know. Let's get out of here now. We've paid our respects."

"You haven't finished paying yours yet," she remarked. "Not by a long shot."

The words just hung in the air. Starting the engine, I pulled from the haunting parking spot and drove back to White Plains, nudging the speed limit all the way.

*   *   *

A week later, the hammer fell again as my close friend Ben Carucci died at forty-four. He and his wife, Lee, were opening their summer home when death struck. I was deeply saddened by the loss and observed from a distant daze as Berkowitz prepared to plead guilty. In a final gesture, I phoned one of his attorneys, Leon Stern, and urged him to confront Berkowitz with the evidence we'd found. A few days later, Stern's associate, Ira Jultak, advised me Berkowitz refused to answer any of the questions.

"We're interested in John Carr, and Michael, too," Jultak told me. "But we're getting no cooperation at all from our client."

The way was finally cleared. There were no options left, and on May 8 Berkowitz stoically entered guilty pleas in Brooklyn before a panel of three judges—one from each borough in which shootings occurred—in a courtroom jammed with spectators, press and victims' families. I couldn't bring myself to attend, but Jim, rousing himself from his own adversity, covered the session for us.

It was, as many noted, a carefully programmed event. No trick or probing questions were put to Berkowitz. His answers were mainly "yes" and "no" responses stipulating that he indeed committed all the crimes. And then it was over.

With summer on the horizon, I retreated to Fire Island for three weeks in July to decide what to do in the future. Our old friends were also there. Along with the socializing, I spent several hours discussing the case with Carl Kelly, an NYPD officer.

He wasn't surprised that the evidence, as we then knew it, was disregarded, and was concerned that the case would eventually tarnish the whole of the NYPD. "The information flowed upward," he said. "There were only a few people at the top who had access to all the details.

"This case is a hornet's nest," he added, indicating the folders he'd read. "It was so big they didn't dare admit they might have screwed it up. A lot of cops would be ticked off to know all this was allowed to go on."

"The precious 'system' strikes again," I responded bitterly. "And Mister District Attorney Eugene Gold is one of its main components."

"Those people aren't going to like you guys at all if you keep on with this," Carl warned.

"So what else is new? Mitteager might end up in prison as it is."

And it was through the beleaguered Mitteager that the initial upswing would come.

At the end of July, Jim sent word to the beach that Allan Wolper, a columnist for the *SoHo Weekly News* in Manhattan, had expressed interest in the *Post*-bribery case. "The photo thing goes hand in hand with the conspiracy angle," Jim explained, when I phoned him from the dock. "I'll tell Wolper about all of it. And if he decides to write it up, maybe both stories can come out."

For the first time since late February a wisp of optimism drifted in the air. Allan Wolper was indeed interested in the photo case and said that he'd reference the search for accomplices in that context. He subsequently devoted numerous columns to the saga of "Sam Sleeps," wondering aloud why the *Post* escaped indictment. And, true to his word, he cautiously raised the conspiracy flag. Finally, someone was listening.

Buoyed by the positive turn, Jim and I sought out several principals in the .44 case, including key Brooklyn witness Tommy Zaino, who observed the Moskowitz-Violante attack from his borrowed blue Corvette. Zaino's statements added more optimism. We were now convinced that Berkowitz wasn't alone that night and almost certain that he didn't shoot the young couple, either.

Zaino also revealed that 10th Homicide Det. Ed Zigo asked him not to talk to us, which only sparked Zaino's curiosity because he had remained inwardly troubled by the police assertion that the long-haired man he saw pull the trigger was Berkowitz. It was Zaino who was told by police that Berkowitz might have drenched his short, curly hair with water to make it appear long and straight.

"Did they say he carried a garden hose with him, or did he just duck under the hydrant he was parked at?" Jim asked incredulously.

"Hey, I didn't buy that, either," Zaino said.

After hearing Zaino's account, which hadn't reached the public, it wasn't difficult to see why Zigo—who knew us from the meeting at the Tenth months before—tried to discourage him from cooperating.

Meanwhile, another important event was dawning on the legal front. After his arrest, the financially strapped Mitteager secured the services of attorney Felix Gilroy, head of Staten Island's Legal Aid Society.

Gilroy, an affable, quick-witted lawyer in his late thirties, listened intently as Jim filled him in on both the bribery case and the Son of Sam investigation. In due course, he came to believe that Berkowitz was part of a conspiracy. During one brainstorming session among the three of us, the groundwork was laid for a unique legal strategy.

Since bribery was often considered a crime of "intent," it was reasonable to seek to establish that Mitteager's intentions were aboveboard. It would also be beneficial to find a witness who could shed some light on the intrigue at Kings County Hospital.

Gilroy then filed a motion before State Supreme Court Justice Ernst Rosenberger in Brooklyn. In early October, he received the judge's ruling and called to tell me what it was.

"Pack your bags and your questions," he said. "We're going to meet the Son of Sam."

PART II

WEB OF CONSPIRACY: THE DOMINOES FALL

The evidence is so overwhelming that only
an idiot could ignore it, deny it, and leave it.

—David Berkowitz

It's as if each time there's a weak link
found someone is there to eliminate it.

—District Attorney John Santucci

He said, "Drink the blood. We always
drink the blood in the cult."

—"Death Mask" killer Bernard LeGeros

Satanism is a by-product. The real
motivation for the leaders is drugs.

—Vinny, a prison source

XII
"Hello from the Gutters"

At 6 p.m. on Wednesday, October 25, I hurried through La Guardia Airport to board an Empire Airlines commuter flight. The destination was Utica and David Berkowitz, who was being held outside the city at the Central New York Psychiatric Center in Marcy. The maximum-security facility was a temporary stop for the Son of Sam, who would soon be transferred to a cellblock at Attica.

After a short and scenic flight at low altitudes, the small jet touched down at about seven fifteen and nosed its way to Utica's generic passenger terminal. The Horizon Motel was adjacent to the airport, and as I registered I was greeted by a clerk who said several people were trying to contact me.

I knew Felix Gilroy had driven up earlier with court reporter Lorraine Woitkowski, so I expected a message from him. But there were also notes from Jim, who'd called to wish us luck, and from a reporter named Joe Kelly, who worked for a Utica newspaper.

Kelly, it developed, had read an Associated Press story about the interview and wanted to talk to us. He would write two articles about our visit. I found him in the motel bar with Gilroy, where we discussed the case for an hour over cocktails. Woitkowski, who was in her thirties, later joined Gilroy and me for dinner.

During the meal, the mood was markedly tense in anticipation of the next day's interrogation. Gilroy, trying to lift our collective spirits, teased a nervous Lorraine by suggesting she might become enamored of Berkowitz.

Parodying the supermarket tabloids, he bit down on his cigar and said, "You can even write an article about it. You can call it 'I Fried Eggs for Son of Sam'—or 'Bride of Berkowitz.'"

Lorraine, who was worried about the prospect of being in the same room with Berkowitz, groaned audibly, and no amount of friendly cajoling eased her tension.

Later, in Gilroy's room, he and I ran through a series of questions I composed for Berkowitz—queries concerning John and Michael Carr, the Son of Sam letters, killer Fred Cowan, the Moskowitz murder and the cult clues. Gilroy had devised his own list, which centered on Berkowitz's relationship with Herb Clarke, the guard who slipped him the conspiracy questions and took the "Sam Sleeps" photos that resulted in Mitteager's indictment.

At about 1 a.m., Gilroy wearily looked up from the pile of papers.

"We're as ready as we'll ever be. I'll be dreaming about German shepherds," he said, and we called it a night.

I, too, had trouble sleeping. Outside, a steady rain fell and a thick fog rolled in. Beyond the window, the blinking lights of the airport haloed in the mist. Everything was morose. I thought about the past fourteen months and how I'd gone from outside the case to the verge of becoming the first nonofficial person to have access to Berkowitz. So many times we'd danced on the brink of failure and now, almost miraculously, I was a few hours away from confronting the man whose life and crimes had so dominated my own existence for more than a year. It was a singular occasion, one I knew would strongly affect my future.

It was a long and nervous night. As I tossed fitfully, I began to dread the possibility that, despite all I'd learned, I was wrong and Berkowitz would pointedly deny everything. It wasn't a comforting thought.

* * *

At 9:15 a.m., after a quick breakfast, we drove about five miles through a drizzling rain to Marcy. The wipers scraped noisily across the windshield, puncturing the silence that pervaded the car. The preparations and background work were done; the strategy was set. There was nothing left to say.

As we drove up the hill to the Center, Marcy loomed ominous and forbidding. Its starkness was overpowering. At the guardhouse, we were joined by Special Prosecutor's assistant Thomas McCloskey and investigator David Campbell. McCloskey was handling the Mitteager case for the state, and he and Campbell made the journey from New York City to observe the questioning. Ironically, McCloskey was formerly an assistant district attorney in Queens and was assigned titular responsibility for the Virginia Voskerichian case before the arrest of Berkowitz. He and I weren't formally introduced, and it would be months before he learned who I really was. Gilroy merely said I was his assistant, which was true.

Once inside the gates, we passed through several checkpoints and were ushered into a waiting room before George Daley, head of security, led us down a corridor and a flight of stairs. We finally entered a small conference room known as "the Courtroom." In the center was a large wooden table with six chairs placed around it. Lorraine Woitkowski was noticeably on edge, and Gilroy, making conversation, asked where she wanted to sit.

"I'll know better when I see where Mr. Berkowitz will be seated," she replied.

Felix looked at her strangely. "What did you say?" he asked. Woitkowski repeated her statement. Nudging her, I gestured over her shoulder and she turned around and froze. Berkowitz was already in the room, sitting at the table and smiling at her like she was crazy. He'd walked in right behind us, unescorted and free of any handcuffs or restraint.

"Oh, I see you're already here," Lorraine stammered, and Berkowitz grinned at her.

Berkowitz was now twenty-five, about five feet eleven and powerfully built. He was wearing scuffed black shoes, green prison trousers and a short-sleeved green shirt. He had a one-day beard. His eyes were bright blue, and very alert. His dark hair was short and curly, and he'd allowed his sideburns to grow long and thick. He appeared relaxed, leaning back in his chair while waiting for us to begin.

On the record, all the questioning would be done by Gilroy, and I sat next to the attorney, prepared to pass comments or follow-up questions as the need arose. We were directly opposite Berkowitz. The others took the remaining seats in the room, moving their chairs away from us. Security chief Daley occupied a seat by the door. And so it began.

Gilroy opened with a series of questions which established that Berkowitz knew and remembered Herb Clarke, and that he indeed answered queries Clarke put to him about the Son of Sam case. Berkowitz stated he answered those questions truthfully.

Gilroy then asked: "Do you know a person named John Carr?"

"Yes."

"How did you know John Carr?"

"I don't want to talk about it."

This was a major confirmation of my suspicions, and I swallowed hard at the disclosure. Gilroy began pressing, and Berkowitz began sidestepping.

Finally, Felix asked: "Are you intentionally not answering my questions?"

"Yes."

"When did you meet John Carr for the first time?"

"I don't remember."

"When did you meet Michael Carr for the first time?"

"I don't remember."

"You remember now that you have met them?"

"Yes."

"You just don't remember when; is that correct?"

"Yes."

"What is your present attitude? Do you think you will ever get out of jail?"

"No."

"Do you think if you gave me the answers to these questions that other people might end up in jail?"

"There is a good possibility, and I wouldn't want that to happen."

"You are protecting somebody, then; is that what you are telling me?"

"I don't know, but I don't want to see anyone else in jail."

With this exchange, my pulse quickened. It was a significant admission from Berkowitz. But he then refused to answer a series of follow-up questions, telling Gilroy that while he didn't want Mitteager to go to prison either, he wouldn't provide any assistance. Gilroy then asked about the word association clues in the Son of Sam Breslin letter.

Q.   In some of these letters there is a code, isn't there? A clever code?

A.   I'd rather not talk about the letters.

Q.   It would be very important to me if you could at least confirm the fact that there is a code in these letters, without going into details.

A. I wouldn't call it a code.

Q. What would you call it?

A. I don't know.

Q. Doesn't the letter that talks about the Wicked King Wicker and the pine box and all—isn't that sort of a couple of clues to where you were living at the time?

A. Yes.

Q. You put that in there intentionally, didn't you?

A. Yes.

Q. . . . Did you have any books to follow or did you read anything in preparation of the code that was in the letter?

A. No.

Q. Did you completely make it up on your own?

A. I'd rather not say.

Q. . . . When you used the term "knock on coffins," that was a reference to Pine Street, wasn't it?

A. It could have been.

Q. Did you use word substitution in your hints?

A. I guess so.

Q. What can you tell me about the conversations [with Clarke] about the hints you put in that letter?

A. Nothing.

Q. You are going to make me ask you all the questions about it; is that right?

A. I am not going to talk about the letters.

Q. Could you talk about the code or hints, if it is not too much trouble? Would that really upset you?

A. Yes, it would upset me.

Gilroy then told Berkowitz that if he refused to cooperate or was intentionally deceptive he could be ordered by the court to testify as a witness. Berkowitz then agreed to be somewhat more forthcoming. He stated that Clarke talked to him numerous times about the clues in the letter, about John Carr and other subjects and that he answered Clarke truthfully. Gilroy then sought to learn what the authorities had done regarding possible accomplices.

Q. Did any of the psychiatrists ever ask you if other people were involved in these crimes?

A. No.

Q. Did *anybody* ever ask you if other people were involved?

A. I don't think so.

Q. Didn't Herb Clarke ask you those questions?

A. I don't remember the exact questions he asked me but they were about the shootings.

Q. If you were to tell all you know about this, there would be other dangerous people who would get in trouble; isn't that so?

A. They might get in trouble. I don't know.

Q. Do you care about society at large?

A. Well, my world is in here.

Berkowitz then said that he knew German shepherd dogs were being killed around Pine Street and that he did not phone Mrs. Florence Larsen to inquire about adopting a German shepherd two days before his arrest. He then evaded another series of questions, to which Gilroy responded: "I have all day to stay here. I can stay here all day." Berkowitz glared at him. "I don't feel like staying here all day," he said. At that point, we recessed for ten minutes. While the others went for coffee, I stayed in the room with Berkowitz, walking around to his side of the table and taking the seat next to his.

"I wasn't expecting these kinds of questions," he said. "Did you have a part in this?"

"Yes. The cops never went into any of this with you, did they?"

"No."

"And I'll bet you're glad they didn't."

Berkowitz smiled.

"It's for the good," I added. "Even yours, though it might not look that way."

"There's not much that can be for my good," he replied. Knowing that he was a sports fan, I then switched to the subject of baseball. He relaxed, and for a few minutes we amiably discussed the recent Yankees-Dodgers World Series, which he'd seen on television. I was amazed at Berkowitz's attitude; his willingness to chat about sports as if we were two people who'd just met and were having a beer together in a neighborhood tavern. He was alert, intelligent and clear as a bell. Being in his presence, I was convinced the "demon dog" story he told the police was every bit the fabrication I'd always believed it to be. Back in the room, Gilroy began by again trying to get to the heart of the matter.

Q. How many people are you protecting by not disclosing everything?

A. I don't know.

Q. Would it be fair to say it is at least eight or ten people?

A. Well, I don't know.

Q. Can you give me an approximate number?

A. I think it is in the hundreds.

Q. Did you meet all these people or did they just operate among themselves?

A. I'd rather not say.

At this point, we didn't know what Berkowitz was alluding to, but in time the implication would become apparent. Gilroy then asked about the Son of Sam graphic symbol, which Larry Siegel and I connected to nineteenth-century occultist Eliphas Levi. The shooting which followed the use of this symbol in the Breslin letter occurred outside the Elephas discotheque in Queens. Berkowitz acknowledged the symbol had "significance." He added: "I believe somebody put it in my mind to write that." Gilroy then brought up Berkowitz's trip to Houston, Texas, in June 1976, where his Army buddy Billy Dan Parker purchased a .44 Bulldog revolver for him. Berkowitz said Parker had "no idea" of the weapon's intended purpose.

Q. You visited John Carr's [former] wife in Houston, didn't you?

A. No.

Q. You are smiling now; does that mean you are kind of not telling the truth?

A. No, I am telling the truth.

Q. What makes you smile? You are hiding something, right? You don't want to be completely honest with me; isn't that so?

A. I'd rather not talk about it.

Gilroy then moved to the reason he asked Berkowitz about Carr's former wife, whom we never believed was visited by Berkowitz in her Beaumont home, near Houston.

Q. Isn't it really true, though, that you knew John Carr's wife lived in Houston?

A. Oh, yeah.

Q. Can you tell us why you went to Houston?

A. I'd rather not talk about it.

Q. Is that for the same reason, that other people may get in trouble?

A. Yes.

Q. If you thought these other people were out hurting society at large, you would care about it, though, wouldn't you?

A. Well, I don't think too much can be done about the situation now.

Q. Is it completely out of control?

A. Yes.

Q. Why do you say that?

A. Well, it is hard to explain. I don't really want to go into it.

Q. Do you know if John Carr was ever in Houston?

A. He might have been.

Q. Do you recall when he came home from Dakota?

A. I understand he died in Dakota.

Q. How did you find that out?

A. Somebody told me.

Q. Do you know how he died?

A. I believe he shot himself in the head.

Q. Do you know why he did that?

A. I might.

Q. You would have an idea why he might have done it? You are smiling now.

A. All right, I am smiling but I don't know why he shot himself in the head.

Q. Is there any chance these other people may be hurting people like you did?

A. There is a possibility.

Q. Do you feel any moral obligation to tell the authorities about that possibility?

A. They are not going to do anything. They are absolutely powerless.

Q. Why are they powerless now?

A. They can't do it; I'd rather not talk about it.

Frustrated, Gilroy turned back to the Pine Street neighborhood.

Q. When you were living there, were people killing dogs and putting them on the aqueduct?

A. Yes.

Q. Did you know who was killing the dogs then?

A. I had an idea.

Q. Would it mean anything to you if I told you they were still killing dogs in that area?

A. I'm not surprised.

Q. You have some idea [who was killing the dogs], is that it?

A. Yes.

Q. Would it be possible that the same people who are killing the dogs could also kill people?

A. It is possible.

Q. Would you help the authorities to stop that if it was going on?

A. There is nothing I can do.

Q. Why do you say that?

A. It is over.

Gilroy then probed the letters Berkowitz sent to Sam Carr complaining about his dog's barking; a get-well card to his former landlord in New Rochelle, Jack Cassara, which contained Sam Carr's return address; and a threatening letter to volunteer sheriff's deputy Craig Glassman, which I just learned contained Cassara's return address. With these notes and return addresses, Berkowitz was circling himself as the writer of the letters and a suspect in the wounding of Carr's dog and other violent incidents in the Pine Street area. Gilroy asked Berkowitz why he had given clues to his identity.

"Well, I wanted the police to come and find me," Berkowitz replied.

Indeed he did. As detailed earlier, he hoped he would be arrested for these relatively minor crimes and off the streets in the event the cult decided, as was discussed, to offer the police a scapegoat for the Son of Sam shootings. Berkowitz didn't want it to be him.

Q. How did you come to live at 35 Pine?

A. It's a long story. I'm not going to get into it.

Q. Who is the Wicked King Wicker?

A. I'd rather not say.

Q. Are you the Wicked King Wicker?

A. No.

Q. Is that actually a person?

A. I'd rather not say.

Q. Did you ever hear of kids finding dogs in plastic bags?

A. Yes, I heard something about it.

Q. You remember before you were arrested that there were a lot of dogs killed in Westchester County?

A. Yes, I think so.

Q. Do you have any idea what that was all about?

A. I have some idea. I'd rather not say.

Q. For the same reason you have been giving all along? It would hurt people you know?

A.   Yes. I guess you could say that.

Q.   Did you ever like Sam Carr?

A.   No.

Q.   Did you ever like his son John Carr?

A.   No. I hated every one of them. I hated their guts.

Q.   What was the reason for that?

A.   I'd rather not say.

Q.   Who was John Wheaties?

A.   I'd rather not say.

Q.   Isn't it true that John Wheaties is John Carr?

A.   It is a strong possibility.

Q   . . . . You deliberately used his name in a letter, didn't you?

A.   Yes.

Q.   Did you do that to kind of point the finger of suspicion at him or at least cause him trouble or harm?

A.   Yes.

Q.   Would you have liked to see the Carrs [John and Michael] get falsely accused of committing some crimes?

A.   No.

Q.   You just wanted the finger of suspicion to point at them?

A.   No, I wanted them dead.

Q.   But you used [John Carr's] name in the letter; is that right?

A.   Yes.

Q.   Did you have a code name for Michael Carr?

A.   I'd rather not say.

Q.   Herb Clarke asked you about John Carr, didn't he?

A.   Yes.

Q.   Did you give him an answer . . . can you tell me what that was?

A.   No.

Q.   Is that because you don't want to? [Berkowitz had turned pale and nearly collapsed when Clarke slipped him a note saying it was known he was involved with John Carr.]

A.   That's right.

Q. Parts of your letter [to Breslin] refer to the Black Mass. Do you know what that is?

A. I have heard of it before.

Gilroy then tried to zero in on the printing style used in the Breslin letter, a style completely different from Berkowitz's own.

Q. Do you know what an illustration studio is?

A. It is where you take pictures.

Q. Were you ever in one?

A. I believe the Carrs have one.

Q. How did you know that?

A. I just did.

Q. Did you ever see any of the Carrs do any illustration work?

A. Well, I know they used to take pictures. They had a studio.

Q. Do you know where the studio was?

A. I believe it was in their house.

Q. Did they have a sign in front of their house—Carr Illustration Studio?

A. No. [There wasn't.]

Q. Was the illustration studio listed in the phone book? [A Carr III Studio was listed in the 1976 phone directory, but not in 1977. The listing did not say it was an illustration studio.]

A. I don't know.

Q. How did you discover it was an illustration studio?

A. I'd rather not say.

Q. Did you know that Sam Carr had a heart condition?

A. Yes.

Berkowitz then became evasive again, and stated he was alone in the killings and denied his earlier responses. We put little credence in his denials, as he fidgeted, eyes darting nervously as he claimed sole responsibility and said he'd lied by implicating others. But the spoken word couldn't capture his expressions of shock and surprise at the nature of some of the questions put to him. Gilroy didn't give up, and threw out a question that caught Berkowitz totally off guard.

Q. Do the words "witches' coven" mean anything to you?

A. I have heard it before.

Q. Were some of these people [suspected conspirators] involved in the witches' coven?

A. I believe they were. Yes.

Q. Were you in that same coven?

A. Yes.

Q. Did you meet regularly?

A. Well, I can't really say. I don't want to say.

Q. Was Mr. Cowan involved in that?

A. I don't want to talk about it.

Berkowitz then said some people had dual natures and were part "spirit," making it difficult to bring them to justice. Gilroy snickered.

Q. Can you tell me if John Carr is a spirit or a person?

A. Well, let's just say he went into the next world. [This reply brought involuntary smiles to our faces.]

Q. Was Fred Cowan a real person when you knew him?

A. Yes.

This was a devastating series of comments. Berkowitz acknowledged that a satanic cult existed and that he belonged to it. Also, he'd earlier stated he only knew of Cowan after his death, but was now admitting he'd actually known him.

As I heard Berkowitz's revelations, I didn't betray any emotion. I reached for a cigarette and glanced at Gilroy, who was now perspiring slightly. He knew the importance of what he'd just heard.

The others in the room shifted nervously in their grandstand seats, as they'd done several times during the session. We heard some low murmurs. Gilroy, realizing he was in treacherous waters, retreated to a safer area so as not to alarm Berkowitz or violate any rights which could render his comments inadmissible.

Shifting his notes around, Felix spent the next ten minutes asking Berkowitz about the relationship he had with Herb Clarke at Kings County Hospital; and then George Daley announced it was time for a lunch break. It was 12:10 p.m., and the interrogation had lasted more than two hours to this point—already longer than three assistant district attorneys spent questioning Berkowitz about all the .44 shootings combined.

As soon as we reached the parking lot, our restrained demeanor evaporated.

"Felix, I don't know what the hell to say," I exclaimed. "He's confirmed everything. He knew John and Michael, there was a cult, a word-game code in the Breslin letter—and he says he knew Cowan."

Gilroy was trying to unwind. "You were right all along. How does that feel? He didn't expect to get hit with that stuff—he was caught flat-footed and let it out before he realized what was happening."

"I thought we were right, but hearing it from the horse's mouth is sort of overwhelming. I'd be lying if I said it wasn't."

"He's clever, isn't he?" Felix said. "The guy is no dummy, and he's not crazy either. We trapped him there, and he tried to wriggle out of it by denying it, but he was too late. And then, sure enough, he comes right back and confirms it all again. I think he wants to tell the truth. This afternoon, we'll try to get it."

Lorraine Woitkowski, who settled into her court stenographer's role like the pro she was once her initial fright subsided, said, "If I never take another job anywhere in the courts, I'll never forget this day as long as I live."

Just then, reporter Joe Kelly approached and showed us a copy of his day's story. He asked if he could join us for lunch, and we drove to a diner in Marcy. Felix was circumspect with Kelly, as he had to be. As would be reported the next day, Gilroy said Berkowitz was evasive, although "some of the answers were surprising. Just leave it at that." I added that Berkowitz didn't request any breaks in the questioning and quoted him as saying the interview "doesn't bother me. I've got nowhere else to go." We told Kelly that Berkowitz "looked alert and in good health" and that he wasn't handcuffed. And that's all we said.

On the return trip to the Center, I asked Felix if he believed Berkowitz was lying. I didn't think he was, but I wanted to hear Gilroy's opinion again.

"No, he knows too much and he didn't want to give it up. It slipped out of him," Felix said. "If he just wanted to lie he'd weave some tale about barking dogs and demons, like he did when he got picked up. Or else he'd laugh at us and say we were full of crap and goodbye. Besides," Felix added, "all this information was dug up first—he's not said anything we can't back up. Hell, the only reason we're even asking him these things is because the evidence was uncovered first."

In a few minutes I'd see how on target Gilroy's assessment was. Felix began the afternoon's session and received an unexpected shock. He asked Berkowitz why he'd used the term "we" when describing the Moskowitz murder to a psychiatrist.

A. Well, I have decided I am not going to talk anymore. I don't wish to talk anymore. I am not going to answer any more questions.

Q. Do you know that by doing that you're prejudicing my client?

A. I am sorry. I am not going to answer any more questions.

Q. Is there a reason you talked this morning and not this afternoon?

A. I'd rather not say.

Q. Can you give me a reason for that?

A. I believe you have some ulterior motives in this.

Q. I have a very ulterior motive: I represent my client. My client was indicted because he had been involved with Herbert Clarke and Clarke was asking information of you. The reason he was asking that information was because he believed you were not the only person involved in this. From the answers you have given this morning, it seems that there were other people involved in this case besides you. If you are going to stop at this point, I am going to come away with the impression . . . that there are other people involved in this case.

A. I can't answer any more questions.

Gilroy then ascertained that Berkowitz didn't have a physical or mental reason for refusing to talk. Then he asked:

Q. Did anybody talk to you or say anything to you?

A. I have spoken to some people.

Q. Was it a result of the conversations you had with people that you are now expressing a desire not to confer anymore?

A. Yes.

Q. Would you identify those people?

A. No.

Q. Did you talk to your psychiatrist between this morning and this afternoon?

A. I don't wish to talk about it.

Q. Can you give me a reason why you don't want to discuss it with me?

A. Some people I have spoken with gave me the idea that you may have some sinister motives to this.

Q. What could that sinister motive be?

A. Perhaps you are trying to write a book or make a movie or something.

Q. Do you know that this interview was court-ordered?

A. Yes.

Gilroy then repeated the legal grounds for the interrogation, and Berkowitz replied by stating that he was alone in committing the crimes and that he'd lied during the morning session. "I don't want any books written about me," he concluded.

Q. When you were talking to Mr. Clarke, did you know that there was somebody else involved besides just Mr. Clarke?

A. He said there were some writers. A former policeman or something like that.

Q. Did he mention more than one person? [At this, I gave Felix a sideways glance.]

A. Yes, I think there were two. I don't remember their names.

Q. There is no reason for you to feel hostility toward the fact that we had to interview you today?

A. No.

Q. There is no reason for you to feel that we are out to take advantage of you, is there?

A. I believe there is.

Q. Because of that feeling, have you deliberately not answered certain questions?

A. Yes.

Q. Would you say you are evasive about answering those questions?

A. Yes.

Q. Do you know what the word "evasive" means?

A. Trying to avoid.

Q. Intentionally trying to avoid?

A. Yes.

Gilroy then told Berkowitz that his refusal to answer left us with a strong impression that he was part of a conspiracy. "I will give you an example. For instance, the question about whether or not somebody called the Elephas disco and detoured the cops away that night—whether you did that or somebody else did that. If you could answer that question for me, we would know. That would be one example. Can you answer that question?"

"It wasn't me," Berkowitz said.

Suddenly, Berkowitz was talking again. I bit my lip and exhaled.

Q. You have told us you know John Carr, and John Carr, in fact, fit the description of some of the people [composite sketches] before you were arrested; isn't that so?

A. Yes. It appears that way. . . . It doesn't really matter, he is dead now, isn't he?

Q. Would you describe him as a friend?

A. No.

Q. Would you describe him as an enemy?

A. Yes.

Q. How did he become your enemy?

A. It is a long story and I don't want to go into it.

Q. But there is no doubt in your mind that as you speak today for this record that the John Carr that was referred to in letters was an enemy of yours?

A. Yes.

Q. It is my understanding that John Carr was not in New York. He was in [North]

Dakota. How did you come to hate a man who was in Dakota?

A.   It is a long story. I don't want to go into it.

Gilroy then tried to establish the circumstances under which Berkowitz and John Carr initially met. Berkowitz said the answer was "nobody's business." He then stated that Mitteager and I shouldn't have gotten involved in his case in the first place.

Q.   Everything should have been left to the police officers?

A.   That's right.

Q.   Do you think you got apprehended because of the ticket that was placed on your car in Brooklyn?

A.   Well, there were other reasons. It wasn't just the ticket.

Q.   You knew that Sam Carr had gone to Queens, to the task force, to turn you in; didn't you?

A.   Yes.

Q.   Did you think that the fact Sam Carr went to turn you in would cause the police to come and catch you sooner than they did?

A.   Yes. [This was another major admission. Berkowitz was saying that *before* his arrest he knew that Sam Carr had turned him in as a Son of Sam suspect.]

Q.   How did you know that [Michael] Carr had camera equipment and the illustration studio?

A.   Just a guess.

Q.   A pretty accurate guess, wouldn't you say?

A.   Yes.

Q.   You are smiling now, aren't you? When did you meet Michael Carr for the first time?

A.   I don't remember.

Q.   Was he a nice fellow?

A.   No.

Q.   Can you distinguish between a person who is—as you would say Michael Carr is—not a nice fellow and an ordinary person?

A.   I'd say anybody who worships the devil is not a nice person. [This answer stunned Gilroy and me, who were not expecting it. It came from out of nowhere.]

Q.   Are you telling me that Michael Carr worshipped the devil?

A.   I believe he did. I believe [John] Carr did.

Q.   What was the basis of that belief?

A.   I'd rather not say.

Gilroy then asked Berkowitz if he possibly was imagining that the Carr brothers worshipped the devil. Berkowitz said, "I am well."

Q.   You recognize there is a "fact" going on in this room? The fact that we are sitting here asking you questions. That is a fact—right?

A.   Yes.

Q.   There is nothing illusionary about that, is there?

A.   No.

Q.   So, you have a definite and concrete reason when you say the Carrs [Michael and John] worship the devil?

A.   I don't want to talk about it.

Gilroy then went through a series of questions trying to ascertain the reasons for Berkowitz's hatred of the Carrs. Berkowitz said, "They made a lot of noise." As Gilroy pressed on, Berkowitz began to fidget. Suddenly, he broke down and began to sob quietly. There was emotion in him, real emotion, and the knowledge affected me. Despite what he'd done or been involved with, I felt empathy for him. It was now apparent he was struggling within his own mind over the subjects we'd covered during the day. It was also apparent his feelings about the Carrs ran deep, and were intense. After a few minutes, George Daley handed him a handkerchief. The moment was poignant and telling. Berkowitz then softly said, "You can go on."

Felix looked at me. "You really felt for him. I could see it in your eyes," he said later. "It got to me, too." Felix began again, slowly, and Berkowitz repeated his comments about the noise made by the Carrs. That didn't satisfy Gilroy.

Q.   What would lead you to believe they [John and Michael] worshipped the devil?

A.   I had my reasons.

Felix then broached the subject of the Moskowitz-Violante shooting. Berkowitz said that he'd taken the ticket off his car before the shooting, that he'd seen the police write the ticket, that he was wearing a short-sleeved shirt with a jacket on over it, but that he did the shooting himself.

Gilroy then returned to Berkowitz's life in the Pine Street area, and asked him again if he'd called to adopt the German shepherd just before his arrest. At that moment, the session was abruptly halted as two men entered the room.

"Gentlemen, my name is Richard Freshour. I am with the attorney general's office. I would like to see the order under which you are authorized to be here."

"I think we mailed a copy," Felix said.

"I did not see it."

"Here is the certified copy," Felix said. Freshour wasn't placated. He introduced Dr. Daniel Uwah, deputy director of clinical staff, and said, "Based on what I have before me here, I am inclined to refuse to allow the interview of Mr. Berkowitz to continue in the absence of his counsel being present."

"I don't know what authority you have for that," Gilroy retorted.

"On the authority that this is a state institution and that I am counsel for the institution."

"That is no authority," Felix snapped.

Freshour answered: "It is the authority to the extent that Mr. Berkowitz does have an attorney, I believe—"

"He has been noticed," Felix cut in. "He was sent a copy of the order. I personally spoke to his office before the court signed it and I advised him the court intended to sign an order on a certain day. This is an assistant from the Special Prosecutor's office," Felix said, indicating Tom McCloskey. "He was noticed. There is a copy and affidavit on file of service on all these people. They were contacted."

Freshour then attempted to confiscate all the material gleaned from Berkowitz. "I am inclined to refuse to allow the interview with Mr. Berkowitz to continue. Additionally, any material which has been obtained up until this time, I am going to request that it be retained here until we obtain—"

"No," Felix fumed. "I won't permit that. I don't think you have any authorization for doing what you are doing at this time and you certainly have no statutory—"

"I don't see you have any authority to be here," Freshour interjected, "and I would request to see the original of the order signed."

"You have a certified copy—certified by the clerk. I just handed it to you. I might add there is a representative from the attorney general's office sitting in this room and he's been sitting in this room all along," Gilroy said.

Freshour, caught somewhat by surprise, asked to see McCloskey's credentials and then requested to speak off the record with all parties—including Berkowitz, who had witnessed the heated exchange with detached interest.

At the conclusion of the discussions, Freshour, over Felix's strong objection, terminated the interview but didn't confiscate the Berkowitz statements. He said he was called to Marcy at the request of Dr. Uwah, who thought Berkowitz was being interrogated for too long a period. (It is my opinion that Uwah tried to stop Berkowitz at the lunch break, and thought he had. But when Berkowitz remained in the interview during the afternoon, he took other steps. But whoever it was, Berkowitz said, tried to poison his mind about our intentions and apparently wasn't concerned with Berkowitz's stamina.)

Gilroy then asked Uwah: "Were you present at any time during my questioning of Mr. Berkowitz?"

"Do I have to answer this question?" Uwah asked Freshour.

"Yes."

"No, I wasn't," Uwah replied.

*   *   *

Outside, both Gilroy and I exploded. "First someone tries to shut him up during the lunch period, and then we get cut off cold and they try to withhold the material," I said. "I smell a rather large rat in the woodpile."

"Screw 'em," Felix stated. "We've got it all on the record. You know one of them said we were going too far, that we went far afield. That we were trying to solve the Son of Sam case!"

"God forbid anyone would want to solve the Son of Sam case," I answered.

Although I'd flown up to Utica, I drove back to Westchester with Felix and Lorraine. On the long trip, we went over the day's events. Lorraine played a tape of the interview, which she'd made as a backup for her court steno notes.

"He did contradict himself," I said. "He gave it up, then took it back and then gave it up again."

"I think we all know where the truth is," Felix replied. "You and I both knew when he was caught and tried to back away. But he kept coming back to the truth. I truly believe he wanted to give it all up. If we didn't break for lunch, I think we could have broken him."

We then analyzed where the investigation stood. Berkowitz's confirmation of the word association "code" in the Breslin letter strongly indicated, as I'd felt all along, that he hadn't written that communication; at least not alone. John Carr, though dead, was almost certainly an accomplice. And Michael Carr also emerged as a top candidate. And then there was Fred Cowan, about whom we could do little at present.

"What about the cult?" Felix suggested.

"That's supported by the allusions in the letters, the dead dogs and the existence of a conspiracy. If there were more than two in this, we're approaching a cult by definition, and the other indications tell us what kind of a cult it was—satanic," I observed. "You notice he didn't even try to deny the Black Mass reference in the Breslin letter."

"What do you think he meant when he said he was protecting what he took to be hundreds of people?" Felix asked. "I didn't know if that was a BS statement or not."

"If he was leveling with us, it means that our neighborhood cult has branches in other places. I've got some ideas, but it's going to take a lot more work to firm them up. But first we've got to try to pinpoint the group's location in Westchester. That's the most important thing to do."

*   *   *

The real significance of Marcy went beyond what we perceived at the time. It would be almost one year to the day later when its true import would emerge.

Back in Westchester, I approached my neighbor Tom Bartley. I couldn't tell him exactly what happened at Marcy, because of court restrictions which, in fact, resulted in the interrogation's specifics being kept under wraps until this writing. But I was able to tell Bartley enough had been learned to warrant a strong pursuit of the case. Tom was interested, and we looked for a way to bring the Son of Sam case into the headlines again. I knew what that way would be, and it would be in a legitimate, newsworthy manner.

It was time to hold the Westchester Sheriff's Department and the Yonkers police accountable for some of their actions in the county—actions which enabled Berkowitz, at least, to remain at large for two months and four shootings longer than he would have been had the most basic investigative procedures been followed.

Berkowitz had been sending a message to local authorities before his arrest. As he said at Marcy, "Well, I wanted the police to come and find me."

But they didn't.

The Gannett Westchester-Rockland chain published a morning paper, *Today*, which served Westchester, Rockland and Putnam counties, southern Connecticut and the north Bronx. The group also printed nearly ten afternoon dailies in the region. In terms of circulation, the papers reached a considerable number of readers.

After several months of further investigation and conferences with Bartley, executive editor Joe Ungaro, and Dave Hartley, editor of the Yonkers *Herald Statesman*, plans were formulated to publish a series describing the failures of local authorities in the Berkowitz matter. We were delayed by official stonewalling, as both Yonkers PD and the Sheriff's Department sought to keep us from documenting what I already knew to be true.

It was public knowledge that volunteer Sheriff's deputy Craig Glassman received four threatening letters from his upstairs neighbor Berkowitz in the months prior to his apprehension. However, no one except Sheriff's officials knew that the first note, penned in early June of 1977, contained Berkowitz's most recent former address on the envelope—that of the Cassara home in New Rochelle. Likewise, no one knew that the second letter, dated July 13, contained a reference to "Captain Carr" and utilized "Command Post 316" as part of the return address. Carr lived at 316 Warburton Ave.

Neither return address was investigated by the Sheriff's Department. If they had been, the department would have walked right into the Cassara and Carr letters beehive and Berkowitz, through the matching handwriting on all the correspondence and other factors, would have been identified immediately as the person who threatened Glassman's life. He could have been arrested by mid-June, two weeks before the Elephas disco woundings and six weeks before the Moskowitz-Violante attack in Brooklyn.

The Sheriff's Department was trying to keep a lid on those return addresses, but I found out what they were and recognized the implications.

Likewise, the Yonkers police, who were handed Berkowitz's name on June 10 as the suspected writer of the Carr letters and a possible shooter of Sam Carr's dog, didn't even question Berkowitz—who also could have been linked to another dog shooting and the firebombings of the Carr and Neto homes in the Pine Street neighborhood.

The Gannett editors thought those were stories worth telling.

Because of Jim Mitteager's legal difficulties, the newspaper staff decided it would be wiser if his name wasn't officially connected to the articles, so Bartley and I shared the byline. The first piece was published on Sunday, February 25, 1979, and, excerpted here, it highlights the discoveries.

> *David Berkowitz could have been jailed on a number of serious charges that would have taken him off the streets two months and four victims before his capture in August 1977 as the Son of Sam killer.*
>
> *. . . New information shows that not only private citizens but Berkowitz himself provided the Yonkers Police Dept. and Westchester Sheriff's Office with all the leads they would have needed to arrest him by at least mid-June 1977, nearly two weeks before the shootings of Judy Placido and Salvatore Lupo and almost two months before the murder of Stacy Moskowitz and blinding of Robert Violante.*
>
> *Indeed, the evidence suggests that Berkowitz was at the very least taunting local police and perhaps even fashioning a deliberate trail of obvious clues. . . .*
>
> *That trail led directly to Berkowitz. . . . From his spacious, seventh-floor studio, Berkowitz says he sallied forth to firebomb neighbors' homes, shoot their dogs and mail letters threatening their lives.*
>
> *And although the Yonkers police and Westchester sheriff's officers say they investigated these crimes, Berkowitz was not arrested. A Gannett Westchester-Rockland Newspapers investigation has found that if all the evidence had been put together it could have led to Berkowitz's arrest in a host of state and federal crimes including arson, attempted murder, reckless endangerment and threatening lives through the mails.*

The article also reported that officials had rebuffed all attempts to gain access to information, including a Freedom of Information Act request filed.

With this scenario, it is not surprising that both agencies were less than willing to cooperate with the newspaper series. It didn't matter; the truth was published anyway.

The series ran in four segments, and the Yonkers Police Department at first threatened to sue Gannett, but the chain, to its credit, stood fast and the articles appeared unencumbered.

The editors had been pleased with the investigative reportage done on the series, and agreed to add a fifth part to it, which was published on March 1, under Tom Bartley's and my bylines.

The story, under the headline "BERKOWITZ: OTHERS COULD GO TO JAIL," was a landmark in that it publicly raised the conspiracy specter for the first time. The headline was based on a sole comment from Berkowitz's Marcy interview four months before, when he said there was "a good possibility" others could be incarcerated if he talked.

The article, which occupied more than a full page, discussed the dead German shepherds, some flaws in the official version of the Moskowitz scene, the varying composite sketches of the killer, an allusion to multiple cars at some .44 crime scenes and an interview with Mrs. Florence Larsen about the call she took from someone calling himself "David Berkowitz of 35 Pine Street," who was interested in adopting a German shepherd two days before the arrest.

Significantly, the story contained an analysis of the authorship of the Son of Sam letters I obtained from renowned handwriting expert Charles Hamilton, who would be the first to expose the "Hitler Diaries" as fraudulent four years later. Hamilton said:

"I've studied much of Berkowitz's writing and many samples of his printing, too. The Breslin letter is a masterpiece by comparison. Berkowitz doesn't write like that; he doesn't print like that; and he doesn't think like that. Further, he's incapable of it.

"Whoever wrote that letter to Breslin is possessed of a high degree of urbanity and wit, is well educated and is able to make words flow together beautifully. Berkowitz can't do it, and his limited education shows in everything he writes.

"The police were duped into believing Berkowitz wrote that letter to Breslin," Hamilton continued, "and then convinced themselves he did it because they wanted to believe he did. But he didn't."

I asked Hamilton about theories which suggested a "split personality" in Berkowitz might have produced a work superior to his known writing, thinking and graphics abilities. Hamilton simply said, "No. You cannot assume or become a personality or intelligence that is so much greater than your own. It can't be done."

A friend of Berkowitz, who'd known him for years, put it another way in the article: "If he had a million years and a million pieces of paper he couldn't have done that thing [Breslin letter]. It's just not him at all. If you knew him like I do, you'd know that, too."

The article received scant media attention, as I had feared, but I was delighted because it represented a major breakthrough in the investigation. The Gannett papers were interested and on board. I got the go-ahead to continue probing the case under their auspices.

But the article had another immediate result. With one phone call, I would find the group we'd been looking for—the Son of Sam cult.

XIII

Minot? Why Not?

The call came on March 2, 1979, the day after the article about the unanswered questions in the .44 case appeared. He was a Yonkers teenager named Richard,* the product of a good home, and he lived near Untermyer Park and frequently took walks through the former estate's desolate, wooded confines and along the path of the aqueduct.

"I don't know if this has anything to do with the dead German shepherds you wrote about, but I found some, too, in the park," he told me. "And I know there's a devil-worshipping group that's been meeting in there for quite a while."

Richard had my attention. Not one word of suspected cult involvement in the case had reached the public. "Where do they meet?" I asked.

"There's an old pump house in the woods called the Devil's Cave. That's one place. And they also had an altar set up on the gutters."

"The gutters?" I asked quickly. "What do you mean, the gutters?"

"The aqueduct. We call it the gutters or the sewers."

"You mean the kids who live around there call it the gutters?"

"Yeah. If you come down, I'll even show you some graffiti with 'NGP' written in a bunch of places—that means 'near gutters' path' around here."

"Really? They had an altar set up there—on the gutters? Were the dogs nearby?"

"Pretty close. . . . A couple of my friends saw the group, too."

The next day, in the company of Dave Hartley, the youngish, soft-spoken editor and general manager of the Yonkers *Herald Statesman,* I met Richard near the park's entrance on North Broadway, barely a mile north of Pine Street. He was a high school sophomore, and a lanky, pleasant-looking youth. Dave Hartley himself was aware a cult had convened on the premises, but he didn't know I was looking for such a group until then.

"The student nurses and some doctors at St. John's Hospital [adjacent to the park] heard the chanting and saw candles and torches around midnight last Halloween; and they'd heard them before that, too," Hartley said. "Security guards went down through the woods to the old pump house and saw them. The guards went back and called the cops, but by the time the police got here the cult had scattered."

But there was evidence left behind. "Some candles and torches," Dave said. "And I came up myself and found a hood and two capes they left when they took off." The outfits, which I later saw, were gray in color and consisted of a full, peaked hood with eye slits and two long capes, or cowls.

"I saw them meeting, too," Richard interjected, "although not on that night. Two of my friends also spotted them."

"Let's check out the place," I said, and we entered the spacious, sprawling park.

Passing through the restored section, which boasted fountains, gardens and elaborate columns and statuary, we walked down toward the river on a long, steep stone stairway known as "the Thousand Steps." At the bottom, on what was once a round, open-air observation point with decorative columns, we turned to the right and groped our way through about a hundred yards of a muddy abandoned vineyard. Finally, hidden in the dense shrubbery, we came to the Devil's Cave.

"This was where they pumped the water for the gardens and vineyards in the old days," Dave explained.

"Yeah, another water reference," I answered. "They're all over the place in the Sam letters."

The pump house was a circular structure about thirty feet in diameter that was built into the side of a hill. It was constructed of stone, and a small doorway allowed access to its dank interior. With flashlights to illuminate the gloom, we walked inside. I was stunned by what I saw.

Built into the far wall was a long stone platform, or bench, which obviously served as an altar, for above and behind it black-painted pentagrams and large, inverted crosses glared grotesquely from the wall in the light beams. To the right, a hideous red painting of the head of Satan appeared; and more inverted crosses, painted in black, leered from other strategic locations in the structure.

On the ceiling, which was damp with moisture, there was a small rendering of the German SS lightning-bolt insignia, along with the numbers 666, the sign of the great biblical beast of Revelation—a satanic symbol. On one of the support columns in the center of the cave, an X-shaped figure with arrow points at the four ends was painted in black.

"That looks just like the Sam symbol," I said. "The arrows are pointing out to the so-called four magical elements: earth, air, fire and water. Each of those was alluded to in the Breslin letter."

The pump-house floor was dirt, and the stagnant air reeked of must and mildew. "We've got to get photos of this," I said to Dave. "But for now, let's get the hell out of here. This place is making me queasy."

"Amen," he replied.

Richard, who had stood by silently as we made our observations, then took us farther down the hill to the aqueduct itself. Through the still-barren trees, the Hudson River shone brightly below, reflecting the dying orange sun, which was setting in the western sky over the Palisades.

Walking the aqueduct path, Richard directed us to the site where he saw the wooden altar assembled. The supporting nails were still embedded in the two trees between which it was suspended.

"It was a long, wide board, and it hung there between the trees about four feet off the ground. They had a wooden chair placed in front of it," he explained.

Continuing down the path, he pointed out several spots adorned with the "NGP" graffiti, which he again said meant "near gutters' path." He next led us to three sites where he'd found dead German shepherds. Two areas were proximate enough to the meeting scenes to appear significant. The third, where a rotted carcass still lay, was too far away to be definitely linked to cult activity.

"So this is the gutters and the sewers?" I asked once more.

"That's what we call it," Richard replied. "Lots of people who live along here, the young people, know it by those names. What's so important about the name?"

"Not much. I'm just curious about it. It's a unique name for a place to have," I said, giving Dave Hartley a sideways glance.

Richard then took us to meet two of his friends, both local teenagers. Each confirmed the "NGP" designation, and one said he'd witnessed a cult meeting one summer night—from a safe distance. "There were about twenty of them, wearing hoods and carrying torches. They were standing in a circle and chanting something I couldn't understand."

"That's what the nurses saw and heard," Dave said, and Richard added a similar story, putting the number of cultists at "around fifteen or twenty."

Dave and I then returned to the pump house alone, where he pointed out small red arrows painted on a series of trees which led up to the back of the hospital property.

"Some of them must have parked somewhere around the hospital and come in this way," he said. "They had a trail marked so they could find their way in here at night. Quite an operation. Put a flashlight on the trees and you end up at the pump house, or you keep going down to the aqueduct."

"You know," I said, "it seems like a fair amount of people knew what was going on in here, but nobody knew the significance of it. About a year ago, Sal D'Iorio of the Sheriff's Department told me there were strong indications of cult activity somewhere in this area. Now I know what he meant."

"Then this must be the spot," Dave stated. "Here and the aqueduct."

"Yes," I answered. "'The wemon of Queens are the prettiest of all. It must be the water they drink.' That's the Son of Sam Borrelli letter—New York City drinking water."

"The pump house," Dave said, "and the aqueduct."

I nodded. "And I've got a better one for you. 'Hello from the gutters of N.Y.C. which are filled with dog manure, vomit, stale wine, urine and blood. Hello from the sewers of N.Y.C. which swallow up these delicacies . . .'"

"The Breslin letter," Dave cut in.

"Which also signs off with 'In their blood and from the gutters,'" I added.

"You've got them, don't you?" Dave asked.

"We sure as hell do."

*   *   *

As a conduit of water, an aqueduct was a gutter or sewer by definition. In this instance, it was literally the "gutters of NYC" since it once carried drinking water to the metropolis. And because "dog manure, vomit, stale wine, urine and blood" referred to the satanic Black Mass, that sentence of the Breslin letter meant, "Black Mass-aqueduct."

The site was but a mile north of the Berkowitz and Carr homes, and one could walk the aqueduct path from Untermyer Park to the Pine and Wicker Street sections, where the other dead shepherds were found, in a matter of fifteen minutes. An adventurous individual with access could also travel that distance underground, with difficulty, through the old pipe itself. Chances were excellent that the Pine Street dogs, carried in plastic bags, were dumped there after rituals further up the path at Untermyer Park.

Putting the puzzle pieces together, there was physical and eyewitness evidence of the cult's existence, and the entire package—including symbols in the pump house—was linked to the Breslin letter, in which Berkowitz at Marcy acknowledged word substitution clues were employed.

Most important, the initial evidence was unearthed before Berkowitz said a word about cult involvement.

More than a year before, when Larry Siegel and I first deciphered the satanic clues in the Sam letters, we drew up a list of three items which, separately or together, could demonstrate the accuracy of what we uncovered.

One of those required the discovery of evidence that Berkowitz or John Carr was in a cult. At Marcy, Berkowitz admitted to just that, and added Michael Carr to the roster. A second step was to locate the cult itself and link it to Berkowitz and the Son of Sam case. That was now done. And the third step was to develop evidence independent of cult activity which demonstrated Berkowitz didn't act alone in the actual .44 incidents. We had made progress there, besides the already known inconsistencies concerning composite sketches and the like, but still had a distance to travel. Handwriting expert Charles Hamilton's analysis of the Sam letters provided a tremendous boost, but I intended to move on by conducting an in-depth investigation of the Moskowitz-Violante shooting. If it could be demonstrated Berkowitz wasn't alone at several crime scenes, the case would be stronger yet—but all we needed to do was to show evidence of a conspiracy in *one* shooting to topple the entire house of cards. Then all the divergent pieces of evidence would mesh, substantiate each other, and the truth would be undeniable.

Before beginning the Moskowitz-Violante investigation, I phoned Tony Catalano, manager of the Yonkers Animal Shelter, to learn if my count of the dead German shepherds was accurate. It wasn't. More had been found subsequent to Berkowitz's arrest, in virtually the same spot on the aqueduct near Pine Street as the earlier three.

"The first one was shot to death," Catalano told me. "It was lying there alone. The other two were together. They were either strangled, shot or poisoned. Because of the condition of the bodies we couldn't tell, but they didn't walk off together and lie down side by side to die. They were murdered."

He added that still another shepherd had been wounded in the immediate neighborhood. "Its ear was sliced off. It wasn't chewed off, like in a dog fight. It was a clean, even cut, like it was done with a knife."

The toll of dead German shepherds stood at ten, at least; and one, minus an ear, was wounded.

* * *

It was, I reasoned, time to explore the Process a bit further. Besides the shepherds, a Process link, we had to consider Berkowitz's Marcy statement that he believed he was protecting "hundreds" by remaining silent. If so, there was no doubt his alleged cult was part of a larger organization, one which likely had branches in different U.S. cities—branches such as those a Process subset, probably with OTO crossovers, could have.

Since the Sam letters contained so many clues, I went back to them and to other Berkowitz writings with which I was now familiar. Doing so revealed definite connections to Process-like terms. For instance, Berkowitz had written he needed a "messenger to earth"; and messenger was a Process rank—as were "father and master," both of which were allusions he made to Sam Carr and Craig Glassman. The Borrelli letter contained the phrase "honour thy father," using the British spelling of "honor." The Process was founded in Britain, as was Aleister Crowley's OTO chapter.

Additionally, the Breslin letter said: "Now, the void has been filled"; and the "bottomless void" was definitely Process terminology. That letter's return address, in part, said: "Blood and Family"; and the Process had referred to itself as "the family." Berkowitz signed a threatening letter to Glassman with "Brother," another Process level, and he'd written "H.H." on the envelope of one of the anonymous letters he mailed to Sam Carr. This, I would later learn, signified "Heil Hitler"—a Process demigod. Regarding Hitler-Process links (which also brought Fred Cowan into the fold), I would learn that an associate of Berkowitz's told police in 1977 that Berkowitz frequented the White Plains Road area of the northeast Bronx and "possessed and wore Nazi insignia." Quote.

In another 1977 police report, a witness stated that Berkowitz was seen in Manhattan with one "Father Lars," who was said to be involved with some offbeat society, supposedly religious in nature. It was a Process offshoot.

Two other phrases, closely associated with the Process via Charles Manson, were also used by Berkowitz. They were: "My children I'm turning into killers", which was written on the wall of Berkowitz's apartment; and "little ones," a phrase used by Berkowitz in a letter to Glassman.

There were other illustrations of this orientation as well. Putting them together, along with the German shepherds and Berkowitz's Marcy comments, I began to realistically believe that a Process subset organization was involved in the .44 caliber shootings. But I still wasn't willing to make the cult connection public. I hoped we could catch some members of the Yonkers group in the act and uncover more evidence of conspiracy in the killings themselves.

* * *

In the next few months, there were various developments in the case. Stacy Moskowitz's father, Jerry, called to thank Tom Bartley and me for the articles specifying the less than professional conduct of the Yonkers police and Westchester Sheriff's Department in the local Berkowitz investigations. The Moskowitz family had filed a $10 million lawsuit against the Yonkers Police Department, charging negligence in Stacy's death. They would lose the suit. Before the articles appeared, they were ignorant of the sheriff's role in the case.

I visited Jerry, his wife, Neysa, and their daughter, Ricki, on a March Sunday and told them I seriously doubted Berkowitz shot Stacy. It was a difficult thing to say, but I was gratified the family trusted the analysis and said they'd stand by as I probed further. Neysa showed me Stacy's room and some personal effects and photos.

"She meant everything to us," Neysa said sadly. "I hate Berkowitz with a passion, as you know. I was all over the place calling for his execution on the spot. But if he didn't do it, I just hope to hell you get the people who did." (At his sentencing, Berkowitz, who was subdued when he pleaded guilty, threw the courtroom into turmoil by chanting "Stacy was a whore" several times. The courtroom erupted, and the sentencing was delayed. Berkowitz, I'd later learn, was motivated by two reasons: he wasn't ready to be sentenced, in his mind; and he had developed an intense dislike for Neysa Moskowitz, who had loudly sought his execution. Berkowitz also knew something else: he hadn't shot Stacy.)

"I went along with what the cops said," Jerry added. "But I always knew he didn't look anything like the sketches. And I got to know a lot of the local police as a result of what happened—and a lot of them aren't convinced it was him either."

On my way home that night, I drove by Pine Street and down the hill to Wicker and Warburton. From the home of the victim to the hangouts of the killers, I thought before slowly driving on. As hard as I tried to avoid emotional involvement in the deaths and the families' sufferings, I wasn't always successful. That night was one of those occasions.

I received another call in the wake of the articles. It had a familiar tone to it. The caller was an anonymous woman who began to tell me about a girl named Jane and a station wagon and Little Neck Bay and a successful accountant named Reeve Carl Rockman. "Cut it out, Veronica. I know just who you are," I said. "I was at your house last year, but you ducked under the bed. Go call Dunleavy—he could probably use a little excitement." Veronica Lueken was at first aghast, and immediately hung up the phone. An hour later she called back, apologizing for her actions of 1978 and admitting she had "made a mistake."

"You sure did, lady," I told her.

Lueken said her information about Staten Island's Meehan family was erroneous because she confused Mike Wollman, a friend of the Meehans' son, with Rockman. "They look alike, and when I saw Wollman going in and out of that house I thought it was Rockman."

"You were paranoid, Veronica."

"I'm sorry, but I thought Rockman was using another alias out there. He already uses aliases—did you at least check that?"

"Yes, we know he had two addresses in Queens and was calling himself Reeve Carl Rockman and Reeve T. Carl. But there's more to this—we interviewed Jane Jacklin and she's not dead at all, as you claimed she was."

"I was told she was murdered," Lueken insisted. "And I even met her a few months before."

"Oh yeah? Then what did she look like?"

Lueken then described a woman other than the Jane Jacklin that Mitteager and I spoke to. Besides obvious appearance differences, the real Jane was the mother of an infant, and would have been noticeably pregnant in June 1977, when Lueken said the meeting occurred.

"No, she wasn't pregnant," Lueken said, and her husband, Arthur, who said he was present that day, came on the line and confirmed the details.

"People come to me, they confide in me," Lueken then explained. "That's how I heard about the cult and Rockman."

"If you're leveling with me this time—and that's a big if—then whoever approached you used the real Jane's name," I said. "And if anyone was murdered, it might have been the Jane impostor."

Lueken then said that a New York City homicide detective was privy to the information and could vouch for its authenticity. She gave me the detective's name, and he called the next day. We arranged to meet for lunch at a restaurant on Central Avenue in Yonkers.

In appearance, Bronx homicide detective Henry (Hank) Cinotti wasn't what I expected. Husky, and about six feet tall with jet-black hair, he sported a mustache and a prominent goatee. Wearing black clothes, with a large gold crucifix draped around his neck, he looked more like an undercover vice or narcotics cop than a homicide detective. His speech was classic New Yorkese.

Cinotti was thirty-seven, and a seventeen-year police veteran who owned several departmental commendations. He also was openly, devoutly religious—to a fault, some said—and acknowledged that he was a follower of Veronica Lueken—an association he would later sever.

Because of his ties to Lueken, I was openly skeptical of Cinotti, who insisted he investigated her claims and found they had considerable validity. He revealed that in June 1977 three young women approached Lueken in a Queens restaurant and told her of a satanic cult which was involved in ongoing murders, apparently the Son of Sam killings. The girls fingered Rockman as a leader of the group. One of the girls gave her name as Jane Jacklin. The others introduced themselves as Wendy Smith* and Nicki,* who didn't offer a last name. The girls expressed fear of Rockman and said they wanted to escape the group's clutches.

Lueken never saw Jane or Wendy again, Cinotti said, but Nicki subsequently came to her and asked to be hidden out, claiming that the group was involved in the .44 case and that Jane had been slain and dumped into Little Neck Bay. Cinotti said that Lueken took Nicki to her residence on Van Duzer Street on Staten Island, where Nicki, a native Haitian, remained for several weeks before flying back to her Caribbean homeland. (I remembered the Meehans reported a black girl lived with Lueken during that period, so this part of the story seemed accurate.)

Two days before Berkowitz's arrest, Lueken, who by then knew what Rockman looked like, claimed she spied him in an old station wagon in the company of a young man with dark, curly hair. Lueken copied the car's license plate number, and gave it to Cinotti, who showed me a dated computer printout proving he ran the plate number that day—August 8, 1977. When Berkowitz was arrested on the tenth, Lueken claimed he was the man in the station wagon with Rockman. The car, the printout showed, was registered to the *real* Jane Jacklin.

"That's simply bizarre," I said to Cinotti. "The real Jane admitted to Jim and me that she owned that car at the time, but said she knew nothing about any of this. Now, we did check with Motor Vehicles, and they told us the car was later junked at an auto wrecker's in Queens. We checked that place, and were told it went out of business in 1971—six years before."

"Ah, hah," Cinotti said. "Maybe Jane isn't involved at all. It could be her husband has some link to all this. He was a laid-off New York City cop at the time. And anyone who knew Jane could have used her name when talking to Lueken."

I asked Cinotti what he knew about Rockman. "He's college-educated, no police record, divorced and now remarried. He did some accounting work at a drug rehab center, and had a dope problem himself at one time. He's also been under a psychiatrist's care, but we can't find out why due to the confidentiality factor. He's working now for a company on Wall Street—actually at 2 Broadway."

"Number 2 Broadway?" I asked. "That's the building where one of the Sam victims worked—Christine Freund."

"Jesus," Cinotti exclaimed. "Rockman works for Acme Limited*—who did she work for?"

"Reynolds Securities," I replied. "That's probably a big building, but it's still a remarkable coincidence. And one of Rockman's addresses is in Forest Hills—only about seven blocks from the Freund killing scene. What kind of car was he driving then, Hank?"

"A small green Fiat."

"Well, at the time of the shooting, the cops had reports that a guy in a small green car dropped off another man at the railroad station there just a few minutes before the shots were fired. They never found the guys or the car."

"He's starting to look better to you, eh?" Cinotti grinned.

"It's an interesting turn of events," I admitted, somewhat reluctantly. "We had written Lueken off as a crackpot. And her Staten Island information was in fact garbage, and the real Jane wasn't killed. I'm not willing to say she really saw Berkowitz either. She was seeing conspirators everywhere. And Lueken made it all worse by refusing to talk to us."

"She's eccentric," Cinotti agreed. "And she was scared."

My interest in Rockman heightened further when I learned that a small business in Manhattan, located in a building where he once worked and his father still maintained an office, utilized Sam Carr's answering service in Yonkers. It was another unlikely coincidence.

Rockman was born in 1947, was about five feet nine, had a medium build and straight, sandy-colored hair. He also had some type of defect or deformity of one of his fingers or thumbs, which caused him to favor the hand and discreetly shield the imperfection from others.

When I discussed Rockman, Lueken and Cinotti with Jim Mitteager, I quickly discovered his appraisal of Lueken's credibility hadn't changed. The situation was worsened on the night of Good Friday, when we planned a midnight stakeout of Untermyer Park in hopes of spotting a cult meeting, an operation that the Yonkers police would attempt months later.

That night, a small group of interested parties gathered at 10 p.m. in the home of Don Starkey, an arson investigator for the Yonkers Fire Department. Starkey had advised me that a series of more than twenty automobile arsons occurred in the general vicinity during Berkowitz's tenure on Pine Street, and that he received reports that a car similar to Berkowitz's—with two people in it on at least one occasion—was observed driving from a scene.

Berkowitz had admitted he was a onetime firebug, and Starkey was also aware of Berkowitz's acknowledged complicity in the firebombings of the Carr, Neto and Glassman homes.

Also present at Starkey's house were Gannett's Tom Bartley, Mitteager and Cinotti. No one except me had met Cinotti before. Hank arrived with two companions wielding baseball bats, handed out religious medals, and began to discuss demonology and religious topics in a manner that caused Bartley to back out of the surveillance and convince Mitteager half the world had gone totally crazy.

Jim almost took to the exit sign with Bartley, but I persuaded him to see the evening through.

At 11:30 p.m., on a cloudy, moonless night, Starkey, Jim, Hank, his two companions and I sneaked into the eerie darkness of Untermyer Park. Jim insisted on letting Cinotti and his friends lead the way. "Somebody could get shot or beaten to death tonight," Jim warned. "I don't like this at all. Somebody might shoot first and worry about it later. I got enough problems—I don't need something like this on top of them."

Don Starkey was also on edge. "If anyone's meeting here, I just want to observe them. I'm not looking for any confrontations," he emphasized.

For ninety minutes, we searched the woods near the pump house and walked along the aqueduct. Each time an animal stirred in the bushes we froze expectantly.

Then, shortly after 1 a.m., it began to rain heavily, and we abandoned the stakeout.

"Never again," Jim said later. "Not under those circumstances. I don't give a shit if Charlie Manson himself was going to be slitting a dog's throat, I just don't know how Hank and those guys he brought would react."

Jim, already skeptical of Veronica Lueken, as was I, now echoed Tom Bartley's distrust of Cinotti. My own faith in the detective wavered, and for several months I didn't speak to him. Our investigation of Rockman also ceased.

*   *   *

In April, I testified at Jim's pre-trial hearing at State Supreme Court in Brooklyn, where I repeated my limited knowledge of the *Post*-Mitteager-Clarke-Berkowitz relationships. Since the Gannett Westchester Newspapers were now involved in the investigation, they sent a reporter to cover the hearing, as did other New York City media (but not the *Post*). In my testimony, I referred to John Carr and the conspiracy hunt, as did Jim, and our comments were reported by the press. We were still trying to get the message out.

On cross-examination, prosecutor Tom McCloskey thought he'd make a big point about clandestine operations by demanding to know if I attended the Marcy interview. Until he saw me in court, I don't believe he knew it was me, by name, who participated in the Berkowitz interrogation. McCloskey attempted to suggest I'd somehow cloak-and-daggered my way into the maximum-security facility. I managed to deflect his allusion by answering: "You know I was at Marcy, Tom. We saw each other there, remember?" McCloskey immediately dropped the subject.

Also that spring, Michael Carr, who had blossomed into a top suspect although he didn't know it, naively sent a press release to the Yonkers *Herald Statesman*. Editor Dave Hartley, who didn't publish it, forwarded the item to me. Dated April 29, it said:

> *Carr's Telephone Answering Service, Inc. is happy to announce the return of Michael Vail Carr III, BvC, M.C.O.S., its secretary and Org. Exec. Sec. from the Flag Land Base—a religious retreat maintained by the Church of Scientology of California in Clearwater, Florida—after completion of the Executive Delegation and Supervision course.*

By now cognizant that the Process had sprung from Scientology, which called itself a "church," I called Mitteager to relate the news to him. Scientology had run into legal difficulties with the Justice Department and was suspected of fostering illicit smear tactics in a number of cities, including Clearwater, Florida, scene of Michael Carr's sabbatical.

"This confirms what we heard about Michael after John Carr's death," I said to Jim. "He's a ranking Scientologist. And regarding the Process, maybe the apple didn't fall too far from the tree."

"Yeah, and maybe some of the apples climbed back into the tree," Jim suggested. "If he's counseling lost souls for Scientology, allegedly helping them discover themselves, he could certainly be working both sides of the street and plucking a few out for recruitment in the Satan stuff. That Scientology movement is fertile ground for latching on to confused people. He'd have his pick of candidates. Even that press release sounds like some recruitment gimmick. It's certainly got nothing to do with answering telephones."

"Not on the surface, at any rate," I cautioned. "We'll have to wait and see if it's the apple and the tree or if he's using his Scientology position for other reasons."

In May, I received word from a source that Berkowitz's life was in danger. I immediately phoned Jim, who contacted Felix Gilroy. Gilroy sent a formal advisement to the Correction Department warning that reliable informants said an attempt might soon be made on Berkowitz's life.

*   *   *

It happened at about 8:15 a.m. on the morning of Tuesday, July 10. Berkowitz, in a segregated Attica cellblock reserved for high-security-risk prisoners, was carrying a pail of hot wash water as part of his inmate's job as a porter when the razor slash came. The cut, which caught Berkowitz from behind, extended from the left side of his throat to the back of his neck. It required fifty-six stitches to close. A bit deeper and he would have been dead.

Berkowitz, with typical aplomb, walked up to a correction guard and said, "I'm sorry, but I've been cut." He was taken to the infirmary for treatment and refused to cooperate with prison officials in their investigation. He never revealed the name of his assailant, who was another inmate.

Writing about the incident to a friend, Berkowitz blamed his inattention and lack of concentration on an *occult* book he'd been reading. He wrote:

> *There were other things. I wasn't sleeping well and I was tossing and turning. I was losing sleep and I walked around all day feeling tired. There were still more things but I can't pinpoint it other than saying I was getting bad feelings in general and bad vibes from everybody else.*
>
> *I admit that I did get somewhat enmeshed in this book and often spent hours inside its pages. However, everything was happening so subtly, so slowly, that I never connected the book to this. Maybe it wasn't the book but just a very common stroke of bad luck. Anyhow, everything culminated with my throat being slashed. I could well have lost my life, yet, it didn't upset me.*
>
> *After the assault, I was sent to an isolation room at the hospital. Being locked alone in that airless room, that solitary soundless room, I started to think and meditate about this close brush with death and everything that led up to it, and the last rotten, depressing month. FINALLY! I put*

*two and two together. I was getting these negative feelings from this book
all along. . . .*

*If you could have seen this book, then you'd understand. It was full of
satanic symbols, prayers, and most of all, pictures. Do you know someone by the name, Eliphas Levi? [He] had this picture drawn up. It was
a picture of a goat head attached to the body of a man. It was called
BAPHOMET. I did stare at this picture for hours on end. . . .*

*In that hospital room, I slept and slept. . . . I realized that I had gotten
careless, I wasn't alert. . . . So out comes the razor blade and swoosh.*

*Immediately upon my return to my own cell a week later, I went strait
[sic] to my bunk, kneeled down underneath it, grabbed that book, and
tore it into shreds.*

Although I can't say with certainty that the attack on Berkowitz was linked to my
source's information, it's definitely possible it was, given the timing of the incident—
although Berkowitz would later imply another motive. That motive, according to a
prison source, involved Berkowitz's cult activities. Nonetheless, a chagrined Gilroy
told the press that he'd formally alerted the Correction Department weeks before
that an attack might be imminent. But only then, in the aftermath of the assault,
were security measures around Berkowitz increased.

As word of the attempted murder was flashed, we were in the final stages of preparing a major report on the Moskowitz killing for the Gannett Westchester-Rockland
Newspapers (WRN). For six weeks, with help from Jim Mitteager and Tom Bartley,
I probed that shooting. We reinterviewed witness Tommy Zaino, who saw the attack
from his borrowed blue Corvette; and located and extensively questioned Cacilia
Davis, whose complete account of what happened that night had never reached the
public.

With stopwatches and multiple re-creations and other analysis of the events of
July 31, 1977, a picture emerged which demonstrated, as I'd long suspected, that
Berkowitz wasn't alone at that scene and apparently wasn't the triggerman either. The
article, which occupied more than an entire page in the large-formatted newspapers,
was published on Thursday, July 19. This time, the editors allowed Jim's name on the
story, and he and I shared the byline.

Whereas the March article, which raised a number of conspiracy-related questions, was largely ignored by the rest of the media, this one wasn't. TV and radio
covered the story, and the Associated Press released a dispatch written by Richard
(Rick) Pienciak, who'd been following our investigation since interviewing Mitteager
nine months earlier. Pienciak had urged us to publish John Carr's suspected link to
the case, but we demurred, waiting for more information before doing so.

Not surprisingly, law enforcement officials denied the article's revelations, which
were far less extensive than the later details that appear in this writing. WCBS radio
reporter Irene Cornell sought out Brooklyn DA Eugene Gold, who refused to speak

with her but hollered that the article was "wild speculation" as he ducked into an elevator. WPIX-TV sent reporter Jeff Kamen to Gold's office for comment, but he was denied access. WPIX would follow the case closely from then on and air extensive coverage of future developments.

Gold, under pressure, finally released a statement, which my colleague Mike Zuckerman reported in the next day's editions of the Gannett papers. The statement charged that his own star witnesses were in error. The story, Gold's office said, was "a wild hypothesis not supported by the evidence." Gold, his spokeswoman, Rhonda Nager, admitted, "hasn't read the story but he knows of its contents."

Then Nager requested that the following comment not be attributed to her by name. "It was night, it was dark, and at the very best [the witnesses'] recollections are hazy and those recollections could be marred by the intensity of the experience."

The DA's office was now trying to destroy the credibility of its own key witnesses, whom the police believed and upon whom much credit was bestowed at the time of the arrest.

The Moskowitz report drew the battle lines. Gold was going to stonewall for as long as he could get away with it; and, because the article concerned Gold's jurisdiction, Queens DA John Santucci and the Bronx's Mario Merola remained silent. The NYPD issued a soft public denial, but was clandestinely operating on a different level.

Regarding the press, it was enlightening to gauge current reaction to new developments in the case that originally was such a media spectacular. The wire services and most TV and radio stations—who were not in direct competition with their print counterparts—paid some attention to the story. The *New York Times* published a small piece reporting our allegations and the official denials. The *Daily News*, which unfortunately had a stake in the sole-killer concept, ignored the issue. This was the same publication that, along with the *Post*, had embraced the Son of Sam story as its own two years earlier.

News columnist Jimmy Breslin, with TV sports reporter Dick Schaap, had penned a novel about the .44 case which depicted Berkowitz as a drooling, demented madman who acted alone. Additionally, the *News*, which had posted reward money for the apprehension of Son of Sam, presented some of that booty to—of all people—the Carr family. So the *News*, whose reporter William Federici was involved in the jumbling of Mrs. Davis's original story, would treat the hunt for accomplices as if it didn't exist. It would be several years before management changes restored the paper's traditional lifeblood.

The *Post*, with problems of its own regarding the Mitteager case, which was about to come to trial, also ignored the Moskowitz article. But later, at the urging of Steve Dunleavy, who was well aware of the subject's validity, the *Post* covered the conspiracy probe.

Once we'd broken the ground, the New York area press might have made a positive impact by transcending the reporting of charges and denials to mount serious inquiries to complement ours. But it wasn't to be, and there were several reasons why we effectively had to go it alone.

First, there was a combination of incredulity and embarrassment. Except for the *Post,* which dropped out due to circumstances described earlier, no one had looked behind the headlines after Berkowitz's apprehension. Reluctant to consider that they might have missed a story of such dimensions, some publications simply accepted the official renunciations as gospel.

Second, no media outlet likes to play "catch-up," and all were unknowing of the sources and leads we had developed. So rather than start from scratch in the middle of a labyrinth or continually publish credited versions of the Gannett pieces, some editors simply disregarded the new developments.

Third, since the press relies on official agencies for material, it can have inherent motives for generally assuming a noncombative posture with the likes of police departments and district attorneys' offices—a position that would have been severely compromised by pursuit of the Sam case. Concurrently, with the days of Watergate-type investigative reporting on the wane—much to the dismay of most reporters and editors—a fair number of media executives, including the then top editor of the *Daily News,* were actively seeking to shed their "watchdog" cloaks and rekindle amiable relationships with government branches.

We, ourselves, didn't relish a battlefield setting for the new Son of Sam investigation. We had made official visits before publishing a word about John Carr or the Moskowitz murder. But when it became evident that authorities wouldn't follow through, we determined that they could read about our findings at the same time everyone else did.

But the Gannett staff, Mitteager and I were basically satisfied with the response to the Moskowitz story. The message was out: there were big problems with the Son of Sam case, and there would be no turning back.

*   *   *

In Minot, North Dakota, far from the New York subterfuge, Jeff Nies, twenty-six, a reporter and native of Ridgewood, New Jersey, was scanning the overnight AP wire at the *Minot Daily News* when he saw the dispatch about the Moskowitz story and its conclusion that Berkowitz wasn't alone in the .44 shootings.

Nies's mind immediately clicked on to John Carr. Nies wasn't working in North Dakota when Carr died seventeen months earlier. But, as his paper's current police reporter, he'd heard stories of Carr's links to Berkowitz from various Minot and Ward County police officers—connections that were unknown by us in New York.

Twice in the months after Carr's death I phoned Dakota authorities, only to be turned away. And New York officials had slammed the lid on us in the East. But Nies, who dealt with the Dakota officers daily, knew explosive facts which had been kept from us.

He phoned Gannett's main office in White Plains and reached Tom Bartley, who told him I was en route to Fire Island but would be checking back with him. Four days later, Nies and I established contact.

"There's a lot of information on John Carr out here," Jeff said. "They know he was involved with Berkowitz and belonged to a satanic cult. They sent it all to New York before Berkowitz pleaded guilty but it was squelched back there."

"What?" I was incredulous. "We were after him before his death and they closed us down. Now you're saying they knew he was tied to Berkowitz all along?"

"Exactly," Nies emphasized.

"And a cult, too?"

"Yeah, they got it all right after Carr died."

"Jeff, you'd have no way of knowing this, but we saw Berkowitz nine months ago and he confirmed knowing Carr and he said there was a cult, too. Now I hear that the cops out there uncovered the same things long *before* we talked to Berkowitz. Damn it, confirmations of everything existed all along. Berkowitz's statements were confirmed before we even met him."

"They didn't really cover it up out here," Jeff said. "They sent it all to New York."

"O.K., O.K. But don't you see, there's no debate on this anymore. Both Carr and Berkowitz admitted to knowing each other and there's cult evidence on both ends. We've got it!"

Nies then began filling in the blanks. Over the next two weeks, the scope of what had been hidden about John Carr was unveiled to me. The information was stunning. Finally, I told Jeff I needed to talk with one of the officers involved in the Carr investigation. Three more days elapsed before Nies persuaded Lieutenant Terry Gardner of the Ward County Sheriff's Department to speak with me. It was Gardner who was quoted in the *Post* story about Carr's death and said the Dakota investigation was complete.

Gardner was initially suspicious, and several conversations ensued before he began to open up at all. When he did, he put Minot police officer Mike Knoop on an extension. Knoop, who'd done undercover work in Minot's drug culture, had himself developed information about Carr.

"Hell, yes," Gardner said. "We said the investigation was done. We didn't owe those papers in New York a thing. Some of them thought they were God almighty because they were from New York, and we didn't take too well to that. In the second place, we were asked to keep it quiet by the Westchester Sheriff's Department because, they told us, there was a confidential investigation going on."

"Who asked you to keep it quiet and what did you do?" I asked.

"The investigator's name was Ken Zajac, and he said they had a case going with John Carr and Son of Sam."

"Yeah, thanks to us, they did," I said. "They didn't know shit until I told them."

"You told them?" Gardner was surprised.

"Yeah, and before them we went to the Brooklyn DA's office."

"Well, we forwarded everything we found to Westchester," Gardner said. "We couldn't believe we never heard from anyone in New York after that. It just died. Someone back there called [our] sheriff—because we kept looking into it—and told us to forget it."

"You're aware they then ignored what you people dug up and let Berkowitz plead guilty as a lone killer three months later?"

"Yeah. We were surprised there wasn't any follow-up, but what could we do?"

"New York had the Son of Sam case, not us," Mike Knoop said.

"That's right," Gardner added. "I'm certain they figured that Carr was Berkowitz's accomplice and he was dead, so they couldn't prosecute him. And to let this out would have blown the whole case against Berkowitz out of the water. All his confessions, everything would go up in smoke."

"Was Carr in a cult?" I asked.

"Yeah," said Gardner. "He was a cultie, and he was involved with Berkowitz. We interviewed a lot of his friends and looked into his life pretty good at the time."

"There was a lot of dope dealing out here, too," Knoop cut in. "And old John Carr was up to his neck in it."

"Do either of you guys know Carr's nicknames?" I asked.

"Sure," Gardner answered. "J.C. was one and Wheaties was another."

"Where'd you get that?"

"His girlfriend, Linda O'Connor, and his drug counselor," Gardner said.

"That's a big piece of information, gentlemen. Berkowitz told us John Carr was John Wheaties."

"Sure," Knoop agreed. "They knew each other. We got that, too."

* * *

The evidence compiled in North Dakota was so compelling I immediately pulled out all the stops in New York to learn just what official agencies were aware of the information. Sal D'Iorio of the Westchester Sheriff's Department, which apparently ran interference for the Brooklyn DA's office, said all information the department received was forwarded to Brooklyn DA Eugene Gold "in a matter of days."

Technically, the Sheriff's Department was blameless. But in effect, it ducked its Son of Sam responsibilities on jurisdictional grounds and laid the accountability on Brooklyn. "They were prosecuting the Son of Sam case," D'Iorio said. "We passed everything we uncovered on to them."

At no time did anyone in the Westchester Sheriff's Department advise me that important information confirming the John Carr, Berkowitz and cult suspicions I'd originated had been unearthed in North Dakota. And neither, of course, did Gold's office in Brooklyn. Without any follow-up investigation, as Gardner and Knoop said, the Brooklyn DA—who kept Queens and apparently the Bronx in the dark—sat back and allowed Berkowitz to plead guilty as a sole killer in early May 1978. And this was the agency that already knew about the VW chase, our information about Carr and a cult, and Mrs. Davis's statement about Berkowitz's Galaxie leaving the area shortly before the Moskowitz-Violante attack.

Queens district attorney John Santucci would later remark: "The information about Carr never reached this office. Five .44 attacks occurred in my jurisdiction and I was uncomfortable with the entire case since the arrest and had been urging a trial, but couldn't convince the other district attorneys [Gold and Mario Merola], who were willing to accept the guilty pleas. If I was aware of the Carr information I would have acted on it then. I only wish you'd come to me instead of Brooklyn. But you had no way of knowing what was going to occur either."

Indeed, eighteen months had elapsed and only now was I learning what really happened after John Carr's death.

*   *   *

When Carr's body was found the night of February 16, 1978, he was in fact termed a probable homicide victim, not the suicide as later told to the *Post.* Said Gardner: "At the time, we didn't really know what happened. We eventually called it an *apparent* suicide, but we never really closed the case. If information was later found to call it homicide or probable homicide again, we'd do so."

What Gardner didn't mention is that a tentative determination of "apparent suicide" eliminated the need for a long, complicated murder investigation which could have failed. As sheriff's investigator Glenn Gietzen later told the *Minot Daily News*: "New York told us Carr was wanted for questioning. I viewed him as a devil worshipper who blew himself away rather than get caught."

Yes, a devil worshipper. Gietzen said he found Carr's tarot cards and occult posters "with X's and O's, upturned [inverted] crosses, and snakes on them." And there was more. On February 21, the day before our *Post* story appeared, Westchester sheriff's investigator Kenneth Zajac contacted North Dakota concerning Carr. He reported to his superior, D'Iorio, the day after I called D'Iorio about Carr's death that he had:

> . . . contacted the Minot, North Dakota, Police Department, speaking to Lt. Hendrickson who revealed to me that John C. Carr, DOB 10/12/46, was in fact found dead in their jurisdiction and that it was being carried as a homicide, possible suicide, but was not classified as suicide as of this writing. He further stated that the Ward County Sheriffs Dept. was investigating the case.
>
> He informed me that a Detective Getson [Gietzen] was working on the case.
>
> I then spoke to Deputy Linn Howe who related to me that John C. Carr was the victim of a homicide, as yet not classified a suicide, and that their investigation into the case was continuing. He did, however, inform me that they were in possession of written statements from friends of John C. Carr in which John C. Carr allegedly told them he was friends of David Berkowitz and he knew him personally for a long time.

> . . . *Also at this time, this writer [Zajac] was informed that Det. Get-*
> *son had interviewed the psychiatrist who was treating John C. Carr who*
> *listed him (Carr) as a "paranoid schizophrenic" and made statements to*
> *Det. Getson of his (Carr's) problems.*
>
> *Det. Getson also ascertained that John C. Carr made, during therapy,*
> *drawings of David Berkowitz, his home, apartment, etc.*
>
> . . . *Det. Getson informed Investigator Zajac that he would be sending*
> *this writer [Zajac] via mail copies of the reports, statements, etc.*
>
> . . . *The undersigned asked Det. Getson at this point if any other*
> *law enforcement agencies had contacted him [yet] regarding this case,*
> *to which he stated that WFAS radio [a Westchester station] had called*
> *him. Other members of his department were contacted by the* New York
> Post. . . . *After the first statement was made by them (Ward County*
> *Sheriffs Dept.) they were hanging up on these people and not discussing*
> *the case further with anyone except the undersigned.*

D'Iorio then authorized a telex, which was sent to North Dakota that afternoon, February 21. Addressed to Ward County deputy Linn Howe, the message was signed by Zajac for the Westchester sheriff, Thomas Delaney.

> *As per our conversation this date. May this serve to . . . request all infor-*
> *mation re: John C. Carr, DOA as of 2/17/78 homicide your jurisdiction.*
> *Request copies of investigation, any photos, or photos found in residence*
> *revealing any connection or possible connection with New York or res-*
> *idents of New York. Also, copies of statements you have from friends.*
> *Official letter of request in mail to your jurisdiction this date.*

Later that same night, as the *Post* presses prepared to roll, another telex was sent to North Dakota from Westchester authorities. This one impounded all of John Carr's effects:

> *This dept. believes family of John C. Carr . . . homicide your jurisdiction,*
> *en route to your jurisdiction in attempt to regain or take possession of*
> *personal property of victim Carr. This property presently impounded by*
> *your department for this department. Do not release to family. If any*
> *difficulty pls call . . . attention Chief Investigator D'Iorio or Investigator*
> *Zajac immediately. Repeat:*
> *Do not release property.*

On February 22, with the *Post* article on the newsstands, Zajac reported to D'Iorio that he'd done an initial check on Carr's brother, Michael, as I'd recommended two days earlier. I advised D'Iorio that North Dakota contacts told us Michael, twenty-five, was a counselor in the Church of Scientology and was professionally involved in photo graphics and illustrations, a possible link to the Breslin letter's printing style. Zajac then switched to the North Dakota probe and dropped a bombshell:

> Detective Getson [Gietzen] stated during this personal conversation with the undersigned that John C. Carr was known to be a member of a satanistic occult group in his jurisdiction that was drug oriented. He (Carr) made statements to Getson that part of the ritual was drinking the leader's urine. This ritual, according to Detective Getson, was satanistically oriented.

Gietzen had been told about the ritual by Carr himself when he was picked up on a Minot street in October 1976. Minot police officer Michael Knoop also heard the urine-drinking comment, and stated Carr said it was consumed from a chalice. Knoop had uncovered evidence of satanic cult activity in the area while working with undercover drug informants; and Carr was known to the police as a drug dealer.

At the time of this incident, Carr, suffering from a drug overdose, had been thrown from a van and found by Gietzen, who was then joined by Knoop. Carr had more than two thousand dollars in cash strapped to his leg and in his wallet, allegedly from drug dealings.

Zajac absorbed more details during his conversations with Ward County and Minot officials that day, and fired off another report to D'Iorio. In it, Zajac stated his professional evaluation of the case. The memo, as usual, was labeled "Son of Sam Investigation."

> It is the opinion of the undersigned that there is a strong possibility that John C. Carr may be involved with David Berkowitz, [in addition to] the fact that the North Dakota Ward County Sheriff's Office informed this writer at 4:30 p.m. . . . that they had statements from John C. Carr's girlfriend in North Dakota, which contained alleged facts that John C. Carr did in fact know David Berkowitz. Also, statements from . . . males verify the fact that John C. Carr knew David Berkowitz personally.

The investigation was at this stage at the moment the *Post* article was being discredited by the authorities in New York City and Westchester. On February 23, with the story we'd put together dead and buried, Zajac wrote:

> Det. Getson, while speaking to [Zajac] via telephone . . . stated that Linda R. O'Connor had made a statement that during John Carr's trips in and out of North Dakota he made statements to her that he knew the police were looking for him in connection with David Berkowitz and he (Carr) was extremely paranoid.

Det. Getson then stated to Linda R. O'Connor: "You knew that he
was being looked for by the police and yet you still harbored him. Do you
realize that is a crime?" She stated, "I had no knowledge that he was a
criminal, so I was not bound by that law."

... (Carr) stated [to Linda] that the cops were hot on his trail and he
had to leave [New York] for a while but he would contact her.

On February 24, Ward County officers interviewed Jeffrey Sloat, an airman and former roommate of Carr's. The report said, in part: "During the period of them being roommates, John C. Carr acted in strange ways, always talking of Berkowitz and stating they were friends." (One of the "strange ways" Carr acted, another report said, was to cover ten-dollar bills with mayonnaise and eat them.)

On February 27, Ward County investigator Glenn Gietzen wrote up another report on an interview with Sloat. In part, it said:

He (Carr) talked a lot of Berkowitz, a lot of Son of Sam, and talked
about his dog Berkowitz had shot. When asked for particular details,
Jeffrey said it was mostly small talk until after the dog was shot.... [The
Carr dog was shot in April; Berkowitz was arrested in August. Accord-
ing to Sloat, Carr was talking about Berkowitz even before April, many
months before his arrest as Son of Sam. The Carr family said they'd never
even heard of Berkowitz until June, when the Cassaras in New Rochelle
named him as a suspect in the wounding of the Carr family's dog in
Yonkers.]

Jeffrey was instrumental in committing John in a mental institution.
When asked why he had done that, he stated: "All the time he lived with
me he acted very crazy."... He stated John would run around beating on
the walls, breaking glass, and screaming something that was incoherent.
John conversed quite often with Abraham Lincoln through a picture,
carrying on lengthy conversations with the past president. He would
write all over the walls the letters XXO and XOX [with an inverted cross
beneath, as drawn by Gietzen later].... He would also write, "There's
only 32 days in a month, so to hell."

Carr, the authorities also determined, owned several guns. In total, police in North Dakota amassed information indicating that Carr knew Berkowitz (in contrast to the official story put forth in New York); was involved in a satanic cult; knew police in New York were looking for him and fled; and used and dealt drugs and owned weapons, including handguns.

A clear picture of Carr's deteriorated mental state also emerged from the interviews, as did the fact that he closely resembled a Son of Sam composite sketch released after the Lomino-DeMasi attack, a time police established Carr was in New York.

And nothing happened. Berkowitz was allowed to plead guilty as a lone killer. There wasn't even a follow-up investigation, as emphasized by the North Dakota police.

* * *

In late August 1979, my conversations continued with Jeff Nies, Gardner and Knoop. One night, while Nies listened in on an extension in the Sheriff's Department, I asked Gardner for the names of people he'd learned were associated with John Carr. The deputy reached into a file and went down a list of names, most of whom were from North Dakota.

He then came to another name. "This guy's supposed to be from New York," he said.

"O.K., that's of interest. Who is it?"

"It's this guy named Reeve Rockman," Gardner replied, and then prepared to continue with his list.

"Reeve Rockman?"

"Yeah, we don't have much on this dude. Just that he was out here with Carr in October of '76, just after John got the boot from the Air Force and went on a druggie binge."

"What else?"

"Nothing much. Rockman showed up out here and John went back to New York with him about October 25 of '76."

"I see."

"Who the hell is he? You know him?" Gardner asked.

"I don't know anymore. I thought he was a figment of somebody's imagination."

* * *

I hadn't spoken to Bronx homicide detective Hank Cinotti since the week after the aborted Good Friday stakeout in Untermyer Park. And it wasn't easy for me to make the call.

"Hank, you remember your boy Rockman—Veronica Lueken's pride and joy? Well, it seems he managed to get himself to North Dakota to visit his buddy John Wheaties."

"No shit!" Cinotti exulted. "I told you he was involved but you didn't want to believe it."

"I knew about his two names and addresses, and I always said he was curious. But I couldn't buy the rest of Lueken's story and neither could Jim," I explained. "Look, what's done is done. The important thing is that he's a live wire again."

"He always was with me." Hank chuckled.

"O.K., I had that coming." I told Cinotti about the North Dakota information and said I was flying to Minot as soon as possible.

"Not without me, you aren't," Hank insisted.

"I've got the interviews lined up. I've got to talk to these friends of Carr. They're expecting me there over Labor Day weekend. I've got a flight that Friday before."

"Will you let me talk to this Gardner?" Hank asked.

I gave Cinotti the deputy's number and began preparing for the trip. I would be going alone. Joe Ungaro, the Gannett papers' executive editor, authorized my expenses, but not Jim Mitteager's. And Mitteager, who was strapped for cash because of his legal problem, couldn't afford to go on his own. His trial date was also approaching and he was occupied with his defense. A third consideration was that Jim remained openly critical of both Cinotti and Lueken.

"I think all the stuff about Carr is great," he said. "And you can bet it's on target. But this Rockman thing—for all I know Lueken called up out there a year ago and Gardner just forgets the information came that way."

"No, he knows right where it came from."

Jim was starting to feel that his input was being back-burnered, and he was dismayed that I'd reached out for Cinotti again. He also resented that Gannett declined to underwrite his trip, although it was merely an economic decision. But Jim still remembered the first series published in March, when editors kept his byline off the articles because of his arrest.

"I don't like what's going on," he said. "I don't blame you, but it seems like things are starting to get out of hand."

"You don't expect me to stay home, do you?"

"Of course not. You dug it up anyway. I hope everything goes great out there. Just call me from Minot and let me know what the hell is happening, will you?"

"You got it."

* * *

As I drove to La Guardia Airport on August 31, I was unaware of a violent event that had recently happened in Queens. Shortly after the Moskowitz article was published—which itself came on the heels of Berkowitz's throat slashing—a rotund young man named Howard Weiss was shot to death in his Flushing apartment.

Months later, Weiss's close male companion—his lover, police say—would be arrested for the killing. His name was Rodriguez. The relevancy of this murder would increase when it became known that Weiss was a friend of David Berkowitz.

Weiss, Berkowitz and a former Yonkers police officer I will call Peter Shane all belonged to a police auxiliary fire rescue unit in the Bronx in 1971, before Berkowitz joined the Army.

Shane, in applying for the Yonkers police position in 1973, listed Weiss as a reference. He would later acknowledge that he gave Weiss two handguns in the spring of 1979, shortly before Weiss's murder. Shane and Berkowitz each owned .44 Bulldog revolvers; and although sources said Weiss also did, none was found in his apartment. But detectives working the Weiss case told a reporter that "most of Weiss's guns were recovered."

The implication was evident: Weiss owned more guns. Both Weiss and Shane held "peace officer" status: Shane as a Yonkers cop and Weiss as a part-time investigator for a Bronx child welfare agency. Thus, firearms registration certificates, through which their gun ownerships could be traced, weren't available.

Shane knew Wheat Carr, sister of John and Michael, from her own post as a civilian dispatcher with the Yonkers Police Department. Therefore, Shane provided a direct link between Weiss, Berkowitz and members of the Carr family. And Shane's tie to Berkowitz wasn't an old one. It would be established that Shane, Berkowitz and Weiss all attended the Maryland wedding of another friend shortly before the Son of Sam killings began.

"There were movies of the wedding reception. They were there," I'd learn from Queens assistant district attorney Herb Leifer.

Shane, for his part, would acknowledge his friendship with Wheat Carr and Weiss, but said he didn't work with Berkowitz in the auxiliary unit. Yet, as Leifer would say, "Those guys were all at the wedding, and Shane and Weiss were friends—and so were Weiss and Berkowitz."

Reporter Dan Diamond later quoted a source as telling him, flat out, that Shane and Weiss were both involved in the cult with Berkowitz. "They are all psychos who are intrigued by blood and death. It's part of their life," the source stated. He added that the three men, as well as other cult members, were "fire buffs" and explained that this common bond influenced their cult activities, some of which involved arson.

Years later, a friend of Berkowitz's would supply me with specifics of the "fire" connection that confirmed the allegations made by the source.

In the meantime, Howard Weiss was dead, and another avenue of investigation was shut off permanently. His ties with Berkowitz and Shane would be firmly established during the coming months. Charter Arms had sold only 28,000 .44 Bulldogs in the entire United States at this time. Yet at least two (and later more) people linked to Berkowitz owned them. It was a curious statistic. If only 28,000 out of 250 million U.S. residents owned .44 Bulldogs, the odds against any one person having one were already high. And the odds against several people, all of whom were connected to one person—Berkowitz—owning them were astronomical.

Before the Weiss link would be uncovered, there was evidence lurking in North Dakota. It was time to pull it from the shadows once and for all.

XIV

A Matter of Murder

A crashing thunderstorm raged in the early-evening darkness as the jet bucked its way toward the small Minot airport. Outside the cabin windows, jagged bolts of lightning stabbed the inky summer sky.

"See that, Hank? They know we're coming. The witches of Minot are out to get us."

Cinotti, trying to balance a teetering glass of wine as the plane shuddered in the buffeting wind, laughed nervously. Until I saw him at the ticket counter in New York, I didn't know if the detective would make the trip. Only at the last minute did he receive his superiors' permission to go. He even held a pre-departure phone conference with Detective Captain John Plansker, not mentioning he was traveling with me. And so once again, as had occurred eighteen months earlier in Westchester, the Son of Sam case was technically reopened.

"Come on," Cinotti chided. "You're not afraid of those witches, are you?"

"Screw the witches. It's this weather that's somewhat unnerving," I answered as the jet dipped again.

The trip had been a long one. We'd changed planes in Minneapolis and stopped at Grand Forks, North Dakota, before encountering the storm. The pilot announced we were circling Minot and would land from the west to escape the frightening weather.

"I wonder what's waiting for us down there," Hank said.

"The ground, I hope. And after that, I don't know. But there's a lot to learn. I just hope to hell we can get it."

Finally, we touched the runway and the plane lurched toward the terminal area.

"I'll bet the Pope took this flight once and ever since then he kisses the ground when he gets off a plane," I said as we braked to a halt.

Ever religious, Hank shook his head at the blasphemy. At the exact moment we stepped into the rainy night, I thought there was some ironic truth to the Pope comment as a brass band began playing in front of the terminal.

"Some covert intelligence trip this is," Cinotti shouted over the din. "They send out an orchestra to meet us."

Actually, the group was assembled to welcome a local politician. Once inside the terminal, I heard a familiar twang.

"Hey, you guys looking for a couple of cops?"

It was Terry Gardner, accompanied by Mike Knoop and Jeff Nies.

"How'd you know it was us?" Hank asked. "The plane was full."

"That's why we're cops." Gardner grinned.

Gardner, twenty-nine, was an Air Force Vietnam veteran who joined the Ward

County Sheriff's Department in 1973. Born in Illinois, he spoke with a pronounced midwestern lilt; and the cowboy hat he wore completed the effect. Cinotti promptly anointed Gardner with nicknames, dubbing him both "McCloud" and "Deputy Dawg," for the cartoon character.

"Well, pa'dner," Hank drawled in Bronxese, "we got a horse named Maverick in the NYPD. You should come on all in to New York and ride him right through the front of One Po-leese Plaza, heah."

"Shit, I should have done that with the Carr file last year," Gardner agreed. "When I get to New York I'll bring Knooper here with me. Need somebody to wade through that mess you guys made back there."

Mike Knoop laughed easily. He was tall, husky and bespectacled. At thirty, he was a veteran Minot police officer. Like Gardner, he spoke with a midwestern flair. But unlike Gardner, he rarely raised his voice above a low decibel.

While the cops bantered, Jeff Nies pulled me aside and we exchanged greetings. His work on the case was extremely helpful, and I thanked him for contacting me after reading the AP dispatch about the Moskowitz article.

"Enough of this stuff," Gardner said. "Let's get the hell out of here and get you folks to your motel."

Minot is a small city, its population about 33,000. It is situated 1,600 feet above sea level on the banks of the Souris River a hundred miles north of Bismarck and about fifty miles south of the Canadian border. Its summers are short and pleasant; its winters, long and bitterly cold. In farm country, Minot is surrounded by miles of open, rolling plains and an occasional large, scenic lake. The Air Force base, where John Carr died, is about thirteen miles north of the city.

In short order we gathered in our motel's cocktail lounge to discuss the case. The two Dakota policemen had lined up several interviews for us: Linda O'Connor, John Carr's girlfriend; her ex-husband, Craig; Tom Taylor and Darlene Christiansen, two close friends of Carr who traveled to New York for his funeral; and Leslie Shago, another friend. Nies also arranged for us to talk by phone with Carr's drug counselor, Lee Slaghter, from his new home in Minnesota.

Over a round of drinks, Gardner and Knoop filled us in on their investigation of Carr.

"He was really tight with an Indian named Phil Falcon, who ran a coffee shop here called the Falcon's Nest. We found some dead German shepherds behind that place," Gardner said. "That goes with what you found in New York. Falcon was into the occult—he's out West now. He left here about a year before Carr became oatmeal."

"There was a group of about eight or nine of them," Knoop continued. "Dope dealing, Satan rituals, you name it. Carr was a dealer and a user."

"Where'd they meet?" I asked.

"Besides the Falcon's Nest, they had rituals at some old farm somewhere out of town," Gardner said. "There's a guy named Donny Boone, who split from here. He was in it. He was decapped in a car wreck in Arizona in '76. And then there's Jerry

Berg, who used to live in Bismarck but came up here to Minot State College and stayed. He and his buddy, Larry Milenko,* were in the cult scene with Carr."

"Along with a guy called the Wiz," Knoop added. "And there were some others, too, who were minor players."

"What about Carr and Berkowitz?" Cinotti asked.

"Our investigation showed they knew each other and Carr admitted it," Gardner answered.

"Well, Berkowitz admitted knowing Carr, too," I said. "And both these admissions came at different times in different parts of the country. That argument is over."

"Besides Carr, could any of these others have come to New York for the Sam shootings?" Cinotti wanted to know.

"It's possible," Knoop replied. "We can't prove it, but it's not off the wall to think they might have. We know John was back there to be available for four or five of the shootings—including that one where the two girls were shot on the stoop."

"Yeah, that's one I'm very interested in concerning John," I said. "He fits the description; he was left-handed and he was in town. They had a witness who saw the shooter split carrying the gun in the left hand."

"What about Rockman?" Hank demanded. "How the hell did you get him?"

Gardner chuckled. "I talked to Craig O'Connor, who told me Carr was afraid of a 'Rockman.' I thought he said, 'rock man.' I even put it in my notes that way: 'Carr said a rock man is going to kill him, apparently a musician.'"

I looked at Gardner. "And you say New York cops are turkeys?"

"Shit, Craig didn't know anything but that statement. Anyway, I then found some local girl named Harliss, who I heard knew Carr and was into the occult. She gave me some cult dope about Carr and said Rockman was a dude who came out here on one occasion in order to see John."

"Why?" Cinotti asked.

"Maybe dope, but we don't know for sure. He spent about a week here and then John went back to New York with him in late October '76—just after he left the service."

"Rock man," I teased again. "Who'd you think it was, David Bowie?"

"Goddamn," Gardner said. "It was just me and Knooper here trying to dig up all this information. Gietzen didn't give a damn once the first week of interviews was over. He said it was New York's problem—and look how they handled it. Down the hatch. But we were curious about what we found, so we just kept going."

"How did the sheriff feel about this?" Hank asked.

"He didn't mind, but after a while he said there was nowhere to go with the information except to use it as intelligence about the dope and cult scene. So we stopped."

"That was the Minot Police Department's response, too," Mike Knoop added.

"It's a good thing you guys kept poking into it," Hank said.

"I'm furious about this whole damned thing," I said. "We were there right after Berkowitz's arrest. All this Carr stuff you guys got confirmed what we were onto all along. And we see Berkowitz, who gives us all this information that you guys had already confirmed, but we didn't know it. We blew a year and a half."

"Look," Gardner said. "We didn't know what you were into back there. We're cops. We hear from the cops back there and we deal with them. They fucked it up, nobody else."

Jeff Nies, who'd been quiet during most of the conversation, put things into perspective.

"At least it wasn't lost forever. It could have been. But now everybody's together here. We can still pull it together," he said.

"A lot of time has gone by," Cinotti replied. "The trail is colder now."

"Well, let's heat 'er up," Gardner said, and ordered another round for the table.

* * *

The first interviews were scheduled for the afternoon of Saturday, September 1. In the morning, we met Sheriff Leon Schwan and Minot police chief Carroll Erickson, visited the now shuttered Falcon's Nest and drove out to the base—where we saw the Liberty Loop home where Carr was found dead and were introduced to Rick Ferron, OSI's chief investigator. We also studied notes and reports compiled by Gardner, Knoop and Gietzen, and Jeff Nies showed us the results of interviews he'd conducted since we established contact in late July.

For the sake of conciseness and clarity, the following are highlights of the information uncovered by us, the North Dakota authorities and investigators for the Queens district attorney's office—who would travel to Minot two months after our visit. In each instance, the information overlapped, as the details provided by Carr's associates and others remained consistent.

That John Carr was nicknamed Wheaties was confirmed in taped statements by Linda O'Connor, counselor Lee Slaghter and Phil Falcon, whom we later reached by telephone. "On one of his jackets he even had a patch with a Wheaties box sewn on the shoulder," Falcon said.

Linda O'Connor added: "Wheaties, breakfast of champions. He liked to eat them. I thought the nickname originated here and not in New York." Slaghter said simply: "John told me one of his nicknames was Wheaties."

Queens investigators later received an additional confirmation from a friend of Carr's in New York. Thus, Berkowitz's statement about the nickname at Marcy was confirmed, and John Carr was identified as an alias of Son of Sam used in the Breslin letter.

That John Carr was involved in satanic cult activity, as stated by Berkowitz at Marcy and crucial to our evaluation of the entire case, was confirmed by Tom Taylor, Darlene Christiansen, Leslie Shago, Harliss, Phil Falcon and Carr's own sister, Wheat. She later told Queens investigators: "John's involvement in the occult I'm not going to deny. There's no way I could deny it. I'd be stupid to deny it."

Counselor Lee Slaghter also said: "John talked about witchcraft in passing, but didn't dwell on it." Airman Jeff Sloat, who roomed with Carr for a time, previously described the "XXO" symbols with inverted crosses beneath that Carr drew on walls. And Deputy Glenn Gietzen recovered occult posters and tarot cards among Carr's effects.

Leslie Shago provided an important link between New York and Minot rituals when she produced a receipt which showed that she brought the ear of a German shepherd to a taxidermist for mounting on August 9, 1977—the day before Berkowitz's arrest. "I didn't know what it meant," she said. "Bobby Dukes,* a friend of John Carr's, asked me to do it for him." (In the Pine Street neighborhood, a German shepherd was later found with an ear "sliced off.")

Tom Taylor, Carr's lanky, long-haired musician friend, said Carr asked him to attend a cult meeting at an old farm outside Minot, but he declined.

But perhaps the most graphic description of Carr's cult activities came from his dark-haired Indian friend, Phil Falcon. In a recorded interview with me, Nies and Jack Graham of the *Minot Daily News,* Falcon said: "He kept a list of the demons of hell on him. And to gain power over people, to put a curse on them, he'd go out and bury shit on their lawns. He thought this was some black magic curse. He was a Satanist."

"These demons he kept a list of—would they include 'Behemoth' and 'Beelzebub'?" I asked.

"Those were two of them."

"And this excrement—was it dog manure?"

"Yeah."

This information provided two more links between Carr and the Son of Sam letters.

Falcon went on to say that Carr belonged to cults in both Minot and Westchester County, New York, an important confirmation of our suspicions. He described the New York group as "very violent, large and underground. They were really into the occult. They'd all get together in like a witches' coven, a witch's church. Their sacrifices went all the way."

Falcon said the Westchester group convened "both indoors and outdoors," and at least one of its meeting sites "was pretty close to [Carr's] house." This fit the description of Untermyer Park, but Falcon couldn't recall the exact location. He described an indoor site also, which he remembered as being an attachment to someone's home or business. He added that he thought there were other locations, too, but said he knew nothing about them. At the time, we didn't think Falcon meant "witch's church" literally. It would later turn out to be just that.

Falcon said that John Carr was "very much" into satanism and that "John read my entire collection of occult books, [from] how to make amulets to the 'third eye.'"

Carr, Falcon said, practiced some satanic rituals in Minot with Donny Boone, whom Falcon didn't know was dead.

"I came to my house and here were Donny and John," Falcon explained in describing one ritual. "When I walked in the door, they were in the kitchen, and Donny had this animal, whatever it was. He had cut its throat and it was bleeding all over the kitchen. He was going to take it into the other room there. There was a [magic] circle drawn and they were sacrificing it. Old Donny Boone was drinking the animal's blood. It was running down his chin."

Falcon said he put a stop to the ritual and threw Carr and Boone out of his house. "It was an unbelievable mess to clean up."

If Falcon knew other details about cult activity in Minot or Westchester, he didn't disclose them. He acknowledged his own occult interests, but avoided saying whether or not he participated in any sacrificial rituals himself. As Gardner noted, several German shepherds were found slain behind Falcon's coffee shop, although there is no evidence that Falcon himself was involved in the deaths of those dogs. The coffee shop was a regular hangout for Carr, Boone and others involved in the Satan scene.

*   *   *

In other areas of inquiry vital to our investigation, Carr's relationship with Berkowitz, which each had confirmed, was paramount.

Counselor Lee Slaghter said: "John told me he looked up to Berkowitz because Berkowitz wasn't afraid to do anti-establishment things. He told me they used to bum around together in Yonkers. But something happened between them. There was bad blood between them after a while." This statement supported Berkowitz's Marcy comment, when he said he "hated" John Carr.

Slaghter added that Carr "had a tremendous amount of detailed knowledge of the [.44] shootings, like the kinds of cars the victims were in and things like that. He said he knew more about the Son of Sam case than the police did. He also alluded to being at crime scenes, but his inference was subtle. He didn't actually say he was." Slaghter then said: "I told all this to a New York detective who called me and asked me about John shortly after his death. I don't remember [the detective's] name."

Phil Falcon made a significant statement: "He never called him David or Dave. I didn't know it was Berkowitz. He just used to talk about his friend Berkie in Yonkers." So, as Berkowitz knew Carr's nickname, so did Carr know Berkowitz's, one of which was in fact Berkie.

Falcon's comment was important for another reason. He left Minot for the Pacific Northwest in March 1977—five months before Berkowitz's arrest and three months before Sam Carr first learned Berkowitz's name from the Cassaras. Yet Falcon said Carr was talking about Berkowitz earlier. Falcon's revelation was strengthened by the fact that he didn't return to Minot after March 1977, hadn't spoken to Carr and actually didn't even know Carr was dead until we told him.

Leslie Shago went further. The young fringe associate of the Carr crowd identified a photo of Berkowitz and said he was in Minot on one occasion. The photo was only a portrait, but Shago correctly described Berkowitz's height and weight. Berkowitz has never written about this alleged trip, but a source close to him later told me

Berkowitz said he was in Minot. And in a letter Berkowitz later wrote, he said North Dakota was one of his "favorite states" and accurately described its terrain and other features. No more is known about the alleged trip at this time.

Even more telling about Carr's involvement in the Son of Sam case were statements from Tom Taylor and Darlene Christiansen, who each said they saw him draw the Son of Sam graphic symbol on the back of a Minot telephone directory in February 1977—four months *before* it first appeared in the Breslin letter, but immediately after Carr returned to North Dakota from an extended stay in Yonkers. Taylor said Carr explained the symbol's meaning to him and Darlene at the time. They didn't know it was later used in a Son of Sam communication.

Linda O'Connor, Carr's auburn-haired girlfriend, added that John once wrote a poem dedicated to her husband, Craig, in appreciation of his acceptance of her relationship with John. The writing, she told Gardner and Knoop, said: "Because Craig is Craig, so must the streets be filled with Craigs."

Those same words appeared in a poem later found in Berkowitz's apartment, in which the original meaning was hatefully twisted and directed at Berkowitz's downstairs neighbor, Craig Glassman. That poem said: "Because Craig is Craig, so must the streets be filled with Craig (Death). And huge drops of lead poured down upon her head until she was dead. Yet, the cats still come out at night to mate, and the sparrows still sing in the morning."

"John Carr wrote the original words saying the streets should be filled with good people like Craig O'Connor long before Berkowitz borrowed them," said Gardner.

Linda O'Connor also reported to Gardner, Knoop and the Queens investigators that she saw a receipt for a .44 revolver in the glove compartment of John Carr's auto. She couldn't recall if the receipt was for a Charter Arms .44 or a Colt model.

Along those lines, Tom Taylor said that he personally picked up and examined .44-caliber ammunition in Carr's Minot apartment. "They were Winchesters," he said. He also stated that Carr had a "large handgun," although he wasn't certain whether it was a .44 or a .45, as he hadn't actually held the weapon. "But I never saw any .45 ammo around," he said. Phil Falcon also said that Carr owned "either a .44 or a .45."

A potentially important link to the .44 ammunition is the fact that Berkowitz, via Billy Dan Parker, purchased .44 Winchester bullets in Houston, according to a federal report. But when arrested, Berkowitz had only Smith & Wesson .44 bullets. In his confession, he claimed the S&W ammunition was that which he purchased in Houston, but it wasn't. Therefore, there were two boxes, a hundred rounds, of Winchester bullets unaccounted for, something that apparently didn't concern the NYPD or the Brooklyn DA's office, which sent investigators to Houston after Berkowitz's arrest. (Berkowitz didn't have any .44 shell casings, cleaning equipment or manuals in his apartment, which he should have, as he had that equipment for his other weapons.)

Whether the .44 Winchester bullets Taylor said he examined in Carr's Minot apartment were those bought by Berkowitz in Houston is not known.

Regarding Houston, the interviews in North Dakota established that John Carr visited that city every summer, since his ex-wife and daughter lived nearby, and he apparently was there at the same time as Berkowitz in June 1976. Linda O'Connor said that Carr's brother, Michael, told her this.

Carr, we learned, was in New York at the time of the .44 attacks on Joanne Lomino and Donna DeMasi on November 27, 1976; the murder of Christine Freund on January 30, 1977; the wounding of Judy Placido and Sal Lupo on June 26, 1977; and the murder of Stacy Moskowitz and Robert Violante on July 31, 1977. He was also thought to have been in New York at the time of the murder of Donna Lauria and the wounding of Jody Valente on July 29, 1976. He was eliminated as a suspect in the October 23 wounding of Carl Denaro in 1976; the murder of Virginia Voskerichian on March 8, 1977; and the killing of Valentina Suriani and Alex Esau on April 17, 1977—although it remained possible he could have made a quick turnaround flight to New York on those occasions.

Carr, according to Tom Taylor, wasn't shy about using a gun on people either. Taylor stated that Carr carried a revolver under the front seat of his auto and that on one occasion he fired shots at an acquaintance in Minot named Whitey.

"[Whitey] ripped him off for some crystal or coke, and he decided to have some fun with this guy. Whitey told me he shot at him; other people told me, too. Whitey was in his Volkswagen, putting speakers in it or something like that, and John just pulled up across the street, pulled out his .22 and started shooting at him. Whitey freaked out and ran into the house."

Lieutenant Gardner said: "Whitey reported the shooting to me. He said it was over some drug deal gone bad. He didn't name Carr as the gunman, however. He just wanted to alert us that his life was in danger. They must have settled it all after that."

Regarding Carr's use of alcohol and narcotics, Taylor, and others, said he "drank heavily" (which was known by Berkowitz). Carr was also hospitalized at least three times for drug overdoses. Taylor said: "He was into coke, pot, LSD, angel dust, crystal or whatever you want to call it." Another strong piece of evidence linking Carr to the Son of Sam case was the discovery that Carr dated thirteen- to fifteen-year-old girls in Minot. At least three friends, including Tom Taylor and Frank Head, reported this proclivity. In the Breslin letter, John Wheaties was called a "rapist and suffocater of young girls."

Moreover, in a note left in his apartment and dismissed by New York authorities, Berkowitz referred to Carr as a "terrible rapist and child molester. You should hear John boast of his perverted conquests," Berkowitz wrote, but the accurate clue was ignored.

In a closing note on Carr's activities, Gardner said an informant named Denise Malcom* said that Carr advised her that "a chain of safe houses for Satanists on the run existed in the United States and Canada. We checked with the Canadian authorities," Gardner said, "and we were told that some kind of network existed up there for bikers and that they heard Satanists also sometimes used the same facilities."

* * *

By the time the extended series of interviews was completed, all the involved parties were certain as to where we stood regarding John Carr.

"Besides what we learned, he and Michael were, in real life, the sons of Sam," I said. "It makes more sense for them to have used the name than Berkowitz. I keep remembering that Borrelli letter, with all its intimate knowledge of Sam Carr and how it sounded like it was written from right inside that house."

And so it was with John Carr, a man who New York officials—without any investigation—first maintained didn't even know Berkowitz and whose suspected involvement in the murders—and that of a satanic cult—was formally reported to authorities by Jim Mitteager and me weeks before his death. A man whose initially uncovered connections to Berkowitz were buried by the office of Brooklyn district attorney Eugene Gold before Berkowitz entered his guilty pleas. A man whose links to the Son of Sam were not fully fleshed out until we traveled to Minot, making the journey no New York officials made before then.

And then there was Reeve Rockman, the other subject of the trip. His photo was identified by Taylor, Christiansen and Leslie Shago, who pointed out: "When he was here he was about twenty pounds lighter than in the picture." Shago also said Rockman "had something wrong with one of his hands," as did Taylor and Falcon. These observations were accurate.

Rockman, a mystery figure and stranger to Carr's friends in North Dakota, was observed at the Falcon's Nest and at a party in Minot in mid-October 1976—shortly after Carr left the Air Force and was hospitalized with a drug overdose after telling Gietzen and Knoop about his urine drinking at a satanic ritual.

The Minot residents said Rockman was introduced as "Reeve, John's friend from New York." They said they understood that Rockman was involved in drug dealings with Carr in New York.

Taylor and Christiansen said Carr carried a photo of Rockman, apparently a newspaper clipping, in his wallet and told them: "This is the guy who wants to kill me." That statement was essentially the same as one made earlier by Craig O'Connor. "John burned the picture right there in the sink," Taylor said.

"J.C. [Carr] also told me that if he stayed in New York the state would have fried him in the electric chair," Christiansen added.

* * *

The Minot interviews were conducted at the Sheriff's Department, with the exception of that with Leslie Shago, who was visited at her home. Carr's friends were given the option of cooperating or not. The work was exhausting, as some were initially reluctant to talk about their knowledge of Carr.

It wasn't until Monday morning, our third day in Minot, that Cinotti got around to asking a question he and I discussed privately during the weekend.

"What makes you so sure Carr committed suicide?" he asked Gardner. "He was afraid for his life; afraid of Rockman and who knows who else. Someone could have come out here to kill him after he cut out of New York. He was here two days—why come all the way back here to kill yourself in your girlfriend's bedroom? He knew he was wanted for questioning, so there's no reason others couldn't have found that out, too."

"Aw, shit," Gardner replied. "I had a feeling this was coming. We're not certain he killed himself. We called it 'apparent' suicide. It looked like he did it himself, but I can't swear that he did. I know Linda and Taylor and the others think it was murder. Based on all this, it does look like we've got a motive for murder as well as suicide. But he knew he was wanted for questioning—that's a damn good motive for suicide, too."

"He was a weak link, Terry," I said. "He was found out. They could have knocked him off to block the trail."

"Yeah," Hank added. "But they try to make it look like suicide so as not to defeat the purpose."

"Don't look at me," Mike Knoop quickly said. "This was the sheriff's case, with some assistance from the Air Force."

"I'll tell you," said Gardner. "I called Michael Carr that night to tell him of the death. Linda told me not to call Sam because he had a heart condition—"

"A heart condition? Now doesn't that sound familiar?" I said.

"The Borrelli letter," Hank said, nodding.

"Let me finish," Gardner remarked. "Michael didn't sound surprised when I told him. He just said, 'Well, I hope he didn't suffer.' That's a strange thing to say."

"A little hard," Jeff Nies agreed.

"Maybe it was just because they knew of his drug problems and all that," I suggested. "But still, it was a very matter-of-fact way to put it."

"There's something else I didn't tell you," Gardner said. "I didn't want to stir anything up about murder. Nosing around after John's death, I got three anonymous long-distance calls. From the connections I knew they were from a ways off. They were all from women, different women. One said, 'We got John and the gun was across his legs and if you don't lay off we're going to get you.'

"Now the gun thing wasn't public, so I didn't dismiss the call," Gardner continued. "The other two were tips. One said John had a .44 Bulldog, and the other said three .44s were bought down in Texas—one by Berkowitz, one for John and one for somebody else she didn't name."

"Put that with what Linda and Taylor said," I stated. "What about it, Hank? More than one .44? John was down there then."

"I don't know," Cinotti replied. "Most of the bullets were pretty smashed up. And any .44 Bulldogs would have similarities. It's possible."

"How'd they get your name?" Nies asked Gardner.

"It was in the *New York Post,* at least. We did the story," I said. Gardner then produced the photos of Carr's death scene. His head was practically blown off, and he lay on his face at the foot of the bed in Linda O'Connor's apartment. The rifle butt was perched across one leg.

"We think he sat on the bed, put the gun butt on the floor, put the other end in his mouth and pulled the trigger," Gardner explained. "The bullet split and there were two holes in the ceiling above the bed."

"Two holes?"

"But one bullet."

"As long as you're sure," I said. "But shouldn't the gun have hit the floor before he did? It's on top of him."

"Maybe it bounced off the wall and came back. There's only a couple of feet there between the bed and the wall," said Gardner.

"And maybe it didn't."

"Man, you guys are causing trouble," Gardner complained.

Cinotti, a veteran homicide investigator, had another observation. "I think the force of the shot with that .30-30 Marlin rifle should have blown him back onto the bed, not forward to the floor. Unless someone was behind him propping him up. There's hardly any blood at all behind where he sat—everything went forward. So the guy wouldn't have been covered with it."

With that, Cinotti demonstrated his theory. Lying prone on the motel bed, facing the foot of it, he told Gardner to take Carr's seated position. Cinotti then placed his hand on the small of Gardner's back, supporting him. He then simulated the gunshot.

"See, he'd start to go back, but the hand behind him would stop his motion and he'd fall forward, face down, and to the left—just like the body did."

"I don't know," Gardner said slowly. "I mean, what's old Johnny going to do—just sit there and say, 'O.K., now you get behind me'?"

"He'd have been knocked out first," Hank answered. "Then propped up. They'd then set the rifle off with a stick or a broom handle or something. His face was blown off; no one would know if he was slugged first."

"And didn't Linda say he got a call at about eight o'clock, before she went out, but he didn't say who he talked to?" I asked.

"Yeah, that's true. They could have found out then that she was going out for the night. Maybe it did happen that way," Gardner conceded.

Then it was time for our flight back to New York. "We'll keep on everything here," Knoop said.

"And we'll also start looking at this murder scenario," Gardner promised.

"Well, my job is to get moving on Rockman," Hank said. "And no leaks," he stated firmly to me. "You've got to swear none of this goes in the papers. We've got to be able to work this without the damn cameras over our shoulders. And I didn't tell the department I was coming here with you. They'd have stopped me if I did, and the investigation would have been dead as far as they're concerned."

"Why?" I asked. "The NYPD didn't even know Rockman was here until I told you. They take information from all sorts of lowlifes every day—they even pay for it. But the press is different; it's taboo. I don't know if I can make that promise. This is significant news, and I've been after this for more than two years. I've seen enough cover-ups."

"This isn't any cover-up," Hank fumed. "You know this case, damn it. You've seen what's happened before. They don't want the press to know *anything*—let alone be the ones who dug this stuff up in the first place. You're right, I piggybacked with you, and it was the right thing to do—but the PD will never accept that."

For a minute the room was silent. I looked at Jeff Nies, who shrugged. "O.K., no publicity," I then agreed. "We don't need the headlines right now. I think we all want to see some arrests. Nobody out here eliminated Michael Carr, and he was my top suspect coming in. So Mitteager and I will get cracking on him."

Jeff Nies nodded his assent. "I'm in, Hank. My partner [Jack Graham] will be back soon. We'll keep doing our bit. I'm sure the paper will go along with whatever you and Maury want to do."

Gardner jumped in. "If you don't, I'll wrap your little weasel butt around a tree," he said half seriously. He and Nies had had a few run-ins over other coverage in the *Minot Daily News,* so this was a fragile alliance for both of them. Indeed, the situation was precarious for everyone.

Nies, who'd absorbed several Gardner barbs over the weekend, didn't let this one pass. His voice rose an octave. "Don't try to threaten me, Terry," he yelled. "There's nothing in the world that says I have to do what you say."

"Jeff, it's only temporary," I soothed. "If we hold off, the whole thing might fall. If we're premature, we may blow it. And we don't need the NYPD's political crap either."

Mike Knoop was a Solomon of reason. "John Carr is dead. No one can prosecute him. We all want the others—Rockman, Michael Carr or whoever. And a couple of them could even be somewhere in Minot. So we'll all keep it quiet, for everybody's sake. Agreed?"

"Yeah, it's agreed," Jeff said. "I never said it wasn't. I just don't like taking instructions from the Ward County Sheriff's Department."

Gardner glared at him, but said nothing.

* * *

With everyone finally in accord, if not completely satisfied, we drove to the airport, and within thirty minutes we were en route back to New York. It was Labor Day,

September 3, 1979.

"It's a lot different than during that storm Friday night," Hank observed as the sleek jet climbed through the marshmallow cumulus clouds. "The witches of Minot didn't get us after all."

As we settled back to doze, we didn't know that other demons, including death, would soon rise up to face us in New York. The fallout from our trip would stretch some 1,800 miles. And in Minot, now far below us in the warming sun, other tragic events would occur.

In more ways than one, all hell was about to break loose.

XV

Inside the Biggest Case

John Plansker, commander of detectives for the NYPD's Seventh Area in the Bronx, was a man held in high esteem by the cops who worked under him. At fifty, Plansker was respected for his professionalism, his fairness, and his confidence in the men and women with whom he'd broken many an important case over the years. When he was promoted to deputy inspector in 1985, he tossed his own party at a Bronx restaurant and invited about a hundred and fifty of his former and current detectives, picking up the tab himself.

On August 31, as Cinotti prepared to board the flight to Minot, the lean, soft-spoken captain, whose reddish hair showed hints of gray, sent a report to Deputy Chief Edwin Dreher, commander of all Bronx detectives. It was titled "Confidential Investigation, Interim Report #1."

Plansker summed up the allegations against Rockman as he then knew them to be, and mentioned that police officials in Minot had advised Cinotti by telephone that Rockman had been in North Dakota with John Carr. Plansker wrote:

> *[It] appears that we will be able to draw an association with Rockman, Berkowitz and Carr. . . . This would raise the possibility that Berkowitz did not act independently or operate alone as originally believed.*
>
> *I fully realize the implications and ramifications of this report and I also understand the need for discretion in this matter. However, I do believe that we must pursue this investigation to the point where we have eliminated any element of conjecture.*

Dreher, who knew Plansker was a first-rate investigator, approved the request, and the Son of Sam investigation was reopened by the New York City Police Department. There was, of course, no public announcement, and even within the ranks only a handful of people knew what was going on.

For a long time, I'd envisioned champagne corks popping if I was ever able to get the case reopened. The impossible had been accomplished; the perseverance rewarded. But there would be no celebrations. Instead, I found myself sworn to secrecy.

Dreher and his superiors, particularly Chief of Detectives James Sullivan, had not been amused by the Moskowitz investigation we'd published in July, and Dreher probably wasn't overjoyed that Plansker also attached our March conspiracy article to his report. But Dreher knew he had no choice but to act; serious questions about Berkowitz's alleged sole responsibility were being raised publicly for the first time. Neither Dreher nor Plansker knew that the person most responsible for those articles was at that moment en route to Minot to interview witnesses.

Hank Cinotti had made his own choice—a decision many would disagree with. He had gauged the Police Department's reaction to the press's butting into the sacrosanct .44 case, and decided the information he'd gleaned was more important than the source of it: the antagonistic media. For a similar reason, he also protected Veronica Leuken's identity, listing her as a confidential informant. He believed, correctly, that the mention of Lueken's name would sink the ship before it left the pier. Some NYPD officials have stated that Cinotti would have fared better had he laid all his cards on the table. No one will ever know.

For my part, Lueken and Reeve Rockman were mainly the NYPD's responsibility. I was long wary of Lueken, but there was no doubt Rockman was identified by Carr's friends in Minot. But what was his role? Was he an active conspirator and cult member, or was his part that of a well-heeled, white-collar dope dealer? As the NYPD was focusing on Rockman, I left that question unanswered and devoted myself to a deeper probe of Michael Carr and the events surrounding John Carr's death.

*   *   *

The reconstruction of the scene and events immediately preceding John Carr's death strongly suggested he was murdered. The position of the body and that of the gun were prominent factors, but there were others.

For instance, Carr's actions on February 15, the day before he died, were decidedly not those of a man contemplating suicide. He rented a postal box, opened a checking account at a local bank and visited the Air Force to ensure continuing payment of a disability check he was receiving because of a service-connected injury. He took each of these steps within twenty-four hours after returning from New York, from where he'd told Linda O'Connor the police were "hot on his trail."

Next, on the night of his death, February 16, he received a phone call at Linda O'Connor's home before she went out for the evening but he didn't reveal the identity of the 8 p.m. caller to her. When Linda returned at about 12:30 a.m., she saw that her two Irish setter dogs were outside the house; they should have been inside.

She also said that a latch lock on the inside of the front door had been turned to open it—an unnecessary action. John Carr, Linda said, knew the door could be opened from the inside without turning the latch.

Linda also said that Carr was in good spirits before she left and that he told her he would wash the dinner dishes. But the dishes were left half done in the sink, as if Carr was interrupted while washing them. The daily newspaper was also missing from the home, and she reported finding a single glove—neither hers nor Carr's—in the residence.

Linda further stated that she borrowed some money from Carr's wallet, leaving several bills in it. Yet the wallet was empty when Gardner went through it.

For years, Carr had worn a good-luck charm he'd acquired overseas—a "rubbing Buddha"—which was on a chain around his neck. But this artifact wasn't on the body and was missing from the house, as was a picture of his daughter Carr kept in his wallet.

Linda O'Connor also said that she found a spot of blood under a living-room table the next morning. Gardner, however, said he saw no such blood when he examined the premises the night before.

The rifle itself contained no fingerprints—not even smudges. It was as if it had been wiped clean.

At my request, Dr. Louis Roh, the deputy medical examiner of Westchester County, examined the Carr autopsy report. (Roh's testimony would be instrumental in the conviction of Jean Harris for the murder of "Scarsdale Diet Doctor" Herman Tarnower.) On the basis of the powder burns on Carr's inner mouth and palate as described in the autopsy report, Roh said he believed the gun had been inserted deeper into the mouth than normally would occur in a suicide of this type.

Combined, these elements pointed to murder.

Roh's opinion supported Cinotti's and my evaluation of the case, which held that an unconscious or semiconscious Carr was propped up and the gun forced into his mouth.

Linda O'Connor would later tell a friend she believed Carr was silenced because "he knew too much." Berkowitz himself would label him "the weakest link" because of his drug and alcohol problems.

* * *

The photos taken of the death scene were merely snapshots. But examining them through a magnifying glass, I noticed several intriguing clues which escaped the attention of North Dakota investigators.

I brought the pictures to Captain Gerry Buckhout of the Greenburgh Police Department in Westchester County. Buckhout and Donald Singer, Greenburgh's chief of police, had been aiding the investigation because of the possible connection of several sniper incidents which occurred in their jurisdiction. Buckhout handed the photos to Greenburgh's police laboratory, where enlargements were made. As I suspected, the results were startling.

First, the blowups clearly showed smudges of blood on the bedroom wall. On top of those smudges, which were caused by someone bumping into the wall, were other splatters—angled right to left. These blood splatters were caused by the rifle shot which ended Carr's life. In other words, the blood smudges on the wall *preceded* the splatters from the head wound. This would have been impossible in a suicide.

Second, on the baseboard of the wall, at floor level next to the body, someone apparently attempted to write a message in blood. The letters weren't clear enough to be conclusively deciphered, but there appeared to be several illegible letters followed by "NY SS." This, we believed, may have represented "New York Son of Sam," but we weren't sure.

Buckhout, Singer, Cinotti and later officials in the Queens DA's office all agreed that some form of writing was evident on the baseboard. Even Gardner reluctantly added his assent.

These two developments led to the belief that Carr may have been knocked out in the living room, which would have accounted for the blood Linda O'Connor said she saw there. Then he could have been dragged semiconscious into the bedroom and thrown to the floor, bouncing off the wall and leaving the first blood smudges on it.

A loaded shotgun in the bedroom closet was bypassed and the .30-30 Marlin rifle next to it—in a box—was chosen instead, perhaps because a rifle was less likely to shower a killer or killers with blood than would a shotgun blast. But that wasn't certain.

Regardless, the rifle ammunition was stored in another part of the house. That is, if Carr was murdered, his killer(s) would have left the bedroom to locate that ammunition. While alone, the semiconscious Carr, bleeding on the floor, could have tried to leave a message in blood, probably about the identity or origin of the killer(s), on the baseboard next to where he lay.

Then the killer(s) would have returned to the bedroom, propped Carr up, put the rifle butt on the floor and its barrel into his mouth and set off the fatal shot. The box which contained the rifle was on the bed, indicating the gun was loaded on the spot.

But there was more. The photographic enlargements also showed that two small numbers, perhaps a half inch in height, were scraped into the drying blood on Carr's right hand. They were sixes. A third number was obliterated except for a faint trace. But it, too, was apparently a six, for, together, the numbers would read 666—the sign of the biblical great beast of Revelation: the mark of the devil. There was no other conceivable significance to the numbers.

It simply wasn't credible that Carr could have scraped those numbers into his own drying blood or that he would have.

Once again, the authorities who viewed the blowups agreed that the numbers were indeed visible. And since they were scratched out of blood, they were erased when the body was washed prior to autopsy. The photographic evidence from the death scene was all that remained.

It was now evident, based on all the circumstances surrounding his death, that John Carr was murdered. There was no doubt in the minds of any of the professionals involved that Carr was killed, and that the slaying was motivated by his connection to the Son of Sam case.

The murder determination in New York reflected the feelings of Linda O'Connor, Tom Taylor and other Carr friends who maintained that Carr, despite his problems, wasn't suicidal.

Since Carr was murdered, who did it? He had expressed fear of Reeve Rockman, but from all indications Rockman wasn't the killer type, at least not personally. But could he or someone else have sent the killer(s) from New York or elsewhere to eliminate Carr, who had become the object of police interest? Yes. But it was also possible that someone from North Dakota did the job. Someone Carr knew, someone he would have allowed into the house. Someone with whom Carr spoke on the telephone at eight o'clock that night. Someone who would have known from that conversation that Linda O'Connor was leaving for the evening.

As far as could be determined, not many people knew Carr had flown back to Minot. So the murderer(s) would have learned his whereabouts from one of the few who did know where he was, or from Carr himself.

Terry Gardner would later say that he believed an outsider committed the murder with the help of a North Dakota accomplice. I share Gardner's opinion, but these are informed judgments, not facts. But it is apparent that the murder, made to look like a suicide, was intended to halt the Son of Sam investigation right there—six months after Berkowitz's arrest. The idea would have been to convince the police that if a .44 conspiracy existed, it was limited to Berkowitz and John Carr. The result: case closed.

When New York's analysis of the nature of Carr's death was relayed to Gardner, he perfunctorily advised his superiors. The conclusion didn't come as a total surprise, since the case was originally labeled a homicide and Gardner and others in the Ward County Sheriff's Department already knew a motive for murder existed. But considerable time had elapsed since the incident and no real suspects were identified. There was little the Sheriff's Department could do. If Carr's killer was to be found, it would be New York that would come across him during the Son of Sam investigation. If that happened, Ward County could actively join the probe again. And that was that.

*   *   *

For a time New York officials weren't even convinced that Carr was dead. The body was too disfigured for visual identification, and at least three sets of fingerprints sheriff's investigator Glenn Gietzen said he obtained from the corpse were missing. When the Queens DA's office later requested proof that Carr was dead, there were no fingerprints available.

Additionally, the autopsy report itself raised some troublesome questions. For instance, the body was listed as being five feet nine inches tall, two inches shorter than Carr's stated height. Estimates of Carr's weight varied widely, some far removed from the corpse's 170 pounds. The corpse's stomach was empty, whereas Linda O'Connor said John had consumed a light dinner. There was no sign of lung damage in the corpse, although Carr had been a heavy smoker of both cigarettes and marijuana for years.

Likewise, chemical tests revealed no traces of drugs in the body's system, although Carr, at the least, was taking the powerful tranquilizer Haldol in the days preceding his death.

And just as puzzling was the fact that the autopsy report failed to note that Carr's left ring finger was scarred as the result of a military accident. It was possible the defect was simply overlooked. But because of the blood on the hands, the photos we enlarged didn't reveal any scarring either.

Most curious, however, was the autopsy report's specific notation that the body was distinctively suntanned, but *only* "between the upper thighs and knees such as might be seen with the wearing of shorts and high socks."

In the first place, the death occurred in North Dakota in February. Before that, Carr was in New York's cold weather. He was in Houston around Christmas of 1977, but that was two months before his death. And as the autopsy noted, the tan was restricted to that portion of the body between the knees and the upper thighs. John Carr's friends said he wasn't the type to wear knee socks and shorts in any weather—let alone in a cold climate in the middle of winter. These mysteries would remain.

Later, one set of fingerprints was located and the FBI matched them to those known to be John Carr's. The discovery didn't settle all the doubts. "He could have mailed them in, for all we know," Queens assistant district attorney Herb Leifer would say later. "He almost certainly is dead, but it remains a small, nagging doubt. It's remotely possible he pulled a body switch and cleared out."

If the body wasn't Carr's, what kind of person would be apt to suntan in such a manner? Possible answers include hikers, backpackers, forest rangers or military personnel who were recently in the tropics.

My own opinion is that Carr is dead. But like Leifer, I retain a lingering doubt. Carr's body has not been exhumed, and dental records weren't checked by North Dakota authorities. And so stands the case of John Carr.

*   *   *

While the Carr analysis was going on in mid-September 1979, Terry Gardner called from North Dakota to report that Michael Carr had become aware of the Minot trip. Linda O'Connor had phoned him with the news.

"She didn't think she was doing anything wrong," Gardner said. "She told him we were checking up on John, and that only a few general questions were asked about him."

"That's just great," I replied. "The cops know about him, but they're working on Rockman first. Now Michael has plenty of time to cover his tail. He's going to be cagey; he isn't a fool."

"Just watch your butt," Gardner advised.

There was reason to be concerned about Michael Carr. The probe had appreciably raised his suspect stock, and we would soon learn even more about the enigmatic other son of Sam Carr. The knowledge would cement his position as a prime suspect and answer a question about Berkowitz that plagued me for years.

The information came from a source close to Berkowitz, and the details were essentially confirmed. He reported that David's all-important entry into the world of killer cults came about in an undramatic, mundane manner.

Already at least somewhat familiar with occult precepts since his acknowledged conversations with his stepmother's daughter—the nomadic "witch" Ann—Berkowitz was lounging outside his Barnes Avenue apartment building in the Bronx one evening in mid-1975 when darkest destiny materialized.

Its name, the source stated, was Michael Carr. Berkowitz, as superintendent James Lynch verified, would frequently "just hang out in front on nice nights."

Michael Carr was attending a party in a certain apartment in the building when he, too, decided to enjoy the evening air. On the sidewalk, the source continued, Michael and Berkowitz struck up a casual conversation, which gradually crossed into areas of spiritualism.

Michael, born in 1952, was a year older than David. He had light brown curly hair, styled into a "perm." He'd had a number of drug- and alcohol-related problems, as did his brother, and later became active in the Church of Scientology.

No fledgling follower, Michael rose to a mid-level position in the church. But he was also interested in other spiritual matters, too—such as the occult and devil worship.

It is an old but insightful parable which advises that when a person is starving he will accept bread from whoever is there to offer it. In Berkowitz's case, the source stated, the slices popped from the toaster that night.

Berkowitz, already hurt from the recent reunion with his natural mother, listened eagerly as Michael Carr chatted about such topics as reincarnation, God, Satan and mysticism. Michael then invited his new acquaintance to join him and the others at the party inside, which the source described as "a floating coven party."

Symbolically, the .44 Bulldog was put into Berkowitz's hands that night.

For a long time, I'd looked for the rhyme and reason behind Berkowitz's moves from the Bronx to New Rochelle and finally to out-of-the-way Pine Street in Yonkers. But when I learned of his sidewalk meeting with Michael Carr, the zigzag wanderings took on a rational meaning. Michael Carr lived two hundred yards behind 35 Pine Street.

Unknown to the source, Berkowitz had labeled Michael a devil worshipper at Marcy. We had another important confirmation, and now the suspect knew we were asking about him in North Dakota.

*　*　*

Meanwhile, Jim Mitteager was disappointed that an agreement to withhold publicizing the NYPD's new investigation was struck. Once more, he felt that decisions were being made without his input, and he also was isolated from the Minot officials and sources. In another move, he replaced Felix Gilroy with Ed Rappaport, a prominent criminal attorney. So it would be Rappaport, and not the colorful Gilroy, who would represent Jim at his trial, which was slated to begin in November.

I called Gilroy to express my regrets, but he was nonplussed about the situation. "We just disagreed on how to present the defense; that's all," he said. "Just keep going and let me know what happens."

"Remember Marcy," I signed off.

"You got it. We learned a lot that day."

In late September, Cinotti and I met for an update at the Westchester home of Joe Basteri, who retired from the NYPD in 1978 after a thirty-year career. Basteri was a homicide detective for twenty years and an original, chosen member of the Son of Sam task force. He and Hank worked some cases together in the past and remained friendly. Both Cinotti and I wanted to discuss the current inquiry with him. Basteri also spoke by phone with Gardner and Knoop in Minot.

"It looks good to me," he said after a two-hour briefing. "But you can't do anything about John Carr now. The PD will never admit it. For what? They'll let the dead dogs lie. You've got to go ahead with Michael Carr and Rockman. And you need something concrete from Berkowitz to bust this wide open. That stuff he said at Marcy was good, but you want him to give you more than that."

"I know," I said. "But John Carr is still important. We can't just say we've got him connected to the biggest case in NYPD history—when no one else is supposed to be involved—and let it go at that."

"I didn't mean *you* should forget him," Basteri explained. "That's the way the department will look at it. They don't want to know about this stuff."

"There are bodies all over the goddamned streets and all they care about is their image," I said.

"No," Basteri said. "You can't blame the whole department for this. The task force didn't know all the details—everything went upstairs. Whatever went down on this case involved the brass and Eugene Gold."

"I have no bitch with the task force guys or the rest of the NYPD," I replied. "Just with those people who knew and did nothing about it."

Basteri was torn by the new developments. He was staunchly loyal to the NYPD, but at the same time he recognized the Son of Sam case was far from settled. The meeting with Basteri marked the beginning of what we'd later jokingly call "the Pine Street Irregulars"—a takeoff on Sherlock Holmes's vagabond "Baker Street Irregulars." In time, a group of current and retired police officers would occasionally convene at one of our homes to compare data and discuss new avenues of investigation in the case. All involved were interested in seeing the true story of the killings exposed. Their assistance would be invaluable.

Included in the group, whose membership varied from time to time, were Basteri and Cinotti, Yonkers Lieutenant Michael Novotny, Greenburgh Captain Gerry Buckhout, Yonkers arson investigator Don Starkey and myself. Chief Don Singer of Greenburgh also provided support, as did several other officers, including FBI agents, for whom anonymity is necessary. Eventually, Ted Gunderson, a retired senior special agent in charge for the FBI, would join the effort from his private investigation agency in Los Angeles. Gardner, Knoop and reporters Jeff Nies and Jack Graham remained in contact from Minot.

"We've got our own informal Omega task force," Buckhout once observed.

* * *

That may have been so, but one of its charter members was nearly lost at 11:15 p.m. on September 24. Terry Gardner, on a routine stop in his unmarked sheriff's car, slowed to a halt at a trailer dealership on U.S. 83 south of Minot.

As he did, a shot rang out and a bullet whizzed over the roof of his car, leaving a hole in the wall of the building behind him. Gardner jumped out, dove under his auto and lay in silence for several minutes. There was no additional gunfire.

A nearby witness said he observed two men acting suspiciously in the area investigators determined the shots came from, and it was believed a blue-and-white car was used in the getaway.

The Ward County police speculated that Gardner, who cruised the lot nightly, may have happened upon teenagers siphoning gasoline. No arrests were made. I learned of the incident from Jeff Nies, who told me the article would appear in the following day's *Minot Daily News*. Later, Gardner phoned and confessed that the attempt rattled him considerably.

"Why," I asked, "would kids snatching gas be carrying guns and fire at a cop who didn't even see them? And when's the last time someone shot at a cop out there?"

"A long time ago," Gardner said. "I don't know what the hell this was all about but you can keep your thrill-a-minute investigations back there."

"Burglars don't usually shoot at people," I said. "They're more apt to run if spotted—and you didn't even see them."

"No, I didn't. But I do go by there every night, usually within a half hour of the same time. But no more."

There was no way of knowing for certain if the attack on Gardner was connected to the ongoing .44 investigation in Minot. We had strong suspicions, but that's all they were. Nonetheless, I called Cinotti immediately and relayed the information to him.

"It's probably related," I said. "Whatever, you and your people are all safe and sound in your secret investigation while someone out on the front lines is getting shot at."

"I don't like this," Hank replied.

"Damn right. It's our work they're doing out there now. And they're getting no help from you guys. If this one didn't involve Sam, the next one might."

"I'll take care of it," Cinotti said, and passed on the details to his superiors.

The detective was alarmed, and I was apprehensive, too. Not a week before, Gardner had cautioned me because Michael Carr had learned of our visit to Minot. Now someone had taken a shot at Gardner. Our flanks were decidedly unprotected.

Two days later, the NYPD reacted by veering from the Rockman road when Detective Captain John Plansker interviewed Mrs. Florence Larsen at the 50th Precinct in the Bronx. Larsen was the animal placement worker who received a call from someone identifying himself as Berkowitz seeking a German shepherd just two days before his arrest. I learned of Plansker's questioning because Larsen called me as soon as she returned home.

Larsen said that Plansker showed her a copy of the March article in which I'd quoted her and asked if the story was accurate.

"He had me read it and I told him it was true," she said. "He told me, 'We're going to investigate this article and all the information that's in it point by point.'"

"I certainly hope so, Florence," I answered.

Larsen said that Plansker "took down all sorts of information about me and my family, the call about the shepherd, and dead shepherds in Yonkers and other people involved in the case that I knew. He had me repeat my whole part in the case.

"He said that you [Gannett newspapers] were stirring up a lot of trouble and that he'd just been assigned to the case and that he'd be getting back to me again."

In his next report to Dreher, dated October 1, Plansker wrote that Mrs. Larsen "remains firm about the details of the telephone call [from "Berkowitz"] and apparently has no reason or motive to fabricate this incident The telephone call is significant because persons associated with John Carr in Minot, North Dakota, have been reported to use German shepherds in connection with rituals and sacrifices. We have a copy of a taxidermist bill dated August 9, 1977, for the mounting of a dog ear."

In terms of publishing, the lions were still at bay. The Gannett Westchester-Rockland papers and the *Minot Daily News* were aware of what was occurring, but agreed to delay publicizing the NYPD's new investigation to honor the arrangement Jeff Nies and I had made with Cinotti. Some will certainly say the news should have been made public immediately; that Nies and I were becoming "part" of the story rather than simply observers of it, as some believe the press should only be.

An Associated Press reporter said, "People want to know if you're a reporter or a detective."

"A little of both," I answered, and within those boundaries I believe any investigative journalist should feel confident of decisions he or she might make. Uncovering the news, conducting investigations, is not the same as chronicling the news. And in the .44 case, my role fluctuated between both poles. I thought it was in the best interests of the overall investigation to withhold certain developments from publication until an appropriate time.

My position was never one of news management or interference with the public's right to know. But from the singular perspective one gains when inside a particular probe, I believe it is beneficial to avoid *premature* disclosures which could compromise the opportunity for success.

I was beginning to feel uncomfortable with the "hold" agreement after Gardner became a target. Jim Mitteager was pressing for full disclosure, and the Plansker interview of Mrs. Larsen added more fuel to the fire. I told Cinotti that as more principals in the case were questioned, the likelihood of leaks to other media branches increased. At the same time, in Minot, sheriff's investigator Glenn Gietzen was angered that he wasn't consulted during our trip to his jurisdiction.

"We met the sheriff, and we were with Gardner, so what's Gietzen's problem?" I asked Nies.

"He says he should have been informed, and that he thinks Carr committed suicide, and he's ticked off badly."

"That's between him, Gardner and Sheriff Schwan. Gardner said Gietzen didn't give a damn after a week of interviews following Carr's death and said it was New York's problem. Gardner and Knoop did most of the work. So Gietzen's opened a vineyard full of sour grapes. He didn't even inventory all of Carr's possessions before sending them to the Eugene Gold crematorium in Brooklyn. He's the last one to bitch about anything."

"O.K.," Jeff said. "But he might go to a TV or radio reporter out here and let it out that the investigation's going on."

"Wonderful," I answered, and got off the phone.

* * *

Ward County police politics was about to become the least of our worries. At 4 a.m. on October 4, Michael Vail Carr III, a prime suspect, was racing toward a rendezvous with infinity. As he sped north on Manhattan's rickety, ancient West Side Highway at 70th Street, something happened. His pale green Buick plowed headlong into a streetlight stanchion at nearly seventy-five miles per hour. The impact dislodged the steering wheel and ripped the engine out of the car.

At twenty-seven, Michael Carr was finished.

Dave Hartley of the Yonkers *Herald Statesman* called me at 8:30 a.m. "I've got a photographer down there now. Maybe the pictures will tell us something."

"Why, Dave?" I asked. "Aren't we sure that this is merely a coincidence?" Actually, I was dazed by the news.

"Too many coincidences," Hartley replied.

Hank Cinotti was on the scene by 10 a.m. He reported no skid marks, indicating Carr never hit the brakes, but said he saw a small crease, which appeared fresh, on the car's rear, passenger-side fender.

"It was there," Hank stated. "Whether or not he got it just then I can't say. But it wasn't there long."

Wheat Carr, Michael's sister, said she talked to him "after ten and before one" that night. She said he was going into Manhattan to meet a friend and "relax and party." Wheat also remarked that Michael "had worked since seven o'clock in the morning" in the Yonkers home. That may somehow have been so, but a receipt found in the demolished auto showed that it had been parked for eight hours that day—until 6 p.m. October 3—at Cousin's Garage on 58th Street in Manhattan. It left the lot at 6:03, ten hours before Carr's death.

What actually happened to Michael Carr may never be known. Both his sister and Linda O'Connor in Minot said he wasn't a "fast driver," yet the car was traveling at a very high rate of speed on a section of decaying, cobblestoned roadway that required considerable caution. Carr, who was a frequent visitor to Manhattan, knew the highway's contours well.

Wheat Carr maintained that Michael, as a member of the Church of Scientology at 10th Street and Sixth Avenue in Greenwich Village, hadn't touched alcohol "in three years." Yet his blood alcohol content was reported to be .15, and a reading of .10 is considered intoxicated under New York State law.

Did Michael Carr violate his Scientology credo, or did someone spike his favored orange-juice drink? Or was he chased and then forced off the road, or did someone shoot out a tire or tamper with his car in some other manner? Or did Michael Carr, who knew for the past three weeks that he was under scrutiny in the Son of Sam case, commit suicide? Or was it only a curiously timed accident?

One thing was bluntly clear: both real-life sons of Sam, named by Berkowitz as cult members, were now dead; and both died violently within weeks of their names being handed to authorities as suspects in the .44 case.

Dave Hartley was right: there were too many coincidences.

Wheat Carr initially said that she believed Michael's death had nothing to do with the Berkowitz investigation. But Yonkers Lieutenant Mike Novotny stated that she later approached law enforcement officials in both Manhattan and Westchester in an attempt to have his demise probed as a *murder.*

Meanwhile, just where Michael Carr spent his final hours remained a mystery.

* * *

Michael Carr was educated in Yonkers schools and graduated from the Rochester Institute of Technology and Photography in upstate New York in 1973. Reportedly married for a brief period, he earned his living as a photographer and graphics illustrator, in addition to duties with the family answering service business.

Michael liked to bounce around the glittery Manhattan disco circuit. He counted among his friends a number of professional photographers, and sources close to Berkowitz state that Michael also socialized with the gay set: uptown, near Columbia University; and elsewhere downtown. Both at work and play, Michael occasionally wore high boots and an earring, according to an attorney whose name is known to Queens investigators.

A Westchester tavern employee, whose name is also known to investigators, stated that at about 1:30 a.m. on October 16, 1976, he threw David Berkowitz, Michael Carr and a companion named Bobby out of a favorite Carr watering hole in Greenburgh: the Candlelight Inn at 519 Central Avenue. The employee knew Michael Carr and said he likewise recognized Berkowitz and Bobby.

Shortly after the rowdy trio were shown the exit, two shots snuffed the Candlelight. One hit the front of the building and embedded in the wall. But the other crashed inside and wounded a young woman in the ankle. Not satisfied, the unknown snipers pegged two more shots into an office building at nearby 455 Central Avenue.

We would consider this incident when analyzing other sniper attacks in Westchester, several of which were mentioned earlier. One of those, which involved the wounding of a young girl, happened within a mile of the Candlelight Inn.

The Candlelight endured a few hard times. Witnesses said a woman connected to the Son of Sam investigation once shot out the tavern's clock.

The ballistics report from the Candlelight and 455 Central Avenue incidents stipulated that all the bullets were fired from "a revolver, possibly of Smith & Wesson manufacture; either .38 special or .357 Magnum."

The following handguns were registered to other members of the Carr household at the time of Michael Carr's death: two Smith & Wesson .357 Magnums, two Colt .38s, a Smith & Wesson .32, a Bower .25, a Colt .25 and a Colt .22.

Besides his Candlelight capers, Michael Carr had the insidious inclination of obtaining credit cards under fraudulent names, some scented with illusions of royalty. For instance, this upstanding Scientology counselor held charge cards from both Gimbels department stores and European Health Spas in the name of "Baron De Czarnkowski." At J. C. Penney he registered as "M. V. Deczarnkowski"; and at Bloomingdale's he purchased his fragrances under the moniker "M. Deccarnowski." Michael Carr fancied himself an exiled Russian nobleman, even to the point of creating his own coat of arms.

When I saw his "Baron" credit listings, and also noticed that the word "czar" was hidden in two of the last names, I was reasonably certain that another of the Breslin letter's aliases was deciphered: "The Duke of Death." I suspected the remaining alias, "The Wicked King Wicker," belonged to a certain other party. We already knew who "John Wheaties" was; and we believed "The Twenty Two Disciples of Hell" referred to the cult itself.

Regarding Michael Carr's pronounced Russian interests and the information that he associated with people at Columbia University: it is interesting to note that Son of Sam victim Virginia Voskerichian was herself a Russian-language student at Columbia, and was even dating her twenty-seven-year-old Russian instructor at the time of her death. It is also known that the killer(s), after being observed in the neighborhood for quite some time before the attack, shot Virginia—who was late—on what was her regular homeward route from Columbia. The link may or may not be substantive, but it has never been checked by any law enforcement agency.

*   *   *

The shock waves generated by Michael Carr's death jolted everyone involved in the investigation. In Minot, the word spread like wildfire among John Carr's associates after Gardner and Knoop phoned several of them with the report. In New York, my own phone rang all day: Tom Bartley, Dave Hartley and Joe Ungaro of Gannett wanted to release the story of the NYPD's investigation as soon as possible. Mitteager, and now Jeff Nies, chimed in. Cinotti, Gardner and Knoop pleaded patience. "Don't do anything now, there's going to be surveillance at the wake," Cinotti explained.

Despite that request, I was leaning toward publication. More importantly, so was Gannett, and they were paying the bills. The broadcast media were reporting the death, and the next day's newspapers would also do so. The *Post,* in fact, would banner it across page one. But since no one knew of the probe and Carr's links to it, the reportage would be superficial.

For their part, the Gannett papers would deliberately play the story modestly. But the publishing dilemma would evaporate that same night, less than twenty-four hours after Carr's demise, when the issue dramatically decided itself. It is impossible to arrive at a reasonable conclusion as to what really happened to Michael Carr without considering his death in the context of what happened next.

*   *   *

Wheat Carr, in her own words, "eloped" with a Yonkers policeman named John McCabe several months after the death of her brother John.

McCabe spent October 4 in Manhattan, gathering Michael Carr's effects and identifying the body. That night, he phoned in sick for his scheduled midnight shift and a substitute patrolman, Carmine D'Ambrosio, took the wheel of McCabe's sector car.

At 2 a.m., while driving McCabe's regular route, on McCabe's scheduled shift and in McCabe's marked radio car, D'Ambrosio headed north on Warburton Avenue on a course that would take him below the darkened woodlands of Untermyer Park, scene of noteworthy cult activity.

At one point, the police car rounded a curve and drove down a straightaway. To D'Ambrosio's right, Untermyer Park was a murky blur rising above him.

But someone was lurking in those shadows.

And then that someone blasted out the passenger-side window of McCabe's sector car with a rifle shot fired broadside from some twenty yards inside the silent recesses of Untermyer. The police car swerved and came to a screeching halt. D'Ambrosio wasn't hit, but the bullet, which ultimately lodged in the molding of the driver's door, barely missed him. Looking toward the sound, the officer saw the outline of a man disappearing into the woods and gave chase, firing two shots in the direction of the fleeing assailant. But Untermyer Park swallowed up the gunman in its gloom.

Yonkers police, responding immediately to the radio call, searched the area. The shooter was long gone, but they did find something else. There were cigarette butts and coffee containers near the spot where the gunman stood—and waited. Waited until he could fire broadside into the passing police car.

That McCabe was supposed to have been driving that vehicle has not been revealed until now.

*   *   *

But this night wasn't over; it was destined to be a long one. At about this same time, 1,800 miles to the northwest in Minot, John Carr's friends Tom Taylor and Darlene

Christiansen, who had cooperated with the investigation, were driving home from a night out. It was approximately 1 a.m. On County Road 12, Darlene was behind the wheel while Taylor dozed next to her in the passenger's seat.

Suddenly, a red Chevrolet Camaro appeared behind them, speeded up and forced them off the road and into a shallow ditch. Neither Taylor nor Christiansen was hurt, and Darlene said the red Camaro kept right on going.

Several days later, Taylor attempted suicide, overdosing on quaaludes. He was comatose when Darlene found him in their shared apartment. Beside him was a note in which he apologized for his act and closed with the words "Believe in God."

But Taylor was still alive, and he was rushed to a local hospital. He survived.

"He was scared out of his wits," Gardner said. "He knew more about what was going on than he ever told us. I don't think he was guilty of complicity, but I'm convinced he had some knowledge that frightened him. He had no money, yet he somehow came up with over a thousand dollars to fly to New York with Darlene for John Carr's funeral. He never gave a consistent answer as to why he went or where the money came from. I think he was a mule of some sort, taking something to New York then or bringing something back without knowing what it was. But we can't prove it."

Within months of the suicide attempt, Taylor and Christiansen left Minot and didn't return.

We ourselves had departed Minot on September 3. And in the course of a ten-day span beginning less than a month later, Gardner was shot at; Michael Carr died; his brother-in-law's sector car was shot up; and two friends of John Carr reported they were run off the road in Minot. That incident was followed by a suicide attempt with a curiously worded note, considering the investigation's probe of satanism.

It was time to act. With input from Mitteager, and editorial guidance from Bartley, Sherman Bodner, and Tom McNamara, the story was bannered across the Gannett Westchester-Rockland papers' front pages on Friday, October 12, which happened to have been John Carr's birthday. The headline read: "NYC POLICE REOPEN SON OF SAM PROBE." The byline was shared by me, Mitteager and Jeff Nies. By arrangement, the *Minot Daily News* broke the story at the same time, and our bylines appeared there as well.

To protect Cinotti, the lengthy article didn't mention that I'd been in Minot, and used Ward County sheriff Leon Schwan as the confirming source of the investigation. "We and the city of Minot police are assisting the investigation New York has begun," Schwan said. "There are some things out here they're very interested in."

With the not-unexpected demurral of the *New York Daily News,* the story received considerable attention. Four days later it was followed by another stating that John Carr was afraid a person from New York (Rockman) was out to kill him and that Carr said if he'd remained in New York, "the state would have fried me in the electric chair."

Neither Rockman's name nor that of Darlene Christiansen, the source of the "electric chair" comment, was published.

Hints about suspected satanic cult activity appeared in both articles, but the evidence supporting a murder scenario in John Carr's death wasn't discussed. Michael Carr's connection also remained secret.

The *New York Post*, as it is prone to do on occasion, rewrote our first story, got an additional quote from Gardner and published it as if the information was its own. Reporter George Carpozi's byline appeared on the article.

In Attica prison in upstate New York, David Berkowitz received a copy of the *Post* before the original story reached him. Commenting on the allegations of satanism, his relationship with John Carr and Carr's suspected complicity in the .44 case, Berkowitz wrote to a friend:

"Everything is here. One neat package. Carpozi has done it. . . . But he doesn't realize it." Berkowitz went on to say the allegations were "absolute facts." He also wrote that he knew John Carr had attended Minot State College. This was true, as he took some night courses there. Berkowitz even knew the name of the school. It was another confirmation of his association with John Carr.

* * *

The New York City Police Department, caught with its hand in the proverbial cookie jar, was suddenly thrust into the limelight as conducting a new investigation of its biggest case—the case on which it slammed the door two years earlier. Captain Plansker had by this time sent two comprehensive reports on the probe to Deputy Chief Dreher since August 31, and Dreher had forwarded them to Chief of Detectives James Sullivan.

On October 17, according to Plansker's next report (dated the eighteenth), Detective Hank Cinotti was, at Dreher's request, asked to reveal how he first learned of Rockman and of Rockman's acquaintance with John Carr. Plansker conveyed that information to Dreher, and wrote that Cinotti "contacted police officials in Minot, N.D, and discovered that the name of Rockman had appeared in police records during the investigation of the death of John Carr. It was at this time [August 10] that Detective Cinotti approached the undersigned for the purpose of conducting an investigation."

While Cinotti's rendering of the scenario to Plansker was true, he omitted two points. He didn't reveal Lueken's name and, still protected in print, he didn't say that he first learned of Carr's involvement with Berkowitz, and allegedly with Rockman, from me.

* * *

While the NYPD was bobbing and weaving from the press on October 17, Queens district attorney John Santucci sat with a number of Gannett newspaper articles on his desk. The dark-haired, forty-eight-year-old prosecutor began his career as an assistant in the very office he now headed. He was later a member of New York's City

Council and a state senator before assuming the district attorney's chair on January 1, 1977. There were more than one hundred assistant prosecutors and a large number of other employees reporting to him.

Five Son of Sam attacks occurred in Santucci's jurisdiction (as compared to two in the Bronx and one in Brooklyn), and he perused the conspiracy articles with considerable interest—as he'd done since the first one appeared in March.

Santucci had never been comfortable with the original resolution of the .44 case. After hearing of Berkowitz's arrest, he and his close aide and press spokesman, Thomas McCarthy, were driven to One Police Plaza in a hair-raising ride on the potholed Brooklyn-Queens Expressway.

While at Police Plaza, Santucci sat in on some of the questioning of Berkowitz and formed the opinion that Berkowitz was lucid and not demon-possessed, as he then claimed, and that the .44 case might well go deeper than it was presented to be. His own evaluation of the evidence left him with nagging doubts concerning Berkowitz's alleged sole responsibility.

Santucci then pressed for a Berkowitz trial, but was persuaded by Eugene Gold in Brooklyn and the Bronx's Mario Merola to allow Berkowitz to plead guilty without any dissidence. Santucci's reluctance to yield to the pressure reached the media, where he was criticized by "sources" for his stance.

But for the past week, since the "John Carr-NYPD Re-opens" article appeared, Santucci's office had been quietly compiling data about the case. After the story was published, some people called us with information; others contacted the police or Santucci's office. The details in our newspaper reports, buttressed by other data he accumulated that week, convinced Santucci that the nearly two million residents of his borough would be best served if he, as its top law enforcement official, probed further into the Berkowitz matter.

From his own contacts, WPIX-TV reporter Jeff Kamen caught wind of Santucci's activities. WPIX, Channel 11 in New York, was also the flagship station for INN, the Independent News, which reached a considerable number of U.S. markets. Ironically, WPIX and the *Daily News* were owned by the same parent company; and WPIX was even headquartered in the large *Daily News* building in midtown Manhattan. But regarding the .44 conspiracy, the attitudes of the two media outlets were as divergent as night and day.

While the *Daily News* had all but ignored the story and would continue to do so, WPIX-TV had followed our investigation in Westchester since the Moskowitz article was published in mid-July. Kamen, an aggressive, quality reporter, was denied access to Eugene Gold's office while trying to follow up on that investigative report. The lockout was filmed and reported on the station's news broadcast.

In the late afternoon of Wednesday, October 17, Jeff Kamen called Santucci's press spokesman, Tom McCarthy. Kamen told McCarthy he heard Santucci reopened the Son of Sam case.

"What kind of funny cigarettes are you smoking, Jeff?" McCarthy asked. "The Son of Sam case? You must be hallucinating."

Kamen was insistent, and McCarthy, who planned to watch a World Series game that night, wanted to go home. But he agreed to walk down the hall to ask Santucci about it.

"You'd better sit down, Tom," the DA said. "And I don't think you'll be seeing the ball game tonight."

As McCarthy later explained: "In this office, I am sometimes deliberately in the dark on sensitive cases, and none was—and is—more sensitive than Son of Sam. This practice is in effect for two reasons. First, I don't want to be put in the position of having to deceive the press to protect matters of extreme confidentiality; and secondly, if I'm not familiar with certain details, I can't inadvertently let them slip out in conversations with journalists. That's why I didn't know what was happening to that point."

But from that moment on, McCarthy knew much of what there was to know about the .44 investigation.

"We were about to begin receiving a deluge of calls from reporters all over the country. It would be an ongoing thing. Some offered tips they heard or other information they thought might be helpful. Because of the scope of it all, I had to learn the case well in order to evaluate the information as it poured in from the press before passing it on."

At home in White Plains that evening, I received a call from WPIX's Monica Rosenschein, with whom I'd spoken the week before about the NYPD story. "John Santucci is reopening the Son of Sam case. Now you've got him and the PD in on it. They've confirmed off the record. We're breaking it tonight. We knew you'd want to know so you could get it in the morning's edition."

To say I was overjoyed would be an understatement. Monica pledged me to secrecy and hung up. I called the Gannett office and said I'd be in to write the story. Five minutes later, Neysa Moskowitz, mother of Stacy, was on the line. She'd been a frequent caller and supporter since March, and we'd spoken several times during the previous week.

"Steve Dunleavy just called me," she said. "He wants to know if you heard anything about Santucci opening up the case. He said he heard a rumor about it."

"Why doesn't Steve call me himself?"

"I think he feels you might be annoyed that the *Post* redid your story."

"No, but they might have given it a one-line credit. Actually, I'm glad they ran with it. This message has to get out."

"Steve says he was involved with you on the John Carr thing at the beginning."

"That he was. But things got screwed up."

"I've got a three-way gizmo here," Neysa said. "Why don't we set up a conference call."

A few minutes later, I heard Dunleavy's unmistakable accent. "How's it going, mate? Long time, no talk. I see you've been busy."

"Yeah, and I see you guys have been reading."

"Ask him about Santucci, Steve," Neysa cut in.

"We got a rumor today, but no one can flesh it out yet. You've been close to this—did you hear anything?"

I couldn't violate Monica's confidence, but I didn't want to deceive Dunleavy either. He would, after all, read the morning issue of *Today* and immediately know if I misled him.

"Well, I heard that rumor, too. I wouldn't be surprised if there was something to it, but who knows?" I said.

I was also dying to tell Dunleavy that his old nemesis, Veronica Lueken, had provided information that was part of the NYPD's probe, but resisted the temptation.

"So you heard it, too," Dunleavy said. "I'm going to call their night number over there, the hotline, and see what we can get. I'll get back to you."

In a few minutes, my phone rang again. "They're reopening, too," Dunleavy gushed. "It's going to be a circus now. They're confirming off the record. If we go with it, they won't deny it, but they're not making formal statements."

"See you on the front page tomorrow, Steve," I remarked, and we said goodbye. It was going to be a busy night for both of us. I called Jim Mitteager and told him I was driving to the paper to write the story. Jim volunteered to phone Queens to learn anything else he could.

At Gannett's offices, I wrote the article and phoned Jeff Nies in Minot so he'd have the wording, too. The papers were cooperating all the way on this case. What Nies didn't know was that some of Carr's friends, who saw him at the interviews, thought he was an undercover narcotics cop posing as a reporter. Gardner was somewhat concerned for Nies's safety, but didn't tell him, so as not to rattle him unnecessarily.

Mitteager then called from his Staten Island home to say he'd received the confirmation from McCarthy, too. "He said it was a serious matter and they don't want to exploit the case. They were attempting to do this quietly, but it leaked. It had to, eventually. We print, and they won't deny."

At 10 p.m., with several other staffers and the article's editors, Alex Poletsky and Tom McNamara, I took time out to watch Channel 11's news broadcast. A muffled cheer went up from the group gathered at the small TV in the newsroom as the story, WPIX's lead item, was aired. The Gannett papers had themselves walked a precarious limb. They touched the untouchable Son of Sam case, and now, along with the earlier news of the NYPD's probe, they were vindicated.

"I wonder if Eugene Gold is watching this," McNamara exclaimed. "He thought he'd made fools of us in July. Let him absorb this for a while. Santucci had five shootings out there and he's in our corner."

"There was never a doubt," I deadpanned. "All we needed was a little time to pull it all together."

Although I tried to maintain a stoic posture, my emotions were strong. As I watched WPIX and heard the words "The Queens district attorney's office has reopened the

Son of Sam case," I shook hands with the others and said a quiet "Thank God." The job was done. More than two years of work—of constant challenge and occasional derision and ridicule—had finally paid off in one of the biggest and most notorious criminal cases in U.S. history. At last, the unmovable mountain had been shaken.

Like Tom McNamara, I too thought of Brooklyn DA Eugene Gold, and of the many others who tried to block the investigation and disclosures. Gold had publicly charged us—me—with "wild speculation" in my reporting, with Jim, of the Moskowitz scenario. Gannett took it on the chin with that one, too. But we kept going.

The press dogs had finally had their day.

*   *   *

The Associated Press and United Press International monitored the WPIX broadcast. Their reports were on the wires in short order, and were promptly picked up by other TV and radio outlets. But no other New York newspapers got the word in time for their deadlines. So it was Gannett and the *Post* which scooped the print media the next morning.

The Gannett headline, which stretched across the front page in large type, said: "QUEENS D.A. ENTERS SON OF SAM PROBE." Jim and I shared the byline. The article stated that Santucci was adding his own resources to those of the NYPD, and summed up earlier information.

The *Post's* front page blared: "SON OF SAM SHOCKER, QUEENS D. A. REOPENS THE CASE." The next day, the *New York Times* reported the investigation in a detailed article by police reporter Len Buder, and other area papers highlighted the story. However, the *Daily News* carried but a brief item on an inside page.

The NYPD was caught off guard by Santucci's action, and Deputy Chief Dreher and Chief of Detectives Sullivan were less than delighted to learn that the DA was now involved. There was embarrassment aplenty. First, the top-secret investigation went public and now Santucci was poking around, too.

At 5 p.m. on October 19, Jane Jacklin's husband, a now rehired NYPD uniformed officer, was interviewed by Dreher, Inspector Charles Rorke and Captain John Plansker at the 48th Precinct in the Bronx. Jane Jacklin was supposed to have approached Veronica Leuken about Rockman and then later to have been cut up and thrown into Little Neck Bay. I had already determined that the woman who allegedly talked to Lueken was not the real Jane Jacklin, whom Mitteager and I met in early 1978.

According to Plansker's report, dated October 22, when John Jacklin* was asked if he knew anyone by the name of Rockman, "there was an apparent nervous reaction, but he stated he did not know anybody by that name. He was presented with a photo of Rockman and first stated it resembled someone he knew a long time ago who was involved with drugs. He then stated it might resemble a reporter who had questioned his wife regarding the Son of Sam killings. He indicated that several reporters had questioned his wife regarding her connections with a group of people who were allegedly associated with Berkowitz." Jacklin then called Jane.

"Jane states she was interviewed by a Maury Terry and a man named Mitteager who represented themselves as reporters and asked if she ever used drugs, ever visited the Blue Dolphin diner or if she knew Reeve Rockman. They also asked if she knew Veronica Lueken and showed her a letter allegedly written by Lueken which described how Jane's body was cut up and thrown into [Little Neck Bay]. . . .

"The interviews of Jane and John Jacklin lead to the presumption that Veronica Lueken is the informant referred to in Detective Cinotti's original report and is the individual who allegedly observed Berkowitz and Rockman together in Jacklin's auto. Veronica Lueken is known to this Department because of her unorthodox religious practices in Queens. Her reliability as a witness or informant is seriously in question and the possibility of independently establishing an association between Rockman and Berkowitz in Queens County during 1977 is doubtful."

This is all the top brass in the NYPD needed to hear. Lueken was bonkers and this embarrassing investigation could be closed down immediately. Santucci could twist in the wind by himself. But Plansker didn't agree:

"Despite this reversal, we have developed information and circumstances that almost demand resolution. I believe that this investigation should be continued, if only for the sake of being able to say that this Department has never ignored or overlooked any information connected with the Son of Sam shootings. Some of the questions and information generated by this investigation are listed below:

A. We have statements that John Carr knew Berkowitz [from Minot].

B. We have statements that John Carr mentioned Berkowitz and Son of Sam before Berkowitz's arrest.

C. We have statements that Rockman was an associate of John Carr.

D. We have statements that Rockman was involved in witchcraft.

E. The Berkowitz letters and writings seem to contain references to witchcraft.

F. We have a statement that John Carr knew some of the victims. [This may have been so despite the fact that the original informant turned out to be unreliable.]

G. Rockman lived near two of the shootings in Forest Hills and worked in the same building as one of the victims.

H. The second Forest Hills shooting [Virginia Voskerichian's] is not consistent with the other shootings in terms of time and type of location."

Rockman was interviewed by Dreher, Plansker and Rorke a few days later and, not surprisingly, denied everything. However, Plansker still wasn't satisfied—but he was overruled. The NYPD dropped out of the probe after two months and prepared to bring up Cinotti on a smattering of charges related to his failure to identify and produce Lueken and his traveling to Minot with me. He would also be charged with providing me with confidential information.

The fact that I uncovered the Carr-Rockman information first and lined up the interviews and that Cinotti joined me in Minot—not the other way around—was irrelevant to Dreher and Chief of Detectives James Sullivan. They were out to portray Cinotti as a rogue, unbalanced cop with an unreliable informant—Lueken. It was their way out of a situation they never wanted to reach the public in the first place.

And they'd see to it that Santucci received little cooperation either.

*   *   *

This same night, October 22, retired homicide detective Joe Basteri called me. For years, Basteri had been friendly with NYPD Lieutenant Remo Franceschini, who currently was in charge of the squad of NYPD detectives assigned to Santucci's office. These detectives assisted the district attorney's investigations but reported through the NYPD chain of command, not directly to the DA. This structuring would soon acquire a special significance. Santucci also had a contingent of Queens County detectives, who did report directly to him.

Franceschini advised Basteri that Cinotti had just been suspended by the Police Department. He added that Santucci sent homicide bureau chief Herb Leifer and Queens County detective George Byrd to interview Cinotti at the 48th Precinct. While there, Dreher refused to allow the Queens representatives to question Cinotti.

Franceschini asked Basteri to locate Cinotti, since Santucci wanted to speak with him immediately. I told Basteri I'd try to track down the elusive Henry Cinotti, and within an hour I got word to him.

"They sent me to a department shrink," Hank said. "And he asks me why don't I give up the name of my informant. Some shrink. I see what's going on. They're going to try to destroy me. I'm not suspended, but I am on modified assignment. Desk duty, no gun, psychiatric evaluation. I saw that Leifer at the Four-Eight—I was there but he wasn't allowed to see me."

"Santucci's people want to talk to you," I said. "They asked to see me, too. Joe is going out with me Wednesday [the twenty-fourth]—why don't you show up yourself?"

"I don't know," Hank said. "I gotta think about it. If I see you, I see you. But don't approach me—I can't be seen with you."

Cinotti turned down my offer to speak with Plansker about the genesis of the Minot trip and my conclusion that Lueken had spoken with a Jane Jacklin impostor. I also told Hank that Michael and John Carr and the cult were getting lost in the shuffle.

"They could care less," Cinotti said. "And if you go to them it will only make my situation worse."

If I couldn't help the beleaguered detective directly, there were other things I could do. It was time to publish the Untermyer Park cult's connection to the Son of Sam letters. I worked that night and the next on the story, consulting frequently with Jim Mitteager. Jack Graham of the *Minot Daily News* located a Michigan college professor who was an occult expert, and he was interviewed for the article. Requesting anonymity because of his job, the academic said he believed the Son of Sam symbol was borrowed from the original Eliphas Levi rendering and that the German shepherd ears were a unique emblem. He added something that would soon cause a bit of a stir:

"I believe you are dealing with a sadomasochistic group with strong undertones of latent homosexuality. This is an evil group that turned to ritualistic killing, using the occult as an excuse for their own latent homosexuality. They borrowed from satanism, from magic and from whatever they saw and liked."

The story was ready to go, and would appear on Wednesday, October 24.

*   *   *

In the newsroom the night before, I got the opportunity to return Monica Rosenschein's recent favor. I called WPIX and, speaking alternately with her and another WPIX employee, Felix Martinez, filled them in on what we were publishing in the morning. The Gannett editors approved the arrangement, since WPIX consented to credit us with breaking the story. Our discussions with Channel 11 ended not five minutes before airtime, and once again we surrounded the TV to watch the broadcast. WPIX was true to its word, and the cult story led off the newscast.

On the twenty-fourth, the article itself hit the newsstands under the front-page headline "SATANIC CULT TIED TO 'SAM' KILLINGS." A large photo of the so-called Devil's Cave accompanied the piece. Channel 11, and others, sent camera crews to Untermyer Park to film follow-ups for the nightly TV news. I was asked to meet the WPIX crew at Untermyer, but was forced to demur. I was due at the district attorney's office in Queens.

*   *   *

As Joe Basteri and I approached the Queens County office complex, we spied Hank Cinotti entering a side door. He ignored us and went to speak with Herb Leifer, the homicide bureau chief. Meanwhile, Basteri and I talked with Lieutenant Remo Franceschini and Tom McCarthy until Leifer and George Byrd arrived.

Santucci was about to dispatch assistant district attorney Michael Armienti and county detective Tom Mulderig to Minot, and his staff wanted to learn about our trip.

"Yes, I was there," I said. "And I didn't try to hide that fact from anyone in Minot—just the NYPD to protect Cinotti. He didn't leak a thing to me; it was the other way around."

I briefed the DA's staff on the findings thus far, and agreed to cooperate with their investigation. "We all want the same thing. Within reason, I'll do what I can. But certain sources will have to be protected."

Leifer didn't go for that idea. But McCarthy, as press liaison, explained my position. Leifer still wasn't pleased, but nodded his reluctant assent. While there, I learned that Santucci had tried to question Berkowitz, but the confessed Son of Sam sent back a message saying he wouldn't cooperate with the DA's new probe.

"That says something, doesn't it?" I asked. "If it was nonsense he'd be the first one to stand up and take sole credit again." I wrote the story of Berkowitz's refusal to cooperate two days later.

The makings of another uneasy situation with Mitteager were hatched that day, as the DA's representatives said they couldn't deal with him because of his imminent trial. "We're not passing judgment—it just wouldn't be appropriate for us under the circumstances," one said. Mitteager said he understood the decision, but was nonetheless unhappy about it. He was isolated from the Minot officials, and now the Queens DA placed him on a shelf as well.

"It's becoming your case," he told me. "I understand why; and you're the one who had John Carr, Moskowitz and the cult in the first place. I'm forty miles away out here and I'm going on trial. So work with Queens as you see fit."

Jim's byline continued to appear on every story we published during the next several months, and his input was helpful. But he and the case were divorcing, mostly due to circumstances and bad timing.

As for Santucci, his office would soon need all the cooperation it could muster. The DA endured a lot of official heat for reopening the Son of Sam case. Eugene Gold lined up against him, and the NYPD was incensed that he dared to challenge its position. Sergeant Joe Coffey, for example, had been a supervisor on the Omega task force. He walked into Santucci's office and pointedly told him: "You're not going to get a thing." He bet Santucci a dinner that the inquiry would fail and stalked out of the room.

Coffey knew that the deck was being stacked. The New York City Police Department withdrew its support and refused to cooperate with Santucci's probe. Because of this major rift, the DA decided not to utilize his own squad of NYPD detectives in the .44 investigation, so as not to compromise their standing in the Police Department. He would instead conduct the inquiry with his assistant district attorneys and county detectives.

There were numerous NYPD detectives who disagreed with the department's position. Some quietly assisted the investigation anyway, and worked clandestinely with me, if not the DA, over the years. But the department's official posture, cast in concrete by those at the top, was that Berkowitz committed all the .44 shootings by himself.

There was to be precious little middle ground on this case. One was either a friend or a foe. Reporter Howard Blum of the *New York Times,* and others, called to warn me that Deputy Chief Edwin Dreher was waging a smear campaign against me and

Cinotti.

"It's pretty pathetic," Blum said. "From the story I heard, Cinotti is supposed to be an insane religious fanatic and a homosexual Nazi. And you and Cinotti are supposed to be homosexual lovers."

"That son of a bitch," I said. "He can't shoot down the case, so he tries this crap. A deputy chief of the NYPD. Maybe my fiancee would be interested in hearing that I'm a fag." (I was soon to be married to Georgiana, the woman I talked with at the Suriani-Esau murder scene in April 1978.)

"He's hurting the PD's position and himself, not you," Blum said. "Nobody believes him—they're appalled. I just wanted you to know."

Dreher didn't stop. In March 1981, WOR-TV aired the first of several syndicated television specials about the case. I served as reporter and host for the segments. Dreher, reading that the initial report was due to air, asked for a preview. According to the executive producer of the newsmagazine series *What's Happening, America,* Dreher previewed the show and "obviously didn't like what he was seeing. As soon as it was over he started calling you a fag and Cinotti's lover. And he said Cinotti was insane and a neo-Nazi. We told him to screw off," the producer said. "He was trying to get us to kill the show."

That time, I didn't ignore Dreher. I immediately called the NYPD's deputy commissioner for public information and told her that if Dreher persisted with his slurs, I was going to file a written complaint against him. Whether Dreher stopped his attacks or not, I don't know. But I heard nothing more about him from reporters after that incident.

Using that approach to attempt to discredit me, and others to impede John Santucci's office, the NYPD brass rolled through the Son of Sam case. Mayor Ed Koch, who would sleep through more corruption scandals than Rip Van Winkle, blissfully ignored the turmoil.

Throughout the probe, I appeared on a number of radio and TV programs. On several occasions, NYPD officials were invited to debate the case with me. Each time, the department declined the offers. It seems as if the power elite was more comfortable with whispered slander than public discussion, which in itself says something.

* * *

The Queens investigation built momentum despite the Police Department's maneuverings. Detectives delved deeply into Berkowitz's life, and interviewed friends and members of his family. The original Minot informants were questioned again by Michael Armienti and Tom Mulderig.

Other investigators talked to the Cassaras, the Carrs, former police auxiliary associates of Berkowitz, surviving Son of Sam victims in Queens and numerous others.

Herb Leifer and Detective George Byrd spent considerable time in Yonkers, and piles of Yonkers Police Department reports, and those of the NYPD, were scrutinized. Investigators even crossed jurisdictional boundaries when they questioned star

Brooklyn witness Cacilia Davis in depth. Mrs. Davis simply retold the story as I'd already published it.

"She was on target as far as we're concerned," Leifer reported. Santucci said: "It's apparent Berkowitz wasn't alone that night in Brooklyn."

The investigators also sought out photos of John Carr. As Leifer and Byrd left Wheat Carr's new residence in Hastings-on-Hudson, she called out to them: "You want to know what John looked like?"

Byrd and Leifer turned around, and Wheat grabbed her shoulder-length hair and pulled it tightly above her neck. "Here's what he looked like," she yelled to the startled investigators.

Detectives also acquired data on .44 purchases and other aspects of the case from Texas, Florida, New Jersey and California. Bit by bit a picture was developing—a group picture. In it were Berkowitz—and some accomplices. At one point Santucci observed: "Whoever said Berkowitz was a friendless loner was dead wrong. This guy had a lot of contacts and connections."

The Queens probers also looked into the Reeve Rockman matter. Their assessment, independent of my own, was that while Rockman was identified in North Dakota, corroboration beyond that provided by Veronica Lueken was necessary in New York. Until then, Rockman was guilty of association with John Carr and perhaps Berkowitz. But it was necessary to fit him into a smaller circle—that of the people directly responsible for the .44 killings.

Lueken, whose story was supported by her husband, said she had three informants who alleged Rockman was involved in satanic cult activity. One of those was the Jane Jacklin impostor. Of the others, Nicki had disappeared in Haiti and Wendy Smith—whose last name was a common one—proved extremely difficult to track down.

Linda O'Connor in North Dakota said that Michael Carr received drug therapy at a large rehabilitation center in New York—a location where, curiously enough, Rockman was once employed as an accountant. But investigators weren't able to confirm Michael Carr's presence there, at least not under his real name.

So the Rockman connection was put on a back burner.

In Westchester, our own probe continued. Sometimes the path crossed that of the DA's investigators. We continued publishing the results throughout the remainder of 1979 and into mid-1980. The public was supportive, and numerous tips were phoned to Gannett and the district attorney's office. Some people, wanting to ensure that their leads weren't bypassed, forwarded them to both places. Members of the press also offered information to Santucci's staff.

An example of a valuable lead given both to me and to Santucci was one which originated with two members of a sheet-metal workers' union to which Berkowitz belonged in late 1976 and early 1977, before he joined the Postal Service. These sources said that Berkowitz showed a .38-caliber revolver to several co-workers while in an apprentice class in Westchester.

At the same time, they reported that Berkowitz was very friendly with a young man named Phil Kahn,* and that Berkowitz and Kahn left the job one day in January 1977 telling co-workers they were driving to an animal shelter to adopt a German shepherd.

No .38 revolver was found in Berkowitz's apartment, but the informants insisted he possessed it at the time. As for Kahn, he admitted his friendship with Berkowitz to the Queens probers, but denied the German shepherd excursion. Again, his fellow workers reported Kahn was lying. Kahn remains under scrutiny.

In time, a list of suspects, including Kahn, emerged. Among the others were ex-Yonkers police officer Peter Shane, of the Howard Weiss-Berkowitz connection; Weiss himself; Michael and John Carr; and Bobby, the man who was ejected from the Candlelight Inn with Berkowitz and Michael Carr. There were other candidates, too.

As for the .44 shootings themselves, my own evaluation at that time was that Berkowitz most likely pulled the trigger in the attacks on Donna Lauria and Jody Valente and on Valentina Suriani and Alexander Esau. These shootings accounted for three murders and one wounding in the Bronx. Mitteager and I were convinced he didn't shoot Stacy Moskowitz and Robert Violante in Brooklyn, Joanne Lomino and Donna DeMasi in Queens, or Virginia Voskerichian in Queens. Three attacks remained questionable: the murder of Christine Freund, the Elephas woundings of Judy Placido and Sal Lupo and the wounding of Carl Denaro. We believed that Berkowitz probably didn't shoot Denaro, because of the assailant's obvious difficulty controlling the weapon, and because three shell casings reportedly were found at that scene. The .44 revolver doesn't eject shells and no casings were found at other sites. This, too, suggested a different shooter and a weapon other than Berkowitz's Bulldog.

But at no incident did we think the shooter acted without support of some type.

* * *

In early November, another cult-related incident occurred near Untermyer Park in Yonkers. This time, the witness was a Westchester County police officer who stumbled onto a ritual being held at the old Stillwell Estate on North Broadway, barely a half mile from Untermyer. The Sheriff's Department tried to keep the incident from reaching the public, but Gannett reporter Ed Trapasso uncovered the details anyway.

The estate was county property, and at dusk on Saturday, November 10, the officer walked through the woods and saw a group of at least five people standing in a circle. One man, dressed in a red cape, was leading the others in a series of chants. The caped "high priest" was also holding two German shepherds on chains.

Seeing the cop, the group scattered and escaped.

Subsequent investigation by the police revealed satanic writings on the interior walls of a decaying carriage house nearby. The phrases said: "Demon," "Welcome to Hell" and "Entering Hell."

The red cape, I told Trapasso, likely indicated that the group was engaged in a fertility or sex-magic ritual at the time.

Sheriff's officials blustered that there was no evidence linking the ritual to the Son of Sam cult meetings up the block at Untermyer. Apparently, North Broadway was becoming Satan Street, U.S.A.

"They have no evidence to say it *wasn't* connected either," I told Trapasso. "These are the people who eighty-six reports and don't know how to investigate a return address on a threatening letter."

"They called it doublespeak in the Watergate days," Trapasso joked.

Our own evaluation was that with the German shepherds in tow and with the incident occurring so proximate to Untermyer it was indeed possible the ceremony was linked to the .44 case.

*   *   *

While the work progressed in Queens and Westchester, someone was watching from a distance, reading the Gannett reports and those written by the AP and the *Post*.

David Berkowitz, incarcerated in Attica prison near upstate Buffalo, had refused to help Santucci. But that didn't mean he was staying out of the fray. Berkowitz had been wrestling with his conscience since we met at Marcy a year before. He decided the time had come. He was going to aid the investigation. But he was going to do it his way—not the way of John Santucci.

An incredible, behind-the-scenes drama was about to unfold.

Its opening act would stretch the Son of Sam conspiracy from coast to coast.

XVI

The Most Unlikely Ally

The public and almost all the media were unaware of the backstage story that was developing. The New York City Police Department was ignorant of it, while the Queens district attorney, who did know what was going on, was forced to view the events from the sidelines.

It is appropriate to let Berkowitz himself introduce the players. As he wrote to Lee Chase,* his self-appointed Christian counselor in a western state: "The following people are involved and working on this:

Gilroy, from Staten Island
Pienciak, from the A.P.
West Coast—you know who!
D.A. Santucci
Middle of Silence Gallery
Sheriff, Minot, N.D.
Maury Terry & Mitteager, the authors of those stories.

"I'm just warning you to be careful, here," Berkowitz continued. "As I say, all of these above mentioned are somehow related, if you know what I mean. Let's use tact and caution and let us remember how fragile the situation is for someone like my father. Oh, yes, something else, the D.A. obtained a copy of my mailing list here. So this is how they will contact you."

Lee Chase would move to another state before Santucci could reach her, but others, including myself, knew where she was.

Felix Gilroy, of course, was Mitteager's attorney and my companion at Marcy. Berkowitz didn't know he no longer represented Mitteager. Gilroy's participation would be pivotal, but brief.

Rick Pienciak was the Associated Press's Son of Sam reporter. He covered the original case, later interviewed Mitteager after his arrest and spoke with me several times by phone. He knew the angle we were pursuing before it was made public. Pienciak, a brown-haired man of twenty-nine, attended a January 1979 press conference at which Berkowitz termed his 1977 "demon" story a hoax. Pienciak then managed to get onto Berkowitz's mailing list—an important consideration since only correspondence from approved parties got through.

Lee Chase, an intelligent, dark-haired woman of forty-one, was an expert in the study of "demonology" who began writing Berkowitz shortly after his arrest, when his mail wasn't screened at Kings County Hospital. Her goal was to convert him to Christianity. She and Berkowitz exchanged letters frequently—sometimes more than once a day. Berkowitz trusted Chase and regarded her as a close confidante.

The "sheriff" in Minot was Lieutenant Terry Gardner, and the Middle of Silence Gallery was a commune or association of artists and poets who literally believed in demonic possession. Before Berkowitz's arrest, MOS sent out press releases saying that Son of Sam was controlled by his demon-familiar, "Sam the Terrible"—which they picked up from the Breslin letter. The Gallery also offered mundane theories about the killer, a number of which were very reasonable. After Mitteager was arrested, a group of MOS people, who were gentle, sensitive throwbacks to the late sixties, rode a bus to Jim's Staten Island home to ask him if any of the letters Berkowitz wrote them from Kings County Hospital were snatched by guard Herb Clarke. The answer was "no."

Berkowitz wanted to see the Son of Sam case solved—to have arrests made, the truth brought out. But he didn't want to make formal statements in a courtroom. He was pledged to secrecy and feared for the life of his adoptive father, Nat, and other relatives in the New York area. So Berkowitz came up with a plan. Using Lee Chase as an assistant, he would send clues and leads to the different people mentioned above. With luck and some guidance from him, he thought the case could be broken wide open without his having to turn state's evidence in a courtroom.

Even operating in the shadows, Berkowitz was taking a risk. He had only to touch his throat to know what already happened to him. But he was angry. Angry that he had taken a fall for others; angry that they were still on the loose. He was also stricken by guilt. He wanted to pay back something for the havoc he helped create.

Since the Marcy meeting a year before, Berkowitz had pondered the case. Until that day, he didn't know that anyone was looking into the conspiracy. He had believed the case was shut down. After Marcy, he waited and watched. In July, after his throat was cut, he heard rumblings about the Moskowitz article we wrote. He didn't have the piece yet, but when he finally received it from a Westchester relative, his reaction, I was told, was one of extreme joy and satisfaction. He sent the clipping to Lee Chase and told her it was right on target. Pienciak also said that Berkowitz "especially liked the Moskowitz article."

When Michael Carr died, Berkowitz clipped a *New York Times* story on the death and mailed it out to Chase with the words "Occultists, the same sad end" written on it.

In mid-October, Berkowitz caught wind of the new NYPD investigation. On October 15, before Santucci's probe was publicized, Berkowitz wrote to Lee Chase:

"Gee, you picked the most godawful time to move. All this time we've been just goofing off when now it's very important. Look, this is very, very important and I think you know what it's about. Now listen to me—I want you to get all the clippings you've got which deal with animal sacrifices, especially dogs and cats (if possible) but any will do. Next, everything you've got on Druids (modern day Druids). Please do this. Also, remember those materials you had on Bundy? I mean about those 'Ted' slayings possibly being related to the occult. And of course any clips or papers you've got on [a satanically linked professor]. Now, make one copy of each article.

"What I must get ahold of are clippings or stories on cult groups or just plain satanic occult groups who sacrifice. [Berkowitz was writing this letter nine days *before* we broke the story about the cult, the dead dogs and Untermyer Park.]

"Look, remember what you said about 'Ted' [killer Ted Bundy] being with the occult (sacrificing)? I know you do. Okay, it's a long story. Damn, Lee, this is what my phone call was going to be about. We've got work to do now, kid."

Berkowitz went on to say that he'd soon have Felix Gilroy's address and that he wanted material sent there. He asked Lee to find out the address of the Ward County Sheriff's Department in Minot. "Will you help me now, or what?" he asked. "If you don't take action now, then it may as well be never. Just prepare the materials and I'll be in touch."

Lee Chase was surprised, but only mildly. Berkowitz had been hinting about his cult involvement for more than a year, but would back away from confirming it. Now the die was finally cast. No sooner was the Chase letter in an envelope than Berkowitz wrote another one. This note, sent to a California preacher, was a flat-out confession:

"I really don't know how to begin this letter, but at one time I was a member of an occult group. Being sworn to secrecy or face death I cannot reveal the name of the group, nor do I wish to. This group contained a mixture of satanic practices which included the teachings of Aleister Crowley and Eliphaz Levi. It was (still is) totally blood oriented and I am certain you know just what I mean. The Coven's doctrines are a blend of ancient Druidism, the teachings of the Secret Order of the Golden Dawn, Black Magick and a host of other unlawful and obnoxious practices.

"As I said, I have no interest in revealing the Coven, especially because I have almost met sudden death on several occasions (once by half an inch) and several others have already perished under mysterious circumstances. These people will stop at nothing, including murder. They have no fear of man-made laws or the Ten Commandments."

Berkowitz, whose "Golden Dawn" reference linked his cult to the OTO, then asked the preacher to send him booklets or articles on satanic killer cults. "I think it is imperative that I educate certain people—the people whose job it is to clean up after this coven. Of course I am talking about the authorities. Actually it is my duty as a citizen of this planet to do so. But it would be up to those concerned people to do their own investigating. Knowing the fearlessness and dedication this group possesses, I fear greatly for my family."

Several days later, Berkowitz would send a similar letter to another minister. In it, he added: "To break away completely is impossible because of a Pact each new member signs in his own blood. Also, each new and carefully screened recruit supplies a picture or pictures of all his or her family members, plus their addresses. These items are used, if necessary, as tools for blackmail, coercion and eventually physical harm should one attempt to betray the group.

"I guess you could say that I mellowed with time and as a result of being away from direct influence. However, I do want to leave it completely and QUIETLY. A woman who lives on the west coast has been counseling me. She is a Christian. To be honest, I'm not."

Berkowitz, who would later add that influences of the Basque witches of Portugal and Spain were absorbed by his group with the other practices he mentioned, then told the reverend: "You also seem trustworthy and reliable. Of course, I could be wrong. If I am, then my family could be harmed." He pledged the pastor to secrecy, and asked for occult-related materials he could send to the authorities on the sly.

* * *

That night, before going to sleep, Berkowitz typed out another note to Lee Chase. "Tonight I feel so haunted. Why? Don't you remember when, quite a while back, I asked you about Arliss [*sic*] Perry. Lee, who killed Arliss Perry? Did you ever wonder? You were surprised and you asked me how I knew of this case. How did I? When you figure out the rest of the riddle, then . . . ? Just do what I asked you to do. Wishing you well. P.S., don't worry. It wasn't me. However, why do you suppose I asked you about this case long ago?"

He signed it: "Love, David."

Two days later, on October 17, Berkowitz again wrote Chase to urge her to expedite the job at hand. He added: "I know a great many things which few would ever believe as it stands now. Of course, and very importantly, many do NOT WISH TO KNOW!" Then, still not telling Chase he heard the case was reopened, Berkowitz said: "The Son of SCratch [Sam Carr and the devil] case is 'closed.' It is closed in the eyes of the public and the authorities. Good! So let it be. It's best this way. . . .

"It is the job of police departments . . . to catch criminals. It ain't my job. Whatever leads and clues they develop [on Son of Sam]—they develop. It ain't my job to do this, either. What I'm trying to say is that in time other criminals will slip up somewhere. Someone will come forward with corroborating information to help solve a given crime. Someone will get caught in the act. Then, it's off to jail."

Still speaking about the Sam cult, Berkowitz added: "The time will come, and it does seem soon, that many cases across the U.S.A. will be marked 'solved.' The more crimes you commit, the greater the likelihood of capture. The more people you include in a group that engages in criminal activity, the greater the chances of someone 'ratting' you out. Things are hot now for some. So I'll just sit back and wait."

* * *

Several days later, in Minot, Lieutenant Terry Gardner received a book, *The Anatomy of Witchcraft,* which Berkowitz spirited out of prison to a friend. The book was mailed anonymously to Gardner from a zip code we traced to a particular post office in lower Manhattan. On the dedication page, in Berkowitz's unmistakable printing, was a message: "The Book of the Black Curse and those not fearful to administer it.

Never to be caught! The evil which has permeated one's soul."

On the title page, Berkowitz wrote: "You wouldn't believe who this book belonged to." He then listed thirty-two pages he wanted Gardner to study. On each of those, Berkowitz highlighted what was, in effect, his story and that of the cult.

He underscored a reference to Dr. Stephen Ward, who died in an apparent suicide in England in the aftermath of the Keeler-Profumo scandal in the early 1960s. "For Ward himself was a dabbler in the occult and on his death there was a great deal of scurrying around among certain London practitioners to cover their traces." (Ward was a close friend of socialite Claus Von Bulow, who was living in England at that time. Von Bulow, who later relocated to Manhattan and Newport, Rhode Island, would be charged with attempting to murder his wife, Sunny, via insulin injections.)

On another page, Berkowitz clearly underlined a passage in which the author, Peter Haining, related that much of his own occult knowledge was derived from the novels of Dennis Wheatley. Berkowitz underscored only "Den Wheat-ey"—the home of John Wheaties Carr. He was saying that much of *his* occult knowledge came from that source.

On another page, Berkowitz underlined an additional passage concerning satanic cults in Britain: "I have good reason for estimating the membership of the cult to run into several thousand men and women." This is precisely what Berkowitz alluded to at Marcy a year earlier. Now the pieces were falling into place.

He also highlighted a reference to a restaurant in Houston, Texas—which would later prove significant, as would a sentence about "bell-ringing" in a satanic service. He was giving us a "church" clue, although we didn't know it then.

It was Berkowitz's highlighting of a chapter called "Evil on the Coast" which set off the rockets, however. There, he underlined a sentence in a section about the Process: "Thou shalt kill. They say they are dedicated to bringing about the end of the world by murder, violence and chaos—but they, the chosen, will survive to build a new world of Satanic glory."

On the same page, with a specially marked asterisk and brackets, Berkowitz zeroed in on a section about the Chingons—which research had shown was a Process off-shoot based in California. And in another letter to Chase, he'd written: "California is the home of Chingon and other foul groups."

We had the cult I had suspected for nearly two years.

But Berkowitz wasn't finished yet. On facing pages in that same chapter, he underlined passages about Charlie Manson's authority over his followers—including the assertion that Manson was a "Christ/Devil"—another Process link. He then underlined just two words, that Manson's disciples acted "under orders." What, we asked, was so important about those two words?

Berkowitz also underscored: "Sunset Strip"—where the Process hawked its wares. Further down, he underlined: "The shade of Aleister Crowley looms large in the area [L.A.], but his excesses pale into insignificance compared to today's devil worshippers."

At the bottom of the page, Berkowitz had written a note but then erased it. We were certain it concerned Manson and the cult, however, considering the context of the pages.

But in the margin, there was another note he didn't erase. In his own hand, he wrote one of the most chilling messages I have ever read: "ARLISS PERRY, HUNTED, STALKED AND SLAIN. FOLLOWED TO CALIFORNIA. STANFORD UNIV."

*   *   *

The book was in Terry Gardner's hands less than an hour when he called me. "Who the fuck is Arlis Perry?" he demanded.

"Goddamn, I don't know. I never heard of her. And what's with this stuff linking her, Manson and all? We've got the group, Terry. It's the Chingons, son of Process, and the Process was in California and here in New York, too. He's tying Manson into it and connecting it all to this Arlis Perry."

"You mean he's saying that his group was the Chingons, that it was tied to the Process and that Manson was in it, too?"

Gardner was awed, as was I. "It seems like that's just what he's saying. As unreal as this sounds, it fits with what we've been working on. He led us to believe a long time ago that the group in Yonkers was part of a bigger picture, and we already had the Process or one of its children under suspicion. Now, out of the blue, he gives it to us," I said.

I repeated the Process's history to Gardner, emphasizing that the group set up cells in a number of U.S. cities in the late sixties and early seventies. I told him how the California group went underground at the time of Senator Robert Kennedy's assassination, and how the Chingons and Four P movements came to be.

"Bugliosi, who prosecuted Manson, believed Manson was in the Process," I said. "So did Ed Sanders, who wrote *The Family*. Rather than being that far-out, what Berkowitz is saying makes sense."

"I'll be goddamned if I don't need some time to absorb this. Hey, this is the Ward County, North Dakota, Sheriff's Department—not the FBI. How the hell can we do anything about this?"

"I think we first better find out who this Arlis Perry person is," I suggested. "From what he's saying, she's dead. You're a cop. Why don't you call around out there and see what's what."

With a resounding "click," Gardner was gone. In two hours, he was back on the line. "Hey, boy, you'd better lie down—not sit down."

"What do you have?"

"Arlis Perry was nineteen years old. Around midnight on October 12–13, 1974 . . . "

"John Carr's birthday, and Aleister Crowley's birthday, too. That fits with what he underlined on that page," I said.

"O.K., but wait a minute. She was murdered—butchered—in the church at Stanford University."

"In a church?"

"More than that," Gardner said. "She'd only been out there for a few weeks."

"Terry, you're busting my horns. What do you mean, 'only out there for a few weeks'?"

"She'd just been married. Her husband was a student at Stanford. She just got there from right down the road here—Bismarck, North Dakota."

"Holy shit." I must have repeated that expletive a dozen times.

"There's more," Gardner said. "The Santa Clara cops just got some newspaper clips in the mail, anonymous. Sent from New Orleans. One of your articles about Carr and Berkowitz was in there, along with a tiny clip from the time about Arlis. They didn't know what the hell it meant."

"We all do now," I whispered. "He said she was 'hunted, stalked and slain' and 'followed' to the Coast. He's saying the killer or killers were from North Dakota! No wonder they couldn't solve the case out there. They were probably looking for some local wacko."

"That's right," Gardner said. "They thought it was some local nut job. Now it's all turned right back east to North Dakota, Carr's group here and Son of Sam in New York."

"Surprise, surprise."

"They can't figure out how Berkowitz ever heard of this case," Gardner said. "But it seems pretty obvious, what with John and the boys here in Minot. If they followed a Bismarck girl to Stanford and iced her, you'd bet your ass David would know."

"I don't think there's any question about it. Now we've got to go like hell to develop more and try to firm this up."

*   *   *

On October 25, two days after Gardner received the book, Berkowitz sat in his cell and typed another letter. He didn't know that Lee Chase had sent the clips to a relative in New Orleans, who then mailed them to the Santa Clara Sheriff's Department. He didn't want that step taken. He would be upset when he learned what she'd done.

Berkowitz would have two reasons for being annoyed with Chase. First, he wanted to deal only with his select contacts, whom he knew were intimately familiar with the Son of Sam–John Carr–cult case. Second, he was approaching this endeavor very seriously, and he didn't want to lose credibility. He was afraid that would happen if anonymous clips showed up at an alien sheriff's department. If his own sources made inquiries, that was one thing, because they could explain the situation to Santa Clara. But not the other way. Berkowitz would soon write Chase to chastise her, but first he had this other letter to get out.

Berkowitz remembered Marcy very well. He had thought about that day for a year now. Until that misty morning, he thought no one was looking into the conspiracy angle since guard Herb Clarke disappeared and Mitteager was arrested. He then waited and watched, and finally put two and two together. He reasoned, correctly, that the people he met at Marcy had to be the ones behind Gardner and Santucci's new investigation. He didn't know that it was me, by name, who was with Felix Gilroy that day and who had supplied Gilroy with the conspiracy questions. But through his friend Denise* in New York City, he'd now obtained Gilroy's Staten Island address. On the twenty-fifth, he sent an astonishing letter to the attorney.

> *A long time ago we met in the Central New York Psychiatric Center because of a court order which required you to question me. I was evasive then and I still am. I always will be.*
>
> *To be honest, you did shock me with how much information you had. You didn't do too bad of a job. However, you still have a long way to go.*
>
> *Another thing which you said to me continues to haunt me until this day. I don't remember it word for word, but it was in reference to helping society—protecting others who might be harmed.*
>
> *I could tell you honestly that a great many people are suffering because of their evil indulgences. There are certain powerful persons who are able to gain entrance into other people's minds and souls.*
>
> *You asked about Satanists. I'm not talking of thrill seekers who hang onto and join every anti-establishment group which comes along. I'm not talking about those who remain on the fringe of such groups. My letter is in reference to the elite and dedicated hardcore members of Occult groups.*
>
> *You see, these people cannot be taken lightly. Please try to understand their philosophy of life and society. They have no fear of man-made laws nor the laws of God. To them, murder comes easy. Being anti-God, they love nothing better than a good kill.*
>
> *These people will stop at nothing in order to fulfill their desires. They have the complete ability to elude the police and to cover their tracks completely.*
>
> *Many members of these hidden and secret groups are participating of their own free wills. Others aren't. Yet, they are there to obey every command and complete every task without question—lost souls, half-mad zombies they are.*
>
> *Mr. Gilroy, there is a very important key that cannot be overlooked—it ALL ends in tragedy! So many people who have followed the Left Handed Path [black magic] have met either sudden death via accident, suicide or murder. Or they have suffered financial loss, the ruination of their reputations, or they just ended up totally insane. It is the same sad story!*
>
> *John and Michael are dead. My life is ruined, too. And I also came close to death several months ago.*

Personally, I think it is best if you leave all this alone—you or whoever else started this investigation. Just drop it! It's for your own good. It is you who started all this, right?

Look, there are people out there who are animals. There are people who are a fearless lot. They HATE God! I'm not talking about common criminals. You know who I am talking about.

There are people who will follow a "Chosen Lamb" throughout the ends of the earth. If they feel that this person is the "next one"—well, they have money. They have brains and hate.

They will even kill in a church. Do you think I'm joking? Do you think I'm just bending your ear? Well, do this—do this quickly (I'm serious):

Call the Santa Clara Sheriff's office (California). This is by Santa Clara University and close to Stanford University. Please ask one of the sheriffs who have been there since late '74 what happened to ARLISS PERRY. Remember this name: Arliss Perry!

Please don't let them give you the "Psychopathic Homicidal Maniac" line or something similar. They know how she was murdered. They cannot tell you who did it or why. It was NO sex crime, NO random murder.

Ask them where she was killed. Ask them how. Ask them how often she wandered into that building of gold, purple and scarlet.

Please ask them for the autopsy report. Let the police provide you with everything—every little detail. Make them tell you what she went through. Don't let them skip one single perverted atrocity that was committed on her tiny, slender, little body. Let the Santa Clara police tell you all . . .

Oh, yeah, lastly (and this is important), make sure you ask them where she lived—I mean where she came from. Doing this will solve the whole case. Back in little, tiny B _____ . This is where the answer lies. The place (state) with the lowest crime rate of anywhere!

Some areas are accessible only by horseback and four-wheel drive. Plenty of open land and fresh, clean air. No crime. No death penalty. Rugged terrain. Buffalo. Grizzly bear. Rattlesnakes. Badlands. Tiny cities. Big lakes, etc. Few police are ever visible—rarely to be seen. Open plains. All wheat and oats.

I'm serious about all this. There is no reason why I shouldn't be. Sir, Satanists (genuine ones) are peculiar people. They aren't ignorant peasants or semi-illiterate natives. Rather, their ranks are filled with doctors, lawyers, businessmen, and basically highly responsible citizens. They are normal on the outside, at least.

They are not a careless group who are apt to make mistakes. But they are secretive and bonded together by a common need and a desire to mete out havoc on society. It was Aleister Crowley who said, "I want blasphemy, murder, rape, revolution, anything bad." Surely you will agree that death literally followed Crowley's footsteps.

Do you still doubt me? Well, listen to this because I'm not through yet. Someone said that I and another individual went to a dog pound shortly before my arrest. Well, to be honest, I didn't go there. Obviously, someone used my name. Yes, I will agree with this.

At one time, I think around late 1976 or early '77, I was supposed to get a job at the Yonkers Animal Shelter. With regards to this alleged visit by me with someone else, I don't know which dog pound or shelter this was. There is a place on Saw Mill River Road that sells guard dogs. Was this the one? Anyway, the shelter I was at was the one near the Motor Vehicles Bureau in Yonkers.

To show you how much I know, this place is a small, one story building. There is a yard attached and north of the main building in which the dogs are exercised in. Some dogs are left out there all day long, but their [sic] few in number. There are very few parking spaces in front of the building. Most of the people who drive to the shelter have to park their cars haphazardly along the front of the building because of only few spaces. Usually, the dogs are let out in the morning for exercise.

Across the street (and this spoiled everything) there is a truck yard. Well, it was some type of yard with vehicles in it. The problem was the guard who was there. A guard was present every twenty-four hours around the clock. Often, he sat in a chair right by the fence. When I went to the shelter the guard who was there was an older man (probably retired from other work) who wore glasses. I believe they were dark black-rimmed glasses. Let me make it clear, this guard didn't work for the shelter but across the street.

The street on which the pound is located is a dead-end street. I can't remember the name of it for anything. Am I correct in saying that it begins with an "F"? [Yes, he was: Fullerton Avenue.] I can't be certain. Facing north it is on the right-hand side of the street and the last building on the block—right at the end.

Inside the building, as soon as you walk in, you can see the individual cages. They are housed one on top of the other like an apartment building. Make it more like a prison. Several dogs have been taken on as pets by the staff. These dogs roam free on the inside of the place. There were two dogs which I became friendly with when I first came there. One was a small, shaggy dog, sort of a terrier. He was grey in color. He sat on the boss's desk. This is the main desk where all the paper work is done. The other dog, a fat German shepherd, was sleeping in the corner of the main office. It was a she. But the keepers wouldn't let me pet her because they said she was very temperamental.

The staff of the shelter was mainly made up of young people (men). One of the guys gave me a tour. He showed me the machine in which they put the dogs to sleep. It looks almost like a washing machine. I believe he told me that they use it every day. Surprisingly, the machine wasn't too far from the main entrance, but it was in sort of a cubicle.

Just about as soon as you enter the building, you turn right to get to the main office. The main office was almost barren. The desk was by the window. There were some file cabinets. The female German shepherd slept in the corner. But the boss was out on a call when I got there. He had a truck and with him went a young helper. They go out on calls often, it seemed. His helper was young, he had black hair, and he was thin. If I'm not mistaken, he also wore glasses. Both of them, the boss and the helper (I might be wrong).

The inside was ugly and dirty. It stank and it was noisy.

To explain all this, my job was going to be cleaning out the cages in the morning and letting the dogs out—feeding them, etc. It wasn't going to pay well. Not more than an amount slightly more than the minimum wage. But I believe that every six months or year you earn a raise. Certainly I wasn't going to be able to pay my rent and bills with it. But there was another way in which I was going to get paid—somebody needed dogs! I guess you understand what I'm trying to say. This whole letter isn't to bend your ear or waste your time. I'm only trying to show you how much of certain facts I know. To prove authenticity I must show you that I possess some knowledge of certain things.

Without providing you with names (I'll never do this) I can safely tell you that I was going to provide the dogs for obnoxious religious purposes. But you were going in that direction beforehand, weren't you?

I filled out the application for the job providing them with former employers, and all the other information they asked for on the form, which was kept in a file cabinet by the desk in the main office. This is where the blank forms were kept. However, despite the application, someone from the inside was supposed to vouch for me. It was all set up for me to get the job. Perhaps they chose someone else. You see, being that I was older than most of the other workers, the idea was that I was quickly going to advance in responsibility and seniority. Then I would have possessed many of the main and important keys. This was to let a few dogs out at night. I mean take them out. Of course this wasn't going to happen during business hours. This is where the problem was. That guard across the street sitting on his silly wooden black chair. The area, consisting of factories and warehouses, was too desolate and remote for this operation. That guard would have busted us easy. In fact, the possibility of abducting the guard was also considered. But at night the fence was closed. The guard was on the other side of the fence, a telephone must have been close by for him, and perhaps he was armed. Anyhow, it never went through. Plans were changed.

Since this was about three years ago, obviously things have changed. Perhaps there is now a new guard for one or all the shifts. These were uniformed guards. I believe their uniforms were blue. But I can't claim 100% accuracy on any of this. The passing of time has blurred my memory. But you'll find all this extremely close. I can guarantee this at least. There is a slight chance that my application form is lying around somewhere. I don't know how long the shelter keeps this stuff. But getting back to this report that I was seen at a dog pound shortly before my capture, well, it isn't quite true. But . . . ! You figure out the rest.

This letter is coming via certified mail. However, let me make it clear that this communicating will not become a habit. Your [sic] on your own. Whatever you find out, then it's yours. But truthfully, I wouldn't recommend probing. Don't forget what I told you earlier in this letter.

Yours truly,
David Berkowitz

Six months before Berkowitz wrote this letter, Tony Catalano, manager of the Yonkers Animal Shelter, told me that at the time of Berkowitz's arrest he and two co-workers believed they had seen him at the shelter. They indeed had. Said Catalano: "Everything he talks about is true. From the guard to the layout to the pay scale to me—I was the assistant then. And one of those 'pets' he talks about was mine; the other was the boss's. He knows this place better than I do—and I'm in charge of it. He was here day and night," Catalano said.

Berkowitz, by this admission, tied himself and the Sam cult to the dead German shepherds. It blended with his neighbor's report of him walking a dog on Pine Street and the other information we'd accumulated. It also cast new light on the call to Florence Larsen from the Berkowitz impostor seeking a German shepherd. That is, Berkowitz, who was to confess to sole responsibility for the .44 shootings, could also be blamed for the dog killings in the area—as originally did happen. The police routinely placed those incidents at his doorstep. Months later, when more dogs were found, no one paid attention—except us.

A later check with other animal shelters in lower Westchester revealed that three German shepherds were stolen—at night—from the Mount Vernon Animal Shelter on different occasions between October and December 1980—a year *after* this unpublished letter was written. There were no signs of forced entry and officials labeled the incidents an inside job. The plan was identical to that Berkowitz described as having been formulated nearly four years earlier by the Sam group.

With regard to the rest of the letter, Berkowitz's words were self-explanatory. We took his warning seriously, and became more cautious than we already were.

In addition to the Arlis Perry specifics which weren't included in the book sent to Gardner, several items particularly stood out. First, the cult's membership, according to the letter, included successful, prominent citizens. Second, Berkowitz's pointed reference to a "Chosen Lamb" was a clear-cut reference to the Process. The Process, as noted earlier, preached the alliance of the lamb of Christ and the goat of Satan. Illustrations of the lamb and goat joined together appeared in their magazines.

Finally, the dog shelter job plan graphically demonstrated Berkowitz's ranking in the cult. He wasn't a leader; not by a long shot. Would someone with authority in the group be chosen to clean out dog cages? And, by extension, would someone picked to do that work be capable of devising the plans which would successfully frustrate the biggest manhunt in NYPD history for so long? And could he, by himself, compose the Breslin letter—as renowned handwriting expert Charles Hamilton insisted he *didn't?*

* * *

In Attica prison, the clue-dissemination effort continued. Unaware that we were scrambling frantically in New York and Minot on the Arlis Perry matter, Berkowitz wrote to Lee Chase on October 26 asking her again to send out material on "Operation Photo," which was the code name the clue program was given. Berkowitz told her: "Remain anonymous. Leave my name out of it. All this material is, are helpmates for someone doing a very important investigation. Here's your chance to help. But leave out anything you've got on the 'Admiral's Daughter' [Arlis Perry]. By the way, I know who did it. Not me, but someone from the past whom I had the privilege of meeting. If you want to call it a privilege. I'm not certain that it was."

Turning from Chase, Berkowitz mailed a packet of occult-related material to Gardner in Minot. The pamphlets, explaining the dangers of satanism, were those he'd just received back from one of the preachers to whom he'd written.

In a note to Gardner, Berkowitz asked: "Sir, are you making any progress? I doubt if you are. I doubt if you can." He added: "This is all just to let you know what you are up against. Forget it. It's a losing battle."

Attached to the satanic material was something that just didn't fit in. It was a newspaper clipping about the 1979 crash of an Air Force F-106 jet in Montana.

"I couldn't understand it," Gardner said. "And then I checked with the Air Force. We learned that when John Carr was stationed in Minot he was a mechanic who worked exclusively on the F-106." Gardner and I were convinced Berkowitz was providing more proof of his association with John Carr.

Gardner sent the confessed Son of Sam a note asking if the F-106 analysis was correct. Berkowitz didn't respond, but he wrote Lee Chase: "I gave him the best of clues and I did it in my own roundabout way. I feel like I've accomplished something. By the few clippings I sent him, I feel that I helped humanity. The news clipping on an air crash in Montana said it all. He's very clever."

*   *   *

On October 27, Berkowitz sent Chase a clipping from the *Post* which reported the Queens investigation was branching out to several states across the country.

> *Obviously, this investigation is serious. . . . The article is pretty clear. You know damn well that these Satanists cover their tracks pretty good. You are aware of their intelligence (businessmen, doctors, military personnel, professors, etc.) . . . Cults, as you know, flourish around college campuses. They flourish around military bases, too. Drugs flow all over these two places (universities and bases). Young servicemen and young college students are involved in sexual relations. So mix the two of them up. Put them near each other and what do you have? You've got a pretty wild, dedicated and nasty bunch of young, zealous, anti-establishment devil-worshippers. And what a deadly mixture it is. My, my. Didn't Miss Perry wander around the Stanford campus frequently? Well, start adding, kid. What have we got here? [Arlis Perry did frequently wander the Stanford campus—but that fact was never made public.]*
>
> *There is an attorney in Staten Island, N.Y., who was ordered by the court to interview me when I was in Marcy. Of course, I could have refused to talk. But something inside me was beckoning me to talk. I beat around the bush and dropped little hints here and there. But he knew too much.*
>
> *It is in the court record that I was in a Holiday Inn. I was staying there when I was in Houston. Houston is a huge, spread-out city. There must be a thousand-some odd motels in this city. Guess what he found out? Guess who was registered in another room at the same Holiday Inn? [Here he named a woman linked to the case.] She was down in Houston when I was. This is why I only stayed at my friend Dan's [Billy Dan Parker] for a few days. I couldn't stay longer because I had other plans. . . . There was my attempt to get a job with the Yonkers Animal Shelter. This guy knew about the cigarettes in my car. Not my pack of butts. [We didn't know.]*
>
> *Oh, so many things. I can't go into it all. All this is unpublished. Truly it is a major coverup. All of this, all that went on in Marcy, has been forgotten by the detectives. But they knew of the numerous inconsistencies, the numerous unanswered questions, etc. God, there is so much! Honestly, I could probably type ten full pages detailing every inconsistency, every known fact that I wasn't alone. That it wasn't me. That gun in my possession is all they've got. But if they only knew the real motive. All this would have driven Sherlock Holmes to drink. This will be another Martin Luther King and Kennedy thing. Lee, I know it ALL! The others are gone. Dead. Took off to the prairies.*

Lee, all this takes is common sense. You've got common sense. Unfortunately, not everyone else does. Let's go back for a moment to when I was first arrested. Remember the hysterics? Not me, the citizens of New York. Remember the demands for my execution? "Kill him." "Die Berkowitz, Die." Remember the district attorneys and their pledges to convict at any cost? You must not forget the pressures, the terror, the madness, the publicity, the pressure on the police to wrap the case up and catch their man, the disgusting press, etc. Keeping all this in mind, it's easy for me to see how they missed so much. Small questions that would gnaw away at an investigator's mind. These little but peculiar stories that began to filter in. Those strange occurrences, etc. ALL OF IT WAS COVERED UP AND DUMPED. It couldn't be explained. There weren't any answers. So they IGNORED it.

But, time is passing. The pressure is off. The wounds are beginning to heal and the hysterical terror is gone. People are "normal" again. . . . So now it is time to recheck everything. It's now time to reorganize and review all the information and evidence that has come in. And NOW the discrepancies can no longer be ignored. Thus, they've discovered that they lacked so very, very, very much. I'm in prison, yet the cops in New York are back where they started from. It's not my fault. Actually, it isn't theirs, either. Nobody was level-headed enough back then to grasp all the evidence.

Well, here we go. Let's see what happens. Guess what? I've just heard over the radio that the detective whose [sic] been investigating the case has been placed under psychiatric care. The [NYPD] has announced a standstill in the investigation because of "this officer's mental state." I swear. I just heard this. Now, I'll have to wait for the newspapers to elaborate. These thirty-second news/radio items don't reveal much detail. More tomorrow.

And so ended the month of October 1979.

*   *   *

As November dawned, Detective Hank Cinotti was on the blocks, the NYPD was out of the case and Santucci's probe surged forward. Gilroy and I made the DA aware of the Arlis Perry matter, which Santucci's office left in the hands of Gardner, Mike Knoop and me. The Santa Clara Sheriff's Department was briefed on the entire investigation. There, Detective Sergeants Ken Kahn and Tom Beck agreed to sit tight. In a conversation with Kahn, I said that Berkowitz was talking somewhat, providing assistance, and recommended that they let matters be. "We don't want to spook him," Gardner chimed in.

The entire backstage effort was conducted out of the public eye. But in early November, I encouraged Gardner to let it be known publicly that Berkowitz sent him the packet of satanic materials.

"That's all we'll let out," I promised. "But it will at least let people know that Berkowitz is aware of what's going on and hasn't denied anything."

Gardner consented, and on Monday, November 5, Gannett and the *Minot Daily News* broke the story. In North Dakota, which now had the Son of Sam case in its backyard, the article was bannered in a huge front-page headline "BERKOWITZ TO GARDNER: YOU FIGHT SATAN'S FORCES." The lieutenant's picture and that of Berkowitz accompanied the piece. In Westchester, we played the story on the bottom of page one.

Once again, the *New York Post* picked up the article, phoned Gardner and rewrote its own version for Tuesday, November 6. In its headline the *Post* said that Berkowitz was sending "taunting mail" to Gardner and that he'd attached a note in "childish" handwriting. I knew why the *Post* used that terminology—to differentiate Berkowitz's writing from the neatly printed Breslin letter—but Berkowitz was doubly miffed.

He told Chase that he wasn't "taunting" anybody; that he was trying to help. "That childish scrawl just so happens to be the way I write. Sorry." Berkowitz was also annoyed that his correspondence with Gardner reached the public. Chase called Gardner, who wrote and assured Berkowitz it wouldn't happen again.

Berkowitz also wryly commented on writing expert Charles Hamilton's evaluation of his penmanship and spelling ability that appeared in our articles: "The Bum! The nerve of him stating that I'm not intelligent enough and that sensible writing is above me. HA. He's got some nerve. Truly, I was kind of insulted. I'm not that dumn, I mean dum, am I?"

Chase, reluctant to photocopy extensive material for Berkowitz, wrote and told him so. He wasn't thrilled. "Okay, I get the hint. So forget about photocopying. This wasn't going to be another 'nothing' venture. These two, one from New York and one from North Dakota, are trying to uncover a Satanic coven. It isn't a wild goose chase. It's for real. Since they really don't know what they're looking for, your stuff would have helped. But, okay, pass it up.

"One of the guys who is trying to uncover this occult group is a man who was investigating this 'satanic angle' . . . just after my capture. If you could only know ALL that he's uncovered, I'm certain you'd flee immediately to help him here in N.Y."

Berkowitz was referring to Gilroy. He still hadn't connected me to the Marcy questions.

Several days later, Berkowitz had a problem he wanted to share with Chase. "Obviously, my father is following this new investigation closely. He is concerned and is continually asking questions. He wants answers. I'm trying to dodge him, but he's persistent. Naturally, he wants me to talk. 'David, tell the truth.' Well, it's not that easy. You understand why. You know the dangers. So forget about operation photo. I could talk tomorrow. But it isn't easy to substantiate what I say—there's the question of what district attorney is willing. None are! Santucci bit off more than he could chew. It's obvious he realizes this now. The evidence is so overwhelming that only an idiot could ignore it, deny it, and leave it. The evidence is there. But who is the guilty party? Who else besides Berk? They need names, dates, places and other witnesses to acknowledge and agree with each other as to the facts."

*   *   *

John Santucci may not have "bitten off more than he could chew," but he was rapidly discovering that the case was a maze of complexities and subplots. Still, the DA's probe moved onward. Herb Leifer, George Byrd, Tom Mulderig, Michael Armienti, Tom McCarthy and other assistants toiled well into the nights.

McCarthy phoned one November morning to tell me that investigators were about to call Berkowitz's friend Denise to question her. I explained that it would be wiser to leave her alone for the time being. "She's very close to him," I said. "And he thinks she's panicky. It could hurt rather than help."

McCarthy turned the phone over to Mike Armienti, and we discussed the matter for ten minutes. In the end, Armienti agreed to let Denise be for the present.

Santucci's probers weren't as compliant on another subject, however. Aware that Berkowitz was writing Chase with specific details, they'd tried to find her—only to learn she'd moved and left no forwarding address—purposely. Berkowitz had tipped her off that Santucci would be looking for her.

Santucci's investigators had unearthed a considerable amount of information about the Carr brothers and others. But more evidence linking those still living to the .44 killings themselves was needed. Accordingly, they wanted to get their hands on copies of Chase's correspondence with Berkowitz.

As a reporter, I was in a minor bind. I knew where Chase was but couldn't reveal her location. However, I also knew there was evidence in the Berkowitz letters and wanted to make them available to Queens if I could. A solution presented itself in North Dakota.

In November, Chase phoned Gardner several times. The North Dakota lieutenant persuaded her to mail him some of Berkowitz's letters. He also encouraged her to get in touch with me, saying that it was I who'd broken the case open in the first place. Chase called me, and we spoke for more than an hour.

"David wants the case solved," she said. "He's tired of being known as the Son of Sam—because he's *not*. There were a bunch of them. But he's petrified about going into a courtroom, and he's afraid the cult will kill his family if he comes forward. That's why he's doing it this way."

Chase urged me to find a way to get on Berkowitz's mailing list, and agreed to send me copies of all her pertinent correspondence with him. "It's yours. Use it as you need to. This has got to be brought out. But don't give up my name or number to anyone there."

Herb Leifer knew Chase's name from Berkowitz's mailing list, and he was disappointed that I wouldn't put him in touch with her. But, with her permission, I supplied him with edited copies of the most relevant letters, omitting all personal details from them. So the DA's office finally had Berkowitz's own frank admissions to ponder and add to the evidence file.

"It's all here," said Leifer. "But who the hell do we arrest? The Carrs and Howard Weiss are dead, and we don't have enough yet on these other people. This is going to be a long, difficult haul.

"We could sure use David's confirmations about them," he added. "And then we could go for independent corroboration. Under New York law, we'd need more than David's statement, since he's a co-conspirator. You can't convict on just the testimony of an accomplice. We've got to put some of these people at the crime scenes or into this group via other evidence, too."

"I see what you mean," I answered. "He's given us John and Michael but he says he won't testify. So, in more ways than one, this independent evidence is crucial."

"Knowing something to be true and being able to prove it in court are two different things," Leifer lamented. "So we just keep working."

Leifer then went through the list of suspects, which had expanded because the public provided some solid leads after the publication of the newspaper articles. "Too many candidates," he said. "If we've got this cult, there are over twenty people involved in one way or another. But who are the shooters, who are the lookouts and wheelmen, and who planned it all?"

"Well," I said, "Berkowitz was a shooter; John Carr; maybe Michael. We don't know who shot Stacy Moskowitz, except the evidence and sketches say it wasn't any of them. We've got Ski Cap at the Voskerichian scene, too, and that wasn't any of them."

"I think Ski Cap might have been a woman," Leifer said.

"Me, too. It was warm that night and yet this hat was worn, and none was worn at any other shootings that we know of. The hat would hide longer hair. And the witness said the person looked to be sixteen to eighteen years old. That could be because of the softer features a woman would have. Berkowitz was there—the other sketch clearly shows that—and yet he confessed to being Ski Cap. Impossible."

"Yes, it is," Leifer agreed. "He was protecting Ski Cap. If only David would come forward."

"Herb, you're starting to call him David," I teased.

"With all the people I've talked to, I feel like I know his life almost as well as my own. How he got away with that demon-dog nonsense is beyond me. They just wanted it to be over. To drink their champagne, take their bows and go home as heroes."

* * *

In Attica prison, Berkowitz wasn't concerned about Leifer. He was still immersed in his clue campaign. He then received a letter from his friend Denise in New York

City. "On the news they say that D.A. Gold knew all about the idea of an occult group in the beginning when you were first arrested but didn't use any of the stuff in court," Denise wrote. "And imagine, Carr, his daughter, Cassara and that woman in Brooklyn who saw you got a reward. It's very funny, don't you think?"

Berkowitz immediately wrote to Chase, telling her: "Lee, Gold knew all the long."

Berkowitz went on to say that he'd written to the preachers requesting occult material. "I had quite a bit to say and I do want to be cautious because I never told anyone (even you) the things I told [them]. Hopefully, [they] can remain trustworthy and concerned. One day you will know the truth. It's difficult to say. Not that I can't find the words, it's my father I'm concerned about—his safety. Regardless, things are moving quickly, yet, I've had nothing to do with it. I'm NOT talking, but the wrong people could possibly think that I am. Either the authorities or someone will learn the truth. If they can't develop anything, then tuff turds. I'm staying buried right here."

Berkowitz also said: "Immediately after I was arrested, Mr. Borrelli, the homicide chief [captain] second to Dowd, personally asked me who else was involved. This is true. He asked me about a certain person because this person called up the police headquarters after I was caught. The telephone conversation bothered Borrelli. This was obvious. He sensed something but was unable to put his finger on it. If you doubt me, then call him. I'm sure the police headquarters and Rockefeller Plaza [Associated Press] would have his new assignment and precinct he works out of."

* * *

On November 8, Berkowitz received our October 24 article on the cult in Untermyer Park and its links to the Son of Sam letters. He quickly sent it to Chase. "I've enclosed a *very* important piece of newsprint. I want this back without delay," he wrote.

On the twelfth, the first sign of trouble appeared on the horizon. Berkowitz had rethought his feelings about his clues to Gardner ending up in print. He castigated the *Post* for distorting his intent, and then told Chase: "I am quite upset with this stuff turning up in the papers. I thought the Sheriff would keep silent. Apparently, he got so excited when he discovered the major clue [about John Carr and the F-106] in that seemingly insignificant article that he just had to tell somebody about it. No doubt, the *Minot Daily News* is bucking for a Pulitzer Prize/Journalism award. Well, it would be the first one in the newspaper's history and certainly the last. Nothing ever happens in Minot!"

But he added: "Fine work was done by the Sheriff because he finally figured it all out—but I left him thinking for awhile before he solved the riddle." Berkowitz then talked about the puzzle in "the first sentence of the Breslin letter" and its "hidden clues" [the Black Mass elements and link to Untermyer Park],

A few days later, Berkowitz opened a note from Denise. Santucci's office reversed its agreement with me and phoned her, as Gardner did earlier when he thought an anonymous call from Chase had been made by Denise. Denise, as I knew well, was reacting nervously.

"Dave, I'm getting frightened. Everybody knows my name and number. . . . Please don't write to anyone about the case. The Queens D.A. called the Gallery [MOS] and asked to see the letters you write them. They don't know what to do and I said not to show them anything."

Berkowitz then told Chase: "Why must she always panic? The District Attorney from Queens tried to contact her. So what did she do? She got hysterical and called the Middle of Silence Gallery and told them not to give the D.A. any of my letters. Too bad, because in it I explained the meaning of the symbol—you know what I mean [the Son of Sam symbol]. I mean, too, that I have been writing the Gallery from time to time and I really wouldn't mind if the D.A. peeked at some of them [the letters]. Of course, Denise told them to hide the letters and not to cooperate." Berkowitz's mild disappointment with Gardner and his realization that Denise was upset were minute considerations compared with what would happen next.

Serious trouble was waiting in the wings.

XVII
"Sam" Speaks

In mid-November, with Justice Ernst Rosenberger presiding, Jim Mitteager's trial opened at State Supreme Court in Brooklyn. The jury would be asked to determine his guilt on two charges: bribery and rewarding official misconduct. Conviction could result in a seven-year prison term for the despairing reporter, whose bylines continued to appear on the numerous .44 articles being published in Westchester.

On November 14, as the legal proceedings unfolded, Berkowitz wrote a letter to AP reporter Rick Pienciak. Pienciak had thus far been frustrated by the reopened case, finding himself mainly restricted to sending out dispatches based on our work or on what little he could glean from Santucci's office.

Since his original statement, in which he credited the newspaper reports for having spurred his entry into the case, Santucci had been publicly silent. This irritated some journalists, who were reliant on the DA's office because they had nowhere else to turn for material. Pienciak also wanted something to publish, and when he received Berkowitz's letter, his sky brightened. In it, Berkowitz confirmed the cult's existence and said: "Two years have elapsed and only recently have they (whoever they are) begun to find hidden meanings in those original letters. I have to give these people credit."

Berkowitz told Pienciak about the Arlis Perry murder and emphasized that neither he nor John Carr was responsible, which deepened the mystery. We knew Berkowitz wasn't even in the cult at that time, but Carr had been an early suspect. Berkowitz, in fact, told Pienciak the Perry case was "very deep" and suggested that Lee Chase could help him out with it and the .44 probe.

He also said that although he was indirectly aiding the Son of Sam investigation, he wouldn't give up names of accomplices to Pienciak or anyone else. "It isn't for my sake, but for my famalies [*sic*]. My father comes first. Then again, he has been encouraging me to talk. However, he has no idea of the dangers involved—the dangers to him."

Next, Berkowitz wrote Chase and recommended that she cooperate with Pienciak. Digressing from the business at hand, Berkowitz offered another observation: "Many housewives need new vibrators. These little buzzing contraptions would certainly keep them occupied with other things than parading outside Kings County Hospital and demanding the execution of SOS. This happened, by the way. A hundred or so marchers (99% housewives) all screaming for my head and being led by that dreadful Mrs. Moskowitz. Boy, speaking of self-righteous sexual frustration. I know that [court-appointed psychiatrist] Abrahamsen and Sigmond Frued [*sic*] would have had a ball analyzing them all."

* * *

Two days later, on the twenty-first, Berkowitz's cynical humor gave way to panic. "Well, now you did it!" he wrote Chase. "Oh, man, you will never guess who dropped in for a surprise visit today. Hint: they came from the west coast. Hint: they got a funny letter from Louisiana. Hint: their [*sic*] from California. Well, who could they be? UFOs? No. Damn it. You know who. That's right. I kid you not.

"If you can recall, I asked you to send nothing. Nothing! But you mailed your little [Sacramento] "Bee" clipping [about Arlis] anyhow. Naturally, [along with] that letter to Badlands [North Dakota], they assumed the letter was from me. Damn, I got blamed for it. This is the honest to God truth. And now my ribbon is acting up again—my typewriter ribbon. [The words began to fade on the paper. Berkowitz was in a quandary.]

"The Santa Clara boys screamed they wasted the taxpayer's money. I guess their [*sic*] on their budget thing out west, too. Like in New York they've taken away the cop cars and given them bicycles. Saving on gas! Oh, great. Now these guys are so pissed that they will never bother to pay attention again. I just knew something like this was going to happen. I just knew it! All these inquiries about Miss P., all these little tips, the strange phone call [an anonymous call from Chase to Gardner], crazy letters, curious Mr. Gilroy. Of course, it was only a matter of time before their curiosity was aroused. What did you expect? They don't fool around with murder. This is serious business and someone could get hurt.

"Look, I'm not mad. But I would like to pinch your butt. Oh, but it would be a nice pinch. You'll like it. Anyhow, now what do I do? Of course, I refused to talk with them."

Berkowitz was mistaken. The Santa Clara sheriff's detectives, Ken Kahn and Tom Beck, hadn't shown up at Attica—yet. But they did phone there and ask to speak to Berkowitz. When the message was delivered to him, he thought they were in the visitors' center and refused to come out. The crisis was momentarily averted.

* * *

On the night before Thanksgiving, the Brooklyn jury acquitted Jim Mitteager of all charges. Bursting with jubilation, he called me from a phone in the hallway outside the courtroom. "This is the *best* Thanksgiving I'm ever going to have!" he exclaimed.

"Thank God for you that it's over," I said. "I was in touch with Marian Roach at the *Times* today. She said Joe Fried was out there covering it for them and was phoning in reports. I know she wishes you well, too. She was nervous about it all day. Remember, she was there the first time we spoke to Cacilia Davis in Brooklyn."

"Yeah," Jim said. "And Joe is here. He's writing the story for tomorrow's *Times*."

"Go home and take Carol out for a few drinks," I suggested. "You've both been through hell."

"I'm on my way," Jim shouted. "Happy Thanksgiving! I feel like I've been born again."

In the next day's *New York Times,* reporter Joe Fried wrote an account of the acquittal in the *Post*-Mitteager-bribery trial. In compiling the article, he solicited comments from members of the jury. One, speaking for the panel, told him in a statement the *Times* published: "The wrong defendant was on trial. The feeling was that the *Post* should have been on trial."

Berkowitz, who felt ambivalent toward Mitteager, had no reaction to the exoneration. He had bigger troubles to deal with.

In late November, Rick Pienciak flew out West to meet with Lee Chase and returned by way of Minot, where he spoke to Gardner. While with Chase, Pienciak obtained copies of some of Berkowitz's letters. Through Chase, word got back to Berkowitz that Pienciak was pursuing a theory that Berkowitz and others in the group were homosexuals. Berkowitz had seen the "latent homosexuality" reference in our article about the cult, but he hadn't reacted badly because the comment wasn't specific. However, he believed Pienciak was about to be very specific.

"I only want to assure you that in this matter he [Pienciak] is incorrect," Berkowitz wrote to Chase. "However, I have met some of these 'strange' persons in the various circles [the cult] that I circulated. But I never 'did it' with them. No way! This isn't for me. Matter of fact, plenty of straight women were present, too. [This was a major revelation.] Probably more women than men. Muff—nuff said?

"Now of course, you must correct Uncle Rick in this matter. If you don't, then I'm dead. The reason, I'm in prison, he isn't. Neither you nor he have no knowledge whatsoever of how the prison gossip system works. It doesn't matter if a certain rumor *isn't* true—here there is no justice. Should the inmates believe this (they will believe it because they want to) then I will be dead within a week. . . . In prison a man survives by his masculinity. So please straighten him out once and for all—him and Maury Terry."

Berkowitz then talked about his inability to turn state's evidence. "I can't do it. I can but I don't want to. I'm in a predicament here where I cannot talk with the press or police. Let a rumor begin that I am a stool pigeon and I'm just as dead as if I was one of those 'strange ones.' Comprende? I sure hope you do because I'm in a dangerous situation. Nobody here hates a 'strange one,' stool pigeon or sex freak more than anything imaginable. I think I just said this wrong. What I mean to say is that those three I just mentioned are hated so very much that they are in constant danger.

"Again, I'm not any of these. But I can't let others think I am."

Berkowitz then switched subjects. "Please read the attached letters and give me an opinion. These letters from Gardner and Terry are questionable—what should I do? I will await your advice. Also, please don't return the letters. . . . Terry is the guy who wrote those stories which you have in your possession now." The articles, sent to Berkowitz by Denise, were read by him and then forwarded to Chase.

I finally had established contact with Berkowitz. Gardner, who was now on his mailing list, sent me his own letter to Berkowitz, and I enclosed mine in the envelope. It got through. In it, I simply told Berkowitz that I'd been at Marcy, composed the conspiracy questions he was asked that day and was working the case since the day of his arrest. Chase later wrote him to encourage his correspondence with me. And he needed it: his anger at Rick Pienciak was suddenly boiling over.

"Shit!" he wrote Chase on November 26. "You see now how I am trying to indirectly help others learn the truth about all of this. Yes, I am now a victim again. This time a victim of stupid investigators who know nothing of the occult or whatever they decided to call these weirdos. Here I am trying to help others and Satan has pulled out his weapon—his secret weapon—should I decide to help Rick or others like him. And now this crazy Rick is going with his 'strange desires' theory. Should I talk with anyone (Rick, Terry, Mitteager, Gardner, Santucci) about this Occult involvement, then out comes this 'strange' theory—which wouldn't sound like a 'theory' in print. Then, after this nonsense circulates, I'd be dead in no time. If not dead, then I'd be a man most miserable. I'll be joked at and laughed at by all the other inmates.

"What god-damn mother fuckin fools these 'investigators' are! What stupid fucks! Meaning well, they will destroy the very one that is helping them in the first place. It is I who is leaving many of the clues. . . . They want clues, yet, they are killing me at the same time. What idiots!"

Berkowitz then said he was thinking of writing to the media to say: "These investigators are foolish and crazy. The investigation will eventually stop because of the lack of further materials and that will be that. No more investigation—no more stupid rumors or stupid fools to spread them. Like the usual, Satan will again be the victor."

To suggest Berkowitz was somewhat distressed with Pienciak would be akin to labeling World War II a water pistol fight. And he wasn't finished. The next day, November 27, he was assailing the AP reporter again:

"[The] blind fool is working on this 'strange desires' theory without the slightest bit of evidence. All guess work. The blind fool is trying logically to figure out why all this [the conspiracy] came about. The pervert! It's his mind that's dirty.

"Lee, I know just what's going to happen. It's the same old story with the N.Y. *Post* and *Daily News*. These two have screwed up every story they ever got on my case. They are the most sensational and ugly (also inaccurate) newspapers in the world. I know just what they will do. I can see the sensational headlines. . . . Even though it isn't true it would certainly made a good and spicy story—which is all the eight million perverts in New York City want to hear. None of these tabloids are the least bit concerned with accuracy. . . . Disgusting bastards.

"I had sensed something was wrong when my father wrote me this huge letter and pleaded with me to ice up. It was so weird because the week before he had asked me to cooperate so that I could perhaps get a reduction in sentence. This, of course, wasn't my purpose. I was going to leave this investigation up to others. To get what my father wanted, I would have to go over to the finest detail every single event, every single detail about the victims, the crimes, my part, etc. No way! I'm not going back down to New York shackled in chains and paraded from courthouse to courthouse and county to county. I'm not going to be paraded around in front of dozens of reporters and the victims' families.

"Yes, I see what weapon Satan has in store for me should this thing really get moving. I can see what horrors await me as I try to explain to my friends here about this 'Homo' headline. I'm not going to be giggled at and cat-called at as if I were a girl. This is what will happen. Yet, it would all be over some stupid [homosexual] theory."

Berkowitz *did* confirm that some of the group members were gay. His gripe was that he would be lumped in with them. The confirmation was a valuable one, giving us more to work with on Howard Weiss, Michael Carr and others. Now, too, women emerged as suspects.

*   *   *

On December 4, Rick Pienciak and I met in Yonkers, where we discussed the case at length. He had agreed to join forces and cooperate—but the next day he would tell Chase not to deal with anyone but him.

During our meeting, Pienciak offered a reason for his willingness to work with me.

"You've been in this from the beginning. Everyone says you must have had hot information to get in so early and stay there. Nobody but us has a chance at this. If the *Times* can't get the story all by themselves, they'll stay out of it. The *News* is embarrassed because they gave a reward to the Carrs and because Breslin wrote that ridiculous fiction about the case. And the *Post* is covering it, but they have no information and don't know which way to turn. That leaves you and me," he said.

No, it didn't. It left me. Unknown to both of us that night, the Berkowitz-Chase alliance was about to sever Pienciak from the investigation.

The next morning, Pienciak told Chase not to provide any information to Gardner, me or Santucci. Chase promptly mailed a note to Gardner in Minot, who was considering a trip to her home.

"Right after I talked to you about coming out here this weekend," she wrote, "I called Rick Pienciak with A.P. and he was very critical of me—almost called me a fool and made it clear that I was at least a 'traitor' to David. He had me bitterly crying when I slammed the phone down on the hook and called the phone company for a disconnect immediately."

Chase reported this incident to Berkowitz, and then wrote to Pienciak telling him her phone and postal box numbers were changed and she was out of the case. She wasn't, of course. But in the short span of three weeks, Pienciak had managed to completely alienate both her and Berkowitz.

Berkowitz wrote Chase the next week saying he'd heard from Pienciak again and the "letter indicates he is a phony." Pienciak was not happy with this turn of events. He became bitter toward Berkowitz and Chase and began to downplay the thrust of the entire investigation. However, he would be heard from again. In 1982, he would be involved in an article which nearly had a disastrous effect on the probe.

Pienciak's participation soured Berkowitz to a considerable degree, and Berkowitz was even more angered by the fact that he himself had originally judged the reporter to be trustworthy. But there was yet another dark cloud on the horizon, as the Queens district attorney's office ventured into a different piece of uncharted, risky ground.

Berkowitz's stepsister, Ann,* the daughter of his adoptive father's second wife, had experienced some personal difficulties of her own in life. The DA's investigators heard about Ann from several of Berkowitz's friends who told them, among other things, that Berkowitz at one time had a close association with her. For that and other considerations Herb Leifer and company decided to find Ann, who was said to be living in a California commune.

The investigators had legitimate reasons, at the time, to be interested in Ann. But apparently no one in Queens considered just how such an inquiry would be received by Nat Berkowitz and his wife, Julia, Ann's mother. The elder Berkowitz had been urging David to cooperate with Santucci, but after he heard that Julia's daughter was being sought for questioning, he changed his mind. Or Julia did.

Nat then wrote to David and asked him to cool his heels. His father's pressure on him was strong. Along with the Pienciak fiasco, Berkowitz's desire to help the investigation was suddenly being severely tested. There was, it would turn out, no evidence linking Ann to the case, but again, damage had been done.

Regarding his father's change of heart, Berkowitz wrote: "My father is dying to see this stuff [the Gannett articles.] . . . He is curious to see what this is all about. First he says, 'Cooperate, cooperate, cooperate.' Now he is saying, 'Silence, silence, silence.' I'm just confused by everything. You ought to see the letter he sent me. Eight full pages—using every inch of paper to write on. There's hardly any white visible—only blue ink. So I've got to give him some answers soon."

Berkowitz was just a few days away from learning that Ann was being sought for questioning. The letter he referred to here didn't mention Ann as a prime reason for his father's about-face. But before that could happen, the roof collapsed from another weight.

*   *   *

Since I first became aware of the intrigue of Attica, I had but two goals in mind. First, to establish my own communication with Berkowitz. And second, to do whatever I could to ensure that the precarious situation wasn't sabotaged—intentionally or innocently—by other parties. Along those lines, I recommended that Queens not approach Berkowitz's friend Denise, whom I knew was high-strung and likely to panic. And, knowing how close Berkowitz was to Lee Chase, I also convinced the DA's office to let her be. I didn't know Pienciak had visited her until he returned—not that he would have listened to my suggestion anyway. Queens knew of the potential relevance of Berkowitz's stepsister, Ann, before I did; so there was nothing I could have done to avert that situation. But had I known, I would have recommended that Ann be left out of the picture, temporarily at least.

I myself had made a mistake in November when I encouraged Gardner to publicize the packet of clues he received from Berkowitz. Fortunately, Berkowitz was more annoyed with the *Post*'s treatment of the story than he was that it became public. But I wasn't going to recommend any further publicity about the Attica situation for quite some time. We had enough material to publish as it was. It was far better to allow Berkowitz to play his cards unencumbered. If push eventually came to shove, fine. But as I saw the situation, that day was a long way off—before the Ann and Pienciak incidents occurred.

And then there was the matter of the Santa Clara Sheriff's Department. Both Gardner and I advised those detectives to let us negotiate the Arlis Perry matter through with Berkowitz, as he knew who we were and had expressly stated he was against Lee Chase's sending any material to California. "Arlis has been dead five years," Gardner said. "It hasn't been solved in all that time. Another few months won't hurt."

But nobody listened. First, after delaying a few weeks, the California detectives phoned Attica—and Berkowitz refused to speak with them. Even at that, they didn't decide that perhaps Gardner and I knew what we were talking about. Santucci's investigators also joined with us and strongly opposed any Santa Clara contact with Berkowitz. But it was to be of no avail.

On December 3, the night before I met with Rick Pienciak, I received a call at 9 p.m. It was Detective Sergeant Ken Kahn of the Santa Clara Sheriff's Department.

"What are your plans for tomorrow?" he asked.

"Work during the day, and I'm supposed to meet somebody at six tomorrow night. Why? What's up?"

"We're in New York and we'd like to get together with you if we could." It took a minute for that to sink in. Kahn and his partner, Tom Beck, were calling from a Holiday Inn near Kennedy Airport in Queens.

"Does Santucci know you're in town?"

"No. We just flew down from Buffalo—Attica."

"What? You didn't—"

"I'm afraid we did," Kahn said slowly.

Kahn explained that Berkowitz initially refused to talk with them, but then felt sorry they'd come such a distance and agreed to acknowledge their presence. He told them that he feared for his father's life; that he had to exist in prison and couldn't be considered an informer; and that inmates would kill him if he was seen talking to cops. He also said he knew Lee Chase sent news clips to Santa Clara without his permission.

"He told us he wasn't lying about the Arlis murder, that he knew who did it and why, but wouldn't give up any names," Kahn said. "He told us that some state college

in Bismarck would provide a key to the solution." Here, Kahn was mistaken. The police assumed Berkowitz meant Bismarck Junior College, which Arlis attended. Only
later, when replaying the tape, did they realize he mentioned another school—Mary
College.

"We're convinced he knows about the killing," Kahn added. "You were right. He
was very sincere. He said he met the killer—or one of them—at a cult meeting in
New York. But that's all he'd give us."

Berkowitz had already written to Chase about where he met one of the killers,
so this wasn't news. The information about the college was new, however, although
Berkowitz had hinted about a school in his letters. The most important outcome of
this meeting was that the Santa Clara detectives saw for themselves that Berkowitz
was leveling with those involved in the case. But there was to be a big price to pay for
this firsthand assessment of the Son of Sam.

"He's going to write to you and Felix Gilroy and say he's through with all of this,"
Kahn said.

"I warned you guys, and so did Gardner," I insisted. "Berkowitz told you everything about his fears—the same things we told you."

"Yes," Kahn acknowledged. "He wasn't at all what we thought he'd be like. He was
friendly, but elusive. He said goodbye with a firm handshake and said he couldn't
help anymore."

I told Kahn that I'd rearrange my schedule and meet him and Beck the next day.
I then called Tom McCarthy at home and filled him in on what had happened.
McCarthy was dismayed.

I next reached Gardner in Minot and asked him to send a letter to Berkowitz
saying that we had nothing to do with the surprise visit and had recommended
against it.

The next morning, Queens assistant district attorney Mike Armienti called to tell
me Kahn and Beck were at the DA's office at that moment. "I walked out on them,"
he said. "George Byrd is also furious, and so was the boss [Santucci]."

"I'm sick and tired of people not listening when we tell them we know how Berkowitz is going to react," I said. "And goddamned Berkowitz tells them he blames
me and Gilroy for this. We had nothing to do with it—I was trying to keep them the
hell away from there."

"They couldn't resist coming to meet the infamous Son of Sam face to face," Armienti fumed. "This is all screwed up now. He'll not only back away on Arlis, he'll back
away on everything."

Apparently finding the Queens climate somewhat frosty, Kahn and Beck flew back
to California without calling me. And I met Pienciak as scheduled, but didn't tell
him what happened. It would be a month before I'd talk to Kahn again. In time, as
the waters calmed, Kahn would become an ally in the investigation. He and Beck
are good detectives, but that day, undoubtedly at the urgings of their own superiors,
they were party to a considerable gaffe. As mentioned earlier, there were enough

miscalculations to go around in this case. The Santa Clara Sheriff's Department couldn't claim sole possession of that tarnished crown.

*   *   *

Berkowitz was nearly done. He wrote to tell Chase that he was unable to trust anyone but his father, and would follow Nat Berkowitz's advice and remain silent. He said he also heard that Santucci's office wanted to reach his stepsister, and came down hard on Chase for sending the clippings to Santa Clara.

But Lee Chase, to her credit, didn't give up. She pleaded with Berkowitz to contact me, telling him it was I who had developed the information in the first place and that I had nothing to do with the Pienciak, Ann and Santa Clara situations. And Berkowitz, despite the immense pressures on him, listened to Chase. He would give it one final try. The letter was dated January 12, 1980.

> *Dear Maury,*
>
> *Yesterday I mailed you a correspondence form. All you have to do is sign it and send it back. . . .*
>
> *Well, I guess it would be okay for us to communicate further. I am agreeing to do this, but within reason. Also, I do not wish a visit at this time. I cannot go into details on this.*
>
> *Thank you for the article . . . enclosed in the letter. [It was the October 26 story saying Berkowitz refused to cooperate with Santucci.] It was only recently that I had an opportunity to read the articles you wrote. Because no one from the Westchester area is watching out for me, I didn't learn of these articles immediately. But now, I've accumulated several clippings, thanks to my friend Denise.*
>
> *As for my letter to Mr. Gardner which found its way into the newspapers, it wasn't so much that the letter became public. This really didn't bother me. . . . The thing that upset me was the nonsensical way that it was presented. I threw out the N.Y.* Post *article long ago but I remember those sensational headlines quite well. So this brings me to another important matter.*
>
> *Maury, I can see by these clippings that you have quoted me often. But why do you keep quoting me? I mean, I'm supposed to be "deranged, crazy insane and a madman." Do you understand what I'm trying to say? Honestly, how do you expect people to believe you when you mention something I was supposed to have said.*
>
> *Look, you cannot build a building without laying the foundation first. So if your [sic] trying to use me as a source of facts and information, then you'll only be wasting everyone's time. Nobody will believe me or you because I have no credibility.*

What does the public think when they see my name mentioned some-where? What does the public (the ones you seem to be trying to convince) see when they view my picture or something. I'll tell you what they think. They think I'm just a crazy madman. What do they see? I'll tell you what they see. They see those odd scrawls on the wall of my apartment. They think and see in their own minds a sick madman who hears voices of destruction and hears barking dogs which tell him to kill.

Maury, the public will never, ever truly believe you no matter how well your evidence is presented. They will never believe you unless you could first convince the public that I was sane all along.

This is really the foundation of your arguements [sic]. The first ques-tion people want to know is one of insanity. If they think me insane, then what good will your articles be? Obviously, this question must be answered first before you begin any investigation in which you are trying to use my words as a reliable source.

Maury, I will tell you now and quite personally that all the things which people saw—the strange writing on the wall, the topsy-turvey [sic] apartment with the letters and books scattered about—the broken wall, etc. This, you see, was all by deliberate design. It was a deliberate act. It was set up this way as a means of feigning insanity.

But this is only part of the story. Yet, I will take the responsibility here and admit that I am in no way insane nor was I ever insane.

The broken wall of my apartment was only knocked in several days before I got arrested. I'm quite certain that any police detective will con-firm to you that there were still numerous pieces of plaster chips on my rug below the hole.

As for the scrawls on the walls [bizarre ravings about Sam Carr and Craig Glassman], if I recall correctly they were done in red magic marker. But if you notice, all those markings were very much alike. Why? Because they were only written on the wall [at the same time] several days before my arrest.

The apartment was the same way in general. The books, magazines, pornographic literature, etc. was left scattered topsy-turvy about my floor only days before my arrest.

I never had very much furniture. But within a week before I was ar-rested I threw out the several good pieces I had. The furniture was loaded into a small van and deposited in front of the Salvation Army warehouse on Columbus Avenue (Route 22) in Mt. Vernon. Early one morning and a few hours before the building opened, the furniture was placed near the front of the building.

All of this may seem unimportant to many and maybe unimportant to you. However, this clearly points to advance planning and, of course, *sanity. Let me also add that no one from the public, police or prosecutor's office knows this. Even if the police found out, all they could do is shake their fists at me and laugh at my being clever. But, it wasn't all my idea and I'm certain you know this.*

So, unless you could first convince the general public that I am a sane and rational person, then those articles you continue to write would amount to nothing. Every time you quote me, every time you say, "Berkowitz said this," "Berkowitz said that . . . " it would mean very little and have no credibility.

My recommendation would be to prove to the general public that I was always sane. How to do this, I don't really know. But surely this would be helpful to you. Furthermore, I would kindly ask you not to inform anybody (except your close associates) that we are corresponding. If you mention anything from the above, say it came from another source and not from me. This would be beneficial to both of us.

Sincerely,
David Berkowitz

It was a remarkable letter, and it was specific. There were numerous statements which could be confirmed from the details Berkowitz provided—and he knew it. But first, I wanted more information. Writing back in a word substitution code to elude the notice of the prison censors who opened his incoming mail, I asked Berkowitz some questions about the van rental and other matters. I also told him that we had accumulated a considerable amount of information we hadn't published. I let him know that I was aware of some of the difficulties he was enduring and that it had all finally narrowed down to him and me. He addressed that subject, too, in his reply:

Dear Maury,

I have your letter of January 19th in front of me now and I also have a receipt from the Correspondence Department, informing me that you are now on my mailing list.

But before we go any further, please let me explain a few things to you. I want to do this so that I don't get you too misled and so you don't get your hopes up.

Since I have been at Attica I have progressed quite well, both emotionally and physically. Things are much different now then [sic] they were two years ago. Now I have a good job, friends, and I'm kept busy with plenty of projects. I type a great deal of the inmates legal work—briefs, appeals, etc. This is a twenty-four hour job. I also write other letters for my fellow prisoners since many of them cannot speak well on paper.

Many haven't had the opportunities of a good education like those on the outside. So again, this keeps me busy.

Next, I am kept busy writing to the Governor and others in Albany with demands for the expansion of the Crime Victims Compensation Board and victims of violent crime in general. Perhaps I will let you read a copy of a lengthy letter I am sending to Hugh L. Carey [the governor of New York]. Just let me know if you want it.

For my views of this new investigation, I have mixed feelings. I can also say that I am guilty of these crimes. You see Maury, even if I could show you that I didn't do it all, I'd still be guilty of conspiracy in some of the cases. I'd even be guilty of second degree murder in others. So, regard-less, I would still have a long prison term, but this dosen't [sic] bother me.

Next, I could safely tell you that one [cult] member, John Carr, is deceased. So this would leave me with only myself to share the guilt or proof of it. [Berkowitz didn't know we'd already zeroed in on Michael Carr and several other suspects. But by itself, this statement said, for the first time, that John Carr was indeed an active, direct accomplice in the Son of Sam killings.] Besides, many others have vanished—scattered about all over the U.S.A. for all I know. So this leaves both you and me alone, once the dust clears.

Furthermore, I am not a stool pigeon and I cannot, no matter how heinous the crime, testify against another individual. Even if a given individual has wronged me, still, I must keep silent because this is the code—this is our code—the inmates of Attica.

I know this seems like something out of a gangster movie, but this place is my home now and I will live by the rules and by the oath. I've made many friends here (believe it or not) and I have no wish for them to lose faith in me.

Neither do I want to go back to court and go through this circus rou-tine again. This was disgusting and stupid so I just refuse to even consider this.

As for your questions, I can tell you that the rent-a-van place is lo-cated in the Bronx. It is on the corner of [here Berkowitz gave the exact location]. A small van was rented and the price was almost one hundred dollars—fifty as a safety payment and thirty-eight dollars or thereabouts as the initial cost. Once the van was returned, the guy gave back the extra money. But I can't remember the exact prices. The van was rented for one day and then returned that [following] afternoon. Also, the owner, an average sized Italian fellow, but heavy set in the middle, said that we had to fill up the gas tank, too. It cost about six bucks to fill the tank back up. The station also carried large trucks, smaller size vans like the one rented and also, hitching trailers.

I'm sorry, but I don't know who was supposed to pull me through for that dog shelter job which I applied for. I was just supposed to fill out the application and turn it in. By the way, did all of the things I said check out—all the details?

Look, Maury, please don't knock yourself out over all this as it isn't worth it. What's done is done and it cannot be undone. So if you can't seem to go further, then I'll understand. Sometimes it just doesn't seem to matter anyhow.

Sincerely,
David Berkowitz

Attached to the letter was a map which provided step-by-step directions to the Bronx gas station. I sent another letter off to Berkowitz and arranged a meeting with the Queens investigators. Just as Berkowitz's "animal shelter" letter was confirmed, so were pertinent details in these.

All the information provided by Berkowitz about the Bronx gas station—the types of vans rented, their prices, the deposit amount required, the tank-refill requirement and the description of the owner—was correct. There wasn't a single mistake or false claim.

As for the apartment itself and the furniture disposal, the following was learned by me and Santucci's probers:

- Berkowitz said all the wall writing was done in red. It was, and color photo enlargements showed the writing to be fresh, or not faded, and all of it appeared—from the style and other factors—to have been written at the same time. Moreover, a fair amount of the writing concerned Berkowitz's downstairs neighbor, Glassman, who hadn't even moved into the building until five months before the arrest. So it obviously wasn't written before then. Supporting that conclusion, and the entire scenario, was the fact that Queens investigators earlier interviewed a friend of Berkowitz's who told them he'd been invited to visit David "two or three weeks before the arrest." The friend had to postpone the visit—but no one believed Berkowitz would have invited him to the apartment if the walls were then in that condition and all the furniture was gone.

- Berkowitz said the hole in the apartment wall was made shortly before his arrest. The plaster chips were indeed still on the floor, as he said. And a neighbor, Edna Williams, whose apartment shared that common wall, said she heard the noise and noticed a resulting crack on her side of the wall "within a short time of the arrest, at about 5 a.m."

- Berkowitz said books, letters, etc., were left scattered about in a deliberate attempt to portray him as a lone, insane killer. Among the items were some bizarre notes claiming sole responsibility for the crimes. One note had been altered to backdate it six months. Berkowitz's personal address book also contained irrational listings such as "Sam's Secret Satanic Service," "FALN Secret Meeting Place" and "The Master." Those entries were haphazardly written in the first nine pages of an otherwise neat, correctly alphabetized address book, and were interspersed with previously written, orderly, routine entries. And the bizarre listings—and only those—were written with the same green felt marking pen. "They were all done at the same time," Herb Leifer stated. Additionally, the FALN, the Puerto Rican terrorist group, had not been in the headlines between February and August 1977. However, in the first week of August—at the same time Berkowitz said the setup occurred—the FALN was in the news after a major bombing incident. In other words, the FALN could well have been on the mind of someone writing that entry during the first week of August.

- Berkowitz said that he never had very much good furniture, and what little he had was removed and dumped in front of the Salvation Army building on Columbus Avenue (Route 22) in Mount Vernon in the pre-dawn hours. From Berkowitz's own father, and others, Santucci's probers learned that David indeed had furniture at 35 Pine Street, including a couch, a large bureau, a dinette set, chairs and a large stereo speaker and tape recorder he purchased in Korea. All of these were gone from the apartment when police walked in on August 10, 1977.

- As for the claimed disposal site of the furniture, the Salvation Army warehouse was located in an isolated section of Mount Vernon, and on Columbus Avenue, as Berkowitz said. And that section of Columbus Avenue was also known as Route 22, just as Berkowitz stated. However, telephone directories listed only the Columbus Avenue address; that is, one had to have been there in order to know the details Berkowitz did. Moreover, Salvation Army officials confirmed that furniture was indeed occasionally left in front of the building overnight, as Berkowitz said his was. It didn't happen often—but it did happen.

- What was obvious about the scenario was that the loading and unloading of heavy furniture from a seventh-floor apartment was not a one-man job. Not that Berkowitz said it was: "It wasn't all my idea and I'm certain you know this," he wrote.

Santucci, Leifer, George Byrd, other Queens investigators and I all agreed Berkowitz was telling the truth about the Great Con-the-Cops Apartment Caper. All the details he provided were either confirmed outright or buttressed significantly by the investigation.

Tom McCarthy said: "Someone could try to nitpick individual items here and there on the Son of Sam case. But the total picture, all the evidence put together, is overwhelming. From the crime scenes, to North Dakota, to the confessions, to Untermyer Park and the Son of Sam letters—and now Berkowitz's own admissions, which are backed up all over the place."

"That's almost exactly the way Berkowitz put it four months ago," I said.

*   *   *

The evidence may have been mounting, but the list of suspects was reduced by one in late December, at the same time the Arlis Perry matter was opening up in North Dakota.

The newly deceased was Jerry Berg, a cult-connected friend of John Carr's whose name surfaced early in the Minot investigation of Carr's satanic associates. Berg, Carr, the now deceased Donny Boone, Phil Falcon, a person known as "the Wiz" and a young man named Larry Milenko* comprised the inner circle in Minot.

Jerry Berg, a short, stocky young man with curly blondish hair, was a native of Bismarck who moved to the Minot area in the mid-1970s to take some courses at Minot State College—where Carr, Falcon and some of the others also studied part-time. An accomplished outdoorsman, Berg had been on the wrestling team while at Bismarck Junior College, from which he graduated in 1972. He was three years older than Arlis Perry, who entered BJC in the fall of 1973.

On December 27, 1979, Berg and Milenko were chopping trees in a wooded area outside Minot. According to Milenko, the pair had separated and were about "an eighth mile" apart. Milenko said the sound of Berg's saw stopped and he then walked over to where Berg was working—and found him crushed to death beneath a large tree. Milenko, ever respectful, then put the body in his truck, drove it to a hospital, dropped it off—and left. He immediately hired a lawyer.

"Berg was an experienced woodsman; he'd been in that business," Gardner said. "It just seemed very strange to have something like this happen to him at all—let alone at the same time we're poking around about John Carr and Arlis Perry."

In searching through Berg's possessions, police found further evidence of his satanic interests. In a letter Berg hadn't yet mailed to two friends in North Carolina, he said he was having difficulties with his brother and was thinking of "putting a black magic curse on him." He also talked of looking up his black magic teacher, "Aquarius Hador," who was "now in Minneapolis. I'm sure he's as evil as he's ever been," Berg wrote. Ironically, he closed the letter by cautioning his friends to "be careful in the woods."

Police were never able to prove that Berg's death was a murder. But the toll of violently dead now included four who were directly linked to Berkowitz or the Son of Sam case: Jerry Berg, John Carr, Michael Carr and Howard Weiss.

Additionally, the Yonkers mailman who committed suicide a month after

Berkowitz's capture, Andrew Dupay, was strongly suspected of having been threatened by the group. And then there were the near-misses: sniper attacks on Gardner and on the police officer substituting for Wheat Carr's husband, John McCabe; and the incident in which Darlene Christiansen and Tom Taylor reported they were run off the road near Minot. There was no absolute proof that the latter incidents were related to the Son of Sam investigation, but strong indications were certainly present.

Another incident, which occurred less than two weeks before Berg's death, was also highly suspicious. This one happened in New York.

*   *   *

A letter I later received said: "Dear Maury Terry. Please look into this double killing. Carol was asking people about the O.T.O. a year prior to the murders. . . . I can't accept that the people responsible for this are still walking around free. I am afraid that the problem will not go away and that minds this unbalanced may perpetrate additional horrors. Forgive me for not signing my name. I haven't gotten over the fear."

The writer was apparently a woman friend of one Carol Marron, thirty-three, a Brooklyn resident. Marron was a secretary at the Pratt Institute in Brooklyn and designed clothing to supplement her income. For seven years, she lived with Howard Green, fifty-three, an abstract painter who drove a cab for his steady paycheck.

As the letter writer said, for more than a year Marron and Green had been delving into the occult. Their small basement apartment at 270 De Kalb Avenue was spiced with various items of satanic significance. Chances are excellent that this paraphernalia was purchased at a certain occult store located not far from their residence; a store that served more purposes than one for certain occult adepts.

In the early evening hours of Saturday, December 15, Marron and Green were spotted by an acquaintance on a subway train in Manhattan. The friend left the train at 59th Street, but Marron and Green kept going. The subway they were riding would carry them past Columbia University before continuing to the end of the line at the Bronx-Yonkers border.

Sometime later that night, Green and Marron returned to their Brooklyn apartment. The next time they were sighted was at 7 p.m. the following evening. They were lying next to each other off Route 80 in West Paterson, New Jersey, not far from New York City. Both were bludgeoned on their left sides, both had right eye wounds and both clutched clumps of hair in their fists—a satanic symbol. And there was one other similarity. Every drop of blood had been drained from the bodies of Carol Marron and Howard Green with a veterinarian's syringe.

"It was definitely a satanic murder," said NYPD Detective Jim Devereaux, who was assisting New Jersey police with the investigation. "And it wasn't a one-man job. In all my years in this business, I've never seen anything like this."

That was precisely the point.

"The only murderous satanic cult I know of in the New York area is the Son of Sam group," I told Devereaux. "But the NYPD won't admit it exists, so we're stymied. A vet's syringe is not a foreign object to people who deal with dogs, you know. If I get any more information that may help tie this in, I'll let you know."

It would be more than two years before that information came my way.

*   *   *

The Son of Sam probe was entering a new phase in the spring of 1980. A large store of information was accumulated during the preceding five months and before, including data provided by Berkowitz. It was time to sort it all through. Berkowitz himself had quieted down. He wrote me several routine letters in the spring of 1980, avoiding additional specifics. Each time, I responded by asking for relevant information. But it was apparent the earlier incidents had taken their toll, and he finally fell silent. Later, he wrote to say why:

> I received two interesting letters today. One from you and another from Lee. Well, I suppose I owe both of you an apology. Really, this business with Pienciak and the investigation has been causing me all sorts of troubles.
>
> The Queens District Attorney was, at one time, bugging my father. My dad was really scared because he sensed the intensity of the investigation and was also fearful for further embarrassment for his wife and himself. Don't forget what occurred after my arrest. Dozens of reporters flocked around him, tailed him to the local store, and camped out on his doorstep. Too, he was the subject of ridicule, hate mail, nasty phone calls, and terrible threats. So he is fearful of further publicity. Therefore, when the investigation turned to him . . . I just clammed up.
>
> Next, the authorities were attempting to locate my step-sister, Ann, who lives out in California. She has had an awful life until recently. Somehow she has managed to . . . pull her life together. Of course she was fearful of the investigation because my father told her that the investigators inquired about her. So my dad again asked me to clam up, and there you have it.
>
> Well, I'm glad that you paid Lee back [photocopying costs] and will soon be sending her her materials [occult literature]. Anyhow, both she and I are trying to pull ourselves together.
>
> I had this big hassle with this guy Pienciak from the Associated Press. . . . [Berkowitz then described Pienciak's dealings with Lee Chase, etc., and mentioned that McGraw-Hill was planning to publish Lawrence Klausner's so-called official book on the case.]
>
> The result of McGraw-Hill's success could mean further harm to my

father, and more publicity as to my being a deranged madman.

Oh yes, this is important. If either you or anyone else receives a phone call from one Ira Jultak, please do not give him any information. He is my former defense attorney whom I fired quite a while ago. I have heard that he has been seeking out information.

Too, he is working with the author of the McGraw-Hill book and is going to share in the profits. So he is out to silence me. He [also] attempted to do this a long time ago by trying to stop a press conference [where Berkowitz repudiated his original "demon" story, which was—and remained—a central focus of that book].

So please don't give him any info.

Sincerely,
David Berkowitz

This was to be the last I'd hear from Berkowitz for almost a year. Once again, we were on our own. But the "we" no longer included Jim Mitteager, who bowed out of the investigation to obtain a full-time job to help support his family and to work on settling the debt he incurred as the result of his arrest and trial.

In Minot, Gardner, Mike Knoop, Jeff Nies and Jack Graham remained active, and in New York, Santucci's probe continued. Our own informal force of "Pine Street Irregulars" kept checking new leads, and Detective Hank Cinotti prepared to face a Police Department trial. In March, Georgiana and I were married, nearly two years after that night we'd talked at the Suriani-Esau murder scene. After a nine-day wedding trip to New Orleans and Cancun, Mexico, it was back to the rigors of the .44 investigation.

Several aspects of the case had progressed markedly. In one instance, we obtained vital information about the yellow Volkswagen that fled the Stacy Moskowitz murder scene in Brooklyn. Several witnesses came forward after I published an article which revealed for the first time that a wild chase of that car had occurred after the shooting.

An attorney, an NYPD police officer and a restaurant employee all stated that Michael and John Carr had driven such a vehicle during the Son of Sam era. Their statements were forwarded to Santucci. Additionally, the Cassara family in New Rochelle, at whose home Berkowitz lived in early 1976 before his move to Pine Street, told us and Queens that while at their home Berkowitz had been driving a yellow or beige Volkswagen. Berkowitz had only his Ford Galaxie registered to him, so it was apparent he borrowed the VW.

A private investigator, Jordan Stevens, also stated that the yellow VW was driven by both John and Michael Carr, but that it wasn't registered in either of their names. Stevens obtained this information from yet another witness who knew John and Michael.

Stevens said the car was between "1970 and 1972 vintage" and "wasn't in great mechanical shape. The front bumper also hung down a bit." The NYPD officer, who reported he was "very familiar" with the car, said it was a 1971 model.

Santucci observed: "I think we can safely say that the VW was accessible to John and Michael Carr."

The Candlelight Inn employee who threw Michael Carr, Berkowitz and their friend Bobby out of the bar shortly before the sniper incident there in October 1976 also said: "The yellow VW was outside the place. And they used to talk about leaving the Inn and going over to Untermyer Park. They never said why—I can see why they didn't."

The fact that a yellow VW was available to the Carr brothers did not mean that either of them was driving it the night Stacy Moskowitz was killed and Robert Violante blinded. In fact, it would soon come to light that neither John nor Michael was the Brooklyn gunman.

At the same time, new evidence about other crimes peripherally linked to the Son of Sam case was uncovered. Specifically, the reports concerned violent acts in Westchester which Berkowitz first claimed to have committed alone. In the case of the firebombing of the Neto home in Yonkers, Sylvia Neto said she was awakened by voices just before the firebomb crashed into the front of their home in the pre-dawn hours of May 13, 1976. "I heard someone calling out, 'Come on, come on, hurry up, hurry up,'" she said. "It sounded like the one voice was calling the other one Eddie," she added. "But I'm not sure if it was Eddie."

The wounding of the Carr dog in daylight on April 27, 1977, was another act Berkowitz took sole credit for. But two witnesses said otherwise. One told Queens investigators that he saw the shooter, who was a blond-haired young man. Another witness was actually stopped near the scene by Yonkers police responding to the shooting call. That man, who was walking his dog, said a man carrying a rifle ran from the aqueduct and passed right by him. The witness said the shooter was tall, thin, and had straight, fairly long, blond hair. The reports of the two witnesses jibed, and the person each described was not David Berkowitz, who didn't remotely resemble the man seen by the witnesses.

From top to bottom, the Son of Sam case, as originally presented to the press and public, was in shambles.

But even as this new evidence was being accumulated privately, Hank Cinotti went on trial within the New York City Police Department. For months, I struggled with the notion of making some of Berkowitz's statements available to Cinotti's defense. But he demurred, saying that "the case itself is more important. Keep it all quiet."

I testified at the trial, as did Joe Basteri, who told the trial commissioner the true story of how Cinotti came to know of the North Dakota information about Carr and Reeve Rockman. Rick Pienciak, reporting for the Associated Press, obtained a quote from Deputy Chief Ed Dreher in which Dreher, ignorant of all the evidence which had been uncovered, said for posterity: "The Berkowitz case is closed. Berkowitz had no helper. I won't change that opinion. I don't think the department will."

Cinotti, who faced dismissal from the force and a loss of benefits, was merely fined thirty days of vacation time and placed on probation for a year. It was, effectively, a partial victory—for the moment. But after the media attention abated, Cinotti was removed from the detective ranks and assigned to a uniformed patrol in lower Manhattan's 1st Precinct. He remained there long enough to reach his twentieth year of service and retired from the force. All the while, he remained quietly involved in the investigation.

Even on his way out of the NYPD, the department challenged his final year's overtime pay, upon which police pensions are partially based. Once again, Cinotti had to fight for his cause. He won.

*   *   *

There were numerous issues to be dealt with in the probe. One of those concerned Arlis Perry. What did the North Dakota cult have to do with the murder of the young Christian newlywed in the church at Stanford University?

As Berkowitz wrote, the case was "very deep." And he rhetorically asked Lee Chase: "Who killed Arlis Perry, and why?" He knew those answers, but we didn't.

It was time to try to find out.

Some of those involved in the cross-country hunt for conspirators are: (top left) Queens, New York, District Attorney John Santucci; (top right) Lt. Terry Gardner, North Dakota; (center left) Det. Mike Knoop, North Dakota; (center right) Jeff Nies, reporter, *Minot Daily News*; (bottom) Jack Graham, reporter, *Minot Daily News*. (Petry; *Minot Daily News*)

Michael Carr and his sister, Wheat. (*New York Times*)

The death auto driven by Michael Carr on October 4, 1979.
(*Gannett Westchester-Rockland Newspapers*)

The "Devil's Cave" at Untermyer Park, Yonkers, scene of satanic rituals.

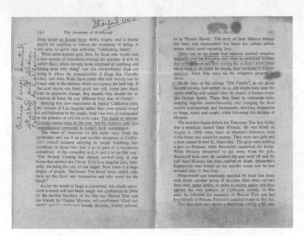

Important page from a witchcraft book marked and
smuggled out of prison by David Berkowitz.

Millionaire producer Roy Radin at 1980 arraignment in Long Island, New York. (*Associated Press*)

The headlines told of a mysterious disappearance in Los Angeles.

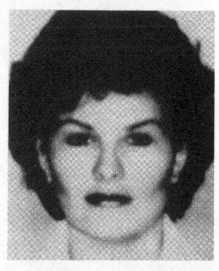

Early suspect: "Bodyguard" Bill Mentzer, shown here after a 1984 altercation in the Venice, California, area, was believed to occasionally change his name and his appearance.

Elaine Jacobs traveled in show business circles and in a limousine allegedly used for a last ride.

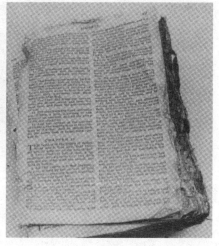

The dirt road in desolate Caswell Canyon, north of Los Angeles, in 1983. Beehives are at the road's end and a body was found nearby. (*Maury Terry*)

At a murder scene, this Bible was opened, as shown, to Isaiah 22. (*Maury Terry*)

The new inquiry showed
the Manson headlines told
only part of the story.

Movie actress Sharon Tate.
(*Associated Press*)

Charles Manson.
(*Associated Press*)

WOE TO YOU O-
Earth and sea, for
The devil sends the
Beast with rath,
Let him who has understand
recon the number of the
beast, For it is a human
number — its number
is Sixhundred and
Sixty Six ...

Frightening satanic warning found at a ritual site in 1985.

Bernard LeGeros is led from Rockland County,
New York, courthouse in late 1985.
(*Sarno; Gannett Westchester-Rockland Newspapers*)

XVIII

"Hunted, Stalked and Slain"

John Carr may have been dead, but his ghost haunted the investigation of the murder of Arlis Perry. Berkowitz specifically said Carr wasn't involved in her death, but he did link her killing to the North Dakota cult scene in this manner:

"Don't worry, because I didn't commit this crime," he wrote to Lee Chase in November 1979. "Nor was I present when it was done. Back in October '74 I was busy and at work as a piss-poor paid security guard. I was here in N.Y. But (and I say BUT) in my travels with different people in this area, I met someone who was involved in her death and spoke freely of the slaying—bragging. He knew many details, and I know that this guy, Manson #2, doesn't bull. I know he killed often, him and his 'crew' [cult]. This is what this new investigation was going to rest on. . . .

"You, as a natural detective, can't help at this time but notice the strange coincidence here. Many months ago I inquired about Arliss [sic] Perry. If you'll note your [newspaper] clip, she hails from Bismarck. Bismarck is just south of Minot. Minot is the second focal point of this investigation, next to Yonkers and Westchester County. This is why I mentioned her to you as compared with the multitudes of other murders of young women. Why her? Simply because I knew beforehand where she once lived. Also, I knew it was a cult thing . . ."

Berkowitz had told Santa Clara detectives Kahn and Beck that he met Manson II at a cult meeting in New York; he told Chase the same thing. I was at first thrown off by the Manson II statement, since it appeared to contradict Berkowitz in another way. He said the man and his cult killed often; and he also said Arlis was "hunted, stalked and slain. Followed to California." If that was so, and the answer to the murder, or the motive, lay in Bismarck, then where were Manson II and the cult doing all these other alleged killings? As Berkowitz himself wrote, North Dakota boasted an extremely low crime rate, and murder was a relatively rare occurrence there.

For quite some time, I was troubled by this problem. Then a source very close to Berkowitz straightened me out. The seeming contradiction was actually a clue, as was the name Manson II. For a moment, I will get ahead of the story to explain the significance of Manson II, as stated by the source, whom I will call Vinny.

"Manson II wasn't from North Dakota," Vinny said. "He was from the L.A. area. That's where the Sam cult has its headquarters. The North Dakota branch wanted Arlis dead, and they called California for help. Manson II went north to Stanford to arrange it. At least one, maybe two people from Dakota came out to help. But it was Manson II's show to run. *He was involved with the original Manson and the cult there in L.A.* That's why Berkowitz used that name as a clue."

This information was so overwhelming it was at first hard to believe. But Vinny wasn't done.

"This guy was an occult superstar. They used him for the most important jobs. Berkowitz met him in New York because he was imported from the Coast to participate in the Son of Sam killings. He's the guy who shot Christine Freund in the Son of Sam case. And he was around for some of the others. He was back and forth. But he did Freund and was in New York for, I think, some of the later ones."

"Are you telling me a guy involved with Charlie Manson and the original cult in California arranged Arlis Perry's murder as a favor to North Dakota and then came to New York for Son of Sam?"

"That's exactly what I'm telling you," Vinny replied.

"Then why is Berkowitz trying to help solve the Perry case?"

"Because he believes Manson II was the guy who had the most to do with picking him to take the fall on Son of Sam. He hates this guy, and fears him."

"So he wants the Perry case broken for a personal reason?"

"He may have a conscience these days but he's got more on his mind than just trying to be a good citizen," Vinny said.

"And you got this from Berkowitz himself?"

"Directly, face-to-face."

According to Vinny's statement, the Sam cult was headquartered near Los Angeles and had branches in Bismarck, Minot, Houston and New York, at least. And these branches (and others, I'd later learn) shuttled killers and "contracts" back and forth.

If any of this statement was true—any of it—it would rank the entire case as one of the most significant criminal stories of all time—bigger than the Son of Sam case already was. Berkowitz, Manson and the Process and its cells set up around the United States—the network already in place. And then the splinter groups spinning off from the Process; among them the Chingons and another faction in New York. And all of them linked as part of an underground web of murder.

How bizarre was this charge by Vinny, who said he was repeating Berkowitz's statements to the letter?

It should be remembered that Arlis Perry was murdered on the fifth anniversary of Manson's arrest—a day which was also the birthday of black magician Aleister Crowley, whom Berkowitz had already tagged as an inspiration for the cult. Further, Arlis Perry's death occurred during a period when elements of the Manson crowd were very active: Lynette (Squeaky) Fromme would attempt to murder President Gerald Ford in northern California sometime *after* the Perry murder.

Berkowitz himself admittedly joined the cult in New York in 1975, just six years after Manson's arrest and less than a year after Arlis Perry's killing. And as for the Process/Chingon groups, it was already established that a network was in place. Process members, using the name "Process," and mingling with existing OTO factions, were seen openly in New York City as late as 1973. The time frame fit.

Moreover, it was already established that strong connections existed between the

Minot and New York cults. All Vinny was doing was extending the pattern to Los Angeles and tying it together.

Vinny's comments were first made to me in 1982, more than two years after Berkowitz first wrote about Arlis Perry. Unknown to Vinny, his statements were consistent with what Berkowitz had said in 1979. Vinny and Berkowitz didn't meet until 1981, in prison. Berkowitz, in other words, told Vinny the same story he'd written about in 1979. The difference was a simple one: in his conversations with Vinny Berkowitz filled in details he only alluded to in 1979.

* * *

The initial step was to try to learn if Berkowitz was telling the truth about his knowledge of the Arlis Perry case. If he was, that fact alone would once more demonstrate the existence of a Son of Sam conspiracy—via the "back door." That is, how else would alleged lone killer Berkowitz know confidential details about the murder of a North Dakota girl in Stanford, California—a murder which he insisted was committed by a satanic cult? And a branch of *his* cult, at that.

* * *

Santa Clara detective Ken Kahn publicly stated that he was convinced Berkowitz was telling the truth about the Perry case. "It's about the best information we've had," Kahn said. "I think it's a very significant lead. I put a lot of credibility behind it." Before that, Kahn explained, "we interviewed about two hundred and fifty potential suspects and it led us nowhere. . . . I believe [Berkowitz] knows what happened."

Berkowitz was very concerned with his credibility on the Perry case. It will be remembered that he didn't want to jeopardize his standing on the matter and thus requested that Lee Chase not send any items on the case to Santa Clara, or elsewhere, for just that reason. Another letter he wrote Chase during this period, mid-November 1979, further illustrates Berkowitz's mindset.

> *If anything reaches this guy in Staten Island [Gilroy] or the Sheriff from N. Dakota on this case, then they'll laugh me out of sight.*
>
> *The investigation will close immediately on receipt of such a clipping. Obviously, they will say, "HOAX, SHAM, CON-ARTIST."*
>
> *If you recall, several months ago and long before you knew of this current [.44] investigation, seemingly out of the blue I asked about Arliss. . . . You wrote back asking me how I heard of this particular case since it was strictly a west coast news item. You acknowledged the fact that this didn't make it to the east coast, at least not in the New York City area. Your [sic] ABSOLUTELY correct! I never read about it in any New York area paper. Neither did I see it in a detective magazine. . . .*
>
> *This is the whole case in a nutshell. The fact that I didn't read about her or her murder is good evidence. . . .*

Two weeks ago, I sent this guy, Gilroy, a four-page typed letter.

One and a half pages dealt with Mrs. Perry. Actually, there isn't too much more, if even this much, that I know about the case as far as facts go. I know who did it and why. But I'm not going to mention this to anyone—not give a name. I just discussed with him the case.

Here is the problem. Gilroy doesn't know that I have a news clipping on her. You sent it to me, remember? [It was a brief clip from a California paper devoid of any detail.] And this is the most important point, I questioned you first about Arliss—and to your surprise. You only sent this one clipping to me only after I mentioned her to you first. Now if you were to send a clipping to Gilroy or N. Dakota about her, then he'll (without a doubt) think that I'm giving him bum information. He'll think that I'm trying to lead him on a wild goose chase to get attention for another crime I'm trying to confess to. . . .

So please don't send anything on her case. This case is reserved for me. If he should get a bunch of Perry-related clippings at the same time that I'm writing him about her, then I'm screwed a hundredfold. . . . This guy is the attorney for Mitteager and Terry. These two were the ones who managed to get photos of me in Kings County. They believed about this Sam Carr business in the literal sense, if you know what I mean. Everyone else thought I was deranged. They didn't understand what I was trying to say. This whole investigation is here because of these three.

Gilroy is unknown to the public. He's never been in the papers in reference to this investigation or the SOS case. He's not after publicity. . . .

Being that Gilroy is thorough, I'm certain he is now checking the New York area newspapers to read about the Perry case. Haha! He'll never find it. This will surprise him and he will investigate this thing further. Gilroy knows that I had an abundance of clippings about killings. Next, he'll contact the Queens D.A. to ask him to look in my collection for the Perry articles. Hence, no articles are in my large collection on Arliss. [He meant, no articles on Arlis were in his collection.] Now, he will realize he is on to something. Understand? "How did Berkowitz know about this? I can't see how he heard of it. Maybe he isn't bullshitting."

So please don't send any photocopies to these two [Gilroy and Gardner], . . . Let me remind you again that I contacted you first about this. But he won't know or believe this. Unfortunately, I don't know much more than was released in the newspapers (west coast). No, he will never believe I knew of the case before I read the clip you sent me.

Berkowitz did in fact query Lee Chase about the Perry case first—in a letter dated June 8, 1979. He asked Chase if she'd ever heard of the case and next hinted that Arlis

Perry was a "true Christian"—a fact not included in the brief clip Chase then sent him the next week. In replying to Berkowitz, Chase asked how he could have heard of the case. Berkowitz answered with another tidbit that didn't appear in newspaper articles: "She sure was a skinny little thing." He later added: "She was so tiny." Both these assertions were true. "I gather the Arlis Perry murder has never been solved," he wrote before receiving the clip from Chase. He was right, of course. Also, *before* he received the short clipping, he spelled Arlis's first name correctly—with one *s*. But after getting the clip, which incorrectly added a second *s*, he abandoned his original accurate spelling and took up the erroneous one.

The Arlis Perry case and Berkowitz's allegations were primarily investigated by me, with assistance from Gardner and Jeff Nies. The Santa Clara police provided some help, as did Santucci. But Santa Clara investigators never returned to North Dakota to mount an investigation. Their reasoning was that the case was now old, but if Berkowitz gave up more information they'd be there to follow it through.

* * *

My first interest was in establishing just what knowledge Berkowitz had which he *couldn't* have possessed if he was lying.

1. Before seeing the brief news clipping Lee Chase sent him, he knew Arlis was a "teenaged" girl and that she was killed in a church at Stanford.

2. He knew from the outset that she was a "true Christian." The clip Chase later sent him didn't contain this information either.

3. He knew she was "tiny," "skinny" and "pretty," descriptions that were not published.

4. He spelled Arlis's first name correctly before adopting the incorrect spelling in the small clip he received.

5. He knew the case wasn't solved as of 1979. "I'd have known if it was solved," he wrote. [The lone clip Chase sent him was a short Associated Press item from two days after the murder. No photo of Arlis accompanied the piece, which was dated October 14, 1974.]

6. He knew Arlis liked to "frequently" take walks around the Stanford campus—an unpublished fact.

7. He accurately described the purple, scarlet and gold interior of the Stanford church at the time.

8. He knew the *exact* location of Arlis's stab wound, behind the ear. Some local San Jose area papers did write that Arlis was stabbed at the base of the neck or skull. Berkowitz was able to pinpoint the precise location, which had been withheld from the public.

9. He emphasized the hideous torture Arlis endured—indicating knowledge that went far beyond any newspaper account.

10. He knew that Arlis had an "interest" in cults. This was a non-published fact confirmed to me by several of her friends in Bismarck. Her curiosity was that of a Christian wanting to know about the "other side."

11. He knew that Bismarck's Mary College existed. Mary was a tiny school that neither we in New York nor the California police had ever heard of.

12. He connected Mary College to cult activity in Bismarck and to Arlis's death. It was firmly established that a satanic cult met in a wooded area right below Mary College during this period.

13. He alleged in his letter to Felix Gilroy that prominent, respected people were involved in the cult. Witnesses in Bismarck stated just that.

14. He saw a photo of Arlis that apparently was not published anywhere until 1981—seven years after her death and two years *after* he sent a photo of another girl out of prison saying that that girl looked just like Arlis. "Almost a twin sister," he wrote. He was right.

15. He said the murder was a cult killing and not a random sex crime. In Chapter I, unpublished details about Arlis's death and the position of her body, etc., appeared for the first time, along with the fact that Arlis's grave marker was stolen in Bismarck two weeks after her death, near Halloween; also that Santa Clara authorities heard from Bruce Perry's parents that

Arlis may have attempted to convert members of a Bismarck cult to Christianity.

16. He wrote that the murder was planned and not random. In Chapter I, the confidential details about the law firm visitor appeared, along with other information which strongly suggested Arlis purposely went to the church the next night—the evening after her "intense" discussion with the law firm visitor. Arlis, it will be remembered, didn't tell her husband about the encounter at the firm.

17. If Berkowitz's known, named accomplice John Carr and his cult branch were nearby in Minot at this time, why *wouldn't* Berkowitz know confidential details about the Perry murder? Indeed, as he wrote to Lee Chase: "Why her? Simply because I knew beforehand where she once lived. Also, I knew it was a cult thing."

In the investigation of the Perry case, I personally conducted more than forty interviews with Bismarck area police and friends, family and associates of Arlis Perry. Numerous sources were interviewed several times. Jeff Nies and Lieutenant Terry Gardner also questioned several people, and Minot officer Mike Knoop provided logistics support. The Santa Clara Sheriff's Department, at the time of the killing, didn't interview any of Arlis's close friends in Bismarck—so convinced were they that the killer or killers were California psychopaths. Then, in 1979, despite their belief in Berkowitz's veracity, they sat tight—with the exception of fresh interviews of Arlis's parents, Bruce Perry and Bruce's parents. We, however, decided to act. Here is the picture which emerged.

In 1971–73, a northern California–based cult, which claimed it wasn't satanic, materialized in Bismarck, the capital of North Dakota, a small town with a population of 36,000. There were six representatives of this cult group in Bismarck. They wore black clerical garb, but adorned their necks with red collars and ribbons instead of religious white collars.

Members of this sect rented a home in Bismarck directly across the street from the residence of Arlis's grandmother. Arlis visited her grandmother regularly and may have contacted group members in that way.

At least two young women Arlis knew actually became involved in this cult. Arlis herself, according to two close associates, expressed an interest in learning about the group. One said he was "almost certain" Arlis attended one of the cult's meetings. These statements about Arlis's "interest" in learning about the occult—and numerous other comments which also detailed her innocent curiosity—confirmed Berkowitz's allegation.

At the time of the killing, the Santa Clara Sheriff's Department heard from Bruce Perry's parents that Arlis and a girlfriend had once gone "across the river to Mandan to try to convert some members of a satanic cult to Christianity." Girlfriends of Arlis told me that she did, indeed, visit a Mandan coffee shop where members of this group were recruiting from the numbers of students who socialized there. The coffee shop's owner eventually barred the cult members from his establishment. I spoke to that former owner, who is now a minister in Ohio, and he confirmed the story.

I then located one of the cult's members, who left the group and now resides in Kansas. He stated that while the group did try to recruit from that coffee shop, and did hold meetings in a rented home across the street from Arlis's grandmother's address, they weren't satanic. He did acknowledge, however, that his former cult espoused mysticism, astrology and the tarot. He also said that he'd encountered members of the Process in Chicago but that his group wasn't connected to the Process.

We remained unsure of this "nonsatanic" claim, and have also considered the possibility that members of the Process or Chingon cults infiltrated the other group or falsely represented themselves in Bismarck as being members of it.

*   *   *

But there was another, definitely satanic cult operating in Bismarck during the 1972–76 time period, at least. Some sources, including police officers, say it is still active today.

Significantly, this secret group matched Berkowitz's statements *exactly:* it was holding its midnight meetings behind Mary College.

The cult's existence in a wooded area behind the school has been confirmed by at least ten people, including police officers, area residents, nuns who taught at Mary College and other Bismarck citizens who were involved in Christian activities. Importantly, the latter sources belonged to the same religious organizations as Arlis did—Young Life and the Fellowship of Christian Athletes.

One nun who taught at Mary told me: "My students knew all about it. They said the cult used to kill dogs back of here. . . . We have a large cross here at the graveyard and the devil worshippers used to creep up the hill to spit on our cross."

Berkowitz, in the satanic book he sent to Gardner in late 1979, underlined the following sentence: "They must be prepared to defile His image and spit upon the Cross."

A married couple who lived in a trailer home near the cult meeting site at Mary told me that they saw torches and heard chanting and that three of their pet dogs were abducted in the middle of the night and later found mutilated inside a circle of stones (a magic circle).

This couple also said that the only access to the cult meeting site was via the Mary campus itself. "The creek—Apple Creek—blocked access from the other direction. They were holding their rituals near an old shed in the woods. The only way to get there was by a trail that led down from the campus."

The cult also met at Hillside Cemetery, as well as behind a Catholic church and a Bismarck synagogue on infrequent occasions.

As mentioned, police and others knew of the Mary cult's existence, as did Arlis Perry. A friend from the Fellowship of Christian Athletes said: "She definitely knew about it. We discussed the cult several times at our FCA meetings."

Arlis's pastor, Rev. Don DeKok, said: "I knew about it, and I might well have mentioned it to her." DeKok offered another important observation: "Right at the time of Arlis's funeral here—either just before, that day or the next—one of my parishioners was awakened before dawn and saw a man wearing a black cape trying to break into the church."

Arlis's grave marker was stolen less than two weeks after this incident.

DeKok also said: "A friend of one of my parishioners went down to Mary and hid out on the hill one night to spy on the cult. I never found out who they were, but she said there were some well-known Bismarck citizens in attendance."

This provided another confirmation of Berkowitz's statements—about both the Mary group's existence and his assertion that prominent citizens belonged to it.

A further confirmation came from Mandan police sergeant Lamar Kruckenberg, who said: "In early '74 an undercover cop was brought to an indoor cult meeting in Bismarck by one of his informants. He was looking for drug activity—there was no suggestion of murder at this time, which was about seven months before Arlis's death. This cop told me the people there were wearing masks because there were supposed to be some respected Bismarck people among them." The undercover officer left the force several years later, and we were unable to locate him.

Closer to Arlis herself were two male acquaintances, both of whom were said to be occult adepts. A girlfriend of Arlis said of one: "He was always trying to invite us girls over to his basement for seances with black candles." Another friend of Arlis recalled: "He carried a satanic bible around with him."

During the interviews, the names of several possible suspects emerged—including at least two successful Bismarck citizens said to be connected to the Mary cult.

One young woman also said: "Right after the murder, a month or so later, I heard that the cult here contacted the California group and that's how it was done."

No one but Santucci, Sergeant Kahn in Santa Clara and I knew of this Berkowitz-Vinny allegation, which wasn't made until the early 1980s and was kept secret. Yet this woman volunteered that identical information to me in December 1985, saying that she heard it shortly after Arlis's death occurred in October 1974. Her statement was a powerful one.

*　　*　　*

When the interviews began, I told each contact that we were looking for a "bridge"—someone who would have had cult contacts but whom Arlis felt she could safely approach to satisfy her curiosity about the subject.

Arlis, the investigation clearly showed, was a sincere young Christian. We found no dark corners in her life. She lived at home, attended school and socialized with her religiously active friends. Shortly before her marriage, she worked in the dental office of Bruce's father, Duncan Perry. Duncan Perry was the "prison dentist"; inmates from the nearby state penitentiary were brought to his office for treatment while Arlis was there. It remained possible that something which occurred in that setting could have offered a motive for her death.

But beyond that possibility, I wanted to establish the means by which this young girl from the "Right-Hand Path" could have learned about the "Left-Hand Path"— the cult scene at Mary. I reasoned that, since Satan cults don't advertise in newspapers or have open attendance at their midnight meetings, Arlis would have sought assistance from someone she thought she could trust—but someone she also knew was connected to the seamier side of Bismarck society.

I already knew that Arlis was aware of the cult's existence, but we had to discover that "bridge," beyond which, we hoped, lurked the motive for her murder.

At least three young men and two young women were identified as the result of this approach. Any one of them, the sources agreed, could have linked Arlis's world with that of the Mary cult. Since the investigation is open, I am not at liberty to discuss specifics concerning these people. But I can say that all were in positions which provided ready access to the Mary cult operation. This evaluation has been corroborated by the Queens DA's office and Sergeant Ken Kahn of the Santa Clara Sheriff's Department.

In previously listed items concerning Berkowitz's knowledge of the Perry case, I referred to a photograph of another young woman which he sent out of prison saying it looked like Arlis's "twin." When I received this picture, I thought Berkowitz was hallucinating. It looked nothing at all like those of Arlis Perry I had seen. At the time of her death, the pictures which appeared in the media were two shots taken of her in high school. In each, she had straight blond hair, wore glasses and had no makeup on.

The picture Berkowitz likened to her, however, was that of a young woman who had carefully styled, curly hair and who was wearing makeup. Also, this woman wasn't wearing glasses. In no way did she resemble Arlis Perry. Berkowitz sent this photo on October 27, 1979.

Two years later, on October 24, 1981, the San Jose *Mercury-News* published a photograph of Arlis Perry to accompany an article about Berkowitz's involvement in the case—portions of which I'd made public a month earlier. This photo of Arlis looked *exactly* like that of the woman Berkowitz likened to Arlis in 1979.

I was stunned. The newspaper said that the picture was the only one of Arlis in its file and that it was a wire service photo they apparently obtained for the 1981 story. "We must have ordered it from Bismarck," I was told. Bismarck.

Arlis's parents, sister and girlfriends studied the picture at my request. They identified Arlis, but said they'd never seen the photo before and couldn't remember her ever looking as she did in the picture. "Without the glasses, I'd say it was taken in her first [and only] year of college here," Arlis's mother said.

It was readily apparent Berkowitz had seen that picture. But where and how?

* * *

In the witchcraft book he mailed to Lieutenant Terry Gardner in October 1979, Berkowitz wrote of a satanic ceremony which involved "a detailed soliloquy directed at the . . . victim, describing *her* (Arliss Perry) annihilation." Here, he was clearly referring to the cult meeting in New York at which he said Manson II told of the Perry killing. Apparently, it was through this dialogue that Berkowitz learned many details, including the extreme tortures performed on her. It is my opinion that Manson II had this photograph of Arlis in his possession at the time and showed it to Berkowitz and others present.

If so, where did this "superstar" satanic killer get it?

Arlis, as the picture showed, was dressed and made up as if posing for a formal photo session. Her family, however, said the picture was not among those taken for her engagement announcement, her wedding, a prom or a similar event. Arlis's parents, and the Santa Clara detectives, also said no such photo session occurred during her brief time in California.

But since Arlis spent only six weeks of her life in California, and the San Jose newspaper said the picture apparently was obtained from Bismarck, the hunt was focused there. And it produced some results.

There was a young man in Bismarck who frequently followed Arlis around—taking pictures of her. Arlis was invited to his house to pose for photographs on several occasions. Some, taken there or elsewhere, she liked well enough to display in her room at home. On one occasion, Bruce Perry and this young man got into an argument when the man called Arlis and invited her to his house to pose. Bruce, in the presence of Arlis's parents, grabbed the phone and told the man to stop bothering Arlis.

But Bruce was away at Stanford during Arlis's freshman year at Bismarck Junior College—which was the time period in which her mother believed the mysterious photo probably was taken.

No evidence directly linking this man to the Mary cult has been uncovered, but several people said a close friend of his was very interested in occult practices. However, it is distinctly possible that a photo he'd taken of Arlis was somehow obtained from him and passed on to the killers for identification purposes. Then another print made from the same or a similar negative could have found its way into the files of the Associated Press or *Bismarck Tribune,* which shared the same building in Bismarck.

Regardless of whether this individual was actually the source of the enigmatic photograph, the picture itself is key to the Perry case.

*   *   *

Another bizarre and frightening clue in the Arlis Perry case came from the hand of Arlis Perry herself. Arlis's own words offered dramatic testimony of the evident preplanning involved in her murder.

On September 27, 1974—fifteen days before her death—Arlis wrote a letter to her close friend Jenny in Bismarck. Jenny and other Dakota friends of Arlis were not interviewed by the California police.

In the letter to Jenny, Arlis wrote: "I had to laugh about your call to Bruce Perry. Mrs. Perry [Bruce's mother] made the same mistake. She called them, too. But the strange part of it is that his name is not only Bruce Perry but it is Bruce D. Perry, and not only that but it is Bruce Duncan Perry and he attends Stanford University, and he just got married this summer. One thing, his wife's name is not Arlis. Anyway, next time you get the urge to call, the number is . . . This time I guarantee you'll get the right Bruce Perry."

A question: was it plausible to believe that there were *two* Bruce Duncan Perrys studying at the same school, at the same time—both of whom had just been married?

There were not—but someone had taken out a phone in that name. And since Arlis was able to recite all that information, she almost certainly talked to that man.

Apparently, with the influx of students arriving for the fall semester, Arlis and Bruce had a considerable wait until their phone was installed. When Jenny and Bruce's mother tried to reach them, they spoke to an information operator who gave them the listing of the other Bruce D. Perry at Stanford. It would have been a university area exchange number, since both Jenny and Mrs. Perry would have told the operator that Bruce and Arlis were living on campus. "I asked for Bruce D. Perry at Stanford," Jenny recalled.

Both then called the other Bruce and were told they had reached a wrong number. Of course, this information reached Arlis, as noted in her letter. Arlis apparently then took the natural step of calling the other Bruce to tell him where she was living and to give him her phone number (after the unit was installed) so that if he received another wayward call he could give the caller Arlis's correct number.

But now the other Bruce—the false Bruce—would also possess Arlis's phone number and, almost certainly, her address. If he'd anticipated any difficulty finding her, his problem—via the fraudulent telephone listing—would have been covered in advance. Through this method, his victim could eventually find *him*—just as Jenny and Mrs. Perry did.

What was it Berkowitz wrote about Arlis? "Hunted, stalked and slain. Followed to California."

The phone listing of a nonexistent Bruce Duncan Perry was a vivid portrayal of the "hunted" allegation. And regarding the word "stalked," it will be remembered that Berkowitz knew the unreleased fact that Arlis frequently took long walks around the campus. In fact, she wrote her parents that Bruce was discouraging her from roaming the area alone.

But how did Berkowitz (and the killers) know of her walking habit? The answer would appear to be that Arlis was followed—stalked. Interestingly, her regular walks ceased by September 30, twelve days before her death, because on that day she began working full-time at a Palo Alto law firm.

For Berkowitz to have known she took long walks around the campus, the killers would have been following her *before* September 30, which meshes with the false phone listing being in place by mid-September.

* * *

I didn't learn of the fraudulent Bruce Duncan Perry until I interviewed Jenny in December 1985. Her husband, reading Arlis's long-stored letter, thought the telephone incident might be relevant, and Jenny sent me a copy of it. A subsequent check with Stanford University by both me and Sergeant Ken Kahn confirmed what we already knew was true: there was no other Bruce Perry at Stanford, let alone another Bruce Duncan Perry who'd just been married.

Another inquiry, this one with the telephone company, led nowhere—records that old weren't in existence. But we did learn that the other Bruce, whose published number the information operator had in September 1974, wasn't listed in the new area telephone book that was distributed several months later. In and out—the other Bruce was gone.

The plan, while ingenious—and chilling—was simple to enact. With an appropriate cash deposit and a false name, it wasn't difficult to obtain the listing. And why not? It is apparent that Arlis was "hunted" and "stalked" for several weeks.

The idea that Arlis Perry evidently spoke on the phone to one of her own killers is horrible to contemplate. But no other plausible explanation for this unsettling chain of events has surfaced—except for the possibility that the listing was obtained in a demonstration of sheer, macabre arrogance and omnipotence.

The existence of the phone listing, which wasn't discovered until late 1985, melded with other information I possessed since 1980, when a source of Minot reporter Jack Graham told me she had heard that the Perry killing involved "someone registering at Stanford under a false name." The lead was impossible to pursue then. But now, its import was established. The information was basically accurate, but it applied to a bogus phone listing, not an actual registration at the school. The source said she had picked up the story from the cult crowd in Minot.

Reviewing the Perry investigation results, Queens homicide bureau chief Herb Leifer said: "If Berkowitz was lying, *none* of this information could have been confirmed—it wouldn't even have existed. And far more information than he spoke about was uncovered. It looks like he knew that once you turned over that rock and started digging, you'd find what he always knew would be there."

If, after examining the broad scope of evidence and confirmations, one believes that Berkowitz was telling the truth, then one has decided that conclusive supporting evidence of a Son of Sam—and much larger—conspiracy has been uncovered.

* * *

Numerous questions about "motive" remain. Berkowitz wrote that one existed, and the entire idea of tracing her to the Coast and planning her slaying also demonstrated that a motive lurked somewhere.

She could have been killed simply because, as an ardent, vocal Christian, she was an automatic enemy of the cult. Its leaders may have ordered her death to provide underlings with an example of their power and prowess. But to have committed the crime in Bismarck—where murder was a rarity—would have been too obvious. The cult, whose existence was known, would have come under immediate suspicion, as would have a number of Arlis's acquaintances who had the means to "bridge" her world and that of the group.

But after Arlis reached California, the killing could be accomplished because, as did happen, the search for the murderer would be conducted there, not in Bismarck. When I interviewed Arlis's friends, I asked each the same question: "Pretend for a moment the killing occurred in Bismarck. Who would the suspects have been?"

Of course, the cult was immediately mentioned, as were Arlis's acquaintances who had contacts on both sides of Bismarck society.

Returning to the question of motive, Arlis also may have tried to convert to Christianity a cult member who later returned to the group and perhaps acknowledged that he (or she) told Arlis certain details the cult deemed confidential. It is also possible she inadvertently learned the identity of a respected citizen involved in the group.

A large amount of drug trafficking was occurring in Bismarck during this period and one does not have a satanic cult without drugs being in evidence. Somehow, in her explorations, Arlis may have stumbled across some knowledge of the group's drug operations.

There are at least two other possible motives, neither of which can be mentioned publicly. But as Berkowitz alleged, the investigation found that motives for Arlis's murder did indeed exist.

Arlis did not appear to be fearful. Her letters from California revealed a young woman who was occupied with adjusting to her new life and interested in what was happening in her hometown. Her correspondence contained no concerns for her safety or indications that any noteworthy troubling matters were left behind in North Dakota. Combined with her serious discussion with the law firm visitor the day before she died, her failure to tell her husband about it, and her unflinching desire to walk to the church alone the next night, it appears that Arlis was set up by someone close to her—someone she didn't fear.

This evaluation was also based on a comment in Berkowitz's letter to Felix Gilroy, in which he said that identifying her hometown would solve the case. That statement strongly suggested that someone obvious, and close to Arlis, was involved.

The Bismarck cult assuredly had more than one leader. It is possible that one of them was a local educator because Berkowitz, in pointing to Mary College, also dropped several clues about "professors." Including teachers, people who relocated to the Bismarck area from Southern California in the early seventies would be worthy of scrutiny because the Bismarck cult would have needed contacts in Los Angeles to enlist that "headquarters" group in the murder plot, as alleged by Berkowitz and the prison informant.

Several such people did settle in Bismarck during those years. Two were young men who were said to have been involved in narcotics distribution and connected to three Bismarck men who spent considerable time on the Coast. The California natives lived in a rented "crash pad," known locally as the "hippie house," that was the scene of numerous drug parties in Bismarck. Curiously, the "hippie house" was said to have been located at the same address later occupied by the California cult group that recruited in Bismarck between 1971 and 1973—the house across the street from Arlis's grandmother's residence.

As two final notes, seven young men whom Arlis knew were identified as matching the general description of the law firm visitor. But since no police sketches of that man were drawn, it wasn't possible to show a rendering to Arlis's friends. Also, it was mentioned earlier that Arlis's jeans were *placed* with their legs positioned on her own, spread-eagle legs in a manner that resulted in a rough, diamond-shaped configuration. Though it isn't certain that was the intent, a study of Mary College yearbooks revealed that a diamond logo appeared on some official school sweaters.

The Arlis Perry murder investigation remains open.

XIX

What's Happening, America?

Throughout the summer of 1980, Berkowitz remained silent. True to his word, as he'd written in May, there was a muted stillness emanating from Attica prison. For the past nine months, he'd been concerned that his involvement in the investigation stay confidential, a position which tended to dispel the remote analyses of some who'd earlier labeled him a publicity seeker. Not this time, if ever. After all, Son of Sam had worked in silence for the first five attacks. Only at the sixth, after the police held their press conference, was a letter left.

While I retreated to Davis Park on Fire Island for a three-week vacation with my wife, District Attorney John Santucci's investigation continued in Queens. A file cabinet containing new evidence uncovered since the probe began decorated a corner of Herb Leifer's office. The list of suspects still alive had grown to seven, but the corroborating evidence needed to arrest any of them was still eluding the best efforts of the investigators. And in this case, there would be no arrests unless Santucci was 100 percent certain he'd obtain convictions.

One of the newest suspects was a young man named Gorman Johnson,* who had been arrested in New York City at the height of the Son of Sam siege with a fully loaded Charter Arms .44 Bulldog in his possession. The gun was purchased in Pennsylvania. A man arrested with Johnson acknowledged an acquaintance with .44 victim Valentina Suriani.

Interestingly, Johnson lived in Berkowitz's neighborhood—barely a block from 35 Pine Street. He'd also resided less than two blocks from Berkowitz when the confessed killer lived in New Rochelle. And when Berkowitz moved to Yonkers, Johnson followed suit several months later.

Like Berkowitz, Johnson had driven a cab in the northeast Bronx. And the similarities didn't end there.

Yonkers arson investigator Don Starkey reported that Johnson was suspected of igniting a fire in a local apartment building where he'd worked as a security guard—two more traits he shared with Berkowitz. Also, a relative of Johnson's was a convicted arsonist, and Yonkers police believed Johnson himself participated in a murder for which yet another of his relatives was arrested and convicted. That relative, however, refused to implicate Johnson, and so he remained free.

Tom McCarthy, Leifer and I discussed Johnson's status during a late-summer meeting in Queens.

"We've got the ex-Yonkers cop Peter Shane with a .44 Bulldog," I said. "And the dead Howard Weiss supposedly had one, too. And we've got both Weiss and Shane tied to Berkowitz, who also had a .44 Bulldog. Now, right around the corner from Berkie, we've got Johnson suspected of committing crimes in just the right categories.

And *he's* got a .44 Bulldog. Want to play those odds?"

McCarthy shook his head. "No, it doesn't take Einstein to work out that equation. But we can't prove it in court. Until we can, he just takes his place on our list. David could really help us out, but he's not talking."

"That's about it. I wrote him several times and he's not saying a thing. And the bastard wouldn't come down to the visitors' room when I went up to see him in August."

"What's going on with him? I thought he was your buddy," Leifer joked.

"He's scared, and he explained why he stopped talking. We're going to have to roll with it. I don't know what the hell else to do. Anybody else that would have been nailed by now is dead."

McCarthy had a suggestion.

"If you could dream up some way to convince him you won't blow his cover, he just might get off his ass and respond to it."

McCarthy's idea had merit. With the exception of the pamphlets he'd mailed to Lieutenant Gardner in Minot, not a word of Berkowitz's comments about the .44 or Arlis Perry case had reached the public.

"We haven't published anything in months," I replied. "We've been into the 'lie in wait' strategy, but maybe the time is now."

"It couldn't hurt," Leifer said.

At Gannett, a plan was formulated among executive editor Joe Ungaro, me and Mike Zuckerman, a quality reporter who would later join the staff of Gannett's *USA Today* newspaper.

Zuckerman and I would prepare a four-part series which would include the data I'd now obtained which proved Brooklyn DA Eugene Gold knew about allegations of John Carr's cult involvement and association with Berkowitz months before Berkowitz pleaded guilty. Another story would reveal that NYPD Captain John Plansker formally urged the continuation of the Police Department's aborted inquiry of the reopened case. Plansker's reports were introduced at Detective Hank Cinotti's departmental trial, after which we were able to acquire them.

In yet another article, a demonstration of trust would appear for Berkowitz to consider. Using the confessed killer as an unnamed source, the story would describe the Pine Street apartment setup. It was hoped that Berkowitz, seeing his confidentiality was protected, would respond with more facts to aid the investigation.

The series was published and received a fair amount of media coverage. But Berkowitz, who received a copy in the mail, remained silent. In this instance, no news wasn't good news. And we'd already just absorbed a heavy dosage of depressing information.

*   *   *

Jack Graham was, at twenty-nine, fondly considered the "bearded giant" of the *Minot Daily News*. The husky, bespectacled, brown-haired reporter and native of Washington, D.C., had joined the Son of Sam fray with an intense passion for ferreting out the Minot links to the case. For a year, he'd worked closely with Jeff Nies and me. Among other contributions, he was instrumental in tracking down John Carr's friend Phil Falcon on the West Coast.

In August and September 1980, Jack and I worked on an investigation of Larry Milenko, John Carr's cult-connected friend who was toiling in the woods with Jerry Berg when the falling tree crushed Berg to death. In early September, at a party he'd managed to infiltrate, Jack had an angry confrontation with Milenko. "We're going to get you, you bastard," Jack told him.

Two weeks later, Jack was vacationing in Michigan, visiting his family in East Lansing and attending Jeff Nies's wedding in a Detroit suburb. On Monday, September 22, he began his return trip to Minot. In the back of his Datsun were packed a number of wedding gifts he was bringing home to North Dakota for the honeymooning Nieses.

At 8:30 on the night of the twenty-second, Jack stopped to visit a Michigan friend, Neil Colburn. Jack's arrival at Colburn's home was delayed because he had car trouble on the way.

"It was stalling out on him," Colburn said. "He had road service before getting here but was still worried about it. He went out later to try the car, and came in and said it was stalling on him again."

Jack and Colburn reminisced for a couple of hours. Jack had a bottle of beer and two Irish coffees before calling it a night at about 11:45. "He was in good spirits," Colburn recalled. "He told me he caught the garter at Jeff's wedding. He said he leaped for it."

But Jack was never to know if that traditional ceremony signified an upcoming marriage for him.

The next morning, after leaving dollar bills for each of Colburn's three children on the kitchen table, Jack was on the road before dawn. Four and a half hours and about 250 miles later, his car crossed the center line on a slight curve on U.S. 2 near the small community of Vulcan, Michigan, and slammed headlong into an oncoming eighteen-wheel trailer, whose driver was unhurt.

Jack was pulled unconscious from the wrecked Datsun and rushed to Dickinson County Memorial Hospital in Iron Mountain. He didn't make it.

The call came to me from a friend of Jack's, a source who was assisting the investigation.

"You know he was after Milenko," she cried. "He said it right to his face. Michael Carr was killed in a wreck—you've got to go after this. You just can't let it go."

We didn't. I phoned Jack's roommate in Minot, a reporter who was already stupefied by the news. "Jack won't be taking any calls tonight, or ever again," he sobbed as he answered the phone.

"I know, Tom. I just heard. I don't know what to say." And I didn't. My instinct had been to act first, and feel later. I learned Neil Colburn's name from Tom and, after reaching him the next morning, reconstructed Jack's final hours as best I could.

Lieutenant Terry Gardner and I went over the itinerary in minute detail, and Gardner contacted the Michigan police to request a close examination of Jack's car. But the Datsun was virtually destroyed, and no signs of tampering were discovered. Any suspicions we may have harbored added up to nothing. It may well have been an accident.

"But if the car was rigged, it could have been done before he left Minot," I said to Gardner. "And if it conked out at a good speed, like it had been doing, Jack would have lost control for a few seconds and his concentration would have been broken."

"That's true," Gardner replied. "He was only over the center line by a couple of feet—but it was enough. There weren't any skid marks. He didn't even hit the brakes."

The matter would remain unresolved, and not being able to shake that lingering doubt was the worst result of all. Whatever happened, another person deeply involved in the Son of Sam investigation was now dead. And he'd been killed just two weeks after confronting a suspect. Jack had departed Minot several days after that party and never returned.

The investigation done, I, along with others whose lives he touched, grieved for Jack Graham. The following night, I tried to explain my churning feelings to my wife.

"There have been so many accumulated emotions because of this goddamned case—ranging from fear to anger and from elation to sorrow and frustration of the worst kind. And they never go away; the feelings just keep piling up. I just don't know where the hell to put them all anymore."

Aimlessly pacing the apartment, I finally dug out two audio tapes Jack sent me which contained interviews conducted for the investigation. Spinning, spinning, the reels erased the present. Playing them, yesterday lived.

There was Jack, in typical form, encouraging Phil Falcon to cooperate during our marathon, three-city, transcontinental conference call. But Jack's exuberant voice, filtered by the events of the past forty-eight hours, now echoed ironic and bittersweet: "It's all coming down, Phil. All coming down."

Yes, Jack, I thought morosely. You dedicated, idealistic son of a bitch. It was all coming down all right. All coming down . . .

* * *

Like a hangover from the previous year, 1981 dawned on an ominous note. As Sheena Easton's "Morning Train" rolled to the top of the charts, another diesel was lumbering down the track. It was the so-called official Son of Sam book which painted Berkowitz as a lone madman. None of those involved in the investigation was oblivious to the fact that the book, inaccurate as it was, could distort the public's perception of the case and make the presentation of the real facts a more difficult endeavor than it already was. Fortunately, we were able to offset the publication's impact.

On a talk show on WMCA radio in New York, host Candy Jones arranged for author Lawrence Klausner and me to meet. Out of that program, listeners, including Klausner's own publishers, heard that he hadn't even interviewed most of the principal characters in the case, including Cacilia Davis and Berkowitz. And although Klausner tried to cut me off at every turn with a filibuster of inanities, I refrained from revealing the Berkowitz letters, which would have blown down his house of straw on the spot. But that moment was at hand.

After the program I told Candy privately that something big was in the wind, and she invited me to appear again on her show when the day arrived. Thus began an association that would include four more interviews on her broadcast.

At the same time, Frank Anthony, the aggressive producer of *What's Happening, America*, a television newsmagazine show hosted by author and former *60 Minutes* regular Shana Alexander, asked me to do a thirty-minute segment on the conspiracy investigation for WHA.

Meanwhile, Berkowitz remained stone-still. I'd finally written and said that unless he began aiding the inquiry again, I'd be forced to publicize his involvement—a secret I'd held for sixteen months. There was no reply. It was quandary time. I knew that if I backed away my credibility with Berkowitz would be destroyed.

I also knew that it was important to deflate Klausner's "lone madman" thesis as much as possible. Plus, the public deserved to know what had been going on. I had withheld the information hoping Berkowitz would step forward to break the case wide open, but he hadn't done so. There was no point in holding back any longer.

But I wanted to effect a double-pronged strategy. I'd been affiliated with the Gannett newspapers for more than two years and wasn't prepared to shun an ally for television's sake. Accordingly, an arrangement was made wherein Gannett would break the story in print on March 19, and WHA would air its comprehensive presentation two nights later.

All was ready, but Berkowitz had to be advised of what was about to happen.

In a letter, I told him that because of his reluctance to cooperate further, I was going public with some, but not all, of the information he'd provided, along with confirmations to back up his assertions. I mentioned it would be clearly stated he was *not* cooperating with Santucci's investigation.

Unfortunately, the *New York Daily News,* in an honest error, published a pre-broadcast article which said Berkowitz was interviewed in his cell, and suggested that he blamed the police for covering up the case—which he didn't. He actually said he understood how, in the hysteria of the moment, important clues were overlooked or ignored. If a cover-up occurred, he didn't blame the police.

And he wasn't interviewed in his cell either. The mistakes were the result of a communications lapse between the *News* and the show's production staff. Berkowitz received my letter before the article reached him. He replied:

I just received your letter of 3/16, a mailgram from Denise and one from the N.Y. Post, *and a letter from my conservator. Aside from your letter, all the others mentioned a program that is to be aired on 3/21.*

At this time I don't know what to say and I am quite nervous about the whole thing. Things were quiet for so long and Klausner's book hasn't been all that successful, I believe. Now this. I noticed you said in your letter that it will be very clear that I am not cooperating. However, both mailgrams said that I said there was a cult and accomplices. This is the opposite of what you said in your letter. [It actually wasn't. I wrote that Berkowitz's refusal to cooperate with the authorities would be stated; not that he hadn't offered other comments.]

Maury, I cannot stop you from plodding away at this investigation. I cannot stop you from publicizing your findings. . . . As I say, whatever you do is your business. But remember that I am in a precarious position. Prison is an unpredictable place and an individual's survival rests on his reputation. And since I will probably be here for quite some time, I do not wish to lose whatever standing I have made for myself.

Whether or not your findings reopen the case is another matter. [It was open, but since Berkowitz hadn't heard anything lately, he erroneously thought Santucci had backed off.] . . . I have not heard from Pienciak or Lee Chase in ages. If they are up to something I know nothing about it. By the way, Lee and I split up quite some time ago. We're still friends, I think.

Lastly, Denise will be watching this program and will be taking notes. If anything is detrimental towards me, I will find out about it.

Sincerely,
David Berkowitz

Once again, despite his anxiety, there wasn't a single denial from Berkowitz. Two days later, after receiving the *Daily News* clip, his tone changed as his fear increased. Still, he made no attempt to withdraw a word. Between the lines, his brief letter spoke volumes:

I just received an article from the Daily News: *"Son of Sam on TV Show, I did not act alone." Oh, really, Maury, how silly can you be. Once you make it appear that I said this or that, then the public will turn a deaf ear to you.*

Society believes that every criminal is a con-artist. For a notorious criminal to admit that he didn't do this or that, the effect will be nil. The public will only feel that I am saying these things to get my sentence reduced and to take the heat off me. This isn't true, of course, but people have a different view.

The News *article says that I had conversations in my cell and blame*

*the police for covering the investigation up. No, you said this! Obviously
you've put many words in my mouth. You also make it appear that I am
bitter no one will believe me and that I am desperately insisting the case
be reopened. Not so.*

Yours,
David Berkowitz

I hadn't put any words in Berkowitz's mouth, but the mistakes in the newspaper
article upset him. Even at this late hour, he'd again confirmed the conspiracy existed.
And aware as I was of the credibility factor he mentioned, his letters would be bolstered by supporting evidence. However, Berkowitz knew none of this. All he had to
go on was a well-intentioned but inaccurate clipping.

In the interim, Berkowitz's friend Denise called me on his behalf to ask that I
stick to the facts and not expose him to danger. I reassured her he would be treated
fairly and asked her to send him a mailgram saying he had my assurance that what
appeared in the newspaper article wasn't a true description of the program's contents.
I also urged her to encourage Berkowitz to come forward once and for all.

"If he did, could they move him to a federal prison and make sure that I could be
near him?" Denise asked.

"I'm sure they can. Santucci is ready to do everything possible."

"I can't promise what David'll say, but I'll tell him I spoke to you and ask him
about coming forward," she said. "And I'll tell him you said the program is O.K."

"It *is* O.K., Denise," I insisted, and we said goodbye.

*   *   *

On Thursday, March 19, 1981, the Gannett newspapers fired the first salvo. The
morning *Today* paper, which reached into New York City, was bannered: "SON OF
SAM: I WAS NOT ALONE."

Inside, a host of articles listing some of the evidence supporting Berkowitz's statements appeared. The only alleged conspirator named was John Carr. Berkowitz's
confirmation of the cult's existence also was published, but we kept the Arlis Perry
case and the Michael Carr connection under wraps. In total, the articles covered
nearly six pages. For Gannett's regional afternoon dailies, the process was repeated.

The report was picked up by the rest of the media. WPIX-TV, WOR and WABC-
TV, along with WINS radio's John Russell—who'd followed the case all along—
interviewed me; as did a few out-of-state radio stations. I was also immediately
scheduled for another appearance on Candy Jones's radio show.

Santucci's office also received a host of calls, including one from WCBS radio
newsman Art Athens, who'd offered information to the Omega task force before Berkowitz's arrest. Athens had maintained his interest in the investigation, but Santucci
wasn't issuing any statements on the Gannett reports.

The next day, Mike Zuckerman reported in Gannett that the NYPD offered absolutely no comment in response to the articles and that the Bronx and Brooklyn district attorneys were sidestepping the issue. In Queens, John Santucci watched his counterparts dive for cover.

As a sidelight to the media coverage, the Associated Press, whose reporter Rick Pienciak was kayoed from the case by Berkowitz and Lee Chase a year earlier, did not write a word about the disclosures. There was little doubt as to why this occurred, and Gannett editors expressed their considerable displeasure to AP executives. From that point on, the AP, perhaps now aware that Pienciak conceivably had an ax to grind, resumed its coverage of the work being published in Westchester.

Saturday night, the second bomb exploded as WOR-TV's thirty-minute report aired on *What's Happening, America*. Along with highlights of the Berkowitz letters and supporting evidence, Lieutenant Gardner and Officer Knoop were interviewed in Minot; Cacilia Davis told her account of the Moskowitz scenario; the yellow VW story was mentioned; the Untermyer Park and animal shelter cult connections were explored; handwriting expert Charles Hamilton stated flat out that Berkowitz wasn't the author of the Breslin letter; and John Carr's drug counselor said that Carr was nicknamed Wheaties and possessed intimate knowledge of the .44 shootings.

Additionally, interviews were conducted with Mike Lauria, father of victim Donna Lauria, and Jerry and Neysa Moskowitz, parents of the slain Stacy. All expressed belief in the conspiracy's existence and called for full disclosure of the truth. Now even victims' families were lining up against the NYPD, Brooklyn DA Eugene Gold and the Bronx's Mario Merola.

Berkowitz, for his part, said nothing. As Denise assuredly advised him, his position was fairly and accurately represented.

* * *

A month later, I hosted another segment of *What's Happening, America*. This time, the chase of the yellow VW through Brooklyn was described and we revealed that Berkowitz had driven a borrowed yellow or beige VW while living in the Cassara home in New Rochelle. Other aspects of the case were also covered, but the focal point of this program was the disclosure of the letter Berkowitz left in his "topsy-turvy" apartment which warned that his cult planned to kill "at least 100" young people in the tri-state area. The note, we stated, was withheld from the public by Gold and top NYPD officials. (This segment would later be honored by United Press International as the best investigative report aired in the New York City area in the year 1981.)

The next day, Friday, April 24, the Gannett papers published my article about the letter. The story, like the TV presentation, emphasized that police officials and Eugene Gold suppressed the note.

This report also contained a significant about-face statement by Gold, who had now acknowledged that "pieces of a puzzle concerning a cult" had indeed existed all along—as Jim Mitteager and I formally advised his office as early as January 1978.

Gold's concession marked a point as close as he could possibly come to falling on his sword. Gone were his 1979 charges which falsely accused me of "wild hypothesis unsupported by any evidence." Gold was caught in a rising tide, a surge he could have avoided had he not attempted to whitewash the case from the outset. If he'd presumed we'd eventually just go away, he was mistaken.

A short time later Gold announced he was stepping down as Brooklyn district attorney. High-level sources in his own office—who had defied Gold by providing me with the cult letter and classified reports of the Moskowitz murder—told me that Gold's decision to retire from office was influenced by a few factors. Among them was the Son of Sam case.

In Westchester, a *Today* editor, tongue firmly in cheek, headlined the story of the abdication "GOLD WILL NO LONGER GLITTER IN BROOKLYN."

Twenty months after Gold retired, he admitted to a Tennessee court that he'd sexually molested a ten-year-old girl while attending a district attorneys' convention after he left office. The victim, Gold acknowledged, was the daughter of a prosecutor who participated in the conference. The charges were dismissed with the stipulation that Gold receive psychiatric treatment.

* * *

On other fronts in the spring of 1981, the newly released Son of Sam evidence continued to ripple the pond. In the Bronx, DA Mario Merola, in response to a question about the two .44 attacks in his jurisdiction, told Gannett's Mike Zuckerman: "Berkowitz was acting alone in the *Bronx* cases." Merola stipulated that he was referring only to the Bronx, and *not* to the Queens and Brooklyn shootings. While Merola was no longer denying the existence of a conspiracy, his conclusion concerning Berkowitz's sole guilt in the Bronx was greeted with considerable skepticism.

In Hollywood, too, people were nervous. The *Daily News* soon reported that production of a major film scheduled to be based on Klausner's book had been scrapped. As the *News* revealed, the movie's executives feared that the current revelations, and future ones, would render the "Berkowitz alone" scenario a fiasco.

The house of cards had finally collapsed.

* * *

John Santucci had issued no progress reports since reopening the case. And despite the concessions now acknowledged by the other DAs, no assistance was forthcoming. At the beginning, he received no support and was forced to go it alone. And that's the way it would remain, which was now fine with him.

For several months, the case dropped out of public view, but the backstage efforts continued. I knew that Santucci and his investigators were convinced a conspiracy existed, but I was obligated to maintain that confidence. Through Tom McCarthy I'd asked if the DA would participate in one of the two television specials. The invitation was politely declined.

"The DA doesn't want to be viewed as using this case to create a major controversy," McCarthy explained.

"That's already happened, Tom. And he joined it when he reopened."

"He reopened based on the evidence. Others created the controversy by lining up against him," McCarthy answered. "It's somewhat absurd when you think about it. We had five of the eight attacks out here—who the hell else is in a better position to make an informed evaluation of the case? And this isn't new; he wanted to resolve this in '78. But Brooklyn and the Bronx bucked him when he wanted a trial."

"Then why not ask him to talk about it now? Damn it, the time has come. Gold is on the way out and Merola's statement was so cute he could sell waffle irons. This is the guy who in '78 tried to claim Berkowitz took time out from shooting people to light three million fires at fifteen-minute intervals throughout the entire city. Even the cops shot that down as bullshit. Now he's doing the best Invisible Man I haven't seen since Claude Rains."

McCarthy chuckled. "Why don't you open the next program with that? They'd love it in the Bronx. But Berkowitz *was* a firebug."

"Yeah, he was a buff and he did torch a few things here and there. He's admitted that. But hell, that was part of their thing—him, Weiss and the rest. That fire log of his even had an August 2 fire written down *before* a July 29 fire. Did you know that?"

"No, I didn't."

"Well, he was either clairvoyant or he simply copied that log from someplace and made a mistake while doing it."

"Interesting," McCarthy said. It was one of his favorite words, one I was sure would be his epitaph someday, when he sailed off to Cagey Spokesman's Heaven.

"Look," he said. "I'll talk to the DA about the next program. When's it going to air—the end of September?"

"Yeah, and it would be great if he was part of it."

* * *

In late August, I flew to California to tape a report on the Arlis Perry murder, which we were now going to air publicly. The majority of the evidence would remain confidential, but an overview of the case, including Sergeant Ken Kahn's comments about his belief in Berkowitz's veracity, would be broadcast.

After I returned to New York, John Santucci, Herb Leifer and I had a private meeting in Queens on the Son of Sam probe.

Besides their legal backgrounds, Leifer and Santucci shared another trait. Each was always "trying to quit" smoking whenever I showed up. Translated: I usually left with an empty pack, foraged by a pair of "reformed" tobacco addicts.

Getting the preliminaries out of the way, I tossed the box of Marlboro Lights onto Santucci's desk and told him I'd just eliminated the middleman. Then it was down to business and the DA didn't mince words.

"I think they've killed before, during and after the .44 incidents," he said. "I don't doubt that for a second. Do you think they're still using Untermyer Park?"

"I don't think so, but I'm not sure. All that publicity should have driven them off. But then, a cop spotted a ritual involving German shepherds at an old estate nearby after that. They might have just moved up the road."

Santucci then ran through a list of names, most of whom have been mentioned in this narrative in one way or another.

"I think they're all part of it," he said. "And I think we've got women involved, too."

"So do we," Leifer agreed.

"Yes," Santucci continued. "But until we get a clearer picture of who the actual shooters were, we'd be risking giving immunity to a gunman if I took this to a grand jury. That's the damned law in this state. Once you put someone in front of a grand jury they've got immunity unless they waive it. And do you think any of these people would do that?"

"Not likely," I answered.

"You're right. And that's what makes this kind of investigation so damned difficult. All the district attorneys are against this law. The feds don't have it, but we're stuck with it. And I just won't take the chance of handing a free ticket to someone who might turn out to be one of the shooters."

"I was wondering what your strategy was," I said. "I think what you're saying is that we're sitting here with so-called negative proof. We can demonstrate the conspiracy exists, but doing so doesn't, by itself, result in automatic arrests of any people suspected of being part of it."

"I would agree with that," Santucci said. "We can lay out all this information and say that it shows Berkowitz wasn't alone. That's one thing. Then you look for who to arrest. You've got people identified, but you don't know which role they played, or if they played several roles. I believe there were lookouts, wheelmen and several different people who were shooters. So to try to find out who did what, you look for your witnesses. But there aren't many witnesses who can help you in this case. So where do you turn? You'd then want to put your suspects in front of a grand jury—but you can't because they've automatically got immunity once you do."

"So what do you need?" I asked.

"I need to discover who the shooters were and who ran this operation."

"We need to turn somebody," Leifer interjected. "We were hoping it would be David. But as you know, he's not talking anymore. We need an insider. We don't have much in the way of 'outside' witnesses to the shootings—people who could say, 'Yeah, I saw Joe Blow do it.'"

"Look at it this way," Santucci continued. "Using Brooklyn as an example, you could put Mrs. Davis on the stand and demonstrate that, based on her observations, Berkowitz wasn't the shooter. And you'd back up her testimony with her friend's, Zaino's, the yellow VW chase and other reconstructed events from that scene. But for all that does, it still doesn't give you the shooter's identity. We know who *didn't* pull the trigger, or hang out in the park, or drive the VW. But we don't know who *did*."

"You're depressing me," I said.

"I don't mean to. This work that's been done is very important because it exposed this operation in the first place, and it would also corroborate the testimony of Berkowitz or someone else involved," Santucci said. "But we need that someone."

"You know what Berkowitz said about having to turn over pictures of family members and all—"

"Yes. That's an added problem. We can take steps to combat that situation, but we'd first have to convince someone we could do it."

"And you can't do a thing about the Carr brothers. I mean, John was a dead ringer for the Lomino-DeMasi sketch," I said.

"It doesn't matter now in terms of prosecution, which is where we're at," Leifer answered. "Nobody can prosecute anybody who is dead."

"Speaking of John Carr, I heard recently that he was the weakest link and would have been the one most likely to break," Santucci said.

"That probably explains his untimely demise," I replied.

"And I also heard that Reeve Rockman wasn't involved—at least not directly—in the shootings. Whatever else he may have had a hand in—drugs or anything else—I don't know."

I caught the drift of Santucci's remarks. "It sounds to me like you might have a little bird on your shoulder. Perhaps a little bird who's tired of taking a fall all by himself?"

"No, not him personally. But there is someone else. You recall that Berkowitz was recently transferred from Attica, right?"

"Yes, to Dannemora."

"Let's just say I wish he was back in Attica and that I have some personal questions as to why he's no longer there."

For a moment, no one spoke. "Are you telling me that you've got an informant and he and Berkowitz were separated just as good information was coming in—is that it?"

"Yes, the move was a curious one. Let's just leave it at that."

"Do you have any other informants?" I asked.

"I'm working on that right now. It's a fragile situation, but there are a few things in the works."

"In Dannemora?"

"And elsewhere," Santucci said. "We were talking about Brooklyn. I also heard recently from an informant that Berkowitz didn't shoot Stacy Moskowitz or the Violante boy. You already put that out there pretty thoroughly. But that's Brooklyn—I need the Queens cases."

"Wait a minute—those damned boundaries don't apply to me. What did you hear about Brooklyn?"

Santucci paused for a second, deciding whether or not to reveal the information.

"I was told that 'the guy from the hospital' did that shooting," he said. The district attorney then mentioned a familiar name.

"No kidding." I whistled. "He does fit into the picture."

"Yes, but I'm not sure it's him," Santucci explained. "I wasn't given the name—I was told the guy from the hospital. But we both know Max's* connections to the case, and he did work in a hospital. But it may be another hospital worker we haven't identified yet. But I wish Max would get pulled over in Queens on some violation so we could use it as an excuse to question him. We'd get nowhere just inviting him in."

"And this comes from inside?"

"Yes."

"And you think it's good?"

"I have no reason to think it isn't. I'd appreciate anything you've got on Max, because it might be him."

"Jeez, I knew the evidence was there on Brooklyn, and I know Berkowitz liked that big Moskowitz report we did. This all fits in—what about the other cases?"

"In Queens, now. I've got serious questions about the Lomino-DeMasi shootings, the Christine Freund murder and the killing of the Voskerichian girl in Forest Hills," Santucci said.

"Yeah, Ski Cap and Berkowitz were both at that scene and Berkowitz tried to claim he was Ski Cap. It's garbage. Herb and I both think Ski Cap may have been a woman."

Santucci looked at Leifer, who nodded his assent.

"It's definitely possible," Santucci answered. "But as far as the other Queens cases go, I just don't know. Nobody saw anything at the Denaro wounding, and at Elephas we've got nothing on the shooter. I'm aware of that yellowish car there and of the guy with the mustache who jumped into it. He allegedly witnessed the incident and then left in the same direction as the shooter—isn't that it?"

"Yeah, and with his lights out."

"But that doesn't give us the shooter," the DA explained. "It's just another example indicating that something was going on out there involving the gunman and someone else."

"Merola had the only witness who was going to ID Berkowitz," I said. "The only one. Jody Valente—who was wounded in the car when Donna Lauria was killed."

"Well, there's no question that Berkowitz is guilty of both murder and conspiracy," Santucci replied. "He was involved in everything, and I'm sure he pulled the trigger a few times."

"He's not even trying to deny that," I said. "He's not trying to get out of anything. I'd say that helps his credibility."

"It's tough to argue with that," Leifer answered.

"What about the Arlis Perry matter?" Santucci asked.

"I just taped a piece out at Stanford with Ken Kahn, the cop on the case. It's eerie.

She was put right beneath a big cross sculpted into the damned church wall. There's symbolism in everything these people do. But Kahn's on the record as saying they believe Berkowitz. How couldn't they? It's all there. . . . You know this means we've got a larger picture than what went on in New York."

"You mean the guy Berkowitz calls Charlie Manson II," Leifer said.

"Well, as I said before, I think they were active before and after the Son of Sam incidents," Santucci agreed. "But my focus has to remain here in Queens. This is an exceptionally complex investigation, but I couldn't ignore it. There were too many unresolved questions, important questions."

"And now?" I asked.

"We've been able to resolve a lot of them, and that's one goal of this inquiry. Arrests are another matter. We need a break, and we need some damned help from Berkowitz or someone else with firsthand knowledge. We're going to try to make that happen, but through nobody's fault here a lot of time has gone by and it won't be easy. But we'll try," the DA said.

"So you'll do the TV show?"

"Yes. I said in our opening statement that when the time was appropriate, and not before then, we'd make the findings of this office public. I know you wanted something before, but we couldn't do it. I can't go all the way, there are still things that are confidential. But I think we'll be able to contribute to the program."

*   *   *

On Saturday night, September 26, 1981, the *What's Happening, America* broadcast was aired. Along with some basic revelations about the Arlis Perry case, Santucci said publicly for the first time that his office's investigation had convinced him Berkowitz didn't act alone. The quote most widely circulated by the wire services and reported by the rest of the media was:

"I believe David Berkowitz did not act alone—that in fact others did cooperate, aid and abet him in the commission of these crimes. In fact, it has crossed my mind that this .44-caliber pistol, which was the weapon used in the shootings, was passed around among a number of people."

"It could have been one gun or there may have been more," Santucci said afterwards. "The ballistics were inconclusive; I don't doubt Berkowitz's gun was used in some of the shootings. But since I couldn't prove more than one gun was used either, there was no purpose to be served by raising the issue then."

But since that time, other informants known to Santucci have alleged that more than one .44 was used, at least in the earlier attacks, a subject that hasn't been raised publicly until this writing. In fact, because of the NYPD's statements, it was assumed Berkowitz's .44 was the only one fired.

But the informants' revelations supported identical comments phoned anonymously to Lieutenant Terry Gardner in Minot following John Carr's death. Significantly, since none of the informants, including those whose names are known, knew about the ballistics reports, they couldn't have been aware that a lack of definitive ballistics proof existed.

I mentioned this aspect to Tom McCarthy, telling him that if I was an informant trying to lie, that was probably the last fabrication I'd try because it was challenging what people accepted as established fact.

"Wouldn't you be afraid of being discredited on the spot if you dreamt something like that up?" I asked.

"You sure as hell have to take what they're saying a lot more seriously because of that," he answered. "One of the police's techniques is to withhold certain keys so that they can gauge the value of information they get. If an informant couldn't have read about some piece of evidence, his credibility goes up. The police kept this ballistics information from the public for other reasons—not for future corroboration. So it's really ironic how it's working out."

The prison sources, incidentally, said their information came directly from Berkowitz, and it was firmly established that they were closely acquainted with him. The bottom line was that, in addition to the other conspiracy evidence and Berkowitz's own flawed 1977 confession, there were now serious questions regarding the gun as well.

"I can see why they tried to sweep this under the rug," I said to Tom McCarthy. "They were willing to let this entire thing get away rather than have the holes in the case against Berkowitz exposed."

"If so, not anymore," McCarthy said simply. "Even if we're never able to arrest anyone else, we can at least let it be known what's been found and maybe we drive these lunatics underground for a while."

*   *   *

McCarthy's optimism was ill founded. There was no proof that the killings had stopped, although it seemed the group's attention had been diverted to silencing its own mistrusted members. But there was still much more to come.

The morning after the TV broadcast, the Gannett newspapers published the entire Santucci interview, along with an article I'd prepared on the Arlis Perry case. In the complete discussion, which had been edited because of television's time constraints, Santucci voiced his long-standing dissatisfaction with the original .44 investigation. "I did want to see a trial because I wanted to determine whether some of these [conspiracy] questions in my mind—and certainly I think in the minds of others—could be resolved. And I think they should be resolved.

"In this case," he continued, "the sketches of the individuals—the composites— were at wide divergence from Berkowitz. That was one problem. Allegations that there was more than one vehicle involved [and] the time frame in the killer getting from one place to another gave us serious questions."

Santucci then cautiously enunciated a facet of the case which troubled him deeply: "If there are people out there who were involved with Berkowitz, they may be doing the same thing today. . . . And I think part of my function is to *prevent* things from happening—and this is the way I have to do it."

I asked the district attorney about the large number of dead suspects.

"We've looked into some of the incidents you've talked about and yes, there is an unusual number of people who are no longer living," he said. "The probe certainly would have been easier if all the principals—or all the people involved peripherally or directly—were still alive. But unfortunately, many are not."

Santucci emphasized that he was certain Berkowitz was guilty of murder—although not by himself. And regarding live suspects, he then said: "I have ideas as to who would be most valuable for me to talk to. There are also people who are no longer available to me. Where each of them is at the present time, I don't know. I also have some people in mind whose whereabouts I know—but who wouldn't be helpful to me."

The DA then addressed the original categorization of Berkowitz as an "insane loner": "The evidence I have available to me indicates that he was perfectly sane, knew exactly what he was doing, and that he did have a circle of friends he was involved with."

Santucci closed by saying that although conspiracy evidence was uncovered, arrests were another matter.

"Whether or not [the probe] would lead to indictments . . . is very debatable. But my principal goal is to find out, to settle the issue. . . . I would try to get enough evidence to prosecute. But that's a little more difficult than just settling the question."

* * *

Now, it was a matter of public record. And the message wasn't missed by people involved in the case. In upstate Dannemora prison, David Berkowitz heard it loud and clear. And he began talking to a number of people—inmates and others connected to the prison. He wanted advice; he was thinking of locating a lawyer to explore what might be done for him and to protect his family.

Now, too, several reporters voiced written agreement with the conspiracy determination, and information from the public began flowing again. Numerous tips were checked but most, despite their sincerity, proved groundless. However, one call to authorities was referred to me for follow-up. His name was Bob Williams,* and he lived in a small Connecticut city.

"I knew a guy named Brian Birch,*" he said. "He was fixing my car at his home in the fall of '76 and he pulled out a .44 and said, 'Don't mess with the Son of Sam.' He was standing on his staircase with the gun in his hand. I asked him what the hell he meant and he told me to forget it."

I could sense Williams was serious, but the story still sounded far-fetched. "Are you sure it was a .44?" I asked, and Williams replied he was certain the gun was a .44 revolver, model unknown.

Williams's allegation was potentially important for another reason: nobody had heard the term "Son of Sam" in the autumn of 1976. It wasn't until April 1977 that the name was used in the Borrelli letter. Williams told me he originally phoned the NYPD during the shooting spree but no one had gotten back to him.

"I know they had a few thousand names to work on, so it probably got lost in the pile. But I don't want you to think I'm just coming out of the woodwork with this," he said.

"How do you know when this incident with Birch occurred?"

"We were working together at the time. It didn't mean anything to me then, but when I heard about Son of Sam later I called the cops."

"Can we somehow prove this happened when you say it did?"

"I don't know. I just know that's when he said it. When I later heard about Son of Sam, it hit me right away. You don't forget a guy saying something like that and flashing a gun around."

Sincere as Williams was, his explanation wasn't good enough. More was needed. "You said he was fixing your car—what kind of car was it?"

"That was my Chevelle—a '69," Williams immediately said.

"How long did you keep that car?"

"I don't recall for certain. I know I got rid of it and bought a '77 Volare, the car I'm driving now."

"Did you buy the Volare when it was new?"

"Yes."

I asked Williams to check his paperwork on the vehicle purchase. In thirty minutes, he called me back. "I bought the Volare in November '76. I have the material right here."

"Then if Birch fixed your Chevelle, and made that Son of Sam comment and waved the .44 at that time, it had to be before November '76."

"Jesus, yes."

Williams was elated, and his statement was forwarded to the district attorney. Brian Birch, however, had left the area and was said to be somewhere in Arizona. He hasn't been found. Birch, although he didn't resemble the Moskowitz-Violante gunman, was a hospital worker. There were hospital and medical connections all over the case, ranging from victims' jobs to other links involving several suspects, including Reeve Rockman, who'd once worked at a Manhattan hospital. The connections were too many to be dismissed as coincidental, and more would soon surface.

Williams also said that Birch was friendly with another man named Chet Brown,* a former Bronx resident who moved to Connecticut. This information was of considerable interest because Chet Brown from that same Connecticut city was observed at the Carr home in October 1977—apparently visiting Michael Carr. I'd copied his license number at the time, and it had been in my file for four years. That Chet Brown and the one Williams knew also had the same middle initial. This information was forwarded to Queens as well.

Birch and Brown remain as possible suspects. And they were about to be joined by a number of others.

The Queens investigators and I were aware that the case was bigger than what we'd thus far been able to root out in New York. There was, of course, the Arlis Perry murder and the mysterious Charlie Manson II. But none of us was prepared for what was about to happen.

The Son of Sam case was poised for a huge upward leap into the ranks of monied society.

And with it would come more murders.

From the Belly of the Beast

In July 1981 an apprehensive David Berkowitz was unexpectedly transferred from Attica to the Clinton Correctional Facility in Dannemora, New York. Located in the northeast corner of the state near the Canadian border, the ancient gray behemoth was the most inaccessible prison in the system. Left behind at Attica, to John Santucci's chagrin, were valuable informants. But ahead at Dannemora were others, more than one of whom was eventually removed from that facility and separated from Berkowitz.

Frankly, the succession of moves was suspicious and would be noted as such by the district attorney's office and myself.

These prisoners, and one prime outside contact, provided important information about the case. All knew Berkowitz well. To each, Berkowitz revealed intimate details, particulars which overlapped and were repeated to us by the informants, who were with Berkowitz during time periods ranging from 1979 to 1985.

To protect these sources, who may someday be asked to testify in a court of law and whose lives may be in jeopardy, the information they provided will be attributed here to two composite characters, whom I will call Vinny and Danny. The real names and letters or statements from each of them are in the possession of the Queens district attorney, who developed two of them. Others were cultivated by me.

As the information contained common elements, the road to confirmations was a single one. This consistency enhanced the informants' credibility and that of Berkowitz, who, it turned out, was relating the same details he first described to us in 1979–80—but with one major difference. With his fellow prisoners, and others, he filled in blanks he'd left for us to decipher as clues. They said he was open with them for several reasons, one of which was his desire to explore the possibility of obtaining legal assistance for himself and protection for his family should he decide to step forward. He thought, in the case of at least two of the informants, that their attorneys might be willing to assist him, and so he briefed the inmates to elicit their opinions on what their lawyers might be able to do for him. He ultimately decided against pursuing the matter.

With both Berkowitz and the informants, it was a relatively simple, although time-consuming, task to compare statements and letters written over a period of years to determine if their versions remained consistent. They did. And the written material was bolstered by more than a dozen visits I made to various prisons around the state, interviewing the sources personally on multiple occasions. Vinny and Danny were repeating the same stories in 1986 that they originally told between 1979 and 1985.

I personally spent many months fleshing out the allegations, and was assisted by the Greenburgh Police Department in Westchester, Yonkers's Lieutenant Mike Novotny, retired NYPD homicide detectives Joe Basteri and Hank Cinotti, and others who requested anonymity because of career considerations.

Information was then compared with that unearthed by the Queens investigators, and it meshed.

With that background, the stage is set.

*   *   *

In October 1981, with the Santucci interview now public, Berkowitz was aware the DA believed the conspiracy existed. He'd earlier told Vinny and Danny that both John and Michael Carr were in the cult and that John Carr, at least, was a triggerman.

He hadn't said whether or not Michael was a gunman, but did tell them that while he was already "drifting" toward satanism at the time, his chance meeting with Michael in the Bronx brought him into the group's clutches when Michael invited him to the party at the Barnes Avenue apartment building. Berkowitz had also revealed that the cult was larger than he thought we in New York were aware of.

Now, in mid-October, he told Vinny that the group planned a murder for Halloween.

Halloween was one of the major satanic holidays and, based on what Vinny heard, the killing would serve a dual purpose: a cult sacrifice and the elimination of yet another weak link. "It is to be an inside, housecleaning thing," Vinny wrote.

He said Berkowitz felt powerless to stop it. But how did Berkowitz know what the group was planning?

According to Vinny, outside contacts monitored Berkowitz and kept him apprised of the cult's activities. This statement has also been supported by independent information. Vinny was shocked to hear that a murder was planned. He wrote the following letter to a close friend, summarizing some of the details he learned:

> *If Santucci cares, you may share all of this with him. I want you to give him all. Most of this means zip to me. But I can tell just reading it over that things are significant that I don't even realize myself. Time is critical. I'll take my chances. This is all true. It's true as I write it, as I see it. I'll try to be objective. The D.A. can take them for what they are worth.*
>
> *I want no deals. No publicity. These sickies have a fetish. Their favorite mode of murder is gunshots. They blow people's heads off. I have a family. I also have a head and want to keep it.*
>
> *Santucci does not have to play games with me. I fully expect he will dissect me and my motives. It's a price I have to pay. I'm not exactly*

eligible for sainthood. All I can do is shut up if some lunatic starts turning this into publicity.

My main concerns here are two things. That October 31 crime they planned, and giving as much as I safely can on the "Group." Because November 30 is the next date. Then New Year's. I am not psychic but already I've "predicted" 3 crimes.

Drugs are involved. I feel the real key to exposing the Group is through drug and porn connections. Illegal weapons are also, but not as good 'cause that's sporadic. And they already have arsenals. But they need steady supplies of drugs for their own "parties" and to make money. And remember, those who head this may not believe this crap about Satan. They believe in how people can be led and used. Used in a very effective way. Sickeningly effective.

They saw a good thing. I don't believe it was always this sophisticated. But they are expanding. And when you touch drugs and porn and call girl type operations and daughters of middle-class people at school, things get hot. 'Cause politicians may be involved. Or influential persons. So I'm scared, to put it mildly. If I get wind they blew someone's head off October 31, I may go catatonic.

Tell Santucci this is real. Screw my inhibitions. Look—whoever heads this isn't from the City. At least, he lives outside. I think Jersey or Long Island. At least, he has some sort of big place. A regular Hugh Hefner place for parties, kinky sex. And people come from all over. Most people there are upper middle class. This group has strong holds in a lot of ways. Besides "dedication" is "intimidation" or "guilt"—but fear is strongest. And Berkowitz' fear is real.

He said to me that if I said certain things he told me he'd just deny it. Not maliciously—but these people blow heads off! Blackmail exists, also. Or people won't talk because they're co-conspirators.

Now listen, you know that coven book where they write their crimes? Can't you see, I'm positive their "Dragon" doesn't write his crimes. (I never asked.) But that book is "insurance." The members figure it's occult but that book is insurance against rats. This is not a nickel-and-dime group of people out for "kicks." Doctors and lawyers do not have to be so flamboyant. This group has got to offer something of substance. Something very "lucrative" for someone.

When was Donna Lauria shot? Cause DL has a special significance. This I verified. They cover certain "target crimes" by unrelated other crimes. To cloud the picture.

This is the type of Group that can move into an unknown area and win "converts" fast. Sex, drugs, homosexuality—many members educated and good-looking. Fun parties. Big "mansions" of sex. They call them mansions. "In their Father's (Satan's) house are many mansions." Or "palaces"—sick people. They go for "retreats," too. I am not nuts. I will just say what I was told.

I have things which lead me to suspect they may have filmed (or videotaped) many of these crimes. I have more than a suspicion. They have certain killings on film.

That revelation alone will get me wasted. I'm destroying my notes. I must. Too dangerous.

They not only ransacked Berkowitz' place to make him look "mad," but he was supposed to "get caught" in a final act. No, I suspect different. He does also. He knows his days are numbered. That's why he came to me. He needs J.S. [John Santucci] 'cause dammit, this insane stuff is true.

Keep these things [coded notes compiled earlier]:

I went to see my fortune story behind the brownstone in Brooklyn Heights, 'cause I went to NYU [New York University] at that time. That night, I met my date in Washington Square Park. Tom, and Ronald, and David were there, too. We had some coke [cocaine] and a hamburger. We then saw a movie: "Frankenstein Meets Mickey Mouse" and "Rodan, the Flying Monster."

Narvoe and Ebee and Sissy Spacek and Rudi Kazooti were there.

Roy Rogers and Dale Evans are my favorite stars. Next to James Camaro who is white but dresses like an Indian.

We were a regular jet set of the occult. Kennedy assassination taught that conspiracy theories are thought of as fairy tales. The insane act solo. . . .

On October 31, look for a kinky or bizarre assassination. Male(s) and female(s). Their heads shot off. . . . And they'll remove the evidence like when they ransacked Berkowitz' place. Or leave misleading clues like in 1977. Just keep this in mind if you stumble on something. A Halloween shooting. That will convince me.

Vinny's letter contained many confirmations of earlier, unpublished information Berkowitz had provided. Among them, of course, was the statement that affluent people were involved with the group. The following facts, in addition to those unearthed in Bismarck, North Dakota, supported that contention:

When Berkowitz was arrested, he possessed a list of telephone numbers, which were barely investigated by the NYPD. No names accompanied these particular numbers, and the NYPD simply dialed them and wrote down notations such as "female answers" or "no answer." That was the extent of the Police Department's work.

However, with the original paperwork in hand, I was able to enlist sources in the telephone company to identify the names behind the mysterious numbers. In light of what Vinny (and, earlier, Berkowitz) wrote about doctors and lawyers being connected to the cult, the results of the Berkowitz phone numbers search were intriguing.

One number was identified as that of an exclusive country club in Long Island's Hamptons area: the Montauk Golf and Racquet Club. Two other numbers were listed to the Long Island summer residences of Yonkers doctors; these were *not* office numbers.

Another number was that of a private residence in East Hampton, another belonged to an unlisted telephone in West Babylon, Long Island, and a final number was listed to a private home on exclusive Shelter Island, Long Island.

There was, simply, no legitimate reason for Yonkers postal clerk David Berkowitz to possess these telephone numbers. Moreover, he didn't list any names next to them.

Berkowitz also had the phone number of the Fort Harrison Hotel in Clearwater, Florida—a facility owned and operated as a major training center by the Church of Scientology. This further cemented his relationship with middle-level Scientology official Michael Carr, at the least.

Regarding the rest of Vinny's letter, he said that—contrary to the official belief at the time—some of the Son of Sam victims were chosen targets, and not randomly selected victims. Santucci had suspected this for some time, and his investigators had been seeking links between some of the victims.

Vinny named Donna Lauria, slain in the Bronx on July 29, 1976, as one of those deliberately selected for death. He further stated that some of the .44 shootings occurred at random to cover up the targeted incidents.

He also said that a major leader of the group lived in a large, freewheeling mansion in either New Jersey or Long Island; that the group was involved in drug, porno and call girl operations involving college-age girls; that shipments of illegal weapons were sometimes part of the picture—and that at least one Son of Sam murder was filmed, or videotaped, by the group.

Without exception, these allegations were explosive, to put it mildly. They were also so complex and elaborate that we immediately suspected there was at least some truth to them.

In the coded section of Vinny's letter, he was, I later learned, describing the murder of Stacy Moskowitz and the blinding of Robert Violante. Some of the coded names were said to refer to participants in that attack—which was alleged to have been videotaped by the cult. As Vinny later wrote me: "Videotapes. Snuff films. The killing of Stacy Moskowitz is on film. It draws a high price. The sick bastards. But this is 'business.' The whole Moskowitz killing was orchestrated. The whole 'capture' was. Analyze the events yourself. [Vinny didn't know Berkowitz had already revealed details of that operation to me.] You'll feel like a fool for ever having believed differently. Sickeningly, this whole nightmare is real. I have a good idea where the films and 'ritual book' [the log of coven crimes] are. But a premature leak could get them 'lost.'"

* * *

"Lost" was one thing; dead was another—as in murdered on Halloween. As Vinny later wrote: "I had two locations, Brooklyn Heights and the Village [Greenwich Village]. I didn't know which was to be the place, except it was to be one of them. Berkowitz didn't know either. And he didn't know it would be that guy. When I sent out that code, I didn't know that the guy who turned out to be the victim was among those names." And why was he killed? "He was afraid he was going down on drug dealing. He was about to help the cops [Santucci]—to tell it all. And he was gonna make a copy of the videotape. And *stills.* They wasted him. It served a double purpose."

The dead man was, logically enough, a photographer. He was referred to twice in the coded Vinny letter. First as "Ronald." Next as "Sissy Spacek." His name: Ronald Sisman, and Vinny had written down his name two weeks *before* the murder, which occurred on the night of October 30, or shortly after midnight on Halloween, in Sisman's Manhattan brownstone at 207 West 22nd Street, on the fringe of Greenwich Village. Technically, the neighborhood was known as the Chelsea section.

In December, Vinny, not even realizing that he'd listed Sisman's name in October, wrote to the same friend to whom he'd sent the earlier letter. "The name, I believe, was Sisseck (sp?). A girl and he were shot. A coed from Massachusetts. Sisseck was [planning] a deal with the D.A. He was gonna produce the videotapes."

Vinny wrote that Berkowitz hadn't told him personally about the motive for Sisman's murder, but that a mutual prison associate had filled him in. Vinny later said to me:

"Berkowitz had told me about Sisseck, and he told me an inside job was in the works for Halloween. But he didn't say that Sisseck was the planned victim. I don't think he knew it. He was getting info from outside, but there was a lag sometimes. But he knew Sisseck before. He'd been to his brownstone with Michael Carr . . . He told me Sisseck was dealing, and that there was a party going on when they got there. He saw the chandelier. Berkowitz waited while Michael Carr got the stuff."

As a confirming note, the building was indeed a brownstone, and there was a chandelier on the premises, along with a hanging Tiffany lamp.

According to Vinny, Ronald Sisman had been at the scene of the Moskowitz-Violante shooting and may have videotaped the attack himself. If not, he assisted whoever operated the camera.

"It was either him or that guy 'Mickey' ["Mickey Mouse" in the coded letter]. I have no idea who he is. I also think Manson II might have assisted the filming, but I'm not sure."

Sisman, thirty-five, was a Canadian native whom police described as a photographer, procurer and dope dealer. He and Elizabeth Platzman, twenty, a Long Island resident and a student at posh Smith College in Massachusetts, were both shot in the back of the head, execution style. Her hands were bound behind her with a cord; his weren't. The apartment, as Vinny also predicted, was totally ransacked.

Police established that the ransacking—at least most of it—occurred after the killings—that is, that sometime between the murders and the discovery of the bodies, the apartment was entered and torn apart.

As Vinny also wrote, and this was confirmed by the police, Sisman, a drug dealer, was paranoid about what he believed was an impending arrest on drug charges related to the sale of large amounts of cocaine. Police theorized that the killings were the result of a dope burn and that the killers may have been looking for a large amount of cash Sisman might have had in the brownstone.

However, as the police conceded a year later, the killings were unsolved, and if the word "tape" was substituted for "cash," the entire scenario fit perfectly.

"We've got a reentry here," I told Herb Leifer. "I think they came in the first time and Sisman told them the tape was in some bus locker or whatever. He thinks that's going to spare him, but they kill him anyway. Then they go to where the tape was supposed to be hidden—only it isn't there. So that's when they come back and tear the brownstone apart looking for it. Apparently, they got it.

"Sisman probably copied the thing for his own insurance before the original left his possession. And he probably then told somebody he thought he could trust that to get out of this feared drug bust, he'd give Santucci the tape in exchange for a ticket out of the country. Only he told the wrong person and was whacked before he could move."

"It seems to fit," Leifer said. "I'm just amazed that people inside that damned prison know all these details about a double murder that went down in Manhattan."

"I don't see how there could be anything but a pipeline," I answered.

Santucci's office viewed the Sisman-Platzman murders from a safe distance. They occurred in Manhattan, not in Queens, and no arrests were made.

"If Sisman was one of them, he can't help us now either," Santucci said. "That list keeps getting longer."

The district attorney wasn't offering a casual opinion. He knew that Vinny previously alleged that college girls were involved in the ring; and the murdered Elizabeth Platzman was an out-of-state student. He also knew about the Berkowitz phone numbers. And he was likewise aware that information which supported the shocking charge that the Moskowitz-Violante shooting was videotaped had been uncovered.

*   *   *

Specifically, in 1979, when Berkowitz was organizing "Operation Photo" with Lee Chase, he requested that a particular news clipping be sent to Lieutenant Gardner and Felix Gilroy. The article reported that the FBI was probing leads that a Philadelphia schoolteacher named Susan Reinert had been slain in a Black Mass ritual and the event *recorded on film*. Until Vinny's letter two years later, we had no idea why Berkowitz wanted that clipping sent out. Now the implication was clear.

Additionally, I delved into the Moskowitz case again, and a close scrutiny of the events surrounding the shooting revealed the following:

—Berkowitz told the police that Tommy Zaino and his date were the original targets but that "plans were changed" when Zaino pulled from beneath the streetlamp. Why? Why abandon Zaino because he pulled to a darker spot, which should have been more desirable? And why shoot Violante and Stacy, who then pulled into the same spot beneath the bright sodium streetlamp? The presence of a camera and optimum lighting conditions would answer those questions.

—In the same vein, why weren't Violante and Stacy attacked in the darkened park, where they'd gone to ride the swings shortly before the shots were fired? They passed right by the killer, who, as Violante stated, was leaning against the restroom building. So why not shoot them at that time, rather than wait until they returned to the brightly illuminated car, which was in clear sight of witness Zaino as well? A camera's presence would also answer those questions.

—And why, as several witnesses reported and the composite sketches showed, was the killer wearing a wig that night? No evidence of wigs surfaced at any other .44 incident. An attempt to conceal one's features from a camera's eye would provide an answer to that question.

—Finally, if a camera was on the scene, where was it located? Mrs. Cacilia Davis, who was at the murder site five minutes before the shooting while walking her dog, told us in 1979 that, in addition to Violante's and Zaino's occupied autos, a Volkswagen "bus" (a van) was parked across the street and slightly behind the victims' car. The killer would pass directly in front of this van en route to the Violante auto. Although it was on the scene minutes before the attack, the van's existence wasn't noted in any police report. While this isn't proof the van contained camera equipment, it does provide a reasonable answer as to where such material may have been situated and why the van left the scene before the police arrived. And for the alleged macabre filming, the vantage point was an excellent one.

It is my personal opinion, based on the evidence and my familiarity with the sources and the case, that the videotape exists.

As for Sisman himself, an association between him and Michael Carr came as no surprise. Sisman was a photographer; Michael Carr, a photographer and illustrator. As the Carr family told Queens investigators in 1979, many of Michael's friends in business and on the Manhattan disco circuit—also traveled by Sisman—were professional photographers.

And on the subject of the videotape, it was clearly established that Sisman was friendly with a man who had a "thing" about bizarre videos—a man who lived in a sprawling mansion in Southampton, Long Island, which, curiously, was the site of Berkowitz's alleged mass-murder-in-a-disco plan. Somehow, all roads were now leading to Rome.

That man was mentioned in Vinny's coded letter as well. He was called both "Roy Rogers" and "Rodan the Flying Monster." Once again, as in the case of Sisman, Vinny had the name of one "Mr. Big"—although he didn't know it then. I wouldn't either, until the spring of 1982.

* * *

In November, the other source, Danny, ventured forth with his information, which was identical to Vinny's. He wrote:

> *Weapons were never carried in cars. They were always conveniently near locales. The weapon (and letter) so conveniently exposed in Sam's [Berkowitz's] car was a set-up. How anyone fell for it is beyond me. It was all planned. The [Son of Sam] letters were dictated. So was the log of arsons. Dr. David Abrahamsen [the court-appointed psychiatrist] almost stumbled on it. He once asked Sam how he "thought up the story."*
>
> *Sam panicked. Not because it would show he was lying, but because he thought the cops had broken the whole plot. Breslin was used—made a fool out of. His ego played right into their hands. Everyone's did. Breslin, Craig Glassman, old man Carr. They could "rely" on these clowns. People like that are predictable. They [the group] could never have spread the lies as effectively as these unwitting "allies" did. The letters were a scam. They were dictated. Even Abrahamsen saw the one to Breslin was out-of-character for Sam.*
>
> *They were "tests." The public was fed a little. All they [the cult] had to do was sit back and watch how the "glory hunters" (the "gory" hunters) wrote a script for them to build on.*
>
> *The irony is that the "Children" [the internal name of the cult] really did not think up this whole elaborate fairy tale [the original version]. The "experts" did. Those who the public trusted. Those supposedly "above" the sensationalism. I could name them, but you know who they are. And each of them can sleep nights knowing that their egotistical greed kept the truth from being found out. And because of that, the list of innocent victims grew.*
>
> *And it still grows. And there is still a cover-up. Ironic, months were spent trying to fit it all together. But once they got one confessor—no one seemed to really care to analyze "why" or "how."*
>
> *There were 22 disciples. You got one. That left 21, if I'm not mistaken.*
>
> *The one good that can come out of all this is that we recognize the weaknesses in our system and clean them up, so maybe these horrors can never happen again unchecked and on this scale.*

Those were the written words of a convict. And Danny went further, into specifics:

> *The motive is drugs. I have all the details. Some [.44 shootings] were "hits." Pornography is also involved. Also: snuff films on videotape. And that, sir, is proof. This is not just "sick." It is big business. Someone has gotten rich off the bloodshed. And I can back up every single word. I'll*

give you facts. What you do with them will determine how much you get. You see, I don't trust you.

I trust what Lincoln said. You can't make assholes out of the people forever. I think that's how he said it.

It's how I say it. The authorities are elected to protect, not to censor and cover up. Gannett [newspapers] is always bullshitting you care about the public's right to know.

Prove it. I've got my ass on the line. We have a deal to talk.

And my writing this letter is a commitment. I'm risking my life. Does that maybe "challenge" you? Even if they waste me, you got a story.

The "Children" were very literally being raised to kill. [This was a reference to wall writing in Berkowitz's apartment: "My children I'm raising to be killers. Wait 'til they grow up."] For very real reasons. There is a "Black Master." Only, he is not an illusion. Dr. Abrahamsen also came close to this realization. Berkowitz feared Abrahamsen knew, that he figured it out. Check the ballistics reports. More than one weapon was used. They can't "argue" around that one.

Those conflicting composites do not prove eyewitnesses are worthless. Perhaps they prove the cop-D.A.-political mentality is dangerously prejudiced. Sam was a "Squeaky Fromme"—nothing more glamorous than a patsy.

He laughed when he was apprehended. Sure, why not? It was orchestrated. Do you believe he actually transported guns like that? No. And the note, left out in the open, the visible gun. It was a set-up. The apartment was a set-up. Made to look like he was nuts.

They [the cult] didn't want a trial, nor an investigation. Things were getting hot, too many experts were involved. If the investigation continued, the truth would have been found out.

The truth. That elusive word we'd been chasing since August 1977 was now in sight. Danny proved he was close to Berkowitz by including a quote from a letter I had sent to the confessed .44 killer.

Later, in a personal interview, Danny amplified what he'd written. "I was told they bought more guns in Texas, at least, around the same time Sam was down there. . . . The cult never planned to have a '.44 killer.' The cops did that. Look at the composites. There were different people using different .44s early on. Then the cops come out with 'one guy and one gun.' The group laughed. That's when they decided to go along with the game. And they played it well—I mean they knew they could count on Breslin; that's why they used him. They sent him that letter with all sorts of clues in it and he creamed all over it. He was so thrilled that he got a fucking letter that he didn't even catch on to what they were really doing. You are not dealing with stupid people at the top of this," he said.

"What about the Borrelli letter and the hatred of Sam Carr and all that stuff that happened to him in Yonkers?" I asked.

"That was Michael Carr's idea. He hated his father so much that he wanted to torment the hell out of him. That's what all that was about. . . . And John Carr, Sam [Berkowitz] told me, also hated the old man because the father liked Michael more than him."

"So the term 'Son of Sam' began there?"

"Yeah, but it had another meaning, too, to the group. Something like 'Servants and Master'—SAM."

"Who did the Breslin letter?"

"It was a group effort. I think it was dictated by a woman. There were a lot of women in this; one was a leader." [Here, Danny was confirming information Berkowitz provided in 1979.]

"How big was this group?"

"In Westchester, there were those twenty-two, but with fringe people the number went higher. The 'Children' were the inner circle; twelve of them, I was told. That's who planned the Sam shootings."

* * *

According to Danny and Vinny, the cult originated in England. They didn't know the names "Process," "Chingon" or "OTO," but the English-origin information was enough to put it over the top. Both the Process and Aleister Crowley's OTO were rooted in England.

The group had a main headquarters near Los Angeles, and both confirmed that Manson II was from L.A. and was involved in the Arlis Perry murder. He was also involved in at least one Son of Sam shooting, they said—that of Christine Freund.

Vinny's description of the cult's philosophy also matched that espoused by the original Process, and generally that of the OTO. He explained the theology in depth to a minister friend of his, who wrote:

> *The cult bases its theology on a strange mixture of apocalypses from Daniel, Revelation, II Esdras, II Adam and Eve, and the Gospel of the Essenes. Of particular interest is the timetable in Daniel and Beast of Revelation whose number is 666. According to Daniel, after a "time, two times, and half a time," there will be a "time of trouble such as has never been since there was a nation until that time."*
>
> *The cult interprets this to be 2,300 years after the Book of Daniel was written, and we are now in that time of trouble.*
>
> *According to Revelation, Satan was an angel who was cast out of heaven and bound on earth. Earth is his realm. God is supreme, and the worship of Christ is elevating a man to the position of deity. This is wrong. Satan is the one who should be worshipped on earth to hasten the*

coming day of the Lord. This day must be preceded by the time of trouble, the Armageddon of Revelation—and one goal of the cult is to help it along by promoting dissension, confusion, and holocaust. They look upon the destruction wrought by Hitler as a warm-up for what's coming—and they want to be in on the big event. They see their murders, etc., as a divine mission.

The reverend wrote that the marks of the cult, its signs, were "666," "HT" and "HH" for "Hitler" and the German SS lightning bolts. "All are marks of the beast, Satan-Hitler, whom they serve."

This information was confirmed by the fact that the initials "HH," never made public, were written on the back of the envelope in which Berkowitz enclosed one of the threatening letters he mailed to Sam Carr. We also possessed information contained in a 1977 police report in which an acquaintance of Berkowitz stated that Berkowitz "possessed and wore Nazi insignia." Of course, along with numerous other items—including at least two guns Vinny and Danny said Berkowitz owned—these articles were missing from his Yonkers apartment at the time of his arrest. One of the missing guns apparently was the .38 revolver Berkowitz showed to the sheet metal workers.

The reverend added that the Sam cult specialized in three types of crime:

> *All rapes, murders and arson jobs take place in the vicinity of coven meetings. In the last Son of Sam murder [the Moskowitz-Violante shooting], the coven members were assigned definite stations according to ritual significance in a nearby playground. Rapes are for the purpose of deflowering a virgin, which has special significance for Satan worshippers. Arson is a symbol of the great conflagration, or Armageddon, and murders are to spread confusion and to fulfill the prophecy in Daniel: "But the wicked shall do wickedly."*
>
> *Before each coven meeting, Satan has to be appeased by the rape of a virgin [young girl], a holocaust [arson], or the ritual murder of a person or animal.*

Berkowitz certainly informed Vinny of some deep, philosophical matters. But there was more. As the reverend reported:

> *There are about 1,000 persons in the cult, nationwide. In the east, a headquarters is in an abandoned church, privately owned, in [a New York area town]. A present and active member of the cult who is still committing crimes worked for [a Westchester automaker]. He is married to the daughter of one of the . . . executives.*
>
> *John Carr and Mike Carr were in David Berkowitz' coven. Other*

murders by the cult: Arlis Perry; a girl in Santa Monica, California, late 1977; John Carr, North Dakota; Mike Carr, New York City." [Berkowitz told Vinny that both Carr brothers were murdered. Our analysis of their deaths had not been made public.]

A girl from Valhalla [Westchester County] stumbled onto a coven meeting [before Berkowitz's arrest]. She was raped and brutalized and told to keep it quiet. She did. One month later she died of a drug overdose. [Vinny also wrote that the cult committed a rape at the time of one of its meetings in Untermyer Park. Yonkers police confirmed that such an assault took place late at night near St. John's Hospital, which adjoined the park.]

So concluded the reverend's report on his pivotal meeting with Vinny. The synopsis was submitted to the Queens district attorney, and later to me, by the minister.

"I doubt anybody could be making this up," Herb Leifer said. "It's just too thorough and specific."

"If I was lying, I'd say John and Michael did it all with Berkowitz and that was that," I responded.

"Yeah," Leifer said. "They *want* the DA to have the information. These guys could testify as to what they were told, but unless Berkowitz himself or some other member backs it up on the stand we're in that hearsay evidence situation again. It's good stuff, but it still doesn't give us what we need to prosecute."

*   *   *

Leifer was correct, unfortunately. But in another sense, the case may have been growing too large for the Queens district attorney's office. The nationwide scope of the group and its origins were now clearly stated. Since neither Vinny nor Danny recognized the words "Process", "Chingon" or "OTO," I suspected Berkowitz hadn't mentioned them, although in his own letters he'd specifically referred to the Chingons.

To me, it was now apparent that whatever name the group used in New York, it had first sprung from the Satan slice of the original Process pie, and then altered its identity to avoid scrutiny. There was no evidence available to demonstrate the parent Process was involved. But it will be recalled that Process members were free to worship either Jehovah, Lucifer or Satan. It was not difficult to see where this offshoot hung its hat, or how it had evolved.

In fact, Berkowitz would soon state that the Sam cult was a "violent offshoot" of Scientology. That remark specified that the original Process fostered the .44 group.

Cults, as many experts confirmed, changed names frequently as circumstances demanded. The actual name wasn't all that important—but the original theology and networking was.

As for the claim that approximately one thousand people nationwide belonged to the cult, this figure, while startling and ominous, was not incredible. Berkowitz, as far back as Marcy in 1978, had said he believed he was protecting "hundreds." And the original Process, with its cells in numerous American cities, stated as early as 1969 that two hundred people in the United States joined the movement. Additionally, the Process actively sought alliances with existing occult groups such as the Crowley-worshipping OTO. So, with expansion and recruitment since then, it was not beyond the realm of possibility that offshoot or related ranks increased their numbers by some seven or eight hundred across the country by 1977. And of course, the figure may have been somewhat exaggerated by those who provided it to Berkowitz.

Vinny and Danny also quoted Berkowitz as saying Charles Manson was a member of the cult. This, too, blended with everything we learned, or would learn, including Berkowitz's "offshoot of Scientology" remark. Author Ed Sanders and Manson prosecutor Vincent Bugliosi both believed Manson was affiliated with the Process. In his book *Helter Skelter,* Bugliosi said that two Process members from Cambridge, Massachusetts, visited him to dissuade him from that belief. Those same two Processans then called on Manson in prison—after which Manson stopped talking about the Process.

Prior to that, Bugliosi had privately asked Manson if he knew Robert DeGrimston (Moore), head of the Process. Manson said he'd met Moore. "You're looking at him," Manson said. "Moore and I are one and the same." Bugliosi believed Manson was saying that his ideas mirrored Moore's. We would find out considerably more than that.

Taking Bugliosi a step further, Sanders strongly suggested in *The Family's* hardcover editions that Manson belonged to a secret Process chapter in southern California. (Threatened legal action by the Process resulted in the removal of direct references to the cult from the American paperback editions. In England, after court action, there were no deletions from the book.)

Sanders was able to carry his investigation one level deeper than Bugliosi. But in a sense, both men were right. I didn't know it yet, but we'd soon begin our own exploration of the Manson-Process relationship.

*   *   *

Since the reverend assumed the important job of documenting the Sam cult's theology, I was able to focus on the crimes themselves. Cult members, the informants said, sometimes told rape victims: "Call Satan your father"; and they added that the group met, depending on cycles of the moon, on Thursdays. This allegation dovetailed with North Dakota reports that John Carr's group there also met on Thursdays.

Cult members were also said to bind themselves with a "symbolic cord" to indicate bondage to Satan just as he was bound to earth. Some victims (perhaps Elizabeth Platzman) were also tied in this manner. The informants further alleged that some cult members were tattooed—sometimes beneath the upper lip—with one of the group's signs. Others, they said, had pierced ears, as did John and Michael Carr.

The informants said Berkowitz's ear wasn't pierced, and they didn't know if he was tattooed. But they said not all members were thusly marked.

The rape allegations complemented the "John Wheaties, rapist and suffocater of young girls" alias; and we'd also earlier established that John Carr dated thirteen-to-fifteen-year-old girls in Minot. Further, the note Berkowitz left in his apartment referred to John as a "terrible rapist and child molestor." Now it was all coming together.

The group reasoned that Hitler was worthy of worship for several reasons. One of which, the informants said, was a numerology timetable in which each letter of the alphabet was assigned a number. Under this system, A equaled 100 and Z was matched with 125. The numbers which corresponded to the letters in Hitler's last name (107, 108, 119, 111, 104, 117) added to 666—the number of the great beast of the biblical book of Revelation. The devil's number.

At a dinner one night on City Island in the Bronx, Tom McCarthy and I discussed the new developments.

"Nothing surprises me anymore," he said. "I find it difficult to believe these sources could be dreaming all this stuff up. It can't really get more bizarre than it already is, right? We've got dead dogs and murder and a dead guy in North Dakota with 666 on his hand. What more do we need to get in Ripley's Believe It or Not?"

"Amen," I answered. "Nobody in the world knows about that writing on Carr's hand, and we get unsolicited word from the slam that 666 is one of their big signs and that they sometimes leave it at crime scenes."

I told McCarthy that I'd called the Westchester medical examiner on a hunch and learned that a young man named Anthony Varisco was slain in the recent past and had 666 tattooed in a triangular pattern on his hand—the same shape in which John Carr wrote "XXO" on the walls in Minot.

"Who the hell killed this Varisco?" McCarthy demanded.

"They said it was some squabble with a woman. It happened in Putnam, just over the Westchester border."

"So what does that mean to us?"

"It means we've got another local murder victim; this one with a damned 666 on him. Maybe he was tattooed under his lip, too, but he's in the ground now."

"Was this 666 thing on him made public?"

"No. And don't forget you've got that '78 Hirschmann case, where he was blasted just above the Putnam line and his wife knocked off in Queens. He had that Process-sounding 'Brother Tom' and swastika tattoo on him—and his name was Robert, not Tom."

"Yes," McCarthy replied. "Still unsolved, along with just about everything else connected to this mess. The only one we got was the Howard Weiss murder, and that involved his gay lover, at that. And this homo stuff is all over the Sam case."

"It's all bizarre," I said. "But not as bizarre as a lone lunatic claiming barking dogs told him to ice people. There were at least *real* motives: dope, porn, snuff films for big bucks."

"I guess so." McCarthy nodded. "Real motives for real crimes."

"Yeah, and how many wars were fought in the name of religion? To these people, at least the lower levels, this *is* some kind of perverted religion. Christ, and I thought the nuns in grammar school were bad."

"I'm not debating with you, for a change." McCarthy grinned. "It's just difficult to absorb it all sometimes."

"Hell yeah, but so was the idea of nine hundred idiots drinking poisoned Kool-Aid because Jim Jones told them to, but they did it. So was the idea that freaking Charlie Manson could hocus-pocus kids into butchering, but that happened, too. And San Francisco had those Zebra killings by that fucked-up band of Muslims who were shooting whitey at random to earn their 'death angel' wings. This isn't quite without precedent."

"That's all true," McCarthy agreed. "I'm just saying this thing keeps expanding and it's the most complicated case I've ever seen. It's like a goddamned maze."

"Don't feel bad," I said, laughing. "I started out thinking it was just Berkowitz and probably John Carr. I didn't ask for this either. But you can't just walk away from it."

"Ah, but don't you sometimes wish you could?" McCarthy asked, lowering his wineglass. "I know I do."

"You're not alone," I said. "And look at it, the NYPD had three hundred cops after Son of Sam. Now it's a much bigger case and we are sorely lacking in manpower. It stinks."

"That's why the DA is keeping focused on the Queens shootings," McCarthy explained. "After that, the rest may start to fall in place, or at least be worked on more. We don't like it any damn bit better than you do." There was little else I could say. As McCarthy noted, the case was mushrooming. And in late December 1981 another crime would be added to the roster of those suspected of being connected to the group's operations.

*   *   *

As the year wound down, the football Giants made the playoffs for the first time since the 1963 championship game, which they lost to the Bears, 14–10. This time, they knocked off the Eagles in the wild-card game before losing to the 49ers in the semifinals. For me, a long-term season-ticket holder, it was a euphoric December as the once great franchise lumbered awake after an eighteen-year hibernation. Also that month, Paul Davis's wistful recording of "Cool Night" played as Christmas trees sparkled. At the same time, WOR-TV broadcast a special *What's Happening, America* program which highlighted its major stories of the year. The three Son of Sam segments were condensed and featured prominently on the show.

Concurrently, we began wondering if yet another prison prediction would come true.

On November 27, Vinny had written:

> *Crimes continue. On October 31 was "something." I have details.*
> *I sent them out prior to then as insurance. But December 31 is the next date to watch out for. Publicity now would be rash, foolish, and lose a greater good. I want no publicity. None. And no "deals" with authorities. Is that enough to show you where I stand? My hope is to prevent any December 31 harm.*
> *If people get killed and then you have an interest—forget it. If you permit more bloodshed before you have the courage to risk your own reputations, you'll never accomplish any good, anyway.*

At this time, Vinny knew only that his information had been received; our face-to-face meetings and other contact had yet to occur. He wasn't aware that details he'd provided were being carefully scrutinized. The climate at Dannemora was too hot and the situation too precarious to permit any overt approaches to informants. Another prisoner, to whom Berkowitz had also spoken, had been removed from the cellblock and would be transferred from the facility. He'd been too openly occupied with the Berkowitz information, and it backfired on him. The other informants noted this and kept their roles secret.

John Santucci's office was cognizant of the December 31 warning, as were the Gannett newspapers' Mike Zuckerman and Yonkers's Lieutenant Mike Novotny. But we had no information as to what, if anything, would happen or where it would occur.

On November 30, a satanic holiday Vinny mentioned earlier, we'd noted several rapes and shootings—any one of which might have been cult-related. But we had nothing to work with; no way of knowing if any real connection existed. Now, on December 31, New Year's Eve, we waited and watched.

In the afternoon, I phoned Mike Novotny. "This is about the creepiest feeling I've ever had," I said. "Wondering if right now as we're talking somebody's about to get killed and others are plotting it while we sit here helpless."

Novotny managed a weak laugh. "I know what you mean. Happy New Year."

"Based on what he wrote, we should be looking for something bizarre involving a gun, and with head shots, if it's murder we're talking about. If it's rape or arson, that's something else," I suggested.

"With any luck, something will go down in our own backyard so we won't miss it," Novotny said. "If it's in the city, or somewhere else, we might not even hear about it. We can't possibly know everything that goes down in the metro area tonight. If it's gotta happen, I hope to hell it's around here."

*   *   *

The lieutenant's words were morbidly prophetic. Not four hours after our conversation, between six and seven p.m., forty-seven-year-old Joseph Carozza was shot to death on his forty-one-foot yacht, the *Sarc,* which was berthed at the Five Slip Yacht Club in New Rochelle—a city with multiple connections to the Son of Sam case.

Carozza, owner of a Bronx auto-body shop, was shot twice with a .38-caliber revolver. He was estranged from his wife, Patricia, a nurse, and had lived in the marina for six years.

A spokesman for the Westchester medical examiner's office said that Carozza, who was belowdecks, apparently began to climb a stairway to the main deck when he spotted his killer and tried to retreat below. One bullet was dug out of the stairway wall. Two others struck Carozza from behind: one in the back, the other in the head. December 31, gunshot, head, bizarre circumstances—the scenario was familiar.

Peter Zari, owner of the marina, told the Gannett newspapers: "To the best of my knowledge, he was never involved with anything underhanded. He's not that type of guy to get himself involved in a heavy—and this is a heavy."

The *New York Daily News* reported that an acquaintance of Carozza said that when word of the murder reached a New Year's party at a country club in the area at about nine o'clock that evening, a woman broke down hysterically and shouted: "I knew they were going to get him."

For its part, the New Rochelle Police Department was stymied—another familiar tune. "We're mystified completely," a department spokesman told Gannett. "I don't know why this guy got blown away. There's no immediate motive."

Maybe not, which in itself said something to us.

Mike Zuckerman, who'd periodically worked with me on the Sam investigation since late 1980, delved into the Carozza killing for more than one reason. In addition to the dire warning about December 31, Mike Novotny and I immediately suspected Carozza might be linked to another suspect in the .44 case. Zuckerman's digging paid off. Searching through old files in a courthouse, he learned that Carozza once underwrote a business loan for the suspect—a man Novotny and I thought could be the "Wicked King Wicker"—the remaining Breslin letter alias.

Zuckerman's research established the link. It didn't prove the cult was involved in Carozza's murder, but it did conclusively demonstrate that Carozza, slain on Vinny's targeted December 31, was tied to a man previously suspected in the .44 case. As such, it was a significant discovery and almost certainly not a coincidence. The reason: if the group didn't commit the crime, who did?

Throughout the .44 probe, I remained in the background while local police investigated the several crimes I suspected were tied to the Sam matter. My reasons for this were simple: I didn't want to be considered a gadfly; and detectives often resent reporters intruding into what they regard as their exclusive domain.

Much later, when it was apparent New Rochelle's investigation was unsuccessful,

I phoned the department and briefly outlined what we'd found, but the information wasn't made public.

The killing of Joseph Carozza remained unsolved.

*   *   *

With Carozza's death out of the headlines in a matter of days, I knew the time had come for meetings with Vinny and Danny. The information they'd provided, while good, was incomplete. It was certain they possessed more knowledge than that contained in the letters they'd written. Through a source, I was able to get a letter into Vinny. As we awaited his reply, the Son of Sam case would explode onto page one again. Berkowitz, silent so long, was about to speak.

His comments would be given in a sworn deposition taken by New York City attorney Harry Lipsig, a legend in Big Apple legal circles. The diminutive, white-haired and slender Lipsig was still, at eighty, a walking dynamo. Some dubbed him the "King of Torts"; I fondly regarded him as the "Mighty Mite." Harry's reputation grew with each case he handled. He counted among his clients a fair number of celebrities, including Roy Innis, head of the Congress of Racial Equality (CORE).

Innis and I developed a working relationship during the Atlanta child murders investigation, when he'd asked me to assist CORE's efforts to help solve that tragic series of slayings. Innis and his staff had unearthed troubling information which raised the distinct possibility that Wayne Williams, convicted of two of the killings, had acted in concert with others. CORE had developed a witness who said she was at one time part of the group.

The Georgia and federal authorities, not surprisingly, chose to disregard CORE's information and, although Williams was found guilty of but two killings out of more than twenty, the books were wiped clean. The CORE witness, whom I interviewed, alleged that drugs and satanism were the motives for the murders. In Atlanta today, a number of interested parties are still probing the case.

In the Son of Sam case, Innis's lawyer, Harry Lipsig, represented two victims—Sal Lupo and Robert Violante—in a multimillion-dollar civil suit filed against the Berkowitz estate. Lipsig and I had spoken several times about the Moskowitz murder and the cult, and Harry was convinced Berkowitz acted in concert with others. Accordingly, he obtained a court order to depose the confessed .44 killer as part of the civil action.

Surprisingly, Berkowitz cooperated to an extent, amplifying somewhat what he'd told me earlier. But he remained evasive, and at no time did he touch on the specifics into which he'd delved with Vinny and Danny. Nonetheless, he remained consistent, and his statements, importantly, coincided with established evidence. The deposition was taken at Dannemora on January 19, 1982. What follows are relevant excerpts.

Berkowitz, typically, began by saying he didn't want to cooperate with Lipsig. "I do not choose to answer a lot of these questions because they hurt me," he said. "As to their [the victims'] health and well-being, I have never challenged the money, so-called monies that are in the estate. They are welcome to that. I have never tried to get it. They can have it. I pled guilty to those crimes and there is nothing more I can say."

Lipsig then pressed. "Do you remember injuring Robert Violante?"

"No comment."

"Do you have any relatives?"

"One, yes. My father. Let's leave him out of this."

"Don't you think you ought to do something so he would have some pride in you, since you are concerned about him, obviously? Won't you do that, please? We can fence this way for days, man. What is the good of it all? Do you mean that you are devoid of all human feeling for these poor devils you injured?"

"It's not a question of feeling."

"You are not helping them when you can. I made it clear to you. You know, you say one thing and do another. Do you like to be in that light?"

"Continue with the questions," Berkowitz answered, and proceeded to claim responsibility for the .44 shootings. But Lipsig wasn't buying the story.

"Do you remember a Virginia Voskerichian shot in the face as she was walking home?"

"Yes."

"Did you do that?"

"No comment."

"Well, did you discharge a bullet that struck her?" He remained silent. "Don't you want to answer that question?"

"I don't want to answer the question."

"Does it move you that you killed her?"

"I know she is dead. There is nothing I can do. I cannot answer these questions anymore."

Lipsig didn't back away. He instead talked about John and Michael Carr. "Were they friends of yours?"

"No comment."

"Is there something with reference to them that you feel should not be told?"

"I would prefer not to say it without legal counsel."

"Do you know that they are both dead?"

"Yes."

"Do you realize that nothing can be done to them?"

"That's true, not to them directly."

"Well, to whom indirectly?"

"I would rather not say."

"Is it that there were other people involved besides Michael and John and yourself?"

"I would rather not say."

"But you are interested in protecting Michael and John—is that right?"

"Well, they have family."

"Did you get together with either Michael or John or both of them at some time before these acts of violence took place?"

"I cannot say, Mr. Lipsig."

Lipsig kept on, and Berkowitz kept dodging, saying he felt "a degree" of loyalty to the Carr brothers. Finally, he said: "This is pointless. I can't say any more without legal counsel." (Berkowitz had approached Vinny and Danny to seek legal help, possibly from their attorneys. His responses here confirmed their statements—he had no lawyer.)

"Were you a member of a cult?" Lipsig asked.

". . . If you keep probing along these lines, I am going to have to refuse to answer any more questions until I have legal counsel."

"Would you like to have counsel represent you?"

"There is no attorney I can think of."

"Suppose you were given a list of names of lawyers that might be interested and willing to represent you. Would you consider such a list?"

"I may."

"Is it then that if you had the benefit of the advice of counsel and if counsel said that it was in your interest to disclose whatever activities there were on the part of Michael . . . or John Carr—you would be willing to discuss it after counsel might have so advised you? Is that right?"

"It is possible."

Lipsig then asked how long Berkowitz had been acquainted with the Carr brothers. "A few years," he replied. Berkowitz then said he had "an idea" as to why John and Michael were dead, but that he wouldn't disclose it.

Lipsig then asked: "Are you in a position to clear them?"

"No."

"Is it then that you are worried about involving them? Frankly, is that it?"

"There is a lot more than that. I can't go into it."

"And when you say, 'It's a lot more than that,' then involving them is one of the things you are concerned about—but it's a lot more than that. Am I correct?"

"Yes . . . Mr. Lipsig, I cannot go further along that line of questioning."

"Without the benefit of counsel—is that it?"

"Without a lot of things."

"Well, what else?"

"A strong drink."

* * *

After a break, Lipsig returned to pertinent matters.

"You had some connection with the Church of Scientology, did you not?"

"It wasn't exactly that. But I can't go into it. I really can't."

"Were you connected in any way or an adherent or convert of the Church of Scientology?"

"No, not that way. It was an offshoot, fringe-type thing."

"Were John and Michael with the Church of Scientology?"

"Well, not really that church. But something along that line. A very devious group."

"Did this devious group have a name?"

"I can't disclose it."

"Roughly, how large would you say its membership was?"

"Twenty."

"Were they all residents of the New York metropolitan area?"

"No."

"Were they spread across the nation?"

"Yes."

"Did they meet on occasion?"

"Yes. But I really can't say more without legal counsel."

"Are you worried about involving people in the group, frankly?"

"I'm worried about my family, too. You know how treacherous some people can be. You don't have to dig it out from there."

"When you say you are worried about your family, who particularly in your family?"

"My father."

"How many of [the cult] would be in New York State, according to your best estimate?"

"Fifteen or so."

"Are they all males?"

"No."

"Could you give us roughly the percentage?"

"No, I couldn't."

"Would it be split pretty even?"

"Yes. Say approximately. I didn't say definite numbers."

"I take it very frankly . . . that since you have clothed this group in anonymity, that included in the group were Michael and John Carr?"

"Yes."

"Do you have any thought that either John or Michael Carr lost their life through the activities of a member of this group?"

"Yes. Definitely."

"Well, don't you think . . . that they should be brought to justice?"

"I don't know where they are."

"What motive could the members of the group have [to kill John or Michael Carr]? Knowledge of your activities?"

"Yes. Violence, fear and rage."

"Desire to accomplish their silence?"

"Yes. And just plain sickness—moral sickness."

"Were [members] dedicated to violence?"

"Yes, and depravity and everything else."

"And the depravity that you speak of would be of what nature?"

"Everything."

"Sex?"

"Yes. The opposite of everything that is good."

"Murder?"

"Yes. God gives life and they take it."

"Have they taken life other than what you have taken?"

"To my understanding, yes."

"How much of it in New York?"

"I cannot say . . . a lot of that occurred before I was there, as far as I know."

"Did they inspire the [.44] shootings?"

"I suppose they were my fault. I am responsible . . . I can't lay blame on anyone but myself."

"Do you know how many members are still alive?"

"Half."

"Was Sam Carr a member of the group?"

"No."

"But John and Michael were?"

"Yes. Could we sort of change the questioning?"

*   *   *

Lipsig then took up the matter of specific Son of Sam crime scenes. Regarding the Moskowitz-Violante shooting in Brooklyn, Berkowitz acknowledged the presence of the yellow Volkswagen.

"Did you know the person in that Volkswagen?"

"Well, I would rather not say."

"Bluntly, was it a member of the group?"

"I cannot say."

"Was any member of the group within the vicinity of these [.44] shootings?"

"Yes."

"How many members of the group were present at all of them?"

"I would say two or three—four."

"Did any of them designate victims?"

"Yes."

"Was it three or four at each incident?"

"Yes. Males and one female."

"Was the idea of a series of [shootings] planned?"

"Yes."

"Did you join in the planning?"

"Yes. . . . Mr. Lipsig, if this is going to be made to the press—"

". . . Was there any underlying name or type of identification that was used in selecting the victims . . . ?"

"I can't say."

"Was it you that left the letter for the police [the Borrelli letter at the Suriani-Esau murder scene]?"

"I would rather not say."

"Was it a member of the cult . . . ?"

"I would rather not say."

"Was the letter in your handwriting?"

"I would rather not say."

"It wasn't in your handwriting, was it?" Berkowitz didn't answer. "Was it?"

"I'd rather not say."

"You hesitated when I asked you whether it was in your handwriting . . ."

"Look, this is a matter for the police. This is a civil court hearing for the police."

"You don't want to be a lawyer in this examination, do you?" Lipsig asked humorously.

"I want to protect my family from harm and avoid adverse publicity, because that is not necessary."

"And the publicity you're concerned about . . . might make clear to the world that there were members of the cult involved and your worry is safety for your father, and possibly others from this group—is that it?"

"Well—"

"Is that it?"

"Yes."

"Did members of the group in their crimes use knives as well as guns?"

"Yes." (This confirmed Vinny and Danny's statements that group members had "ritual knives," as did Berkowitz.)

"Did somebody else pick the name 'Wicked King Wicker'?"

"Mr. Lipsig, let's—can we deal with your client, please?"

"If it weren't for the possibility of harm to your father, would you feel that the other members of the group should be brought to justice?"

"Yes."

"You have told us that there were three or four [cult members] present on each occasion. Did they cooperate in any way?"

"Yes."

"How?"

"I would rather not say. I didn't really want to talk about this from the beginning, you see. But you were very insistent. I would have preferred to say nothing, because I just can't talk—get into this anymore. . . . I meant to ask you, who was your other client besides Violante? You said you had two."

"Lupo," Lipsig answered. He then asked about the circumstances of that shooting near the Elephas disco. "Of the three or four present . . . how many of those are still alive?"

"I believe one."

"So John and Michael were of the [other] three present?"

"Not always." (This statement was supported by the evidence, since John Carr's travels to New York were dated.)

"When Lupo was selected?"

"I believe so. I can't recall." (If so, the remaining accomplice who was still alive was almost certainly the sandy-haired, husky man with a mustache who watched the shooting and drove from the scene in the same direction as the shooter. He was driving a yellowish compact-sized car with its lights extinguished.)

"Shouldn't [the group] be brought to justice in view of what you indicated was their depravity and their addiction to violence?"

"Yes, but—"

"And if your father were given protection, would you then disclose and help to bring to justice these creatures addicted to violence and depravity?"

"I would like that. I can't obligate myself now. I have no legal counsel."

"I take it that all of the prior references to being inspired [by] demons and so forth was just a cover to protect them?"

"Indirectly, I guess."

"Why did you suggest that [the shootings were] inspired by demons? Did you have them in mind—the members of the group—as demons?"

"That was the general idea. But the idea to make it look like it was the act of a deranged madman."

"Did you ever feel that your life is in danger here?"

"Yes."

"How do you counter that danger?"

"You don't. You just—there is no—you just—I can't say."

"You live with it—is that the answer?"

"Yes."

* * *

Lipsig then turned his attention to the group again.

"Did you have any interest in any of the female members?"

"Yes. There were a few nice ones, physically."

"Would I be intruding too much on your personal life if I asked you if they were available to you physically?"

"Yes. I really don't want to talk about it."

"Did you ever hear the name Arlis Perry?"

"Yes. But again, this is not—you are going across the state. You're going across the United States. Let's deal with this, please."

"Didn't that involve, or wasn't there a member of the group involved in that?"

"Yes, there was."

"Now that [killing] was of somebody out of the state, [but] it's part and parcel of the whole picture of the conduct of a particular group—isn't that so?"

"True."

"What was the general idea of the group? Was it some kind of devil cult or—"

"I'm sorry. I can't get into this. It's too much to talk about."

"And I take it you have a concern for human beings?"

"Yes."

"And don't you think that concern should carry with it the idea of eliminating anything such as this cult engaged in?"

"Yes."

"Did you wear one of their costumes?"

"It wasn't exactly a costume . . . I suppose a costume would be fitting, but I don't wish to discuss it."

"Included in it, was there a particular type of hat and a particular type of gown?"

"For some."

"Would the officers have a special type of garment?"

"Yes."

"And what was the chief officer called . . . his title?"

"There were several, but—"

"Of the [approximately twenty in Westchester] how many were officers?"

"Three."

"And one of the three was a woman—am I right?"

"Yes."

"The big chief was a man?"

"Mr. Lipsig, please."

"How often did they meet?"

"I can't say right now."

"You have written about a number of these things to people."

"Very vaguely. I suppose it was a mistake."

"Coming back to Arlis Perry . . . don't you feel that . . . whoever was responsible for that innocent human being should be brought to justice?"

"Well, yes. But I'm in no position to talk right now." (It will be remembered that Berkowitz wanted Manson II arrested.)

"If your father were given absolutely unequivocal protection that would give you peace of mind, would you then disclose and bring to justice these individuals who engaged in murder and—"

"I might."

* * *

Lipsig then ascertained from Berkowitz that the group was mainly composed of white-collar workers; that it practiced its own rituals and killed animals as well as human beings. He then asked:

"Don't you feel that it's unreasonable that you have been the one that has been given up as the sacrifice?"

"Well, it's more to it than that. I can't elaborate."

"Did the group have a particular community as its . . . main base?"

"Well, there is, but I don't wish to say anything at this time regarding that."

"Was it in Yonkers?"

"In that vicinity."

"So that the officers were of that vicinity, obviously?"

"Yes."

"Was it the cult that sold you the idea of using the demons as a cover?"

"It could have been."

"Did you discuss the cult with any of the psychiatrists that interviewed you?"

"No."

"Did you avoid the subject with them?"

"Yes."

"Did you use the same gun every time or different time?"

"Just what is in my testimony in Queens—in the district attorneys' offices."

"I didn't hear you."

"Just what is in my testimony." (Berkowitz was hedging on the number of guns used.)

"What did you say there?"

"I was involved in this. I had the gun and I used it."

"Was it the same gun every time?"

"I fear getting into this. I know this is going to go to the media before it goes anywhere else and I don't want that. I don't need this. This type of publicity."

"So if it does, it's gone and it's finished. Someday it will come out. . . . Do you believe there is a possibility of their killing again when they feel safe?"

"This group, I can't say."

"Was there more than one group?"

"I have heard that there were others."

"Where did they get the animals they used in their rites?"

"I can't say."

"Would you say that you answered all my questions honestly?"

"To a degree. I mean, there are certain ones that I didn't wish to answer."

Lipsig then said: "I am convinced that you weren't the only person that injured this list of people involved in this case. Now, besides being present at the scenes and in the vague way you have indicated they were involved, didn't some of them at one time or another either supply a gun or themselves use a weapon with one or another of these victims?"

"It could be."

"Did the three or four that were present at each occasion always use more than one vehicle?"

"It was more than one."

"Besides the yellow Volkswagen, what other make vehicle?"

"Mine."

"And how many [accomplices] came with you to the Stacy Moskowitz-Robert Violante scene?"

"I believe it was three." (Vinny and Danny said there were more, if one counted the alleged camera setup.)

"How many were in your vehicle?"

"Two."

"And one in the Volkswagen?"

"Yes."

"Was that a male?"

"Yes."

"And was it a male or female in your car? My view of it was that it was a male."

"No comment."

"What weapon did that male have?"

"I don't know."

"Where did you get the bullets for your gun?" (Although Lipsig didn't know it then, the bullets in Berkowitz's possession when he was arrested were *not* those he purchased with his .44 in Houston, as he claimed in 1977.) Berkowitz now answered Lipsig with silence.

"The gun you got in Texas. Where did you get [the ammunition]?"

"The ammunition was purchased with gun," Berkowitz finally said.

"There was enough ammunition for all these shootings in that one trip to Texas?"

"As far as I know, yes."

"And when you say as far as you know, then somebody else got that [other] ammunition, since it's something you're not sure of in your own knowledge, isn't that so?"

"Yes."

"And that person who got the ammunition—that ammunition was supplied to you not all at one time but at various times as needed, isn't that so?"

"Yes."

*　*　*

With that final statement, Berkowitz asked that the session be brought to a close. Lipsig had done an excellent job, but all the good was about to be nullified.

Outside the prison, Lipsig met Associated Press reporter Rick Pienciak and gave him carefully selected details of Berkowitz's statement. The information was sketchy, but the resultant publicity backfired. Berkowitz had specifically stated he didn't want his comments to reach the media, and he also said he would consider cooperating with Santucci's probe if his father was protected and he found a suitable lawyer.

Berkowitz was enraged that any of his comments ended up in the press. He filed a complaint against Lipsig with the Bar Association (later dismissed) and refused to talk further. The aftershock was even more distressing because Berkowitz, before the deposition, had written Lipsig indicating a respect for the attorney and a desire to see justice served.

The offending material was essentially that which I'd already published and broadcast previously, with the exception of Berkowitz's inclusion of women in the group (which I'd known) and his statement that three or four cult members were at each crime scene. Lipsig kept the newest details secret. But it wasn't *what* was released that enraged Berkowitz then—it was that *anything* was released.

Rick Pienciak, who'd tried to downplay the investigation since Berkowitz showed him the exit two years earlier, now had his own story to write, and he did so either unknowing or uncaring of the fuse he was helping to light. Pienciak was functioning as a reporter, which was his job, but there would seem to be times when tomorrow's headline might defer temporarily to a potentially greater good. Lipsig, too, had the opportunity to reveal nothing.

But perhaps thinking the publicity would pressure Berkowitz to come forward, he chose otherwise. In any case, the news exploded, and in Queens, so did John Santucci's staff.

Executive assistant Tom Russo called me immediately. "Why the hell did this happen?" he demanded. "It's all over the front page of the *Post,* and God knows where else. This is going to drive Berkowitz right back into his hole. And there's nothing really new here in the papers; you put most of this out last year."

"Well, Gannett and WOR are putting it in perspective," I said. "But the rest of the media are just reading the AP wire. I don't know who did what, but Harry isn't averse to publicity and Pienciak's had the rag on for the case since he got the old Berkie boot."

"We can't do anything about him," Russo said. "But we've got to bring Harry on board. You know him—can you see if he'd be willing to come over for a meeting?"

"I'm sure Harry will come," I answered.

*   *   *

On January 25, six days after the deposition, Lipsig and I sat in the DA's office with Santucci and Russo, who'd recently joined the .44 investigation.

Santucci wasted no time in laying his cards on the table. "Nobody knows more about this case than Maury, myself and Herb Leifer, who can't join us today," he told Lipsig. "Anybody else you may have been talking to is uninformed. So I'm going to bring you up to date, and if you're willing, we'd like you to assist us from here on. Berkowitz has consistently refused to see me—but you saw him and you may have the opportunity to do so again," the DA explained.

"I will file the papers immediately," Lipsig said, and described his session with Berkowitz. "I'd known about this cult, but Berkowitz impressed me with his intelligent, matter-of-fact demeanor. He was sincere, and I'm convinced he was telling the truth.

The man is sound as a dollar."

"We know," Santucci responded, and then told Lipsig about the difficulties he'd encountered with the NYPD on the investigation—calling some of the department's top brass "obstructionist." He also mentioned his suspicion that certain prison transfers might have been motivated by a desire to isolate Berkowitz from informants.

"This is outrageous," Lipsig angrily said. "I thought the DA's office was all-powerful."

"Not in this case, it isn't," Santucci replied. "I have suspicions, Harry, but no proof. And as far as the PD is concerned, they need to obtain permission from above before they give us any Berkowitz material we need."

"Everywhere you look there are roadblocks, Harry," I explained. "And based on what I've been hearing from my sources, there's big money somewhere in this picture. Drug money, at least. And power and connected people. I'm just saying what I hear, that's all."

"I'll tell you," Lipsig answered. "When I examined him last week he was fearful, looking about to watch the guards who were at the ends of the room. He wanted to see who was listening in, and he asked me to lower my voice a number of times. He was in obvious fear for his safety. He was concerned about the changing guard shift—you'll see that in the transcript. He said his 'safe' time ended when the shift changed."

"Every time something hits the papers on this case, I get a little apprehensive," Santucci said. "Too many unusual occurrences have transpired. It's just a simple advisement, Harry."

"How many suspects do you have?" Lipsig asked.

"On the streets or in the cemetery? There are two categories," I answered, forcing a smile.

"About seven or eight still alive," Santucci responded. "But I don't have enough to arrest any of them. We need inside corroboration."

"Berkowitz said he might be willing to cooperate," said Lipsig. "If I get the approval to go back up, I'll take Maury with me and if Berkowitz gives the go-ahead, I'll call you immediately."

"That's all we can ask," Tom Russo said.

*   *   *

In December of 1982, I accompanied Lipsig and Mark Manus, a member of his firm, on a return trip to Dannemora. While I waited outside so as not to tip off my presence there, Berkowitz sat stone-still in a conference room and refused to answer questions for several hours. Lipsig, frustrated, then attempted to elicit a reaction from Berkowitz by mentioning names of people he knew were *not* connected to the conspiracy. He succeeded. Berkowitz erupted in anger.

"He stood up, pounded the table and started cursing out the boss for trying to drag his friends into the case," Manus said. "He was furious. He was leaning over the table and shouting—for a minute I was afraid he was coming right over the table. That's how angry he was. He then stalked out of the room."

"We were getting nowhere," Lipsig said. "Any reaction was better than none at all at that point. The only thing he said all day was that his accomplices would get theirs in time, and that he had to live his life in prison and justice would catch up to them eventually even without his help."

Lipsig also wrote to Governor Hugh Carey and the Bronx and Brooklyn district attorneys urging a full-scale, coordinated investigation. "I was ignored," he said.

The Bronx posturing was typical of Mario Merola's stance throughout the investigation. In Brooklyn, Eugene Gold was gone. The new DA, Elizabeth Holtzman, had distinguished herself as a U.S. representative during the Watergate hearings, but she knew nothing about the Son of Sam case.

Sources told me that members of Gold's old guard, particularly a ranking assistant named Dale Campbell, failed to recommend that she investigate the case. Campbell, transcripts showed, was in attendance on the night in August 1977 when Berkowitz originally confessed to the Moskowitz-Violante shooting.

No one was to know how Holtzman—an avowed adherent of ferreting out suspected Nazi war criminals in the United States—would have reacted if told that Moskowitz and Violante were allegedly struck down by a cult of Hitler-worshipping Satanists who were said to have set up housekeeping in Brooklyn Heights—barely a stone's throw from her office.

XXI

A Coast-to-Coast
Conspiracy

What about your children? You say there are just a few?
There are many, many more, coming in the same direction.
They are running in the streets—and they are coming right at you!

—Charles Manson, testifying at his trial

"That's right," Vinny said, warily glancing about the dreary visiting center in maximum-security Dannemora prison. "The Children—that's what the inner circle of twelve called themselves. Just like Manson's group. It was all part of the same setup, going from New York to L.A., and to Texas and North Dakota—with Texas weapons shipped up through Tampa, Florida. They also had some stuff in Massachusetts and Connecticut, and I think in Jersey."

Mike Zuckerman and I listened in silence while Vinny recited the scope of the cult's operations as whispered to him by Berkowitz. Later, we'd ask countless questions. But I was already mentally comparing Vinny's remarks with Berkowitz's 1977 "cult warning" to police in the tri-state area. Now I knew what he meant.

"The Children were the core in the East; in Westchester, anyway," Vinny went on. "Counting fringe people, there were sometimes as many as forty. But twenty-two was the official number of the cult itself, with the twelve planning and doing the killings."

It was late spring 1982. Vinny was first on the visiting list, and would be followed by Danny a month later. For five straight hours Vinny spoke, not once leaving his seat at the small table. The story was compelling, and would later be supported by months of street investigation. The road to Dannemora had been a tricky one; it took a while to convince Vinny of my sincerity. But he finally wrote:

Just got your letter. You aren't bullshit. You do know. Did Berkowitz tell you, or do you (like I) have evidence? Berkowitz is probably scared of me now, but I never violated his trust. As a fact, all I know would only make things better for him.

The fat cat on Long Island? That's easy—R.R. I know where the L.I. house is. My notes with the name of the town were burned, but I can remember it. Here is the guy's face. [Vinny drew a rough sketch of a round-faced man with curly hair, a beard and a mustache.] I know that looks absurd but I've seen his photo. I can recognize him anywhere.

There is a "church" in Westchester. We must locate it. They hold meetings. I can tell you enough to find it. There is a fat cat in Westchester that's really significant. It gets complicated. Eventually, I'll give you arsons, and crimes in other states, too. I'll give you info on others. The final chart will prove itself undeniably. There are drugs involved, and interstate transport of weapons. That's FBI domain—and maybe only the FBI can be objective (and effective) enough. I'll give you a few names when you come—and locations.

One is the "church" in Westchester. You'll find it OK. But the real fat cat lives on L.I. I had the name of the town—two-word place. But I know his name, and lots more. He lives in some sorta mansion, and I can describe it to a "T." I used three or four sources to double-check.

Drugs, transported from Hawaii. The weapons come from Texas, via Florida. They are taken up in vans by outlaw bikers.

I've sent these facts out secretly to five separate sources. None know what they have. This is not a game. I must be vague in print. Written stuff can be lethal.

How do we know these facts are sound? Shit, tell Santucci to go through the shit I have. How do I know? Maury, if I gotta waste time on that crap, fuck it. Just give him the facts. I got enough shit to deal with, let alone having to gift-wrap it for him, also.

Berkowitz said D.L. [Donna Lauria] was hit. Yes, he said that.

His reactions on that were complex, obscure. Christine Freund was a hit. He was not vague on that one. A hit.

I'm gonna have my contact contact you. We'll have a voice communication. I'll mail this out. If you can send stamps, I'll use 'em for our letters. Hit Gannett for them. Hang in there. Write all you need to. Chew my head off if you disagree. We're on the same side.

I'm not a cop, or a D.A. How the hell did I get into this situation? I feel like a fucking cop sometimes—that turns me off. Peace.

I'm not a hero, and you ain't immune to bullets, either. Bear this in mind.

Eventually, my Vinny and Danny file would grow to more than a hundred letters that were enhanced by over a dozen personal visits spanning the years 1982–86. All the information was marked by a common trait: consistency. Vinny and Danny also agreed to submit to polygraph tests, but Tom Russo in Queens said they weren't necessary. "We've got enough details here," he said. "If we need to test anybody in the future, we will."

But now, in the spring of 1982, right under Berkowitz's unknowing nose, Vinny laid out the cult scenario for me and Mike Zuckerman. As we began, I stipulated some ground rules: "One lie, one tiny lie, and you're done. We're going to be out there in the streets checking all this out, so if you shaft us, we'll never listen to another word again."

"Hey, I *want* you to check it," Vinny said. "That's why I agreed to talk. Berkowitz wanted it checked, too. That's why he talked to me in the first place. He wanted legal help. I challenged him left and right and told him my lawyer would dump *me* if I fed him any shit. So he went into this thing in heavy detail, and I asked him all sorts of questions about it. I can just tell you as best I know it," Vinny said. "Then you go check it out."

"How is he these days?" I asked.

"Pissed at the publicity. He was almost convinced to write you to set up a meet with Santucci—but he changed his mind. He's scared. He knows he could get zapped anytime, and he does want the truth out—but he doesn't trust anybody anymore. And that includes you. But he told me you were there from the start."

"Yes, from the first freaking day after he was nailed."

"Well, he thought you'd be able to understand this shit, but he just stopped trusting and later said he didn't want you to know any of it. But fuck him. He's getting torn all sorts of ways. . . . He showed me your letters, written in code, right? He told me what you were asking about."

"Yeah, they were in code. No use letting the censors in on it."

"That's how I sent out my stuff," Vinny said. "Hidden in books, written in sound-alike names and nicknames. I made it sound like jokes and gibberish, but it all meant stuff."

"What about Sisman?" I asked. "You had his name before he was knocked off."

"Shit, neither me or Berkowitz knew it was gonna be him. I just knew something was going down Halloween, and that it was gonna be either in the Village or Brooklyn Heights. I tried to stop it."

As he talked about the Sisman murder, tears welled in Vinny's eyes. "That was bad shit," he finally said. "Knowing about something like that ahead of time but not being able to do anything. This is all bizarre, but I swear to you it's true as I heard it, and you gotta get Santucci and investigate it."

"Why don't you just tell us what you know?" Zuckerman asked quietly. And Vinny did just that.

The information was concise and involved. It also included names—names of people who, it turned out, did exist. Berkowitz himself provided Vinny with the specifics about the .44 shootings, the cult, Ronald Sisman and others. In some instances, other prison contacts confirmed or supplemented Berkowitz's general familiarity with the group's drug and porn links in New York City, drawing on their own more precise knowledge of that apparatus.

In fact, the informants explained that an alliance existed between the cult and related narcotics and pornography enterprises. This arrangement blended at least two independent franchises which had united for mutual benefit: they could use each other.

It is helpful to remember that the informants emphasized that crossovers between groups occurred. And since an understanding of the Son of Sam shootings would be incomplete without first looking at the overall picture, the sources' description of the entire interwoven operation will be discussed first. Fleshed out by subsequent interviews and letters, here is Vinny's account, which was later substantially corroborated by Danny.

*   *   *

The Westchester group, whom we will call the Children for identification purposes, planned and carried out the Son of Sam attacks. The cult was an offshoot of a parent group which originated in England. As such, it did not exist in a vacuum. The Children were linked to similar groups in the United States, with Houston, Los Angeles and the Dakotas prominently mentioned. The cult maintained a primary headquarters near Los Angeles.

In New York, the Westchester Children interacted with another satanic operation in Brooklyn and Manhattan, and a certain occult shop within the city limits functioned as a clearinghouse and rendezvous point for cult members from Westchester and elsewhere, who intermingled. As an example of the cross-connections, at least one New York City female occultist was said to have been on the scene of a Son of Sam shooting, which blended with what Berkowitz told Harry Lipsig.

Westchester and New York City members also convened occasionally in a brownstone, occupied by a woman, in Brooklyn Heights—a trendy neighborhood where still another woman involved with the city faction also lived. The brownstone was said to be located on Henry Street, between Love Lane and Atlantic Avenue, which was a number of blocks south. The other Brooklyn woman resided about a block west of Atlantic and Henry. Additionally, another spot near Love Lane was described as a cult meeting site. (Vinny later provided a map of the area, which was accurate down to the most intricate detail—including the location of trees on a block.)

"They work the colleges," Vinny said. "They recruit for the cult and the prostitution on campuses. One of those Brooklyn women was involved in the college coordination." He provided two names, saying he believed the woman in question was one of them. Both exist.

David Berkowitz, Michael Carr and other Westchester members knew and were known by the New York City group. Michael Carr, whom Vinny and other sources categorized as gay, also associated with cult-connected people who were affiliated with Columbia University, and some of those acquaintances lived in that area of uptown Manhattan. Vinny said that many of Michael Carr's companions were homosexual or bisexual. This proclivity, he said, was a common thread which, even beyond cult links, wove a considerable number of members and associates together.

Vinny (and Danny) said the Children counted women among their members, as Berkowitz also told Harry Lipsig.

The top leader of the Children, not surprisingly, was said to be a lawyer who dealt in real estate, or a real estate man who also held a law degree. He was said to have been middle-aged, perhaps forty-five to fifty-three years old, in 1977. He was described as balding and thin and was said to wear glasses, at least on occasion.

This leader was said to have maintained an office in the White Plains vicinity during the Son of Sam era, and perhaps still did in 1987. The office, rather than being in a high-rise building, was described as then being in a "residential-type" dwelling in or near White Plains.

The leader's home was said to have been somewhere other than White Plains, in a location unknown to the informants. But he was described as having been active in local politics, "town board or something," either in his hometown or in connection with his business. This leader, who may have been divorced, allegedly had a son or son-in-law who also was an attorney and who was perhaps in his mid-twenties at the time. The leader also may have had a daughter, who would have been of "college age" in the 1977 time frame.

The Children's leader was further said to be a Mason, rank unknown, and to have owned or kept dogs. "Berkowitz occasionally watched the guy's dogs for him," Vinny said. This major cultist also owned a boat during these years. "Not a yacht, but a pretty big boat," Vinny explained.

This man—about whom multiple, intricate details were provided—is allegedly responsible for directing the group which committed the Son of Sam murders and other violent crimes.

Berkowitz offered no information about the other Westchester leaders, the informants said. But he did reveal that one group member was then employed at a large Westchester automotive facility, where he held an administrative, sales liaison or dealer coordination post. He was said to have been married to the daughter of one of the company's executives or managers. The informants were given a first name for this member, which will be withheld here.

Regarding other Westchester members, Vinny said Berkowitz told him: "A couple of Yonkers cops are involved. I don't know if they were present or former cops." Vinny didn't have their names, but prior investigation had unearthed three suspects, including former Yonkers officer Peter Shane.*

Some cult members, in both Westchester and New York City, were said to own or work in "art stores. Small, artsy-craftsy places," Vinny said. "Like throwbacks to the hippie days."

*　*　*

In Westchester, the group met at Untermyer Park, which confirmed our own investigation; an old mansion in Greenburgh, central Westchester, which was said to have been "burned out"; and an abandoned church—which was said to be located near Central Avenue in the White Plains vicinity. The church, Vinny wrote, was "near the old mansion."

The cult leader, via his real estate or other dealings, allegedly learned of this church's existence and obtained access to it in some manner. The church, no longer in use by a congregation, was said to be devoid of pews; and the group allegedly stored satanic material in a small shed attached to the building. (Vinny later sent me a drawing of the church.)

Another abandoned church offered yet one more meeting site. This edifice was said to have been an "eastern headquarters" for the group. The informants said it was privately owned (perhaps partially converted) and was located in the vicinity of the northeast corner of Westchester County, somewhere near (and possibly over) the adjoining Putnam County and Connecticut borders. Vinny couldn't pinpoint the exact location but, quoting Berkowitz, he mentioned "Salem" and "Brewster."

North and South Salem, with their historical witchcraft names, were in Westchester, and the village of Brewster lay a few miles north in Putnam County. The area was largely rural, with homes, estates and some farms and stables hidden from the few main roads by thickets of trees. It was a perfect cult site, and a difficult, extensive setting in which to try to locate the old church.

Vinny said the church's interior (in 1976–77) was adorned with a silver pentagram on one wall; and silver-wire inlays, some in the form of the German SS lightning bolts—a symbol of the cult—appeared on the ends of some pews.

Vinny also said that besides the Son of Sam and other murders, the group committed rapes in Westchester and set a number of fires.

One particular fire involved a considerable loss of life, and an investigation into the alleged cult participation in that crime is ongoing. But data supporting the Vinny-Berkowitz allegation *have* been uncovered. Another cult-ignited fire allegedly occurred in or near Brooklyn Heights.

The Children's murders, while cloaked in satanic "theology," occasionally also served to eliminate weak links or enemies, Vinny stated. And except for major satanic holidays, the group met on Thursdays that coincided with cycles of the moon.

Danny later remarked: "This is a whole subculture the cops don't know about or understand. That's why these idiots can get away with all they do. If somebody gets caught, he shuts up—so they think it's just an isolated thing. And they don't get caught too much in the first place. They got smart people heading it."

Danny and Vinny were very clear as to why they were willing to assist the probe. First, if arrests were made, Santucci could ease their plights with recommendations to the parole board. Second, there is a caste system within every prison population. Robbers, dope dealers, even killers are repelled by the types of crimes the Sam cult engaged in: the murders and rapes of innocent young women. Accordingly, the informants preferred an uneasy alliance with law enforcement and me to sitting back silently with the information they gathered—some of which concerned the cult's drug connections.

* * *

The Children and the New York City cults, or their leaders, were said to be involved in the drug business on a medium scale. This brought the Children into an alliance with the simpatico Ronald Sisman, who, while not a cult member, was known to the cult (and the police) as a dope dealer with porno connections aplenty. Sisman, Vinny said, was directly tied to R.R., the wealthy Long Island overlord.

Into this upper stratum of the cults' drug and kinky-sex operations walked other professional and white-collar types: doctors, lawyers and businessmen. Some were satanically bent, most likely in elitist OTO directions; some weren't. But there was a considerable amount of money to be made and sexual savoring to sample even if one's interests were limited to narcotics and porn.

"They keep looking for bigger kicks," Vinny said. "They got everything, but it ain't enough. So they get into weirdness. And it ain't exactly a secret that doctors get hooked on drugs and start dealing, too. And they all think they can get away with anything—that they're above the cops. If not, they try to buy them. There's a lotta money in coke."

Vinny said that R.R. was perched atop this kink-and-cultic social whirl—using middlemen, underlings and other contacts to fill in whatever blanks he couldn't personally inscribe. Enter Sisman and one James Camaro, whose name Vinny also mentioned in the notes he compiled before Sisman's murder. Camaro wasn't the man's actual name, Vinny believed, trying to remember. "But the real name is close to that."

Camaro was an olive-skinned Caucasian or Hispanic, who Vinny said, "dressed like an Indian," because "he wore a headband and stuff like that. I saw his picture." Camaro was in his late twenties to mid-thirties, Vinny thought, and had dark hair.

Vinny described Camaro as R.R.'s "insurance, but I don't think he was as close to him as Sisman was." He added that Berkowitz and other Westchester cultists feared Camaro, who acted as a go-between from R.R. and Sisman to the Children. Camaro, Vinny reported, also had some "loose organized crime connections," which wasn't surprising for one involved in pornography and upscale prostitution.

Camaro and Sisman, as R.R.'s operatives, administered a porno enterprise which involved, the informants said, a call girl ring which utilized college girls and produced private sex films, stills and videotapes. Some coeds, first enticed by the New York City cult's innocent come-on, were later fed to the call girl network, Vinny remarked.

While Camaro specialized in this area, Sisman branched out and handled a fair amount of drug dealing. The Children in Westchester used drugs provided by the R.R.-Sisman link and, to some extent, were part of the dope distribution network. (A Yonkers resident has said he occasionally picked up hard drugs from David Berkowitz's apartment.) This narcotics pipeline, Vinny stated, accounted for the presence of Berkowitz and Michael Carr at Sisman's brownstone.

The drug operation, while not large by organized crime standards, managed to accomplish its purpose. Coke was its prime substance and was said to have arrived in New York from South America, via Florida.

Heroin from Southeast Asia was also shipped, Vinny said. "They used hospital and medical connections. [Name withheld] told me they used a hospital and another company in Hawaii as two places that got the shit ready to come to the U.S.—to New York and maybe other places. The heroin was supposed to go into blood or plasma shipments and other hospital accomplices would then handle it here."

Once again, we were looking at medical links.

Vinny, incarcerated in a New York prison, sent me the names and phone numbers of several Hawaiian locations, including a large hospital and a quarrying company. An FBI agent confirmed via the Bureau's Honolulu office that the addresses and phone numbers were in fact accurate. The list did not originate with Berkowitz.

Vinny was uncertain of R.R.'s role in the heroin operation. "But it fits somewhere in the picture," he said. "He's involved with other people besides the cult. Maybe that part was someone else's more than his. You've got to understand that the Children and the city cult were one thing—they had their own links. R.R. and his crowd, at least some of them, were not in the cults. But they used them and formed partnerships. That's how it worked."

Vinny explained that Berkowitz "didn't let on that he knew a lot of the particulars about the dope and porn stuff. But he knew names and some basic stuff. And he'd been to R.R.'s house, and Sisman's, and he knew Camaro. But other people knew more details than he did. Berkowitz said what he knew, and other people confirmed it. . . . If R.R. and them were meat wholesalers, you don't think they're only dealing with you, right? They got other customers, too. A couple of other customers have been in this place [prison]. Berkowitz knew what he knew, and they knew other things."

*   *   *

Regarding the porno and call girl system, blackmail was sometimes employed to keep the girls in line, Vinny said, adding that Camaro sometimes used the Auto Pub restaurant in Manhattan's General Motors Building as one location where well-heeled clients and collegiate call girls met.

Enter the world of television. Vinny wrote that Camaro appeared in a "home porno flick" with a woman who held a responsible production post with a TV network in Manhattan. The woman's title and network were specified.

Vinny didn't know her name, but he did have her description—which was so precise I identified her after just one phone call to a friend in the television industry. Since the woman was not an on-camera personality, Vinny couldn't have picked up her description from a TV screen.

This story, in conjunction with Berkowitz's fascinating list of phone numbers, illustrates how people connected to the cult's upper echelons seemed to fraternize easily in prestigious, though bizarre, social circles.

*   *   *

The call girl operation, Vinny said, was responsible for at least two murders in

Manhattan—both linked to Columbia University. One victim was a male medical or graduate student (name unknown) who was slain after learning a young woman he was dating was involved with the ring. Vinny said she told the victim about it, and he was killed either because he raised a fuss trying to wean her away from the group's clutches or simply because he'd acquired inside knowledge of the operation.

"Camaro had something to do with that," Vinny wrote. "I think they tried to make it look like a robbery."

Subsequent investigation revealed that at least two unsolved homicides bore similarities to the slaying to which Vinny referred. A Columbia grad student was slain in the immediate area of the school in February 1981. After dropping off his girlfriend, he returned to the street and his killer tossed some money to the pavement and said, "Hey, pal, you dropped this." When the student turned around, he was shot dead. Police said the victim's girlfriend witnessed at least part of the incident.

Another victim was a medical resident at Columbia-Presbyterian Medical Center, which was affiliated with the university. He was shot dead while walking on a street near the hospital in the autumn of 1981.

The other murder Vinny specified was said to have been that of a coed—probably a Columbia or Barnard student—who was slain in Manhattan after trying to extricate herself from the call girl network. Vinny, quoting sources other than Berkowitz, said that Camaro also played a role in this murder and said he thought the victim was disfigured in some way by her killer or killers.

If Camaro indeed had a hand in those murders, he didn't operate alone, Vinny said. "He had his own guy, a landscaper or gardener. He was a Puerto Rican or some kind of Hispanic. I was told this jerk worked at [a northern Manhattan park] and also did some part-time gardener work at Columbia."

Vinny went on to say: "There's a fag named Fred Reese,* who does secretarial-type shit—he's in this, too. He's the fag boyfriend of Lenora Stein,* who's part of that cult shop crowd. It's all one large circle. They come and go and mix it up with each other."

I asked Vinny if Berkowitz (or another source) ever spoke of the horrible December 1979 murders of Brooklyn residents Howard Green and Carol Marron, who had all the blood drained from their bodies with a veterinarian's syringe. Green and Marron were occult devotees, according to the police. Specifically, they were into a sex-magic group which, as the letter I received stated, shared an umbrella "theology" with the Process, and assuredly its offshoots.

"Nobody ever spoke of that," Vinny said. "But they lived in Brooklyn? Who would *you* nominate? Who else is there around New York that would do that to a couple of devil worshippers except some of their own? That wasn't any one-man operation that did them in."

I also asked if Vinny later heard who was responsible for the Sisman-Platzman homicides. He said he hadn't, but "Camaro would be a top choice for either doing it or having it done. Sisman went down over that Moskowitz tape, which was made for R.R. on Long Island. And from what I know, Camaro was one of his goons. So I'd say Camaro was somehow involved."

Vinny then brought the entire scenario into focus. "I was told directly by Berkowitz that Camaro was on the scene of the Moskowitz thing and also acted as a go-between on the Christine Freund murder—which wasn't a random shooting. And neither was Donna Lauria's."

Mix and mingle again. With these explosive charges, we were now back to the .44 shootings.

*   *   *

But before examining those attacks, the following supporting data, in addition to what I have already listed, were uncovered during the investigation of the Vinny and Danny statements:

The abandoned church in central Westchester, which Vinny accurately sketched, was immediately identified by Captain Gerry Buckhout of the Greenburgh Police Department, as was the nearby "burned-out" mansion, which turned out to be the former Warburg-Rothschild estate. Vinny's precise drawing of the church was remarkable in that the building was torn down in the mid-seventies—more than seven years *before* he sketched it from a description provided by Berkowitz.

The church, abandoned at the time, was dismantled after a suspicious fire destroyed its adjacent parish hall. Before that, it stood empty since the late fifties, when its congregation moved to another edifice—taking the original pews with them. Vinny had said the church contained no pews.

Buckhout interviewed the man who subsequently purchased the old church and its adjoining buildings—the parish hall and a rectory.

"When he came in during the seventies, a woman who claimed to be a witch was on the site. She had a business there, selling paintings and arts and crafts out of the parish hall," Buckhout explained. "There were also strange hippie types living upstairs in the former minister's house. It was something of a crash pad, and was painted purple. The 'witch' was a suspect in the fire that later destroyed the parish hall."

The owner's revelation that the "witch" sold paintings, etc., supported Vinny's allegation that some cult members owned or worked in "art stores." The woman was in her mid-forties and had sons who'd run afoul of the law, Buckhout learned.

"One was arrested in Yonkers for public lewdness and another was picked up in Long Beach, California—near L.A.—for cursing out a cop," he said. "One of them also worked in a lower Manhattan design place; he was in the same field as Michael Carr."

Buckhout also discovered that one of the woman's sons was later killed in an apparent accident. As for the "witch" herself, she had left the area and has not been located. "This church was the place," Buckhout said. "Your prison guys are on the money."

Three years earlier, John Carr's friend Phil Falcon had told us that the Westchester group met in a "witch's church." At the time, the significance of the statement escaped us. Falcon had meant his comment to be taken literally. Berkowitz, too, had underlined a church clue in the book he mailed to North Dakota in 1979.

*   *   *

There were more than a dozen abandoned or converted houses of worship in the rural northern Westchester-Putnam-Connecticut sector, any one of which might have been the "eastern headquarters" Vinny described. By itself, the very existence of numerous abandoned churches was something of a confirmation, since other sections of Westchester didn't have any to speak of. In other words, one would have to know they existed in that area in order to make an accurate claim. But for our purposes, surveilling such a large number of locations around North Salem was impossible because our manpower was limited and no one knew how frequently the church was used by the secretive group.

Interestingly, in 1979 this region was the scene of documented satanic rituals. In one instance, a Ridgefield, Connecticut, police officer heard chanting in a wooded thicket near the Westchester-Connecticut border. While investigating, he was attacked and beaten. The cultists fled.

"They must have had guards there, and they weren't afraid to jump a cop," Sergeant Bernie DePrimo of the Connecticut State Police told me in mid-1986. "Nuns at a nearby convent also heard chanting and saw torches on occasion. There was a group there all right. There was scattered cult activity around the area."

In the wake of the assault, DePrimo said, the State Police developed confidential information which led them to a curious location: the *same* New York City occult store later targeted by Berkowitz, Vinny and Danny.

DePrimo also offered another startling piece of information. "We heard that whoever headed this around here was a successful guy involved in real estate."

This dovetailed precisely with the prison allegations about the occupation of the leader of the Children. It was a significant development in the case.

Moreover, at the time of the Connecticut border incidents—which happened nearly three years before the Vinny-Danny statements and months before the Son of Sam case was reopened—David Berkowitz wrote to Lee Chase and pointedly mentioned satanic rituals occurring near North Salem.

*   *   *

Another intriguing series of events happened in this same region in 1979. Keith Richards of the Rolling Stones was then ensconced in a secluded rented home in the immediate vicinity of the cult activity. In fact, it was reported that scorch marks were found on an isolated section of his property.

Richards, who'd lived in the home since about 1977, was frequently touring with the Stones while his girlfriend, Anita Pallenberg, remained at the house. A number of publications, including biographical sketches of the band, described Pallenberg as a student of the black arts. During the 1979 cult era, while Richards was away, a teen-aged boy was found shot to death in Pallenberg's bedroom. Authorities determined that the youth committed suicide.

Keith Richards, who had known Pallenberg since the sixties, was a guest at the 1968 London wedding of noted film director Roman Polanski and the beautiful young actress Sharon Tate. Among his many credits, Polanski directed the famous devil epic *Rosemary's Baby* for Paramount Pictures. Paramount's vice president of production, Robert Evans, who later was caught in a cocaine bust, was deeply involved with the film and became closely acquainted with Polanski. At the time Rosemary's devil-child was born (1967–68), Evans was back in Hollywood from a London assignment as head of Paramount's European production team.

In Beverly Hills, Evans, Polanski and Sharon Tate were friendly with John Phillips, songwriter and lead singer of the Mamas and the Papas rock group. A decade later, Phillips would be an occasional visitor at the home of his friend Keith Richards, hidden away in Satanville. Phillips himself was leasing a house nearby in Connecticut at this time.

Phillips's late-sixties relationship with Polanski and Tate was an intimate one. He was frequently in their company and was entertained in their rented Benedict Canyon home at 10050 Cielo Drive—scene of oncoming slaughter—on several occasions. In fact, both Phillips and Polanski have acknowledged that Polanski, while married to Tate, conducted a brief affair in London with Phillips's wife, Michelle, who also sang with the Mamas and the Papas. This liaison transpired several months before Sharon Tate and four others were butchered by Charles Manson's killers in August 1969.

Because of his affair with Michelle, Polanski at first suspected an angry John Phillips was involved in the murders—to the point of holding a knife to his throat before slinging it into a wall.

Ironically, Phillips has admitted to a passing acquaintance with Manson himself, to whom he was introduced by drummer Dennis Wilson of the Beach Boys. Manson and some followers even lived at Wilson's Sunset Boulevard estate for a time in 1968, before the friendship soured. Wilson subsequently occupied a slot on Manson's enemies list.

Manson moved easily in show business circles and developed a close relationship with Terry Melcher, son of singer-actress Doris Day and the producer of her TV show and other ventures. Melcher, to Manson's great interest, was also a record producer—and Charlie was determined to make it big as a singer. He was anxious to ingratiate himself with Melcher, from whom Roman Polanski sublet 10050 Cielo Drive.

Melcher, too, was acquainted with John Phillips. And in tune with Phillips's association with Manson, author Ed Sanders reported that he uncovered information indicating Manson attended a 1968 New Year's Eve party at Phillips's Los Angeles home.

Phillips, Sanders also said, apparently referred members of the Process to a Los Angeles real estate operator named Artie Aarons in 1968, when the English occultists were seeking to pitch tent in that city. Sanders obtained this information from Jonathan de Peyer, known as Father Christian to his fellow Processans.

There were also stories about which held that Phillips contributed some cash to the Process, with the reported amounts ranging from the ten dollars Phillips said he gave to "some cult dressed in black" to a figure much higher. In any case, Father Christian said that with Phillips's recommendation Artie Aarons found lodging for a Process contingent at a large home he managed at 1882 South Cochrane in Los Angeles.

Neither Sanders nor I imply that Phillips was directly affiliated with the Process. From all indications, his interests—by his own account—were elsewhere: music and drugs. But, the interweavings and connections among people and events in the Son of Sam and Manson cases are provocative—especially in light of Manson II's alleged involvement in the .44 killings, the further contention that Charlie Manson belonged to the same satanic organization Berkowitz later joined, and the North Salem cult link to the Sam case.

And the Process itself was even located in that area. In the mid-seventies members of the cult occupied a house off Salem Road in Pound Ridge, a rural community several miles south of North Salem. It was as if the players and environment from the Los Angeles scene of 1968–69 had been magically transported to the specific area Berkowitz and the prison informants referred to.

The reason for this interest in the California and New York connections case is simple. According to Vinny, Manson II was involved with the original Charles Manson. And more than that, Vinny said: "When Manson had the Tate murders done, he was not just doing it out of some Helter Skelter fantasy. That was part of it, he believed in that shit. *But there was a real motive, Berkowitz told me. He said Manson was working for somebody else when those crimes were committed. He said Manson 'volunteered to do the killings' for somebody else.*"

This was an incredible charge. Vinny said Berkowitz got the information from: "Who else? Manson II."

* * *

But to return to the Vinny-Danny information about the Son of Sam operation in New York: the allegation that John and Michael Carr's disdain for their father, Sam, sparked incidents of violence against him and inspired his inclusion as an object of hatred in the Borrelli letter was essentially confirmed by an ex-boyfriend of their sister, Wheat—and by Wheat herself.

The boyfriend told me: "The brothers hated the old man. I knew each of them somewhat when I was dating Micki [Wheat's nickname]. I was told Sam used to severely punish them and even locked them in closets and things like that."

In a recorded interview with Santucci's probers, Wheat simply said: "O.K., there was a lot of bad feeling between both John and Michael and my father."

As I'd noted as early as September 1977, the Borrelli letter read as if it was written from inside the Carr house—not by Berkowitz from his apartment high on the hill above it. The later confirmations put vital pieces of the puzzle in place.

In other categories, the names, locations and people Vinny and Danny described or named turned out to be real. Beyond that, two New York City women they identified were positively tied to OTO cult activity. The investigation also established that one of them, as Vinny said, indeed "worked the colleges"—recruiting for the cult on various campuses. "She also knows R.R.," Vinny said.

At every turn taken by the probe, the credibility of Berkowitz and the informants was bolstered.

But in the case of James Camaro, since Vinny said the man's name apparently wasn't Camaro but "close to it," we were stuck. Berkowitz had offered the real name, which Vinny failed to remember when he saw his own coded substitution for it months later. Although he did have an approximate Manhattan address where he said Camaro once lived, we were unable to locate him. We needed the real name.

Once, however, we thought we'd found him. In early 1985 a motor vehicles computer run led Hank Cinotti and me to a freezing, midwinter stake-out of an apartment on the ocean in Long Beach, Long Island. For three days, while we shivered and complained in Cinotti's drafty van, the suspect, smarter than we were, remained indoors. Finally, at eight o'clock one morning, he emerged to lead us on a wild trip at high speeds all the way to Staten Island—to a funeral home.

Since Vinny had seen a photo of Camaro and could identify him, our goal was to obtain his picture. So we followed the line of cars to a cemetery and blended in with the crowd at the gravesite, waiting for the photo opportunity, which didn't come.

After the service, the suspect and two companions drove to a distant section of the graveyard to place flowers at another tomb—which they couldn't find. Cinotti and I watched their search from the van. Suddenly, "Camaro" walked right to us. It was a tense moment. Fortunately, because of the van, he assumed we were cemetery workers.

As he stood near the passenger's door asking me for directions, Cinotti lowered the camera out of the suspect's line of vision and snapped his photo. "Click, click."

"Camaro" heard the camera, looked startled, but probably imagined he was hearing things. After steering him to the section he was seeking, Cinotti and I leisurely drove away.

Two days later, I visited Vinny and showed him the snapshot.

"It's not him," he immediately said.

"Look again," I pleaded. "Hold it upside down, turn it sideways; close your eyes and feel it like it's Braille—shove it up your ass. You don't know what the hell we went through to get this damned thing."

"It's just not him," Vinny said again.

It was not one of my better days.

The informants didn't have the name of "Mr. Real Estate" either, since Berkowitz hadn't given it up. But the details they did supply led us to several possible suspects who could have functioned as the leader of the Children. That investigation continues. Similarly, several possible choices were identified as Camaro's alleged accomplice, the Hispanic gardener.

*　　*　　*

Berkowitz cautiously held back several key cards while dealing to the informants, including the names of most of the Son of Sam shooters. He did offer a first name for the elusive Manson II. The name Vinny gave me was Frank, but we didn't know if Berkowitz revealed an accurate name or if Manson II assumed an alias in New York.

Berkowitz, according to the informants, had further stated that John Carr was a triggerman and that Michael Carr, if not a shooter, was on the scene of some .44 attacks. This complemented what Berkowitz told Harry Lipsig in a portion of the deposition withheld from the public.

Berkowitz also named a New York City female cultist who Vinny said was at one .44 scene, at least—as were Manson II, Sisman, Mickey and someone named Tom. Mickey and Sisman, as noted, allegedly participated in the Moskowitz videotaping, and Camaro also was said to have been at that attack.

Regarding women at crime scenes, Vinny had the names of two—both of whom exist. He said the woman in question was one of them. (Santucci had uncovered the name of a third suspect.) Vinny also said that someone named Rudy was involved with the cult in either Westchester, New York City or Long Island.

His original coded note included the names of a few others, who were also said to be affiliated with the group. He explained that his allusion to New York University in the letter meant that some young women connected to the New York City group had attended school there. "Something like photography and drama courses," he recalled. Out of the blue, we had another photo link, of which there were many in the investigation.

*　　*　　*

Sources are as valuable as the verifiable information they provide. The Vinny and Danny comments, which were thoroughly investigated, helped their stock rise appreciably. Additionally, their relationships with the prime source—Berkowitz—were proven.

The initial stage of the Vinny-Danny investigation, which is still monitored today, lasted more than a year and was coordinated by me, with assistance from Santucci's office and the police officials and others previously listed.

The "big picture" of the cult's operations was valuable for intelligence purposes, but DA John Santucci's attention necessarily remained on the .44 shootings themselves. Other facets of the group's activities weren't in his jurisdiction, although he remained apprised of developments.

In mid-1983, we convened in his office and analyzed an extensive report I'd prepared on the investigation of the informants' charges.

"A considerable amount of support has been found," he said. "And many allegations as to the existence of people, places and the like have been confirmed directly. Of course, from where I stand, the ultimate test would occur in a courtroom, if we can ever carry the damned case to that point. But I agree there's substance to what these people have been saying."

"It's all been checking out," I said. "Talk about 'smoke and fire.'"

"Yes, but we can't lose sight of the earlier work on the .44 incidents. That's what I need to bring somebody to trial. Half the people we're interested in are dead, and we don't know who this Manson II is either. I need a Queens shooter."

* * *

Santucci was right. The Son of Sam attacks also remained my prime concern. It would have taken an interstate task force to dent the rest of the operation. But like the informants' statements about the drug and porn activity, information they offered on the Sam shootings was enhanced by buttressing details.

And once again, the charges were sensational.

The sources said that David Berkowitz, while an active conspirator in all the shootings, had pulled the trigger in only *two* of the eight Son of Sam attacks. Whom did Berkowitz actually shoot?

"Here's a direct quote," Danny said. "'The Bronx was my territory—only the Bronx.'"

"And that's directly from him?"

"Yes. He wanted out after the first one but couldn't get free."

Based on this information, which was supported in various ways, Berkowitz murdered Donna Lauria and wounded Jody Valente on July 29, 1976; and killed both Valentina Sudani and Alex Esau on April 17, 1977.

"That's all he did," Danny insisted. "Not that it isn't a lot, but it's nowhere near being the so-called Son of Sam."

Vinny added: "He was able to handle that lovers' lane thing [Suriani-Esau] because he said he was conceived illegitimately in a car and he was against that shit. But he said he wouldn't have anything to do with shooting nobody on a street or a porch or anything."

This was a reference to the Virginia Voskerichian slaying and the wounding of Joanne Lomino and Donna DeMasi in Queens.

The sources also said, as Berkowitz told Lipsig, that several cult members were at each crime scene. And they added that two Son of Sam shootings were done by *women.*

Women were also present at scenes because, Danny said, "the cops were looking for one guy. They could breeze through roadblocks with girls in the cars—or even with two guys. And there was always more than one car."

"What kinds of cars?" I asked.

"Well, the VW, for one. He didn't say who drove it. And there was a yellowish or tan compact and a small red car, too."

"Any more?"

"That's all I know about."

"How big was this yellow or tan compact?"

"Like the size of a Chevy Nova."

This was a direct hit. This type of auto had been spotted near the Elephas disco, driven away with its lights off by the man with the mustache. A similar vehicle was also spied across the street from Donna Lauria's home by her father not five minutes before that shooting. It was occupied by a lone white male. A car fitting this description also followed Brooklyn cyclist Michelle Michaels shortly before the Moskowitz-Violante shooting. It, too, was occupied by a lone male, who had a "pinched face," high cheekbones, and wore sunglasses—even though it was the middle of the night.

And the same-size yellowish or tan vehicle would soon surface at still another .44 site—bringing the total to four.

"Where was the small red car used?" I asked.

"Manson II used that in the Freund murder," Vinny said. Confidential police reports would soon show that an identical vehicle sped from that scene moments after the shots were fired.

The informants didn't know which victims were shot by women, but their statements considerably strengthened the original suspicion held by Santucci, Herb Leifer and me that the killer of Virginia Voskerichian—who wore a ski or watch cap—was a woman. By process of elimination, I then reasoned that the Queens wounding of Carl Denaro—during which the assailant fired wildly as if unsure of the gun and unable to control its recoil—was most likely the other female-perpetrated attack.

Regarding weapons, Vinny said: "They weren't always carried from Westchester. Sometimes they were able to store them nearby, at 'safe houses' or something." And as previously noted, the informants insisted that different .44s were used, at least in the earlier attacks before the NYPD announced it was searching for one gun and one gunman.

Danny wrote: "Yes, more than one instrument [gun] was gotten in Texas. Yes, all gotten at once. Yes, yes, yes. If no one looked into that possibility it's simply because they are morons."

* * *

The statement that Berkowitz shot only the Bronx victims was heavily supported by the composite sketches and other information gleaned from extensive study of the other crimes—all of which has been outlined earlier. His so-called detailed knowledge of various crime scenes was easily explained by his presence at them. And even in the Bronx, the existing evidence demonstrated the conspiracy was active there as well.

And then, in 1986, a witness came forward to say he was on "personal business" in the area when Valentina Suriani and Alex Esau were slain on the Hutchinson River Parkway service road at about 3 a.m. on April, 17, 1977. The witness, Will Levine,* said he remained silent out of fear and to protect his own interests—which doesn't make him eligible for Man of the Year accolades.

Levine said he was on the block when he heard the shots, turned around and saw a stocky man with dark hair peering into the victims' car while holding "something white" in one hand—apparently the Borrelli letter, which was dropped at that scene.

Levine said he then saw the shooter walk east on an intersecting block, St. Theresa Avenue, where he met up with another man at the second corner. The shooter then handed what Levine thought was the gun to the other man, who then entered the passenger's side of a waiting auto—which drove from the scene.

The shooter, meanwhile, climbed into the passenger's side of another car, Levine said. That vehicle then drove off—followed closely by a third car. The third auto, Levine said, appeared to be an *unmarked police car.*

"All three cars were involved together," Levine said. "One of them was blue. I was trying to get plate numbers, so I didn't pay much attention to the makes. But that last one looked just like an unmarked cop car. I got a good view of that."

And the shooter? "It looked like Berkowitz to me."

Levine, saying he fears reprisals, has refused to speak to authorities, but Queens DA John Santucci was informed of his statement. If Levine's account is accurate, the presence of an unmarked police vehicle wouldn't be surprising: three former or present Yonkers officers were previously suspected to be members of the cult.

An unmarked police car, tuned to official frequencies, could also help explain the group's remarkable success in eluding massive dragnets. In Brooklyn, witnesses said the yellow VW contained a CB radio as well, and Berkowitz may have carried a hand-held scanner at that scene.

*   *   *

But for all the knowledge we'd now assimilated, there were still several important questions to be answered. What actually happened to Donna Lauria and Christine Freund? Who was the wealthy R.R. from Long Island? And who was Manson II, and how did he tie in to Charles Manson—who himself was alleged to have committed the Tate murders by "volunteering" his services to another party?

The answers were now in sight.

XXII

A Call to Copco

It had been six years and forty miles of bad road, but from Gravesend Bay in Brooklyn to the old aqueduct in Yonkers the story was the same: evidence demonstrating a conspiracy had been uncovered in every crime first attributed to David Berkowitz alone. Now, even the basic police belief that all the .44 shootings were random acts of violence was challenged by the informants. But was there any truth to these allegations?

Pretty, dark-haired Donna Lauria was the first Son of Sam victim. She was slain deliberately, the informants said.

"Berkowitz was very weird and vague talking about this one, which he admits he did," Vinny reported. "But he said she knew something about the group, or about someone in it, and started talking. She was killed because she talked too much. He wasn't specific, but her killing had special significance."

That part made sense. Of all the victims, only Donna was named in the Breslin letter—crowned a "very, very sweet girl" in the cynical, taunting prose that spewed from the printer's pen. But what about the rest of the story? Could it be supported?

It could.

Donna, a medical technician, and Jody Valente, a student nurse, were attacked on a weekday. With the exception of the Voskerichian slaying, the .44 assaults happened on weekends. So why was Donna shot at 1:10 a.m. on a Thursday?

"They always went to the Peachtree disco on Wednesday nights," Donna's father, Mike Lauria, had told me.

The glitzy Peachtree was in New Rochelle, a city with multiple links to the .44 case. Habitual Wednesday visits there could well have explained the timing of a deliberate attack. Moreover, it was established that members of the Carr family, at least, occasionally patronized the Peachtree.

As reported earlier, a suspicious yellow car was seen cruising Donna's block shortly before she went out that last night. And later, just minutes before the shooting, Mike Lauria spied a yellow, Nova-sized car occupied by a lone male parked across the street and behind Jody's car. Additionally, the police themselves originally believed that the shots were aimed only at Donna.

Perhaps one of the most pertinent pieces of the Donna Lauria puzzle was hidden in a long-forgotten, confidential police report. In it, a male acquaintance of Donna's was quoted by a young woman Donna knew. According to the woman, the man had said shortly before Donna's death:

"Donna has one week to live."

Although the information was secondhand, its import cannot be downplayed: within ten days of the statement, Donna was indeed dead.

The NYPD didn't disregard it either. This youth was a prime suspect until he provided an alibi and Jody Valente said he wasn't the gunman. Of course the alibi was valid: Berkowitz committed the crime. But did this man, who had a checkered past, know something was coming?

I also recalled the Laurias sadly telling me that Jody Valente, whom they regarded "almost like a daughter," seemed to avoid them in the months after the murder. "We could never understand that," Mike Lauria explained.

Perhaps Jody experienced unsettling reminders of the tragedy when she saw Donna's parents. But maybe, as one of Donna's closest friends, she herself had heard something and tried to suppress her suspicions. I don't have that answer yet. But what *is* certain is that nine months after Donna's slaying Valentina Suriani and Alex Esau were gunned down in a car parked barely a hundred yards from Jody's front door. Another coincidence? Only the killers know for certain.

But the initial question was: did information exist to fortify the jailhouse charges that Donna was an intentional victim? The answer: yes.

*   *   *

"Target crimes," Vinny labeled them, saying that the cult, to cloud issues and disguise motives, would commit random shootings to hide the fact that some victims were purposely marked for death. Like Donna Lauria, the beautiful, twenty-six-year-old Christine Freund was said to have been slain in such a "target crime."

In 1984, the now retired NYPD veteran Hank Cinotti and I sought out Christine's boyfriend of seven years, John Diel.

Christine and Diel were seated in his car in Forest Hills, Queens, on January 30, 1977, when the fatal shots were fired at about 12:30 a.m. Fortunately, Diel wasn't hit.

Christine was by far the oldest Son of Sam victim, and we wanted to determine if more than coincidence was at play in that regard. We also had other allegations to work with, courtesy of Vinny.

Now thirty-six, the short, athletic, curly-haired Diel was a bartender by trade. When we found him, he was serving customers in a friendly Queens grill. Ironically, Christine Freund's younger sister, Eva, dropped by while we were talking with Diel. Her presence may have been an omen, because the case began to unravel that evening when I posed a question Diel said no one had asked before.

"Did anything unusual happen *earlier* that night?" I wanted to know. That opened the floodgates: the police hadn't covered the entire evening. Now, through Diel's statement and supporting official documents, the true story of Christine Freund's final hours emerged.

It was an eerie tale, one which stirred images of the chilling Arlis Perry operation.

The story actually began two nights before the murder, when Chris received *two* calls from an anonymous man who asked: "Are you Christine Freund? Do you live on Linden Street?" Frightened, Chris told the caller she was married to a cop, hung up and phoned Diel. (This information also appeared in confidential police reports.)

The next evening, Chris remained late in Manhattan, socializing with her girl-friends. On Saturday night, with the temperature locked at a frigid fourteen degrees, Diel picked Chris up at her home in the Ridgewood section of Queens at about eight o'clock. On Metropolitan Avenue, as they were en route to Forest Hills to see the film *Rocky,* a yellowish-colored car pulled abreast of Diel on the passenger's side. The driver, whom Diel couldn't describe, peered at them before speeding off. Diel didn't know if another person was in the car.

"It was an unusual thing," Diel recalled. "He passed us on the wrong side on a street that was icy and narrow. There was snow piled at the curbs. After slowing down to look at us, he drove off at maybe forty miles an hour. The conditions weren't good for that. But I can't remember what model or size the car was."

A few minutes later, Diel and Chris arrived in front of the Forest Hills Theatre on Continental Avenue (71st Street). The movie was going to be crowded, and the narrow street was swarming with people and cars.

"I was stopped in the middle of the street," Diel explained. "It was cold and I knew I'd have trouble parking. So I told her to go inside and get the tickets and I'd meet her there. So Chris got out there in the middle of the block."

Diel then circled the neighborhood unsuccessfully. There were no parking spaces to be found. He next drove east on Austin Street, turned south at the first inter-section and traveled west on Burns, heading back toward Continental and Station Plaza, less than two blocks south of the theater. There, in Station Plaza, Diel noticed a parking spot—some three car lengths in from the corner of Continental—and parallel-parked, backing into the space. His car was facing Continental.

As he turned off the engine, a pale yellow, light tan or off-white compact the size of a Chevy Nova or Ford Fairlane suddenly stopped about thirty feet behind him in the middle of the street. The car, which was between five and eight years old, was occupied by two men and was unnaturally angled so that its headlights shone on Diel's blue Firebird.

As Diel idly watched, the passenger in the compact jumped out and leaned against its open door while gazing intently at the Firebird. The man appeared to be thin and had dirty-blond or sandy-colored hair that was styled in a blow-dry cut. He looked to be in his twenties, and his face seemed "pinched," said Diel, whose vision was somewhat restricted by the headlights' glare.

Diel, now out of his car, locked the Firebird and—being late—began to jog north to the theater. The other man then climbed back into the compact, which drove away.

Four hours later, the murder would occur in this exact spot.

After the movie, at about 11 p.m., Diel and Chris walked about a quarter mile through the biting cold to the Wine Gallery restaurant on Austin Street, where they lingered until about 12:20 a.m. While there, Chris remarked that two men seated behind Diel and near the door were staring at her and making her uneasy. Diel turned around and stole a quick look at them. One, whom Chris termed "creepy," had brown hair and severe acne scars. The other, Diel reported to police in 1977, had sandy-blond hair parted in the center. He also wore a mustache and appeared to be in his early thirties.

When the couple left the Wine Gallery, the two men were nowhere around. But someone else was lurking.

Outside the restaurant, Diel bumped into a man he positively identifies as—David Berkowitz. Berkowitz was dressed in a beige raincoat (the same garment he was seen wearing just two blocks away at the Voskerichian killing six weeks later) and had one or both hands stuffed into his pockets. "Sorry, sorry," Diel apologized to Berkowitz, who merely replied: "O.K., O.K."

Leaving David behind, Diel and Chris began the quarter-mile trek to their car. Now the streets were empty as the numbing cold gripped the night. Street signs rattled in the wind and steam clouds rose skyward from the manhole covers that speckled the snow-lined Austin Street. Diel pulled Chris close to him as they walked.

At the corner of Continental and Austin, they noticed a solitary young man, with an orange knapsack, who appeared to be hitchhiking in a curious direction—right into the middle of exclusive Forest Hills Gardens. It was an unlikely route to be traveling at that hour, in that weather. Regardless, the man slowly made his way south, staying in the middle of Continental, and Diel and Chris passed him by.

The couple then cut diagonally across Continental and hurried beneath the Long Island Rail Road trestle to the corner of Burns. Their car was parked about fifty feet in from the intersection. When they reached the Firebird, which faced Continental, Diel opened his door, climbed in and leaned over to unlatch the passenger's door for Chris.

Diel then started the engine, revved it and put on an Abba tape while the car warmed up. "God, it's cold," Chris said, and Diel hugged her briefly and gave her a light kiss. "We had been going out a long time. We weren't making out in the car," he explained.

Accordingly, he said it was "impossible" that anyone approached them from the front. But as he prepared to pull away, three shots were fired through the passenger's window, shattering the glass. Two of the slugs hit Chris, one in the head, and she died a few hours later.

Across the street, a woman heard the gunfire and looked out from her room to see a red car speeding from the scene. Diel himself leaped from the Firebird and began shouting: "They shot her! They shot my girlfriend!" witnesses reported.

"Why," I asked Diel, "did you use the word 'they'?"

"I don't know," he replied. "It was just an expression."

Maybe so.

*   *   *

Were the prison informants accurate? Was Christine Freund a deliberately targeted victim shot by Manson II rather than Berkowitz?

After visiting the scene with Diel and Cinotti and meticulously reenacting the events of that fatal night, I showed Berkowitz's confession to Diel. Like other key figures, Diel wasn't interviewed by authorities after the arrest. Reading the transcript, Diel immediately labeled Berkowitz's version as "totally false" in critical areas.

"I bumped into him all right," Diel said, pointing at the confession. "But it was way back at the Wine Gallery—not where he said. And he was facing the other way; away from the direction we were going [the eventual crime scene]."

But Berkowitz had indeed confessed to bumping into Diel. There was no argument there. So what was the problem? The problem was that Berkowitz, trying to get himself away from the restaurant and back to the crime scene, erased nearly a quarter mile by claiming he nearly "touched shoulders" with Diel as the couple diagonally crossed Continental Avenue near the railroad trestle—only about 125 feet from their car.

"That's pure bullshit," key witness Diel told me; and he later repeated his entire statement to Tom Russo in DA John Santucci's office.

Diel further explained that Berkowitz lied again when he confessed to being "four or five feet" away from the couple as they entered their car. Berkowitz later tried to enhance this claim when he told a psychiatrist that he was able to watch from such a close distance by hiding behind a tree. If so, he must have lugged a spruce from Yonkers, because there wasn't any tree; not *there*.

Diel added: "Nobody passed us up either. The only person we saw was the hitch-hiker, and *we* passed him." Then how did Berkowitz pull the trigger, as he first claimed to have done? He was well behind the couple, whose car was facing forward. And the gunman, as Berkowitz confessed, did approach from *the rear*. So if it was Berkowitz, he would have walked right by as Diel warmed up the car, turned around and came back to fire.

"He did not walk past us," Diel said.

Berkowitz didn't say he did either. He just left an unchallenged gaping hole in his confession; perhaps purposely. Nobody caught these major discrepancies in 1977 because no one analyzed the crime scene, paid attention to the direction the Firebird faced or interviewed Diel after the arrest. Nobody wanted to.

Together, these contradictions comprised what might politely be termed "significant flaws" in the Freund confession. But then hadn't the prison informants, quoting Berkowitz, said he shot only the Bronx victims? Another important allegation was now supported.

* * *

But what about the "deliberate hit" and Manson II? Simply stated, the entire series of events bolstered the charge that Christine Freund was purposely chosen for death.

Berkowitz, in his confession, did make one claim which seemed to be supported by the facts. When asked why only three shots were fired, he replied there was only "one person to shoot." Which was exactly the point the informants were making.

Here is my analysis of the Freund murder:

First, to ascertain they had the right girl and address, the killers anonymously phoned Chris twice to ask if she was Christine Freund on Linden Street. Two nights later, on her first evening out in Queens since the calls, Chris and Diel were passed by the yellow car in the "unusual" manner Diel described. This act suggested that they were followed from the Freund home and that the killers pulled ahead on the passenger's side to visually identify Chris. Turning off a block or two up the road, they probably fell in behind again and tailed the couple to the theater.

But there, with the congestion of cars and people, they missed seeing Chris as she left the Firebird in the center of the street. That wasn't surprising because the assassins were locked in on the car itself, which was still sitting in traffic. Believing Chris was still in the Firebird, they stayed with Diel as he searched for a parking spot.

When Diel parked, they readied to do the hit there and then. The yellowish compact, a familiar sight at .44 scenes, pulled up and aimed its headlights at Diel's car. Ready to strike, the shooter hopped out—only there was no Christine.

So they waited. In the interim, a small red car (specified by the prison informants) replaced the yellow one; a feat easily accomplished because multiple cars were an intrinsic part of the operation. In fact, the killers had time to drive back to Westchester if necessary.

Leaving the theater, the young couple was shadowed to the Wine Gallery, where Christine eyed two conspirators, including Manson II, and called them to Diel's attention. The men then left the restaurant, leaving Berkowitz to monitor the young lovers.

The accomplices returned to Station Plaza and waited in the red compact—which a witness observed there a few minutes before the attack. He told police the car's engine was running and that it was occupied by *two* people.

Diel and Chris then left the Wine Gallery. After the "bumping" incident, Berkowitz followed them to the shooting site, saw them diagonally cross Continental Avenue and watched the murder from behind a tree on the opposite, northwest corner of Continental and Station Plaza.

From that vantage point, which was in front of Diel's car, Berkowitz fled to his own auto, which was parked on a "winding street"—probably Tennis Place—while the killer escaped in the small red car. This auto, which was precisely described as to color and size by the prison informants, was observed racing from the block by a second witness. The car's presence was not revealed to the public.

On the basis of all the circumstances and evidence, I believe the murder occurred in the manner just described.

The hitchhiker may or may not have been involved with the killers. Since he never came forward, that question remains unresolved.

As for the men in the Wine Gallery, Berkowitz's presence outside and his desire to distance himself from that location strongly suggested they were part of the setup. Moreover, the acne-scarred man was soon tentatively identified as an associate of his—and the companion's description was very similar to the one Vinny provided for Manson II.

"He had an athletic build, was maybe five-ten and had sandy-blond hair which was straight or wavy rather than curly," Vinny said. "I think he would have been about thirty in 1977."

"So he would have been in his early twenties when he was allegedly involved with the original Manson?"

"Yeah, that's right. And they brought him in to shoot Freund."

"Did he have a mustache?"

"I don't know. I don't recall that, but those things come and go easy," Vinny replied.

The description was also similar, though not precisely so, to that of the man who jumped from the compact. John Diel, however, couldn't say if that man and the one seated near the door in the Wine Gallery were the same person.

"Nothing about that compact meant anything to me until you asked me about the whole night," Diel explained. "So I never gave that possibility a thought until now. It's been several years, so I just can't say if they were the same guys."

Vinny's portrayal of Manson II also matched that of the man who reportedly watched the Elephas shooting and drove off in a yellow car with its lights extinguished. Moreover, the description was similar to that of two men connected to the Arlis Perry case—the law firm visitor and the man who entered the Stanford church minutes before her death.

There were numerous common denominators. But without eyewitness identification, which we couldn't try to obtain unless we learned who Manson II was, no positive conclusions could be drawn.

*   *   *

The question of motive remained in the Freund killing. "Berkowitz knew it was a hit. He was very clear on that," Vinny said. "But he said he didn't know the motive. Someone else did, though. Berkowitz only knew that someone had a connection to Camaro or R.R. and that Camaro acted as the middleman. Camaro got the Children to do it and they hid the motive in the so-called random .44 shootings that were going on."

Vinny provided the name of the person who supplied him with the motive, and said it was someone who had knowledge of the drug-porn phase of the operation. The motive, Vinny said, was as old as time itself.

"It involved her boyfriend and another woman."

"John Diel? He was about to become engaged to Christine," I countered. "What the hell are you talking about?"

"He was fooling around with another woman and toes were stepped on. That's the way I got it."

"Whose toes? And who had the damned connection? Was it the woman herself or did she have another boyfriend who was pissed?"

"Triangles are messy," Vinny answered. "I know part of it was a warning to the boyfriend [Diel], but Christine herself may have done something to set it off, too. Shit, I can't interrogate people around here when I feel like it. I was told the answer was in that triangle and that at least some of it was a warning to him. I don't know if the woman had it done or a boyfriend." In fact, since the Freund killing occurred before the .44-Caliber Killer was "born," the NYPD was searching for a motive in the shadowy recesses of John Diel's clandestine affair with a married Queens woman who, with her husband, had temporarily relocated to Germany. The information was not made public.

Diel was in love with Christine Freund. But he was occasionally tempted by after-hours opportunities. He told Cinotti and me that three such liaisons happened in the fall of 1976, a few months before the murder.

The intent here is not merely to examine John Diel's private life. Rather, murder is a public crime; Christine Freund was dead; and serious allegations had surfaced concerning another woman in Diel's world.

Of the affairs Diel acknowledged, he classified two as "one-nighters." But the other was more serious. Christine learned of the deeper affair when she borrowed Diel's car and a love letter from the married woman fell from the visor. Christine then took steps to disrupt the relationship, even though the woman was then in Germany for a time.

After laying down the law to Diel, Chris mailed a note to the woman (police found a draft copy and the woman's reply) threatening to expose the relationship to her husband unless she stayed away from John. According to police reports, the woman remained in love with Diel despite the letter.

But on the surface, the matter appeared to be settled.

However, the woman did have three possible motives for murder. First, to preserve her marriage, which she apparently wanted to do. Second, to hit Diel with a message that he should consider coming back to her. And third, to eliminate Chris because Chris intended to marry John Diel.

The woman's husband also had a motive. He approached Diel one day and asked if he was having an affair with his wife. Diel denied it, but that didn't mean the husband believed him. Nor did it mean that the woman couldn't have had still another boyfriend—someone else who wanted Diel to stay away for his own reasons.

After the murder, the NYPD spent several weeks interviewing Chris's friends, some of whom knew about the affair and her letter. But on March 3, the police—for the first time—interviewed a friend of the woman herself.

Five days later, Virginia Voskerichian was shot to death barely a block from the Freund scene. The shooting, which occurred at about 7:30 p.m. on a Tuesday, broke both the weekend and time-of-day patterns of the .44 attacks.

* * *

The Voskerichian murder had a fascinating impact. Police immediately linked the two slayings and announced that a lone, deranged madman was stalking the city. All investigations of motive in the Freund killing ceased on the spot.

Was it possible the Voskerichian shooting occurred when and where it did to deliberately deter the police probe of the triangle motive in the Freund murder? It was distinctly possible.

The entire picture could have explained Diel's enigmatic "They shot her!" cry at the scene of Christine's killing, which he maintained was "just an expression."

"Was he warned ahead of time?" I asked Vinny later.

"I don't know if he was or not. I just don't know if the whole thing was to send him a message or if some of it was to get back at her, or both."

And I don't know yet either. But I do have a suspicion. However, as Vinny said, someone had the means of contacting, directly or indirectly, either R.R. or Camaro, who allegedly then solicited the Children.

"I think all involved did it as a favor to their connections," Vinny said. "It was important enough to somebody that Manson II was brought in."

Whatever the final outcome of the Freund case, John Diel is an innocent man. Aware of the prison statements, he cooperated with the probe. Secretive dalliances with women doesn't place responsibility for Christine's death on his shoulders. Apparently, he didn't know what he was involved with. And Christine may have partly contributed to her own demise. The waters remain murky.

I also am not accusing either Diel's lover or her husband of complicity in murder. That has yet to be proven.

To return to the original prison allegation: Vinny's report that Christine Freund's murder was sparked by a situation which concerned "her boyfriend and another woman" was strongly supported, as was the concurrent, and complementary, charge that the murder was a deliberate hit.

* * *

On the basis of all available evidence, it was now possible to arrive at a full analysis of the .44 attacks.

VICTIMS	APPARENT SHOOTER
Lauria-Valente	Berkowitz
Denaro	Quite possibly a woman; three potential suspects identified
Lomino-DeMasi	John Carr, the chief suspect

Freund	Manson II
Voskerichian	Quite possibly a woman; three potential suspects identified
Suriani-Esau	Berkowitz
Placido-Lupo	Unknown, but not Berkowitz
Moskowitz-Violante	The hospital worker; two possible suspects identified

Others said to have belonged to the cult or suspected of participating in Son of Sam shootings or related crimes were mentioned earlier. The roster wasn't complete; some group members remained unidentified.

In 1986, I asked Vinny to summarize, in his own words, the Westchester-New York City-Long Island relationships. Years after he first stepped forward, this was his written reply:

> When Berkowitz and me first met, I told him I thought his original "demon" story was bullshit. He afterwards showed me those Gannett articles and your letters to convince me his satanic story was credible, had some basis in fact.
>
> I questioned him about the Westchester group—for specifics. When they met, who was who, names, etc. He had told me all about the Carr brothers, etc., and now I was asking about Mr. RE [Real Estate] and that cult. I wanted to get info to find Mr. RE and get that [coven] book of deeds done, etc.
>
> He began to tell me about Camaro. And how RE really got orders from someone bigger—how some of the "incidents" [.44 attacks] were not random but "contracted."
>
> Camaro was the go-between—where was he from? Go-between from where and between who? That's when he told me about the place "in the Village" and about Sissik [Sisman]. This intrigued me—how did he know that? Sounded like B.S. to me.
>
> He had been there, he said, along with Michael Carr. He saw the place. Saw the chandelier. Went to a party there. At least a party was going on. David waited in the foyer. They had to "pick something up." And that's how he began to tell me about "Mr. Big."
>
> Mafia? That was my first thought. No—drugs and sex and "entertainment"—kinky shit.
>
> Big lived on Long Island—a mansion. Had David been there? He

hesitated. Denied being there—eventually admitted he had been there.

Berkowitz explained what he knew (or what he was willing to let up he knew) about "Mr. Big." He said he didn't know the guy's name—just "Mr. Big." Shades of Rocky and Bullwinkle.

I sent out feelers. It was [name withheld] who verified what David said about the Chelsea setup. Drugs? You bet your ass—cars out front like it was Sunday and this was a church service. Did the cops know? Hell, they directed the traffic so there'd be no hassles for the "paying customers." [Vinny was writing about events which preceded Ronald Sisman's killing. Two years after that murder, a Police Department scandal erupted in the 10th Precinct, where Sisman lived. Several officers were removed for alleged collusion with owners of "after-hours" clubs. Payoffs were involved, the NYPD ruled.]

Ironically, Berkowitz did let the name slip [of R.R.; "Mr. Big"]. It was on my lists [as both "Roy Rogers" and "Rodan the Flying Monster"], but it was among many names and at first I couldn't tell who was who.

R.R. was into drugs. He was into a lot, but as I understand it, it was drugs which was his real link to Sissik and Mr. RE. I wonder how he became involved with RE. I know RE was prominent to some degree in Westchester law and political circles, and that Chelsea place was a hangout for political types from all over.

I'm sure Mr. RE organized the Children on his own—and Sissik/R.R./ Camaro were their suppliers. I believe RE was intimately tied to R.R./ Sissik—and his Children were merely a mechanism for "distribution" in Westchester and environs.

The group in Westchester had existed for some time. Berkowitz said that when he joined it, a "small circle" of a dozen members had long planned the events which later came about. It was planned long before Berkowitz entered the picture—various dastardly deeds had been done all along [as Berkowitz also told Harry Lipsig], building up to the crescendo of violence which later ensued.

R.R. never personally came to Westchester, as I understand it. Sissik didn't, either. Camaro was the "angel" for them.

The real reason for [the shootings] was a need of R.R. et al. The group had been itching for ultimate violence. Perhaps the first event [Donna Lauria's murder] was even a natural, sick culmination of their hype. But most certainly Mr. RE capitalized on his Children's enthusiasm very quickly.

It is almost incredible how R.R. then capitalized and organized the whole operation. It was actually very organized. In retrospect, it is obvious no lone nut could have carried it out as smoothly and methodically as it was—movement, arms procurement, strategy for locating victims, hours, etc., were all carefully planned out. As were escape routes.

In Berkowitz' own words, Camaro came [to some .44 scenes] as an "adviser, a coordinator" of events. And he did not always come alone. Manson II came and was an actual actor [shooter]—a "special guest weirdo," so to speak.

We both know how fantastic it really got—right down to videotapes of the action. R.R. originated the original Friday the 13th Homebox Channel right there in New York City.

You know how much of a "net" there was. We still see evidence of it. To anybody as knowledgeable as we are of the "workings and efficiency" of the policing machine, it is not incredible to see how all this went on undetected. I mean, had Ford's Theater been on Central Avenue when Lincoln was shot, and had the whole Westchester PD been present, and had they all seen Booth jump from the balcony—they probably would have arrested an old lady in the third row mezzanine as their suspect.

R.R. needed some "chores" taken care of. He needed those chores done for other persons to whom he was indebted, or for whom he did things. I believe drugs was the real link between R.R. and the Children. The "events" were a natural consequence of the relationship. It finally got out of hand.

It got too hot. So they decided to put an "end" to it. Publicly, at least. But the paranoia did not stop. Mistrust led to Sissik's demise. To summarize, R.R. was into a big, kinky scene. He controlled money, people, and drugs. And he used all of them in a very calculated fashion. It boomeranged. That much I know.

So, who was R.R., called both "Rodan" and "Roy Rogers" and linked in a coded sentence to "Dale Evans"? "Roy Rogers and Dale Evans are my favorite stars. . . . We were a regular jet set of the occult," the 1981 letter read. "Stars"; "jet set." Vinny seemed to be talking about high rollers and the entertainment business. Perhaps about a lofty meshing of drug, kink and cult activities in show business?

Maybe so.

In the spring of 1982, when Mike Zuckerman and I first met with Vinny at Dannemora, we asked him about Dale Evans and R.R. Berkowitz wasn't talking at the time, so Vinny had to give it his best shot alone. "I can't remember if the key word is 'Dale' or 'Evans' in that one. Whichever, him and Roy Rogers are the biggies."

"Then what about Roy Rogers—Rodan? Who the hell is he?" Zuckerman asked.

"His first name is Roy," Vinny replied. "And he lives in a big mansion in a town with two names on Long Island. Shit, I can't quite come up with the damn town, but it begins with an *S*."

"Sands Point?" Zuckerman tried.

Vinny looked thoughtful. "That may be it. But he's into all sorts of weird shit with whips and chains and kinky crap."

"What's his last name?" I asked quietly. The visiting room wasn't crowded, and Zuckerman and I were dressed as downbeat as possible to resemble nothing more than street friends of Vinny. Still, we didn't want to call any attention to ourselves by appearing to interrogate him. Serious questions were asked with relaxed smiles.

"Damn, it's something like Rodan, or Rudin, or Rodin," Vinny said, pressing his thumb and forefinger to his forehead. He was under a strain, and it occasionally showed. "I'm sorry, but I'm a little nervous here. But this guy beat the shit out of some actress and took videotapes of it. At the mansion. Berkowitz was at his place once—and in Minot, too."

"So he did go to Minot," I muttered. "He was throwing hints all over the place. And we had a girl ID him there."

"Yeah." Vinny nodded. "But I thought you already knew that—he thought you did. You know a lot of stuff but some shit escaped you, huh?"

"Sure it did. That's why we're here. But we know enough to see if you're bullshitting—don't forget that."

"You don't have to play Mr. DA with me," Vinny said. "Can't you just listen and tell those fucks back in New York to shove it? They all screwed this up in the first place, not me. You gotta worry more about their bullshit than mine. If I was gonna bullshit I'd have talked to some reporter who didn't know anything—not you, for Christ's sake." Vinny looked exasperated.

"What about this Long Island moneyman?" Zuckerman cut in, blanching at a swallow of Dannemora vending-machine coffee. "Berkowitz was at his place once?"

"Yeah. This guy had a lotta parties for all sorts of idiots. Dopers, bikers, big shots. I don't even know if he knew Berkowitz's name. I mean there were a lot of people always at this jerk's place."

"So why was Berkowitz there?"

"Because of the tie-ins with the cult and all. I don't know who he went there with, but it was for one of those big parties."

"And what about the Moskowitz tape?" I asked.

"That was made for this Rodan. Sissik [Sisman], some guy Mickey and whoever else. And Camaro was there that night, too. Either Mickey or Sissik made the thing—I believe it was Mickey, as I got it."

"O.K., but what was the big guy's name?"

"It's Roy, whatever—Rodan. It sounds like that code name." Throughout the day, we kept returning to Rodan, but Vinny couldn't remember the actual name. On the way back to the airport, Zuckerman and I were mouthing the possible names aloud. Suddenly, we both had it.

"Roy Radin!" we simultaneously shouted.

"And it's Southampton, not Sands Point," I said. "Goddamned Vinny not only couldn't remember the place, he thought it was two words. 'It begins with an S,' he says. Shit, he's been inside too long. But it does sound like two words."

"Yeah," Zuckerman answered. "And Berkowitz's last shoot-'em-up in a disco was supposed to be in Southampton, too."

"That's right. Damn, talk about your chickens coming home to roost. I'll bet that was a deliberate clue. Rodan is right—freaking Roy Radin."

"That actress thing happened out there a couple of years ago," Zuckerman remembered. "Melonie Haller, I think her name was. She was on *Welcome Back, Kotter* or something. She said they doped her up, stripped her, raped her and videotaped it at some weekend orgy Radin was running."

"Yeah, now I remember that. And they put her on a train to New York all spaced out and the cops were called by the train people."

"Whips, bondage and videotapes." Zuckerman smiled. "You like that part about the taping, right?"

"Hell, yes. It's a fetish of Radin's. Just like at Stacy's murder. I'll tell you, there are some things at that scene that a camera's presence could explain. I think that tape does exist, but finding it is another thing—look what Sisman appears to have gotten for his interest in it."

"You know, that thing could be for Radin's private collection," Zuckerman said. "But if you ever wanted to sell a few copies to your rich buddies—can you imagine the price of the most famous Son of Sam murder on tape?"

"At least fifty grand each," I speculated. "But like you say, this is like some collector of art who has a masterpiece stolen. He can't tell anybody he's got it, but he gets off knowing he does and revels in sneaking into his vault to look at it."

"A monster ego trip," Zuckerman agreed. "And if you ever needed cash, sell a few copies to your millionaire pals."

"Yeah, we've got that 'jet set of the occult' and 'stars' stuff he put in that letter now. But who the hell is this Dale Evans character?"

"Got me," Mike replied. "But Radin produces concerts and shows with big names in them. And he's definitely into all this far-out crap. I think that's enough to start with."

"Colonel Kink and his own Hell's Heroes," I said. "Suddenly all this mondo bizarro stuff makes sense. Radin's in the same age bracket as Berkowitz and the Carr boys. The damned thing is *actually logical*. Crazy logic; but still logic."

*   *   *

The scenario made even more sense when I learned that the murdered Ronald Sisman, whom Vinny kept calling "Sissik," was a close associate of Radin. Sisman was allegedly slain over the Moskowitz tape. In fact, Radin was interviewed by detectives after the October 30, 1981, murders of Sisman and Smith College coed Elizabeth Platzman. And Sisman, to complete the loop, had been dubbed the "personal" lensman for Melonie Haller, who in April 1980 was the star of a video scandal at Radin's Atlantic beachfront estate in exclusive Southampton, Long Island—a seventy-two-room palace on Dune Road called Ocean Castle.

Radin's lavish home was known locally as a haven for sex and dope parties, some involving the rich and famous. A month before the 1980 S&M blast, Haller posed for *Playboy* magazine, trying to capitalize on her small "sweathog" role in Mr. Kotter's television classroom. And a month after the Southampton soiree, she accused Sisman of attempting to force drugs into her. Sisman told police he merely tried to offer her a tranquilizer, and the charges were dropped. Seventeen months later, it was Sisman who was dropped.

This was a crowd in which murder, drugs and depravity were commonplace. It was like seeing a reflection of the Sam cult. Vinny's statements, rather than straining credibility, could more appropriately be answered by: "Of course."

I also learned that police, raiding Ocean Castle on that wild Haller weekend, confiscated a sex video starring none other than Radin himself. The sex tape immediately brought to mind James Camaro's alleged performance in a similar epic with the woman producer from the TV network. And at more than six feet tall and 280 pounds, the bearded Radin also matched the description Vinny provided of "Rodan," right down to the glasses he usually wore.

Once more, the informants were leading us down a corridor of confirmations and complementary details.

Other articles seized in the Haller raid included a quantity of drugs, a .38 handgun and a set of privately posed photos of a nude young woman wearing a Nazi cap—an adornment I noted with interest.

"He had a whole harem out there," said attorney Stephen Siegfried, who defended Radin in the Haller case. The lawyer's comment, made to the *New York Times* long after Vinny's statement, blended with what the informants said about the cult and collegiate call girl network.

Actually, Haller's railroading, so to speak, was the second time police attention was directed to Ocean Castle that 1980 weekend. They first investigated a report that Radin's assistant, Michael Deans De Vinko—known as Mickey De Vinko to the inner circle—had overdosed on drugs. Before linking up with Radin in various enterprises, Mickey De Vinko had been the husband of the famed singer-actress Judy Garland at the time of her death in 1969 and night manager of the upscale Arthur disco in Manhattan.

In the Haller case, Radin was charged with criminal possession of LSD and cocaine, unlawful possession of a handgun and menacing the twenty-three-year-old starlet. Radin's girlfriend, and later second wife, Toni Fillet, was accused of third-degree assault. The assault charges against both were later dismissed, but Radin was fined $1,000 and placed on probation for the unlicensed .38 revolver.

Additionally, Robert McKeage IV, a forty-five-year-old New Jersey businessman who was Haller's date that weekend, pleaded guilty to assault and was sentenced to thirty days in jail.

A similar tidal wave washed through Ocean Castle in 1981—on the night of

Radin's wedding there to Fillet. After the reception, aspiring model Jacey (J.C.) Layton was lying nude in a sauna at 2 a.m. when Radin, she said, entered and demanded sex from her. Layton—who would become the girlfriend of appliance heir Christopher Maytag, who died of cocaine abuse in 1987—told police that Radin assaulted her when she refused to comply. Authorities couldn't corroborate Layton's story, which Radin denied, but they again removed pills and drug paraphernalia from the estate.

Drugs were everywhere in the Radin portrait, and he was a known heavy user of cocaine—sometimes spending more than $1,000 a week on the trendy white powder. Radin was also closely allied with Sisman, whom we, and the police, knew was dealing coke. According to Vinny, Radin had a piece of that action and influenced Sisman's operation. But I wasn't completely satisfied as to the extent of Radin's alleged dealing until I learned that he was a top target of a secret federal probe of coke trafficking among New York's social and show business elite. It was believed organized crime involvement lurked somewhere in the network, perhaps in the form of a fringe relationship.

"Bingo," I said to Hank Cinotti as we met one afternoon in a Bronx diner. "The Feds couldn't get enough to indict him, but with what our guys know, maybe they could have. We already knew about his amigo Sisman's dealing, and now we've got Radin himself in there, too."

"His relationship with Sisman would've been enough," Hank replied. "This just adds to it. The whole sex and dope scene is falling in just the way your boys upstate said it did."

Yes, it was. But despite his troubles with the Southampton authorities, Radin was still big trouble for us. He had *many* police connections, a fact which may have answered a number of questions which were swimming in my mind for years. I couldn't prove it, but I'd always suspected a leak—besides our own activities—may have been a contributory factor in the curiously timed deaths of the Carr brothers.

I'd also wondered if the door was slammed on the Son of Sam case for reasons beyond politics, career enhancement and face-saving. Radin had the money, friends and other connections to buy someone if he needed to. It was possible that several elements, combined, were at play. It wouldn't have been the first time. But a suspicion wasn't proof.

*   *   *

Roy Alexander Radin was but thirty-two years old in 1982, when Mike Zuckerman and I first learned he was an alleged overlord of the operation we were investigating. Despite his youth, Radin had accumulated a fortune. Ocean Castle alone was worth an estimated three million.

Radin was a theatrical and concert producer, and much of his wealth was earned via the production and staging of large benefit shows for police unions and associations throughout the country. As such, his official links were numerous and widespread.

Radin's shows were star-studded events, with vaudeville and other luminaries, some fading, headlining his bills. Milton Berle, Red Buttons, Donald O'Connor, Jan Murray, Tiny Tim, Eddie Fisher, George Jessel and others were professionally associated with Radin—who also assumed a role in the management of actor Demond Wilson's career. Wilson had co-starred as Redd Foxx's son on the hit TV series *Sanford and Son* and in the short-lived *New Odd Couple* and *Baby, I'm Back.*

But for all his acumen, the SS *Radin* ran aground temporarily in 1975, when New York's attorney general filed a civil suit charging that Radin routinely pocketed 75 percent or more of police benefit proceeds. Radin denied the accusation and the matter was resolved when he agreed to stop organizing police fundraisers in New York State. It may have been then that he decided to show up the establishment.

In any case, Radin reportedly sidestepped the local restriction by arguing that police agencies were labor unions and not charities. Therefore, no one could claim he was bilking police widows and children. And so the beat went on.

Show business blood flowed through Radin's veins since birth. His mother, Renee, was an ex-showgirl and his father, "Broadway Al" Radin, owned speakeasies and nightclubs during New York City's golden age. Al Radin's connections cut across the New York scene. When his parents divorced, Roy Radin lived with his father in Florida for a time. He later dropped out of high school to create a traveling show which starred the venerable J. Fred Muggs, the chimpanzee who cavorted with Dave Garroway during the early days of NBC's *Today* show.

From that Darwinian genesis, Radin evolved into rock music production, theatrical management and the nomadic vaudeville extravaganzas which made him a millionaire by the age of twenty-five.

But success went to Radin's head; badly. His world spun erratically through a galaxy of parties, drugs, overindulgence, big spending and oft-observed cruelty to women. On one sadistic weekend at Ocean Castle, Radin's guests were invited to pack dog collars and leashes in their overnight bags—and not because he was hosting the Suffolk County Kennel Club either. A local merchant on Hampton Road was puzzled by the number of people who stopped by to stock up for canine capers.

The bicoastal Radin maintained offices in New York and on Sunset Boulevard in Los Angeles, City of Fallen Angels. Back and forth he shuttled, his jet-set life an amalgam of champagne, coke, women, limos and lechery. As the power trip and drugs took him over, Radin sank ever deeper into depravity. He became a glassy-eyed caricature of the 1930s Hollywood mogul, strutting through Southampton—bodyguards in tow—flaunting a devilish black cape and twirling a cane.

Water has been known to seek its own level. Radin counted among his many friends one Paul Hill,* a wealthy Manhattan heir whose town house was nicknamed "the Nursery" because he was passionately attracted to pubescent girls; a trait he shared with a certain law enforcement official and with John Carr and the Sam cult—to whom the rape of a young girl was a sacred satanic symbol.

Hill had a special technique. He'd hook the kids on dope to ensure their dependency on him. There may be some justice, for it appears that Hill himself became a junkie by 1985; bitten by his own snake.

But Hill wasn't the only Radin associate to ferment in a vile vat. Radin's guests and parties became wilder and seedier. Videotapes reigned. On one occasion, a local delivery boy told of seeing biker types, baring knives and guns, prowling the halls of Ocean Castle. Standing tall at center stage, the youth reported, was Radin. The story meshed with what Vinny said much earlier about elements of the cult crowd dropping by the mansion now and then.

As Radin and his companions regressed, the power-obsessed Radin began questing for the ultimate thrill, and the informants maintained he found it in the ultimate evil.

By the end of 1982, Radin's marriage to Toni Fillet was done, RIP'd after barely more than a year. Ocean Castle was up for sale, and Radin was pondering a move into Manhattan or out to L.A. We now had an alleged leader in sight, and the information I'd compiled did nothing but strengthen the informants' statements. But it wasn't enough. Without corroborating evidence to arrest him, there was nothing anybody could do but wait and watch.

And in light of the history of the case, we were sure the volcano would erupt again sooner or later.

*   *   *

The outside world wasn't on hold while the Radin investigation progressed. On May 8, 1982, tragedy struck once more. On the fourth anniversary of David Berkowitz's guilty pleas, his chief counsel at the time, Leon Stern, was shot to death when he and his wife apparently surprised two burglars who broke into their Roslyn Harbor, Long Island, home.

Returning from an evening out, Stern, fifty-six, and his wife, Laura, were jumped in their garage. Mrs. Stern was taken upstairs and bound, but Stern was killed when he struggled for an intruder's gun.

Berkowitz had spoken to attorney Harry Lipsig four months earlier, and now his own former lawyer was murdered. Because of that fact and the date of the shooting, those probing the Son of Sam case kept a watchful eye on the Stern matter. Two Queens men were subsequently arrested by Nassau County police, and from all appearances Stern was indeed killed by burglars. Still, it marked the violent death of yet another person closely tied to the .44 case.

At about this same time, Lipsig and I became targets of an intended smear campaign by the Church of Scientology. They were unnerved because one of its mid-level counselors, Michael Carr, was linked to the case—although no public disclosure of his involvement had been made. The group also feared that Lipsig and I intended to lay responsibility for the .44 murders at its doors.

The Church, of course, didn't know that Berkowitz termed the Sam cult a violent Scientology offshoot, or that he possessed the telephone number of their Florida headquarters, the Fort Harrison Hotel in Clearwater, or that I knew the Borrelli letter's allusion to victims as "fair game" was a lift from Scientology founder L. Ron Hubbard's notorious "Fair Game" memo on the treatment of enemies. That phrase, I was sure, was courtesy of Michael Carr.

But from the available evidence, Scientology itself wasn't involved in the .44 killings. An offshoot didn't prove that Scientology was a willing parent, and we viewed the phone number as evidence of Berkowitz's link to Michael Carr, who had been to Clearwater.

It was true that the Church was fertile ground from which a devious member could pluck recruits for the satanic movement. It was true that the Process sprang from Scientology when the DeGrimstons set sail on their own. It was true that Charles Manson, before the Tate-La Bianca murders, received Scientology counseling from a fellow inmate in a federal prison in the mid-sixties. And it was true that Berkowitz's named accomplice Michael Carr was a Scientologist.

But beyond those links, there was nothing with which to accuse the group of complicity. But that didn't stop Scientology from plotting against Lipsig and me. Only I found out about it.

Harry and I weren't the first citizens of Smear City. The FBI had an extensive file on the group's activities and raided its Los Angeles and Washington, D.C., headquarters in July 1977. In the aftermath, nine Scientologists pleaded guilty to one count each of either conspiracy to burglarize or obstruction of justice. Mary Sue Hubbard, wife of L. Ron Hubbard, was among the guilty. She was sentenced to five years in prison and fined $10,000 for obstructing justice.

In 1984, a *New York Times* report on the cult stated it was "long a subject of government investigation." The article further said: "Several former officials of the church who were disenchanted with [L. Ron Hubbard] had admitted helping him divert more than $100 million in church funds to foreign bank accounts."

Scientology isn't a religion based on worship of any god. Rather, it holds that one can discover inner peace through self-awareness and a counseling program known as "auditing." Budding Scientologists will sometimes pay up to three hundred dollars an hour for auditing, during which a "counselor" gauges their responses to life questions through a device called an E-Meter. The process purports to enhance one's ability to soul-search.

Author Paulette Cooper, whose book title *The Scandal of Scientology* speaks for itself, was targeted for an intelligence operation, as was Boston attorney Michael Flynn, who sued the Church at least twenty times on behalf of former members. "He was our number one enemy. We were always trying to set up an operation against Michael," former Scientology official Laurel Sullivan told the *Times*.

In 1980, the *Miami Herald* published a comprehensive report which found that Scientology orchestrated smear campaigns and employed other covert tactics to gain a strong foothold in Clearwater. "A wing of the church had undertaken a systematic program of spying and burglary that went on for years," reporter John Dorschner wrote. Reporters for the St. Petersburg, Florida, *Times,* the *Clearwater Sun* and other publications also have investigated the group.

*   *   *

Geoff Shervell. Dick Storey. Debbie Ward. If exposure renders intelligence operatives useless, then those three Scientologists may wish to short-circuit their E-Meters. Storey, in L.A., and Shervell and Ward in New York were among the Church members who plotted against Harry Lipsig and me. Scientology has its own spy network all right, and it is known as the Guardians.

Through a confidential source, certain Scientology documents fortuitously came into my possession in mid-1982. They are now in the hands of law enforcement, where they remain accessible to me. One thick folder immediately caught my attention. It was labeled "Lipsig Estimate," and it detailed the Church's plot of the month.

Geoff Shervell, whose immigration status was unknown—he apparently is British—ran the operation out of New York, where Ward and others assisted him. Storey was the major honcho in L.A.

In short, the group feared that a major effort was underway to hang the Son of Sam murders on it, and that Lipsig also was going to employ the .44 connection as a weapon in another case he was handling against the Church. So they drew up a plan of action against Lipsig and me, designed to discredit us. They infiltrated Lipsig's large firm and removed legal documents, interviewed the Carr family, and planned to utilize various media contacts to blacken our reputations.

Here are some excerpts from the report:

> *Replacement of Terry. The idea is to have our friend replace Terry as the OL [main contact] for Lipsig. . . . Terry and Lipsig may be so closely involved together . . . that it would be dangerous to try to split them up. We may have to handle them as a team rather than two individuals. Notwithstanding, we should at least . . . see if it is possible for our person [operative] to become indispensable to Lipsig in a greater degree than Maury Terry. This will be achieved by our person having more to offer Lipsig in the way of contacts in the religious field which is what Lipsig is going to need . . . to push this anti-cult attack.*
>
> *Expose on Terry: At some point we are going to have to do an expose on Terry and his false reports and do a full invalidation of his investigation into this whole Berkowitz affair. He is the mouthpiece for Berkowitz and . . . he has to be discredited. This would preferably be done off of their lines. The reason for this is obvious. If we do it, then we have such a vested interest that it will simply be our word against Maury Terry's, so some credible source will have to be found. This is something which should be researched immediately.*
>
> *Expose on Lipsig: This activity will also be conditional on his relationship*

with Terry. If they are really tight, then we will have to expose them both
together. . . . The value of this expose on Lipsig will be enhanced by any connec-
tion we can prove to any government agency and of course any psych agency.

In another section, the following was written:

Lipsig wants to connect Scn. to the Son of Sam case. He has depo'd Ber-
kowitz who supposedly told him that there existed this death cult. Lipsig's
connection is of course the fact that Michael Carr was a Scientologist and
he is going to try to blow that out of proportion.

It was heard that Lipsig told his secretary to note down that he wants
to get supporting data that confirms the identifying of the bodies of John
and Michael Carr. Lipsig says there are people who do not want this
[civil suit against Berkowitz] to go to trial. The police commissioner is
one. . . .

. . . It was heard today that Berkowitz was raised a Jew but . . . was
a born-again Christian. When giving the above data the secretary in
Lipsig's office said it came from a Mr. Ter . . . She stopped in the middle
of the guy's name. When asked if she meant Mr. Terry, she gave a "no"
answer.

The report also contained some twenty marked Son of Sam stories and an assessment: "There are press lines which can be utilized to counter the Black PR Campaign
[my articles and Lipsig's public comments]."

So the Scientologists probably had friends in the media. Nice thought to
contemplate.

I immediately alerted Lipsig, who took steps on his end, and we were put on guard
for the future. It would be too easy—and a mistake—to dismiss the Scientologists
as merely paranoid. They are of much more concern than that, as anyone who has
crossed swords with them can attest.

I, and many others, endorse official efforts to root out any illegal activities conducted by this so-called Church. I regard the group as an abhorrent stain on the
American landscape—a mind-bending cult of which parents and educators should
be aware, and to which young people should give the widest berth possible.

*   *   *

As 1983 bowed in, the Son of Sam investigation was still focused in New York. In
Minot, Jeff Nies and Mike Knoop remained alert, but activity there all but ceased
because the prime players had left Ward County. Lieutenant Terry Gardner was gone
from the Sheriff's Department to new work in corporate security. From Santa Clara,
Sergeant Ken Kahn called periodically to learn what he could about Manson II's
identity. My correspondence with Vinny and Danny continued, and John Santucci's

office in Queens remained frustrated by the refusal of Berkowitz or another participant to turn state's evidence.

In January, producer Frank Anthony, who coordinated the several *What's Happening, America* programs in 1981, asked if I'd do an update on a special documentary,
"The War Within," which would be hosted by prominent attorney F. Lee Bailey.
The syndicated hour-long show, which would air in June, would highlight the Son
of Sam and Atlanta child murders cases. I readily agreed and we started production.

Roy Radin's role and the larger scope of the case would remain secret, but I consented to allude to a 1981 Manhattan murder without naming Sisman or releasing
any particulars. That part of the report would be picked up by the wire services, along
with Santucci's restated comments on the conspiracy's existence.

In early February, after months of persuasion, Vinny consented to make a formal
statement about Radin to authorities. In my presence, he recited the tale for three
hours.

Two months later, Roy Radin told his half sister, Diane Dorr, that he had to vacate
the New York scene for a time. "I'm going away for a while. I have to go away," she
quoted him as saying. "He was very strange about it."

Shortly afterward, John Santucci and I met in his office to discuss the matter of
Roy Radin, lord of Southampton.

"I have nothing to base a warrant on," the DA explained. "Vinny says the tape
allegedly was made *for* Radin, but I can't tell a judge we have evidence it's in that
damned mansion of his. We don't know where it's supposed to be. And no one says
Radin was a direct participant. He wasn't at any crime scenes, or even at any of these
meetings in Westchester and wherever else."

"That's true," I reluctantly agreed. "He's insulated himself pretty well. This James
Camaro was at crime scenes, but we can't find him. Everyone else he's talked about
is real, so I'm sure Camaro is, too. It'd obviously help if we had the exact name, but
we don't."

"What about this real estate lawyer?" Santucci asked.

"Several possibles, but no one we can say for sure. That church up there existed,
but the witch who was in it is long gone."

"I've got nothing but problems with this case," Santucci complained. "I'd give
anything to be able to convene a grand jury, but my hands are tied. I know you don't
like that, and you don't want to accept it—but it's true. I still need independent
corroboration or firsthand testimony from Berkowitz or someone else."

"Vinny and Danny said they'd testify," I tried.

"Not good enough. Whatever they say may be golden, but it would still net out
as hearsay in a courtroom."

"So what in hell do we do about Radin?"

"We wait. I can't do anything about him right now. At this moment, he's
untouchable."

No, he wasn't.

Roy Radin disappeared on Friday, the thirteenth of May, in Los Angeles—said to be the home of the Sam cult's national headquarters.

* * *

It took a week for the news to trickle out, but when it did chaos ruled the lives of those immersed in the investigation. For days, my phone rang off the hook as contacts and sources called to find out if I knew anything. From Dannemora, Vinny wrote: "Tell me, when a person dies, to whom does he bequeath his videotape collection? Remember the meeting? They asked if I thought they could just go put handcuffs on a millionaire. I'll bet even he wishes they did so now."

Vinny had pronounced Radin dead, but officially he'd just vanished into thin air. My own initial fear was a four-letter word spelled l-e-a-k. John Carr, Michael Carr and now Radin. They had one thing in common: their names were handed to authorities shortly before they died or disappeared. Queens had nothing to do with the prior information on the Carrs, and Brooklyn didn't know about Radin. So a leak wouldn't have sprung from the prosecution. But prosecutors' offices routinely deal with police. So if there had been a leak, I reasoned some police agency would have been the source.

Slowly, sketchy details of the disappearance became known. Radin had been on the Coast working on a movie deal with producer Bob Evans—friend of Roman Polanski et al. On the night of the thirteenth Radin entered a limousine outside Hollywood's Regency Hotel with a woman named Elaine Jacobs, whom East Coast papers dubbed a "mystery woman." An uneasy Radin had asked actor Demond Wilson, armed with a handgun, to trail them.

Wilson followed the limo for a time, but said that another car moved between them on Sunset Boulevard and that he lost both vehicles in traffic. Radin and Jacobs were supposed to have dinner at the La Scala restaurant, but they never made it. Or at least Radin didn't.

Jacobs told two stories about what happened. First, she claimed she and Radin argued and he left the limo on Sunset. Next, she said it was she who got out of the car after the heated discussion.

He hadn't been seen since.

Radin's 1983 dealings with both Jacobs and Evans were sparked by a film Evans wanted to produce: *The Cotton Club*. Short of cash, Evans, whom Jacobs allegedly introduced to Radin, agreed to enter into a partnership with the Southampton squire, who said he could raise $35 million to finance *The Cotton Club* and two subsequent projects.

Through a spokesman, Evans told the *New York Post* that there wasn't any deal with Radin. That wasn't true. On April 26, seventeen days before Radin disappeared, he and Evans signed a contract which allocated to each a 45 percent share of *The Cotton Club* and the subsidiary projects. The remaining 10 percent was assigned to Puerto Rican banker Jose Alagria, whose government was to provide Radin's contribution.

In other words, since inking the contract Evans no longer had controlling interest in his own project.

"I couldn't believe Evans signed it," Alagria later told *New York* magazine. "I told Roy, 'The day will come when this guy realizes he's not in control.'"

For her part, the dark-haired, thirty-seven-year-old Jacobs, also known as Elaine Delayne and Karen Goodman, formerly was romantically linked with reputed Miami cocaine king Milan Bellechasses. Jacobs was promised a $50,000 finder's fee from Radin on the *Cotton Club* deal. But she suspected that Radin was somehow involved in the alleged theft of eleven to sixteen kilos of cocaine from her rented home in Sherman Oaks, California, an L.A. suburb. Jacobs allegedly believed that Radin had conspired with her dope runner, Talmadge (Tally) Rogers, who hadn't been seen since the purported rip-off occurred in March.

So there it stood. Evans, Jacobs, drug deals, Hollywood films and a missing Roy Radin.

*   *   *

At 11 a.m. on June 10, beekeeper Glen Fischer entered a desolate, dusty canyon some sixty miles north of L.A. On this warm morning, Fischer was searching for a suitable location to set up his hives. Down a rutted, dirt path he walked into the yawning hole known as Caswell Canyon. To his right, a dried creek bed blanched in the blistering June sun. Sagebrush, tumbleweed and desert foliage splashed patches of color on the grainy, hilly landscape, and clumps of hardy trees flaunted their green resilience to the sizzling sky.

At his feet, Fischer noted fragments of shattered clay targets; someone had used the area for skeet practice. Whoever it was, the beekeeper thought, didn't belong to any Hollywood rod and gun club. Nobody but a desert rat would know about this forsaken place. Behind him to the west, Fischer faintly heard the infrequent whiz of a passing car on Highway 5.

To reach the canyon, one drove an hour north from L.A. and exited Route 5 at Hungry Valley Road. Turning east, a driver would then swing north again to traverse the dead-end Copco Canyon service road, which paralleled the highway before abruptly ending at a metal barrier.

Beyond the rail, hidden behind a small thicket of underbrush, lay the narrow dirt road on which the beekeeper now walked. The path could be negotiated by car—but only by someone who knew it existed in the first place.

Several hundred yards into the canyon, a hot breeze filled Fischer's nostrils with an unfamiliar, pungent aroma somewhat akin to flavored pipe tobacco. Across the creek bed, Fischer noticed a large green shrub, which looked almost like a wide fir tree. It was thick; its full branches hugged the ground, and tall grass further hid its base from view. The beekeeper thought he saw something on the earth beside the shrub.

Crossing the dry creek, Fischer hopped up the south bank and walked eight feet to the dense branches. Looking down, he saw it.

It was dressed in a dark blue suit, and a vest, dress shirt and tie. Four buttons were torn from the vest and two from the shirt, which was laid open. The suit's front pockets were turned out. Someone had removed the identification from whatever this had been.

It was lying on its back. A Gucci loafer remained on the right foot; the other shoe was next to the body. The left hand was raised upward, grotesquely grabbing a low branch of the shrub. The body was mummified, and there was a large hole where the front of the skull should have been. Beetles swarmed in the hollow stomach cavity.

It was, the horrified Fischer saw, the shriveled, baking corpse of what was once a large, well-dressed man. Now its weight was a mere sixty-nine pounds, and it languished in the moisture of its own fluids, which *still* seeped into the earth beneath it. Fischer now knew what the bittersweet odor was.

It was Roy Radin.

* * *

"We're going to the Coast," I excitedly told Georgiana. "We've got our week at Fire Island and we'll go right from the beach to the airport. Ted Gunderson is expecting us in L.A., and he's arranging a meeting with the Sheriff's Homicide people."

"I'm already packing two wardrobes," she said, laughing. "I knew there was no way you'd stay home on this one."

Vinny knew it, too. He wrote:

> *When you go to the coast, look out for souvenirs. Understand?*
>
> *You know what to look for, even if everyone else doesn't. Look for those signs we've discussed in the past [ritual objects at crime scenes]. And if you get to view anything about the dead Flying Monster, see if you can identify any marks, etc. Comprende?*
>
> *The question I pose to you is this—they know the victim, but do they realize what people were hunting for? It involves movies—videotapes. That I've verified for sure. In October 1981 they acted to preserve those tapes. I'm not sure yet if this was purely over that—there could be other motives, too—but from every source I have, it's about the things we're interested in. And it definitely involved the same cast of actors.*
>
> *It's just a hunch, but I say Manson II, or Frank, if that's his name. I believe this was his pet assignment. Do you honestly think the Flying Monster traveled all the way to the Sunshine State and didn't visit any of his old acquaintances? Well, if he didn't plan to, they certainly did plan on visiting him.*
>
> *Bleed the coast for all you can. I'm glad the East is staying out. Because you can probably get info from the West that they don't even realize is valuable. It's the SUBTLE things we need—they will break this thing eventually.*

Maury, when will they learn that I've only told the truth? Yes, it sounds fantastic—but so many true things sound fantastic. Let's see— what number victim is this now? One by one, everyone is disappearing. You know, in another two years there won't be anyone left to capture.

Except for Manson II. Do you realize that L.A. is now the hottest place in this investigation? I'd say the hottest people left are Manson II, Camaro and Mr. Real Estate. Camaro seems to be nowhere. [Mr.] RE is there, but nobody seems to be able to put their finger on him yet.

Ironic, people are dropping like flies around me. I'm not Houdini. I can't predict deaths in advance by magic. We've both paid a high price in years of effort and frustration. I'm sick and tired of handing gems to assholes and watching them bury it in bureaucratic inanities.

You will note I'm as humble and soft-spoken as ever. When you go, listen very closely and look for ties. This one was kept tight. Seems to have been a surprise to all as it came down. Except for one interesting bit of info—seems a certain person [Radin] was advised very heavily against a vacation to that place.

So, it was "about the things we're interested in," Vinny wrote. Drugs, big money and, somewhere in the picture—a videotape or movie. Perhaps, as he suggested, several motives converged at once. And once I heard that Radin was dealing with Bob Evans, I immediately wondered if the "Dale Evans" Vinny referred to in his 1981 letter had been identified.

The week at Fire Island was a good one. All the old friends were there, including George Austin, who'd moved across the walk to share a home with Martin and Pat Burke. Coincidentally, Marty Burke was a close friend of Joe Walsh, a writer I knew well from Westchester. Walsh had summered in the Hamptons for years and heard the stories about Radin and Ocean Castle.

"He was something of a local legend for his weirdness out there," he said. "All sorts of bizarre nonsense was supposed to be going on. Some Hamptons people knew about it. And now he got his."

And we were going to try to find out why. Just as importantly, we were going to see if the still-unidentified Manson II might have participated in the killing.

I had a description of Manson II, and I also knew he would somehow trace back to the original Charles Manson—he would appear somewhere in the Manson "family" or in the show business or drug circles Manson himself inhabited. And perhaps we'd find out for whom Manson "volunteered" to commit the Tate murders—and why.

It was an almost impossible mission, but we had to try. In that, I was fortunate to have the assistance of Ted Gunderson. The gray-haired, fifty-two-year-old Gunderson was a retired FBI senior special agent in charge. Before leaving the Bureau, he'd headed offices in Dallas, Philadelphia and elsewhere before assuming command of some eight hundred agents in southern California. After retiring in 1979, he opened a successful private investigation agency in L.A.

Through producer Frank Anthony, Gunderson and I had earlier made contact by telephone. And now Roy Radin was murdered on Ted's home turf. In that respect, I was lucky: the highly qualified Gunderson was willing to assist the investigation for no fee. He knew what was at stake.

* * *

Aboard a Pan Am flight on Sunday afternoon, July 17, I busied myself with notes on the case while Georgiana watched a film. Our plan was to spend three days in L.A. before driving up the coast to Monterey; then to Stanford University in Palo Alto on the Arlis Perry case; and on into San Francisco for a long weekend of relaxation. I had a feeling we'd need it.

We touched down at L.A. International at about 7 p.m. With a waiting rental car, we were but a short drive from the Marina International Hotel in Marina Del Rey, a few blocks from Venice Beach and the rolling Pacific. Stepping from the terminal into the gathering dusk, I was struck by the thought that the man whose murder we were probing had walked through those same doors for the last time two months before.

"Welcome to L.A.," I said to Georgiana. "We're right back where all this lunacy really began in the late sixties. And now it's gone across the damned country and come home again."

"And so have we," she answered.

Sliding our luggage into the back of the car, we pulled into light traffic on Lincoln Boulevard as we drove north toward the Marina. "I can't help thinking about Manson II, the deadliest of all of them," I said, pointing toward the hazy L.A. skyline to the east.

"He's right around us now, either somewhere over there in the city or in one of these suburbs along the coast. Venice, the Marina, Santa Monica, Torrance, Manhattan Beach. Somewhere here. Damn, the whole freaking headquarters or whatever is here."

"What do you suppose that is?" Georgiana asked, as the Beach Boys' "I Get Around" piped from the car radio, making me wish it was the summer of '64 again. "Do you think it's an old church or a private club or house?"

"Yeah, one of the three. None of the informants knew which."

It was twilight and the colors and sounds of Marina Del Rey beckoned us.

"It's beautiful here," I said. "Thousands of boats, great restaurants, and right off the ocean. The hotel is also done with a nautical flair."

"Some of these places look familiar," Georgiana noticed. "They use this area a lot for TV backdrops, don't they?"

"Yeah, they do. Hey, after we check in and eat, let's hit the beach and walk a little. In the Atlantic this morning and the Pacific tonight—bicoastal beach bums.

Tomorrow's time enough to worry about Radin. Ted's coming for breakfast at nine and we've got the cops at eleven."

"And we're going out to the scene, right?"

"Absolutely. That area's got to be searched. I'm sure the cops will give us directions."

"You're into the upper levels of this now," Georgiana remarked. "The TV show worked fine, and you were still able to keep this part out."

"We had to. There'd be no way of getting anywhere at all on this otherwise. Nobody knows a damn thing, so we're going to be able to sneak in the back door here."

I refrained from bringing up the fear factor. Secrecy about Radin and Manson II also helped us sleep better, and was especially important now that we'd landed in Manson II's backyard. He had no reason to be worried about us, and that's the way I wanted to keep it—particularly since the previous month's TV report also aired in L.A. I was certain he and his friends had seen it.

*   *   *

Later, after a quiet dinner of prawns and shrimp Louie at a seaside restaurant in Venice, we wandered the darkened beach. Beside us, the Pacific waves crested majestically and slapped the shore.

"I've got to thank Berkowitz for this someday," I said. "It's a perfect night in a perfect spot. Finally, they've done a crime that didn't take me out to Minot or to another of those godforsaken max prisons in the wilds of New York State. Maybe I'll ask him if they have another branch in Tahiti."

"You like to joke your way through these things," Georgiana chided. "But you're just trying to play Mr. Cool. This is probably the most important trip of the whole case."

"Which case? You know how many killings we've had to look into? But yeah, this trip may be for the whole enchilada."

I stopped walking and gestured toward the invisible inland hills. "Just think, we've now got a real Hollywood drama—and *shot* on location, too."

"Very funny." Georgiana laughed weakly. "It's after two a.m. in New York—I think your jets are lagging."

"Screw it. I really do know how important these next few days are. It's been a long haul; so many people have come and gone. The case kept moving and we kept moving with it. We've got Gerry Buckhout left, and Hank Cinotti and Joe Basteri, and Mike Novotny when he can do it."

"And Santucci," Georgiana added.

"Ah, yes. Those people are prosecutors and they think like prosecutors. They're worried about the courtroom, which is their job. The rest of us think in terms of the investigation itself. The hunt. Queens is still waiting on somebody to turn. I'm not of a mind to count on that, and I've got no jurisdictional boundaries to be concerned with either. Maybe we can make something happen our way. And so here we are in California, lady."

"Queens knows we're here, don't they?"

"Yeah, they knew we were coming out two days after we did. I told Tom McCarthy. They just said good luck and want to be filled in when we get back. For a while McCarthy had thoughts of coming with us."

"Well, let's just hope something happens out of this week," Georgiana said. "Ted'll be here early. Let's call it a night. I think we're both exhausted."

We hiked back to the car, which was parked at the end of the nearly deserted Washington Street. Dishes clinked through the open windows of restaurant kitchens as clean-up crews drew the curtain on another night. Two Chicanos on Harleys lingered in front of a convenience store and gulls picked at discarded french fries in the gutter.

It was almost tomorrow.

The coming days would make a difference. But no one could have anticipated that a stark, unnerving confirmation of what force was behind Roy Radin's murder would be discovered in less than seventy-two hours.

The Ultimate Evil had risen from the depths of the River Styx and struck once again.

XXIII

In Death's Valley

"It's a long trail of murders, and all that's gone down before is why we've come three thousand miles to be here today," I said quietly. "They're all dead. Radin, Sisman, the Carr brothers, and more. And all were linked to this setup before they went down. In that context, the Radin case wouldn't appear to be an isolated event."

To one side, a file cabinet marked "Hillside Strangler" caught my eye. It was 11:15 a.m. on a sunny Monday, July 18, 1983, in the offices of Sheriff's Homicide in downtown Los Angeles's Hall of Justice. Around a back-room table, Detective Sergeants Carlos Avila and Willie Ahn listened and asked questions as we laid out the Radin scenario as we knew it to be. The husky, tanned Ted Gunderson, conservatively dressed in the manner of his former profession, had placed his mini-recorder between us. Avila and Ahn, who were working the Radin case, took longhand notes.

"We're aware you didn't come all this way on a lark," Avila said, smiling. It was five weeks after Radin's body was found, and the forty-eight-year-old investigator knew well that the probe was a difficult one. "Tell us what you've got on this Manson II or Frank, if that's his name."

"My prison people think he may have had a hand in this. And it makes sense that he would. He was their star shooter, he's from this area, and their so-called headquarters is supposed to be here, too."

"Do you know where?"

"Not exactly. I was just told it was somewhere in Venice."

"That's a likely spot." Willie Ahn nodded. The dark-haired detective was middle-aged and of Asian descent. "Lots of strange characters there."

"I think we want your help on all this as much as we hopefully can fill in a couple of blanks for you, at least in a background sense," I explained. For two hours, the various cases were discussed. The talk was of Hollywood films, drug deals; of Ronald Sisman, Berkowitz; of Christine Freund; of Arlis Perry's killing up the coast at Stanford.

"So the NYPD never told you Radin and Sisman were buddies?"

"No, and we were back there, too," Avila replied.

"That doesn't surprise me. Well, Sisman was dealing coke and the dope came from Colombia through the Miami area, and you've got Miami links in this case. I know there's a lot of coke out of Miami, but there may be a round-robin. My prison people say the same cast of characters appear all over this picture in one way or another—and they haven't been shown to be wrong yet."

"You said there was heroin, too?" Willie Ahn asked.

"That may be somebody else's whom Radin knew. Maybe some organized crime link. Hawaii."

"Sounds right. There's a lot of Asian heroin," Ahn answered.

Ted pulled out a copy of Vinny's note on the Hawaiian operation and read off some addresses.

"Yeah," Ahn said. "That hospital is real and so is that office complex."

"That's what I mean," I interjected. "We've been dealing with confirmations up and down the line on this."

I then gave the detectives a copy of Vinny's coded "jet set" prison notes. "These were written before Sisman's murder. I think you'll see a familiar name or two in there."

"Yep." Avila nodded, and passed the paper to Ahn.

"And he also saw a private photo of Radin with some woman. Here's her description." I showed Avila another letter.

"That's Radin's ex, Toni Fillet," Avila said. "That fits her perfectly. And he saw a personal photo?"

"Yeah. I saw Fillet's picture last year. I didn't think he was talking about her because of the hair color."

"No, he's talking about her all right. Her hair comes out dark, but it's really blondish, like he says."

"Well, he also says Berkowitz was at Radin's house once."

"Is that so? That's interesting," Ahn replied.

"We can't tell you who our suspects are," Avila said. "But there is a small circle of people in L.A. connected to this case. But we have no idea if any of them are in a cult."

"It probably doesn't matter as far as your case goes," Ted remarked.

"No, it really doesn't," Avila answered. "We've got to get somebody first and then worry about what their other connections may be."

"There's a snuff film in here somewhere?" the soft-spoken Willie Ahn questioned.

"Somewhere," I said. "But my people don't claim that's the only motive. And maybe they heard 'movies' and assumed it was the snuff tape but it was really *The Cotton Club* being referred to. That could be, too. But look, you've got drugs and big bucks all over this thing—and that's just like back in New York. And so is blowing somebody's head off—it's a favorite MO of theirs. And it's the same crew of people. And while you can have drugs without a cult, you will not have a cult without drugs."

"I think they know that," Ted offered. "What with Manson and all, you guys have seen your bizarre killings and cults."

"I don't know a lot about cults, but we do have 'em," Avila said.

"These people do other things in the nine-to-five world," I said. "And we're into the executive suite here, not the lower levels. Radin wasn't even in the Westchester cult itself, although some big-money people *are* into this satanic stuff. We've already got links to Long Island money, and Radin dealt with the Westchester leaders and everybody did favors for everybody. I think we're suggesting, really, that there may have been a working alliance here like the informants said was set up in New York."

"Radin might have known all about this headquarters here, and about this Manson II guy," Ted remarked. "But maybe not by name."

Ahn agreed.

"All this sounds familiar," I said. "Dope, big money, murder and upper-class links. We're just saying that when you look at suspects, you may very well be looking at cult-connected people and this Manson II, or Frank or whoever he is."

"But we don't know that yet," Avila said.

"I know. But you've got notes from prison there that are rather titillating, I'd say."

"Right. They're interesting."

"How long did Radin know Bob Evans? He had a coke bust, didn't he?"

"Yeah, he did. A few years ago," Avila answered. "He supposedly didn't meet Radin until early this year. Elaine Jacobs knew both of them and she allegedly put them together. And she apparently didn't meet Radin herself until early this year. Or Evans either. But she got an attorney and has refused to speak with us."

"So who says she didn't know Evans all that long—Evans?"

"Yeah."

"I see. And who was this 'circle of people' you mentioned?"

"They were people Lanie [Jacobs] knew."

"Young guys—thirties?"

"Some."

"Can you give us any names?"

"No, we can't do that," Avila said.

"Is it possible a couple of those people could have known Radin or anybody else, too?" I asked.

"Sure." Willie Ahn nodded.

"Has *anybody* been cleared?" Ted Gunderson asked.

"Not a one."

We were all playing a subtle game, and we knew it. The police couldn't give up sensitive information on a very active investigation; nor did we expect them to. Our aim was to learn as much as we could to ascertain whether the cult shadow fell over the Radin case. All the signs were there; plus Vinny's formal statement was made shortly before Radin's death. And we hoped we might help the investigation by alerting the detectives to the bigger picture.

The police were very clear on their position. First, an arrest; then they'd try to determine if cult connections existed.

"I wish I had more on this Manson II—but it's just the description, a possible first name and the fact that he was supposed to be in Torrance as of two years ago," I said. "We assume he's still around because he's lived in this area for years."

"But we've also got the Florida drug links with Radin's friend Sisman and with Jacobs, too," Ted said. "Those are common denominators. And so is the fact that Radin was wasted, that the headquarters is here, and that letter in code from the can—when was that written?"

"In 1981. About eighteen months before Radin literally went west."

"This is all fine," Avila said. "But this cult thing has to be down the road."

"Yes, we're with you there," I answered. "But don't you think Jacobs would have been incredibly stupid to have herself be the last person Radin was seen with? Hell, it'd be like setting herself up. Is it possible she was used, or just thought he was going to be leaned on—but it was murder instead?"

"Yeah," Avila responded. "It's possible something else was going on, but sometimes people do dumb things, too. But I don't know since she's not talking to us."

"Is she still alive?"

"Yeah. She's still alive."

"And Demond Wilson just lost that limo and a black car that was behind it?" Ted asked.

"That's what he says," Avila replied.

"We heard Jacobs had a kid by this Milan Bellechasses in Miami," I said. "If he's this coke king, do you think he'd set it up this way, putting the mother of his kid in the middle of it? I mean, if the coke rip-off happened and was the motive, Radin could have been offed on a street corner without involving Jacobs at all. So why go through this elaborate setup? A blessing may have been given, but I'd say 'local' on the actual setup."

"That's a valid point," Gunderson agreed. "If there's big-time organized crime or something they could have hit him anywhere—but to use a woman?"

"And why here and not back in New York?" I cut in. "And why a disappearance? Who had something to gain by a disappearance rather than a straight-out hit?"

"These are things we're looking at, too," Ahn said. "But sometimes logic goes out the window. But without a body there's no homicide investigation."

"O.K., but Radin's secretary—this Lawson guy—says Radin got calls that week saying he's got a big mouth and using the name Mike Scalese. Shit, no mob guy's going to do that using an Italian name."

"We have no evidence of any OC [organized crime] involvement," Avila agreed.

"Who did Radin fear enough to ask Wilson to tail the limo that night?" I asked.

"He wasn't afraid of Jacobs herself," Avila said. "But he didn't trust her local or Florida connections, or Evans."

"Interesting."

"That canyon's pretty far out in God's country," Ted stated. "Would Jacobs's friends you mentioned know about it?"

"I'd say that's a good possibility," Avila answered.

"Well, that's pretty relevant, isn't it?" Ted asked. "We'd like to go there. Can you show us how to find it?"

"Be glad to," Avila replied, and drew a detailed map for us.

"Was he shot there or dumped?" I asked.

"There, but we can't go into why we know that."

"So they take a live guy sixty miles. Even in the middle of the night, that's risky.

Jeez, they didn't want him found," I said.

"What was the weapon?" Ted wanted to know.

"Large-gauge shotgun," said Ahn.

We had learned from sources in New York that Radin would sometimes drop from sight for a couple of weeks without telling anyone where he was. We mentioned that if someone used that knowledge, then someone who knew Radin or his quirks might have been involved. I also noted that the New York prison sources said Radin was warned not to travel to Los Angeles.

"I've got that in writing," I said.

"That's a pretty good pipeline," Avila answered. "But you don't mean the actual killers knew his habits?"

"Not necessarily. But whoever set it up may have been able to find that out. Maybe they already knew it, or maybe they had someone in Radin's camp. And then a disappearance would work for someone's advantage, maybe for a reason beyond the fact that there's no homicide investigation without a body. At least that's how we see it. But who the hell knows?"

"We'll have to wait and see," Avila said.

It was time to go. The meeting was cordial, the detectives as helpful as possible under the circumstances. Police like to take information, not give it, so we had to do most of the talking. Nonetheless, we learned some valuable facts, some of which were hidden in what wasn't said. And besides Manson II, we named another individual—whose name we did know—as a suspect, and still another as a possible suspect.

Ted rose, and I nodded at Georgiana, who, except for a few pleasant exchanges with the police, silently observed the session.

"We don't want to complicate this," Ted said at the door. "Dope and Hollywood deals are legit motives, and our snuff film thing is probably secondary. But it could be the informants meant 'movies.' Regardless, we're on exactly the same path. We just think your actual triggermen are cult-connected and into an arrangement here like there was in New York."

"We appreciate the information," Avila replied, and then we were gone, emerging into the hot afternoon in downtown L.A. Gunderson couldn't accompany us to the crime scene. He had a 3 p.m. flight to Denver to testify in a case there, but said he'd be back to have dinner with us the next night.

"Then we can hit the canyon on Wednesday—how's that?" he asked.

"We're leaving that morning and taking the coast highway up to Monterey; and Copco is inland. So we'll go up now and you can get there whenever you can, O.K.?"

Ted consented, and we said goodbye.

*　*　*

After changing into casual clothing back at the hotel, we found our way to Route 5, heading north. Beyond the San Fernando Valley the terrain turned stark and craggy as we climbed into the mountains. Passing Magic Mountain and the picturesque Pyramid Lake, we finally rolled on to the isolated Hungry Valley Road exit.

With Avila's map in hand, we skirted the barrier at the end of Copco Canyon Road, bounced across the brush and slowly turned onto the suddenly visible dirt path. Three-tenths of a mile in, we spied the tall, thick shrub across the dried creek bed and stopped the gray Citation wagon. The late-day sun was searing; there wasn't a hint of breeze; and Glen Fischer's new hives stood but fifty yards from the car. The steady droning of thousands of bees was the only sound we heard.

"This is the eeriest place in the world," Georgiana whispered. "And what a site for a cult to meet."

"Yeah, I was thinking that, too. We'll get out of here as fast as we can and try not to disturb those damned bees."

The sickly-sweet smell of death still lingered, and we crossed the creek bed to the shrub. Circling around it, we suddenly looked down at a large damp spot by the outer branches. It was where the body had festered for nearly a month.

"I wasn't expecting to see this," Georgiana slowly said.

"Yeah," I replied. "After him for so long and we finally meet up like this in a barren inferno three thousand miles from home."

"It's horrible. It's like he's still here," she said quietly, averting her eyes from the ground and staring apprehensively into the canyon, where the droning bees hummed a winged eulogy.

"Yes, still here . . . only the dead can't die," I answered, and turned away, Radin's presence now a very real emotion.

Scanning the immediate area, I noticed a small bush a few feet to the right of where the body had been. Some of its stems were freshly clipped.

"The cops took something from here," I said, and dug into the branches. I came up with clumps of Radin's brown hair.

"Here's how they knew he wasn't dumped. He got it at ground level right here." Georgiana cringed.

For the next hour, ever mindful of the swarming bees, we searched the area, looking for the cult signs to which Vinny alerted me or for other evidence. There were numerous weathered, circular clay targets—mostly shattered—which we later established were no longer manufactured. We also found several duck-pheasant shotgun shell casings.

"Target practice," I said. "With shotguns. So Radin got it with a shotgun in a place that was known by people who practiced with shotguns."

Near our car, we found a broken taillight we later determined came from a 1974 Volkswagen. "Maybe them; maybe not. But two cars bumped here not long ago. No rust or corrosion."

"Only somebody who knew this place could ever find it," Georgiana offered. "They sure didn't come up in that limousine or just stumble into here from the highway."

"Right on both counts."

Finally, we'd had enough. With the wafting scent of death, the humming bee chorus and the desolation, the canyon made us uneasy. We took some final photos and, dry and dusty, drove back to Marina Del Rey. The next day we relaxed, did some sightseeing and joined Ted Gunderson and his daughter for dinner at the Marina.

"Bob Duffy and I will go up to the canyon tomorrow," Ted reported over a tender steak. "We work together now and then. He's good on these things. But you won't come?"

"No more," I answered. "It's Highway One for us—going back to Big Sur, as Johnny Rivers sang it. Maybe you guys will be luckier, although we did all right. You've got to see it for yourself to get the idea of what they went through to get in there. They knew exactly where they were going."

"Wish you were coming, but you folks are now on vacation."

"Yes, sir. We'll be in Monterey tomorrow, Stanford on Thursday and into San Francisco that night. Then R and R till Monday morning."

Or so I thought.

"This is your case," Georgiana admonished back at the hotel. "I don't think it's fair to just take off and let them go up there alone tomorrow."

"But we already saw it. They're good, and their own observations will be valuable. I wanted you to see Highway One—it's a great drive. And besides, you were afraid of the place."

"We can check out, take everything with us and get over to the coast farther up; that's all. They volunteered to help, so I think you should go back. I'll be fine. It'll be four of us—and Ted has a gun."

"Nobody's going to . . . O.K. O.K."

I called Gunderson at 9 a.m., and by one o'clock we were back at the canyon. The same strong scent, the same stillness and the same droning bees greeted us.

"Christ, this place is creepy," said Duffy.

"The valley of death," Ted agreed.

Duffy put his emotions aside and soon made an important discovery. In a patch of grass on the north bank of the dry creek, near where we'd parked our cars, he reached down and came up with a shiny 12-gauge, .00-Buck shotgun shell. It was about thirty yards from where Radin fell. It wasn't a typical target shell; it hadn't been there long and it wasn't a reload—it had been fired but once.

Now, since Gunderson had managed to obtain a copy of the autopsy report, we could try to re-create the murder. The consensus was that Radin was pulled from a car, struggled briefly and—with buttons torn from his vest and shirt—ran for his life through the creek bed. One shot, fired from where Duffy found the shell, missed the fleeing millionaire in the dark.

Desperately climbing the south bank of the creek, Radin sought the cover of the large, fir-like shrub. But with his leather-soled Gucci loafers, he slipped on the sandy earth and fell on his back; one shoe landed beside him.

Trying to get up again, he reached for a low branch. And his killer caught him just as he found it. He was shot in the back of the head (not the face, as widely reported) and fell back dead on the spot, his left hand still grasping the branch.

On the basis of the evidence we had, which didn't include crime-scene photos, we were reasonably certain Roy Radin was slain in that manner. Even for him, it was a horrid way to die.

* * *

We were about to leave when I found it. On both excursions to the canyon I'd avoided crawling over the moist spot where Radin lay to forage through the grass beneath the dense branches of the shrub he'd held while dying. I don't know why I finally decided to do it. I can only remember thinking I'd never be there again and didn't ever want to wonder about it back in New York.

So in I crawled.

It was hidden in the grass near the base of the tangled shrub, about eight feet in from the outer branches. It had sunk about two inches into the sandy soil, apparently the result of a wash.

It was a King James Bible.

And it was deliberately folded open, bent at the spine so that its left-hand pages were beneath those on the right. To ensure that it remained open to the intended passage, the front cover and the first few hundred pages had been torn off.

Peering through the branches on hands and knees and parting the grass which covered it, I looked at it lying there. I saw, in good condition, Isaiah, Chapter 22, staring back at me. Nervously, I began to read it. It sounded like a description of Radin's death canyon:

> *The valley of vision . . . crying to the mountains . . . gathered together waters . . . ditch between two walls for the water.*

And there was more:

> *. . . toss thee like a ball into a large country and there thou shalt die . . . And behold, joy and gladness, slaying oxen, and killing sheep, eating flesh and drinking wine; let us eat and drink, for tomorrow we shall die.*

I was staring into the face of homicidal madness.

"Ted! Gi! Bob! Somebody get the hell over here with the goddamned camera. Quick!"

"What do you have, amigo?" Ted called from the creek bed.

"Just a minute, just a minute."

Backing out to reach the camera, I crept back in and took the photos—of the Bible, the grass around it and then the shallow hole it had sunk into. Finally, I crawled from the dense foliage and held it aloft gingerly. The wash had packed caked dirt into it and damaged the spine.

"Now—why the hell do you suppose this little treasure was hidden under the same tree our victim was grabbing sixty miles out here in the middle of god-blasted nowhere? I tend to doubt it fell from a passing 747."

There were congratulations all around.

"That damned Vinny—he told me," I said. "He told me a long time ago and he put it in a letter again. 'Look for a sign—you know what to look for.' Damn, and here I didn't want to come back to this stinking place. We'd have been over in Santa Barbara by now. You know what this thing means? It confirms *everything;* and this on top of all the other years of building evidence on evidence."

"For all my years in this business, I'll tell you you're absolutely right." Gunderson beamed. "We all make a good team, buddy. Fucking cops can't even do a thorough crime-scene search."

"Yeah, but we all missed it, too, Ted. We were about to leave now, and Gi and I were here on Monday and missed it. I just didn't want to grope through all that stuff. And I'm sure the cops didn't either. I'm just as guilty as them—maybe even worse, because I knew something might be here."

"Not quite," Duffy said. "You *did* go in there. Screw the cops. God, I won't ever forget this one." He grinned.

"Goddamned reporter, too." Ted laughed. "Not even a Bureau guy."

"That's why I'm able to be open-minded," I answered. "Maybe we should keep looking around here—we might find Jimmy Hoffa. You FBI turkeys sure couldn't."

*   *   *

After a quick lunch at a small roadside restaurant a few miles north of the canyon in tiny Gorman, our group split up. Gunderson and Duffy drove south to L.A. and we began our delayed journey to Monterey.

Suddenly, being thrown off schedule didn't matter. Isaiah 22, which we read carefully in the restaurant parking lot, seemed to describe a power struggle, with someone casting out another. But whether there was any relevance to that message, we didn't know.

I'd kept the Bible, wanting to run some tests on it in New York before sending it to the L.A. police. But red blotches we thought might be bloodstains would turn out to be a dye, perhaps from a flower.

The next morning, I called Avila from a Monterey motel room and told him of the discovery. He didn't know what to make of it.

"You've got four witnesses willing to testify if it's ever needed, Carlos. And like we said the other day, it doesn't impact the motives you're looking at. It just not so subtly suggests that your actual perps were part of this cult setup. A three-thousand-mile net has now dropped over all these cases. But that may mean more to us in New York than to you."

"Well, I can't deal with whether anybody's in a cult now—we told you that," Avila said.

"No, but we can. At some point the paths may meet. I'll send this to you in a couple of weeks, along with the shotgun shell and some photos. And I'm not going to publish anything now. There's too much to lose by that."

Two hours later, we dropped in to see Sergeant Kahn at the Santa Clara Sheriff's Department in downtown San Jose. As I took the prized Bible from a bag, chunks of dirt decorated the sheriff's conference table.

"Sorry about that, but this may be as close as we've all come to Mr. Manson the second, the alleged engineer of Arlis's murder. It appears he may still be very much in business." I then briefed the startled Kahn on the developments in Los Angeles.

Later, when the glow subsided, we pondered the implications of the Bible and the Radin murder. They were frightening.

*   *   *

While we visited the Stanford church, drove down curling Lombard Street in San Francisco, toured Alcatraz, crossed the Golden Gate to shop in Sausalito and celebrated with a Saturday-night Chateaubriand dinner at the Mark Hopkins Hotel, Ted Gunderson went right to work in Los Angeles.

We were confident the cult participated in the Radin murder, but we didn't know *who* pulled the trigger or why it was done. Vinny, who may have been confused on the films in question, mentioned the Moskowitz tape as a partial motive; and then there was the alleged coke rip-off and the *Cotton Club* movie deal.

We were also specifically trying to identify Manson II, whom we strongly suspected had a hand in the murder. Initially, Ted Gunderson's job was to find suspects and see if they matched the Manson II profile. Back in New York, I was to work on motive. And like the police, I examined the drug scene and the film arrangements—the two major events in Radin's last months of life.

*   *   *

Robert Evans, fifty-two, was a movie giant, although it was said the luster was tarnished after a 1981 conviction in New York for possession of several ounces of cocaine. Then, too, recent Evans projects such as *Players* and *Popeye* had turned more stomachs than heads. But before that, Evans was a skyrocket. As Paramount's head of production in the late sixties and early seventies, the native New Yorker and former actor had brought films such as *Rosemary's Baby, Love Story, The Odd Couple* and *The Godfather* into the studio's fold.

Seeking the individual credit he couldn't garner with the studio, Evans became an independent producer. Working again with Roman Polanski, he produced *Chinatown,* a highly successful and widely acclaimed film which starred Jack Nicholson, Faye Dunaway and John Huston.

But then, after mixed reviews were sprinkled on his *Black Sunday,* a terrorism story filmed in Miami at Super Bowl X in 1976, the slide began. *The Cotton Club,* a gangster and music epic about Harlem's famous nightclub of the Roaring Twenties, was anointed as Evans's return from limbo. And Evans desperately wanted to own the film. "The whole inspiration is to *own* something," he told *New York* magazine.

Accordingly, Evans shunned the studios and searched for private investors. He said he backed out of a potential deal with billionaire Adnan Khashoggi because the Arab asked for 55 percent of the film. Then, in the autumn of 1982, Evans linked up with brothers Ed and Fred Doumani, and their associate, Victor Sayyah. The Doumanis were sons of a Lebanese father who became a successful Las Vegas builder, and the brothers themselves built and operated that city's Tropicana Hotel and El Morocco Casino. Sayyah was a wealthy insurance executive from Denver.

In January 1983, the Vegas contingent entered into a partnership arrangement with Evans after reading a *Cotton Club* script prepared by *Godfather* author Mario Puzo. Evans's choice for a leading man—Richard Gere—didn't like Puzo's effort. Neither did Richard Sylbert, a production designer and longtime Evans adviser. Respecting Sylbert and cognizant of Gere's box office appeal, Evans redid the script himself—to no one's satisfaction. So in early March, he enlisted *Godfather* director Francis Ford Coppola, now an independent filmmaker, to rewrite the Puzo-Evans screenplay.

On April 5, Coppola finished his first draft, which Evans took to Las Vegas a week or two later. The exact date is uncertain, but it was in mid-April. In Vegas, the Doumanis—who'd approved the original script—didn't like the rewrite. Significantly, although they remained in the project, they suspended further financing. And Evans was already into early production in New York.

Here, stories begin conflicting. One version holds that only now did Elaine Jacobs introduce Radin and Evans, who was delving deep into his own pockets to keep *The Cotton Club* in business. But another account—that of people connected to Radin—alleges that Radin and Evans actually met through Jacobs at least two months earlier—in February at Le Cirque restaurant—and began their dealings then. Jacobs, according to this account, was romantically involved with Evans and also was helping him raise funds for *The Cotton Club.*

If so, was Evans—by linking up with Radin—double-dealing on the Las Vegas investors?

Maybe not, because the Radin arrangement might have included a percentage of Evans's share only, and also was structured to encompass a studio in Puerto Rico and pre-production financing of two subsequent films—one of which was to be *Jake Two,* the sequel to *Chinatown.* (That film apparently would be made minus Roman Polanski, who skipped the United States after a late 1970s conviction for a close encounter of the first kind with a thirteen-year-old girl.)

Regardless, Evans maintained that he barely knew Elaine Jacobs, telling *New York* magazine's Michael Daly: "If I knew who she really was, I would have run out of town." But Carol Johnston, a Radin friend who introduced the Long Island millionaire to Jacobs in early January 1983, told another story. Johnston said Jacobs revealed that she and Evans planned to marry and go into business together.

There also are suggestions from two sources that Radin and Evans knew each other in New York several years before Jacobs brought them together in L.A.

Evans and Radin signed that 45-45-10 contract on April 26, 1983, with Jose Alagria, representing Puerto Rican government interests, assigned the smaller figure. It was Radin who brought banker Alagria into the project after Alagria negotiated to obtain $35 million from his government to fund the deal.

And it was Alagria who said he later told Radin that Evans would one day realize he'd lost control of his own enterprise.

*   *   *

Now Radin's world began to tilt on its axis. In early April, before the movie contract was signed, Elaine Jacobs—who'd been promised a $50,000 finder's fee by Radin—accused him of having a hand in the theft of $1 million in cocaine and cash from her Sherman Oaks, California, home.

Radin's secretary, Jonathan Lawson, and a woman friend of Radin, Anna Montenegro, both said they heard Jacobs accuse Radin of urging her own runner, Tally Rogers, to pull off the job. Lawson said he was present in Radin's Regency suite when Jacobs made the charges to the millionaire's face in early April.

Montenegro, who knew Jacobs before Radin did, said she was at Jacobs's home the day before Radin disappeared and heard her make the same accusations to male acquaintances Montenegro described as "bodyguards," one of whom would soon emerge as an important figure in our investigation. Jacobs supposedly believed Radin used Rogers to engineer the heist because Radin was strapped for cash.

According to Lawson and Sergeant Carlos Avila, Radin was indeed buying coke from Rogers—as much as $1,000 worth per week between January and April 1983. However, Radin paid Rogers with personal checks made out to Elaine Jacobs, some of which the police obtained. And, said Lawson, Radin stopped payment on a $4,000 April check after Jacobs accused him of the Tally Rogers conspiracy, which Radin vehemently denied. Rogers disappeared at that time, and police believe he set sail for the Midwest.

Avila is not convinced the theft itself actually occurred. Others believe it did.

Beyond Radin's alleged dope difficulties with Jacobs, there was another problem. She desired more than the $50,000 finder's fee Radin promised for putting him and Evans together on *The Cotton Club*. She wanted a percentage of the entire package—and she wanted it from Radin's cut; not Evans's.

Here, too, ambiguity reigns. Anna Montenegro reportedly told Radin that Jacobs *already* had been dealt a share of the three-way arrangement without Radin's knowledge. If so, the points certainly weren't Radin's or Jose Alagria's.

Like careening locomotives rushing headlong on the same track, another Radin-Jacobs confrontation, this one over *The Cotton Club,* occurred in Evans's Manhattan town house on May 5, 1983—eight days before Radin's disappearance. At that moment, the Las Vegas financing was suspended and Radin, Evans and Alagria were signed at 45-45-10.

Radin and Alagria had come to Evans's East Coast abode to hammer out the final details of their arrangement. And then, to Radin's surprise, Elaine Jacobs arrived from California. It was an interesting coincidence.

She and Radin then argued wildly over her percentage demand, while a blasé Evans lingered upstairs in the library. Chagrined, Radin charged up the stairs to talk to Evans. According to both Alagria and Evans, Evans, for unfathomable reasons, urged Radin to give in to Jacobs. But not Roy Radin. With Alagria in tow, he stormed from the town house. Outside, Alagria told *Newsday*'s Steve Wick, Radin said he believed drug money was involved in *The Cotton Club*.

Within days of the Manhattan-on-the-rocks episode, Alagria said, he received phone calls from Evans, Radin and Miami lawyer Frank Diaz, who said he represented *both* Jacobs and Evans.

The messages were all the same: Evans was offering Radin $2 million to buy him out of the deal.

Alagria said Evans encouraged him to persuade Radin to accept the buyout and then to deal with him. But Radin wouldn't budge. Alagria found Evans's comments fascinating. Not a week before, Alagria said, Evans had been in financial straits, saying he couldn't afford to post a performance bond required by the Puerto Rican government before it would construct a studio there, which was part of the agreement.

So where did Evans suddenly find $2 million?

*   *   *

Throughout this period, Evans continued his efforts to develop an acceptable *Cotton Club* script. The Las Vegas investors were still on hold, the Puerto Rican money had yet to change hands and technicians, support people and others were at work in Astoria Studios in Queens, where the film would be shot. The bills were piling up, and Evans still didn't have a workable screenplay for his all-important project.

Radin, meanwhile, had but a day to simmer before flying back to L.A., where he signed into the Regency on Saturday, May 7. Radin confidants in New York had warned him not to return to California: Vinny's prison letter to me had been right on target.

Radin went West to attend the bar mitzvah of Adam Buttons, son of entertainer-actor Red Buttons. In a remarkable irony, Buttons would deliver Radin's eulogy and say: "He had the devil on one shoulder and an angel on the other, and was in a perpetual tug-of-war."

In L.A., Radin also hoped to placate Jacobs—while not surrendering to her demands—and to iron out this now precarious movie deal. And it indeed was precarious. On Tuesday, May 10, Lawson said, he overheard an Evans phone call to Radin during which Evans again offered to buy out Radin's share. And again Radin refused, insisting he wasn't relinquishing his 45 percent.

Now, too, anonymous warnings were telephoned to the Regency suite by someone attempting to leave the impression he was Mafia-connected.

Time was running out for Roy Radin.

On Thursday, May 12, Elaine Jacobs called the Regency and made arrangements to meet Radin for dinner the following evening. Anna Montenegro later arrived at the suite in a fearful state of mind. Visibly upset, she told Radin and Lawson that she'd been to Jacobs's house and Jacobs was railing about the alleged drug-cash theft to her "bodyguards."

And so the stage was set for Friday, the thirteenth of May.

As previously noted, Jacobs called for Radin that evening in a limousine. The car had been rented without a driver, and extra money paid for that variation from the norm.

With Demond Wilson allegedly waiting outside the Regency with a registered gun in a shoulder holster, Radin and Jacobs left for La Scala restaurant, which the nervous Radin selected because its layout and popularity offered a secure setting to resolve matters with Jacobs.

As the limo drove from the Regency, another black car—apparently a Cadillac—also pulled out behind it. With Wilson bringing up the rear, he said, the lead cars swung onto Fairfax and then turned on Sunset Boulevard. There, Wilson said, both cars sped through a pair of red lights before turning left on Highland, leaving him lost in traffic. The cars were headed north—in the direction of Sherman Oaks and Route 5. Wilson then went to La Scala, waited, and was reached there by Lawson at 11:30 p.m. He told Lawson he'd lost the limo and the follow car in traffic.

Lawson said he didn't locate Wilson again for two days. He eventually found him at a Marina Del Rey condominium where he'd gone to hide, fearful of what he'd seen. But if Wilson was so petrified by what he'd witnessed involving his close friend Radin—why didn't he phone Lawson when Radin failed to appear at La Scala? Why did Lawson, instead, have to find him—both at La Scala and again two days later?

Wilson knew Radin was concerned for his safety. According to Lawson, the prearranged plan was for Wilson to follow the limo and observe Radin from another table in the restaurant. Then Radin was either to come back to the Regency with Wilson or to call Lawson if the plan was changed.

Ted Gunderson learned that an exhausted Lawson instructed the Regency desk clerk to phone him—in case he inadvertently fell asleep—if Radin didn't return by 11 p.m.

Wilson had been in Radin's suite, armed, at 6 p.m. before eventually going downstairs to assume a position outside the hotel. It was about 8:45 when Radin left with Jacobs. Lawson watched from the hotel lobby as the limo pulled away, and he also noticed another car pull out behind it. He didn't see Wilson's car, but Wilson may have been parked out of Lawson's line of vision.

Shortly after Radin's body was found, Demond Wilson—whom Lawson said

Radin would sometimes inexplicably drop from sight with—left Hollywood and became a traveling evangelist. Today, outside of acknowledging his former drug addiction problem, he refuses to speak to the press about his prior years in the entertainment business.

A week before I left for Los Angeles in July 1983, a prison note I received from Vinny contained a reference to "bodyguards" other than Jacobs's. Its context was revealed to sheriff's investigators at that time.

*   *   *

Meanwhile, on the night of Friday, the thirteenth of May, Jacobs later kept a *prearranged* social engagement at the apartment of an attorney. Evans said she also called him during the evening to say she and Radin had argued. This was the same story she told Lawson, who located her in Florida several days later. Incidentally, Jacobs's young son and a maid were flown to Miami shortly before Radin's disappearance.

In fact, Gunderson discovered that Jacobs put her house at 3862 Sherwood Place in suburban Sherman Oaks on the market on May 12—the day before Radin vanished. And a few weeks later, before the body was found, a Lancer's moving van removed furnishings from the home.

Jacobs, *prior* to May 12, also spoke to a neighbor about her future plans. "She said she was going to New York to be a producer or director," the neighbor told Gunderson.

The Cotton Club would indeed be filming in New York. But where did Jacobs ever get the idea that she was going to be a producer? Certainly not from Radin or Jose Alagria.

Subsequently detoured from the stages of Astoria Studios, Jacobs apparently flew to Miami in the early morning hours of May 14, shortly after Radin's aborted supper. When Lawson found her there she delivered conflicting versions of what happened. Denying she knew where Radin was, she first claimed they'd argued and he left the limo on Sunset Boulevard. Lawson challenged her, saying the limo hadn't stopped on Sunset. She then said it was she, not Radin, who left the car.

*   *   *

In the meantime, Robert Evans went about the business of polishing an acceptable *Cotton Club* script, apparently resigned to the fact that his partner was among the missing. But even before Radin's disappearance became public, Lawson said, Evans never called back to see if Radin had reconsidered his $2 million buyout offer of Tuesday, May 10. And even after Radin's vanishing act reached the media, Lawson reported, he didn't hear from Evans then either.

But Bob Evans was busy. He had it in mind to persuade the Las Vegas investors to lift their month-long suspension of funds and resume financing Bob Evans's film. While Roy Radin went to Caswell Canyon, Bob Evans went to Napa, California, north of San Francisco.

There, for a period of ten days commencing Sunday, May 15, according to *New York* magazine, Evans labored in solitude with other *Cotton Club* principals at the estate of Francis Ford Coppola. Also in attendance were Richard Gere, actor-dancer Maurice Hines and Marilyn Matthews, a black actress Evans met several months earlier in New York.

Matthews viewed *The Cotton Club* as an important employment opportunity for black performers. Therefore, *New York* reported, she was troubled when—about a week before the Napa meeting—Evans told her *The Cotton Club* wouldn't be made unless Coppola rewrote the script in two weeks.

Why Evans allegedly made this comment is curious, because Alagria said the Puerto Rican government was preparing to announce the Evans-Radin agreement at a press conference which was to be scheduled soon.

Regardless, on May 15 the clan gathered at Napa. Night and day they worked in seclusion, and by May 25 a script approved by both Evans and the recalcitrant Richard Gere was hammered out. The following weekend, May 27–28, Evans reportedly flew to Las Vegas with the rewritten screenplay. At first, the Doumanis and Sayyah were still displeased. But the next day they agreed to resume financing the film. An ecstatic Evans could now proceed into full production.

About twelve days later, on June 10, beekeeper Glen Fischer finally located the missing Roy Radin in desolate Caswell Canyon. If not for Fischer, Radin might have decayed undiscovered for another six months or more. *The Cotton Club* hit the theaters eighteen months after Fischer's find—in December 1984—and was a critical and box office failure.

Elaine Jacobs hired an attorney, who refused to allow the police to question her, which was her constitutional right. By early 1987 she was remarried and dividing her time between Miami and Colombia. Milan Bellechasses was said to be living in Colombia and operating a casino there.

Frank Diaz, the Miami attorney who said he represented both Jacobs and Evans on the film deal with Radin, told *Newsday* that he met Evans through Jacobs, adding that Jacobs sought his help in raising funds for the film. Diaz said he was going to "kick in one and a half million dollars"—but after Radin's body was discovered, all bets were off.

Diaz himself is "off" somewhere. The attorney, who frequently defended Colombian drug suspects, was due in a Miami federal court in June 1985 to respond to obstruction of justice and fraud charges he was facing on matters not related to Radin. But the day before his scheduled court appearance, Diaz was kidnapped by two men described as gun-wielding Colombians. His exposure to Hollywood and the shoot-'em-up *Cotton Club* project may have affected Diaz: authorities believe he might have staged his own abduction.

Robert Evans—whom Diaz termed "a friend" in his interview with *Newsday*—was questioned for several hours about the Radin case by Sheriff's Homicide investigators in L.A. According to Sergeant Avila, Evans acknowledged knowing Jacobs—labeling her a casual acquaintance—and also confirmed knowing Roy Radin. Evans denied having any information about what happened to Radin.

And as the producer downplayed his relationship with Jacobs, he similarly characterized his association with Radin as inconsequential. But Avila noted that the signed, multimillion-dollar contract between the two elevated their interaction from the realm of the superficial.

As of 1987, Evans was back working for Paramount.

Finally, Radin's secretary, Jonathan Lawson, adios'd America in fear of his life (with police concurrence) and is now living secretly in Europe. Apparently, Lawson wasn't overreacting. He said that when Jacobs entered Radin's suite that final night, she suggested to Lawson that he drive to her house and return with some cocaine she'd stashed there. Jacobs, Lawson said, told him they could all enjoy the drugs when she and Radin returned from La Scala. Fearing a setup (Lawson said he remembered the "bodyguards" Anna Montenegro said were at Jacobs's house the day before) or an attempt to separate him from Radin, Lawson declined the offer.

In late 1986, Sergeant Carlos Avila broad-brushed the status of the case. "Until it is solved, everyone connected to it remains under scrutiny." Which was another way of saying no one has been exonerated.

I believe Roy Radin's murder was intended to serve the purposes of more than one master, whoever they may be.

*   *   *

But beyond the immediate "why" of Roy Radin's murder lurked the question of *who* the actual killers were. Gunderson and I searched for the cult connection, and the inquiry was lengthy. Concurrently, we sought to learn if the mysterious Manson II was involved. Simply put, we believed that whoever ordered the murder was acquainted with someone, perhaps Manson II, who was aligned with the L.A. headquarters of the Son of Sam "umbrella" cult.

For want of a better word, we believed a "contract" to kill Roy Radin was taken by these cult elements. We thought the alliance mirrored that in New York.

Curiously, this type of arrangement would also match one alleged to have occurred in the Manson case, which happened in the Radin scenario's backyard.

Berkowitz, Vinny said, revealed that Manson II claimed the original Charles Manson "volunteered" to commit the Tate murders, at least, for someone else, and that a very real motive—beyond "Helter Skelter"—existed somewhere in the labyrinth of that investigation.

The potential cross-connections were compelling.

The Bible in the canyon clearly signaled a cult connection to the Radin killing—an obvious conclusion strongly bolstered by what we'd previously learned about Radin's life in New York. Effectively, the Bible's presence was a calling card, a sign of satanic triumph. I, and Queens DA John Santucci, had heard nearly two years earlier that certain symbols were usually left at the Sam cult's crime scenes. The Bible was one—a mockery of Christianity when put to that use.

Gunderson and I agreed with the drug-movie slant of the police investigation, but we were just as certain of cult connivance somewhere. Almost certainly, one of the actual killers was cult-connected, and perhaps someone higher up the ladder was as well.

If we could tie a Radin shooting suspect to the days of Sharon Tate et al., our belief that he could be Manson II would strengthen appreciably. We'd be looking to see if the suspect matched the physical description of Manson II that Vinny provided, which we already knew was identical to that of an individual observed at the Christine Freund murder scene in New York.

Once into the original Manson circle, especially that of the social set, we'd also look for someone *else* who—perhaps having known Manson II from the late sixties—was also a player in the 1983 Radin case. In other words, we planned to go down and back up the ladder of time—looking for parallels in the lives of at least two particular people.

The odds against us were immeasurable. But if we couldn't find and identify Manson II, then perhaps we'd find suggestions of another association of long standing between people connected to the Radin case. That, too, would be of great significance to the investigation.

But who were the Radin shooting suspects? The police weren't cooperative, but well before I learned of Anna Montenegro's statement about the "bodyguards" at Jacobs's house the night before Radin vanished, Gunderson's own inquiry unearthed a fascinating lead.

"His name is Bill, but I don't have the last name," Ted told me. "But he's directly affiliated with Jacobs and has been at her house a lot. I believe he was there the night before Radin got it. And he was driving a black Caddy—which is similar to the kind of car that followed the limo. He had told my source he was some sort of car dealer."

"Do you have a description of this guy?"

Ted indeed did, and incredibly, the description closely approximated the one Vinny provided of Manson II: about five feet ten, athletic build, sandy-brown hair, and age approximately mid-thirties in 1983. "Remember," Gunderson advised, "Manson II would be a hit man and he could change hair color and the like from time to time on different jobs. And you can bet he'd use aliases too."

"I'm aware of that. But you apparently got this 'Bill' in his natural surroundings, and Berkowitz probably did also. This guy wouldn't need to alter his features among his own kind, but his real name would be another thing."

Gunderson didn't have Bill's last name, so I phoned Willie Ahn to ask him about it and to see if the police themselves had located a black Cadillac. If so, I wanted to determine if they believed the follow car on the night of Radin's death had also been a Caddy. Other information suggested it might have been a Lincoln. The date of the call was October 6, 1983.

"We know about Bill," Willie said. "He's very much a part of the Jacobs crowd.

But I can't give you his last name. We're now trying to obtain warrants on two cars—one is his."

Gunderson had struck paydirt.

Ahn also told me, as Avila had previously, that the police were pursuing the drug motive for the murder. I stressed my belief that the movie deal was of more relevance.

"Look, Willie," I said, "it's become clear to Gunderson and me since July that the prison informant confused the snuff film with *The Cotton Club*. A movie is a movie and he told me he simply presumed it was the snuff flick when he heard a movie was the reason this went down. He was right on Radin's being warned to stay away from California; he was right about that 'bodyguard' business to the extent that there's some legitimate suspicion there; and that 1981 'jet-set' letter won't go away no matter how hard we try to discount it."

"I'm not in disagreement with you," Ahn replied. "We've got a long way to go here. We haven't eliminated the movie angle yet."

And then for a moment it didn't matter. Willie Ahn told me he was ill, and the prognosis wasn't encouraging. I hung up saddened. And I never did get to speak to Willie Ahn again. Within months, the personable homicide investigator died.

* * *

It wasn't until June 6, 1984, that Carlos Avila released Bill's last name to me. It was Mentzer. After being stalled for eight months, our inquiry resumed. Gunderson, along with investigator Judy Hanson, journalists Dee Brown and Dave Balsiger, and others—including law enforcement contacts—assisted the probe, which I coordinated daily out of New York. As time passed, a remarkable picture of Mentzer developed.

Mentzer had an arrest record. One of those incidents involved possession of a handgun which he threatened to use during an argument in a bar in one of the beach communities—either Marina Del Rey or Venice. Venice, which borders the Marina, was said to be the headquarters of the so-called Sam cult. Mentzer, we also learned, frequented a gym in Venice, and a television reporter advised us that there was talk of someone known as "Charlie Manson II" in the Venice area. Significantly, Mentzer also had been arrested in Torrance, California, just south of Los Angeles, during the same time period in 1981 that Vinny—in writing—had said Manson II was in that particular town.

So we now had a man who was a suspect in the Radin case and matched the description of Manson II, used handguns in a menacing manner and was in the right towns at the right times.

We also discovered that Mentzer and an individual named Bob Lowe had been arrested at Los Angeles International Airport shortly after the Radin killing and charged with possession of a large amount of cocaine. The case was subsequently dismissed, but Mentzer had hired a Miami attorney to represent him—an attorney who also was connected to Elaine Jacobs.

Although we didn't know it, the detectives had been moving in the same direction and were able to establish a romantic involvement between Jacobs and Mentzer, further cementing the link between the two. Bob Lowe remained a mystery figure to us, but the police had privately connected him to a car that had been transferred to him from Elaine Jacobs via a middleman on May 13, 1983—the day of Radin's death.

In an attempt to put Mentzer in Caswell Canyon, I asked Avila in June of 1984 if the suspect was familiar with it. "He or somebody else, a friend, knew about it," Avila said.

"Would that friend happen to have been a target shooter?"

"Yes, a shooter."

"Do you think Mentzer was there the night Radin was killed?"

"He quite possibly was there."

"If he wasn't there himself, I'm certain he had a hand in the operation," I said. And Avila offered no denial—Mentzer was a suspect.

But there was still much more to be learned.

We next established that Mentzer had been a regular visitor to Miami, home of people tied to the Radin case. He also traveled to Houston—city of .44 revolver purchases and, authorities said, a metropolis with a known population of satanic cultists. Moreover, in 1979 Berkowitz referenced a restaurant in Houston in the context of occult activities. He named a particular establishment—one that was directly tied to OTO activities in New York. Mentzer, we learned, was affiliated with another Houston establishment that was opened to cater to those with occult interests.

Bit by bit, the case against Mentzer was building.

And then our sources put him right into the middle of Charles Manson's social set.

Because of the sensitivities of an open investigation, the details provided here will be of necessity somewhat oblique. Mentzer, sources said, was a friend of Mama Cass Elliot, the singer with the Mamas and the Papas rock group. After the band split in the late sixties, Cass went on to a successful career as a solo artist before being found dead in a London hotel room in 1974, seemingly of natural causes.

But Mentzer apparently had known Cass in Los Angeles in the 1968–1971 time frame, when, out of loneliness and vulnerability, much of which was due to her extreme overweight condition, she began to "collect" an unsavory entourage of hangers-on and dope dealers and entertain them in her home off Woodstock Road in the Hollywood Hills, near Mulholland Drive.

Of Cass's associates, John Phillips, lead singer of the Mamas and the Papas, wrote in his 1986 book, *Papa John*: "At home, [Cass] was surrounded by losers and cruel users. . . . They were just hustlers, music industry leeches. If she came to visit us, she came alone, without her retinue. They were sometimes drugged-out, belligerent [dope] dealers, in leather with weapons, chains and cycles. . . . They were like muggers."

Phillips went on: "They were part of a clique that hung around Cass in the hills or around the house that Terry Melcher sublet to Roman Polanski on Cielo Drive in Bel Air. Among them were Jay Sebring, who was a popular hairdresser to the stars;

and Wojtek Frykowski, a longtime friend of Roman's from Poland; and the same boyfriend of Cass's who had been sought by Scotland Yard [on suspicion of drug smuggling]."

Sebring, thirty-five, and Frykowski, thirty-two, would be among those slain by Charles Manson's hordes shortly after midnight on Saturday, August 9, 1969, in the Tate-Polanski home at 10050 Cielo Drive in Benedict Canyon.

This was the composition of the smaller Cass Elliot circle in that summer of 1969, and apparently in it, remarkably, was Bill Mentzer. Primarily through Frykowski, the Cass Elliot group was linked to the extended Roman Polanski circle, which included Phillips and his wife, singer-actress Michelle Phillips; actor Warren Beatty; Robert Evans; production designer and Evans confidant Richard Sylbert; actor Jack Nicholson and others.

Additionally, Frykowski and his girlfriend, coffee heiress Abigail (Gibby) Folger, twenty-five, lived across the street from Mama Cass and knew her well—along with some of her "retinue," as Phillips phrased it. One of Mama Cass's boyfriends, Pic Dawson, whose father worked for the U.S. State Department, even lived in the Frykowski-Folger home in the summer of 1969, while Frykowski and Folger house-sat for the Polanskis on Cielo Drive.

The climate was certainly favorable for Mentzer to have known Frykowski, Folger, and others in the circle, possibly including Evans. But did he?

"He definitely knew Gibby Folger," a Los Angeles contact said. "I knew both of them then, and saw them together at lunch in a restaurant in Newport Beach with a couple of other people not long before the murders."

I found support for that account by locating a person who claimed he shared the Mentzer-Folger table that day. "I was with them on that occasion," said the source, who was an undercover operative for the FBI.

The source wasn't an FBI agent, but he was recruited by the Bureau in the late sixties to infiltrate the anti-war and drug scenes in California.

"Folger knew Mentzer," he said simply.

This was explosive information. Mentzer allegedly knew one of the Tate victims and Berkowitz had said Manson II told the New York group that a real motive for the murders existed. Mentzer apparently would have been in a position to have known that.

Frykowski was a narcotics user, as was Jay Sebring. Mescaline, LSD, cocaine and marijuana were among their sampled favorites. Author Ed Sanders reported that a man named Joel Rostau—murdered in New York in late 1970—made a coke and mescaline delivery to Sebring on Cielo Drive on the night of the murders. Rostau was the boyfriend of a Mrs. McCaffery, an employee of Sebring's who told Sanders about the visit.

Frykowski was said to have been deeper into the drug scene than Sebring—to the extent of being closely allied with Mama Cass's crowd and doing some dealing for and with them. An artist friend of Frykowski's told police that Frykowski was offered an opportunity to wholesale the drug MDA (an amphetamine) in the L.A. area and that friction later developed between him and the dealers.

Our own sources confirmed this arrangement.

Beyond question, the dope distributors were part of Mama Cass's unsavory group of associates. And they also were regular visitors to 10050 Cielo Drive, where Frykowski entertained them while Polanski and Sharon Tate were abroad from March 1969 until Tate returned alone on July 20. Pregnant, she arrived in Los Angeles to prepare for the birth of her child. Polanski was scheduled to fly back on August 12. One of Mama Cass's dope-affiliated friends admitted to police that he was at Cielo Drive twice during the week of the murders, the last time on August 7—barely thirty hours before the slaughter.

So Radin suspect Bill Mentzer allegedly appeared in this galaxy of stars as an associate of Abigail Folger and a friend of Mama Cass. And even if Mentzer turned out not to be Manson II, we were now certain that he was at least knowledgeable of that dangerous killer because—beyond his social links to Cielo Drive—we also obtained information which, if accurate, put Mentzer into the heart of the L.A. cult scene.

* * *

The Los Angeles occult underground was, and remains, a maze of shadowy connections and subterranean byplay. As in New York, there are regular trade-offs with narcotics traffickers, and recent exposure of ritualistic child-abuse cases in southern California has brought to the surface indications of links between the satanic subculture and child pornography.

There are numerous cult factions still operating in Los Angeles. In 1986, authorities familiar with the network noted that pockets of Druids, OTO, former Process elements and many others slithered beneath the landscape. As did the Chingon cult, whose current existence there was stipulated by two law enforcement officers and two former Satanists themselves.

These revelations supported the Vinny-Danny-Berkowitz information, which held that the Sam cult's overall headquarters was nestled in the L.A. environs.

And where did Radin/Manson II suspect Bill Mentzer fit in?

From four different sources, we learned of his occult ties, which appeared to remain constant through the mid-eighties. Investigator Judy Hanson, working on an unrelated matter, jotted down his license plate number several times while probing a case in 1982. Mentzer, she said, occasionally visited the home of a man known to be a member of a Los Angeles satanic coven.

"This other guy used to go out late at night dressed totally in black—like the old Process costume—and he had occult symbols in his home," Hanson reported. "A neighbor of his told me that he belonged to a cult and was having some kind of difficulty with its leaders. While working this other case, which didn't involve a cult at all, I wrote down plate numbers of this individual's visitors—and Mentzer's car showed up a few times."

This was more than a year before Roy Radin disappeared.

Two other Los Angeles contacts also linked Mentzer to cult activity. One of them was involved in the occult, and the other, while not part of the Satan scene, described Mentzer's connection to it and correctly identified one of his daylight lines of business. Mentzer, it seemed, had his hand in various enterprises—including a rental car dealership, real estate, and frequent work as a professional bodyguard for some well-known L.A. residents, including Larry Flynt, the publisher of porndom's *Hustler* magazine. In his spare time, the evidence began to indicate, he may have worked as a hit man for various contractors—cultic and otherwise.

Another informant, who knew Mentzer personally, linked him to a private social club in the L.A. area that was formed specifically to cater to mystical interests. Whether backroom activities there, said to include dope dealing and sadomasochistic sex, were those of the cult per se, we didn't know. But since the club also had a branch in Houston, we believed we probably had located a link to the headquarters of the Sam group. If not active behind the walls of the club itself, we strongly suspected that at least some of the club's organizers were part of the Sam operation.

Mentzer was identified as being a club member, and the informant claimed that he was instrumental in obtaining occult paraphernalia for the establishment. Southern California police sources also stated that Mentzer was a "honcho" in the club.

One major piece of the puzzle may have been put in place by both the FBI informant and another source. The federal contact placed Mentzer in the San Francisco area during the time period when Arlis Perry was murdered, although that alone wasn't sufficient to connect him to the killing. The other source hit closer to home by saying: "He and a couple of his friends used to like to go up to Stanford and hang around the campus occasionally." Still, the evidence wasn't substantial, and even Berkowitz, while claiming Manson II "engineered" the Perry killing, didn't specify whether he was actually in the Stanford church that night in October of 1974.

But there was more. A Los Angeles man who once worked with Mentzer and whose information had proven to be entirely credible said: "There was a rumor, talk among the guys, that he'd done a murder. I had my own contacts in law enforcement, including someone in the intelligence community in the federal government. I asked if he'd ever heard of Mentzer. He said: '*Bill Mentzer? We have it that he did a hit in Son of Sam.*'"

Los Angeles police sources subsequently confirmed in 1987 that information in their possession held that Mentzer was a member of "some kind of hit squad."

By then, Gunderson and I knew what kind of "hit squad" it was. We also learned that Mentzer was considered a "prime suspect" in the Radin case. But by that time the police investigation of Radin's killing was effectively dead in the water, and had been for some time. Sergeant Carlos Avila, who headed the original inquiry with the late Willie Ahn, had assumed a new assignment in the sheriff's office. Avila had continued to resist the apparent cult link to the case—perhaps because the official crime-scene search failed to uncover the Bible and shotgun shell and because we alone had endeavored to trace Mentzer back to the Manson days. Avila, to his credit, came to regard the *Cotton Club* motive to be at least as likely as the initial belief that the killing was drug related. Gunderson and I had continued to maintain that the film deal was the prime reason for the hit. I'd also tried to explain to Avila that we didn't regard Radin's death as a "cult killing," merely that at least one of the suspects, apparently Mentzer, did have connections into the occult underground and may well be the Manson II we'd been hunting.

Regardless, as of January 1, 1987, new investigators, Sergeants William Stoner and Charles Guenther, took responsibility for the case while Avila toiled at a temporary assignment for the Sheriff's Office at the FBI Academy in Quantico, Virginia. As a matter of routine, Guenther and Stoner read the existing Radin file to familiarize themselves with it and made a series of phone calls, trying to trace the history of a Cadillac that had once been owned by Elaine Jacobs and signed over to Bob Lowe—who was later arrested with Mentzer on cocaine charges at L.A. International Airport—on May 13, 1983, the day of Radin's disappearance. Stoner and Guenther suspected that Lowe might have received the Caddy as payment for a role in the Radin murder.

Barely a week after the detectives began their inquiries, I was in Los Angeles to attend the Giants-Denver Super Bowl game on January 25. A few days after the game, on January 29, I met with Ted Gunderson and one of our informants on the case. Six months before, I'd come up with the names of about seven known associates of Mentzer but hadn't forwarded them to Avila because both Gunderson and I had grown frustrated by the lack of progress in the case and by a related conflict that had arisen with the detective. Gunderson and I lacked the authority to pursue Mentzer further, but we agreed to bypass the Sheriff's Office and provide the information we had to a deputy district attorney who was overseeing the case for the D.A.

And so it was that I phoned Deputy District Attorney David Conn and arranged to see him later that afternoon. I told Conn that I would bring one of the informants with me.

We arrived late, having been delayed by the afternoon rush hour's crunch of cars on the freeway. I introduced Conn to the informant, who described his association with Mentzer in the late sixties. I then emphasized to Conn that I was convinced Radin was killed over *The Cotton Club* financing, and that the purported drug ripoff was a small consideration. I also stated that Gunderson and I thought that more than one person was involved in ordering the hit—and I named the two people we believed were responsible. One of them, Elaine Jacobs, was already a police target. The other was more elusive, but Conn, and earlier Carlos Avila, had eyed him warily.

I then provided Conn with the list of Mentzer associates I'd accumulated. Among them: Robert Lowe, Robert Deremer, Alex Lamota (Marti) and William Rider. I read a quote to Conn: "Mentzer, Lowe, Rider and Lamota [Marti] are the big four."

Conn listened intently, and scribbled down notes as we talked. Before leaving, I told him I had completed a book that would include a section on the Radin case, and that it would be published—with considerably publicity—in June. The book in question was the original hardcover edition of *The Ultimate Evil.*

Leaving Conn's office at about 6:30 p.m., I had no idea that the meeting we had would emerge as significant nearly two years in the future.

*   *   *

That, of course, left the matter of Charles Manson himself.

The questions were two: Was Manson II telling the truth when he told the New York group that Charles Manson "volunteered" to kill the Tate victims for a real motive beyond the nightmarish Process-like Armageddon of Helter Skelter?

And if so, who was Manson working for?

But the investigation wouldn't tarry too long in the past. At the same time the Tate inquiry was underway, the Roy Radin-cult probe was ready to leap back across the country to New York in 1985—in a vicious, conclusive manner. There were still more murders on the menu.

XXIV

Murder Reigned in
Southern California

By 1985, David Berkowitz's credibility and that of the prison informants was in good standing. And Manson II, as the Arlis Perry inquiry demonstrated, didn't lie to the New York cult when recounting that horrid tale. The Christine Freund setting was also bolstered solidly, and joined the innumerable other facts uncovered about the various cases since I began the tortuous journey in August 1977. With that background, and what we'd learned about Bill Mentzer, it would have been foolish to dismiss the claim about a real motive in the Tate murders.

Many years had crawled by since those killings occurred, which made any investigation a difficult proposition. But the effort was important to the Son of Sam case and others we'd probed. All were said to be linked, and the discovery of a motive in the Tate murders would further cement the existence of the satanic network that operated between New York, Texas, California and the Dakotas. The evidence would reveal that the Manson case went far deeper than originally believed.

There were two elements to work with: Was the allegation of a "hit" credible? And if so, what was the motive and for whom did Manson "volunteer" to commit the crimes? In this context the "why" of the killings also included Manson's own motivation—what did *he* stand to gain from his alleged voluntary enlistment?

The Helter Skelter motive presented in court was based on Manson's theology, heavily inspired by Process teachings, that a wave of violence should sweep across the world to bring on "the end." In Manson's mind, Helter Skelter (the name came from a Beatles song Manson twisted) would ignite a black-white race war. By leaving suggestive clues at slaughter scenes, his disciples would deceive the establishment into blaming a radical group, such as the Black Panthers, for the crimes. The blacks would taste victory in the resulting war, but would founder trying to govern the new order. Then Charlie and the Family would emerge from hiding in the desert and assume command.

Prosecutor Vincent Bugliosi built an admirable case on that premise, and it is one I don't dispute completely. The prison informants amplified on Helter Skelter, contending there were at least two motives for the killings. Put another way, Manson was said to be a ticking bomb, and somebody knew it. That somebody then tossed the bomb into the right house—10050 Cielo Drive in Benedict Canyon, northwest of downtown Los Angeles.

The Tate-La Bianca murders occurred on consecutive weekend nights, August 9 and 10, 1969. There were seven victims. Actress Sharon Tate, who was eight months pregnant; Roman Polanski's friend Wojtek Frykowski; coffee heiress Abigail Folger;

prominent hairdresser Jay Sebring; and Steven Parent were slain shortly after midnight on Cielo Drive.

Parent, eighteen, had been visiting young caretaker William Garretson, who occupied the guest cottage on the rented Polanski property. He was shot dead by Charles (Tex) Watson, twenty-two, as his Rambler neared the exit gate. Inside the house, the others were shot, stabbed and beaten.

Frykowski and Folger, his girlfriend, were chased from the home and died on the lawn. Sebring and Tate were killed in the living room; a length of rope around their necks bound them together. There is evidence that after the killers left someone—Manson and a companion—arrived at the house and tried to hang Sharon Tate and Sebring from the front porch, but were unsuccessful and dragged them back to the living room.

Mastermind Manson—while not a participant—was convicted, as were the actual killers: Watson, Patricia Krenwinkel and Susan Atkins—who admitted tasting Tate's blood.

The next night, in L.A.'s Los Feliz section, wealthy supermarket president Leno La Bianca, forty-four, and his wife, Rosemary, thirty-eight, were stabbed to death inside their home at 3301 Waverly Drive. Manson, who initially tied up the couple, was convicted here as well, along with actual killers Watson, Krenwinkel and Leslie Van Houten.

After several months of investigation, the cases—which the Tate detectives didn't link—broke when Atkins, in jail on another charge, talked to her cellmates, in a manner similar to Berkowitz's conversations with Vinny and Danny. To build its case against the others, the L.A. prosecution eventually granted immunity to Linda Kasabian, who was at both scenes but was not a killer.

The police investigation of the murders—especially the Tate killings—left much to be desired, as Bugliosi pointed out in his book *Helter Skelter*. And it is the Tate murders to which the New York informants directed their comments. But there were a number of intriguing facts surrounding the La Bianca slayings, too.

*   *   *

At the time of his death, Leno La Bianca, president of the Gateway Markets chain, was about $230,000 in debt—apparently a result of his addiction to horses. That is a motive for murder. La Bianca not only bet the ponies, he owned nine thoroughbreds. He had also served on the board of directors of a Hollywood bank police believed was Mafia-connected. Several of the bank's board members were convicted of fraudulent financial dealings. La Bianca, however, had no criminal record. Somewhere in that maze another motive may have lurked.

His wife, Rosemary, had herself accumulated a considerable fortune by the time she died. Divorced and the mother of two young children, she had worked as a car hop and cocktail waitress to support herself. At the time of her 1959 marriage to Leno, she was a waitress at the Los Feliz Inn. However, she subsequently became a partner in a dress shop, Boutique Carriage, and put some cash into the stock market. A waitress in 1959, Rosemary La Bianca herself left an estate ten years later valued at $2,600,000—more than five million in 1986 dollars. It was, to put it mildly, a remarkable success story.

In the weeks before the murders, there were problems in the La Bianca home. Rosemary told a neighbor the house was entered more than once while she and Leno were away on weekends. Their telephone was also bugged. Ed Sanders reported that a rare coin collection, possibly taken from the home, was later discovered in another house on Waverly; one said to be owned by a bookmaker, who abandoned the residence about a week after the murders. There was a concurrent story which held that one of Manson's top lieutenants, Bruce Davis, took a valuable collection of silver dollars to England about nine months before the killings.

Davis did make the trip, and spent time with the Process in London, according to L.A. homicide sources. Whether or not he actually had the silver dollars is unknown, but Leno La Bianca was indeed an avid coin collector.

Nonetheless, it was determined that the La Biancas were randomly slain by Manson's "children." But could the La Biancas have been under someone's scrutiny? Yes, they were. And it also remains possible that a connection to Manson lay somewhere in the abyss, for Manson was a career criminal and con man with a multitude of contacts on both sides of the Los Angeles tracks.

Linda Kasabian testified that Manson had her drive indiscriminately around L.A. before specifically directing her to the La Bianca home on the night of the killings. The La Biancas, who purchased 3301 Waverly Drive from Leno's mother in 1968, lived next door to a home formerly occupied by friends of Manson. So Manson knew the layout of that house, 3267 Waverly. Yet he instead chose to enter the La Bianca home at 2 a.m. with the lights on and the couple still up; and he and Tex Watson did so without leaving any signs of a break-in. And then, without any indication of a struggle, they tied up the couple. Manson then left and instructed the others, who were waiting outside, to join Watson and kill them.

Curiously, Leno La Bianca's boat, which was hitched to his car, was found on the street outside the house, not in the long, private driveway. A coin collection was in the car's trunk and Leno's wallet was in the glove compartment. On the street, the boat and car were almost inviting theft.

It's not that Leno was careless; he was concerned about the boat and stored it in the garage of his mother's home. So its presence on the street—at a point beyond his driveway—was unusual. Also, water skis were removed from the boat that night; they were found behind the house, leaning on the fender of Rosemary's own car. Is it reasonable to have been worried enough about water skis to lug them at least forty yards up the driveway to the house while leaving behind in plain view a boat hitched to a year-old Thunderbird?

Then, too, Leno was slain in his pajamas while Rosemary was found wearing one of her favorite expensive dresses over a pair of "shorty" pajamas. She hadn't worn it earlier in the evening—the couple had just returned from a casual day at Lake Isabella. Manson has said he told her to put the dress on, but the combination of Rosemary's attire and the boat and car in the street may signify that Rosemary went out alone shortly before the murders and didn't want to pull the rig into the long driveway, which was Leno's task, when she returned. The wallet and coins might have been left in the car because the auto and boat were parked in the driveway when the couple arrived home about an hour before the killings. If Rosemary went out, she may have used the T-Bird or backed that car and the boat from the driveway and used her own vehicle, which was parked behind the house. Her keys and house keys were reportedly found in the ignition of her unlocked car; another enigma. Rosemary had been concerned about the house being entered. Would she have gone to Lake Isabella leaving her house keys and car keys in plain view in an unlocked vehicle? Or had she actually just driven the car right before the murders and upon her return left them behind for some reason?

Combined with the absence of signs of a break-in or a struggle inside the house, it is conceivable that such events occurred. If so, and combined with the other puzzling factors, they would indicate a possible connection between Manson and the La Biancas. If one existed, it probably was in the narcotics area. But police reportedly found no evidence of such activity on the part of either victim. However, a Los Angeles source told me in early 1987 that Rosemary La Bianca was indeed involved in LSD dealing. The statement has not yet been corroborated.

Putting aside a potential link to Manson, the La Biancas may have been killed in a "cover crime"—to use Vinny's term about cult MO in New York—intended to divert police attention from real motives the night before on Cielo Drive.

At both residences—and at the home of musician Gary Hinman, a Manson acquaintance slain July 27 over what Manson later admitted was a botched dope deal—common elements appeared, among them variations of the word "pig" written in blood. There was no attempt by the killers to disassociate the crimes.

Does that fact tend to bolster the Helter Skelter motive and discount the charge of real motive on Cielo Drive? No, it doesn't. Because if Helter Skelter was the only reason for Tate-La Bianca, why did the notorious public murders *stop* after the La Bianca slayings? Two consecutive nights and Manson's master plan was terminated? Tex Watson split for Texas, Patricia Krenwinkel for Alabama and Kasabian for New Hampshire.

Why didn't they do it again and again in just such a vicious, publicity-garnering manner? They didn't. Manson moved his minions deep into the desert.

"Manson," Vinny wrote from Dannemora, "was a puppet."

The questions about the short-lived Helter Skelter are significant, and so is the fact that Manson crimes in the summer of '69 were not motiveless: Hinman, killed over dope; Bernard Crowe, a black dope dealer wounded by Manson over a drug burn; Donald (Shorty) Shea, a hand at the Spahn movie ranch, where the clan lived, slain because he had knowledge of Tate-La Bianca; and the Tate slayings themselves, for which we'd soon discover a motive.

In that context, it would appear that there may also have been a real motive for the La Bianca murders as well. But if not, it is almost certain that they were killed to confuse the issue of legitimate motive on Cielo Drive. It should be remembered that Manson did believe in Helter Skelter, so he had his own reasons for directing the butchery, even if his marching orders were issued elsewhere.

Manson prosecutor Vincent Bugliosi, hampered by inefficient detective work on the Tate killings particularly, acknowledged that he only went with the Helter Skelter motive in court because the police investigation failed to unearth another. Maybe they didn't look hard enough.

* * *

To find another reason for the Cielo Drive slayings, one has to search through the original police investigation and the extended social and narcotics circle populated by *both* Manson and the residents of the Tate house.

At the beginning, Los Angeles authorities focused on drugs as the impetus for the killings. And four of the LAPD's top suspects were none other than people tied closely to Mama Cass Elliot and her crowd. To the best of our knowledge, Roy Radin and Manson II suspect Bill Mentzer wasn't among them, but the fact is that these four men were prime targets during the investigation's first month. All were cleared of *direct* complicity when they provided alibis and passed polygraph tests. One, however, was tested twice.

The four, who were known to police and others as reputed drug dealers, were frequent guests at Cielo Drive while Frykowski and Folger house-sat for the Polanskis from April 1, 1969, until the night of the murders. And even after Sharon Tate returned from abroad in mid-July, the visits continued. One of the men acknowledged being in the house twice during the week of the murders—including the day before they occurred.

One of Cass's entourage, Pic Dawson, the jet-setting son of a State Department official, actually lived in Frykowski's home when he and Abigail relocated to Cielo Drive.

As friends of Frykowski, Dawson, Ben Carruthers, Tom Harrigan and Billy Doyle crashed Roman Polanski's housewarming party at 10050 Cielo in mid-March 1969 and were ejected after a scuffle. They weren't happy about that. But after the Polanskis left for Europe their visits resumed, at Frykowski's invitation.

Billy Doyle, who was close to Mama Cass, also knew Roy Radin suspect Bill Mentzer, said a Los Angeles source who was acquainted with both men. "I was in the same room with them. They were part of the same scene; they know each other," the informant reported. So Mentzer not only knew one of the Tate victims—Folger—he also knew Billy Doyle.

We were getting ever closer to Manson II and the hidden secrets of the Cielo Drive nightmare.

*   *   *

According to police reports, friends of Frykowski and our own sources, Frykowski became involved in LSD dealing and also was offered a wholesale distributorship of the amphetamine MDA—which was found in both his and Folger's systems the night they died.

Frykowski, a recent immigrant to the United States, didn't have the money to make wholesale drug purchases; he was unemployed. This was a subtlety the police apparently missed. But his girlfriend had the funds. Coffee heiress Abigail Folger had the cash to support Frykowski's endeavor, and our sources say she did just that.

"Folger was backing Frykowski in the drug business," said the former FBI operative, who knew Folger personally. "And your guy Mentzer got around in that scene all the time. It was what they were all into."

As so often happens in narcotics merchandising, friction sparked a feud between Frykowski and the suppliers, and a member of Cass's crowd pulled a gun and threatened Frykowski's life not long before the murders. Additionally, one individual from this same group became incensed when, also shortly before the killings, Frykowski threw him out of his Woodstock Road address. The eviction occurred because this friend of Cass's allegedly choked Wojtek's friend, artist Witold Kaczankowski (Witold K.), who was temporarily living in the house while Wojtek and Folger were residing at Cielo Drive.

Frykowski, some said, got in way over his head without even recognizing that he was careening toward white water. Four from the Cass group were later turned in as suspects in the Tate murders by associates of both Frykowski and Mama Cass—including John Phillips, Witold K. and gossip columnist Steve Brandt.

But it would be misleading to limit these men to Mama Cass. They were known to others in the social network, too. And there is no telling exactly how far and in what directions the drug pipeline extended.

*   *   *

And now, into the week of the murders. As stated, one of Cass's friends visited the Cielo Drive house twice and was introduced there to Sharon Tate the day before the killings. Frykowski also received a new MDA shipment that week, and was concurrently said to be "in the midst of a ten-day mescaline experiment."

John Phillips said in 1986 that Frykowski showed up at his Bel Air Drive home during those final days and demanded to be let in. Phillips said that he turned Wojtek away because he seemed incoherent. So the purpose of the unexpected visit remains unexplained.

Also that week, Ed Sanders reported, a large party was held on Cielo Drive at which Billy Doyle, acquaintance of Bill Mentzer, was allegedly whipped as the result of a dope burn involving about $2,000 worth of cocaine which was perpetrated on Jay Sebring, who was present at the affair.

Investigating, Sanders heard only silence from those said to have attended the party, whose roster apparently included John Phillips. But actor Dennis Hopper, quoted by an L.A. newspaper, did comment publicly on the matter: "They had fallen into sadism and masochism and bestiality—and they recorded it all on videotape, too. The L.A. police told me this. I know that three days before they were killed twenty-five people were invited to that house for a mass-whipping of a dealer from Sunset Strip who'd given them bad dope."

The party was held to honor French film director Roger Vadim, who was then married to actress and anti-war activist Jane Fonda. But at what point in the proceedings the alleged whipping-taping occurred is unknown. However, Sanders reported that Sebring did bring undeveloped film to a photo lab on Wednesday, August 6, and the Polanski maid was off the night before. The party, then, apparently occurred on Tuesday night, the fifth.

On the night of the killings, as noted previously, a man named Joel Rostau, the boyfriend of an employee of Sebring's, delivered some drugs to 10050 Cielo Drive. Rostau would be murdered in New York about fifteen months later, and another of Sebring's associates would be slain in Florida about a month after that.

The name of that game was narcotics, not Helter Skelter.

And then there was the subject of witchcraft, black hoods and leather aprons. While it should be recalled that Frykowski and Folger were in temporary residence at Cielo Drive, it is known that British warlock Alex Saunders, who participated in a film Sharon Tate shot in England before her marriage, said he initiated Sharon into witchcraft.

Saunders, who said he studied under master black magician Aleister Crowley himself, was connected to OTO and other cult activity in Britain. It is not known if he was involved with the Process there. But Alex Saunders said he possessed photos of Sharon standing inside a ritual magic circle.

Police denied that black hoods and leather aprons were found in the loft above the living room at 10050 Cielo Drive. However, Ed Sanders told me in July 1985 that FBI sources informed him those items were indeed there—along with "an inverted ace of spades," said to be a form of cultic life sign. Doris Tate, Sharon's mother, also said that a white cape was found in the house.

*   *   *

Thus, there appears to have been no lack of real motives to supplement Helter Skelter, ranging from dope to revenge to occult-related matters. There was no evidence to demonstrate the New York prison informants were wrong—and I don't think they were.

Manson himself has alleged that the "true" motive remains secret, that a major scandal would erupt if it was revealed. Various members of his Family have echoed those sentiments. Among them are: Venice, California, biker Danny De Carlo, whom Sanders said police linked to a Process offshoot in Santa Barbara; convicted Gary Hinman killer Bobby Beausoleil, who had been affiliated with a San Francisco

Satan cult; Catherine (Gypsy) Share; Vern Plumlee; and others. Most have ascribed the motive to a dope burn.

In a 1987 interview with an associate of mine, Manson added a twist to the narcotics motive. "Don't you think those people deserved to die—they were involved in kiddie porn," he alleged, but didn't say just who in the Tate-La Bianca cases he was referring to.

Another source close to Manson told Sanders that a "real millionaire" friend of Manson's, whose large black car Manson wrecked around the time of the murders, was involved. This source added that an $11,000 LSD burn was in the picture. The millionaire's name wasn't revealed to Sanders, but the information narrowed the field. And there are several reasons to believe the statement had a basis in fact. One of those is an incident which occurred just two nights after the La Bianca slayings.

At approximately 1 a.m. on August 12, Manson arrived at the home of a friend, Melba Kronkite, who lived in the Malibu area. Manson asked Kronkite for $825 to bail out follower Mary Brunner, who'd been jailed several days before on a stolen credit card charge. Melba couldn't provide the cash, and watched as an angry Manson drove off behind the wheel of a large black car, apparently the same one referred to by Sanders's source.

The "millionaire" allegation also blended with Manson's reference to a major scandal—as does a mysterious trip he made, which will be discussed shortly.

Vern Plumlee told a reporter that the killers went to Cielo Drive to get dope purveyor Frykowski and anyone else present. This comment is both logical and supportable. It may also mesh with the millionaire-LSD burn information because Frykowski, as Roman Polanski's friend, was traveling in some select circles.

Beyond that, Frykowski emerges as a likely target by process of elimination. The pregnant Sharon Tate, who was overseas during four of the five previous months, would be an unlikely candidate. Abigail Folger likewise, to an extent. She was a shadow of the controlling Frykowski, who primed her narcotics usage, and, the sources say, she was also financing his dope distribution enterprise. On the surface, Jay Sebring may have appeared to be a plausible intended target. His cocaine habit was known to friends, and police learned of it soon after his death.

But Sebring was a client rather than a dealer, and he didn't *live* at Cielo Drive. While a frequent visitor, he usually slept at home, where he was into a mild bondage scene with willing female partners whom he'd tie up and photograph before culminating the sex act. Moreover, although Sebring's intent to visit the Tate house that final night was known by some in the crowd, there wouldn't appear to have been any guarantee that he'd still be there at about 12:20 a.m., when the killers arrived, since he was scheduled to fly to San Francisco the next day and may well have intended to go home earlier.

A Los Angeles source who was knowledgeable about the Manson set in 1969 said: "Frykowski was the motive. He had stung his own suppliers for a fair amount of money and that didn't go down well at all with the people at the top of the drug scene here. And to make it worse, he was upsetting the structure of the LSD marketplace by dealing independently, outside the established chain of supply. He was a renegade."

The source knew Abigail Folger and others in the circle.

The "fair amount" of money the source described may have been the $11,000 Sanders reported, but my informant said the total sum was "probably a lot higher."

However, the source confirmed the relevance of the black car Manson was seen driving two days after the murders. According to information we uncovered, the black car apparently was a Mercedes-Benz that was owned by a wealthy individual who lived part-time in Berkeley, California, during the Manson era. Sources say that the car owner, whom I will call Chris Jetz, was a narcotics "middleman" who distributed hallucinogenic drugs from secret LSD and MDA laboratories to drop-off points for pickup by elements of the Hell's Angels biker gang, who controlled most of the street-level distribution of chemical narcotics in the L.A. area at the time.

The source's name and Jetz's real name have been turned over to authorities. And the biker connection, from the Process and Manson to the New York prison statements, had now appeared several times during the overall investigation.

Sources also said that Jetz had ties, in the form of funding, to the upscale, self-awareness Esalen Institute in Big Sur, California.

*   *   *

The Los Angeles drug scene in 1969 could be likened to a field of pyramids which roughly divided the marketplace into various specialized segments. Near the top of one pyramid, the chemical dope edifice, was a man connected to Jetz; a superior, so to speak. This man was said to have been a former Israeli who had strong links to the international intelligence community. He wasn't employed by U.S. or Israeli intelligence, at least not at the time of the murders. Rather, he was regarded as a rogue who, in addition to his elevated narcotics ranking, was suspected by some of being an operative for the Soviet Union, perhaps freelance.

This information, which I unearthed in 1986, apparently explained something Ed Sanders earlier told me: "There were so many investigations going on out there after the murders that I began to wonder if the Process was a front for some intelligence operation."

Sanders said that the FBI, Israeli intelligence, the California Beverage Control Board, the Los Angeles DA's office, as well as the LAPD and the Los Angeles Sheriff's Department, all mounted probes of the Tate murders, with the Treasury Department involved peripherally. And those were the ones he knew about.

Whatever clandestine bonds may have existed on top of Dope Mountain, the inquiry we conducted resulted in the determination that Frykowski was the primary target, with Folger secondary, and that LSD dealing and market control was the principal motive.

Mansonite Vern Plumlee added an intriguing gem to his own Frykowski comment: he said the killers had received information that Sharon Tate wasn't supposed to be home that night. Interestingly, it appears that Sharon did plan to spend the evening at the home of a girlfriend, Sheila Welles, but then changed her mind.

But if Manson in fact received that tip it could only have emanated from a handful of people—those who, directly or indirectly, were in contact with Sharon, Jay Sebring, Folger or Frykowski within forty-eight hours of the murders.

And one of them would have wanted people dead on Cielo Drive.

Could Manson himself have known any of Mama Cass's crowd, others in the extended group, or even one of the victims? The prosecution and police didn't pursue this angle successfully, but the answer is decidedly *yes*.

Manson Family associate Charles Melton said: "I've heard that Charlie used to go down to Mama Cass's place and they were all sitting around and she'd bring out the food. Squeaky [Fromme, who later tried to shoot President Gerald Ford] and Gypsy [Catherine Share] were down there. Everyone would jam and have fun and eat."

Manson also was closely linked to record and TV producer Terry Melcher; his young assistant, Gregg Jakobson; and Beach Boys drummer Dennis Wilson.

Wilson and Melcher were good friends of John Phillips, and Cass was associated with Bill Mentzer, among others. Phillips said that Melcher and Wilson frequently tried to interest him in Manson's music and philosophy. Talent manager Rudy Altobelli, the actual owner of 10050 Cielo Drive, testified at Manson's trial that Melcher and Jakobson often praised Manson to him.

But whereas Altobelli and Phillips said they declined these suggestions, Sanders reported that Manson's bus was observed parked at Phillips's Bel Air home in the autumn of 1968, and that Manson apparently also attended a 1968 New Year's Eve party there.

Whether or not this was so, the links between Manson, Wilson, Cass, Phillips, Melcher and Jakobson are evident.

*   *   *

The Manson-Melcher relationship was instigated by Dennis Wilson. In the summer of 1968 he introduced Manson to Melcher and Jakobson while Charlie and some followers were in residence at Wilson's Sunset Boulevard estate. Wilson paid dearly for his hospitable attitude: the Family scrounged him out of considerable money and wrecked one of his cars. One of the Beach Boys' gold records ended up at the Spahn movie ranch.

But Wilson, Jakobson and Melcher were in tune with Charlie Manson, and a Manson song, rewritten by the Beach Boys, was released as a Beach Boys' flip side in December 1968. The "A" side was a remake of Ersel Hickey's "Bluebirds Over the Mountain," and Manson's backing tune was originally titled—honestly—"Cease to Exist." But the group changed those words to "cease to resist" and added a new title, "Never Learn Not to Love," which wasn't quite what Manson had in mind.

In the spring of 1969, Wilson told a British rock magazine that the Beach Boys might release a Manson album. He called Manson "the Wizard."

During the 1968 "Cease to Exist" period, Terry Melcher was living with actress Candice Bergen in the future death house, 10050 Cielo Drive. And Tex Watson and Manson follower Dean Moorehouse were said to have passed a lot of hours at that residence during that summer of '68. In fact, Moorehouse actually lived in the house, with Melcher's concurrence, after Melcher moved to Malibu and before his subtenants, the Polanskis, occupied the premises on February 15, 1969.

Moorehouse provides a curious twist to this story. The middle-aged former minister moved to California in 1965 from North Dakota. He was a native of Minot, of all places, went to college there and worked several jobs in the city before finding God. He then headed congregations in two North Dakota towns, one of which was near both Bismarck and Minot. In light of the Arlis Perry scenario in Bismarck and other doings in Minot, these links are provocative. Though he was gone from North Dakota by the seventies, it is certain native son Dean Moorehouse had contacts there.

Dean's daughter, Ruth Ann (Ouisch), was herself a hard-core Manson follower to the end. Though barely seventeen, Ruth Ann was no shrinking violet: she was implicated in the attempted murder of defector Barbara Hoyt. Ouisch fed her an LSD-laced hamburger in Honolulu, where Hoyt had gone to hide during the Manson trial.

* * *

After Manson's arrest, a number of his society contacts, not surprisingly, tried to downplay their interaction with him. Among them was Terry Melcher, who had a show business image to consider. But, Sanders reported, Melcher's relationship with Manson was more extensive than generally believed. For instance, Sanders wrote that Manson and others in the Family occasionally borrowed Melcher's car and were given permission to use his credit card while on the road. It was love and flowers in those early days.

In addition, Manson became quite friendly with a young divorcee, Charlene Cafritz, who was a close friend of Melcher confidant Alan Warnecke. Like Melcher, Cafritz was a person with considerable wealth. She also was a friend of Sharon Tate, and attended her funeral.

Manson met Cafritz at Dennis Wilson's beach house in 1968. Later, Charlie and three of his female followers visited, at Cafritz's expense, a luxury resort in Reno, Nevada, where she was staying. While in Reno, in December 1968, Cafritz—who was awaiting a divorce settlement there which would net her about $2 million—tried to buy Manson a Cadillac, Sanders reported. Interestingly, she was also said to have purchased a number of thoroughbred horses, which were then resold or given away.

In Reno, Charlene Cafritz took a series of private films of Manson and the girls. The whereabouts of these perhaps sensual epics is unknown. But the Cafritz connection, which some close to the Manson case consider a "good lead" for anyone interested in following through on the investigation, is now minus Charlene herself. She died about two years later of an overdose.

*   *   *

Moving forward to the summer of slaughter: Terry Melcher and Gregg Jakobson visited Manson at the Spahn ranch on June 3. Earlier, Jakobson and Dennis Wilson recorded Manson for an album audition but Melcher, who sat in on the session, wasn't too impressed. The music business was career goal number one for Manson, who wasn't thrilled that Melcher was lagging on the deal. A certain animosity was brewing.

But now the talk was of a documentary film which would depict the daily life of the Family. Stills and tapes for a presentation were already shot. Manson, however, wanted machetes and gore, whereas the others sought to portray the soft side of communal living, then in vogue in America.

Melcher had previously come to the ranch on May 18, when he listened to Charlie and the girls sing. He'd heard better. But he returned on June 3 with Jakobson and sound engineer Mike Deasy, who had a rolling recording studio in his van.

Melcher was also accompanied by a young starlet named either Shara or Sharon who'd apparently been to Spahn before, wearing wigs to disguise her identity. While at the ranch, Manson and Melcher got into a heated argument as Jakobson and the starlet stood by. Its origin was unknown, but it apparently concerned the focus of the film.

Mansonite Edward (Sunshine) Pierce saw them arguing but was unable to over-hear any particulars. However, about thirty minutes later he knew something was up. Manson walked over to Pierce, pledged him to secrecy and asked if he'd help murder somebody.

"He said he had one person in particular he wanted me to help him kill and said there might have to be some other people killed," Pierce later said. "He said he could probably round up maybe five thousand dollars or more and give it to me if I helped him pull this job."

Manson didn't name anybody, but Pierce had some clouded insight into why Charlie wanted to accomplish the crime(s). Paraphrasing Manson, Pierce said: "If you ever want to get anything and you want it bad enough, you can't let anybody come between you when you are going to do something."

Pierce believed Manson was serious, so he called his family in Texas and they wired money to him. Sunshine Pierce flew home the next day.

Both Jakobson and Melcher were familiar with Manson's philosophies. Jakobson, for instance, told prosecutor Bugliosi that over the course of the year preceding the murders, he had a hundred hours of in-depth conversations with Manson.

It is somewhat perplexing that neither Wilson, Jakobson nor Melcher thought of Manson immediately after the carnage at Melcher's former residence. In any event, they didn't call the police. But perhaps they were frightened or simply didn't make the connection.

Melcher, for example, professed great fear of Manson during the trial, asking if he could testify through a loudspeaker in a side room rather than face Charlie head on. The request was denied. But, as it turned out, he needn't have worried. Manson's defense attorney didn't cross-examine Melcher. Prosecutor Bugliosi said that this strategy was "probably at Manson's request."

Also, Paul Fitzgerald, first Manson's attorney and later the representative of Patricia Krenwinkel, announced to the press that John Phillips and Mama Cass would be called as defense witnesses. But for some reason plans were changed, and the two former members of the Mamas and the Papas never took the stand.

*   *   *

As noted, various motives for the killings were evident both on and beneath the surface. Pertinent activities at Cielo Drive immediately prior to the murders have also been discussed, but Manson's own actions just before and after the slayings may provide an important piece of the puzzle.

After having been around L.A. all summer, Manson left town early on Sunday morning, August 3, just days before the murders. After purchasing gas at a station in nearby Canoga Park, he made a beeline for the coast and Highway 1. Up the coastline he drove, heading for Big Sur, about three hundred miles away.

The following morning, at about four o'clock, he picked up Stephanie Schram, a seventeen-year-old hitchhiker, at a gas station somewhat south of Big Sur, apparently in Gorda. Where Manson was earlier in the day isn't known for certain, but he may have been at the Esalen Institute in Big Sur—a well-known sensitivity center whose seminars attracted affluent knowledge seekers of the day. Its sessions were hosted by philosophers, psychiatrists, meditation proponents—and even prominent Satanists. Robert DeGrimston, head of the Process, reportedly lectured there.

But if Manson wasn't positively placed at Esalen on August 3, he indeed was two nights later. Schram, who stayed with Manson and was initiated to LSD by him, told prosecutors that Manson left her outside Esalen in his truck, took his guitar and went inside. When she awoke in the morning, he was back. And, she said, his mood wasn't good. It was now August 6, about sixty-six hours from murder.

Why was Manson at Esalen? There is no clear answer. He'd told some followers at the Spahn ranch that he was heading north to look for new recruits. He later told another associate, Paul Watkins, that he played his guitar for top people at Esalen who rejected his music.

It is also quite possible that he was there for a reason which involved chemical narcotics dealer Chris Jetz, who sources say provided a degree of financial backing for Esalen. However, Esalen officials refused to acknowledge Manson's presence there.

Big Sur isn't far from Santa Cruz, home of Chingon cult activity. And when Manson picked up Stephanie south of Big Sur at 4 a.m. on August 4, he had two male companions with him. Stephanie testified that these unidentified men were hitchhikers who soon left the truck. At least that's what she thought they were.

Regardless, Manson and Stephanie drove south from Big Sur on August 6, stopped overnight at the Spahn ranch outside L.A. and then drove to the home of Stephanie's married sister in San Diego on the seventh. That night, Manson frightened the sister by predicting: "People are going to be slaughtered. They'll be lying on their lawns dead." And within thirty hours, they indeed would be.

Was Manson's alleged rejection at Esalen the final straw, compounded by his learning on August 8 that Bobby Beausoleil had been bagged for the Hinman murder? It is impossible to say with certainty. Manson was the only source for what happened at the institute. If he'd been there for another reason, he wasn't likely to inform stranger Stephanie or Paul Watkins, who was not considered part of the insider murder machine.

But the New York informants *hadn't* said Manson lacked his own reasons for committing the crimes. The point made was that someone took advantage of Manson's madness and guided him to Cielo Drive.

In that sense, whether Manson was spurned at Esalen is irrelevant. It's only if he wasn't that matters.

After the killings, Manson's actions indicate that if he was under orders on the murders, it wasn't in exchange for money. He first showed up at Dennis Wilson's house with Stephanie. Wilson later said Manson wanted $1,500 so he could get out to the desert. So much for Helter Skelter. It was at this time, Stephanie testified, that Wilson told Manson the police had questioned him about someone who'd been shot in the stomach. This was Bernard (Lotsa Poppa) Crowe, a black dope dealer who lived near Mama Cass. Manson had wounded him July 1 over a marijuana burn, and one of Wilson's friends was there at the time. Wilson turned down Manson's request for money, and Charlie then issued a veiled threat against Wilson's son.

Charlie also sought out Gregg Jakobson and was again unsuccessful in his quest for cash. He handed Jakobson, of all things, a .44 bullet and advised him to tell Wilson there were more where that one came from. Manson also dropped in on Melba Kronkite in the Malibu area driving the big black car and seeking bail money for Mary Brunner. Whoever else Manson may have called on is unknown.

Arrested on other charges on October 12, Manson never left jail again. Susan Atkins talked in prison, and the case broke in December.

*   *   *

The preceding scenario isn't intended to be the final word on the relevant issues of the Manson case. My interest in it was based on the alleged relationship between Manson II and the original Charlie; and in the charge that Manson, said to be a member of the Son of Sam "umbrella" cult organization, acted on the request of another. Bill Mentzer's appearance in the web added more impetus to search through the haze of sixteen years.

Prosecutor Vincent Bugliosi was faced with a difficult endeavor as it was. He proved that Manson, although not a direct participant, had ordered the Tate-La Bianca killings. The idea of picking through that puzzle to see who may have pulled Manson's strings—and why—would have been beyond a reasonable expectation at that time.

But the biggest connection was one missed by authorities, and that link fused other bombshells which also evaded the police and the district attorney's office.

*   *   *

The summer of love, 1967, in San Francisco. Throughout the United States, flower power reigned but San Francisco was Mecca. In a song written by his close friend John Phillips, Scott McKenzie advised people coming to the city by the bay to wear flowers in their hair because "summertime will be a love-in there." Eric Burdon of the Animals sang about warm "San Franciscan Nights." The hometown Jefferson Airplane wanted "Somebody to Love" and told about Alice when she was ten feet tall in the acid-laced "White Rabbit."

It was Haight-Ashbury, the Grateful Dead, Quicksilver Messenger Service, the Monterey festival, drugs, sex, Vietnam War resistance and hippiedom. It was the summer the Beatles' "Sergeant Pepper" marched into the United States dropping hints about sugar-cube highs and The Doors' "Light My Fire" rocketed to number one. It was also the era when Charles Manson met up with the Process.

And the time when he first met one of the eventual Tate victims.

Vincent Bugliosi suspected Manson had contact with the Process in San Francisco. But the prosecution didn't pursue that suspicion. Similarly, the district attorney's office said it sought but was unable to find a link between Manson and a Cielo Drive victim, which would have significantly altered the perception of the case.

But we learned that Charlie and Abigail Folger were friends for a time in San Francisco and that Manson hooked up with the Process there as well.

The Folger information comes from a reliable informant who knew both Folger and Manson. The source said he had dinner one night in September 1967 with Manson, Folger and two other individuals at a small seafood restaurant near Golden Gate Park, not far from the Haight.

One of the others at the table was an aspiring actor and stuntman named Donald (Shorty) Shea. He later headed south to Los Angeles and found work at the Spahn movie ranch.

Shorty Shea was murdered by the Family in the fallout from the Tate-La Bianca slayings, allegedly because he knew too much.

He indeed did. Unknown by the police and prosecution, Shea had known Manson and Folger in San Francisco two years before the murders and actually went down to L.A. in Manson's company, according to the source. This revelation also seriously impacts the case. Two people seated in that seafood restaurant that night in 1967 were later murdered on the instructions of a third.

The source's statement—which was supported by that of another California informant who said Shea also knew Bill Mentzer's associates—destroys Helter Skelter as the only motive for the slayings and clearly demonstrates there were other factors involved. The New York informants had hit the target again.

Ed Sanders had heard that Manson attended a fundraising event in San Francisco that was chaired by Abigail Folger's mother. He also knew that in 1967 Manson met disciple Mary Brunner at the University of California, Berkeley, where Brunner worked in the library and Folger at the university's art museum. And he had received information that Manson met Folger at Mama Cass's home. But Sanders wasn't able to flesh out the Folger connection. We were.

"Gibby had more money than she knew what to do with," the source states. "She was into finding herself and new directions, and she was always investing in things, including a surfboard shop in Encinitas [near San Diego]. And not long before the murders, about six weeks, she got involved in putting up some cash for a small recording studio. It's possible that Terry Melcher, who knew Manson well, had a link into that studio." This was another twist; Melcher wasn't believed to have been associated with Folger, but the source says he might have been.

"That night in San Francisco, she loaned ten grand to a small theater," the informant continues. "And she had also given money to Charlie from time to time."

But then she stopped.

"Manson turned against her when she refused to lay out any more bucks for him, and also because she wouldn't come across for him sexually. Charlie wanted to make it with her, but she shot him down."

So Charles Manson, who would soon orchestrate orgies and command sex at will from his young followers, was spurned by Abigail Folger. Add another item to Charlie's own list of reasons for willingness to oversee butchery on Cielo Drive.

"It made sense that Shea was killed after that," the contact says. "He knew both of them, and he could tie things together that nobody wanted tied."

*   *   *

From another informant, it was learned that the $10,000 Folger agreed to advance that 1967 night was to help out a San Francisco arts house known as the Straight Theater, which was located on the corner of Haight Street and Cole. Not coincidentally, Manson lived at 636 Cole during this period, and the Process was ensconced at No. 407 on that block.

On September 21, 1967, a rock group called the Magick Powerhouse of Oz (with the word "magic" deliberately spelled with Aleister Crowley's k on the end) played the Straight Theater to celebrate something occultish known as the "equinox of the gods," September 21 being the first day of autumn.

Lead guitarist and sitar player for the Powerhouse was none other than Bobby Beausoleil, who became a Mansonite and participated in the 1969 Gary Hinman murder. Manson, Folger, the Straight Theater and Beausoleil; the connections are fascinating.

Beausoleil was tightly woven to author and bizarre-film maker Kenneth Anger, who was into the biker mystique and later conducted a magic ritual involving a satanic pentagram during an October 1967 march on the Pentagon. Anger was in the process of filming an occult movie that autumn; it was called *Lucifer Rising*. Beausoleil, twenty, played the part of Lucifer in the picture and his group was to perform the movie's music, such as it was.

So, Sanders reported, Anger was present at the Straight Theater that night to film the soiree.

Following the path a step further: Anger, LSD guru Timothy Leary and others were involved in the formation of the Himalayan Academy, which a source described to me as "a new-age research foundation of altered states of consciousness." The academy was stocked with various types of expensive equipment, such as oscilloscopes and electronic measuring devices. It was a mind-bending experiment of the first kind.

Sources say the academy was comprised of at least fifty members, plus another hundred or so hangers-on. There was considerable wealth on the academy's roster of sympathizers, and informants report that Abigail Folger contributed money here as well. Folger had also attended sessions at Esalen, which was neither geographically nor philosophically far from the Himalayan Academy.

In fact, Folger may have been at Esalen on August 2 or 3, 1969, just before Manson arrived there. A phone call, probably made by Folger, was placed to Esalen from 10050 Cielo Drive on July 30, the Wednesday before the weekend of August 2–3. If Folger went to Esalen, her reason may have been simply to attend a sensitivity seminar, or it may have been related to other matters connected to the oncoming murders. However, no one has discovered if she even visited the facility at that time. But she was not in Los Angeles. Sanders reported that Frykowski entertained another young lady at Cielo Drive that Friday night, demonstrating that Abigail was away.

Regardless, the sources say that Folger put some capital into the Himalayan Academy—and that Charlie Manson was also connected to the society.

"Folger donated to the place, and it was there that Manson was first exposed to the Process," an informant says. "The academy was into all sorts of things and the Process was invited to speak there. That's how it happened."

The source didn't know if Folger was associated with the cult. But according to the informant, *Manson joined the cult* and later convened with the group in Mill Valley and at a dwelling in San Anselmo occupied by a well-known personage aligned with the LSD scene. Both cities are in the Bay Area.

This scenario raised an inevitable question. Los Angeles sources earlier said that Roy Radin/Manson II suspect Bill Mentzer frequently traveled to the San Francisco area, the Stanford campus in Palo Alto, and stipulated that he knew Abigail Folger.

"Mentzer knew Manson and all the cult people," the other informant said.

Another crucial piece of the puzzle was now in place.

And what about the relationship between Manson and the doomed Shorty Shea?

"They knew each other well enough in San Francisco to travel up to Seattle together to visit a commune started there by Brother Love Israel," said the informant, who dined with them. "They were tight long before the Spahn ranch and the murders."

Authorities had placed Manson in Seattle, but they apparently didn't know why he was there—or whom he was with.

*   *   *

From Son of Sam in New York to the plains of North Dakota. From a Bible in Caswell Canyon to Benedict Canyon in 1969. And from the grizzled faces of prisoners in maximum-security jails in New York to the mellowed-out summer of love in San Francisco in '67. The journey was almost completed.

So what happened at Cielo Drive? Like Ed Sanders, I believe a dope burn was the primary motive, and the evidence supports that conclusion. It is also apparent that Manson harbored animosity toward Abigail Folger. And I believe Manson's own race war fantasy, fed by cult mentors, was another component. There may be more. But several things seem very clear. For one, no lower-rung dope purveyor could have ordered the killings. Because of the intense heat such public and celebrity murders generate, approval would have come from on high, although the grudge itself may have originated lower on the ladder.

Manson didn't commit the Tate-La Bianca murders for financial rewards. Was his own Helter Skelter motivation enough for him to accept the assignment? It's possible, but very doubtful. As unglued as Charlie became, he was still a jail-hardened, street-smart, smooth operator. I, and others who assisted the 1985–86 Manson probe, believe that Manson stood to gain something beyond fulfillment of Helter Skelter or a modicum of revenge against Folger; something that mattered to him personally.

A jailed Manson killer whom I interviewed in early 1987 agreed that, "Charlie never did anything that didn't benefit Charlie, himself. I think he used 'Helter Skelter' to turn us on. There had to be another motive for the killings, and he was going to get something for himself out of it."

What that something was cannot be said with certainty, although suspicion abounds. But it might be beneficial to envision that chemical drug pyramid. Perhaps there was someone in it who knew of Manson's volatile mindset. Someone who, as part of that pyramid's structure, could have agreed to offer Manson something he wanted as a favor to those ranked higher. That remains to be proven.

Manson, certainly, was a member of a secret satanic cult. All the evidence and source information points to that, and it is an evaluation I share with others, including Sanders. Bugliosi himself stopped just short of calling Manson a member of the Process, and he didn't have access to the information we uncovered. But Bugliosi did point out that two Process representatives flew from Cambridge, Massachusetts, to visit Manson in jail. After that session, Manson stopped talking about the group.

The Process went underground in the summer of 1968, and offshoots sprang up in its stead. There, the evidence shows, Manson remained and was primed for violence in the company of cult leaders who cross-connected liberally with the drug and celebrity sets. It was startling to see how closely the entire operation reflected the one in New York. But then, it should have: as the prison informants said, the same organization was behind both movements.

XXV

Death Mask

She disappeared from a nighttime street in Oceanside, Long Island, on March 26, 1985. She was just nineteen. It was a Tuesday evening and she'd come from a girl-friend's home and was walking along a side road to her job at a nearby Burger King. Across the street from Burger King, at Nathan's, it was "bike night," a Tuesday ritual. Although it was just 7:40 p.m., the weekly leathered hordes were revving their Harleys in the parking lot.

But Jacqueline Martarella wouldn't see the bikers; would never reach her job. Jacqueline Martarella vanished in the early spring darkness.

As soon as I read of the disappearance, I suspected foul play. I knew Jacqueline wasn't a runaway. Nothing fit. But I knew more than that. I was already involved in a probe of possible cult complicity in another disappearance and a murder, both involving young girls, in the village of Lynbrook, a few miles from Oceanside. When the Martarella disappearance was announced, I, and some in law enforcement, thought the cases were probably linked.

In early March, Harry Daley, a writer and stunt coordinator for films, called me at my new residence in Jersey. Aware of what was going on around his community, he asked if I'd come to Long Island to look into the cases. Daley was a friend of Denis Dillon, the Nassau County district attorney. Dillon, Harry said, was concerned about the matter and would be willing to discuss the situation with me. And so I went.

Two teenagers, Kelly Morrissey and Theresa Fusco, had recently vanished from the streets of Lynbrook in the early evening hours. Morrissey, fifteen, was still missing, but Fusco's body was later found buried beneath pallets in a wooded area near the Long Island Rail Road tracks in Lynbrook. She'd been raped, strangled and dumped nude in the cold November air. She lay there a month before her body was discovered. Theresa Fusco was sixteen.

Denis Dillon explained that there'd been a series of incidents in recent months in Nassau County. At some, witnesses spotted a van, apparently occupied by more than one person, cruising the areas from where victims vanished.

"By definition, any conspiracy of more than two people engaged in multiple killings is a cult," I said. "What kind of cult it is remains to be seen."

"I'm concerned about these incidents," Dillon said. "I'm aware of what you've done on Berkowitz and if you've got any ideas here I'd be glad to hear them."

I told Dillon I'd like to visit the Fusco scene, and he gave Harry and me directions to find it. At the site, we examined the pallets which had covered Theresa's body. On one, there was faded writing in Magic Marker. The word "Rush" appeared—the name of a heavy-metal rock group. Beside it was a symbol the group used: the satanic pentagram. On another part of the same panel, a message was written. Some words were obliterated, but what we could decipher said: "Sex . . . No . . . virgin devil . . . allow."

We didn't have to be hit over the head. For years I'd known that the rape of a young "virgin" was an important satanic ritual—and so was murder.

Pulling the planks from the pallet, we turned them over to Dillon.

"Somewhere out here, there's probably a cult working," I said. "I find it hard to believe she just happened to be covered with a pallet that had that crap written on it by accident. But maybe, on a long shot, it is a coincidence. I think we have to learn more."

Dillon readily agreed. He wasn't prepared to call it a cult killing either. But Harry Daley, who'd carefully scouted the village of Lynbrook, pointed out that an unusual abundance of satanic and Nazi graffiti peppered certain hangouts in the town. He thought there was significance in that fact, and there was. Much of the graffiti was sophisticated, and the Nazi connection was important. I was beginning to envision a link to the biker crowd in Oceanside. Many bike gangs are satanically oriented, a fact not lost on the Process and Charles Manson, both of whom actively sought to recruit bikers as the advance troops of Armageddon. And in large letters, the word "rise" appeared among the occult graffiti at one location in Lynbrook. Manson's killers wrote that word in blood in the La Bianca home. I also remembered Vinny's comment about the Sam cult using bikers to transport illegal weapons.

Still, neither Dillon, Daley nor I knew if we were dealing with an organized cult, a few satanically bent young men or a coincidence. An arrest was in the offing in the Fusco case, and John Kogut, twenty-two, was picked up on March 25. His apprehension was announced the next day—and Jacqueline Martarella vanished eight hours later in Oceanside, about four miles from the Fusco scene in Lynbrook.

*   *   *

While the police searched for Martarella, Harry Daley and I went to work on John Kogut's background. Two other men were believed to have been his accomplices in the Fusco killing, and authorities were building toward their arrests. Kogut had named them in his confession.

But Kogut himself had a history which contained some fascinating clues. A landscaper, he'd been a street kid most of his life. In and out of minor trouble, he was typical of the genre. But there was something else. A witness told us Kogut had once "burned a cross into his arm" and had shown the witness pornographic snapshots of himself.

"He said he was involved in porno stuff," the witness explained.

Shortly afterwards, *Newsday* reporter Sid Cassese, who'd been working with Harry and me, found out about Kogut's porno connection. He apparently was arrested as a male prostitute in New York City while still in his teens. Homosexuality, porn and New York City tie-ins. I was beginning to discern a familiar pattern.

But the most important development was still to come. Seeking information,

Cassese was loitering outside a Lynbrook video games emporium when he ran into a teenaged friend of Kogut's named Bob Fletcher, who was en route to a Friday-night party with a companion. Stopping to talk for a few minutes, Fletcher told Cassese that Kogut was indeed into the pornography business in Manhattan and had even starred in a private, underground child-porn film. Its title was *Five to Nine*—a perverted play on the movie *Nine to Five*.

Cassese wanted to interview Fletcher again, but he never got the chance. Several hours after talking to the reporter, Fletcher was blown away by a shotgun blast to the head outside his cousin's home in nearby Rosedale, Queens. Fletcher was dead, and Sid Cassese was a shaken man.

The incident occurred at about 4:30 a.m., and it happened in the middle of the street. No gun was found. Yet authorities thought Fletcher, who had a history of emotional difficulties, might have taken a shotgun from the house, walked into the roadway and killed himself. As for the missing shotgun, police suggested someone in the house may have taken it from its place near the body.

The other possibility was that Fletcher was murdered. The matter was unresolved, but Cassese said Fletcher was in good spirits when he spoke to him hours before.

And then Jacqueline Martarella was found. Like Theresa Fusco, she was nude, ligature-strangled and apparently raped. Her body was found in late April 1985 hidden in tall reeds adjacent to the seventeenth hole of the Woodmere Country Club in exclusive Lawrence, Long Island, about five miles west of the spot from which she disappeared.

In a day, I was at the scene. And there in the reeds, about fifteen feet deeper into the rushes than the body, I found it. It was one of the signs left at crime scenes by the Sam cult. I'd known about this proclivity since 1981, and Denis Dillon knew it, too, because I'd shown him a prison letter listing this and a few other objects this group often left at murder sites. For investigatory reasons, the object must remain unidentified, but it was not an item one would expect to find hidden near a murder victim.

The object had been carefully placed, and it was apparent it was there for about the same length of time as the body—approximately a month. Its presence told me all I needed to know, and it telegraphed once again what I'd realized all along: the cult hadn't disbanded. Elements of it were still active.

I also recalled something Berkowitz had written in 1979: "They will just replace me. There are others."

Yes. Others like Berkowitz who, if arrested, would say nothing about their cult activities and assume sole responsibility for the crimes. Over the years, police undoubtedly had apprehended people they believed were solo operators but were actually connected to the cult underground. But nobody knew it.

I called Denis Dillon from a nearby restaurant and he drove to the scene from his office in Garden City. It was a cold, blustery April day and the wind blew hard off the inlet water which lapped at the golf course.

"This is it," I said, handing him the object. "Now we know what we're dealing with, on Martarella at least. I don't see how this can possibly be a coincidence. And I'd say there's probably some kind of link to Kogut's crowd, even if it's a loose one. This thing is a magical symbol for them," I explained, pointing at the object. "But nobody else would think it was the slightest bit relevant."

"I know what you're saying." Dillon nodded. "But this is a police case to solve. I'm the prosecutor. We'll just have to wait and see what they come up with."

I understood what Dillon meant. Outside investigators, even if welcomed by a district attorney, are not appreciated by police departments, whose job it is to solve cases in their jurisdictions. Anything viewed as interference, however slight, is met with resentment.

* * *

However, within a week Denis Dillon was back at the Martarella scene. And, as before, it was a telephone call that brought him there.

Harry Daley, "interfering" in police business, was asking questions in the neighborhood surrounding the golf course. He learned from a mailman that behind the course, in a secluded wooded section about six hundred yards from where the body was found, a small cave sat in a clearing. The postman had never looked inside, but he thought we might be interested in knowing it existed. We were.

Inside the cave, which was actually an abandoned root cellar from an estate that had stood on the property years before, we found shocking evidence. The walls were emblazoned with satanic symbols: pentagrams, upturned crosses and other satanic slogans. Outside the cellar, which resembled a bunker, were a white half-glove and leotard undergarment that Jacqueline's father, Marty Martarella, soon identified to us as "very similar" to articles Jacqueline owned. When he looked in his daughter's room, her "similar" clothing was nowhere to be found.

"Now we can make a pretty good call on why she was taken about five miles from where they nabbed her," I later said to Harry.

"You mean they took her to that place, killed her there—if she wasn't already dead—and then just drove her out onto the golf course and hid the body in the reeds."

"It looks that way," I agreed. "And they left their calling card near the body."

"These cops have got to be blind," Harry said. "They missed all of this."

But the satanic cellar contained another secret, one we ourselves missed at first. It was buried in a pile of leaves on the musty dirt floor. It was a hand-printed note—one composed by a serious Satanist. It was a bastardization of the book of Revelation—one of the sources of the Sam cult's "theology," and Charles Manson's as well. Gingerly picking up the damp, aging paper, we read the note:

> *Woe to you O earth and sea, for the devil sends his beast with wrath. Let he who has understanding reckon the number of the beast. For it is a human number. Its number is six-hundred-sixty-six.*

"Good God," Harry whispered.

"Hello, John Carr's hand. This is big-league stuff," I replied. "And one of their favorite symbols, too. Take a look over your head. That's not General MacArthur up there."

Harry peered upward through the gloom, and the message really began to sink in. Next to a black pentagram and a painted upturned cross were the chilling words: I WILL RETURN.

"That's Satan's return to earth," I said quietly. "Like the note, it's a warning. The same thought was conveyed in the Son of Sam Borrelli letter eight freaking years ago—'I'll be back.'"

"I feel like I'm on some Hollywood set," Harry muttered nervously.

"I only wish we were."

The note was turned over to Denis Dillon, who drove down from Garden City to examine the bunker himself. The letter's existence and that of the cellar weren't made public—although a local weekly newspaper, learning of the bunker from its own sources, later wondered if it might have some link to the slaying.

*   *   *

In May 1986, John Kogut was convicted of the Theresa Fusco murder. In the interim, we learned that a close friend of his from nearby Long Beach was a Satanist, but there was no evidence linking him to any crimes. Kogut, in his confession, said Fusco was raped and strangled in a Lynbrook cemetery before being placed beneath the pallets in the woods near the railroad tracks, only blocks from where she disappeared. Two alleged accomplices, whom Kogut named in his confession, were later arrested and convicted in that case.

Also in the spring of '86, someone close to Theresa Fusco said Theresa had knowledge of a satanic cult that was operating in Oceanside and Long Beach.

Kelly Morrissey, who was an acquaintance of Fusco and one of the other men accused of that murder, was still missing and presumed dead. Besides her knowing Fusco, entries in Morrissey's diary revealed that she had dated John Kogut. There was little doubt that the Morrissey and Fusco cases were linked, along with that of Jacqueline Martarella, whose family said she was acquainted with members of Kogut's circle.

At the same time, other murders of young girls continued to occur in the Nassau County region. And as of early 1987, the slaying of nineteen-year-old Jacqueline Martarella remained unsolved.

*   *   *

Similar vicious crimes continued throughout that journey of nine years, which brought us from coast to coast and back again. And then, once more it was summer. For eleven months each year the world I now inhabited was too often strafed by the depraved and the tragic. But in July, as always, I sought out one of the few constants in my life.

In Davis Park on Fire Island, precious little changed from summer to summer. No matter what wars were waged between August and June, the open arms of the ocean always beckoned in July. The sea, the sparkling beach, the people and a tranquil waterside mood were perennially waiting. There, it seemed, time stood still. And with the Atlantic crashing beside me, I could once more dance through a world of never was and dream and tell myself that none of it had happened. If only that was so.

On July 31, 1986, the anniversary of the shooting of Stacy Moskowitz and Robert Violante, I aimlessly walked the night beach alone. Nine years before, a brilliant orange moon hung low in the summer sky and shimmered off a quiet sea. That night, Stacy's tragic end, had been my own beginning. Now, I needed to reflect . . .

In the years since that summer of Sam, I'd roamed a netherworld I wouldn't have believed existed then. That was my age of innocence, and it was gone forever. I'd never wanted to discover that such a terrifying subculture menaced America. But it lived; and it thrived. And it was growing. I'd come to know that very well, as did the many others who traveled parts of that precarious road with me. Together, we ventured into that nightmare world and out again. And it changed us all, in one way or another.

With few exceptions, those people were strangers to me on July 31, 1977. Now, although many remained behind as the hunt moved through and beyond their states and jurisdictions, a bond remained. For that I was grateful. Those people—prosecutors, press, police and others—defied the system. They cared. They cared a hell of a lot. And their contributions were invaluable.

And so, too, were those of the unexpected partisans—the several convicts who, at considerable personal risk, reached out to convey information they knew was too important to languish, as they did, behind prison walls.

The roster of the dead was never far from my mind. So many people connected to the case who were alive that night in 1977 had been murdered or died violently since. And some of those had been under our close scrutiny when the end came. Arrests were not in my realm, but I couldn't help but recall a comment Lieutenant Terry Gardner once made: "You get them one way or another, don't you?"

If that was so, the satisfaction was slim. But maybe, in my own way, I had managed to influence a justice that was beyond the reach of the courts. If so, the verdict was fate's: it was meant to happen as it did.

In various jurisdictions, investigations continued. In Queens and California, especially, authorities still sought answers to questions which plagued them for years. The hope was that some final pieces might soon fall in place.

I believed arrests were possible in some of those cases. As I wandered past the lonely dune house that marked the western border of Davis Park, I inventoried the murders. Yes, I thought, persistent investigation could still bring killers to justice in the slayings of Christine Freund, Virginia Voskerichian, Stacy Moskowitz, Arlis Perry and Roy Radin. And success in any of those areas would certainly open the door to others.

It is imperative that one of those portals swing open soon. From every indication and piece of evidence I'd gathered, the ominous signs pointed to a burgeoning cult movement in and around New York, Houston and Los Angeles, at the least. These cities were part of the organized network, and its membership ranks, I learned, were steadily growing—populated to a large extent by young and successful people from professional walks of life. These, in turn, would align with the successors of David Berkowitz and the Carr brothers.

And beyond the umbrella, parent group, independent cults were springing to life in virtually every state in the U.S.A. In many instances, these groups would seek alliances with the old order, and some would do so successfully.

In my own investigation, things kept happening right into July 1986. Just weeks before we arrived on Fire Island, the Los Angeles area social club we'd linked to the Sam cult was torched. Arson. And the blaze was ignited at the same time inquiries about the club were being made.

Of the many highlights during the years of investigation, the work done on Bill Mentzer was one endeavor which would forever occupy a prominent place in my mind. We didn't have a name; we didn't have an address. We had my analysis of the Radin, Freund and Perry scenes, and information provided by Vinny in Dannemora. And yet, out of some 250 million people, we traced one man across nearly two decades and made the impossible link a reality.

But such efforts extracted a toll. I, for one, was weary. Walking the night beach, I wanted to step away from it all and never look back. The path I'd traveled was one marked by persistent tension; and always, there lurked the shadow of danger. Moreover, when one infiltrates the darkness for so long it is easy to forget the sun is still shining somewhere.

I'd spent too many years living on the edge: it was time to search for a safe harbor. By year end 1986, every meaningful bit of information we had developed on any of the cases or suspects would be in official hands.

It was probably good that I would soon complete my involvement in the various investigations. But again, that's why I came to Fire Island—to ease some frustrations and to think things through and work them out. I'd been there nine days, and my reason was beginning to rhyme again.

After an hour on the sand, I felt better. It was time to turn east and head back to the house. Into the wind now, I felt invigorated and relaxed. I inhaled deeply as a gust of salty night air blew in from the sea, pushing a rising tide of optimism; of hope. Family and friends were waiting at the beach house, among them the same group that had gathered on the dune stairs to discuss the ongoing Son of Sam case nine years before.

And it was still ongoing.

With that recollection, my mind cleared and I wasn't tired any longer.

* * *

The focus remained on the West Coast. New information which made its way to me in mid-July of 1986 was specific: not only was the Chingon cult still active; it had now established strong financial ties with a private college in the Los Angeles area. *The cult's wealthy leaders were said to be funding the institution, and satanic activity was in fact flourishing on the campus.*

At the same time, police in the Los Angeles area and two former L.A. Satanists sent word that an East Coast cult branch allied with the Chingons—the Black Cross—was operating as an elite "hit squad" for various U.S. satanic groups involved in drug and pornography enterprises. Obviously, the narcotics and child-porn details further confirmed earlier New York prison allegations. And as for the Black Cross itself, it appeared to be closely linked to the Sam cult in New York and existed for one purpose: murder.

Its function, the California contacts said, was the elimination of defecting cult members or other enemies, including innocent people who inadvertently learned about a given group's illegal activities. Murder, anywhere in the country, was now but a phone call away for the cults tied to the Chingon network.

As mentioned earlier, when I traveled to Los Angeles in late January 1987, I was aware that the official Roy Radin investigation was effectively stalemated for about two years. Sidestepping the Sheriff's Office, I met with Deputy District Attorney David Conn and supplied him with a list of people I'd come to learn were close associates of Bill Mentzer. Among them, I told Conn, were "the big four": Bill Rider, Bob Lowe, Alex Lamota (Marti), and Bob Deremer.

Unknown to me at the time, about a week earlier L.A. sheriff's investigators Charles Guenther and William Stoner, who had just been assigned to monitor the case, had begun tracing the transfer of a Cadillac from Elaine Jacobs to a middleman and finally to Lowe on May 13, 1983—the very day of Radin's disappearance. The car, they suspected, may have been awarded to Lowe as payment for participation in the murder.

The day after my meeting with Conn, Guenther and Stoner phoned Sergeant Carlos Avila, who had originally handled the Radin matter but was currently on temporary assignment at the FBI Academy in Virginia. Avila advised the detectives that all the information on the Radin case was contained in the office's files, but added that he'd also discovered a curious coincidence had occurred. Avila reported that Los Angeles Police Department Sergeant Glen Sousa—who was LAPD's lead investigator on the Radin case for its missing persons unit during the month before Radin's body was found and the probe turned over to Sheriff's homicide—had left the LAPD shortly afterward to take a job offered him by none other than Bob Evans.

Guenther and Stoner would soon learn more: Even before Radin's body was discovered, Sousa was the beneficiary of an Evans-arranged, star-spangled complimentary weekend in Las Vegas. Fred Doumani, who along with his brother, Ed, provided the initial financing for *The Cotton Club* deal but later suspended funding the film, stated to police that Evans had called him "sometime prior to Memorial Day 1983" and asked that Doumani arrange a gratis stay for Sousa at the Golden Nugget. According to the official report, Evans advised Doumani that "Mr. Sousa had been very good to him and please take care of him while he was visiting Las Vegas."

It was heartwarming to note Evans's concern for the well-being of key members of the LAPD.

Throughout the coming months, the detectives delved deeper into the investigation, now aware of both the names and relevance of Rider, Deremer, and Alex Lamota Marti, in addition to the confirmation I'd provided for their original belief about the nature of Lowe's relationship with Mentzer. Nonetheless, Stoner attempted to dismiss my involvement in the case during a telephone call he received from a police official in New York. It then became readily apparent that if the probe developed to the point of arrests, the Sheriff's investigators would be disdainful of acknowledging the documented roles played by an East Coast journalist and Ted Gunderson, a former FBI supervisor from southern California. In fact, a Sheriff's detective would later accuse us of "interfering" with their inquiry—an inquiry that had accomplished nothing between 1983 and 1987.

But then, I had gone over the detectives' heads to Conn, and I'd also pointedly told the deputy district attorney that I was less than enthralled that arrests hadn't been made by the Sheriff's Office between 1983 and 1987 when, in my opinion, there were numerous solid leads to pursue. Fortunately, Conn wasn't as parochial as the police, who conceivably had an ax or two to grind. He returned each of the handful of calls I made to him during the late winter and early spring of '87.

Regardless, as the investigation progressed, the detectives gained further confirmations about the suspects when, for the first time, they interviewed Mentzer's ex-wife on March 23, 1987. Deborah (De De) Mentzer, who had remarried, stated that Mentzer's "best friends were men named Don Davidson* and a Robert Lowe, and that he also ran around with a man named Bill Rider . . . Debbie then stated that Bill Mentzer had a running partner named Alex . . . and added that he was very mean and acted like he liked to go around hurting people." (Eight months earlier, my own source had said Alex was a "violent person who had claimed to be a member of a hit squad in Argentina at one time.") The former Mrs. Mentzer also put a name and face together when she identified Bill Rider from a photograph that investigators had removed from Mentzer's apartment after he and Lowe were arrested on the cocaine rap not long after Radin's murder.

Rider, whose name and close connection to Mentzer apparently were unknown by authorities until my meeting with Conn, was pictured with Mentzer in "a remote, desert-like area," the police report of the session with Deborah Mentzer stated.

The locale would turn out to be Caswell Canyon, the scene of Radin's demise.

When shown still another photo gleaned during the 1983 search of Mentzer's abode, his ex-wife identified the man she knew only as "Alex," who was standing with Mentzer in that particular picture.

*   *   *

On April 14, 1987, the L.A. detectives learned that Talmadge (Tally) Rogers—Elaine Jacobs's dope runner who disappeared after an alleged coke and cash ripoff of Jacobs shortly before Radin's death—wasn't missing after all. He was safely ensconced in a Louisiana prison following his conviction on child molestation charges.

On May 6, in a jailhouse interview with the police, Rogers admitted that he'd helped himself to ten kilos of Jacobs's cocaine and some $260,000 in cash as well. He said he did so because Jacobs was short-changing him on his commissions for transporting dope from Florida to Los Angeles. Rogers also remarked that Radin was not involved in the heist. He went on to describe Radin's heavy use of cocaine and revealed details of the alleged Florida-based coke distribution system Jacobs was operating in concert with her former lover, Milan Bellechasses. The police would soon learn that Bellechasses had been arrested recently and was being held on federal drug charges in Fort Lauderdale.

Rogers's ex-wife also spoke to the California detectives and told them that she accompanied Jacobs to Bob Evans's Beverly Hills home one night in March 1983—a night when "two male Latins" subsequently arrived and engaged in a private conversation with Evans and Jacobs. Rogers himself had told police of a meeting at Evans's home between Jacobs and the producer—after which Jacobs said, according to Rogers, that a discussion was held about financing Hollywood films with drug profits. According to Rogers, Jacobs reported that "there were approximately eight to ten movie people interested in producing movies using narcotics money."

In the meanwhile, investigators learned from a source close to Demond Wilson that the actor, who was supposed to be Radin's bodyguard on the night he disappeared, "may possibly know more than what he is telling the police." That report seemed to coincide with the suggestion that was mailed by my informant Vinny from a New York prison as far back as July 1983 about a Radin "bodyguard." Wilson, it may be worth noting, occupied an office at Paramount Studios during the 1982–83 time period when he was co-starring in the TV series *The New Odd Couple*. And it was Wilson, a weekly tabloid would report in 1988, who was on the run from a hit man from a satanic cult. The paper, quoting associates of Wilson, said the actor-turned-evangelist was fearful he'd be killed because of some knowledge he allegedly possessed about the Radin case.

For all the advances achieved in the police investigation in early 1987, the eventual biggest break didn't come until May. It was then that the detectives spoke to Bill Rider for the first time. To quote from the official report:

> *In May of 1987 investigators contacted William Rider via telephone. He told investigators that he knew William Mentzer and Alex Marti. He agreed to fly to Los Angeles and assist . . . with this investigation. . . . Investigators showed him a photograph of himself and William Mentzer, and a photograph of Mentzer and Alex Marti. . . . Mr. Rider stated the*

*photographs were taken possibly in 1982 [in] a remote canyon some-
where north of Los Angeles off Interstate 5. Mr. Rider had been to the
location on that day only, and added Mentzer spoke of using the location
for target practice. . . . While driving on Interstate 5, Mr. Rider directed
investigators to exit the Hungry Valley road turnoff . . . to where a dirt
road begins. He then directed investigators to drive up the dirt road into
a canyon. After traveling several hundred yards on the dirt road, Mr.
Rider stated, "This is where the photographs were taken." . . . We were
standing within a few hundred yards of where victim Radin's body was
recovered.*

Rider informed the police that he was the brother-in-law of *Hustler* magazine publisher Larry Flynt, and that he had employed Mentzer, Lowe, and Marti as security
guards in 1982–83, which is exactly what I'd told Deputy District Attorney David
Conn four months earlier. Rider also said that he was afraid of the unholy trinity,
"and if they knew he was cooperating with the police they would kill him and his
family."

Rider didn't mention Bob Deremer in this conversation, but he also knew him
from security work at Flynt's. However, Rider did say that he was playing poker with
Mentzer, Marti, and others in 1983 "when Marti and Mentzer began bragging about
killing victim Radin. . . . Rider recalled that they tried to sell him Radin's Rolex
watch and a ring [which had been taken from the body], but he declined." Also,
according to the police report, "Mentzer told Mr. Rider that Bob Evans was involved
in the hit along with Mentzer's girlfriend, Lanie [Jacobs]."

Rider wasn't through. He also said that after leaving the Flynt operation he em-
ployed Lowe on a security job in Texas in 1986. One night, during a drinking bout,
Lowe told him that Mentzer had also murdered a "black transvestite" in the San
Fernando Valley and that he, Lowe, drove the getaway car on that sordid occasion.
Lowe allegedly told Rider it was a "contract" killing, and that the victim's companion
had been wounded during the attack.

When authorities investigated Rider's story, they found that a prostitute named
June Mincher was slain on May 3, 1984, on Sepulveda Boulevard in the San Fernando Valley community of Van Nuys. Mincher's companion, a transvestite, was indeed
wounded during the foray. Mincher had been shot seven times in the head with a
silencer-equipped .22 pistol.

At the time of her death, Mincher was suspected of trying to extort money from
an Italian-American family that had then hired a friend of Mentzer's to handle their
security. Mentzer's buddy in turn employed Mentzer, Lowe, Marti, Bob Deremer,
and another man to help him out.

By now, the L.A. detectives knew they were on to something valuable, so they
asked Rider if he'd cooperate further. Citing a reasonable concern for life and limb,
Rider opted to ponder the offer for a while.

Meanwhile, in New York, we'd been doing some additional work of our own on Mentzer, discovering that he once had a Maryland driver's license and an address in that state's city of Cumberland—where we learned Bob Deremer also had resided. Even more significantly, we pieced together fragmented bits of information that led to the strong suspicion that Mentzer could be classified as a suspect in the April 1977 disappearance and apparent murder of a Washington, D.C., area disc jockey. The music man had operated a restaurant on the side and apparently ran into some difficulties with creditors who may have been linked to organized crime. A few weeks before he disappeared, a man using the name of "Mentzes" obtained a job at the deejay's establishment. When the disc jockey vanished, so did "Mentzes." If valid, the scenario would have placed Mentzer on the East Coast, just two hundred miles from New York, during the ongoing Son of Sam spree and less than two months after Christine Freund was allegedly slain by Manson II in a "hit" that was hidden in the string of supposedly random .44 killings.

* * *

As 1987 drew to a close, Los Angeles detectives continued to build their case against the Mentzer crowd and Elaine Jacobs. They learned that Jacobs had married for at least the third time in 1985, was living in Florida, and that the new lucky (though soon to be unlucky) man was a suspected major league cocaine dealer from Florida named Larry Greenberger. Greenberger, whom some dubbed the "Meyer Lansky" of cocainedom, was said to be a top lieutenant in the dope trafficking empire of the notorious Carlos Lehder, who was doing two life terms on federal narcotics dealing convictions. Lehder was widely believed to have been the kingpin of perhaps the most powerful coke cartel in the U.S.

In April 1988, Bill Rider surfaced again, this time telling the Los Angeles Sheriff's Office that he'd resume assisting the investigation. It is not yet known what enticed Rider to reconsider his earlier position, but it is safe to assume that he probably had more impetus than a simple desire to function as a good citizen.

As an initial act of good faith, Rider turned over a .22 Ruger semiautomatic pistol that was enhanced with a silencer, telling the police—as he had done in 1987—that Mentzer had once borrowed the weapon from him. Rider suspected that the Ruger might have been used to kill prostitute June Mincher. The police suspected the same and shipped the gun off for a ballistics comparison that, an official report says, determined a match existed between bullets fired from Rider's .22 and casings and slugs recovered at the Mincher scene.

At about this time, the Sheriff's detectives learned that Bob Lowe and Bob Deremer had moved to Maryland. Rider agreed to fly east with the police and allow himself to be wired in an attempt to record incriminating conversations with the pair. A meeting was arranged at the Crystal City Marriott hotel in Arlington, Virginia, on May 10, 1988. Lowe bowed out beforehand, stating a schedule conflict, but Deremer arrived and allegedly told the tape recorder listening in on him and Rider that Mentzer had indeed shot June Mincher and that he, Deremer, had remained at a bar to alibi himself for the time of the slaying.

Deremer then allegedly stated that when Mentzer and Lowe returned to the tavern, Mentzer asked him to drive him back to the crime scene so that he, Mentzer, could observe what the police were doing. Deremer purportedly acceded to Mentzer's request and saw that detectives were still at the site when they drove past. Deremer also allegedly said that he was living with Mentzer and Lowe at the time and received a few months free rent for his gracious aiding and abetting. The recorded conversation also allegedly revealed that Deremer knew Mentzer had borrowed and used Rider's .22 in the Mincher killing.

During his meeting with Rider, Deremer, according to police reports, also discussed the Radin murder on tape, quoting Lowe as telling him that he received a black Cadillac Seville (the car transferred to him by Elaine Jacobs) and some additional cash for his part in the kidnap-murder.

The Los Angeles detectives, who were assisted by the Virginia State Police in this phase of the investigation, were now on a roll. The next night, May 11, Maryland State Police joined in when they provided Rider with another body wire to use during a meeting scheduled with Lowe for that evening in the Scoreboard Cafe in Frederick, Maryland.

According to a police report, Lowe told Rider that he'd driven the escape car during the Mincher homicide and complained that he encountered difficulty in getting hit man Mentzer back into the auto because Mentzer "was yelling at and kicking the victim after the shooting."

And Bob Lowe kept on talking, perhaps reserving a future seat for himself on death row. According to the official report, Lowe admitted that he drove Jacobs's limousine on Friday the 13th of May, 1983—and to being behind the wheel when Roy Radin stepped inside on his final night on earth. (Mentzer, witnesses said, had arranged for the limo rental and put up some extra cash to obtain the car minus the usual company driver.)

Interestingly, Lowe also said that Mentzer and Alex Lamota Marti planned to shoot Radin thirteen times because it was Friday the 13th. Would Mentzer also have thought to plant a Bible at the site opened to Isaiah Chapter 22—with a very significant thirteenth verse? The answer to that question isn't known, but strong suspicion certainly abounds at this point.

In his recorded conversation with Rider, Lowe also allegedly admitted that he received the Elaine Jacobs Cadillac plus $17,000 in cash for his services. And he further said, according to official documents, that "the Radin contract hit was paid for by Lanie Jacobs and Robert Evans."

* * *

Two months later, back in Los Angeles, the Sheriff's detectives rented a pair of rooms at a Holiday Inn on Church Lane. Both rooms were wired for sound. On July 7, the occupant of one of those rooms, Bill Rider, phoned Mentzer while the customers in the adjoining room—the police—listened in. Mentzer agreed to drop by for a visit with Rider early that evening.

Arriving at the hotel, Mentzer made his way to Rider's room and apparently proceeded to make his own "hit" record, so to speak. According to the official report, Mentzer revealed that sometime before June Mincher was slain he, Alex Marti, and another man broke into the hooker's apartment and pistol-whipped her. Mentzer, who had termed Mincher a "transexual," also described how he planted a bomb under the gas tank of Mincher's car, but the explosive was a dud. He further stated that he wasn't worried about the pistol-whipping of Mincher because the statute of limitations had run out on that possible charge.

Indeed, but not on the murder charge.

Obviously feeling relaxed with his old friend Rider, Mentzer got around to discussing Roy Radin's murder, allegedly stating that he and Alex Marti were in the follow car while Bob Lowe drove the Jacobs-Radin limousine. At some point, the details of which are not clear in the report, Mentzer allegedly described that he and Marti entered the limo and had Radin seated between them, with Lowe still at the wheel as the auto sped down an unspecified stretch of Sunset Boulevard.

What happened to the follow car is also not certain, but it is believed that the group probably switched back to it a short time later, as the person who rented the limo to Mentzer told authorities the car had only about sixty-seven miles on it when it was returned early the next morning. The round trip to Caswell Canyon alone would have accounted for approximately 130 miles, exclusive of the mileage accumulated between the rental office in the Bel Air Hotel and the Hollywood Regency, where Radin was picked up. Moreover, the rental agent told police that the limo had been returned with about three-quarters of a tank of gas in it—too much if the vehicle had made the journey to the canyon.

The alleged follow car, a Lincoln, also was tentatively traced to a friend of Mentzer, whom police believed loaned the auto to the suspect. The Lincoln had been searched as far back as July 25, 1983, and the examination revealed plant material was in the front seat on both the driver's and passenger's sides, under the backseat and hood, and in the trunk and undercarriage—possibly indicating that the car had been driven into rugged terrain such as Caswell Canyon, and that its passengers had climbed out at such a location.

At any rate, as Mentzer and Rider continued chatting in the Holiday Inn, Mentzer allegedly stated on tape that Radin was killed over *The Cotton Club* deal and that, in yet another arrangement, Alex Marti had hired him to eradicate an Iranian dope competitor but he'd returned the money when he couldn't carry out the job. Mentzer also allegedly told of how he, Lowe, Deremer, Marti, and another individual assured a friend who purportedly had knowledge of the Mincher killing that they would provide financial assistance to his wife and family if he kept quiet about the prostitute's death while spending time in prison on federal drug charges.

The police wanted more, and Rider said he thought he could provide it if Mentzer could be led to believe that his old amigo was himself involved in criminal activity. No problem. A phony dope deal was arranged for which Mentzer was hired to provide strongarm protection. The "deal" was consummated on August 5, 1988, with Mentzer being introduced to an undercover cop who represented himself as a narcotics trafficker.

A few weeks later, on September 7, Mentzer and Rider convened again. This time the pair rendezvoused at Prezzo's restaurant; and this time Mentzer was accompanied by a man he introduced as Vincent Angelo from Miami. After dinner, Mentzer and Rider stepped into the recording studio that was disguised as Rider's car.

During the conversation, Rider suggested that the "narcotics dealer" Mentzer met a few weeks before might want to utilize him to kill somebody. Mentzer allegedly replied that he'd be happy to comply if the price was right, and went on to say that Vincent Angelo had recruited him to deep-six a Miami couple and offered him $100,000 for the doubleheader. Mentzer then allegedly said that he'd split the take with Rider if Rider helped him pull off the job.

Mentzer also allegedly said that Vincent Angelo was a top dog in Carlos Lehder's drug pyramid, and that he had still another arrangement in mind for Mentzer: to torch or bomb a Florida home owned by Angelo and his wife that had been leased to an elderly man who'd "trashed" it. Rather than bother remodeling the house, Angelo wanted it to disappear so he could collect the insurance money. Accordingly, Mentzer was to ensure that the blaze appeared to be accidental.

Shortly after leaving Mentzer that night, Rider identified a police photo of Vincent Angelo. Only he wasn't Vincent Angelo. He was Larry Greenberger, the latest husband of Elaine Jacobs.

*   *   *

Sometimes justice maneuvers in unusual ways. Exactly one week later, on September 14, Larry Greenberger was dead, courtesy of a bullet in his brain. Greenberger expired on the front porch of the house he shared with Karen Elaine Jacobs Delayne Greenberger, etc., in Okeechobie, Florida. His widow told authorities that her husband committed suicide with his own gun. It may have been his own gun, but suicide was another matter.

"We're looking at it as a homicide," Sheriff O. L. Raulerson said. And Okeechobie County Medical Examiner Dr. Frederick Hobin added: ". . . As the case continues and the investigation continues, it becomes apparent that it was a homicide rigged to look like a suicide. He was shot and then the gun was placed in his hand."

Somehow, Hobin's scenario reminded me of a similar one that was played out ten years before in Minot, North Dakota.

In the week preceding Greenberger's death, Bill Rider and Mentzer got together once more in Los Angeles. Mentzer had told Rider about a storage locker he kept in Van Nuys to stash an arsenal of weapons and explosives. Rider indicated that he had a safe he wanted to store, and Mentzer offered the use of another locker in the same facility. And so it was that detectives learned of Mentzer's mini-armory.

While at the storage facility, according to the police, Mentzer told Rider that he had organized the Radin killing and that a book had been published calling it "a perfect crime." Mentzer was referring to the original hardcover edition of *The Ultimate Evil*, which did anything but describe the murder as a work of art. At the same time, Mentzer allegedly told Rider that he had been involved in numerous other murders throughout the United States. That revelation would come as no surprise when I learned of it.

Mentzer didn't know it then, but his days were numbered. Shortly afterward, when Larry Greenberger fell dead in Florida, local authorities began digging into both his and Elaine's backgrounds. Apparently, the couple had lived a quiet, respectable existence in the community and residents were stunned when the sordid details began to accumulate. Soon, Los Angeles detectives heard the news. Just who shot Greenberger wasn't immediately known, but it was time to bring down the curtain.

Arrest warrants were issued for Mentzer, Bob Lowe, Alex Lamota Marti, and Karen Elaine Jacobs-Greenberger for the murder of Roy Radin. In addition, Mentzer, Lowe and Bob Deremer were flagged for the slaying of prostitute June Mincher.

In early October, Mentzer and Marti were seized in L.A., Greenberger in Florida, and Lowe in Rockville, Maryland. A short time later, Deremer was arrested in Cumberland, Maryland.

In announcing the apprehensions, a Sheriff's spokesman said that at least some of the suspects may have been involved in other killings across the United States.

As for Bob Evans, Deputy District Attorney David Conn did not directly implicate him in the Radin murder, but said that Evans was "one of the people who we have not eliminated as a suspect."

Among the numerous weapons seized that allegedly belonged to Mentzer—including TNT, cluster bombs, and various automatic pistols—was a .44 Smith and Wesson revolver.

Also found with Mentzer's possessions was a highlighted, underscored copy of a hardcover book: *The Ultimate Evil*.

* * *

In New York too—where David Berkowitz has remained silent for several years—there were new developments. On two successive weeks in November 1988 NBC television's *Unsolved Mysteries* aired segments on the Son of Sam conspiracy. Numerous tips and leads were phoned in to the program, some of which were promising and are currently under investigation.

At the same time, a former counselor at Columbia University in New York City came forward and identified a suspect the prison source Vinny had known only as "Rudy." The counselor stated that he had seen Rudy in the company of Michael Carr on several occasions in a bar near the university—and we'd long known that Michael

Carr used to associate with people from the school and imbibe in local pubs. The counselor said that Rudy was "either a Tex-Mex or Hawaiian guy who used to pick up work as an extra or a driver in films or TV shows from time to time." Rudy's exact whereabouts are unknown at this time, but the tavern he frequented with Michael Carr was called The West End. The counselor's report constituted yet another of the many confirmations we'd obtained during the investigation of the information the New York prison sources had provided.

And as noted earlier, James Camaro, whom the informants had named as a key figure in the .44 and related cases, was identified and located in mid-1987. Camaro remains uncharged because there is not yet enough corroborating evidence to hold him.

Of other developments in late 1988, one was especially ominous. Yonkers residents who lived near Untermyer Park state that the cult—or offshoots of it—was active there once again, and had been since early 1987. The group was observed by several witnesses, including three off-duty Yonkers police officers who investigated the park one night in the summer of '88. Neighbors also supplied me with recent photos of mutilated dogs and said they'd learned that the cult had been using another location in Yonkers too.

The group's return brought to mind another disturbing aspect of the entire investigation: the realization that the cult movement, which had been bent toward violence since at least the late 1960s, was still expanding while law enforcement remained virtually powerless. Few police understood this type of conspiracy; most couldn't relate to it. Mimicking law enforcement, Vinny once wrote: "The 'insane' always act solo—the group is well aware of this cop attitude and uses it to their advantage."

Through experience, I knew that Vinny was essentially correct. Police departments tend to rapidly close the books after arrests. Seldom were they inclined to delve beneath the surface. That posture had, beyond question, figured in the expansion of the satanic cult movement. Thus, the occasional arrest of an isolated, supposedly lone criminal had little perceptible impact on the groups' master plans.

But there are indications that a change might be in the wind. On February 26, 1987, the Interfaith Coalition of Concern About Cults conducted a day-long seminar on satanism for members of law enforcement. The conference, which was held at the Archdiocese of New York in Manhattan, was attended by 120 police officials from the New York tri-state area.

And in 1988, I addressed police seminars on cult crimes that were held in Providence, Rhode Island; Binghamton, New York; Richmond, Virginia; and Decatur, Illinois. Attendance exceeded 225 in Decatur and 150 in Rhode Island and Virginia. Other official conferences on the subject have been scheduled for 1989 in various parts of the country.

Throughout the U.S., it is evident that many police departments are now focusing on the potential dangers of satanic cult activity. In a like manner, there has been an increased awareness of the problem on the part of educators, clergy, and mental health professionals.

Whoever intervenes, the involvement is necessary. There is compelling evidence of the existence of a nationwide network of satanic cults, some aligned more closely than others. Some are purveying narcotics; others have branched into child pornography and violent sadomasochistic crime, including murder. I am concerned that the toll of innocent victims will steadily mount unless law enforcement officials recognize the threat and face it.

Unlike some of those authorities, I've been there. I know how serious the situation is. The torch that was put into Manson's hand in 1969 was never extinguished. It was instead passed to Berkowitz and others, and the violence and depravity continued. The evidence demonstrates that the force behind that carnage was in place both before and after the Manson and Son of Sam slayings. And, lurking in various guises, it is still there.

A letter Vinny sent me in the wake of the Roy Radin murder in 1983 said: "When will they learn that I've only told the truth? Yes, it sounds fantastic—but so many true things sound fantastic. Let's see—what number victim is this now? . . . You know, in another two years there won't be anyone left to capture."

Oh yes, there will. And their numbers are growing.

And this time, there is no insulating Middle America. This time it isn't an inner-city eruption that can be written off as the inevitable fallout from poverty and slums. No, this battleground is elsewhere: the list of the dead tells that story. The killer cults were born and nurtured in the comfort zone of America and are now victimizing it at will.

Manson's haunting testimony and a later warning from David Berkowitz echo loudly across the years. Two statements, made on opposite coasts nearly a decade apart. Yet the dire message is the same.

"What about your children?" Manson challenged a Los Angeles courtroom as the 1970s began. "You say there are just a few? There are many, many more, coming in the same direction. They are running in the streets—*and they are coming right at you!*"

In New York, Berkowitz would write: "*There are other 'Sons' out there—God help the world.*"

Sometimes, late at night, one can know the truth of their words. Through the darkness, a foreboding wail can be heard. Faintly at first, then more insistent and nearer, the reverberations ring through urban canyons, roll across the shadowed byways of Scarsdale and Bel Air, and are carried on the night wind to the remote reaches of rural countrysides.

It is a mournful, curdling cry.

It is the sound of America screaming.

Epilogue

The 1990s would see dramatic advances in the investigation. But as the decade began, some things remained as they were. For instance, Joseph Borrelli, once second in command of NYPD's Son of Sam task force, reprised a familiar tune: "I am strongly convinced he acted alone." However, this time the predictable Borrelli wasn't crooning about David Berkowitz.

Borrelli, whose ascent to the rank of NYPD's chief of detectives was boosted by stonewalling the .44 case, was referring to the gunman who murdered radical rabbi Meir Kahane in 1990. Later, Borrelli swallowed this refrain when federal probers neatly tied his "lone killer" to the same conspiracy of terrorists who subsequently bombed New York's World Trade Center in 1993, killing six and wounding hundreds.

It seemed as if Borrelli's investigative techniques formed a distinctive pattern—one that might serve as a roadmap for predicting future tragedies. That point was already brought home by the roster of deaths that followed Berkowitz's arrest, and we'd soon learn of more.

In 1991, events continued to cascade over the extended Son of Sam investigation. Bill Mentzer, Bob Lowe, Alex Lamota Marti and "Lanie" Jacobs-Greenberger were convicted of the Roy Radin murder and sentenced to life terms. Mentzer also was guilty of killing transvestite June Mincher in 1984.

At a pretrial hearing in the Radin case, Hollywood producer Robert Evans—whom Mentzer named as a conspirator on a police wire worn by witness Bill Rider—pleaded the Fifth Amendment. However, the Los Angeles district attorney's office was unable to secure corroborating evidence, so Evans was not indicted.

Mentzer also remained the top "Manson II" suspect—the label awarded the so-called occult superstar who allegedly killed Christine Freund in a 1977 Son of Sam attack and earlier engineered Arlis Perry's ritual murder in California's Stanford Memorial Church.

In 1992, another ghost from the past materialized, this time in the New York phase of the Son of Sam inquiry. He described himself as "an old alley cat with seven of its nine lives gone."

He was called Brother John, and in the 1960s he was a close friend and classmate of none other than John Carr. He was also the first admitted member of the Westchester cult to step forward. He said he was part of the group's early era before he fled New York "to save my life" in early 1973—three years before the .44 shootings began.

According to Brother John, the Westchester cult was spawned far back in the early 1950s, courtesy of a Nazi-sympathizing doctor who traveled from England to north Yonkers in the postwar years. "It started as a ritual magic club that specialized in sex with children and drug dealing, and it grew from there," Brother John said.

"The heavy satanism came later—but they were doing stuff long before Berkowitz came along. It was well organized, and they had some big connections in Yonkers and Manhattan." Brother John, who also spoke to the police, explained that John Carr recruited him and several other adolescents into the group in 1961, when all were high school freshmen in Yonkers. He emotionally described how he and three other youths were raped during an initiation ritual in Untermyer Park—a ceremony at which dogs were sacrificed.

"After that, the leaders turned me and some other kids into teenaged prostitutes," he continued. "They operated out of a bar near the Carr house—and from there they sent us to big hotels and parties in Manhattan, where we turned tricks with their rich friends and other clients. They were all money people."

Brother John revealed that he saw still another phase of the enterprise.

"I personally know that in Manhattan they had some cops and politicians on their payroll, and a few of those guys were also my clients. There were also tie-ins to the Mob through the gay bars, the pornography and the sex shops."

Brother John, whose statements were heavily researched and corroborated by others, including retired NYPD detectives, said he continued to attend rituals held in Untermyer Park and a handful of stately old homes in north Yonkers, two of which were later demolished. All were within a mile of the Carr residence and Berkowitz's eventual address on Pine Street.

"A Yonkers judge and a couple of lawyers and doctors were involved in it then. They were all into sex with kids," Brother John recalled. Of considerable interest, he added that he once helped remove two bodies from a then-wooded area not far from Untermyer Park. The location was across the street from the home of a doctor—*a doctor whose Long Island summer home telephone number would appear in Berkowitz's records a decade later.*

"It was about 1967, and me and another young guy were told to dig them up. They were wrapped, but from the weight I'm sure they were kids," Brother John said. "They were put in a van and we dumped them in the Hudson River."

Brother John also said he witnessed a murder—the 1965 rifle death of a twenty-seven-year-old high school teacher that was written off as an "apparent suicide." Her body was found deep in the woods of spacious Van Cortlandt Park, which was located on the Bronx-Yonkers border. For years and continuing into the late 1970s, Van Cortlandt and Untermyer functioned as outdoor meeting sites for the cult.

"I knew her well, and so did John [Carr] and some of the others because she'd taught us in school. She'd heard about the group and was asking questions. So to protect themselves they set her up and killed her. I liked her a lot, and I was sickened by what they did. To this day I have nightmares about it."

Brother John said he attended his last Yonkers ritual in 1968. "I'd seen enough to know how awful it was, so after that I remained in Manhattan and Brooklyn Heights." But before his relocation, he inadvertently made an acquaintance who years later provided a conclusive link between Berkowitz and the cult.

Unaware of the import of his anecdote, Brother John spoke of a teenager he once met in the Carr home—a young cultist he later drove to the northeast Bronx. He described him well, but couldn't recall the name. However, he did remember dropping off the youth at a specific bakery on Buhre Avenue—several blocks from the residence of future Son of Sam victim Donna Lauria. "It was a German place, and his parents owned it," Brother John said.

In fact, and unknown by Brother John, the German bakery was then owned by the parents of one of David Berkowitz's best friends. Berkowitz and this youth maintained their relationship from Berkowitz's mid-teens until his arrest. In other words, although Berkowitz says he didn't join the cult until 1975, he and the "bakery boy" were close friends at the same time the other teen was already involved with the group and present in the Carr home—*eight years before the Son of Sam shootings began.*

Closing the circle, just weeks before the first .44 attack in 1976, several cult members at Untermyer—including one identified as John Carr—attempted to recruit a young Bronxite who visited the park after hearing rumors about what was transpiring there. The man, a budding artist who was then eighteen, returned several times and learned the nicknames of those he met. One of those was "Eggs," the nickname of that same Berkowitz friend whom Brother John drove to the Bronx bakery in 1968. He was still a cult member in the Son of Sam years.

Brother John's last encounter with the group took the form of a rendezvous with his old pal John Carr in a Manhattan bistro in the summer of 1972. Carr was in the air force, and the pair hadn't talked for several years. Brother John was better served by the lack of communication because what Carr told him that night would propel Brother John from the sidewalks of New York to a new life in the Midwest.

"He said a new leadership had taken over in Westchester and that it was a very violent 'satanic' element that was now in charge," Brother John told me. This was a reference to the Process, which had aligned with the Westchester group by 1970.

"John was scared," Brother John continued. "He kept talking about 'virgin blood' and how important it was. He then said that some kids nobody would ever miss were taken from an orphanage and killed in rituals. He also told me there was now a pyramid structure in the group, and that for him to get to another level he was going to have to kill someone."

That was enough for Brother John. "I got out of New York a few months later, and I never spoke to John Carr again." By 1978 Carr and others linked to the conspiracy were dead, the Son of Sam shootings had ripped the heart from New York and David Berkowitz was locked away for life.

As 1993 dawned, it was ten years since Berkowitz had bowed out of the picture. Although much evidence had been discovered and valuable information had seeped from prison informants, it couldn't equal what I might glean from a face-to-face conversation with Berkowitz himself. But I had long surrendered any hope that he would discuss the case with me.

And then it happened. A friend of Berkowitz's reached out to say the Son of Sam had become a born-again Christian in 1987 and that his faith had prompted a willingness to meet with me.

* * *

It was the spring of 1993, and the man who walked briskly into the visiting room at the upstate Sullivan Correctional Facility was a markedly different person than the one I'd met fifteen years earlier at Marcy. He was smiles and amiability, relaxed and forthcoming. I was amazed—but cautious. Over time, I'd learn his demeanor was genuine.

Berkowitz was nearly forty. He was husky; his hair had receded, and he wore fashionable aviator-style glasses. "It's been a very long time," he said easily. "I'm prepared to talk about some main parts of the case—but I can't talk about all of it or about any of these people who are still alive."

I asked if he'd sit for a television interview, and he agreed. A month later—accompanied by coproducer Wayne Darwen, three camera crews and a traveling prison minister named Don Dickerman—I listened and asked questions as Berkowitz told his story. The highlights were broadcast nationally on *Inside Edition*.

In brief, Berkowitz said he joined the cult in the spring of 1975, after meeting Michael Carr and others at a party on Barnes Avenue in the Bronx—the street on which Berkowitz then lived. "I was lonely, looking for friends, and I'd always been intrigued by the occult," he recalled. "They presented all this to me in a harmless way—just witchcraft and seances and so forth. Plus, there were a few attractive girls in it. I had no idea what was in store. I never dreamed I'd eventually become a murderer."

Berkowitz said he began to associate with the group at parties, at various bars in New Rochelle and the Bronx, and also at late-night meetings in the marshes near Orchard Beach and the woods of Van Cortlandt Park in the Bronx.

"I didn't realize it then, but now I can see that I was being brought along slowly. In time, they took me to Untermyer," Berkowitz explained, adding that there were "slightly less than two dozen, both males and females, involved in the main part of the group." He also acknowledged that this number later appeared as the "Twenty Two Disciples of Hell" alias in the Son of Sam Breslin letter.

"I was initiated at Untermyer," he said. "I recited a prayer to Lucifer and then pricked my finger to draw a little blood. I also gave information about my family, which was stupid of me to do. After that, the whole thing got more serious. There were animal sacrifices and some small arsons in Yonkers and the Bronx. There was also drug dealing and some illegal weapons around."

In February 1976, Berkowitz, who by then was deeply immersed in the group, moved to the Cassara house in New Rochelle. "I was told there was a room there, and I'd get it," he said. "Shortly after that, I was told to move to Pine Street. Things were heating up, and the center of activity had shifted to that part of Yonkers, and they wanted me nearby."

In June, Berkowitz drove to southern Florida, where he visited his adoptive father. He then traveled to Houston, Texas, where he obtained a .44 Bulldog revolver. I reminded Berkowitz of a letter he wrote in 1979. In it, he alleged that a named woman from Westchester—a woman previously associated with the case—stayed in the same Houston motel as he did. He said his allegation was true.

Later, off camera, I asked how this woman arrived in Texas. His answer surprised me. "We met up in Clearwater [Florida], and we drove together from there." Berkowitz also acknowledged that "she went to a place in Clearwater" (not Scientology's Fort Harrison Hotel) in an attempt to procure a .44. He claimed he didn't know if her mission was successful. Nonetheless, he said that while his own .44 was used in some of the shootings, "there were two or three others that were around."

Here is how Berkowitz, who said he was present at each of the eight scenes, describes the Son of Sam attacks:

—*Donna Lauria.* "I did shoot Donna, and I'm very sorry about doing it. She was known by some in the group, and so it actually wasn't random, although the public believed it was," Berkowitz said. He later added it was "very possible" Donna and her girlfriend Jody Valente were "followed that entire evening." He also said three other accomplices were at the scene—including Michael Carr. "I was with Michael," Berkowitz said. "The other two were in a tan car" (the auto spotted by Donna's father minutes before the shots were fired).

The tan car, I later determined, was a Ford—the same type of auto sighted at some other .44 scenes. My investigation found that it was a livery service car used by Gorman Johnson,* who was mentioned earlier in this story. He lived very near Berkowitz in Yonkers and was arrested with a loaded .44 Bulldog in June 1977. I also learned that Yonkers police detained Johnson when he tried to ditch that same vehicle in the Hudson River nine days before Stacy Moskowitz was slain.

—*Carl Denaro.* "A woman shot him. There were several of us there that night," Berkowitz said, adding that three of those "several" conspirators were women. The shooter is believed to be one of two prime suspects.

—*Joanne Lomino and Donna DeMasi.* "That was John Carr," Berkowitz said of the man whose likeness was accurately depicted in a police sketch drawn from a description provided by the two wounded victims. Berkowitz later acknowledged that "a Yonkers police officer who belonged to the group was also there and at a couple of other scenes, too."

It is virtually certain the Yonkers cop was Peter Shane,* a long-standing suspect who matched the second police sketch from the Lomino-DeMasi attack based on a description provided by a witness. Shane, who was referenced earlier in this book, quit the Yonkers police when my first conspiracy articles were published in 1979. He was friendly with the Carrs and with Berkowitz's longtime pal Howard Weiss, who was murdered that same year. "Howie was connected to the group, but he wasn't at any of the shootings," Berkowitz later told me.

—*Christine Freund.* "I believe there was a motive to this, but I don't know what it was," Berkowitz revealed, explaining that "at least five" conspirators were present that night. "It was different because they brought someone in from out of town to do it," he said of the triggerman. Berkowitz later acknowledged "Manson II" was the shooter. He added, "There was another guy with him when he came to New York, and that person was also out there that night," and, "They did use a red car in this shooting." This red auto, which has now been traced to a close friend of Berkowitz, was observed by a witness at the scene.

Berkowitz also alleged it was "Manson II" who bragged about intimate details of Arlis Perry's murder "at a meeting in a house in the Bronx. This guy had a photo of Arlis, and that's how I knew what she looked like," he explained. I later showed Berkowitz two pictures of Arlis. He identified the one that first sparked my interest—the photo that wasn't made public until 1981. This picture was taken in Bismarck not long before her death. It was the one in which she wasn't wearing eyeglasses.

Later, off camera, I asked Berkowitz if Bill Mentzer was "Manson II." "I can't talk about that," he answered. "But I will say that I heard this guy later got in some big trouble."

—*Virginia Voskerichian*. "A woman from Westchester did it," Berkowitz stated. "I was there, too, but it was her who wore that watch cap." Berkowitz didn't recall jogger Amy Johnson* or how he managed to move ahead of her. "The person who did the shooting was driving around a bit before it happened, so maybe she dropped me off," he offered. He also said he didn't know why the Voskerichian killing occurred when and where it did. "I wasn't told a lot of what was in their minds," he explained. There is one prime suspect in this murder.

—*Valentina Suriani and Alexander Esau*. "I did this one, and I'm very sorry about it," Berkowitz said. "There were several of us there that night." He also stated that reluctant witness Will Levine* was "essentially correct" when he reported that Berkowitz walked two blocks from the scene and handed the gun to an accomplice, and that both left the area in cars driven by others.

—*Judy Placido and Sal Lupo*. "Michael Carr did that one," Berkowitz told me. "They had been watching that Elephas disco for a while. They wanted to do something out there because it had some significance." At the very least, that "significance" was ritual in nature, as described earlier in this story.

—*Stacy Moskowitz and Robert Violante*. "After I got the ticket, I tried to stop it from happening," Berkowitz said. "I went over to the park but they [his accomplices] wouldn't listen, so I drove off. I did return to the area a bit later because I figured I'd try once more to get them to call it off," he added, confirming all of Cacilia Davis's account. "But I didn't get there in time. I heard the shots and went back to my car and left."

Berkowitz verified that the triggerman escaped in the infamous yellow VW. He later said the auto "belonged to the Carrs," an allegation confirmed by at least five witnesses, including two police officers. He also revealed it was the same vehicle the Cassaras saw him driving when he lived at their home in New Rochelle. "It was like a community car," he explained.

Berkowitz later supplied some major surprises about the Moskowitz attack. "The person who did it was a friend of John Carr's who came in from North Dakota," he alleged. "However, it wasn't him who actually drove the VW away from there. I guess he ducked down in the seat. But a woman drove it."

The sketch of the VW driver, drawn from the recollection of witness Alan Masters,* led me and everyone else to assume the person was a man in a wig. Not so, Berkowitz said. "It was a woman from Westchester and that was her own hair." He added cryptically: "If you think about it, it makes perfect sense that she was driving that car."

Indeed it did.

Berkowitz said that he spent his last days of freedom preparing for the police. "I knew the ticket would be checked. So several days before I got arrested, we rented a van and got rid of my furniture and other heavy things to make the place look like a madman lived in it." He said that he and three others accomplished the move. "One of them was the guy who did the Brooklyn shooting, another was that woman—and the third was Mike Carr."

Berkowitz also said he knew when the police were on the immediate horizon. "I was aware Sam Carr went to the authorities and so forth, so I knew they'd be coming very soon. It's not hard to see how I knew this—and so everything was arranged."

Berkowitz explained that he confessed to sole culpability for a simple reason: he knew he was guilty. "I did do two of the shootings—that's three deaths—and I played a role in the rest. So what's the difference if I said I did all of them? I knew I was going to jail for life no matter what, and I deserved to. Plus, I was sticking loyal to the others in the group."

But there was even more to the drama behind Berkowitz's capture. In 1997, two witnesses stated that cult members named John DiFrenza and "Richie" actually removed some "last-minute" odds and ends from Berkowitz's apartment on the very day of his arrest. One witness, who was DiFrenza's roommate, said DiFrenza returned that night with Berkowitz's mail and other items. "I told him to get that junk out of here," the witness reported.

When confronted with the witnesses' statements, Berkowitz confirmed the accounts. "Both Richie and John were there that last day. But John wasn't at any of the crime scenes," he said. However, he wouldn't comment on Richie's degree of guilt.

John DiFrenza was murdered in Yonkers in 1989. His death, which reportedly occurred during a sex ritual gone awry, apparently was not connected to the Son of Sam case. In late 1998, Richie—an admitted close friend of Berkowitz and the owner of a red car in 1977—was said to be seriously ill. He has refused to cooperate with the investigation.

*   *   *

The *Inside Edition* broadcasts, which were augmented by a front-page series in the *New York Daily News,* hurtled the story to the forefront again.

Then, in 1996, the Yonkers Police Department quietly opened its own probe of the case. Its aims: to determine if the alleged conspiracy was hatched in its jurisdiction, to learn if any related murders occurred there and to discover if elements of the group were still active locally.

Also in 1996, the successful professional called "Mr. Real Estate," whom the prison informants singled out years before as the leader of the Westchester cult, was finally identified. This crucial door, which also led straight to the Process, was opened by the teenage artist the group attempted to recruit at Untermyer in 1976.

The cultists didn't know that this young man, whom I will call Billy, sketched several of their portraits after he returned home from his handful of excursions to the heavily wooded park. Besides knowing nicknames, Billy kept the drawings, which were uncannily precise. They enabled us to identify a number of members and were subsequently shown to Berkowitz, who validated the identifications. Among them were:

—A man Billy knew as "Pete," who later served time for a Westchester murder. Pete, whose true first name was Pedro, was a close friend of Berkowitz's neighbor Gorman Johnson,* who owned a .44 Bulldog and frequently drove the relevant tan Ford.

—A young woman Billy knew as "Marie" or "Maria." She was positively identified as Maria Cortina, the alias of Suzette Rodriguez, who was gunned down on a Westchester street soon after Berkowitz's arrest.

—A bearded man Billy described as "Ken from Australia, who was always with Marie." Significantly, Ken—whose last name I am obligated to withhold for investigative reasons—was positively identified as a leading member of the Process. Among other established facts, Berkowitz called Ken "one of the elders and a recruiter for the Process," and official files proved Ken's Australian heritage. These corroborations were backed by a photo of Ken that matched Billy's sketch and placed a prominent Process member in Untermyer Park with members of the Westchester cult just a month before the Son of Sam shootings began.

Billy's 1976 sketches isolated yet another individual. It was a stroke of luck the portrait existed because its subject seldom appeared at Untermyer. His true name must be withheld for investigative reasons, but he was the man we now believe was the wealthy "Mr. Real Estate." However, fate intervened before authorities could interrogate him.

I spotted the tiny death notice in early 1996. He had succumbed to death by natural causes at the age of seventy-six—one of the few who didn't meet a bizarre or violent end. I alerted the police, and within hours a detective was at the funeral home. Posing as a mourner and with Billy's old drawing as a reference, the detective identified the deceased in his coffin.

The detective also noted that the rosary in "Mr. Real Estate's" hands was deliberately positioned so that the crucifix was inverted. He further observed that the only flowers in the room were "black or deep purple roses" and that the standard holy picture mementos were replaced by cards imprinted with a Celtic cross—a cross which in this instance represented Druidism.

The police needed to take one more step—a first-person identification. It was accomplished when they brought Billy the artist to the funeral parlor. Billy, who also acted as a mourner, knelt at the coffin and verified that the deceased was indeed the man he'd sketched at Untermyer two decades earlier. "He didn't change much, and his features were so distinct it was easy to know it was him," Billy said. "At Untermyer they called him 'Zoltan,' or something like that."

Actually, the name was "Moloch." It was a cult name the dead man chose for himself—the title of an ancient deity who was worshiped by the sacrifice of children. But there was more to Moloch's singular role in the Son of Sam case, and it related to his interactions with the Process.

By 1997, we had accumulated much new data about the British cult's activities in the United States and its immersion in the .44 shootings. It is not possible to explore the depths of that investigation here, but I will list a few highlights. For example, an admitted former Process member named Linda Harrison came forward to say she saw Michael Carr at a 1970s Process meeting in Chicago. "It was definitely Michael," she said. "And knowing what I came to know about the Process's real purpose, I also believe Berkowitz was nothing more than one of their hitmen."

In addition, Berkowitz verified a report that had languished in NYPD's files since the days following his arrest—when a witness stated she saw him with one "Father Lars" at the Process's Manhattan headquarters. "It's true. I was there with him," Berkowitz said of the report, which was ignored by the NYPD.

Berkowitz said he had a reason to visit the group's headquarters: "They had a big role in all of it." Specifically, he charged that the overall plan for a series of shootings was brainstormed during a surreal meeting at Moloch's White Plains–area home in the spring of 1976. Present at the meeting, Berkowitz said, were at least eight Process leaders and members, along with "some friends of theirs" and "at least two" lower-ranked members of the Westchester cult—including himself.

"They tossed different ideas around," Berkowitz said. "One of them was to kidnap young girls and kill them in cemeteries. Another was to copy the Manson thing in rich neighborhoods. But the goal was to paralyze New York, and they eventually decided on the .44 shootings."

"Did they ever say they were involved in the Manson killings?" I asked. "Yes, they did," he replied.

Berkowitz didn't know it, but I'd surfaced new evidence connecting Manson to the Process. A jailed Manson killer told me Charlie's "family" met Process leaders at the "Spiral Staircase" house near Los Angeles in 1968. Manson himself confirmed this statement in his autobiography. In a clear reference to the English group, he wrote that he met individuals who worshiped "multiple devils" at the very house in question.

Additionally, I viewed a letter Manson wrote in 1989. In his own hand, he described another occasion where he met named Process leaders. Incredibly, he said this gathering actually took place at the Tate home—the scene of future slaughter.

Manson has also claimed a child pornography element bubbled somewhere in the Tate tableau. This factor was also present in the Son of Sam operation, a phase Berkowitz addressed when I interviewed him again in 1997 for New York's WABC-TV. The program, a four-part series coordinated by news director Bart Feder and reporter Sarah Wallace, was expanded to a one-hour special which later aired nationally on the A&E network's *Investigative Reports*.

"The Process was very sophisticated and dedicated," Berkowitz told me. "They had their hands in a lot of things, including drugs and that disgusting child pornography. They also provided kids for sex to some wealthy people, and I did see some of those people at parties."

According to Berkowitz, these sex and drug soirees were held at upscale private residences in Westchester, Manhattan, Connecticut and Long Island's Hamptons. His telephone records, which documented calls to the Hamptons and to the Long Island summer homes of two Yonkers doctors, partially supported his statement. Further, two witnesses maintained that occasionally present at these parties were a Yonkers judge, at least two Westchester County politicians, a high-ranking New York state politician, a celebrated but later-murdered physician, a Nobel Prize-winning doctor, and two aides (one prominent) to then-mayor of New York City Abraham Beame.

Berkowitz also revealed that he met Roy Cohn, the powerful and notorious attorney who once represented—besides numerous other "high-society" clients—the owners of the glamorous but scandal-ridden Studio 54 discotheque.

"I was at a party at that big house he had in Greenwich [Connecticut]," Berkowitz said of Cohn, who died of AIDS in 1986. "I didn't know him, but other people did, and that's how I went to a party there."

Berkowitz also said he attended a party at Roy Radin's mansion in Southampton, Long Island. "I hardly knew him on a personal basis, but I did know some other people who knew him," he remarked. Berkowitz added that two of those "other people," close associates of Radin, were in fact at the final Son of Sam attack in Brooklyn, as alleged by the prison informants.

"There were three people in a van across the street, and they did film the shooting," Berkowitz said, confirming the sensational "snuff film" allegations. "And it's true that two of them were good friends of Radin. One of them was Ron Sisman. He was the one with the camera."

Sisman, the cocaine dealer and pornographer, was executed in his Manhattan brownstone on Halloween 1981. His companion, coed Elizabeth Platzman, was also shot dead. "I knew Sisman, and I had been at his place with Mike [Carr]," Berkowitz said. "Some of the group also hung out at a bar near there." This pub, which Sisman also frequented, was called the Angry Squire.

Berkowitz's claim was corroborated by a young man who also dropped by the

Angry Squire now and then. Jesse Turner, a jailed bank robber, was an admitted Process associate. "In the early '70s, I lived with some of them in a house in the French Quarter in New Orleans," he said. "They were brokering kids, and their rituals were wall-to-wall sex and drugs. I also witnessed a murder they did in Bayou St. John. It was one of their own. They bled him to death and got rid of the body."

Turner said he continued his interactions with the British group in New York. "I was also a good friend of Michael Carr," Turner stated. "About halfway into it I learned the Process was behind Son of Sam. They called it one of their 'Apocalyptic Trials,' which meant a major public display of violence."

Turner was also a close associate of Robert Mapplethorpe, the controversial photographer and sculptor who died of AIDS in 1989. "I lived with Robert and [rock singer] Patti Smith for a while when they were a couple," Turner said. "Robert thought he was the devil. He was affiliated with the Process, but not strictly a member. But they used each other."

Turner, who was debriefed extensively by NYPD and Yonkers detectives in 1996, stated that Mapplethorpe approached him for a favor in 1981. "It was for the Process. Robert told me Sisman had some snuff films, and they wanted them back. I knew the Moskowitz [Son of Sam] film was one of them."

Turner said he recruited two gunmen, who killed Sisman and Platzman and retrieved five snuff films, one of which was Sisman's copy of the Moskowitz tape. NYPD detectives questioned the two alleged killers in 1996. According to official sources, one of them "miserably failed" a polygraph test and the other was graded "deceptive" because he "tried to beat the machine."

The pair then hired lawyers, but the probe suddenly screeched to a halt. NYPD authorities said they lacked enough evidence to make arrests. However, an unidentified federal agent advised WABC-TV that the department's brass shut down the investigation when they discovered it led to the Son of Sam case.

Meanwhile, the Yonkers police found their own efforts hampered by the NYPD. Law enforcement sources in Manhattan revealed that NYPD officials ignored a top-level Yonkers request for access to its Son of Sam files.

Nonetheless, the Yonkers police made considerable progress. More cult members and associates were identified, and witnesses placed Berkowitz with others in Untermyer Park. The Yonkers inquiry also cast light on the group's "business interests." Specifically, despite the occult flavoring and the satanic fervor demonstrated by Berkowitz and others on the lower rungs of the ladder, the police determined that perks from the sex and drug businesses were of far more significance to the hierarchy.

I agreed with that evaluation, which was an avenue initially paved by one of the prison informants in 1981 when he wrote that the group's drug and porn connections were key. So, what finally emerged was a loose confederation of allies—including the Process, the aligned preexisting Westchester cult, biker elements, perverse political and society types and assorted hangers-on. Additionally, a contingent of pimps, many of whom have now been identified, served up young runaways and other wayward adolescents for use at monied sex parties.

In other words, the Son of Sam killings and a litany of other offenses grew out of a subculture melded together—at varying times for overlapping reasons—by sex, drugs, violence, weapons dealings and occult practices.

In 1997 and 1998, I asked Berkowitz about some other crimes I suspected were tied to the cult group and referenced earlier in this book. Here is a brief summary of his replies:

—The May 1976 firebombing of the Neto home on Wicker St. in Berkowitz's neighborhood. A witness had told me she heard one participant calling to another. "I was involved in that with someone else," Berkowitz said. He also said he had a hand in shooting the Neto family's dog on Christmas Eve of that year. "Someone was with me," he said, confirming witnesses' accounts.

—The October 1976 wounding of a young woman by shots fired into Westchester's Candle Light Inn. A bartender told me he threw out Berkowitz, Michael Carr and their friend "Bobby" minutes earlier. The bullets were fired from the same model of revolver owned by the Carrs. "Yeah, we did it," Berkowitz said.

—The wounding of the Carr dog in April 1977. "It wasn't me, but someone else in the group did it," Berkowitz said. At the time, a witness said the shooter had blondish hair.

—The sniper wounding of sixteen-year-old Lisa Gottlieb in her Westchester home in May 1977. "I wasn't involved in that, but I believe another one of the group was," Berkowitz said.

—The suicide of Yonkers mailman Andrew Dupay six weeks after Berkowitz's arrest. "I just knew who he was, and I'm sorry to hear about it," Berkowitz commented. "But I'm not surprised to hear he was threatened. Delivering mail in that neighborhood, the poor guy could have seen things he shouldn't have."

—The Westchester murder of Maria Cortina (Suzette Rodriguez) two months after Berkowitz's arrest. She was sketched by Billy the artist the year before. "I knew her from Untermyer," said Berkowitz, who also identified the drawing.

—The November 1977 sniper slaying of thirteen-year-old Natalie Gallace and wounding of thirty-eight-year-old Susan Levy in New Rochelle. The chief suspect, Frank Signorelli, died in 1980 while in jail on another charge. "I knew Frank from here and there," Berkowitz said. "And I think you might find out he knew Sue Levy from parties or whatever."

—The murder of Robert Hirschmann in Dutchess County, New York, in early 1978. The body of Hirschmann's wife was found in Queens. "His name is very familiar, but not hers," Berkowitz stated.

—The murder of Joseph Carozza on his yacht in a New Rochelle marina on New Year's Eve 1981. "I knew him. I was on his yacht, and so were some others in the group," Berkowitz said.

Besides those cases, others also died violently, their connections to the cult not known until the 1990s. Among them:

—*William Fitzgerald.* Six days before Berkowitz's arrest, Fitzgerald was slain in an apparent murder-suicide by James McIntyre in a Yonkers apartment located several blocks from Pine Street. "I knew Billy somewhat," Berkowitz remarked. "But I'm not sure about the other guy."

—*Dawn Koons.* A former north Yonkers bartender, Koons was murdered in Bakersfield, California, in early 1979. The case remains unsolved. "I knew Dawn from Untermyer," Berkowitz said.

—*Ralph Marcel.* A Yonkers resident whom witnesses placed in the group, Marcel was called "Brother Ed," a Process title. Marcel was run down by a car in Jacksonville Beach, Florida, in June 1981. The auto was driven by a Long Island resident. The case was ruled an accident. "I knew Ralph from around Yonkers and Untermyer," Berkowitz stated.

—*J. D. Cann.* A Yonkers resident who lived in Berkowitz's apartment building in 1977, Cann committed suicide in late 1998. A witness told police that Cann occasionally drove the yellow Volkswagen. According to the witness, after Berkowitz's arrest Cann told coworkers he needed to obtain a gun because people were after him. "It's going to be them or me," the witness quoted Cann as saying. Berkowitz remarked: "Cann belonged to the group, but he wasn't at any of the .44 shootings."

It is highly doubtful that this list, augmented by the names of others noted previously in this book, is complete.

Meanwhile, as time moves forward, the faint hoofbeats of oncoming eternity echo slightly louder with the passing of each year. It is perhaps the only eventual rendezvous one can gauge with certainty. The arrival of truth, however, is sometimes more fluid, more subject to interpretation. But not in this instance.

In 1998, the Yonkers Police Department reached a foreboding determination in its contemporary Son of Sam investigation. The verdict, which mirrored my own conclusion and that of the former Queens district attorney, can be summed up in one word. It is a single word, but it enunciates volumes about the true story behind one of the biggest cases in the annals of modern crime.

It is a word that will stand. It is a word that will not be altered by future events as it resonates through the corridors of criminal history in America.

The word is *conspiracy.*

Acknowledgments

There are those without whom I might not have been able to sustain this investigation. Some, because of sensitive positions they occupy, cannot be named—but they have my appreciation for their professional insights and cooperation.

Others to whom I am indebted are my family and friends, who listened and offered support when it mattered most. Among those friends are George Austin, Joe Walsh, Scott Hammon, Bob and Larry Siegel, Lee Carucci, George and Roger Young, Kyle and Nina (Betty) Rote, Pete Lebhar and the circle at Olliver's.

Special thanks to the Queens District Attorney's Office, particularly John Santucci, Herb Leifer and Tom McCarthy; and to Gannett Westchester Newspapers—especially Joe Ungaro, Dave Hartley, Sherman Bodner and Tom Bartley.

My appreciation is extended to former Lt. Terry Gardner and Det. Mike Knoop in Minot, North Dakota; and to Sgt. Ken Kahn in the Santa Clara, California, Sheriff's Department.

I would also like to note the contributions of reporters Jeff Nies and Jack Graham of the *Minot Daily News* and thank Marv and Jean Dykema and friends of Arlis Perry who assisted me in Bismarck.

A singular acknowledgment to reporter Jim Mitteager, who was there at the beginning; and to reporter/author Marian Roach, who helped in the early years.

My gratitude extends to retired NYPD detectives Joe Basteri and Hank Cinotti, to Lt. Mike Novotny and Lt. Marty Harding of the Yonkers Police, and to Lt. Don Starkey of the Yonkers Fire Department's arson squad. I would also like to note the assistance of police instructor Fred Patterson, who joined some stakeouts and incorporated my work into a seminar for law enforcement officers, and that of the late Joseph Pearlman, an exemplary private investigator.

I also thank the Greenburgh, New York, Police Department, particularly Capt. Gerry Buckhout and Chief Don Singer. My added appreciation to Nassau County, New York, District Attorney Denis Dillon, the Connecticut State Police, the Los

Angeles Sheriff's Department, and the Federal Bureau of Investigation.

A special word of appreciation to people close to the Son of Sam case: Jerry and Neysa Moskowitz, Mike and Rose Lauria, Mr. and Mrs. Frank Suriani, Robert Violante, Cacilia Davis, Tom Zaino, John Diel, Mrs. Nann Cassara, Steve Cassara and the Neto family.

Singular gratitude is expressed to the West Coast investigators, including Ted Gunderson, Judy Hanson, Dee Brown and Dave Balsiger. Their assistance was extremely valuable.

I am grateful to a woman who I will call Lee Chase, who was close to David Berkowitz and whose assistance was timely and informative.

My thanks go to attorneys Felix Gilroy and Harry Lipsig, and to producer Frank Anthony and the staff of WOR-TV's *What's Happening, America* and *The War Within* programs.

An acknowledgment to the work of reporters Mike Zuckerman and Ed Trapasso of Gannett, Newsday's Steve Wick, and author Ed Sanders.

For assistance in the 1990s, I would like to thank the Immigration and Naturalization Service, the Yonkers Police Department, and retired NYPD detectives Al Sheppard, Jim Tedaldi, Jim Rothstein and Richard Johnson.

My appreciation for contributions in the '90s is also extended to: Barbara C., Dale Griffis, Sam Diego, Donald Ripp, Ray Segal, Steve Segovia, Mark Ness, Bart Feder, Sarah Wallace and Wayne Darwen.

My gratitude is also extended to those in the print and broadcast mediums who believed in the relevance of the investigation and offered information or followed through with reports on the work.

And finally, an important acknowledgment to the many private citizens, and others, who either came forward with vital information or gave hours of their time when I sought their cooperation. It made a difference.